Rover 400 Series
Service and Repair Manual

Mark Coombs and A K Legg LAE MIMI

Models covered

(3453 - 344 - 3AC1)

Rover 414, 416 and 420 Hatchback and Saloon models with petrol and turbo-diesel engines

Does not cover automatic transmission models with 1590 cc D-Series (Honda) engine

ABCDE
FGHIJ
KLM

Printed in the USA

Haynes Publishing
Sparkford, Yeovil, Somerset BA22 7JJ, England

Haynes North America, Inc
861 Lawrence Drive, Newbury Park, California 91320, USA

Editions Haynes
4, Rue de l'Abreuvoir
92415 COURBEVOIE CEDEX, France

Haynes Publishing Nordiska AB
Box 1504, 751 45 UPPSALA, Sweden

Contents

LIVING WITH YOUR ROVER 400

Roadside Repairs

Weekly Checks

Lubricants and Fluids

Tyre Pressures

MAINTENANCE

Routine Maintenance and Servicing

Contents

REPAIRS & OVERHAUL

Engine and Associated Systems

Transmission

Brakes and Suspension

Body Equipment

Wiring Diagrams

REFERENCE

Index

The New Rover 400 was launched in the UK in May 1995, being styled on the five-door Honda Civic Hatchback.

The original range comprised Hatchback models fitted with 1.4 and 1.6 litre petrol engines, with automatic transmission available as an option on models fitted with the Honda 1.6 litre engine (not covered in this Manual). 2.0 litre petrol and diesel engine models were added in December 1995 and Saloon models followed in March 1996.

All models have front-wheel-drive with fully-independent front and rear suspension.

Power steering (PAS) is fitted as standard to all models, and all 420 models are equipped with an Anti-lock Braking System (ABS). All models have a driver's airbag with an optional passenger airbag, an immobiliser, alarm and remote central locking. Air conditioning is available as an option on all models.

For the home mechanic, the Rover 400 is a straightforward vehicle to maintain and most of the items requiring frequent attention are easily accessible.

Rover 416S

Rover 414

The Rover 400 Team

Haynes manuals are produced by dedicated and enthusiastic people working in close co-operation. The team responsible for the creation of this book included:

Authors	Mark Coombs A.K. Legg
Sub-editor	Sophie Yar
Editor & Page Make-up	Steve Churchill
Workshop manager	Paul Buckland
Photo Scans	John Martin Paul Tanswell
Cover illustration & Line Art	Roger Healing
Wiring diagrams	Matthew Marke

We hope the book will help you to get the maximum enjoyment from your car. By carrying out routine maintenance as described you will ensure your car's reliability and preserve its resale value.

Your Rover 400 manual

The aim of this Manual is to help you get the best value from your vehicle. It can do so in several ways. It can help you decide what work must be done (even should you choose to get it done by a garage). It will also provide information on routine maintenance and servicing, and give a logical course of action and diagnosis when random faults occur. However, it is hoped that you will use the manual by tackling the work yourself. On simpler jobs it may even be quicker than booking the car into a garage and going there twice, to leave and collect it. Perhaps most important, a lot of money can be saved by avoiding the costs a garage must charge to cover its labour and overheads.

The manual has drawings and descriptions to show the function of the various components so that their layout can be understood. Tasks are described and photographed in a clear step-by-step sequence. The illustrations are numbered by the Section number and paragraph number to which they relate - if there is more than one illustration per paragraph, the sequence is denoted alphabetically.

References to the "left" or "right" of the vehicle are in the sense of a person in the driver's seat, facing forwards.

Acknowledgements

Thanks are due to the Champion Spark Plug Company who supplied the illustrations of various spark plug conditions and to Duckhams Oils, who provided lubrication data. Thanks are also due to Sykes-Pickavant Limited, who provided some of the workshop tools, and to all those people at Sparkford who helped in the production of this manual.

This manual is not a direct reproduction of the vehicle manufacturer's data, and its publication should not be taken as implying any technical approval by the vehicle manufacturers or importers.

We take great pride in the accuracy of information given in this manual, but vehicle manufacturers make alterations and design changes during the production run of a particular vehicle of which they do not inform us. No liability can be accepted by the authors or publishers for loss, damage or injury caused by any errors in, or omissions from, the information given.

Project vehicles

The main vehicle used in the preparation of this manual, and which appears in many of the photographic sequences, was a Rover 420 SLi 5-door Hatchback fitted with a T16 1994 cc petrol engine.

Working on your car can be dangerous. This page shows just some of the potential risks and hazards, with the aim of creating a safety-conscious attitude.

General hazards

Scalding

• Don't remove the radiator or expansion tank cap while the engine is hot.
• Engine oil, automatic transmission fluid or power steering fluid may also be dangerously hot if the engine has recently been running.

Burning

• Beware of burns from the exhaust system and from any part of the engine. Brake discs and drums can also be extremely hot immediately after use.

Crushing

• When working under or near a raised vehicle, always supplement the jack with axle stands, or use drive-on ramps. *Never venture under a car which is only supported by a jack.*

• Take care if loosening or tightening high-torque nuts when the vehicle is on stands. Initial loosening and final tightening should be done with the wheels on the ground.

Fire

• Fuel is highly flammable; fuel vapour is explosive.
• Don't let fuel spill onto a hot engine.
• Do not smoke or allow naked lights (including pilot lights) anywhere near a vehicle being worked on. Also beware of creating sparks (electrically or by use of tools).
• Fuel vapour is heavier than air, so don't work on the fuel system with the vehicle over an inspection pit.
• Another cause of fire is an electrical overload or short-circuit. Take care when repairing or modifying the vehicle wiring.
• Keep a fire extinguisher handy, of a type suitable for use on fuel and electrical fires.

Electric shock

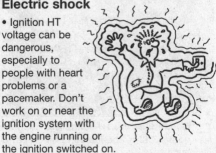

• Ignition HT voltage can be dangerous, especially to people with heart problems or a pacemaker. Don't work on or near the ignition system with the engine running or the ignition switched on.

• Mains voltage is also dangerous. Make sure that any mains-operated equipment is correctly earthed. Mains power points should be protected by a residual current device (RCD) circuit breaker.

Fume or gas intoxication

• Exhaust fumes are poisonous; they often contain carbon monoxide, which is rapidly fatal if inhaled. Never run the engine in a confined space such as a garage with the doors shut.

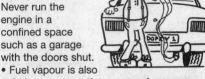

• Fuel vapour is also poisonous, as are the vapours from some cleaning solvents and paint thinners.

Poisonous or irritant substances

• Avoid skin contact with battery acid and with any fuel, fluid or lubricant, especially antifreeze, brake hydraulic fluid and Diesel fuel. Don't syphon them by mouth. If such a substance is swallowed or gets into the eyes, seek medical advice.
• Prolonged contact with used engine oil can cause skin cancer. Wear gloves or use a barrier cream if necessary. Change out of oil-soaked clothes and do not keep oily rags in your pocket.
• Air conditioning refrigerant forms a poisonous gas if exposed to a naked flame (including a cigarette). It can also cause skin burns on contact.

Asbestos

• Asbestos dust can cause cancer if inhaled or swallowed. Asbestos may be found in gaskets and in brake and clutch linings. When dealing with such components it is safest to assume that they contain asbestos.

Special hazards

Hydrofluoric acid

• This extremely corrosive acid is formed when certain types of synthetic rubber, found in some O-rings, oil seals, fuel hoses etc, are exposed to temperatures above 400°C. The rubber changes into a charred or sticky substance containing the acid. *Once formed, the acid remains dangerous for years. If it gets onto the skin, it may be necessary to amputate the limb concerned.*
• When dealing with a vehicle which has suffered a fire, or with components salvaged from such a vehicle, wear protective gloves and discard them after use.

The battery

• Batteries contain sulphuric acid, which attacks clothing, eyes and skin. Take care when topping-up or carrying the battery.
• The hydrogen gas given off by the battery is highly explosive. Never cause a spark or allow a naked light nearby. Be careful when connecting and disconnecting battery chargers or jump leads.

Air bags

• Air bags can cause injury if they go off accidentally. Take care when removing the steering wheel and/or facia. Special storage instructions may apply.

Diesel injection equipment

• Diesel injection pumps supply fuel at very high pressure. Take care when working on the fuel injectors and fuel pipes.

⚠️ *Warning: Never expose the hands, face or any other part of the body to injector spray; the fuel can penetrate the skin with potentially fatal results.*

Remember...

DO

• Do use eye protection when using power tools, and when working under the vehicle.

• Do wear gloves or use barrier cream to protect your hands when necessary.

• Do get someone to check periodically that all is well when working alone on the vehicle.

• Do keep loose clothing and long hair well out of the way of moving mechanical parts.

• Do remove rings, wristwatch etc, before working on the vehicle – especially the electrical system.

• Do ensure that any lifting or jacking equipment has a safe working load rating adequate for the job.

DON'T

• Don't attempt to lift a heavy component which may be beyond your capability – get assistance.

• Don't rush to finish a job, or take unverified short cuts.

• Don't use ill-fitting tools which may slip and cause injury.

• Don't leave tools or parts lying around where someone can trip over them. Mop up oil and fuel spills at once.

• Don't allow children or pets to play in or near a vehicle being worked on.

The following pages are intended to help in dealing with common roadside emergencies and breakdowns. You will find more detailed fault finding information at the back of the manual, and repair information in the main chapters.

If your car won't start and the starter motor doesn't turn

☐ If it's a model with automatic transmission, make sure the selector is in 'P' or 'N'.
☐ Open the bonnet and make sure that the battery terminals are clean and tight.
☐ Switch on the headlights and try to start the engine. If the headlights go very dim when you're trying to start, the battery is probably flat. Get out of trouble by jump starting (see next page) using a friend's car.

If your car won't start even though the starter motor turns as normal

☐ Is there fuel in the tank?
☐ Is there moisture on electrical components under the bonnet? Switch off the ignition, then wipe off any obvious dampness with a dry cloth. Spray a water-repellent aerosol product (WD-40 or equivalent) on ignition and fuel system electrical connectors like those shown in the photos. Pay special attention to the ignition coil wiring connector and HT leads. (Note that Diesel engines don't normally suffer from damp.)

A Check the security and condition of the battery connections

B Check that the fuel injection system component wiring is secure

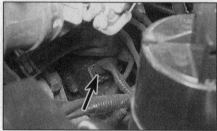

C Check that the ignition coil low tension wiring is securely connected to the coil on petrol engines

Check (with the ignition switched off) that all electrical connections are secure and spray them with a water-dispersant spray (such as WD40) if you suspect a problem due to damp

D Check that the HT leads are securely connected to the spark plugs on petrol engines. To do this, remove the cover first

E Check that the HT leads are securely connected to the ignition coil on petrol engines

Jump starting

Jump starting will get you out of trouble, but you must correct whatever made the battery go flat in the first place. There are three possibilities:

1 *The battery has been drained by repeated attempts to start, or by leaving the lights on.*

2 *The charging system is not working properly (alternator drivebelt slack or broken, alternator wiring fault or alternator itself faulty).*

3 *The battery itself is at fault (electrolyte low, or battery worn out).*

When jump-starting a car using a booster battery, observe the following precautions:

✔ Before connecting the booster battery, make sure that the ignition is switched off.

✔ Ensure that all electrical equipment (lights, heater, wipers, etc) is switched off.

✔ Take note of any special precautions printed on the battery case.

✔ Make sure that the booster battery is the same voltage as the discharged one in the vehicle.

✔ If the battery is being jump-started from the battery in another vehicle, the two vehicles MUST NOT TOUCH each other.

✔ Make sure that the transmission is in neutral (or PARK, in the case of automatic transmission).

1 Connect one end of the red jump lead to the positive (+) terminal of the flat battery

2 Connect the other end of the red lead to the positive (+) terminal of the booster battery.

3 Connect one end of the black jump lead to the negative (-) terminal of the booster battery

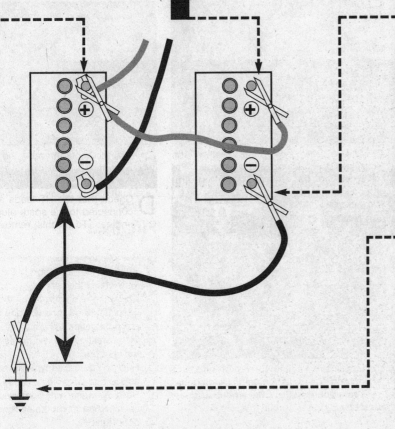

4 Connect the other end of the black jump lead to a bolt or bracket on the engine block, well away from the battery, on the vehicle to be started.

5 Make sure that the jump leads will not come into contact with the fan, drive-belts or other moving parts of the engine.

6 Start the engine using the booster battery and run it at idle speed. Switch on the lights, rear window demister and heater blower motor, then disconnect the jump leads in the reverse order of connection. Turn off the lights etc.

Wheel changing

Some of the details shown here will vary according to model. For instance, the location of the spare wheel and jack is not the same on all cars. However, the basic principles apply to all vehicles.

Warning: Do not change a wheel in a situation where you risk being hit by another vehicle. On busy roads, try to stop in a lay-by or a gateway. Be wary of passing traffic while changing the wheel - it is easy to become distracted by the job in hand.

Preparation

- ☐ When a puncture occurs, stop as soon as it is safe to do so.
- ☐ Park on firm level ground, if possible, and well out of the way of other traffic.
- ☐ Use hazard warning lights if necessary.

- ☐ If you have one, use a warning triangle to alert other drivers of your presence.
- ☐ Apply the handbrake and engage first or reverse gear (or Park on models with automatic transmission.

- ☐ Chock the wheel diagonally opposite the one being removed – a couple of large stones will do for this.
- ☐ If the ground is soft, use a flat piece of wood to spread the load under the jack.

Changing the wheel

1 The spare wheel is beneath a cover in the luggage compartment. Remove the mat and lift up the hardboard panel. The jack and tool kit are in front of the spare wheel well; remove the tools **before** removing the spare.

2 Unscrew the clamp and lift the spare wheel from the well in the floor.

3 On steel wheels, prise off the wheel trim using the wheel brace. On alloy wheels, remove the locking wheel nut cover with the special tool provided.

4 Loosen each wheel nut by half a turn. Use the special adapter on the locking wheel nut.

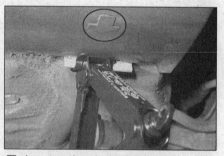

5 Locate the jack head below the reinforced jacking point nearest the wheel to be changed, and on firm ground. The jacking point is indicated by an arrow pressed in the sill.

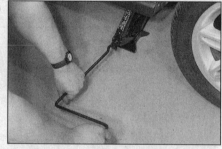

6 Turn the handle to raise the vehicle until the wheel is clear of the ground. If the tyre is flat make sure that the vehicle is raised sufficiently to allow the spare wheel to be fitted.

Finally...

- ☐ Remove the wheel chocks.
- ☐ Stow the jack and tools in the correct locations in the car.
- ☐ Check the tyre pressure on the wheel just fitted. If it is low, or if you don't have a pressure gauge with you, drive slowly to the nearest garage and inflate the tyre to the right pressure.
- ☐ Have the damaged tyre or wheel repaired as soon as possible.
- ☐ Have the wheel nuts tightened to the specified torque at the earliest opportunity.

7 Remove the nuts and lift the wheel from the vehicle. Place it beneath the sill as a precaution against the jack failing. Fit the spare wheel and tighten the nuts moderately with the wheel brace.

8 Lower the vehicle to the ground and tighten the wheel nuts in a diagonal sequence. Refit the wheel trim if applicable.

Identifying leaks

Puddles on the garage floor or drive, or obvious wetness under the bonnet or underneath the car, suggest a leak that needs investigating. It can sometimes be difficult to decide where the leak is coming from, especially if the engine bay is very dirty already. Leaking oil or fluid can also be blown rearwards by the passage of air under the car, giving a false impression of where the problem lies.

 Warning: Most automotive oils and fluids are poisonous. Wash them off skin, and change out of contaminated clothing, without delay.

 The smell of a fluid leaking from the car may provide a clue to what's leaking. Some fluids are distinctively coloured. It may help to clean the car carefully and to park it over some clean paper overnight as an aid to locating the source of the leak.
Remember that some leaks may only occur while the engine is running.

Sump oil

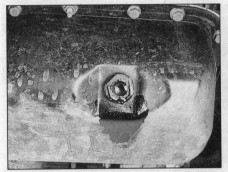

Engine oil may leak from the drain plug...

Oil from filter

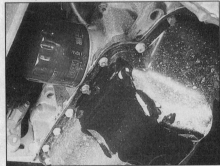

...or from the base of the oil filter.

Gearbox oil

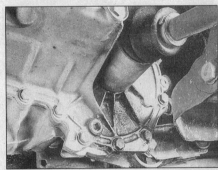

Gearbox oil can leak from the seals at the inboard ends of the driveshafts.

Antifreeze

Leaking antifreeze often leaves a crystalline deposit like this.

Brake fluid

A leak occurring at a wheel is almost certainly brake fluid.

Power steering fluid

Power steering fluid may leak from the pipe connectors on the steering rack.

Towing

☐ Lashing eyes are provided at the front and rear of the vehicle as a means of securing the vehicle onto a break-down truck. Rover state that the eyes **must not** be used to tow the vehicle or as a means of towing another vehicle.

Front lashing eye

Introduction

There are some very simple checks which need only take a few minutes to carry out, but which could save you a lot of inconvenience and expense.

These "Weekly checks" require no great skill or special tools, and the small amount of time they take to perform could prove to be very well spent, for example;

☐ Keeping an eye on tyre condition and pressures, will not only help to stop them wearing out prematurely, but could also save your life.

☐ Many breakdowns are caused by electrical problems. Battery-related faults are particularly common, and a quick check on a regular basis will often prevent the majority of these.

☐ If your car develops a brake fluid leak, the first time you might know about it is when your brakes don't work properly. Checking the level regularly will give advance warning of this kind of problem.

☐ If the oil or coolant levels run low, the cost of repairing any engine damage will be far greater than fixing the leak, for example.

Underbonnet check points

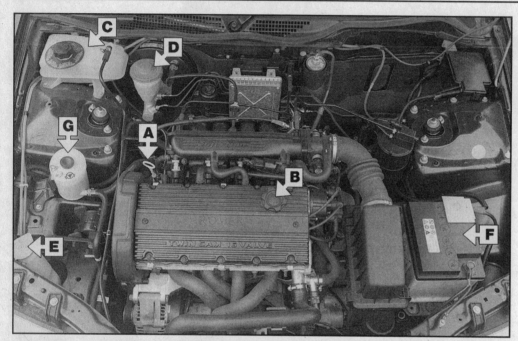

◀ **1.4/1.6 litre petrol**

A *Engine oil level dipstick*
B *Engine oil filler cap*
C *Coolant expansion tank*
D *Brake fluid reservoir*
E *Screen washer fluid reservoir*
F *Battery*
G *Power steering fluid reservoir*

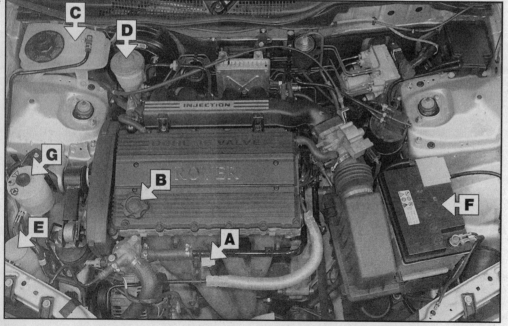

◀ **2.0 litre petrol**

A *Engine oil level dipstick*
B *Engine oil filler cap*
C *Coolant expansion tank*
D *Brake fluid reservoir*
E *Screen washer fluid reservoir*
F *Battery*
G *Power steering fluid reservoir*

A   *Engine oil level dipstick*
B   *Engine oil filler cap*
C   *Coolant expansion tank*
D   *Brake fluid reservoir*
E   *Screen washer fluid reservoir*
F   *Battery*
G   *Power steering fluid reservoir*

Engine oil level

Before you start

✔ Make sure that your car is on level ground.

✔ Check the oil level before the car is driven, or at least 5 minutes after the engine has been switched off.

 HAYNES HiNT *If the oil is checked immediately after driving the vehicle, some of the oil will remain in the upper engine components, resulting in an inaccurate reading on the dipstick!*

The correct oil

Modern engines place great demands on their oil. It is very important that the correct oil for your car is used (See "Lubricants and fluids").

Car Care

● If you have to add oil frequently, you should check whether you have any oil leaks. Place some clean paper under the car overnight, and check for stains in the morning. If there are no leaks, the engine may be burning oil (see "Fault Finding").

● Always maintain the level between the upper and lower dipstick marks (see photo 3). If the level is too low severe engine damage may occur. Oil seal failure may result if the engine is overfilled by adding too much oil.

1 The dipstick is located on the right-hand rear of the engine on 414 and 416 petrol models. On 420 petrol and all diesel models it is located on the front of the engine. It is brightly coloured for ease of location. See "*Underbonnet Check Points*" on pages 0•10 and 0•11 for the exact location of the dipstick.

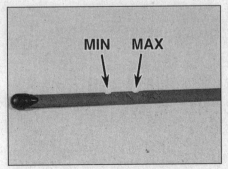

3 Note the oil level on the end of the dipstick, which should be between the upper MAX mark and the lower MIN mark. Note on 1.6 litre engines, the dipstick has HI and LO markings. Approximately 1.0 litre of oil will raise the level from the lower mark to the upper mark.

2 Withdraw the dipstick. Using a clean rag or paper towel, wipe all the oil from the dipstick. Insert the clean dipstick into the tube as far as it will go, then withdraw it again.

4 Oil is added through the filler cap on top of the engine. Rotate the cap through a quarter-turn anti-clockwise and withdraw it. Top-up the level. A funnel may help to reduce spillage. Add the oil slowly, checking the level on the dipstick often. Do not overfill.

Coolant level

 Warning: DO NOT attempt to remove the expansion tank pressure cap when the engine is hot, as there is a very great risk of scalding. Do not leave open containers of coolant about, as it is poisonous.

Car Care

● With a sealed-type cooling system, adding coolant should not be necessary on a regular basis. If frequent topping-up is required, it is likely there is a leak. Check the radiator, all hoses and joint faces for signs of staining or wetness, and rectify as necessary.

● It is important that antifreeze is used in the cooling system all year round, not just during the winter months. Don't top-up with water alone, as the antifreeze will become too diluted.

1 The coolant level varies with the temperature of the engine. When the engine is cold, the coolant level should be on the MAX mark on the side of the expansion tank located in the right-hand rear corner of the engine compartment. When the engine is hot, the level will rise slightly.

2 If topping-up is necessary, **wait until the engine is cold**, then slowly unscrew the expansion tank filler cap anti-clockwise, to release any pressure in the system, and remove it.

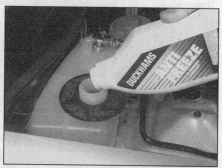

3 Add a mixture of water and antifreeze through the expansion tank filler neck, until the coolant is up to the MAX level mark. Refit the cap, turning it clockwise as far as it will go until it is secure.

Brake fluid level

 Warning:
● **Brake fluid can harm your eyes and damage painted surfaces, so use extreme caution when handling and pouring it.**
● **Do not use fluid that has been standing open for some time, as it absorbs moisture from the air, which can cause a dangerous loss of braking effectiveness.**

HAYNES HINT • **Make sure that your car is on level ground.**
• **The fluid level in the reservoir will drop slightly as the brake pads wear down, but the fluid level must never be allowed to drop below the "MIN" mark.**

Safety First!

● If the reservoir requires repeated topping-up this is an indication of a fluid leak somewhere in the system, which should be investigated immediately.

● If a leak is suspected, the car should not be driven until the braking system has been checked. Never take any risks where brakes are concerned.

1 The brake master cylinder and fluid reservoir are mounted on the vacuum servo unit in the engine compartment on the right-hand side of the bulkhead. The MAX and MIN level marks are indicated on the side of the reservoir and the fluid level should be maintained between these marks at all times.

2 If topping-up is necessary, wipe the area around the filler cap with a clean rag before removing the cap. It's a good idea to inspect the reservoir. The fluid should be changed if dirt is visible.

3 Carefully add fluid, avoiding spilling it on surrounding paintwork. Use only the specified hydraulic fluid; mixing different types of fluid can cause damage to the system and/or a loss of braking effectiveness. After filling to the correct level, refit the cap securely. Wipe off any spilt fluid.

Screen washer fluid level

Screenwash additives not only keep the winscreen clean during foul weather, they also prevent the washer system freezing in cold weather - which is when you are likely to need it most. Don't top up using plain water as the screenwash will become too diluted, and will freeze during cold weather. **On no account use coolant antifreeze in the washer system - this could discolour or damage paintwork.**

1 The reservoir for the windscreen and rear window (where applicable) washer systems is located in the front right-hand corner of the engine compartment. If topping up is necessary, open the cap.

2 When topping-up the reservoir a screenwash additive should be added in the quantities recommended on the bottle.

Power steering fluid level

Before you start:
✔ Park the vehicle on level ground.
✔ Set the steering wheel straight-ahead.
✔ The engine should be turned off.

HAYNES HiNT *For the check to be accurate, the steering must not be turned once the engine has been stopped.*

Safety First!
● The need for frequent topping-up indicates a leak, which should be investigated immediately.

1 The power steering fluid reservoir is located in the front right-hand corner of the engine compartment. 'UPPER' and 'LOWER' level marks are moulded into the translucent wall of the reservoir. The fluid level should be checked with the engine cold and stopped.

2 Check that the fluid is on the upper level mark in the translucent reservoir. Where topping up is necessary, first wipe clean the area around the filler cap.

3 Remove the cap then top up the fluid level using the specified type of fluid (do not overfill the reservoir). On completion refit the filler cap.

Tyre condition and pressure

It is very important that tyres are in good condition, and at the correct pressure - having a tyre failure at any speed is highly dangerous. Tyre wear is influenced by driving style - harsh braking and acceleration, or fast cornering, will all produce more rapid tyre wear. As a general rule, the front tyres wear out faster than the rears. Interchanging the tyres from front to rear ("rotating" the tyres) may result in more even wear. However, if this is completely effective, you may have the expense of replacing all four tyres at once! Remove any nails or stones embedded in the tread before they penetrate the tyre to cause deflation. If removal of a nail does reveal that

the tyre has been punctured, refit the nail so that its point of penetration is marked. Then immediately change the wheel, and have the tyre repaired by a tyre dealer.

Regularly check the tyres for damage in the form of cuts or bulges, especially in the sidewalls. Periodically remove the wheels, and clean any dirt or mud from the inside and outside surfaces. Examine the wheel rims for signs of rusting, corrosion or other damage. Light alloy wheels are easily damaged by "kerbing" whilst parking; steel wheels may also become dented or buckled. A new wheel is very often the only way to overcome severe damage.

New tyres should be balanced when they are fitted, but it may become necessary to re-balance them as they wear, or if the balance weights fitted to the wheel rim should fall off. Unbalanced tyres will wear more quickly, as will the steering and suspension components. Wheel imbalance is normally signified by vibration, particularly at a certain speed (typically around 50 mph). If this vibration is felt only through the steering, then it is likely that just the front wheels need balancing. If, however, the vibration is felt through the whole car, the rear wheels could be out of balance. Wheel balancing should be carried out by a tyre dealer or garage.

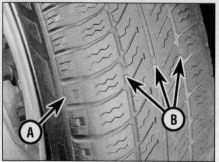

1 *Tread Depth - visual check*

The original tyres have tread wear safety bands (B), which will appear when the tread depth reaches approximately 1.6 mm. The band positions are indicated by a triangular mark on the tyre sidewall (A).

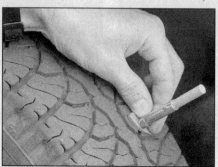

2 *Tread Depth - manual check*

Alternatively, tread wear can be monitored with a simple, inexpensive device known as a tread depth indicator gauge.

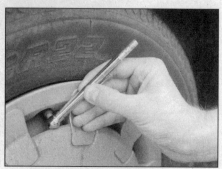

3 *Tyre Pressure Check*

Check the tyre pressures regularly with the tyres cold. Do not adjust the tyre pressures immediately after the vehicle has been used, or an inaccurate setting will result.

Tyre tread wear patterns

Shoulder Wear

Underinflation (wear on both sides)
Under-inflation will cause overheating of the tyre, because the tyre will flex too much, and the tread will not sit correctly on the road surface. This will cause a loss of grip and excessive wear, not to mention the danger of sudden tyre failure due to heat build-up.
Check and adjust pressures
Incorrect wheel camber (wear on one side)
Repair or renew suspension parts
Hard cornering
Reduce speed!

Centre Wear

Overinflation
Over-inflation will cause rapid wear of the centre part of the tyre tread, coupled with reduced grip, harsher ride, and the danger of shock damage occurring in the tyre casing.
Check and adjust pressures

If you sometimes have to inflate your car's tyres to the higher pressures specified for maximum load or sustained high speed, don't forget to reduce the pressures to normal afterwards.

Uneven Wear

Front tyres may wear unevenly as a result of wheel misalignment. Most tyre dealers and garages can check and adjust the wheel alignment (or "tracking") for a modest charge.
Incorrect camber or castor
Repair or renew suspension parts
Malfunctioning suspension
Repair or renew suspension parts
Unbalanced wheel
Balance tyres
Incorrect toe setting
Adjust front wheel alignment
Note: *The feathered edge of the tread which typifies toe wear is best checked by feel.*

Wiper blades

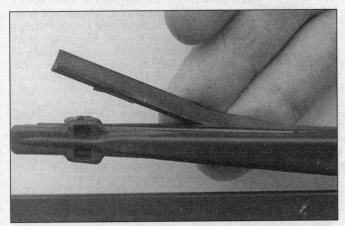

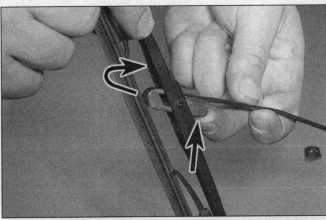

1 Check the condition of the wiper blades. If they are cracked or show any signs of deterioration, or if the glass swept area is smeared, renew them. For maximum clarity of vision, wiper blades should be renewed annually, as a matter of course.

2 To remove a wiper blade, pull the arm fully away from the glass until it locks. Swivel the blade through 90°, then depress the locking tab with a screwdriver or your fingers. Slide the wiper blade out of the hooked end of the arm, then feed the arm through the hole in the blade. When fitting the new blade, make sure that the blade locks securely into the arm, and that the blade is orientated correctly.

Battery

Caution: *Before carrying out any work on the vehicle battery, read the precautions given in "Safety first" at the start of this manual.*

✔ Make sure that the battery tray is in good condition, and that the clamp is tight. Corrosion on the tray, retaining clamp and the battery itself can be removed with a solution of water and baking soda. Thoroughly rinse all cleaned areas with water. Any metal parts damaged by corrosion should be covered with a zinc-based primer, then painted.

✔ Periodically (approximately every three months), check the charge condition of the battery as described in Chapter 5A.

✔ If the battery is flat, and you need to jump start your vehicle, see ***Roadside Repairs***.

1 The battery is located on the front left-hand side of the engine compartment. The exterior of the battery should be inspected periodically for damage such as a cracked case or cover.

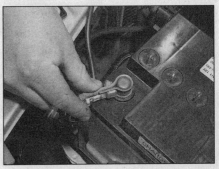

2 Check the tightness of the battery cable clamps to ensure good electrical connections. You should not be able to move them. Also check each cable for cracks and frayed conductors.

HAYNES HINT

Battery corrosion can be kept to a minimum by applying a layer of petroleum jelly to the clamps and terminals after they are reconnected.

3 If corrosion (white, fluffy deposits) is evident, remove the cables from the battery terminals, clean them with a small wire brush, then refit them. Automotive stores sell a tool for cleaning the battery post . . .

4 . . . as well as the battery cable clamps

Electrical systems

✔ Check all external lights and the horn. Refer to the appropriate Sections of Chapter 12 for details if any of the circuits are found to be inoperative.

✔ Visually check all accessible wiring connectors, harnesses and retaining clips for security, and for signs of chafing or damage.

HAYNES HiNT *If you need to check your brake lights and indicators unaided, back up to a wall or garage door and operate the lights. The reflected light should show if they are working properly.*

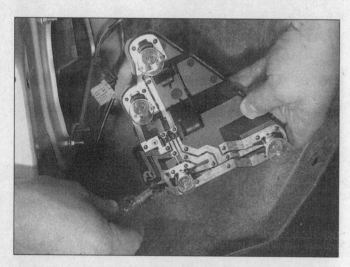

1 If a single indicator light, brake light or headlight has failed, it is likely that a bulb has blown and will need to be replaced. Refer to Chapter 12 for details. If both brake lights have failed, it is possible that the stop-light switch operated by the brake pedal has failed. Refer to Chapter 9 for details.

2 If more than one indicator light or headlight has failed, it is likely that either a fuse has blown or that there is a fault in the circuit (see Chapter 12). The main fusebox is located behind the driver's storage compartment located in the facia beneath the steering wheel. A further fusebox is located in the rear left-hand corner of the engine compartment for engine related fuses. On models with ABS and/or diesel engine models, additional fuses for the ABS and glowplugs are located on the left-hand side of the engine compartment. To access the fusebox located beneath the steering wheel, first open the storage compartment then lift it upwards slightly and release it from the lower pivots. Pull the compartment outwards away from the facia; the fusebox can then be viewed behind the facia.

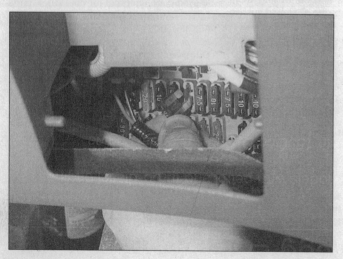

3 To replace a blown fuse, pull it out directly from the fusebox. Fit a new fuse of the same rating, available from car accessory shops. It is important that you find the reason that the fuse blew (see *"Electrical fault finding"* in Chapter 12).

Lubricants and fluids

Engine:

Petrol . . . . Multigrade engine oil to specification ACEA A2
(Duckhams QXR Premium Petrol Engine Oil)

Diesel . . . . Multigrade engine oil to specification ACEA B2
*(Duckhams QXR Premium Diesel Oil, or
Duckhams Hypergrade Diesel Engine Oil)*

Cooling system . . . . Antifreeze to spec. BS 6580 and BS 5117. Ethylene-
glycol based with non-phosphate corrosion inhibitors,
containing no methanol. Mixture 50% by volume
(Duckhams Antifreeze and Summer Coolant)

Gearbox:

1.4 and 1.6 litre engines . . . . Gear oil, viscosity SAE 75W-80W, to API GL5
(Duckhams Hypoid PT 75w-80w)

2.0 litre engines . . . . Special gearbox oil - refer to your Rover dealer
*(Duckhams QXR Premium Petrol or Diesel Engine Oil
may be used for topping-up only)*

Braking system . . . . Hydraulic fluid to DOT 4
(Duckhams Universal Brake and Clutch Fluid)

Power steering system . . . . For topping up, use automatic transmission fluid (ATF)
to Dexron II D specification *(Duckhams Unimatic)*.
For a complete refill, use fluid to specification PSF-V

General greasing . . . . Multi-purpose lithium-based grease to NLGI
consistency No 2 *(Duckhams LB10)*

Choosing your engine oil

Engines need oil, not only to lubricate moving parts and minimise wear, but also to maximise power output and to improve fuel economy. By introducing a simplified and improved range of engine oils, Duckhams has taken away the confusion and made it easier for you to choose the right oil for your engine.

HOW ENGINE OIL WORKS

• Beating friction

Without oil, the moving surfaces inside your engine will rub together, heat up and melt, quickly causing the engine to seize. Engine oil creates a film which separates these moving parts, preventing wear and heat build-up.

• Cooling hot-spots

Temperatures inside the engine can exceed 1000° C. The engine oil circulates and acts as a coolant, transferring heat from the hot-spots to the sump.

• Cleaning the engine internally

Good quality engine oils clean the inside of your engine, collecting and dispersing combustion deposits and controlling them until they are trapped by the oil filter or flushed out at oil change.

OIL CARE - FOLLOW THE CODE

To handle and dispose of used engine oil safely, always:

OIL CARE
FOLLOW THE CODE
OIL BANK LINE
0800 66 33 66

• **Avoid skin contact with used engine oil.** Repeated or prolonged contact can be harmful.
• **Dispose of used oil and empty packs in a responsible manner in an authorised disposal site.** Call 0800 663366 to find the one nearest to you. Never tip oil down drains or onto the ground.

Tyre pressures (cold) - bar (psi)

Note: *Pressures apply to original-equipment tyres, and may vary if any other make or type of tyre is fitted; check with the tyre manufacturer or supplier for correct pressures if necessary. The pressures are given on the inside of the fuel filler flap.*

	Front	Rear
Up to 4 passengers and luggage		
414 and 416 models	2.1 (30)	2.1 (30)
420 petrol models	2.2 (32)	2.1 (30)
420 diesel models:		
Steel wheels	2.1 (30)	2.1 (30)
Alloy wheels	2.2 (32)	2.1 (30)
Full load		
414 and 416 models:		
Steel wheels	2.1 (30)	2.1 (30)
Alloy wheels	2.3 (33)	2.3 (33)
420 petrol models	2.4 (35)	2.2 (32)
420 diesel models:		
Steel wheels	2.2 (32)	2.1 (30)
Alloy wheels	2.4 (35)	2.2 (32)
Speeds in excess of 100 mph (160 km/h)		
414 and 416 models	2.4 (35)	2.4 (35)
420 petrol models	2.6 (38)	2.5 (36)
420 and 420 SD models	2.1 (30)	2.1 (30)
420 SDi and 420 SLDi models:		
Steel wheels	2.4 (34)	2.4 (34)
Alloy wheels	2.5 (36)	2.4 (34)
420 GSDi models	2.5 (36)	2.4 (34)
Towing		
414 and 416 models:		
Steel wheels	2.1 (30)	2.4 (34)
Alloy wheels	2.1 (30)	2.5 (36)
420 petrol models	2.2 (32)	2.2 (32)
420 diesel models:		
Steel wheels	2.1 (30)	2.1 (30)
Alloy wheels	2.2 (32)	2.2 (32)

Chapter 1 Part A:
Routine maintenance and servicing - petrol models

Contents

Degrees of difficulty

Easy, suitable for novice with little experience

Fairly easy, suitable for beginner with some experience

Fairly difficult, suitable for competent DIY mechanic

Difficult, suitable for experienced DIY mechanic

Very difficult, suitable for expert DIY or professional

Lubricants and fluids

Refer to *"Weekly checks"*

Capacities

Engine oil

Including oil filter*:
1.4 and 1.6 litre engine	4.5 litres
2.0 litre engine	5.0 litres
Difference between MIN and MAX on dipstick (approximate)	1.0 litre

Capacities shown are for refilling after draining, if the engine is being filled from dry add a further 0.3 litre

Cooling system

1.4 and 1.6 litre engine*:
Models without air conditioning	4.3 litres
Models with air conditioning	4.6 litres
2.0 litre engine*	4.6 litres

Capacities shown are approximate capacities for refilling after draining. If the cooling system is being filled from dry, another 0.7 litres of coolant will be required on 1.4 and 1.6 litre engines, and another 2.9 litres on 2.0 litre engines.

Transmission

1.4 and 1.6 litre engine*	1.8 litres
2.0 litre engine*	2.0 litres

Capacities shown are for refilling after draining, if the transmission is being filled from dry add a further 0.2 litre

Washer fluid reservoir (all models)	6.5 litres
Fuel tank (all models)	55 litres
Power steering system (all models)	0.35 litres

Engine

Auxiliary drivebelt deflection (under a force of 98N) - 1.4 and 1.6 litre engines:

Power steering pump drivebelt*:
New belt	5.5 to 8.5 mm
Used belt	7.5 to 8.5 mm

Alternator drivebelt:
Models not fitted with air conditioning	6 to 8 mm
Models with air conditioning	9 to 10 mm

Rover definition of a new belt is one that has been used for less than 5 minutes

Cooling system

Antifreeze mixture:
50% antifreeze	Protection down to -37°C
55% antifreeze	Protection down to -45°C

Note: *Refer to antifreeze manufacturer for latest recommendations.*

Ignition system

Spark plugs:
Type	Champion RC9YCC

Electrode gap:
1.4 litre engine	0.8 mm
1.6 and 2.0 litre engines	0.9 mm

The spark plug gap quoted is that recommended by Champion for their specified plug listed above. If spark plugs of any other type are to be fitted, refer to their manufacturer's recommendations.

Brakes

Friction material minimum thickness:
Front and rear brake pads	3.0 mm
Rear brake shoes	2.0 mm

Torque wrench settings

	Nm	lbf ft
Alternator bolts - 1.4 and 1.6 litre engine	25	18
Engine sump drain plug:		
1.4 and 1.6 litre engine	42	31
2.0 litre engine	25	18
Fuel filter fuel pipe union nuts	30	22
Power steering pump pulley clamp bolt	25	18
Right-hand lower mounting bolts - 1.4 and 1.6 litre engine:		
Mounting-to-body bolts	45	33
Bracket-to-engine bolts	60	44
Roadwheel nuts	110	81
Spark plugs:		
1.4 and 1.6 litre engine	27	20
2.0 litre engine	25	18
Transmission oil filler/level plug:		
1.4 and 1.6 litre engine	25	18
2.0 litre engine	40	30

The maintenance intervals in this manual are provided with the assumption that you, not the dealer, will be carrying out the work. These are the minimum maintenance intervals recommended by us for vehicles driven daily. If you wish to keep your vehicle in peak condition at all times, you may wish to perform some of these procedures more often. We encourage frequent maintenance, because it enhances the efficiency, performance and resale value of your vehicle.

If the vehicle is driven in dusty areas, used to tow a trailer, or driven frequently at slow speeds (idling in traffic) or on short journeys, more frequent maintenance intervals are recommended.

When the vehicle is new, it should be serviced by a factory-authorised dealer service department, in order to preserve the factory warranty.

Every 250 miles (400 km) or weekly
☐ Refer to "Weekly Checks"

Every 6000 miles/10 000 km or 6 months, whichever comes first
☐ Renew the engine oil and filter (Section 3)

Note: Rover recommend that the engine oil and filter are changed every 12 000 miles or 12 months. However, oil and filter changes are good for the engine and we recommend that the oil and filter are renewed more frequently, especially if the vehicle is used on a lot of short journeys.

Every 12 000 miles/20 000 km or 12 months, whichever comes first
☐ Renew the engine oil and filter (Section 3)
☐ Check the body and underbody for corrosion protection (Section 4)
☐ Check the power steering fluid level (Section 5)
☐ Check the manual transmission oil level (Section 6)
☐ Check all components, pipes and hoses for fluid leaks (Section 7)
☐ Check the crankcase ventilation hoses and valves (Section 8)
☐ Check the air conditioning compressor, hoses and sight glass (Section 9)
☐ Check the condition and tension of the auxiliary drivebelts (Section 10)
☐ Check the condition of the exhaust system and heat shields (Section 11)
☐ Check the front/rear brake pads and discs for wear (Section 12)
☐ Check the rear brake shoes and drums for wear (Section 13)
☐ Check the brake pipes and hoses (Section 14)
☐ Check the front/rear brake calipers and rear wheel cylinders (Section 15)
☐ Check the steering and suspension components for condition and security (Section 16)
☐ Check the wheel bearings (Section 17)
☐ Check the condition of the driveshafts and gaiters (Section 18)
☐ Check the operation and adjustment of the handbrake - adjustment at first 12 000 miles/ 20 000 km only (Section 19)
☐ Lubricate all door locks and hinges, door stops, bonnet lock and release, and tailgate lock and hinges (Section 20)

Every 12 000 miles/20 000 km or 12 months, whichever comes first (continued)
☐ Check the operation of all electrical systems (Section 21)
☐ Check the seat belts and airbag module (Section 22)
☐ Exhaust emission test (Section 23)
☐ Check the operation of the oxygen sensor (Section 24)
☐ Renew the pollen filter (Section 25)
☐ Carry out a road test (Section 26)

Every 24 000 miles/40 000 km or 2 years, whichever comes first
☐ Renew the manual transmission oil - 2.0 litre engine only (Section 27)
☐ Renew the air filter element (Section 28)
☐ Renew the spark plugs and check the ignition system components (Section 29)
☐ Renew the handset batteries (Section 30)

Every 48 000 miles/80 000 km or 4 years, whichever comes first
☐ Renew the fuel filter (Section 31)

Every 60 000 miles/100 000 km or 5 years, whichever comes first
☐ Renew the timing belt (Section 32)
☐ Renew the auxiliary drivebelt - 2.0 litre engine only (Section 33)

Every 2 years, regardless of mileage
☐ Renew the coolant/antifreeze (Section 34)
☐ Renew the brake fluid (Section 35)

Every 10 years, regardless of mileage
☐ Renew the airbag module and rotary coupler (Section 36)

Underbonnet view of a 1.6 litre petrol engine model

1 Engine oil filler cap
2 Washer fluid reservoir
3 Power steering fluid reservoir
4 Cooling system expansion tank
5 Brake fluid reservoir
6 Engine oil level dipstick
7 Engine management ECU
8 Fuel filter
9 Engine compartment fusebox
10 Charcoal canister (fuel evaporative system)
11 Front suspension upper mounting
12 Battery
13 Air cleaner
14 Ignition coil
15 Radiator
16 Top hose
17 Alternator

Underbonnet view of a 2.0 litre petrol engine model

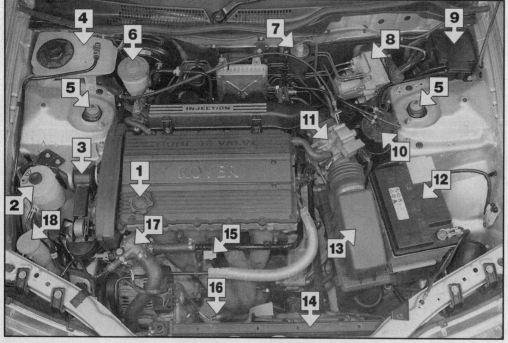

1 Engine oil filler cap
2 Power steering fluid reservoir
3 Engine mounting
4 Cooling system expansion tank
5 Front suspension strut upper mounting
6 Brake fluid reservoir
7 Fuel filter
8 ABS unit
9 Engine compartment fusebox
10 Fuel evaporative charcoal canister
11 Throttle body
12 Battery
13 Air cleaner
14 Radiator
15 Engine oil level dipstick
16 Oxygen sensor
17 Thermostat housing
18 Washer fluid reservoi

Front underbody view of a 2.0 litre petrol engine model

1 Steering track rod
2 Front suspension lower arm
3 Driveshaft
4 Front brake caliper
5 Oil filter
6 Engine mounting
7 Engine sump oil drain plug
8 Auxiliary drivebelt
9 Radiator
10 Exhaust downpipe
11 Bottom hose
12 Manual transmission
13 Steering gear
14 Gearchange rod
15 Front suspension anti-roll bar

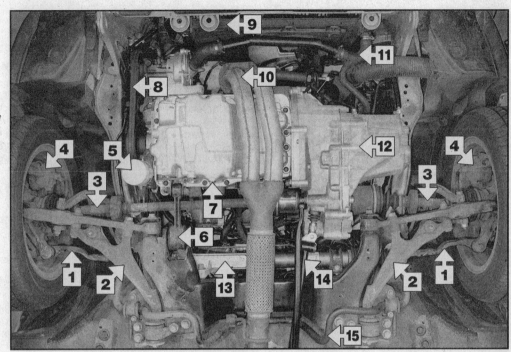

1A

Rear underbody view of a 2.0 litre petrol engine model

1 Rear suspension trailing arm
2 Handbrake cable
3 Rear suspension lower link
4 Rear suspension coil spring/strut
5 Rear suspension anti-roll bar
6 Fuel tank
7 Exhaust system
8 Rear suspension trailing arm front compensator link

1 General information

This Chapter is designed to help the home mechanic maintain his/her vehicle for safety, economy, long life and peak performance.

The Chapter contains a master maintenance schedule, followed by Sections dealing specifically with each task in the schedule. Visual checks, adjustments, component renewal and other helpful items are included. Refer to the accompanying illustrations of the engine compartment and the underside of the vehicle for the locations of the various components.

Servicing your vehicle in accordance with the mileage/time maintenance schedule and the following Sections will provide a planned maintenance programme, which should result in a long and reliable service life. This is a comprehensive plan, so maintaining some items but not others at the specified service intervals, will not produce the same results.

As you service your vehicle, you will discover that many of the procedures can - and should - be grouped together, because of the particular procedure being performed, or because of the proximity of two otherwise-unrelated components to one another. For example, if the vehicle is raised for any reason, the exhaust can be inspected at the same time as the suspension and steering components.

The first step in this maintenance programme is to prepare yourself before the actual work begins. Read through all the Sections relevant to the work to be carried out, then make a list and gather all the parts and tools required. If a problem is encountered, seek advice from a parts specialist, or a dealer service department.

2 Intensive maintenance

If, from the time the vehicle is new, the routine maintenance schedule is followed closely, and frequent checks are made of fluid levels and high-wear items, as suggested throughout this manual, the engine will be kept in relatively good running condition, and the need for additional work will be minimised.

It is possible that there will be times when the engine is running poorly due to the lack of regular maintenance. This is even more likely if a used vehicle, which has not received regular and frequent maintenance checks, is purchased. In such cases, additional work may need to be carried out, outside of the regular maintenance intervals.

If engine wear is suspected, a compression test (refer to Chapter 2A) will provide valuable information regarding the overall performance of the main internal components. Such a test can be used as a basis to decide on the extent of the work to be carried out. If, for example, a compression test indicates serious internal engine wear, conventional maintenance as described in this Chapter will not greatly improve the performance of the engine, and may prove a waste of time and money, unless extensive overhaul work is carried out first.

The following series of operations are those most often required to improve the performance of a generally poor-running engine:

Primary operations

a) Clean, inspect and test the battery (refer to "Weekly checks").
b) Check all the engine-related fluids (refer to "Weekly checks").
c) Check the condition and tension of the auxiliary drivebelts (Section 10).
d) Renew the spark plugs (Section 29).
e) Check the condition of the air filter, and renew if necessary (Section 28).
f) Renew the fuel filter (Section 31).
g) Check the condition of all hoses, and check for fluid leaks (Section 7).

If the above operations do not prove fully effective, carry out the following secondary operations:

Secondary operations

All items listed under "Primary operations", plus the following:
a) Check the charging system (refer to Chapter 5A).
b) Check the ignition system (refer to Chapter 5B).
c) Check the fuel system (refer to Chapter 4A).

Every 6000 miles/10 000 km or 6 months

3 Engine oil and filter renewal

Note: *To avoid any possibility of scalding, and to protect yourself from possible skin irritants and other harmful contaminants in used engine oils, it is advisable to wear gloves when carrying out this work.*

1 Frequent oil and filter changes are the most important preventative maintenance procedures which can be undertaken by the DIY owner. As engine oil ages, it becomes diluted and contaminated, which leads to premature engine wear.

2 Before starting this procedure, gather together all the necessary tools and materials. Also make sure that you have plenty of clean rags and newspapers handy, to mop up any spills. Ideally, the engine oil should be warm, as it will drain more easily, and more built-up sludge will be removed with it.

Caution: Take care not to touch the exhaust or any other hot parts of the engine when working under the vehicle.

3 Firmly apply the handbrake then jack up the front of the vehicle and support it on axle stands (see *"Jacking and Vehicle Support"*).

4 On 2.0 litre engines, undo the bolts securing the oil pump/filter cover to the cylinder block and sump and remove the cover from the right-hand end of the engine, noting the correct fitted locations of the spacers. Note that it may be necessary to unbolt the rear steady rod bolts and pivot it away from the sump (see Chapter 2B) in order to gain the clearance necessary to remove the cover. Remove the foam sleeve from the oil filter **(see illustrations)**.

5 On all engines, using a spanner or a suitable socket and bar, slacken the drain plug about half a turn **(see illustration)**. Position the draining container under the drain

3.4a On 2.0 litre engines, unbolt and remove the oil pump/filter cover . . .

3.4b . . . then slide off the foam sleeve from the oil filter

3.5 Removing the sump drain plug - 1.4 and 1.6 litre engines

HAYNES HINT

As the drain plug threads release, move it sharply away so the stream of oil issuing from the sump runs into the container, not up your sleeve!

3.9 If necessary, use an oil filter removal tool to unscrew the old filter (1.4 litre engine shown)

3.11 Fit the new filter and tighten it by hand only (2.0 litre engine shown)

plug, then remove the plug completely **(see Haynes Hint)**.

6 Allow some time for the oil to drain, noting that it may be necessary to reposition the container as the oil flow slows to a trickle.

7 After all the oil has drained, wipe the drain plug and the sealing washer with a clean rag. Examine the condition of the sealing washer, and renew it if it shows signs of scoring or other damage which may prevent an oil-tight seal. Clean the area around the drain plug opening, and refit the plug complete with the washer and tighten it to the specified torque.

8 Move the container into position under the oil filter on the right-hand end of the cylinder block. On 1.4 and 1.6 litre engines the filter is located at the front of the cylinder block and on 2.0 litre engines the filter is at the rear.

9 Use an oil filter removal tool to slacken the filter initially, then unscrew it by hand the rest of the way **(see illustration)**. Empty the oil from the old filter into the container.

10 Use a clean rag to remove all oil, dirt and sludge from the filter sealing area on the engine.

11 Apply a light coating of clean engine oil to the sealing ring on the new filter, then screw the filter into position. Screw the filter on until its sealing ring contacts the filter housing then tighten firmly through another half-a-turn by hand only - **do not** use any tools **(see illustration)**.

12 On 2.0 litre engines, slide the foam sleeve onto the new filter. Refit the oil pump/filter cover to the engine, ensuring the washers and spacers are correctly positioned, and securely tighten its retaining bolts. Where necessary, refit the engine steady bar and tighten its retaining bolts to their specified torque settings (see Chapter 2B).

13 Remove the old oil and all tools from under the vehicle then lower the vehicle to the ground.

14 Fill the engine through the filler hole, using the correct grade and type of oil (refer to "Weekly Checks" for details of topping-up).

Pour in half the specified quantity of oil first, then wait a few minutes for the oil to drain into the sump. Continue to add oil, a small quantity at a time, until the level is up to the lower mark on the dipstick. Adding approximately a further 1.0 litre will bring the level up to the upper mark on the dipstick.

15 Start the engine and run it for a few minutes, while checking for leaks around the oil filter seal and the sump drain plug. Note that there may be a delay of a few seconds before the low oil pressure warning light goes out when the engine is first started, as the oil circulates through the new oil filter and the engine oil galleries before the pressure builds up.

16 Stop the engine, and wait a few minutes for the oil to settle in the sump once more. With the new oil circulated and the filter now completely full, recheck the level on the dipstick, and add more oil as necessary.

17 Dispose of the used engine oil safely with reference to "General repair procedures".

1A

Every 12 000 miles/20 000 km or 12 months

4 Body corrosion check

This work should be carried out by a Rover dealer in order to validate the vehicle warranty. The work includes a thorough inspection of the vehicle paintwork and underbody for damage and corrosion.

5 Power steering fluid level check

Check the power steering fluid level as described in "Weekly checks".

6 Manual transmission oil level check

1 Position the vehicle over an inspection pit, on vehicle ramps, or jack it up, but make sure that it is level (see "Jacking and Vehicle Support"). The oil level must be checked before the car is driven, or at least 5 minutes after the engine has been switched off. If the oil is checked immediately after driving the car, some of the oil will remain distributed around the transmission components, resulting in an inaccurate level reading.

2 Remove all traces of dirt from around the filler/level plug which is located on the left-hand side of the transmission, where it is situated behind the driveshaft inner joint **(see illustrations)**. Unscrew the plug and recover the sealing washer.

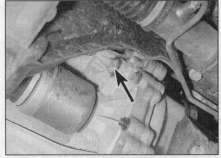

6.2a Transmission filler/level plug - 1.4 and 1.6 litre engines

6.2b Transmission filler/level plug - 2.0 litre engines

6.4 Top-up the transmission oil level using only the specified type of oil

3 The oil level should reach the lower edge of the level plug hole. A certain amount of oil will have gathered behind the filler level plug and will trickle out when it is removed; this does not necessarily mean that the level is correct.

4 To ensure that a true level is established, wait until the initial trickle stops then add oil, via the filler/level plug hole, until a new trickle of oil can be seen emerging **(see illustration)**. The level will be correct when the flow ceases. Add only good quality oil of the specified type (see "*Lubricants and fluids*").

5 Wipe the filler/level plug and the sealing washer with a clean rag. Examine the condition of the sealing washer, and renew it if it shows signs of scoring or other damage which may prevent an oil-tight seal. Clean the area around the filler/level plug opening then refit the plug, complete with the washer, tightening it to the specified torque. Where necessary, lower the car to the ground.

7 Hose and fluid leak check

1 Visually inspect the engine joint faces, gaskets and seals for any signs of water or oil leaks. Pay particular attention to the areas around the cylinder head cover, cylinder head, oil filter and sump joint faces. Bear in mind that, over a period of time, some very slight seepage from these areas is to be expected -

A leak in the cooling system will usually show up as white- or rust-coloured deposits on the area adjoining the leak

what you are really looking for is any indication of a serious leak. Should a leak be found, renew the offending gasket or oil seal by referring to the appropriate Chapters in this manual.

2 Also check the security and condition of all the engine-related pipes and hoses, and all braking system pipes and hoses and fuel lines. Ensure that all cable ties or securing clips are in place, and in good condition. Clips which are broken or missing can lead to chafing of the hoses, pipes or wiring, which could cause more serious problems in the future.

3 Carefully check the radiator hoses and heater hoses along their entire length. Renew any hose which is cracked, swollen or deteriorated. Cracks will show up better if the hose is squeezed. Pay close attention to the hose clips that secure the hoses to the cooling system components. Hose clips can pinch and puncture hoses, resulting in cooling system leaks. If the crimped-type hose clips are used, it may be a good idea to replace them with standard worm-drive clips.

4 Inspect all the cooling system components (hoses, joint faces, etc) for leaks **(see Haynes Hint)**. Where any problems are found on the system components, renew the component or gasket with reference to Chapter 3.

5 With the vehicle raised, inspect the fuel tank and filler neck for punctures, cracks and other damage. The connection between the filler neck and tank is especially critical. Sometimes a rubber filler neck or connecting hose will leak due to loose retaining clamps or deteriorated rubber.

6 Carefully check all rubber hoses and metal fuel lines leading away from the fuel tank. Check for loose connections, deteriorated hoses, crimped lines, and other damage. Pay particular attention to the vent pipes and hoses, which often loop up around the filler neck and can become blocked or crimped. Follow the lines to the front of the vehicle, carefully inspecting them all the way. Renew damaged sections as necessary. Similarly, whilst the vehicle is raised, take the opportunity to inspect all underbody brake fluid pipes and hoses.

7 From within the engine compartment, check the security of all fuel, vacuum and brake hose attachments and pipe unions, and inspect all hoses for kinks, chafing and deterioration.

8 Check the condition of the power steering fluid pipes and hoses.

8 Crankcase ventilation component check

Check the breather hoses linking the inlet manifold to the camshaft cover for signs of damage or deterioration, renewing any hose as necessary.

9 Air conditioning component check

1 The refrigerant condition and level is checked via the sightglass on the top of the receiver drier. The receiver drier is situated in the engine compartment where it is located just to the left of the radiator.

2 Start the engine then switch on the air conditioning system and allow the engine to idle for a couple of minutes whilst observing the sightglass. If the air conditioning system is operating normally then occasional bubbles should be visible through the sightglass.

3 If a constant stream of bubbles is visible, the refrigerant level is low and must be topped up. If the sightglass has become clouded or streaked, there is a fault in the system. If either condition is present, the vehicle must be taken to a Rover dealer or suitable professional refrigeration specialist for the air conditioning system to be checked further and overhauled.

4 Check the air conditioning hoses and refrigerant lines for signs of leakage. Also check the compressor and auxiliary drivebelt. Where necessary have the system checked by a refrigeration specialist.

10 Auxiliary drivebelt check and renewal

1.4 and 1.6 litre engine

Checking

1 Due to their function and material makeup, drivebelts are prone to failure after a long period of time and should therefore be inspected regularly. There are two drivebelts, one for the power steering pump and the other for the alternator and (where fitted) the air conditioning compressor.

2 Firmly apply the handbrake then jack up the front of the vehicle and support it on axle stands (see "*Jacking and Vehicle Support*"). To improve access to the belt, undo the retaining screws and fasteners and remove the plastic undercover from underneath the engine and transmission.

3 With the engine stopped, inspect the full length of the drivebelt(s) for cracks and separation of the belt plies. It will be necessary to turn the engine (using a spanner or socket and bar on the crankshaft pulley bolt) in order to move the belt(s) from the pulleys so that the belt can be inspected thoroughly. Twist the belt(s) between the pulleys so that both sides can be viewed. Also check for fraying, and glazing which gives the belt a shiny appearance. Check the pulleys for nicks, cracks, distortion and corrosion.

4 If a belt shows signs of wear or damage it must be renewed. If the belts are in good condition, check the tension as follows.

5 On models where the power steering pump belt is manually adjusted, check the tension of the power steering pump belt at the mid-point between the crankshaft and pump pulleys on the upper run of the belt. Apply a force of 98 N (equivalent to 10 kg) to the belt and check the belt deflection is within the limits given in the Specifications. If adjustment is necessary, adjust the tension as described in the drivebelt renewal procedure. **Note:** *On later models the power steering pump belt has an automatic spring-loaded tensioner and this check is not necessary.*

6 Check the tension of the alternator drivebelt in the same way. On models without air conditioning apply the specified force and check the belt deflection at the mid-point of the upper run of the belt, and on models with air conditioning apply the specified force and check the belt deflection at the mid-point of the lower run of the belt, between the crankshaft and air conditioning compressor pulleys. If adjustment is necessary, adjust the belt tension as described in the belt renewal procedure.

7 Once the belts have been checked, refit the undercover then lower the vehicle to the ground.

Power steering pump drivebelt renewal - models with a manually-adjusted tensioner

8 Firmly apply the handbrake then jack up the front of the vehicle and support it on axle stands (see *"Jacking and Vehicle Support"*). To improve access to the belt, undo the retaining screws and fasteners and remove the plastic undercover from underneath the engine and transmission.

9 Slacken the tensioner pulley clamp bolt nut by a couple of turns then unscrew the adjuster bolt to release the belt tension **(see illustrations)**. Slip the belt from its pulleys and remove it from the vehicle.

10 Manoeuvre the belt into position, routing it correctly around the pulleys; if the original belt is being fitted use the marks made prior to removal to ensure it is fitted the correct way around. Tension the belt by rotating the adjuster bolt and check the tension as follows.

11 Apply a force of 98 N (equivalent to 10 kg) to the belt at the mid-point of the upper run of the belt and check the belt deflection is within the limits given in the Specifications. Note that the Rover definition of a used belt is one that has been used for more than 5 minutes. Position the pulley as required by rotating the adjuster bolt then tighten the pulley clamp bolt nut to the specified torque.

12 Start the engine and turn the steering from lock-to-lock a few times. If a new belt has been fitted, run the engine for at least 5 minutes to allow the belt to settle in position.

13 Stop the engine then recheck and, if necessary, adjust the belt tension as described in paragraph 11.

14 Once the belt tension is correct, refit the undercover and lower the vehicle to the ground.

10.9a On 1.4 and 1.6 litre engines with a manually-adjusted tensioner, slacken the tensioner pulley clamp bolt nut . . .

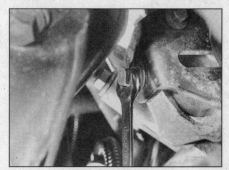

10.9b . . . and slacken the adjuster bolt to release the drivebelt tension

Power steering pump drivebelt renewal - models with an automatic tensioner

15 Firmly apply the handbrake then jack up the front of the vehicle and support it on axle stands (see *"Jacking and Vehicle Support"*). To improve access to the belt, undo the retaining screws and fasteners and remove the plastic undercover from underneath the engine and transmission.

16 Using a suitable spanner or socket fitted to the tensioner pulley backplate hexagonal section, lever the tensioner away from the belt until there is sufficient slack to enable the belt to be slipped off from the pulleys. Carefully release the tensioner pulley until it is against its stop then remove the belt from the vehicle.

17 Manoeuvre the belt into position, routing it correctly around the pulleys; if the original belt is being fitted use the marks made prior to removal to ensure it is fitted the correct way around.

18 Lever the tensioner roller back against is spring, and seat the belt on the pulleys. Ensure the belt is centrally located on all pulleys then slowly release the tensioner pulley until the belt is correctly tensioned.

Caution: Do not allow the tensioner to spring back and stress the belt.

19 Refit the undercover then lower the vehicle to the ground.

Alternator drivebelt renewal - models without air conditioning

20 Remove the power steering pump

drivebelt as described in this Section.

21 Slacken and remove the bolts securing the engine/transmission right-hand lower mounting to the vehicle body and the two bolts securing the mounting bracket to the engine. Manoeuvre the mounting and bracket assembly out of position.

22 Slacken the alternator upper and lower mounting bolts then release the belt tension using the adjuster bolt on the lower mounting bracket **(see illustrations)**. Slip the drivebelt off from the pulleys and remove it from the engine.

23 Manoeuvre the belt into position, routing it correctly around the pulleys; if the original belt is being fitted use the marks made prior to removal to ensure it is fitted the correct way around. Tension the belt by rotating the adjuster bolt and check the tension as follows.

24 Apply a force of 98 N (equivalent to 10 kg) to the belt at the mid-point of the upper run of the belt and check the belt deflection is within the limits given in the Specifications. Position the alternator as required by rotating the adjuster bolt then tighten the alternator mounting bolts to the specified torque.

25 Refit the right-hand lower mounting assembly to the engine and tighten its mounting bolts to their specified torque settings.

26 Refit the power steering pump belt as described in this Section then start the engine and allow it to idle for a few minutes to allow the belts to settle in position.

10.22a On 1.4 and 1.6 litre engines without air conditioning, slacken the alternator upper . . .

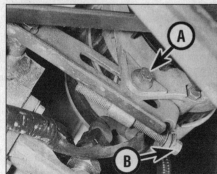

10.22b . . . and lower (A) bolts then slacken the adjuster bolt (B) to release the belt tension

1A

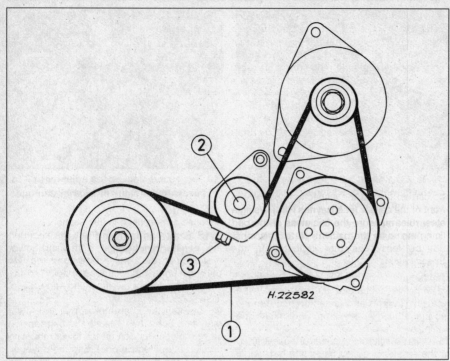

10.31 Alternator drivebelt adjustment - 1.4 and 1.6 litre engines with air conditioning

1 *Drivebelt tension*
   checking point

2 *Tensioner pulley clamp*
   bolt nut

3 *Adjuster bolt*

27 Stop the engine then recheck and, if necessary, adjust the belt tension as described in paragraph 24. Also check the power steering pump belt tension (where necessary).
28 Once the belt tensions are correctly set, refit the undercover and lower the vehicle to the ground.

Alternator drivebelt renewal - models with air conditioning

29 Remove the power steering pump drivebelt as described in this Section.
30 Slacken and remove the bolts securing the engine/transmission right-hand lower mounting to the vehicle body and the two bolts securing the mounting bracket to the engine. Manoeuvre the mounting and bracket assembly out of position.
31 Slacken the tensioner pulley clamp bolt nut by a couple of turns then unscrew the adjuster bolt to release the belt tension **(see illustration)**. Slip the belt from its pulleys and remove it from the vehicle.
32 Manoeuvre the belt into position, routing it correctly around the pulleys; if the original belt is being fitted use the marks made prior to removal to ensure it is fitted the correct way around. Tension the belt by rotating the adjuster bolt and check the tension as follows.
33 Apply a force of 98 N (equivalent to 10 kg) to the belt at the mid-point of the lower run of the belt and check the belt deflection is within the limits given in the Specifications. Position the tensioner pulley as required by rotating the adjuster bolt then tighten the pulley clamp bolt nut to the specified torque.

34 Refit the right-hand lower mounting assembly to the engine and tighten its mounting bolts to their specified torque settings.
35 Refit the power steering pump drivebelt as described in this Section then start the engine and allow it to idle for a few minutes to allow the belts to settle in position.
36 Stop the engine then recheck and, if necessary, adjust the belt tension as described in paragraph 33. Also check the power steering pump belt tension (where necessary).
37 Once the belt tensions are correctly set, refit the undercover and lower the vehicle to the ground.

2.0 litre engine

Checking

38 Due to its function and material makeup, the drivebelt is prone to failure after a long period of time and should therefore be inspected regularly.
39 Firmly apply the handbrake then jack up the front of the vehicle and support it on axle stands (see "*Jacking and Vehicle Support*"). To improve access to the belt, undo the retaining screws and fasteners and remove the plastic undercover from underneath the engine and transmission.
40 To gain access to the crankshaft pulley, undo the bolts securing the oil pump/filter cover to the cylinder block and sump and remove the cover from the right-hand end of the engine, noting the correct fitted locations

of the spacers. Note that it may be necessary to unbolt the rear steady rod bolts and pivot it away from the sump (see Chapter 2B) in order to gain the clearance necessary to remove the cover.
41 With the engine stopped, inspect the full length of the drivebelt for cracks and separation of the belt plies. It will be necessary to turn the engine (using a spanner or socket and bar on the crankshaft pulley bolt) in order to move the belt from the pulleys so that the belt can be inspected thoroughly. Twist the belt between the pulleys so that both sides can be viewed. Also check for fraying, and glazing which gives the belt a shiny appearance. Check the pulleys for nicks, cracks, distortion and corrosion.
42 If a belt shows signs of wear or damage it must be renewed. The belt tensioner is spring-loaded and therefore the belt tension is automatically adjusted and does not require checking.
43 On completion, refit the oil pump/filter cover to the engine, ensuring the washers and spacers are correctly positioned, and securely tighten its retaining bolts. Where necessary, refit the engine steady bar and tighten its retaining bolts to their specified torque settings (see Chapter 2B). Refit the undercover then lower the vehicle to the ground.

Renewal

44 Carry out the operations described in paragraphs 39 and 40.
45 Prior to removal make a note of the correct routing of the belt around the various pulleys. If the belt is to be re-used, also mark the direction of rotation on the belt to ensure the belt is refitted the same way around.
46 Using a suitable spanner or socket fitted to the tensioner pulley centre bolt, lever the tensioner away from the belt until there is sufficient slack to enable the belt to be slipped off from the pulleys **(see illustration)**. Carefully release the tensioner pulley until it is against its stop then remove the belt from the vehicle.
47 Manoeuvre the belt into position, routing it correctly around the pulleys; if the original belt is being fitted use the marks made prior to removal to ensure it is fitted the correct way around.

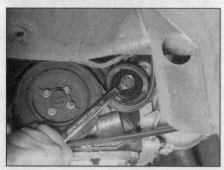

10.46 Pivot the tensioner pulley away from the auxiliary drivebelt then slip the belt off the pulleys

48 Lever the tensioner roller back against is spring, and seat the belt on the pulleys. Ensure the belt is centrally located on all pulleys then slowly release the tensioner pulley until the belt is correctly tensioned.
Caution: Do not allow the tensioner to spring back and stress the belt.
49 On completion, refit the oil pump/filter cover to the engine, ensuring the washers and spacers are correctly positioned, and securely tighten its retaining bolts. Where necessary, refit the engine steady bar and tighten its retaining bolts to their specified torque settings (see Chapter 2B). Refit the undercover then lower the vehicle to the ground.

11 Exhaust system check

1 Park the vehicle on a level surface and switch off the engine. Chock the front wheels and select first gear, then raise the rear of the vehicle and rest it securely on axle stands (see "*Jacking and Vehicle Support*").
2 With the engine cold (wait at least an hour after switching off the engine), check the complete exhaust system from the engine to the end of the tailpipe.
3 Check the exhaust pipes and connections for evidence of leaks, severe corrosion and damage. Make sure that all brackets and mountings are in good condition, and that all relevant nuts and bolts are tight **(see illustration)**. Leakage at any of the joints or in other parts of the system will usually show up as a black, sooty stain in the vicinity of the leak.
4 Rattles and vibrations can often be traced to the exhaust system. Tap the silencer units with a soft mallet and listen for noises caused by corroded or displaced baffle material.
Caution: Do not strike the catalytic converter, as this may damage the ceramic block inside.
5 Carefully rock the pipes and silencers from side to side on their mountings. If the components are able to come into contact with the body or suspension parts, look for broken or worn rubber mountings.
6 Extra clearance can be gained by slackening the clamps between adjacent sections of the exhaust pipe to loosen the joints (where possible - refer to Chapter 4A) and twisting the pipes as necessary to provide the additional clearance. Re-tighten the clamps on completion.

12 Front/rear brake pad and disc check

1 Note that the inner front brake pads are fitted with audible warning wear indicators which emit a high pitched 'scraping' sound when the linings are worn to the minimum thickness. The indicators consist of a bent piece of metal attached to the pad which contacts the disc when the linings are worn and set up a vibration when the brakes are applied. Although this will warn the driver of worn brake pads, a visual check must be carried out at the required interval.
2 Firmly apply the handbrake, then jack up the front of the vehicle and support it securely on axle stands (see "*Jacking and Vehicle Support*"). Remove the front roadwheels.
3 For a quick check, the pad thickness can be carried out via the inspection hole on the front of the caliper **(see Haynes Hint)**. Using a steel rule, measure the thickness of the pad lining including the backing plate. This must not be less than that indicated in the Specifications.
4 The view through the caliper inspection hole gives a rough indication of the state of the brake pads. For a comprehensive check, the brake pads should be removed and cleaned. The operation of the caliper can then also be checked, and the condition of the brake disc itself can be fully examined on both sides. Chapter 9 contains a detailed description of how the brake disc should be checked for wear and/or damage.
5 If any pad's friction material is worn to the specified thickness or less, *all four pads must be renewed as a set*. Refer to Chapter 9 for details.
6 On completion, refit the roadwheels and lower the vehicle to the ground.

13 Rear brake shoe and drum check

Refer to the detailed description given in Chapter 9.

14 Brake pipe and hose check

1 Jack up the front and rear of the vehicle and support it on axle stands (see "*Jacking and Vehicle Support*").
2 Check the security and condition of all the braking system pipes and hoses. In particular, check the flexible hoses for signs of cracking by carefully bending them at several points along their lengths. Check the rigid brake lines for corrosion, especially at exposed locations on the underbody.
3 Ensure that all hose and pipe securing clips are in place, and in good condition.
4 Renewal of the brake pipes and hoses is described in Chapter 9.
5 On completion lower the car to the ground.

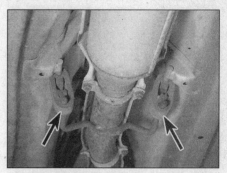

11.3 Check the exhaust mountings (arrowed) for signs of wear or damage

15 Brake caliper and wheel cylinder check

1 Jack up the front and rear of the vehicle and support it on axle stands (see "*Jacking and Vehicle Support*"). Remove the front and rear wheels.
2 For a thorough check of the front brake calipers, remove the brake pads as described in Chapter 9. Carefully clean the brake pad locations in the caliper body and mounting bracket taking care not to inhale the brake dust as it may contain asbestos which is a health hazard. Check the caliper for signs of brake fluid leakage. If this is evident at the flexible hose connection, renew the copper washers with reference to Chapter 9. If leakage is evident at the piston, renew the internal sealing ring or renew the caliper complete with reference to Chapter 9.
3 To check the wheel cylinders, remove the drums with reference to Chapter 9, then clean away dust and dirt from the brake shoes and wheel cylinder. Check the wheel cylinders for signs of brake fluid leakage by temporarily lifting the rubber boots with a screwdriver. If evident, renew the wheel cylinder complete as described in Chapter 9.

1A

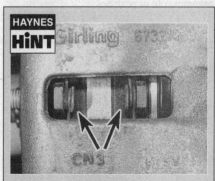

For a quick check, the thickness of friction material remaining on the brake pads can be measured through the aperture in the caliper body

16.4 Check for wear in the hub bearings by grasping the wheel and trying to rock it

16 Suspension and steering check

Front suspension and steering check

1 Raise the front of the vehicle, and securely support it on axle stands (see "*Jacking and Vehicle Support*").

2 Visually inspect the balljoint dust covers and the steering rack-and-pinion gaiters for splits, chafing or deterioration. Any wear of these components will cause loss of lubricant, together with dirt and water entry, resulting in rapid deterioration of the balljoints or steering gear.

3 On vehicles with power steering, check the fluid hoses for chafing or deterioration, and the pipe and hose unions for fluid leaks. Also check for signs of fluid leakage under pressure from the steering gear rubber gaiters, which would indicate failed fluid seals within the steering gear.

4 Grasp the roadwheel at the 12 o'clock and 6 o'clock positions, and try to rock it **(see illustration)**. Very slight free play may be felt, but if the movement is appreciable, further investigation is necessary to determine the source. Continue rocking the wheel while an assistant depresses the footbrake. If the movement is now eliminated or significantly reduced, it is likely that the hub bearings are at fault. If the free play is still evident with the footbrake depressed, then there is wear in the suspension joints or mountings.

18.1 Checking the driveshaft outer CV joint rubber gaiter

5 Now grasp the wheel at the 9 o'clock and 3 o'clock positions, and try to rock it as before. Any movement felt now may again be caused by wear in the hub bearings or the steering track-rod balljoints. If the outer balljoint is worn, the visual movement will be obvious. If the inner joint is suspect, it can be felt by placing a hand over the rack-and-pinion rubber gaiter and gripping the track-rod. If the wheel is now rocked, movement will be felt at the inner joint if wear has taken place.

6 Using a large screwdriver or flat bar, check for wear in the suspension mounting bushes by levering between the relevant suspension component and its attachment point. Some movement is to be expected, as the mountings are made of rubber, but excessive wear should be obvious. Also check the condition of any visible rubber bushes, looking for splits, cracks or contamination of the rubber.

7 With the car standing on its wheels, have an assistant turn the steering wheel back and forth, about an eighth of a turn each way. There should be very little, if any, lost movement between the steering wheel and roadwheels. If this is not the case, closely observe the joints and mountings previously described. In addition, check the steering column universal joints for wear, and also check the rack-and-pinion steering gear itself.

Rear suspension check

8 Chock the front wheels, then jack up the rear of the vehicle and support securely on axle stands (see "*Jacking and Vehicle Support*").

9 Working as described previously for the front suspension, check the rear hub bearings, the suspension bushes and the strut/shock absorber mountings for wear.

Shock absorber check

10 Check for any signs of fluid leakage around the front and rear shock absorbers, or from the rubber gaiter around the piston rod. Should any fluid be noticed, the shock absorber is defective internally, and should be renewed. **Note:** *Shock absorbers should always be renewed in pairs on the same axle.*

11 The efficiency of the shock absorber may be checked by bouncing the vehicle at each corner. Generally speaking, the body will return to its normal position and stop after being depressed. If it rises and returns on a rebound, the shock absorber is probably suspect. Also examine the shock absorber upper and lower mountings for any signs of wear.

17 Wheel bearing check

1 Excessive wear of the wheel bearings will normally be evident as a rough-sounding noise from the offending wheel as the car is

being driven. If a front wheel bearing is worn, the noise may only be evident on corners.

2 To check for worn wheel bearings, jack up the front or rear of the car and support on axle stands (see "*Jacking and Vehicle Support*"). Spin the wheel by hand and listen for any roughness from the wheel bearing.

18 Driveshaft and gaiter check

1 With the vehicle raised and securely supported on stands (see "*Jacking and Vehicle Support*"), turn the steering onto full lock then slowly rotate the roadwheel. Inspect the condition of the outer constant velocity (CV) joint rubber gaiters while squeezing the gaiters to open out the folds **(see illustration)**. Check for signs of cracking, splits or deterioration of the rubber which may allow the grease to escape and lead to water and grit entry into the joint. Also check the security and condition of the retaining clips. Repeat these checks on the inner CV joints. If any damage or deterioration is found, the gaiters should be renewed as described in Chapter 8.

2 At the same time check the general condition of the CV joints themselves by first holding the driveshaft and attempting to rotate the wheel. Repeat this check by holding the inner joint and attempting to rotate the driveshaft. Any appreciable movement indicates wear in the joints, wear in the drive-shaft splines or loose driveshaft retaining nut.

19 Handbrake check

1 The handbrake should be capable of holding the parked vehicle stationary, even on steep slopes, when applied with moderate force. The mechanism should be firm and positive in feel with no trace of stiffness or sponginess from the cables and should release immediately the handbrake lever is released. If the mechanism is faulty in any of these respects then it must be checked immediately.

2 To check the handbrake setting, first apply the footbrake firmly several times to establish correct shoe-to-drum clearance. Applying normal, moderate pressure, pull the handbrake lever to the fully-applied position whilst counting the number of clicks emitted from the handbrake ratchet mechanism. If adjustment is correct, there should be 6 to 10 clicks before the handbrake is fully applied. If this is not the case, then adjustment is required as described in Chapter 9.

20 Hinge and lock lubrication

1 Work around the vehicle and lubricate the hinges of the bonnet, doors and tailgate/bootlid with a light machine oil. Also lubricate the bonnet lock located on the engine compartment front crossmember.
2 Lightly lubricate the bonnet release mechanism and exposed section of the inner cable with a smear of grease.

21 Electrical system check

1 Check the operation of all electrical equipment, ie, lights, direction indicators, horn, wash/wipe system etc. Refer to the appropriate Sections of Chapter 12 for details if any of the circuits are found to be inoperative.
2 Visually check all accessible wiring connectors, harnesses and retaining clips for security, and for signs of chafing or damage. Rectify any faults found.

22 Seat belt and airbag check

1 Check the webbing of each belt for signs of fraying, cuts or other damage, pulling the belt out to its full extent to check its entire length.
2 Check the operation of the belt buckles by pulling the belt hard to ensure that it remains locked in position.
3 Check the inertia reel retractor mechanism by pulling out the belt to the halfway point and jerking hard. The mechanism must lock immediately to prevent any further unreeling but must allow free movement during normal driving.
4 Ensure that all belt mounting bolts are securely tightened. Note that the bolts are shouldered so that the belt anchor points are free to rotate.
5 If there is any sign of damage, or any doubt about a belt's condition, then it must be renewed. If the vehicle has been involved in a collision, then any belt in use at the time must be renewed as a matter of course and all other belts checked carefully.
6 The airbag/SRS warning light on the instrument panel should extinguish 3 seconds after the ignition switch is turned to position "II". If this is not the case, have the system checked by a Rover dealer. No attempt should be made to carry out repairs to the airbag components. Note that the airbag unit and slip ring must be renewed every ten years, regardless of condition.

23 Exhaust emission check

1 Rover specify that this check should be carried out annually or every 12 000 miles. The check involves checking the engine management system operation by plugging an electronic tester into the system diagnostic socket to check the electronic control module (ECM) memory for faults (see Chapter 4A).
2 In reality, if the vehicle is running correctly and the engine management warning light in the instrument panel is functioning normally, then this check need not be carried out. On cars over 3 years old, the exhaust emissions will be checked every year during the MOT test.

24 Oxygen sensor check

1 Rover specify that the operation of the oxygen sensor should be checked annually. The check involves the use of a special electronic tester which is plugged into the system diagnostic socket (see Chapter 4A).
2 In reality, if the vehicle is running correctly and the engine management warning light in the instrument panel is functioning normally, then this check need not be carried out.

25 Pollen filter renewal

1 The pollen filter (if fitted) is located beneath the left-hand side of the facia, in the heater inlet system. To remove the filter, first remove the glovebox as described in Chapter 11.
2 Remove the felt trim panel from under the heater inlet duct, then release the cover from the bottom of the pollen filter housing.
3 Lower the pollen filter from its housing.
4 Fit the new filter using a reversal of the removal procedure.

26 Road test

Instruments and electrical equipment

1 Check the operation of all instruments and electrical equipment.

2 Make sure that all instruments read correctly, and switch on all electrical equipment in turn, to check that it functions properly.

Steering and suspension

3 Check for any abnormalities in the steering, suspension, handling or road "feel".
4 Drive the vehicle, and check that there are no unusual vibrations or noises.
5 Check that the steering feels positive, with no excessive "sloppiness", or roughness, and check for any suspension noises when cornering and driving over bumps.

Drivetrain

6 Check the performance of the engine, clutch, transmission and driveshafts.
7 Listen for any unusual noises from the engine, clutch and transmission.
8 Make sure that the engine runs smoothly when idling, and that there is no hesitation when accelerating.
9 Check that, where applicable, the clutch action is smooth and progressive, that the drive is taken up smoothly, and that the pedal travel is not excessive. Also listen for any noises when the clutch pedal is depressed.
10 Check that all gears can be engaged smoothly without noise, and that the gear lever action is not abnormally vague or "notchy".
11 Listen for a metallic clicking sound from the front of the vehicle, as the vehicle is driven slowly in a circle with the steering on full-lock. Carry out this check in both directions. If a clicking noise is heard, this indicates wear in a driveshaft joint (see Chapter 8).

Check the operation and performance of the braking system

12 Make sure that the vehicle does not pull to one side when braking, and that the wheels do not lock prematurely when braking hard.
13 Check that there is no vibration through the steering when braking.
14 Check that the handbrake operates correctly, without excessive movement of the lever, and that it holds the vehicle stationary on a slope.
15 Test the operation of the brake servo unit as follows. Depress the footbrake four or five times to exhaust the vacuum, then start the engine. As the engine starts, there should be a noticeable "give" in the brake pedal as vacuum builds up. Allow the engine to run for at least two minutes, and then switch it off. If the brake pedal is now depressed again, it should be possible to detect a hiss from the servo as the pedal is depressed. After about four or five applications, no further hissing should be heard, and the pedal should feel considerably harder.

1A

28.2 Release the retaining clips . . .

28.3 . . . then lift up the lid and withdraw the filter element from the air cleaner housing

28.4 Wipe clean the housing then seat the new filter element in position

Every 24 000 miles/40 000 km or 2 years

27 Manual transmission oil renewal - 2.0 litre engine

Refer to Chapter 7, Section 2.

28 Air filter element renewal

1 The air filter is located in the engine compartment, on the left-hand end of the engine.
2 Release the retaining clips, and lift the air

filter cover sufficiently to enable removal of the filter element from its housing **(see illustration)**.
3 Lift out the filter element, noting which way up it is fitted, then wipe out the casing and the cover **(see illustration)**.
4 Fit the new filter, making sure it is the correct way up, and seat it in the housing **(see illustration)**. Locate the cover on the housing and secure it in position with all the retaining clips.

29 Spark plug renewal and ignition system check

Spark plug renewal

1 The correct functioning of the spark plugs is vital for the correct running and efficiency of the engine. It is essential that the plugs fitted are appropriate for the engine; suitable types are specified at the beginning of this Chapter, or in the vehicle's Owner's Handbook. If the correct type is used and the engine is in good condition, the spark plugs should not need attention between scheduled replacement intervals. Spark plug cleaning is rarely necessary, and should not be attempted unless specialised equipment is available, as damage can easily be caused to the firing ends.

2 On 16-valve engines, undo the retaining screws and remove the spark plug cover from the top of the engine **(see illustration)**.
3 On all engines, if the marks on the original-equipment spark plug (HT) leads cannot be seen, mark the leads to correspond to the cylinder the lead serves. Pull the leads from the plugs by gripping the end fitting, not the lead, otherwise the lead connection may be fractured **(see illustrations)**.
4 It is advisable to remove the dirt from the spark plug recesses using a clean brush, vacuum cleaner or compressed air before removing the plugs, to prevent dirt dropping into the cylinders.
5 Unscrew the plugs from the cylinder head using a spark plug spanner, suitable box spanner or a deep socket and extension bar **(see illustration)**. Keep the socket aligned with the spark plug - if it is forcibly moved to one side, the ceramic insulator may be broken off. As each plug is removed, examine it as follows.
6 Examination of the spark plugs will give a good indication of the condition of the engine. If the insulator nose of the spark plug is clean and white, with no deposits, this is indicative of a weak mixture or too hot a plug (a hot plug transfers heat away from the electrode slowly, a cold plug transfers heat away quickly).
7 If the tip and insulator nose are covered with hard black-looking deposits, then this is

29.2 On 16-valve engines, undo the retaining screws and remove the spark plug cover (2.0 litre engine shown)

29.3a On 1.4 litre 8-valve the spark plugs are situated at the front of the cylinder head

29.3b Disconnect the plug caps and position them clear of the spark plugs

29.5 Unscrew the spark plugs using a socket and extension bar

29.10a Measure the spark plug electrode gap using a feeler blade . . .

29.10b . . . or a wire gauge . . .

29.10c . . . and if necessary adjust the gap by bending the outer electrode

indicative that the mixture is too rich. Should the plug be black and oily, then it is likely that the engine is fairly worn, as well as the mixture being too rich.

8 If the insulator nose is covered with light tan to greyish-brown deposits, then the mixture is correct and it is likely that the engine is in good condition.

9 The spark plug electrode gap is of considerable importance as, if it is too large or too small, the size of the spark and its efficiency will be seriously impaired. The gap should be set to the value given in the Specifications at the beginning of this Chapter.

10 To set the gap, measure it with a feeler blade and then bend open, or closed, the outer plug electrode until the correct gap is achieved. The centre electrode should never be bent, as this may crack the insulator and cause plug failure, if nothing worse. If using feeler blades, the gap is correct when the appropriate-size blade is a firm sliding fit **(see illustrations)**.

11 Special spark plug electrode gap adjusting tools are available from most motor accessory shops, or from some spark plug manufacturers.

12 Before fitting the spark plugs, check that the threaded connector sleeves are tight, and that the plug exterior surfaces and threads are clean **(see Haynes Hint)**.

13 Remove the rubber hose (if used), and tighten the plug to the specified torque using the spark plug socket and a torque wrench. Refit the remaining spark plugs in the same manner.

14 Connect the HT leads in their correct order. Where necessary, refit the spark plug cover to the top of the engine and securely tighten its retaining screws.

Ignition system check

1.4 and 1.6 litre engine

15 Label the HT leads (if the original marks are not visible) and disconnect them from the spark plugs, as described in the previous sub-section.

16 Check the inside of the end fitting of each lead for signs of corrosion, which will look like a white crusty powder. Remove any such deposits with a stiff brush, or fine grade emery

paper. Push the end fitting back onto the spark plug, ensuring that it is a tight fit on the plug. If this is not the case, remove the lead again and use long-nosed pliers to carefully shape the metal connector inside the end fitting, until it fits securely on the end of the spark plug.

17 Using a clean rag sprayed with a little penetrating oil, wipe the entire length of the lead to remove any built-up dirt and grease. Once the lead is clean, check for burns, cracks and other damage.

Caution: Do not bend or kink the lead excessively, or stretch the lead lengthwise, as this may break the conductors inside the lead.

18 Disconnect the other end of the lead from the distributor cap. Again, pull only on the end fitting. Check for corrosion and security as described earlier. If an ohmmeter is available, check the resistance of the lead by connecting the meter between the spark plug end of the lead and the segment inside the distributor cap. Refit the lead securely on completion.

It is very often difficult to insert spark plugs into their holes without cross-threading them. To avoid this possibility, fit a short length of rubber hose over the end of the spark plug. The flexible hose acts as a universal joint to help align the plug with the plug hole. Should the plug begin to cross-thread, the hose will slip on the spark plug, preventing thread damage to the aluminium cylinder head.

19 Check the remaining leads one at a time, in the same manner.

20 If new HT leads are required, purchase a set for your specific car and engine. Renew the leads one at a time to ensure the firing order is preserved.

21 With reference to Chapter 5B, remove the distributor cap. Wipe it clean, and carefully inspect it inside and out for signs of cracks, black carbon tracks (tracking) and worn, burned or loose contacts.

22 Check that the cap centre carbon brush is in good condition and is free to move against spring pressure, allowing it to make good contact with the top of the rotor arm.

23 Inspect the metal terminals on the inside the cap. Surface corrosion and light deposits can be removed with fine-grade emery paper, but more serious wear will mean the renewal of the distributor cap.

24 Inspect the rotor arm closely. Light deposits can be removed with fine-grade emery paper, but if the contacts are badly pitted, the rotor arm should be renewed. If the rotor arm is to be removed a new retaining screw will be needed; the screw should be replaced whenever it is disturbed.

1A

> **HAYNES HiNT** *When fitting a new distributor cap, transfer the HT leads from the old cap to the new one in sequence, one at a time, so that the firing order is preserved.*

2.0 litre engine

25 Check the HT leads as described in paragraphs 15 to 20. Ignore all references to the distributor, the HT leads are connected directly to the ignition HT coil.

30 Handset battery renewal

1 The alarm system handset contains a battery which should last for approximately 3 years. When it requires renewal, the indicator warning lights on the front doors will flash rapidly before the doors are opened and the operating range will reduce considerably.

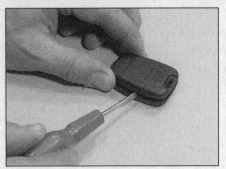

30.2a Carefully insert a screwdriver into the slot . . .

30.2b . . . and prise off the handset cover

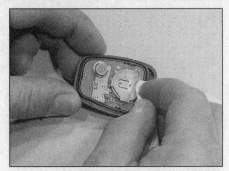

30.3 Ensure the new battery is installed the right way around

2 To renew the battery, use a small screwdriver or coin to prise off the handset cover then remove the battery from its clip **(see illustrations)**.

3 Press each button for a minimum of 5 seconds to drain any remaining power from the handset, then fit the new battery taking care not to touch the contact surfaces with the fingers. Make sure the new battery is correctly located with the positive (+) side facing upwards **(see illustration)**.

4 Press on the cover, then unlock the car using the key and operate the lock button on the handset at least four times.

Every 48 000 miles/80 000 km or 4 years

31 Fuel filter renewal

⚠️ **Warning: Refer to the warnings given in the "Safety first!" Section at the start of this manual before carrying out the following procedure.**

1 The fuel filter is mounted on the engine compartment bulkhead.

2 Depressurise the fuel system as described in Chapter 4A and disconnect the outlet union from the top of the filter **(see illustration)**.

3 Retain the lower end of the filter with an open-ended spanner then slacken the union nut and disconnect the inlet pipe from the filter. Mop up all the spilt fuel and safely dispose of the fuel-soaked rags.

4 Release the retaining clip then slide the fuel filter upwards and out of its mounting bracket, noting which way around the filter is fitted **(see illustration)**.

5 Slide the new filter into position in the mounting bracket ensuring the arrow on the filter, which indicates the direction of fuel flow, is pointing upwards **(see illustration)**.

6 Ensure the filter is clipped securely in position then reconnect the inlet and outlet fuel pipes. Hold the filter with an open-ended spanner and tighten the fuel pipe union nuts to the specified torque.

7 Start the engine and check the fuel pipe unions for signs of leakage. If leakage is evident, stop the engine immediately and rectify the problem without delay.

31.2 Depressurise the fuel system and disconnect the outlet pipe from the filter

31.4 Release the retaining clip and lift the filter out of the mounting bracket

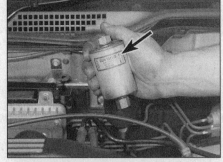

31.5 Ensure the new filter is installed with the arrow (arrowed) pointing upwards

Every 60 000 miles/100 000 km or 5 years

32 Timing belt renewal

Refer to the Chapter 2A (1.4 and 1.6 litre engine) or 2B (2.0 litre engine).

33 Auxiliary drivebelt renewal - 2.0 litre engine

Renew the drivebelt as described in Section 10.

Every 2 years, regardless of mileage

34 Coolant/antifreeze renewal

Cooling system draining

 Warning: Wait until the engine is cold before starting this procedure. Do not allow antifreeze to come in contact with your skin, or with the painted surfaces of the vehicle. Rinse off spills immediately with plenty of water. Never leave antifreeze lying around in an open container, or in a puddle in the driveway or on the garage floor. Children and pets are attracted by its sweet smell, but antifreeze can be fatal if ingested.

1 With the engine completely cold, remove the expansion tank filler cap. Turn the cap anti-clockwise, wait until any pressure remaining in the system is released, then unscrew it and lift it off.

2 Where applicable remove the undershield, then position a suitable container beneath the left-hand side of the radiator.

3 Position the heater temperature control on its maximum setting.

4 On 1.4 and 1.6 litre engines, remove the air cleaner as described in Chapter 4A for access to the radiator bottom hose connection.

5 Loosen the clip and disconnect the bottom hose from the radiator, and allow the coolant to drain into the container.

6 When the flow of coolant stops, refit the bottom hose and tighten the clip.

7 If the coolant has been drained for a reason other than renewal, then provided it is clean and less than two years old, it can be re-used, though this is not recommended.

Cooling system flushing

8 If coolant renewal has been neglected, or if the antifreeze mixture has become diluted, then in time, the cooling system may gradually lose efficiency, as the coolant passages become restricted due to rust, scale deposits, and other sediment. The cooling system efficiency can be restored by flushing the system clean.

9 The radiator should be flushed independently of the engine, to avoid unnecessary contamination.

Radiator flushing

10 Disconnect the top and bottom hoses and any other relevant hoses from the radiator, with reference to Chapter 3.

11 Insert a garden hose into the radiator top inlet. Direct a flow of clean water through the radiator, and continue flushing until clean water emerges from the radiator bottom outlet.

12 If after a reasonable period, the water still does not run clear, the radiator can be flushed with a good proprietary cleaning agent. It is important that the manufacturer's instructions are followed carefully. If the contamination is particularly bad, insert the hose in the radiator bottom outlet, and reverse-flush the radiator.

Engine flushing

13 Remove the thermostat as described in Chapter 3 then, if the radiator top hose has been disconnected from the engine, temporarily reconnect the hose.

14 With the top and bottom hoses disconnected from the radiator, insert a garden hose into the radiator top hose. Direct a clean flow of water through the engine, and continue flushing until clean water emerges from the radiator bottom hose.

15 On completion of flushing, refit the thermostat and reconnect the hoses with reference to Chapter 3.

Cooling system filling

16 Before attempting to fill the cooling system, make sure that all hoses and clips are in good condition, and that the clips are tight. Note that an antifreeze mixture must be used all year round, to prevent corrosion of the engine components. Make sure the heater controls are set to maximum heat.

17 Remove the expansion tank filler cap. On 1.4 and 1.6 litre engines, unscrew the bleed screw from the coolant rail on the right-hand end of the cylinder head.

18 Slowly fill the system until bubble-free coolant comes out of the bleed screw on 1.4 and 1.6 litre engines, then tighten the screw.

19 Fill the cooling system until the coolant reaches the MAX mark on the expansion tank, then refit and tighten the filler cap.

20 On 1.4 and 1.6 litre engines, refit the air cleaner as described in Chapter 4A.

21 Refit the undershield beneath the engine compartment.

22 Start the engine, and allow it to run until it reaches normal operating temperature (until the cooling fan cuts in and out). **Do not** operate the air conditioning at this stage.

23 Stop the engine, and allow it to cool, then re-check the coolant level with reference to *"Weekly checks"*. Top-up the level if necessary and refit the expansion tank filler cap.

Antifreeze mixture

24 The antifreeze should always be renewed at the specified intervals. This is necessary not only to maintain the antifreeze properties, but also to prevent corrosion which would otherwise occur as the corrosion inhibitors become progressively less effective.

25 Always use an ethylene-glycol based antifreeze which is suitable for use in mixed-metal cooling systems. The quantity of antifreeze and levels of protection are given in the Specifications.

26 Before adding antifreeze, the cooling system should be completely drained, preferably flushed, and all hoses checked for condition and security.

27 After filling with antifreeze, a label should be attached to the expansion tank, stating the type and concentration of antifreeze used, and the date installed. Any subsequent topping-up should be made with the same type and concentration of antifreeze.

Caution: Do not use engine antifreeze in the windscreen/tailgate washer system, as it will cause damage to the vehicle paintwork. A screenwash additive should be added to the washer system in the quantities stated on the bottle.

35 Brake fluid renewal

 Warning: Brake hydraulic fluid can harm your eyes and damage painted surfaces, so use extreme caution when handling and pouring it. Do not use fluid that has been standing open for some time, as it absorbs moisture from the air. Excess moisture can cause a dangerous loss of braking effectiveness.

1 The procedure is similar to that for the bleeding of the hydraulic system as described in Chapter 9.

2 Working as described in Chapter 9, open the first bleed screw in the sequence, and pump the brake pedal gently until nearly all the old fluid has been emptied from the master cylinder reservoir. Top-up to the "MAX" level with new fluid, and continue pumping until only the new fluid remains in the reservoir, and new fluid can be seen emerging from the bleed screw. Tighten the screw, and top the reservoir level up to the "MAX" level line.

> **HAYNES HINT** *Old hydraulic fluid is invariably much darker in colour than the new, making it easy to distinguish the two.*

3 Work through all the remaining bleed screws in the sequence until new fluid can be seen at all of them. Be careful to keep the master cylinder reservoir topped-up to above the "MIN" level at all times, or air may enter the system and greatly increase the length of the task.

4 When the operation is complete, check that all bleed screws are securely tightened, and that their dust caps are refitted. Wash off all traces of spilt fluid, and recheck the master cylinder reservoir fluid level.

5 Check the operation of the brakes before taking the car on the road.

1A

Every 10 years, regardless of mileage

36 Airbag module and rotary coupler renewal

1 The airbag module and rotary coupler must be renewed every 10 years.
2 Renewal procedures are described in Chapter 12.

Chapter 1 Part B:
Routine maintenance and servicing - diesel models

Contents

1B

Degrees of difficulty

Easy, suitable for novice with little experience	**Fairly easy,** suitable for beginner with some experience	**Fairly difficult,** suitable for competent DIY mechanic	**Difficult,** suitable for experienced DIY mechanic	**Very difficult,** suitable for expert DIY or professional

Lubricants and fluids

Refer to "*Weekly checks*"

Capacities

Engine oil

Including oil filter . . . . 4.9 litres*
Difference between MIN and MAX on dipstick (approximate) . . . . . . 1.0 litre
Capacity shown is for refilling after draining, if the engine is being filled from dry add a further 0.3 litre

Cooling system

Approximate . . . . 7.0 litres*
Capacity shown is for refilling after draining. If the cooling system is being filled from dry, another 0.7 litres of coolant will be required

Transmission

Approximate . . . . 2.0 litres*
Capacity shown is for refilling after draining, if the transmission is being filled from dry add a further 0.2 litre

Washer fluid reservoir

All models . . . . 6.5 litres

Fuel tank

All models . . . . 55 litres

Power steering system

All models . . . . 0.35 litres

Engine

Oil filter . . . . Not available at time of writing

Cooling system

Antifreeze mixture:
50% antifreeze . . . . Protection down to -37°C
55% antifreeze . . . . Protection down to -45°C
Note: *Refer to antifreeze manufacturer for latest recommendations.*

Fuel system

Air filter element . . . . Not available at time of writing
Fuel filter . . . . Not available at time of writing

Brakes

Friction material minimum thickness:
Front/rear brake pads . . . . 3.0 mm
Rear brake shoes . . . . 2.0 mm

Torque wrench settings	Nm	lbf ft
Auxiliary drivebelt tensioner pulley nut	25	18
Engine oil filter	17	11
Engine sump drain plug	25	18
Transmission filler/level plug	40	30
Roadwheel nuts	110	81

The maintenance intervals in this manual are provided with the assumption that you, not the dealer, will be carrying out the work. These are the minimum maintenance intervals recommended by us for vehicles driven daily. If you wish to keep your vehicle in peak condition at all times, you may wish to perform some of these procedures more often. We encourage frequent maintenance, because it enhances the efficiency, performance and resale value of your vehicle.

If the vehicle is driven in dusty areas, used to tow a trailer, or driven frequently at slow speeds (idling in traffic) or on short journeys, more frequent maintenance intervals are recommended.

When the vehicle is new, it should be serviced by a factory-authorised dealer service department, in order to preserve the factory warranty.

Every 250 miles (400 km) or weekly

☐ Refer to "Weekly Checks"

Every 6000 miles/10 000 km or 6 months, whichever comes first

☐ Renew the engine oil and filter (Section 3)

Note: Rover recommend that the engine oil and filter are changed every 12 000 miles or 12 months. However, oil and filter changes are good for the engine and we recommend that the oil and filter are renewed more frequently, especially if the vehicle is used on a lot of short journeys.

Every 12 000 miles/20 000 km or 12 months, whichever comes first

☐ Renew the engine oil and filter (Section 3)
☐ Check the body and underbody for corrosion protection (Section 4)
☐ Check the power steering fluid level (Section 5)
☐ Check the manual transmission oil level (Section 6)
☐ Check all components, pipes and hoses for fluid leaks (Section 7)
☐ Check the crankcase ventilation hoses and valves (Section 8)
☐ Check the air conditioning compressor, hoses and sight glass (Section 9)
☐ Check the condition and tension of the auxiliary drivebelt (Section 10)
☐ Drain water from the fuel filter (Section 11)
☐ Check the condition of the exhaust system and heat shields (Section 12)
☐ Check the front/rear brake pads and discs for wear (Section 13)
☐ Check the rear brake shoes and drums for wear (Section 14)
☐ Check the brake pipes and hoses (Section 15)
☐ Check the front/rear brake calipers and rear wheel cylinders (Section 16)
☐ Check the steering and suspension components for condition and security (Section 17)
☐ Check the wheel bearings (Section 18)
☐ Check the condition of the driveshafts and gaiters (Section 19)

Every 12 000 miles/20 000 km or 12 months, whichever comes first (continued)

☐ Check the operation and adjustment of the handbrake - adjustment at first 12 000 miles/20 000 km only (Section 20)
☐ Lubricate all door locks and hinges, door stops, bonnet lock and release, and tailgate lock and hinges (Section 21)
☐ Check the operation of all electrical systems (Section 22)
☐ Check the seat belts and airbag module (Section 23)
☐ Exhaust emission test (Section 24)
☐ Renew the pollen filter (Section 25)
☐ Carry out a road test (Section 26)

1B

Every 24 000 miles/40 000 km or 2 years, whichever comes first

☐ Renew the manual transmission oil (Section 27)
☐ Renew the air filter element (Section 28)
☐ Renew the fuel filter (Section 29)
☐ Renew the handset batteries (Section 30)

Every 72 000 miles/120 000 km or 6 years, whichever comes first

☐ Renew the timing belt (Section 31)

Every 2 years, regardless of mileage

☐ Renew the coolant/antifreeze (Section 32)
☐ Renew the brake fluid (Section 33)

Every 10 years, regardless of mileage

☐ Renew the airbag module and rotary coupler (Section 34)

Underbonnet view of a 2.0 litre diesel engine model

1 Engine oil filler cap
2 Washer fluid reservoir
3 Power steering fluid reservoir
4 Cooling system expansion tank
5 Brake fluid reservoir
6 Engine oil level dipstick
7 Engine management ECU
8 Fuel filter
9 Engine compartment fusebox
10 Front suspension upper mounting
11 Airflow meter
12 Battery
13 Air cleaner
14 Radiator
15 Top hose
16 Alternator

Front underbody view of a 2.0 litre petrol engine model - diesel similar

1 Steering track rod
2 Front suspension lower arm
3 Driveshaft
4 Front brake caliper
5 Oil filter
6 Engine mounting
7 Engine sump oil drain plug
8 Auxiliary drivebelt
9 Radiator
10 Exhaust downpipe
11 Bottom hose
12 Manual transmission
13 Steering gear
14 Gearchange rod
15 Front suspension anti-roll bar

Rear underbody view of a 2.0 litre petrol engine model - diesel similar

1 Rear suspension trailing arm
2 Handbrake cable
3 Rear suspension lower link
4 Rear suspension coil spring/strut
5 Rear suspension anti-roll bar
6 Fuel tank
7 Exhaust system
8 Rear suspension trailing arm front compensator link

Maintenance procedures

1 General information

This Chapter is designed to help the home mechanic maintain his/her vehicle for safety, economy, long life and peak performance.

The Chapter contains a master maintenance schedule, followed by Sections dealing specifically with each task in the schedule. Visual checks, adjustments, component renewal and other helpful items are included. Refer to the accompanying illustrations of the engine compartment and the underside of the vehicle for the locations of the various components.

Servicing your vehicle in accordance with the mileage/time maintenance schedule and the following Sections will provide a planned maintenance programme, which should result in a long and reliable service life. This is a comprehensive plan, so maintaining some items but not others at the specified service intervals, will not produce the same results.

As you service your vehicle, you will discover that many of the procedures can - and should - be grouped together, because of the particular procedure being performed, or because of the proximity of two otherwise-unrelated components to one another. For example, if the vehicle is raised for any reason, the exhaust can be inspected at the same time as the suspension and steering components.

The first step in this maintenance programme is to prepare yourself before the actual work begins. Read through all the Sections relevant to the work to be carried out, then make a list and gather all the parts and tools required. If a problem is encountered, seek advice from a parts specialist, or a dealer service department.

2 Intensive maintenance

If, from the time the vehicle is new, the routine maintenance schedule is followed closely, and frequent checks are made of fluid levels and high-wear items, as suggested throughout this manual, the engine will be kept in relatively good running condition, and the need for additional work will be minimised.

It is possible that there will be times when the engine is running poorly due to the lack of regular maintenance. This is even more likely if a used vehicle, which has not received regular and frequent maintenance checks, is purchased. In such cases, additional work may need to be carried out, outside of the regular maintenance intervals.

If engine wear is suspected, a compression test or leakdown test (refer to Chapter 2B) will provide valuable information regarding the overall performance of the main internal components. Such a test can be used. as a basis to decide on the extent of the work to

be carried out. If, for example, a compression or leakdown test indicates serious internal engine wear, conventional maintenance as described in this Chapter will not greatly improve the performance of the engine, and may prove a waste of time and money, unless extensive overhaul work is carried out first.

The following series of operations are those most often required to improve the performance of a generally poor-running engine:

Primary operations

a) Clean, inspect and test the battery (refer to "Weekly checks").
b) Check all the engine-related fluids (refer to "Weekly checks").
c) Check the condition and tension of the auxiliary drivebelt (Section 10).
d) Check the condition of the air filter, and renew if necessary (Section 28).
e) Renew the fuel filter (Section 29).
f) Check the condition of all hoses, and check for fluid leaks (Section 7).

If the above operations do not prove fully effective, carry out the following secondary operations:

Secondary operations

All items listed under "Primary operations", plus the following:
a) Check the charging system (refer to Chapter 5A).
b) Check the pre-heating system (refer to Chapter 5C).
c) Check the fuel system (refer to Chapter 4B).

1B

Every 6000 miles/10 000 km or 6 months

3 Engine oil and filter renewal

Note: *To avoid any possibility of scalding, and to protect yourself from possible skin irritants and other harmful contaminants in used engine oils, it is advisable to wear gloves when carrying out this work.*

1 Frequent oil and filter changes are the most important preventative maintenance procedures which can be undertaken by the DIY owner. As engine oil ages, it becomes diluted and contaminated, which leads to premature engine wear.

2 Before starting this procedure, gather together all the necessary tools and materials. Also make sure that you have plenty of clean rags and newspapers handy, to mop up any spills. Ideally, the engine oil should be warm, as it will drain more easily, and more built-up sludge will be removed with it.

Caution: Take care not to touch the exhaust or any other hot parts of the engine when working under the vehicle.

3 Firmly apply the handbrake then jack up the front of the vehicle and support it on axle stands (see *"Jacking and Vehicle Support"*).

4 Undo the retaining screws and remove the small access panel from the engine/transmission undercover panel to gain access to the sump drain plug and oil filter.

5 Using a spanner or a suitable socket and bar, slacken the drain plug about half a turn **(see illustration)**. Position the draining container under the drain plug, then remove the plug completely **(see Haynes Hint)**.

6 Allow some time for the oil to drain, noting that it may be necessary to reposition the container as the oil flow slows to a trickle.

7 After all the oil has drained, wipe the drain plug and the sealing washer with a clean rag. Examine the condition of the sealing washer,

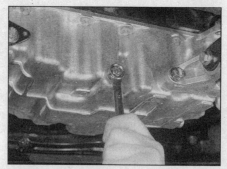

3.5 Unscrew the sump drain plug (shown with undercover completely removed)

and renew it if it shows signs of scoring or other damage which may prevent an oil-tight seal. Clean the area around the drain plug opening, and refit the plug complete with the washer and tighten it to the specified torque **(see illustration)**.

8 Move the container into position under the oil filter on the right-hand end of the cylinder block at the rear.

9 Use an oil filter removal tool to slacken the filter initially, then unscrew it by hand the rest of the way **(see illustration)**. Empty the oil from the old filter into the container.

10 Use a clean rag to remove all oil, dirt and sludge from the filter sealing area on the engine.

11 Apply a light coating of clean engine oil to the sealing ring on the new filter, then screw the filter into position. Screw the filter on until its sealing ring contacts the filter housing then tighten firmly through another complete turn. If the special oil filter tool (a socket which fits over the end of the filter) is available, tighten the filter to the specified torque.

12 Refit the access cover to the undercover and securely tighten its retaining screws.

13 Remove the old oil and all tools from under the vehicle then lower the vehicle to the ground.

HAYNES HiNT

As the drain plug threads release, move it sharply away so the stream of oil issuing from the sump runs into the container, not up your sleeve

14 Fill the engine through the filler hole, using the correct grade and type of oil (refer to *"Weekly checks"* for details of topping-up). Pour in half the specified quantity of oil first, then wait a few minutes for the oil to drain into the sump. Continue to add oil, a small quantity at a time, until the level is up to the lower mark on the dipstick. Adding approximately a further 1.0 litre will bring the level up to the upper mark on the dipstick.

15 Start the engine and run it for a few minutes, while checking for leaks around the oil filter seal and the sump drain plug. Note that there may be a delay of a few seconds before the low oil pressure warning light goes out when the engine is first started, as the oil circulates through the new oil filter and the engine oil galleries before the pressure builds up.

16 Stop the engine, and wait a few minutes for the oil to settle in the sump once more. With the new oil circulated and the filter now completely full, recheck the level on the dipstick, and add more oil as necessary.

17 Dispose of the used engine oil safely with reference to *"General repair procedures"*.

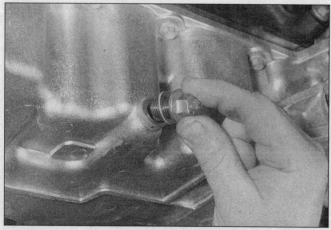

3.7 Refit the drain plug and sealing washer to the sump and tighten to the specified torque

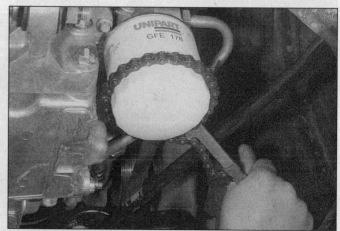

3.9 Using an oil filter removal tool to unscrew the oil filter (shown with undercover completely removed)

Every 12 000 miles/20 000 km or 12 months

4 Body corrosion check

This work should be carried out by a Rover dealer in order to validate the vehicle warranty. The work includes a thorough inspection of the vehicle paintwork and underbody for damage and corrosion

5 Power steering fluid level check

Check the power steering fluid level as described in "Weekly checks".

6 Manual transmission oil level check

1 Position the vehicle over an inspection pit, on vehicle ramps, or jack it up, but make sure that it is level (see "Jacking and Vehicle Support"). The oil level must be checked before the car is driven, or at least 5 minutes after the engine has been switched off. If the oil is checked immediately after driving the car, some of the oil will remain distributed around the transmission components, resulting in an inaccurate level reading.
2 Remove all traces of dirt from around the filler/level plug which is located on the left-hand side of the transmission, where it is situated behind the driveshaft inner joint **(see illustration)**. Unscrew the plug and recover the sealing washer.
3 The oil level should reach the lower edge of the level plug hole. A certain amount of oil will have gathered behind the filler level plug and will trickle out when it is removed; this does not necessarily mean that the level is correct.
4 To ensure that a true level is established, wait until the initial trickle stops then add oil, via the filler/level plug hole, until a new trickle

of oil can be seen emerging **(see illustration)**. The level will be correct when the flow ceases. Add only good quality oil of the specified type (see "Lubricants and fluids").
5 Wipe the filler/level plug and the sealing washer with a clean rag. Examine the condition of the sealing washer, and renew it if it shows signs of scoring or other damage which may prevent an oil-tight seal. Clean the area around the filler/level plug opening then refit the plug, complete with the washer, tightening it to the specified torque. Where necessary, lower the car to the ground.

7 Hose and fluid leak check

1 Visually inspect the engine joint faces, gaskets and seals for any signs of water or oil leaks. Pay particular attention to the areas around the cylinder head cover, cylinder head, oil filter and sump joint faces. Bear in mind that, over a period of time, some very slight seepage from these areas is to be expected - what you are really looking for is any indication of a serious leak. Should a leak be found, renew the offending gasket or oil seal by referring to the appropriate Chapters in this manual.
2 Also check the security and condition of all the engine-related pipes and hoses, and all braking system pipes and hoses and fuel lines. Ensure that all cable ties or securing clips are in place, and in good condition. Clips which are broken or missing can lead to chafing of the hoses, pipes or wiring, which could cause more serious problems in the future.
3 Carefully check the radiator hoses and heater hoses along their entire length. Renew any hose which is cracked, swollen or deteriorated. Cracks will show up better if the hose is squeezed. Pay close attention to the hose clips that secure the hoses to the cooling system components. Hose clips can pinch and puncture hoses, resulting in cooling

system leaks. If the crimped-type hose clips are used, it may be a good idea to replace them with standard worm-drive clips.
4 Inspect all the cooling system components (hoses, joint faces, etc) for leaks **(see Haynes Hint)**. Where any problems are found on the system components, renew the component or gasket with reference to Chapter 3.
5 With the vehicle raised, inspect the fuel tank and filler neck for punctures, cracks and other damage. The connection between the filler neck and tank is especially critical. Sometimes a rubber filler neck or connecting hose will leak due to loose retaining clamps or deteriorated rubber.
6 Carefully check all rubber hoses and metal fuel lines leading away from the fuel tank. Check for loose connections, deteriorated hoses, crimped lines, and other damage. Pay particular attention to the vent pipes and hoses, which often loop up around the filler neck and can become blocked or crimped. Follow the lines to the front of the vehicle, carefully inspecting them all the way. Renew damaged sections as necessary. Similarly, whilst the vehicle is raised, take the opportunity to inspect all underbody brake fluid pipes and hoses.
7 From within the engine compartment, check the security of all fuel, vacuum and brake hose attachments and pipe unions, and inspect all hoses for kinks, chafing and deterioration.
8 Check the condition of the power steering fluid pipes and hoses.

8 Crankcase ventilation component check

Check the breather hoses linking the camshaft cover to the crankcase pressure limiting valve on the inlet duct for signs of damage or deterioration. Renew the hose if it shows signs of damage.

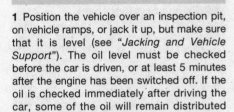

6.2 The transmission oil filler/level plug (arrowed) is located behind the left-hand driveshaft inner joint

6.4 Top-up the transmission oil level using only the specified type of oil

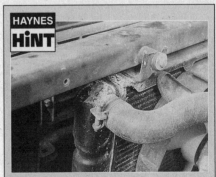

HAYNES HiNT

A leak in the cooling system will usually show up as white- or rust-coloured deposits on the area adjoining the leak

1B

9 Air conditioning component check

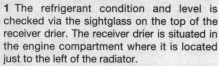

1 The refrigerant condition and level is checked via the sightglass on the top of the receiver drier. The receiver drier is situated in the engine compartment where it is located just to the left of the radiator.
2 Start the engine then switch on the air conditioning system and allow the engine to idle for a couple of minutes whilst observing the sightglass. If the air conditioning system is operating normally then occasional bubbles should be visible through the sightglass.
3 If a constant stream of bubbles is visible, the refrigerant level is low and must be topped up. If the sightglass has become clouded or streaked, there is a fault in the system. If either condition is present, the vehicle must be taken to a Rover dealer or suitable professional refrigeration specialist for the air conditioning system to be checked further and overhauled.
4 Check the air conditioning hoses and refrigerant lines for signs of leakage. Also check the compressor and auxiliary drivebelt. Where necessary have the system checked by a refrigeration specialist.

10 Auxiliary drivebelt check and renewal

Checking

1 Due to its function and material makeup, the drivebelt is prone to failure after a long period of time and should therefore be inspected regularly.
2 Firmly apply the handbrake then jack up the front of the vehicle and support it on axle stands (see "Jacking and Vehicle Support"). To improve access to the belt, undo the retaining screws and fasteners and remove the plastic undercover from underneath the engine and transmission.
3 With the engine stopped, inspect the full length of the drivebelt for cracks and separation of the belt plies (see illustration).

10.3 Check the drivebelt for signs of damage or deterioration and renew if necessary

It will be necessary to turn the engine (using a spanner or socket and bar on the crankshaft pulley bolt) in order to move the belt around the pulleys so that the belt can be inspected thoroughly. Twist the belt between the pulleys so that both sides can be viewed. Also check for fraying, and glazing which gives the belt a shiny appearance. Check the pulleys for nicks, cracks, distortion and corrosion.
4 If a belt shows signs of wear or damage it must be renewed. The belt tensioner is spring-loaded and therefore the belt tension is automatically adjusted and does not require checking.
5 On completion, refit the undercover then lower the vehicle to the ground.

Renewal

6 Carry out the operations described in paragraph 2.
7 Prior to removal make a note of the correct routing of the belt around the various pulleys. If the belt is to be re-used, also mark the direction of rotation on the belt to ensure the belt is refitted the same way around.
8 Using a suitable spanner or socket fitted to the tensioner pulley centre bolt, lever the tensioner away from the belt until there is sufficient slack to enable the belt to be slipped off from the pulleys. Carefully release the tensioner pulley until it is against its stop then remove the belt from the vehicle.
9 Manoeuvre the belt into position, routing it correctly around the pulleys; if the original belt is being fitted use the marks made prior to removal to ensure it is fitted the correct way around.
10 Lever the tensioner roller back against its spring, and seat the belt on the pulleys. Ensure the belt is centrally located on all pulleys then slowly release the tensioner pulley until the belt is correctly tensioned.
Caution: Do not allow the tensioner to spring back and stress the belt.
11 Refit the undercover then lower the vehicle to the ground.

11 Fuel filter water draining

Caution: Be careful not to allow dirt into the fuel system during this procedure and do not allow fuel to contaminate components such as the alternator and starter motor, the coolant hoses and engine mountings, or any wiring.
1 Wipe clean the exterior of the fuel filter then connect a tube to the outlet of the knurled drain screw on the base of the fuel filter. Place the other end of the tube in a clean jar or can and cover the area around the fuel filter with absorbent rags.
2 Slacken the bleed screw on the top of the filter then unscrew the drain screw and allow

the filter to drain until clean fuel, free of dirt or water, emerges from the tube (approximately 100 cc is usually sufficient).
3 Securely close the drain screw and remove the tube and container from under the filter.
4 Refill the filter with fresh fuel using the priming pump in the filter inlet hose. When fuel free of air bubbles starts to flow from the bleed screw hole, squeeze and hold the pump then securely tighten the bleed screw before releasing the pump. Remove the rag from around the filter and mop up any spilt fuel.
5 Turn on the ignition switch and gently squeeze and release the pump until resistance is felt. Once the lines are full of fuel (indicated by the resistance felt when the pump is squeezed), stop pumping and turn off the ignition.
6 On completion, dispose safely of the drained fuel and soiled rags. Check carefully all disturbed components to ensure that there are no leaks (of air or fuel) when the engine is restarted.

12 Exhaust system check

1 Park the vehicle on a level surface and switch off the engine. Chock the front wheels and select first gear, then raise the rear of the vehicle and rest it securely on axle stands (see "Jacking and Vehicle Support").
2 With the engine cold (wait at least an hour after switching off the engine), check the complete exhaust system from the engine to the end of the tailpipe.
3 Check the exhaust pipes and connections for evidence of leaks, severe corrosion and damage. Make sure that all brackets and mountings are in good condition, and that all relevant nuts and bolts are tight. Leakage at any of the joints or in other parts of the system will usually show up as a black, sooty stain in the vicinity of the leak.
4 Rattles and vibrations can often be traced to the exhaust system. Tap the silencer units with a soft mallet and listen for noises caused by corroded or displaced baffle material.
Caution: Do not strike the catalytic converter, as this may damage the ceramic block inside.
5 Carefully rock the pipes and silencers from side to side on their mountings. If the components are able to come into contact with the body or suspension parts, look for broken or worn rubber mountings.
6 Extra clearance can be gained by slackening the clamps between adjacent sections of the exhaust pipe to loosen the joints (where possible - refer to Chapter 4B) and twisting the pipes as necessary to provide the additional clearance. Re-tighten the clamps on completion.

13 Front/rear brake pad and disc check

1 Note that the inner front brake pads are fitted with audible warning wear indicators which emit a high pitched 'scraping' sound when the linings are worn to the minimum thickness. The indicators consist of a bent piece of metal attached to the pad which contact the disc when the linings are worn and set up a vibration when the brakes are applied. Although this will warn the driver of worn brake pads, a visual check must be carried out at the required interval.

2 Firmly apply the handbrake, then jack up the front of the vehicle and support it securely on axle stands (see "*Jacking and Vehicle Support*"). Remove the front roadwheels.

3 For a quick check, the pad thickness can be carried out via the inspection hole on the front of the caliper **(see Haynes Hint)**. Using a steel rule, measure the thickness of the pad lining including the backing plate. This must not be less than that indicated in the Specifications.

4 The view through the caliper inspection hole gives a rough indication of the state of the brake pads. For a comprehensive check, the brake pads should be removed and cleaned. The operation of the caliper can then also be checked, and the condition of the brake disc itself can be fully examined on both sides. Chapter 9 contains a detailed description of how the brake disc should be checked for wear and/or damage.

5 If any pad's friction material is worn to the specified thickness or less, *all four pads must be renewed as a set.* Refer to Chapter 9 for details.

6 On completion, refit the roadwheels and lower the vehicle to the ground.

14 Rear brake shoe and drum check

Refer to the detailed description given in Chapter 9.

15 Brake pipe and hose check

1 Jack up the front and rear of the vehicle and support it on axle stands (see "*Jacking and Vehicle Support*").

2 Check the security and condition of all the braking system pipes and hoses. In particular, check the flexible hoses for signs of cracking by carefully bending them at several points along their lengths. Check the rigid brake lines for corrosion, especially at exposed locations on the underbody.

3 Ensure that all hose and pipe securing clips are in place, and in good condition.

4 Renewal of the brake pipes and hoses is described in Chapter 9.

5 On completion lower the car to the ground.

16 Brake caliper and wheel cylinder check

1 Jack up the front and rear of the vehicle and support it on axle stands (see "*Jacking and Vehicle Support*"). Remove the front and rear wheels.

2 For a thorough check of the front brake calipers, remove the brake pads as described in Chapter 9. Carefully clean the brake pad locations in the caliper body and mounting bracket taking care not to inhale the brake dust as it may contain asbestos which is a health hazard. Check the caliper for signs of brake fluid leakage. If this is evident at the flexible hose connection, renew the copper washers with reference to Chapter 9. If leakage is evident at the piston, renew the internal sealing ring or renew the caliper complete with reference to Chapter 9.

3 To check the wheel cylinders, remove the drums with reference to Chapter 9, then clean away dust and dirt from the brake shoes and wheel cylinder. Check the wheel cylinders for signs of brake fluid leakage by temporarily lifting the rubber boots with a screwdriver. If evident, renew the wheel cylinder complete as described in Chapter 9.

17 Suspension and steering check

Front suspension and steering check

1 Raise the front of the vehicle, and securely support it on axle stands (see "*Jacking and Vehicle Support*").

2 Visually inspect the balljoint dust covers and the steering rack-and-pinion gaiters for splits, chafing or deterioration. Any wear of these components will cause loss of lubricant, together with dirt and water entry, resulting in rapid deterioration of the balljoints or steering gear.

3 On vehicles with power steering, check the fluid hoses for chafing or deterioration, and the pipe and hose unions for fluid leaks. Also check for signs of fluid leakage under pressure from the steering gear rubber gaiters, which would indicate failed fluid seals within the steering gear.

4 Grasp the roadwheel at the 12 o'clock and 6 o'clock positions, and try to rock it **(see illustration)**. Very slight free play may be felt, but if the movement is appreciable, further investigation is necessary to determine the source. Continue rocking the wheel while an

For a quick check, the thickness of friction material remaining on the brake pads can be measured through the aperture in the caliper body

assistant depresses the footbrake. If the movement is now eliminated or significantly reduced, it is likely that the hub bearings are at fault. If the free play is still evident with the footbrake depressed, then there is wear in the suspension joints or mountings.

5 Now grasp the wheel at the 9 o'clock and 3 o'clock positions, and try to rock it as before. Any movement felt now may again be caused by wear in the hub bearings or the steering track-rod balljoints. If the outer balljoint is worn, the visual movement will be obvious. If the inner joint is suspect, it can be felt by placing a hand over the rack-and-pinion rubber gaiter and gripping the track-rod. If the wheel is now rocked, movement will be felt at the inner joint if wear has taken place.

6 Using a large screwdriver or flat bar, check for wear in the suspension mounting bushes by levering between the relevant suspension component and its attachment point. Some movement is to be expected, as the mountings are made of rubber, but excessive wear should be obvious. Also check the condition of any visible rubber bushes, looking for splits, cracks or contamination of the rubber.

7 With the car standing on its wheels, have an assistant turn the steering wheel back and forth, about an eighth of a turn each way.

17.4 Check for wear in the hub bearings by grasping the wheel and trying to rock it

1B

19.1 Checking the driveshaft outer CV joint rubber gaiter

There should be very little, if any, lost movement between the steering wheel and roadwheels. If this is not the case, closely observe the joints and mountings previously described. In addition, check the steering column universal joints for wear, and also check the rack-and-pinion steering gear itself.

Rear suspension check

8 Chock the front wheels, then jack up the rear of the vehicle and support securely on axle stands (see "*Jacking and Vehicle Support*").
9 Working as described previously for the front suspension, check the rear hub bearings, the suspension bushes and the strut or shock absorber mountings (as applicable) for wear.

Shock absorber check

10 Check for any signs of fluid leakage around the shock absorber body, or from the rubber gaiter around the piston rod. Should any fluid be noticed, the shock absorber is defective internally, and should be renewed. **Note:** *Shock absorbers should always be renewed in pairs on the same axle.*
11 The efficiency of the shock absorber may be checked by bouncing the vehicle at each corner. Generally speaking, the body will return to its normal position and stop after being depressed. If it rises and returns on a rebound, the shock absorber is probably suspect. Also examine the shock absorber upper and lower mountings for any signs of wear.

18 Wheel bearing check

1 Excessive wear of the wheel bearings will normally be evident as a rough-sounding noise from the offending wheel as the car is being driven. If a front wheel bearing is worn, the noise may only be evident on corners.
2 To check for worn wheel bearings, jack up the front or rear of the car and support on axle stands (see "*Jacking and Vehicle Support*"). Spin the wheel by hand and listen for any roughness from the wheel bearing.

19 Driveshaft and gaiter check

1 With the vehicle raised and securely supported on stands (see "*Jacking and Vehicle Support*"), turn the steering onto full lock then slowly rotate the roadwheel. Inspect the condition of the outer constant velocity (CV) joint rubber gaiters while squeezing the gaiters to open out the folds **(see illustration)**. Check for signs of cracking, splits or deterioration of the rubber which may allow the grease to escape and lead to water and grit entry into the joint. Also check the security and condition of the retaining clips. Repeat these checks on the inner CV joints. If any damage or deterioration is found, the gaiters should be renewed as described in Chapter 8.
2 At the same time check the general condition of the CV joints themselves by first holding the driveshaft and attempting to rotate the wheel. Repeat this check by holding the inner joint and attempting to rotate the driveshaft. Any appreciable movement indicates wear in the joints, wear in the drive-shaft splines or loose driveshaft retaining nut.

20 Handbrake check

1 The handbrake should be capable of holding the parked vehicle stationary, even on steep slopes, when applied with moderate force. The mechanism should be firm and positive in feel with no trace of stiffness or sponginess from the cables and should release immediately the handbrake lever is released. If the mechanism is faulty in any of these respects then it must be checked immediately.
2 To check the handbrake setting, first apply the footbrake firmly several times to establish correct shoe-to-drum clearance. Applying normal, moderate pressure, pull the handbrake lever to the fully-applied position whilst counting the number of clicks emitted from the handbrake ratchet mechanism. If adjustment is correct, there should be 6 to 10 clicks before the handbrake is fully applied. If this is not the case, then adjustment is required as described in Chapter 9.

21 Hinge and lock lubrication

1 Work around the vehicle and lubricate the hinges of the bonnet, doors and tailgate/bootlid with a light machine oil. Also lubricate the bonnet lock located on the engine compartment front crossmember.
2 Lightly lubricate the bonnet release mechanism and exposed section of the inner cable with a smear of grease.

22 Electrical system check

1 Check the operation of all electrical equipment, ie, lights, direction indicators, horn, wash/wipe system etc. Refer to the appropriate Sections of Chapter 12 for details if any of the circuits are found to be inoperative.
2 Visually check all accessible wiring connectors, harnesses and retaining clips for security, and for signs of chafing or damage. Rectify any faults found.

23 Seat belt and airbag check

1 Check the webbing of each belt for signs of fraying, cuts or other damage, pulling the belt out to its full extent to check its entire length.
2 Check the operation of the belt buckles by pulling the belt hard to ensure that it remains locked in position.
3 Check the inertia reel retractor mechanism by pulling out the belt to the halfway point and jerking hard. The mechanism must lock immediately to prevent any further unreeling but must allow free movement during normal driving.
4 Ensure that all belt mounting bolts are securely tightened. Note that the bolts are shouldered so that the belt anchor points are free to rotate.
5 If there is any sign of damage, or any doubt about a belt's condition, then it must be renewed. If the vehicle has been involved in a collision, then any belt in use at the time must be renewed as a matter of course and all other belts checked carefully.
6 The airbag/SRS warning light on the instrument panel should extinguish 3 seconds after the ignition switch is turned to position "II". If this is not the case, have the system checked by a Rover dealer. No attempt should be made to carry out repairs to the airbag components. Note that the airbag unit and slip ring must be renewed every ten years, regardless of condition.

24 Exhaust emission check

1 Rover specify that this check should be carried out annually or every 12 000 miles. The check involves checking the electronic diesel control (EDC) system operation by plugging an electronic tester into the system diagnostic socket to check the electronic control module (ECM) memory for faults (see Chapter 4B).
2 In reality, if the vehicle is running correctly and the engine management warning light in

the instrument panel is functioning normally, then this check need not be carried out. On cars over 3 years old, the exhaust emissions will be checked every year during the MOT test.

25 Pollen filter renewal

1 The pollen filter (if fitted) is located beneath the left-hand side of the facia, in the heater inlet system. To remove the filter, first remove the glovebox as described in Chapter 11.
2 Remove the felt trim panel from under the heater inlet duct, then release the cover from the bottom of the pollen filter housing.
3 Lower the pollen filter from its housing.
4 Fit the new filter using a reversal of the removal procedure.

26 Road test

Instruments and electrical equipment

1 Check the operation of all instruments and electrical equipment.

2 Make sure that all instruments read correctly, and switch on all electrical equipment in turn, to check that it functions properly.

Steering and suspension

3 Check for any abnormalities in the steering, suspension, handling or road "feel".
4 Drive the vehicle, and check that there are no unusual vibrations or noises.
5 Check that the steering feels positive, with no excessive "sloppiness", or roughness, and check for any suspension noises when cornering and driving over bumps.

Drivetrain

6 Check the performance of the engine, clutch, transmission and driveshafts.
7 Listen for any unusual noises from the engine, clutch and transmission.
8 Make sure that the engine runs smoothly when idling, and that there is no hesitation when accelerating.
9 Check that, where applicable, the clutch action is smooth and progressive, that the drive is taken up smoothly, and that the pedal travel is not excessive. Also listen for any noises when the clutch pedal is depressed.
10 Check that all gears can be engaged smoothly without noise, and that the gear lever action is not abnormally vague or "notchy".

11 Listen for a metallic clicking sound from the front of the vehicle, as the vehicle is driven slowly in a circle with the steering on full-lock. Carry out this check in both directions. If a clicking noise is heard, this indicates wear in a driveshaft joint (see Chapter 8).

Check the operation and performance of the braking system

12 Make sure that the vehicle does not pull to one side when braking, and that the wheels do not lock prematurely when braking hard.
13 Check that there is no vibration through the steering when braking.
14 Check that the handbrake operates correctly, without excessive movement of the lever, and that it holds the vehicle stationary on a slope.
15 Test the operation of the brake servo unit as follows. Depress the footbrake four or five times to exhaust the vacuum, then start the engine. As the engine starts, there should be a noticeable "give" in the brake pedal as vacuum builds up. Allow the engine to run for at least two minutes, and then switch it off. If the brake pedal is now depressed again, it should be possible to detect a hiss from the servo as the pedal is depressed. After about four or five applications, no further hissing should be heard, and the pedal should feel considerably harder.

1B

Every 24 000 miles/40 000 km or 2 years

27 Manual transmission oil renewal

Refer to Chapter 7, Section 2.

28 Air filter element renewal

1 The air filter is located in the engine compartment, on the left-hand end of the engine.
2 Release the retaining clips and detach the airflow meter from the air filter housing. Recover the sealing ring from the air cleaner housing lid, it must be renewed if it shows signs of damage or deterioration.
3 Release the retaining clips then lift the air filter housing cover sufficiently to enable removal of the filter element from its housing. Where necessary, unclip the accelerator cable from the lid.
4 Lift out the filter element, noting which way up it is fitted, then wipe out the casing and the cover **(see illustration)**.
5 Fit the new filter, making sure it is the correct way up, and seat it in the housing. Locate the cover on the housing and secure it

in position with all the retaining clips.
6 Ensure the sealing ring is in position then refit the airflow meter to the air filter and secure it in position with the retaining clips. Where necessary, clip the accelerator cable back into position.

29 Fuel filter renewal

Caution: Be careful not to allow dirt into the fuel system during this procedure and

28.4 Unclip the air cleaner housing lid and remove the filter element

do not allow fuel to contaminate components such as the alternator and starter motor, the coolant hoses and engine mountings, or any wiring.

1 Wipe clean the exterior of the fuel filter and cover the area around the fuel filter with absorbent rags. Have ready a couple of suitable plugs to plug the fuel hoses whilst the filter is removed.
2 Release the retaining clips and disconnect the fuel hoses from the filter **(see illustration)**. Plug the hose ends to minimise fluid loss and prevent the entry of dirt into the system.

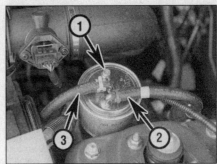

29.2 Fuel filter bleed screw (1), inlet hose (2) and outlet hose (3)

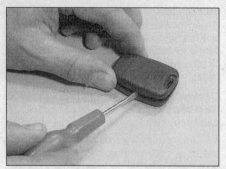

30.2a Carefully insert a screwdriver into the slot . . .

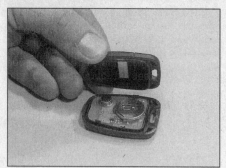

30.2b . . . and prise off the handset cover

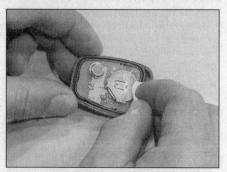

30.3 Ensure the new battery is installed the right way around

3 Unclip the filter mounting bracket from the body and remove the filter assembly from the engine compartment, keeping the filter upright as it is removed to prevent fuel spillage. Slacken the clamp bolt then separate the filter and bracket, noting the correct fitted position of the filter in the bracket.

4 Slide the new filter into the mounting bracket and securely tighten its clamp bolt, ensuring the filter unions are correctly positioned in relation to the bracket (the arrows stamped on the top of the filter must point in the direction of fuel flow). Manoeuvre the assembly into position and clip the mounting bracket securely onto the body.

5 Remove the plugs from the hoses and connect both inlet and outlet hoses to the filter, securing them in position with the retaining clips.

6 Slacken the bleed screw which is fitted to the top of the fuel filter. Gently squeeze and release the pump until fuel which is free of air

bubbles is flowing out of the filter. Once all traces of air have been removed, squeeze and hold the pump then securely tighten the bleed screw before releasing the pump. Remove the rag from around the filter and mop up any spilt fuel.

7 Turn on the ignition switch and gently squeeze and release the pump until resistance is felt. Once the lines are full of fuel (indicated by the resistance felt when the pump is squeezed), stop pumping and turn off the ignition.

8 On completion, dispose safely of the drained fuel and soiled rags. Check the filter to ensure that there are no leaks (of air or fuel) when the engine is restarted.

30 Handset battery renewal

1 The alarm system handset contains a

battery which should last for approximately 3 years. When it requires renewal, the indicator warning lights on the front doors will flash rapidly before the doors are opened and the operating range will reduce considerably.

2 To renew the battery, use a small screwdriver or coin to prise off the handset cover then remove the battery from its clip (see illustrations).

3 Press each button for a minimum of 5 seconds to drain any remaining power from the handset, then fit the new battery taking care not to touch the contact surfaces with the fingers. Make sure the new battery is correctly located with the positive (+) side facing upwards (see illustration).

4 Press on the cover, then unlock the car using the key and operate the lock button on the handset at least four times.

Every 72 000 miles/120 000 km or 6 years

31 Timing belt renewal

Refer to Chapter 2C.

Every 2 years, regardless of mileage

32 Coolant/antifreeze renewal

Cooling system draining

 Warning: Wait until the engine is cold before starting this procedure. Do not allow antifreeze to come in contact with your skin, or with the painted surfaces of the vehicle. Rinse off spills immediately with plenty of water. Never leave antifreeze lying around in an open container, or in a puddle in the driveway or on the garage floor. Children and pets are attracted by its sweet smell, but antifreeze can be fatal if ingested.

1 With the engine completely cold, remove the expansion tank filler cap. Turn the cap anti-clockwise, wait until any pressure remaining in the system is released, then unscrew it and lift it off.

2 Where applicable remove the undershield, then position a suitable container beneath the radiator.

3 Position the heater temperature control on its maximum setting.

4 Loosen the clip and disconnect the bottom hose from the radiator, and allow the coolant to drain into the container.

5 When the flow of coolant stops, refit the bottom hose and tighten the clip.

6 If the coolant has been drained for a reason other than renewal, then provided it is clean and less than two years old, it can be re-used, though this is not recommended.

Cooling system flushing

7 If coolant renewal has been neglected, or if the antifreeze mixture has become diluted, then in time, the cooling system may gradually lose efficiency, as the coolant passages become restricted due to rust, scale deposits, and other sediment. The cooling system efficiency can be restored by flushing the system clean.

8 The radiator should be flushed independently of the engine, to avoid unnecessary contamination.

Radiator flushing

9 Disconnect the top and bottom hoses and any other relevant hoses from the radiator, with reference to Chapter 3.

10 Insert a garden hose into the radiator top inlet. Direct a flow of clean water through the radiator, and continue flushing until clean water emerges from the radiator bottom outlet.

11 If after a reasonable period, the water still does not run clear, the radiator can be flushed with a good proprietary cleaning agent. It is important that the manufacturer's instructions are followed carefully. If the contamination is particularly bad, insert the hose in the radiator bottom outlet, and reverse-flush the radiator.

Engine flushing

12 Remove the thermostat as described in Chapter 3 then, if the radiator top hose has been disconnected from the engine, temporarily reconnect the hose.

13 With the top and bottom hoses disconnected from the radiator, insert a garden hose into the radiator top hose. Direct a clean flow of water through the engine, and continue flushing until clean water emerges from the radiator bottom hose.

14 On completion of flushing, refit the thermostat and reconnect the hoses with reference to Chapter 3.

Cooling system filling

15 Before attempting to fill the cooling system, make sure that all hoses and clips are in good condition, and that the clips are tight. Note that an antifreeze mixture must be used all year round, to prevent corrosion of the engine components. Make sure the heater controls are set to maximum heat.

16 Remove the expansion tank filler cap.

17 Slowly fill the cooling system until the coolant reaches the MAX mark on the expansion tank, then refit and tighten the filler cap.

18 Refit the undershield beneath the engine compartment.

19 Start the engine, and allow it to run until it reaches normal operating temperature (until the cooling fan cuts in and out). **Do not** operate the air conditioning at this stage.

20 Stop the engine, and allow it to cool, then re-check the coolant level with reference to "*Weekly checks*". Top-up the level if necessary and refit the expansion tank filler cap.

Antifreeze mixture

21 The antifreeze should always be renewed at the specified intervals. This is necessary not only to maintain the antifreeze properties, but also to prevent corrosion which would otherwise occur as the corrosion inhibitors become progressively less effective.

22 Always use an ethylene-glycol based antifreeze which is suitable for use in mixed-metal cooling systems. The quantity of antifreeze and levels of protection are given in the Specifications.

23 Before adding antifreeze, the cooling system should be completely drained, preferably flushed, and all hoses checked for condition and security.

24 After filling with antifreeze, a label should be attached to the expansion tank, stating the type and concentration of antifreeze used, and the date installed. Any subsequent topping-up should be made with the same type and concentration of antifreeze.

Caution: Do not use engine antifreeze in the windscreen/tailgate washer system, as it will cause damage to the vehicle paintwork. A screenwash additive should be added to the washer system in the quantities stated on the bottle.

33 Brake fluid renewal

⚠ *Warning: Brake hydraulic fluid can harm your eyes and damage painted surfaces, so use extreme caution when handling and pouring it. Do not use fluid that has been standing open for some time, as it absorbs moisture from the air. Excess moisture can cause a dangerous loss of braking effectiveness.*

1 The procedure is similar to that for the bleeding of the hydraulic system as described in Chapter 9.

2 Working as described in Chapter 9, open the first bleed screw in the sequence, and pump the brake pedal gently until nearly all the old fluid has been emptied from the master cylinder reservoir. Top-up to the "MAX" level with new fluid, and continue pumping until only the new fluid remains in the reservoir, and new fluid can be seen emerging from the bleed screw. Tighten the screw, and top the reservoir level up to the "MAX" level line.

Old hydraulic fluid is invariably much darker in colour than the new, making it easy to distinguish the two.

3 Work through all the remaining bleed screws in the sequence until new fluid can be seen at all of them. Be careful to keep the master cylinder reservoir topped-up to above the "MIN" level at all times, or air may enter the system and greatly increase the length of the task.

4 When the operation is complete, check that all bleed screws are securely tightened, and that their dust caps are refitted. Wash off all traces of spilt fluid, and recheck the master cylinder reservoir fluid level.

5 Check the operation of the brakes before taking the car on the road.

Every 10 years, regardless of mileage

34 Airbag module and rotary coupler renewal

1 The airbag module and rotary coupler must be renewed every 10 years.

2 Renewal procedures are described in Chapter 12.

1B

Notes

Chapter 2 Part A:
1.4 and 1.6 litre petrol engine in-car repair procedures

Contents

Degrees of difficulty

Easy, suitable for novice with little experience	**Fairly easy,** suitable for beginner with some experience	**Fairly difficult,** suitable for competent DIY mechanic	**Difficult,** suitable for experienced DIY mechanic	**Very difficult,** suitable for expert DIY or professional 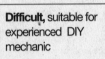

Specifications

General

Engine type	Four-cylinder in-line, four-stroke, liquid-cooled	
Designation:		
8-valve engine	K8	
16-valve engine	K16	
	1.4 litre engine	**1.6 litre engine**
Bore	75.0 mm	80.0 mm
Stroke	79.0 mm	79.0 mm
Capacity	1396 cc	1589 cc
Firing order	1-3-4-2 (No 1 cylinder at timing belt end)	
Direction of crankshaft rotation	Clockwise (seen from right-hand side of vehicle)	
Compression ratio:		
1.4 litre engine:		
8-valve engine	9.9:1	
16-valve engine	10.0:1	
1.6 litre engine	10.5:1	

Camshaft

Bearing journal running clearance:	
Standard	0.06 to 0.094 mm
Service limit	0.150 mm
Camshaft endfloat:	
Standard	0.06 to 0.19 mm
Service limit	0.300 mm
Follower outside diameter	32.959 to 32.975 mm

Lubrication system

System pressure - at idle	1.7 to 3.5 bar
Pressure relief valve opening pressure	4.1 bar
Low oil pressure warning light comes on	0.3 to 0.5 bar
Oil pump clearances:	
Outer rotor-to-body clearance	0.28 to 0.36 mm
Inner rotor tip-to-outer rotor clearance	0.05 to 0.13 mm
Rotor endfloat	0.02 to 0.06 mm

2A

Torque wrench settings

	Nm	lbf ft
Camshaft bearing carrier bolts	10	7
Camshaft cover bolts	10	7
Camshaft sprocket bolt:		
M8 bolt	35	26
M10 bolt	65	48
Connecting rod big-end bearing cap bolts:		
Stage 1	20	18
Stage 2	Angle-tighten a further 45°	
Crankshaft pulley bolt	205	152
Cylinder head bolts:		
Stage 1	20	15
Stage 2	Angle-tighten a further 180°	
Stage 3	Angle-tighten a further 180°	
Engine/transmission mountings:		
Left-hand upper mounting:		
Retaining bolts	80	59
Through bolt	75	55
Right-hand upper mounting:		
Retaining nuts	100	74
Through bolt	75	55
Mounting bracket bolts	60	44
Rear mounting:		
Retaining bolts	65	48
Through bolt	80	59
Mounting bracket-to-transmission bolts	100	74
Exhaust camshaft cover plate bolts - 16-valve engine	25	18
Flywheel bolts	85	63
Flywheel cover plate bolts	9	6
Main bearing ladder-to-cylinder block bolts:		
Stage 1	5	4
Stage 2	15	11
Oil pump retaining bolts	10	7
Oil rail-to-main bearing ladder bolts	5	4
Roadwheel nuts	110	81
Spark plugs	25	18
Sump bolts:		
M6 bolts	10	7
M8 bolts	25	18
Sump drain plug	42	31
Timing belt cover bolts:		
Lower and rear cover bolts	10	7
Upper cover bolts	5	4
Timing belt tensioner:		
Backplate bolt	10	7
Pulley bolt	45	33

1 General information and precautions

How to use this Chapter

This Part of the Chapter describes those repair procedures that can reasonably be carried out on the engine whilst it remains in the vehicle. If the engine has been removed from the vehicle and is being dismantled as described in Part D of this Chapter, any preliminary dismantling procedures can be ignored.

Note that whilst it may be possible physically to overhaul items such as the piston/connecting rod assemblies with the engine in the vehicle, such tasks are not usually carried out as separate operations and usually require the execution of several additional procedures (not to mention the cleaning of components and of oilways). For this reason, all such tasks are classed as major overhaul procedures and are described in Part D of this Chapter.

Engine description

The 1.4 and 1.6 litre engines are from the Rover K-series engine family, and are four-cylinder, in-line units, mounted transversely at the front of the vehicle with the clutch and transmission on the left-hand end. Two versions of the engine are available, an 8-valve single overhead camshaft (SOHC) engine and a 16-valve double overhead camshaft (DOHC) engine. All engines are very similar, except for the obvious differences in cylinder head design.

The main structure of the engine consists of three major castings - the cylinder head, the cylinder block/crankcase, and the crankshaft main bearing ladder.

The three major castings are made from aluminium alloy, and are clamped together by ten long cylinder head bolts; the bolts also perform the task of crankshaft main bearing bolts as they actually screw into the main bearing ladder. An oil rail is fitted under the main bearing ladder, and to avoid disturbing the bottom end of the engine when removing the cylinder head bolts, the oil rail is secured independently to the main bearing ladder (by two nuts), and the main bearing ladder is secured to the cylinder block/crankcase (by ten bolts).

The crankshaft runs in five main bearings. Thrustwashers are fitted to the centre main bearing (upper half) to control crankshaft endfloat.

The connecting rods rotate on horizontally-split bearing shells at their big-ends. The pistons are attached to the connecting rods by gudgeon pins which are an interference fit in the connecting rod small-end eyes. The aluminium alloy pistons are fitted with three piston rings, comprising two compression rings and an oil control ring.

The cylinder bores are formed by replaceable liners which locate in the cylinder block/crankcase at their top ends. There are two different types of liner, on early engines "wet liners" are used and on later engines "damp liners" are used. To prevent the coolant escaping into the sump the base of each liner is sealed. On wet liner engines the liner-to-cylinder block joint is sealed using sealing rings and on damp liner engines the joint is sealed with sealing compound.

The inlet and exhaust valves are each closed by coil springs and operate in guides pressed into the cylinder head. The valve seat inserts are pressed into the cylinder head and can be renewed separately if worn.

The camshaft(s) is/are driven by a toothed timing belt, and operate the valves via followers. Each follower incorporates a hydraulic self-adjusting valve which automatically adjusts the valve clearance. The camshaft rotates in bearings which are line-bored directly into the cylinder head and the (bolted-on) bearing carrier. This means that the bearing carrier and cylinder head are matched, and cannot be renewed independently. The distributor is driven from the left-hand (flywheel end) of the camshaft (inlet camshaft on 16-valve engines). The fuel pump is electrically-operated.

The coolant pump is driven by the timing belt.

Lubrication is by means of an eccentric-rotor type pump driven directly from the right-hand (timing belt end) of the crankshaft. The pump draws oil through a strainer located in the sump. It then forces it through an externally-mounted full-flow cartridge-type oil filter into galleries in the oil rail and the cylinder block/crankcase, from where it is distributed to the crankshaft (main bearings) and camshaft. The big-end bearings are supplied with oil via internal drillings in the crankshaft, while the camshaft bearings and the followers receive a pressurised supply via drillings in the cylinder head. The camshaft lobes and valves are lubricated by oil splash, as are all other engine components.

Repair operations possible with the engine in the car

The following work can be carried out with the engine in the vehicle:

a) Compression pressure - testing.
b) Camshaft cover - removal and refitting.
c) Crankshaft pulley - removal and refitting.
d) Timing belt covers - removal and refitting.
e) Timing belt - removal, refitting and adjustment.
f) Timing belt tensioner and sprockets - removal and refitting.
g) Camshaft oil seal(s) - renewal.
h) Camshaft(s) and followers - removal, inspection and refitting.
i) Cylinder head - removal and refitting.
j) Cylinder head and pistons - decarbonising.
k) Sump - removal and refitting.
l) Oil pump - removal, overhaul and refitting.
m) Crankshaft oil seals - renewal.
n) Engine/transmission mountings - inspection and renewal.
o) Flywheel - removal, inspection and refitting.

Caution: Note that a side-effect of the K-series engine design is that the crankshaft cannot be rotated once the cylinder head bolts have been slackened. During any servicing or overhaul work, the crankshaft must always be rotated to the desired position before the cylinder head bolts are disturbed.

2 Compression test – description and interpretation

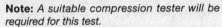

Note: *A suitable compression tester will be required for this test.*

1 When engine performance is down, or if misfiring occurs which cannot be attributed to the ignition or fuel systems, a compression test can provide diagnostic clues as to the engine's condition. If the test is performed regularly it can give warning of trouble before any other symptoms become apparent.

2 The engine must be fully warmed up to normal operating temperature, the battery must be fully charged and the spark plugs must be removed (see Chapter 1A). The aid of an assistant will be required.

3 Disable the ignition system by disconnecting the ignition HT coil lead from the distributor cap and earthing it on the cylinder block. Use a jumper lead or similar wire to make a good connection.

4 Fit a compression tester to the No 1 cylinder spark plug hole. The type of tester which screws into the plug thread is preferred.

5 Have the assistant hold the throttle wide open and crank the engine on the starter motor. After one or two revolutions, the compression pressure should build up to a maximum figure and then stabilise. Record the highest reading obtained.

6 Repeat the test on the remaining cylinders, recording the pressure in each.

7 All cylinders should produce very similar pressures; a difference of more than 2 bars between any two cylinders indicates a fault. Note that the compression should build up quickly in a healthy engine; low compression on the first stroke, followed by gradually-increasing pressure on successive strokes, indicates worn piston rings. A low compression reading on the first stroke, which does not build up during successive strokes, indicates leaking valves or a blown head gasket (a cracked head could also be the cause). Deposits on the undersides of the valve heads can also cause low compression.

8 Although Rover do not specify exact compression pressures, as a guide, any cylinder pressure of below 10 bar can be considered as less than healthy. Refer to a Rover dealer or other specialist if in doubt as to whether a particular pressure reading is acceptable.

9 If the pressure in any cylinder is significantly low, carry out the following test to isolate the cause. Introduce a teaspoonful of clean oil into that cylinder through its spark plug hole and repeat the test.

10 If the addition of oil temporarily improves the compression pressure, this indicates that bore or piston wear is responsible for the pressure loss. No improvement suggests that leaking or burnt valves, or a blown head gasket, may be to blame.

11 A low reading from two adjacent cylinders is almost certainly due to the head gasket having blown between them and the presence of coolant in the engine oil will confirm this.

12 If one cylinder is about 20 percent lower than the others and the engine has a slightly rough idle, a worn camshaft lobe could be the cause.

13 If the compression reading is unusually high, the combustion chambers are probably coated with carbon deposits. If this is the case, the cylinder head should be removed and decarbonised.

14 On completion of the test, refit the spark plugs (see Chapter 1A) and reconnect the HT lead to the distributor cap.

3 Engine assembly/ valve timing marks – general information and usage

1 The crankshaft pulley, crankshaft and camshaft sprocket(s) all have timing marks which align when the crankshaft is at 90° BTDC. This positions the pistons half-way up the bores, ensuring there is no danger of the valves contacting the pistons when refitting the cylinder head/timing belt.

2 Disconnect the battery negative terminal. If necessary, remove all the spark plugs as described in Chapter 1A to enable the engine to be easily turned over.

3 To gain access to the camshaft sprocket timing mark(s), remove the timing belt upper cover as described in Section 6.

4 Firmly apply the handbrake, then jack up the front of the vehicle and support it securely on axle stands (see "Jacking and Vehicle Support"). Remove the right-hand front roadwheel to improve access to the crankshaft pulley.

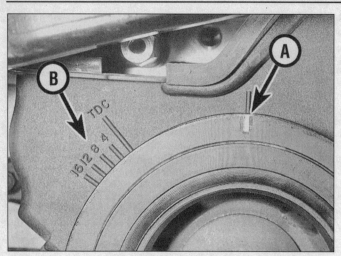

3.6a Align the camshaft sprocket timing (EX) marks (A) with the cylinder head upper surface (B) . . .

3.6b . . . and the crankshaft pulley timing notch with the mark (A) on the timing belt lower cover. Ignore the timing marks (B) on the cover (where present)

5 Using a socket and extension bar on the crankshaft pulley bolt, turn the crankshaft whilst keeping an eye on the camshaft sprocket(s).

6 On 8-valve engines, rotate the crankshaft until the timing ("EX") mark is at the front (exhaust manifold side) of sprocket and is correctly aligned with the cylinder head upper surface. Once the camshaft sprocket mark is correctly positioned, align the notch on the crankshaft pulley rim with the mark on the lower timing belt cover (see illustrations).

7 On 16-valve engines, rotate the crankshaft until the "EXHAUST" mark is at the rear (inlet manifold side) of each sprocket and the "IN" mark is at the front and all timing marks are correctly aligned with the mark on the timing belt rear cover (representing the cylinder head upper surface) (see illustration). Once the camshaft sprocket marks are correctly positioned, align the notch on the crankshaft pulley rim with the mark on the lower timing belt cover.

8 With the crankshaft pulley and camshaft sprocket timing marks positioned as described, the engine can safely be dismantled.

4 Camshaft cover – removal and refitting

8-valve engine

Removal

1 Disconnect the battery negative lead.
2 Release the retaining clips and disconnect the breather hoses from the rear of the camshaft cover.
3 Working progressively and in the reverse of the tightening sequence (see illustration 4.7), slacken and remove the cover retaining bolts.
4 Carefully remove the cover, complete with the gasket. Check the gasket for signs of damage or deterioration and renew it if damaged. Note: Do not separate the camshaft cover and gasket unless the gasket is to be renewed.

Refitting

5 If the gasket has been removed from the cover, remove the crankcase ventilation system filters, wash them in solvent and dry them before refitting them to the cover. Ensure the cover is clean and dry then fit the new gasket, making sure it is correctly located.
6 Make sure the mating surfaces are clean and dry then refit the cover to the cylinder head, ensuring that the gasket remains correctly seated.
7 Refit the cover retaining bolts and tighten them all by hand. Once all bolts are in position, go around in the sequence shown and tighten them to the specified torque setting (see illustration).
8 Reconnect the breather hoses, securing them in position with the retaining clips, and reconnect the battery negative lead.

3.7 Position the sprocket EXHAUST and IN marks correctly and align the timing marks (A) with the timing mark (B) on the rear cover

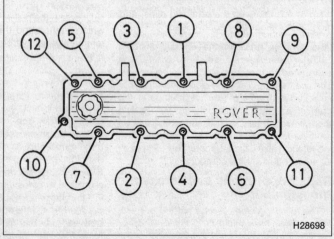

4.7 Camshaft cover bolt tightening sequence - 8-valve engine

16-valve engine

Removal

9 Disconnect the battery negative lead.

10 Release the retaining clips and disconnect the breather hoses from the rear of the camshaft cover.

11 Undo the retaining screws and remove the spark plug cover from the centre of the camshaft cover.

12 Disconnect the HT leads from the spark plugs then unclip the leads from the cover and position them clear.

13 Working progressively and in the **reverse** of the tightening sequence **(see illustration 4.17)**, slacken and remove the camshaft cover retaining bolts.

14 Carefully remove the cover, complete with the gasket. Check the gasket for signs of damage or deterioration and renew it if damaged. **Note:** *Do not separate the camshaft cover and gasket unless the gasket is to be renewed.*

Refitting

15 If the gasket has been removed from the cover, remove the crankcase ventilation system filters, wash them in solvent then dry them before refitting them to the cover. Ensure the cover is clean and dry then fit the new gasket, making sure its "EXHAUST MAN SIDE" marking is pointing towards the exhaust manifold.

16 Make sure the mating surfaces are clean and dry then refit the cover to the cylinder head, ensuring that the gasket remains correctly seated.

17 Refit the cover retaining bolts and tighten them all by hand. Once all bolts are in position, go around in the specified sequence and tighten them to the specified torque setting **(see illustration)**.

18 Reconnect the HT leads securely to the spark plugs. Ensure the leads are clipped correctly into their clips then refit the spark plug cover, tightening its retaining screws securely.

19 Reconnect the breather hoses, securing them in position with the retaining clips, and reconnect the battery negative lead.

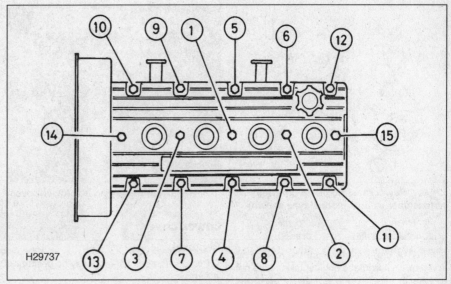

4.17 Camshaft cover bolt tightening sequence - 16-valve engine

5.6 Ensure the crankshaft pulley notch is correctly engaged with the sprocket lug (arrowed) then refit the retaining bolt and washer

5 Crankshaft pulley – removal and refitting

Removal

1 Firmly apply the handbrake then jack up the front of the vehicle and support it securely on axle stands (see *"Jacking and Vehicle Support"*). To improve access, remove the right-hand front roadwheel.

2 If further dismantling is to be carried out, align the engine assembly/valve timing marks as described in Section 3.

3 Remove the auxiliary drivebelt(s) as described in Chapter 1A.

4 Slacken the crankshaft pulley retaining bolt. To prevent crankshaft rotation, have an assistant select top gear and apply the brakes firmly. If the engine is removed from the vehicle it will be necessary to lock the flywheel (see Section 16).

5 Unscrew the pulley bolt and washer, noting which way around the washer is fitted, then remove the pulley from the crankshaft.

Refitting

6 Fit the pulley to the crankshaft, aligning the notch in the pulley with the locating lug on the sprocket, then refit the retaining bolt and washer **(see illustration)**. Make sure that the tapered face of the washer is facing away from the pulley.

7 Lock the crankshaft using the method used on removal, and tighten the pulley retaining bolt to the specified torque setting.

8 Refit and tension the auxiliary drivebelt(s) as described in Chapter 1A.

9 Refit the roadwheel then lower the vehicle to the ground and tighten the wheel nuts to the specified torque.

6 Timing belt covers – removal and refitting

Upper cover

Removal

1 Slacken the lower bolt securing the upper cover to the engine then unscrew the upper bolts securing it to the rear cover **(see illustration)**.

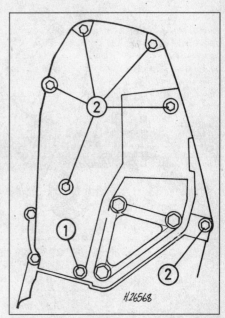

6.1 Timing belt upper cover retaining bolts - 8-valve engine

1 Upper cover-to-engine bolt (cover hole should be slotted)
2 Upper cover-to-rear cover bolts

2A

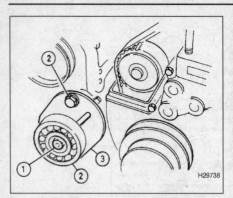

6.7 Power steering pump drivebelt tensioner fixings (manual type shown)

1 Pulley nut   *3 Mounting*
2 Bracket bolts   *bracket*

2 Free the upper cover from the rear cover and remove it from the engine, taking care not to lose the seal which is fitted around the engine mounting bracket. Inspect the seal for signs of damage or deterioration and renew if necessary.

Refitting

3 Refitting is a reversal of removal. Ensure that the rubber seal is positioned correctly and tighten the cover bolts to the specified torque.

6.8 Removing the timing belt lower cover

Lower cover

Removal

4 Remove the crankshaft pulley as described in Section 5.
5 Remove the upper timing belt cover as described previously in this Section.
6 Slacken and remove the retaining bolts and remove the bracket which connects the right-hand lower mounting to the engine mounting bracket.
7 On 16-valve engines, remove the power steering pump drivebelt tensioner assembly. On models with a manual tensioner, slacken

6.12 Timing belt rear cover retaining bolts - 16-valve engine

and remove the tensioner pulley retaining nut and washer then remove the pulley to allow the tensioner bracket to be unbolted **(see illustration)**. On models with an automatic tensioner, unbolt the tensioner pulley assembly and remove it from the engine.
8 On all engines, unscrew the three retaining bolts and remove the lower cover from the engine **(see illustration)**. Check the cover seals for signs of damage or deterioration and renew if necessary.

Refitting

9 Refitting is the reverse of removal ensuring that the seals are correctly fitted. Tighten all bolts to their specified torque settings (where given).

Rear cover

Removal

10 Remove the timing belt as described in Section 7.
11 Remove the camshaft sprocket(s) and the timing belt tensioner as described in Section 8.
12 Undo the retaining bolts securing the cover to the cylinder head/block and remove the cover from the engine **(see illustration)**.

Refitting

13 Refitting is a reversal of removal, refitting the timing belt tensioner, sprockets and belt as described in Sections 7 and 8.

7 Timing belt –
removal and refitting

Removal

Note: *If a new timing belt is to be fitted, the tensioner spring and sleeve should also be renewed.*

1 Disconnect the battery negative lead.
2 Align the engine assembly/valve timing marks as described in Section 3.
3 Remove the crankshaft pulley as described in Section 5, ensuring that all timing marks remain correctly aligned.
4 Remove the timing belt lower cover as described in Section 6 **(see illustrations)**.

7.4a Timing belt and associated components - 8-valve engine

1 Upper cover	*10 Bolt*	*18 Tensioner spring*
2 Seal	*11 Bolt*	*19 Spring sleeve*
3 Bolt	*12 Crankshaft pulley*	*20 Spring stud*
4 Bolt	*13 Washer*	*21 Timing belt*
5 Bolt	*14 Pulley bolt*	*22 Crankshaft sprocket*
6 Shouldered bolt	*15 Tensioner pulley*	*23 Camshaft sprocket*
7 Lower cover	*16 Tensioner pulley bolt*	*24 Sprocket bolt*
8 Seal	*17 Tensioner backplate*	*25 Washer*
9 Seal	*bolt*	

5 Remove the right-hand upper engine mounting as described in Section 17. On 8-valve engines, it will also be necessary to unbolt and remove the engine mounting bracket from the end of the cylinder block **(see illustration)**. **Note:** *This is only necessary if the belt is being renewed; if the belt is being removed as part of another procedure and is not to be renewed, there is no need to disturb the mounting.*

6 On 16-valve engines, a suitable tool should be used to lock the camshaft sprockets together, so that they cannot move under valve spring pressure when the timing belt is removed. Rover technicians use service tool 18G 1570 which slots in between the sprocket teeth, but an acceptable substitute can be fabricated from a length of steel square-section tube cut to fit as closely as possible around the sprocket spokes **(see illustrations)**.

7 Slacken both the timing belt tensioner pulley and the backplate bolts through half a turn each then push the tensioner pulley fully downwards to remove all the tension from the timing belt **(see illustration)**. Hold the tensioner pulley in this position by tightening the backplate clamp bolt securely.

8 Slide the timing belt off from its sprockets and remove it from the engine. If the belt is to be re-used, use white paint or similar to mark the direction of rotation on the belt **(see illustration)**. **Do not** rotate the crankshaft or camshafts until the timing belt has been refitted.

9 Check the timing belt carefully for any signs of uneven wear, splitting or oil contamination, and renew it if there is the slightest doubt about its condition. If the engine is undergoing an overhaul and has covered close to 60 000 miles or it was more than 5 years since the original belt was fitted, renew the belt as a matter of course, regardless of its apparent condition. If signs of oil contamination are found, trace the source of the oil leak and rectify it, then wash down the engine timing belt area and all related components to remove all traces of oil.

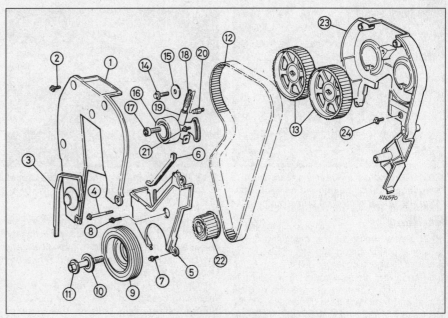

7.4b Timing belt and associated components - 16-valve engine

1 *Upper cover*	9 *Crankshaft pulley*	17 *Tensioner pulley bolt*
2 *Bolt*	10 *Washer*	18 *Tensioner spring*
3 *Seal*	11 *Pulley bolt*	19 *Spring sleeve*
4 *Bolt*	12 *Timing belt*	20 *Spring stud*
5 *Lower cover*	13 *Camshaft sprockets*	21 *Tensioner backplate bolt*
6 *Seal*	14 *Sprocket bolt*	22 *Crankshaft sprocket*
7 *Bolt*	15 *Washer*	23 *Rear cover*
8 *Bolt*	16 *Tensioner pulley*	24 *Bolt*

2A

7.5 On 8-valve engines, remove the right-hand engine mounting bracket from the end of the cylinder block

7.6a A sprocket locking tool can be made by cutting a square-section tube as shown . . .

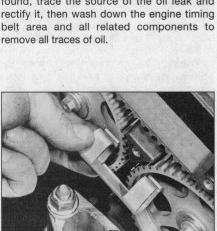

7.6b . . . so that it engages with the sprocket spokes and locks the sprockets together

7.7 Tensioner pulley bolt (A) and backplate (B)

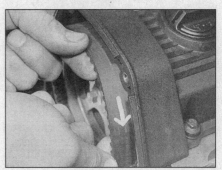

7.8 If the timing belt is to be re-used, mark the direction of rotation on the belt prior to removal

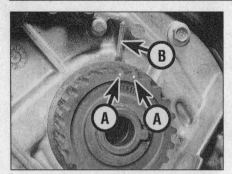

7.11 Timing dots (A) on the crankshaft sprocket must be positioned on each side of the rib (B) on the oil pump housing

7.12 Fit the timing belt making sure that all slack is on the tensioner side of the belt

Refitting

10 If a new timing belt is being fitted, the tensioner pulley spring and sleeve should be renewed (if a genuine Rover belt is being fitted, the spring and sleeve should be supplied as part of a kit). Carefully unhook the original spring and remove it from the engine. Fit the sleeve to the new spring then hook the lower end of the spring onto the tensioner backplate and locate the upper end in the stud groove.

11 Thoroughly clean and dry the timing belt sprockets and check that the camshaft(s) and crankshaft are still correctly positioned. The camshaft sprocket timing mark(s) must still be aligned with the cylinder head surface (see Section 3) and the crankshaft sprocket timing dots must be positioned on each side of the raised rib on the oil pump housing **(see illustration)**.

12 Fit the timing belt over the crankshaft and camshaft sprocket(s), ensuring that the belt front run is taut (ie, all slack is on the tensioner side of the belt), then fit the belt over the coolant pump sprocket and tensioner pulley **(see illustration)**. Do not twist the belt sharply while refitting it. Ensure that the belt teeth are correctly seated centrally in the sprockets, and that the timing marks remain in alignment. If a used belt is being refitted, ensure that the arrow mark made on removal points in the normal direction of rotation, as before.

13 Slacken the timing belt tensioner backplate bolt to release the tensioner and tension the timing belt.

8.7 Remove the sprocket noting the locating pin (arrowed) in the camshaft end (8-valve engine shown)

14 Check the sprocket timing marks are still correctly aligned. If adjustment is necessary, release the tensioner again then disengage the belt from the sprockets and make any necessary adjustments.

15 On 8-valve engines, refit the engine mounting bracket to the cylinder block and tighten its retaining bolts to the specified torque.

16 On all engines, refit the timing belt lower cover to the engine, ensuring its sealing strips are correctly positioned, and tighten its retaining bolts to the specified torque.

17 Fit the pulley to the crankshaft, aligning the notch in the pulley with the locating lug on the sprocket. Refit the retaining bolt and washer, ensuring the tapered face of the washer is facing away from the pulley, then lock the crankshaft (see Section 5) and tighten the retaining bolt to the specified torque.

18 Remove the sprocket locking tool (16-valve models - where fitted) then, using a socket on the crankshaft pulley bolt, rotate the crankshaft smoothly through two complete turns (720°) in the normal direction of rotation to settle the timing belt in position.

19 Check that both the camshaft sprocket and crankshaft pulley timing marks are correctly realigned (see Section 3). Ensure that the belt front run is taut (ie, all slack is on the tensioner side of the belt), then tighten the tensioner backplate bolt and pulley bolts to their specified torque settings.

Note: *On some engines, it will be noticed that the tensioner pulley backplate has an alignment mark on it. If the original belt that was fitted in production is being re-used, position the tensioner so that its backplate mark is aligned with the punch mark on the cylinder head then tighten the tensioner backplate and pulleys bolts to their specified torque settings. Once the original belt has been replaced and a new belt has been fitted, the marks should be ignored.*

20 Refit the right-hand engine mounting as described in Section 17.

21 Refit the timing belt upper cover, ensuring the seal is correctly positioned, and tighten its retaining bolts to the specified torque.

22 Refit the auxiliary drivebelt(s) as described in Chapter 1A.

23 Refit the roadwheel, and lower the vehicle to the ground, and tighten the wheel nuts to the specified torque. Reconnect the battery negative lead.

8 Timing belt tensioner and sprockets – removal and refitting

Camshaft sprocket(s)

Removal

1 Disconnect the battery negative lead.

2 Align the engine assembly/valve timing marks as described in Section 3.

3 Slacken both the timing belt tensioner pulley and the backplate bolts through half a turn each then push the tensioner pulley fully downwards to remove all the tension from the timing belt. Secure the tensioner pulley in this position by tightening the backplate bolt securely.

4 Position the timing belt clear of the camshaft sprocket(s), taking care not to twist the belt too sharply; use only your fingers to move the belt. **Do not** rotate the crankshaft until the timing belt is refitted.

5 On 8-valve engines, slacken the camshaft sprocket retaining bolt and remove it, along with its washer. To prevent the camshaft from rotating, Rover technicians use service tool 18G 1521, but an acceptable substitute can be fabricated from two lengths of steel strip (one long, the other short) and three nuts and bolts. One nut and bolt should form the pivot of a forked tool with the remaining two nuts and bolts at the tips of the forks to engage with the sprocket spokes **(see illustration 8.13a)**.

6 On 16-valve engines, slacken and remove the camshaft sprocket retaining bolt(s), along with the washer(s). To prevent camshaft rotation, Rover technicians use the locking tool 18G 1570 which fits in-between the sprocket teeth. In the absence of the special tool, fabricate a suitable alternative (see Section 7, paragraph 6) or use the forked tool described in paragraph 5 **(see illustration 8.13b)**.

7 Remove the sprocket(s) from the camshaft(s) taking care not to lose the sprocket locating pin(s) **(see illustration)**. If a pin is a loose fit in the end of the camshaft, remove it and store it with the sprocket for safe-keeping.

8 Check the sprocket(s) for signs of wear or damage and renew if necessary.

Refitting

9 Prior to refitting, check the oil seal(s) for signs of damage or leakage. If necessary, renew as described in Section 9.

10 Ensure the locating pin(s) is in position in the camshaft end(s). Note that the pin(s) should be fitted with the split facing inwards.

11 On 8-valve engines, refit the sprocket to the camshaft end, aligning its cutout with the locating pin, and refit the washer and retaining bolt

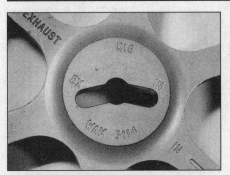

8.12 Engage the exhaust camshaft locating pin with the EX cutout and the inlet camshaft locating pin in the IN cutout

8.13a Using the holding tool to prevent sprocket rotation as the retaining bolt is tightened to the specified torque - 8-valve engine

8.13b Using the locking tool to prevent sprocket rotation as the retaining bolt is tightened to the specified torque - 16-valve engine

12 On 16-valve engines both inlet and exhaust camshaft sprockets are the same but each one is equipped with two locating pin cutouts. If the sprocket is being fitted to the inlet camshaft, engage the locating pin in the "IN" cutout, and if the sprocket is being fitted to the exhaust camshaft, engage the locating pin in the "EX" cutout **(see illustration)**. Ensure the camshaft locating pin is engaged in the correct sprocket cutout then refit the washer and retaining bolt.

13 On all engines, retain the sprocket(s) by the method used on removal, and tighten the pulley retaining bolt(s) to the specified torque setting **(see illustrations)**.

14 Ensure the crankshaft pulley mark is still correctly aligned with the mark on the lower cover and the camshaft sprocket mark(s) are correctly aligned with the cylinder head upper surface (see Section 3).

15 Ensure that the belt is correctly engaged with the crankshaft sprocket then fit it over the camshaft sprocket(s), ensuring that the belt front run is taut (ie, all slack is on the tensioner side of the belt). **Do not** twist the belt sharply while refitting it and ensure that the belt teeth are correctly seated centrally in the sprockets, and that the timing marks remain in alignment.

16 Slacken the timing belt tensioner backplate bolt to release the tensioner and tension the timing belt. Check the sprocket timing marks are still correctly aligned. If adjustment is necessary, release the tensioner again then disengage the belt from the sprockets and make any necessary adjustments.

17 Tension the timing belt as described in paragraphs 18 and 19 of Section 7.

18 Refit the timing belt upper cover, ensuring the seal is correctly positioned, and tighten its retaining bolts to the specified torque.

19 Refit the roadwheel, and lower the vehicle to the ground, and tighten the wheel nuts to the specified torque. Reconnect the battery negative lead.

Crankshaft sprocket

Removal

20 Remove the timing belt as described in Section 7.

21 Slide the sprocket off from the end of the crankshaft, noting which way around it is fitted.

Refitting

22 Refit the sprocket to the crankshaft, engaging it with the crankshaft flattened section. Check that the sprocket timing marks align - the two dots on the sprocket must be positioned on each side of the raised rib on the oil pump body.

23 Refit the timing belt as described in Section 7.

Tensioner assembly

Removal

24 Disconnect the battery negative lead.

25 Align the engine assembly/valve timing marks as described in Section 3. On 16-valve engines, if possible, lock the camshaft sprockets in position with the locking tool (see Section 7, paragraph 6).

26 Using a pair of pliers, carefully unhook the tensioner spring and remove it from the backplate and locating stud **(see illustration)**.

27 Unscrew the tensioner pulley and backplate bolts then manoeuvre the tensioner assembly away from the engine.

28 Clean the tensioner assembly but do not use any strong solvent which may enter the pulley bearing. Check that the pulley rotates freely on the backplate, with no sign of stiffness or free play. Renew the assembly if there is any doubt about its condition or if there are any obvious signs of wear or damage. The same applies to the tensioner spring, which should be checked with great care as its condition is critical for the correct tensioning of the timing belt.

Refitting

29 Ensure the crankshaft pulley mark is still correctly aligned with the mark on the lower cover and the camshaft sprocket mark(s) are correctly aligned with the cylinder head upper surface (see Section 3).

30 Ensure that the belt is correctly engaged with the crankshaft, camshaft and coolant pump sprockets and the belt front run is taut (ie, all slack is on the tensioner side of the belt).

31 Manoeuvre the tensioner pulley assembly into position and refit the pulley and backplate bolts. Pivot the pulley fully downwards and lightly tighten the backplate bolt to hold it in position.

32 Hook the tensioner spring onto the backplate and over its locating stud.

33 Carry out the operations described in paragraphs 16 to 19 of this Section.

9 Camshaft oil seals – renewal

Right-hand (timing belt end) seal

Note: *If the seal is to be renewed with the timing belt still in place, then check that the belt is free from oil contamination. Renew the belt if signs of oil contamination are found. Cover the belt to protect it from contamination while work is in progress and ensure that all traces of oil are removed from the area before the belt is refitted.*

1 Remove the camshaft sprocket as described in Section 8.

2 Punch or drill two small holes opposite

2A

8.26 Timing belt tensioner assembly

1 *Tensioner pulley*
2 *Backplate bolt*
3 *Tensioner spring and sleeve*
4 *Spring locating stud*

9.4 Using a socket to tap a camshaft oil seal into position

each other in the oil seal. Screw a self-tapping screw into each hole, and pull on the screws with pliers to extract the seal.

3 Clean the seal housing and polish off any burrs or raised edges which may have caused the seal to fail.

4 Lubricate the lips of the new seal with clean engine oil and drive it into position. Use a suitable tubular drift, such as a socket, which bears only on the hard outer edge of the seal **(see illustration)**. Take care not to damage the seal lips during fitting and note that the seal lips should face inwards.

5 Refit the camshaft sprocket as described in Section 8.

Left-hand (flywheel end) seal – 8-valve engines

6 Remove the distributor, rotor arm and shield as described in Chapter 5B. To further improve access, remove the air cleaner housing as described in Chapter 4A.

7 Renew the oil seal as described in paragraphs 2 to 4.

8 Refit the distributor components (see Chapter 5B) then, where necessary, refit the air cleaner housing (see Chapter 4A).

Left-hand (flywheel end) seal – 16-valve engines

9 Remove the air cleaner assembly as described in Chapter 4A and proceed as described under the relevant sub-heading.

Exhaust camshaft seal

10 Release the coolant hose from its clip then unscrew the retaining bolts and remove the exhaust camshaft cover plate from the cylinder head **(see illustration)**.

11 Renew the oil seal as described in paragraphs 2 to 4.

12 Ensure the mating surfaces are clean and dry and apply a smear of sealant to the cover plate. Refit the cover plate, tightening its retaining bolts to the specified torque.

13 Clip the coolant hose back into position then refit the air cleaner housing (see Chapter 4A).

Inlet camshaft seal

14 Remove the distributor, rotor arm and shield as described in Chapter 5B.

15 Renew the oil seal as described in paragraphs 2 to 4.

16 Refit the distributor components (see Chapter 5B) then refit the air cleaner housing (see Chapter 4A).

10 Camshaft(s) and followers – removal, inspection and refitting

Note: *Rover produce a sealant kit which consists of a plastic scraper, gasket removing compound and the recommended sealant for the camshaft carrier joint. It is recommended that this kit is used during the following procedure. New camshaft oil seals will also be required.*

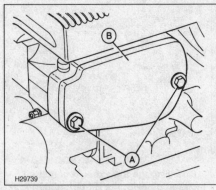

9.10 To gain access to the exhaust camshaft oil seal undo the retaining bolts (A) and remove the cover plate (B)

Removal

1 Remove the camshaft cover as described in Section 4.

2 Remove the distributor cap, rotor arm and shield, as described in Chapter 5B.

3 Remove the camshaft sprocket(s) as described in Section 8.

4 On 16-valve engines, unscrew the retaining bolts and remove the cover plate from the left-hand end of the exhaust camshaft.

5 On all engines, working in the correct sequence shown, slacken the camshaft bearing carrier retaining bolts evenly progressively, by one turn at a time, to gradually release the pressure of the valve springs **(see illustrations)**.

Caution: If the bearing carrier bolts are carelessly slackened, the carrier might break. If the carrier is broken, the complete cylinder head assembly must be renewed; the carrier is matched to the head and is not available separately.

6 Lift the camshaft bearing carrier away from the cylinder, noting the correct fitted positions of the locating dowels **(see illustration)**. If the

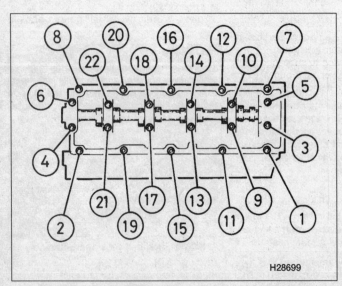

10.5a Camshaft bearing carrier retaining bolt slackening sequence - 8-valve engine

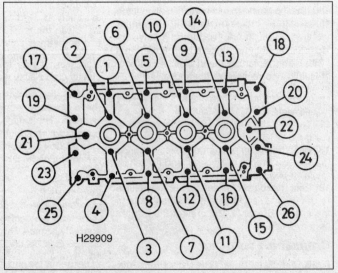

10.5b Camshaft bearing carrier retaining bolt slackening sequence - 16-valve engine

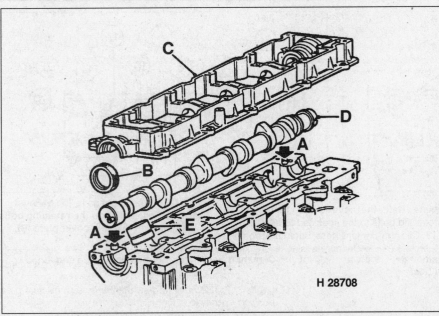

10.6 Camshaft and bearing carrier - 8-valve engine

A *Locating dowels* C *Bearing carrier* E *Follower*
B *Right-hand oil seal* D *Camshaft*

10.8 Removing a camshaft follower

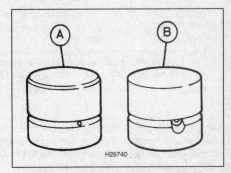

10.10 Camshaft follower identification

A *Original type*
B *Modified type (with drilling leading to oilway)*

dowels are loose, remove them and store them with the bearing carrier for safe-keeping.
7 Carefully lift the camshaft(s) from the cylinder head. Remove the oil seals and discard them; new ones should be used on refitting. On 16-valve engines, the inlet camshaft is easily identified by the distributor rotor arm drive spindle so there is no need to mark the camshaft for identification.
8 If necessary, obtain eight or sixteen (as applicable) small, clean plastic containers, and label them for identification. Alternatively, divide a larger container into compartments. Using a sucker or magnet, withdraw each follower in turn, invert it to prevent oil loss and place it in its respective container, which should then be filled with clean engine oil **(see illustration)**. **Do not** interchange the followers, and do not allow the followers to lose oil, as they will take a long time to refill with oil on restarting the engine, which could result in incorrect valve clearances.

Inspection

9 Examine the camshaft bearing surfaces and cam lobes for signs of wear ridges and scoring. Renew the camshaft if any of these conditions are apparent. Examine the condition of the bearing surfaces both on the camshaft journals and in the cylinder head. If the head bearing surfaces are worn excessively, the cylinder head will need to be renewed.
10 Examine the follower bearing surfaces which contact the camshaft lobes for wear ridges and scoring. Check the followers and their bores in the cylinder head for signs of wear or damage. If a micrometer is available, measure the outside diameter of each follower and compare it to the results given in the Specifications. If the engine's valve clearances have sounded noisy, particularly if the noise persists after initial start-up from cold, then there is reason to suspect a faulty follower. If any follower is thought to be faulty or is visibly worn it should be renewed.

Note: *Modified followers have been introduced by Rover* **(see illustration)**. *Where the modified followers are already fitted, then each follower can be renewed individually. However, if the original type followers are installed and renewal of any follower is necessary, then all the followers must be renewed as a set. Rover no longer supply the original type follower and it is not permissible to have a mixture of original and modified followers fitted to the same engine.*

Refitting

11 Where removed, lubricate the followers with clean engine oil and carefully insert each one into its original location in the cylinder head **(see illustration)**. Proceed as described under the relevant sub-heading.

8-valve engine

12 Liberally oil the camshaft bearings and followers then refit the camshaft. Position the shaft so that the sprocket locating pin is in the 4 o'clock position when viewed from the right-hand end of the engine **(see illustration)**.
13 Ensure the mating surface of the camshaft bearing carrier and cylinder head are clean and dry. Apply a bead of sealant to the bearing carrier mating surface as shown **(see illustration)**. Spread the sealant to an even film taking care not to allow any sealant to enter the oilway grooves.

10.11 Lubricate the followers with clean engine oil and insert them into the cylinder head

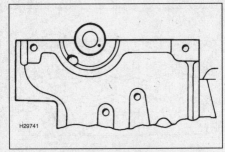

10.12 Position the camshaft so that the sprocket locating pin is positioned in the 4 o'clock when viewed from the right-hand end of the head

2A

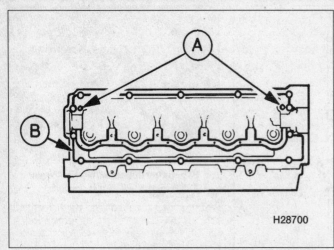

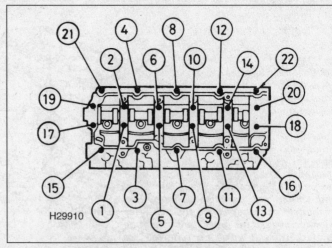

10.13 Ensure the locating dowels (A) are in position then apply a bead of sealant (B) to highlighted area of the bearing carrier mating surface

10.15 Camshaft bearing carrier bolt tightening sequence - 8-valve engine

Use bolts 1, 2, 13 and 14 to draw the carrier squarely into position - see text

14 Ensure that the locating dowels are in position and refit the camshaft bearing carrier to the cylinder head. Ensure the carrier is correctly located then refit the retaining bolts, tightening them all by hand only at this stage.
15 Working in a diagonal sequence, evenly and progressively tighten bolts numbers 1, 2, 13 and 14 in the tightening sequence **(see illustration)** to draw the bearing carrier squarely down into contact with the cylinder head. Once the carrier is in contact with the head, go around in the specified sequence and tighten the retaining bolts to the specified torque.
Caution: If the bearing carrier bolts are carelessly tightened, the carrier might break. If the carrier is broken the complete cylinder head assembly must be renewed; the carrier is matched to the head and is not available separately.
16 Fit new camshaft oil seals as described in Section 9.
17 Refit the camshaft sprocket as described in Section 8.
18 Refit the camshaft cover as described in Section 4 then refit the distributor components as described in Chapter 5B.

16-valve engine

19 Liberally oil the camshaft bearings and followers then refit the camshafts to the cylinder head; the inlet camshaft is easily identified by the rotor arm drive spindle.
20 Position the camshafts so that the camshaft sprocket locating pins are positioned as shown **(see illustration)**. When viewed from the right-hand end of the engine, the inlet camshaft sprocket pin should be in the 4 o'clock position and the exhaust camshaft sprocket pin should be in the 8 o'clock position.
21 Ensure the mating surface of the camshaft bearing carrier and cylinder head are clean and dry. Apply a bead of sealant to the bearing carrier mating surface as shown **(see illustration)**. Spread the sealant to an even film taking care not to allow any sealant to enter the oilway grooves.
22 Ensure that the locating dowels are in position and refit the camshaft bearing carrier to the cylinder head. Ensure the carrier is correctly located then refit the retaining bolts, tightening them all by hand only at this stage.
23 Working in a diagonal sequence, evenly

and progressively tighten the retaining bolts to draw the bearing carrier squarely down into contact with the cylinder head. Once the carrier is in contact with the head, go around in the specified sequence and tighten the retaining bolts to the specified torque **(see illustration)**.
Caution: If the bearing carrier bolts are carelessly tightened, the carrier might break. If the carrier is broken then the complete cylinder head assembly must be renewed; the carrier is matched to the head and is not available separately.
24 Fit new camshaft oil seals as described in Section 9.
25 Ensure the mating surfaces are clean and dry and apply a smear of sealant to the exhaust camshaft cover plate. Refit the cover plate to the left-hand end of the cylinder head, tightening its retaining bolts to the specified torque.
26 Refit the camshaft sprockets as described in Section 8.
27 Refit the camshaft cover as described in Section 4 then refit the distributor components as described in Chapter 5B.

10.20 On 16-valve engines, position the camshaft sprocket locating pins (arrowed) as shown

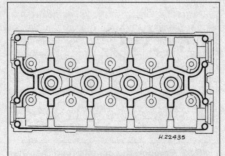

10.21 Apply a bead of sealant to highlighted area of the bearing carrier mating surface as shown

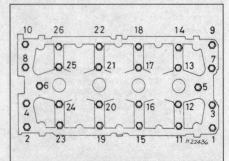

10.23 Camshaft bearing carrier bolt tightening sequence - 16-valve engine

11 Cylinder head –
removal and refitting

Caution: Before commencing any servicing or overhaul work on the engine, the crankshaft must always be rotated to the desired position before the cylinder head bolts are disturbed. Due to the design of the engine, it will become very difficult, almost impossible, to turn the crankshaft once the cylinder head bolts have been slackened. The manufacturer accordingly states that the crankshaft will be "tight" and should not be rotated more than absolutely necessary once the head has been removed. If the crankshaft cannot be rotated, then it must be removed for overhaul work to proceed. With this in mind, during any servicing or overhaul work, the crankshaft must always be rotated to the desired position before the bolts are disturbed.

Removal

1 Disconnect the battery negative lead.
2 Drain the cooling system, as described in Chapter 1A.
3 Remove the air cleaner housing as described in Chapter 4A.
4 On 16-valve engines equipped with air conditioning, remove the alternator and upper mounting bracket as described in Chapter 5A.
5 On all engines, remove the camshaft sprocket(s) and the timing belt tensioner as described in Section 8.
6 Slacken and remove the bolts securing the timing belt rear cover to the cylinder head; there is no need to remove the cover completely.
7 Remove the exhaust manifold as described in Chapter 4A. If no work is to be carried out on the cylinder head, the head can be removed complete with the manifold once the exhaust front pipe has been unbolted and the oxygen sensor wiring connector has been disconnected (see Chapter 4A).
8 Remove the inlet manifold as described in Chapter 4A. If no work is to be carried out on the cylinder head, the head can be removed complete with the manifold once the following operations have been carried out (see Chapter 4A).

  a) *Depressurise the fuel system and disconnect the fuel feed and return hoses from the manifold/fuel rail.*
  b) *Disconnect the various wiring connectors from the manifold components and free all wiring from the manifold.*
  c) *Disconnect the various vacuum, breather and (where necessary) coolant hoses from the manifold, noting each one correct fitted location and routing.*
  d) *Disconnect the accelerator cable from the throttle housing.*
  e) *Unbolt the manifold support bracket (where fitted).*

9 Release the retaining clips and disconnect the coolant hoses from the outlet elbow on the front, left-hand end of the cylinder head. Disconnect the wiring connectors from the coolant temperature sensor(s) which are screwed into the elbow.
10 Disconnect the ignition coil HT lead from the centre of the distributor cap and free the lead from its retaining clips. If the cylinder head is to be dismantled, remove the distributor, rotor arm and shield as described in Chapter 5B.
11 Remove the camshaft cover as described in Section 4.
12 Working in the **reverse** of the tightening sequence **(see illustrations 11.28a and 11.28b)**, progressively slacken the cylinder head bolts by a third of a turn at a time until all bolts can be unscrewed by hand. Withdraw the bolts, and store them in order, so that they can be refitted in their original locations. The bolts can be stored by pushing them through a clearly-marked cardboard template.
13 The joint between the cylinder head and gasket and the cylinder block/crankcase must now be broken without disturbing the cylinder liners. Although these liners are better located and sealed than some wet liner engines, there is still a risk of coolant and foreign matter leaking into the sump if the cylinder head is lifted carelessly. If care is not taken and the liners are moved, there is also a possibility of their seals being disturbed, causing leakage after refitting the head.
14 To break the joint, obtain two L-shaped metal bars which fit into the cylinder head bolt holes and gently rock the cylinder head free towards the front of the vehicle **(see illustration)**.
Caution: Do not try to swivel the head on the cylinder block/crankcase as it is located by dowels as well as by the tops of the liners.
15 When the joint is broken, lift the cylinder head away, using assistance if possible as it is a heavy assembly, especially if complete with the manifolds. Remove the gasket and discard it. Support the cylinder head on wooden blocks or stands – do not rest the lower face of the cylinder head on the work surface. Note the fitted positions of the two locating dowels, and remove them for safe keeping if they are loose.
16 Note that further to the warnings given in the note at the beginning of this Section, **do not** attempt to rotate the crankshaft with the cylinder head removed, otherwise the liners may be displaced. Operations that require the rotation of the crankshaft (eg: cleaning the piston crowns) can be carried out after fitting cylinder liner clamps. The manufacturer's liner clamps are secured by the cylinder head bolts as shown **(see illustration)**.

HAYNES **HiNT**	*Equivalents can be improvised using large washers and tubular spacers.*

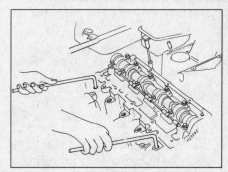

11.14 Using two cranked bars to break the cylinder head joint by rocking

17 If the cylinder head is to be dismantled, remove the camshaft(s), as described in Section 10, then refer to the relevant Sections of Part D of this Chapter.

Preparation for refitting

18 The mating faces of the cylinder head and cylinder block/crankcase must be perfectly clean before refitting the head. Use a hard plastic or wood scraper to remove all traces of gasket and carbon. Also clean the piston crowns. Take particular care, as the soft aluminium alloy is damaged easily. Also, make sure that the carbon is not allowed to enter the oil and water passages – this is particularly important for the lubrication system, as carbon could block the oil supply to any of the engine components. Using adhesive tape and paper, seal the water, oil and bolt holes in the cylinder block/crankcase. To prevent carbon entering the gap between the pistons and bores, smear a little grease in the gap. After cleaning each piston, use a small brush to remove all traces of grease and carbon from the gap, then wipe away the remainder with a clean cloth. Clean all the pistons in the same way. Take great care not to move the pistons during this procedure.
19 Check the mating surfaces of the cylinder block/crankcase and the cylinder head for nicks, deep scratches and other damage. If slight, they may be removed carefully with a file, but if excessive, machining may be the only alternative to renewal.

2A

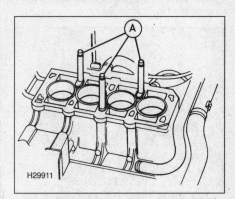

11.16 Rover cylinder liner clamps (A) in position on the cylinder block

11.21 Checking the condition of the cylinder head bolts threads - cylinder head removed

11.24 Ensure the locating dowels (arrowed) are in position then fit the new head gasket . . .

11.25 . . . making sure the TOP mark is upwards and the FRONT arrow points towards the timing belt end

20 If warpage of the cylinder head gasket surface is suspected, use a straight-edge to check it for distortion. Refer to Part D of this Chapter if necessary.

21 Check the condition of the cylinder head bolts, particularly their threads. Keeping all bolts in their correct fitted order, wash them and wipe dry. Check each bolt for any sign of visible wear or damage, renewing as necessary. Note that if cylinder head bolts have been used to secure the cylinder liner clamps, each bolt and clamp should be removed one at a time for checking, and refitted immediately the bolt has been tested. Lightly oil the threads of each bolt, carefully enter it into its original hole (**do not** drop the bolt into the hole) and screw it in, by hand only until finger-tight. Measure the distance from the cylinder block/crankcase gasket surface to the lower surface of the bolt head **(see illustration)**.

22 If the distance measured is under 97 mm, the bolt may be re-used. If the distance measured is 97 mm or more, the bolt must be renewed. As a precaution, we recommend that the bolts are renewed as a complete set, regardless of their apparent condition.

Refitting

23 Remove the cylinder liner clamps (where fitted) and wipe clean the mating surfaces of the cylinder head and cylinder block/crankcase.

24 Ensure that the two locating dowels are in

position at each end of the cylinder block/crankcase surface **(see illustration)**.

25 Position a new gasket on the cylinder block/crankcase surface so that its "TOP" mark is uppermost and the "FRONT" arrow points to the timing belt end **(see illustration)**.

26 Carefully refit the cylinder head, locating it on the dowels.

27 Keeping all the cylinder head bolts in their correct fitted order, wash them and wipe dry. Lightly oil under the head and on the threads of each bolt, carefully enter it into its original hole and screw it in, by hand only, until finger-tight. **Do not** drop the bolts into their holes.

28 Working progressively and in the sequence shown, first tighten all the cylinder head bolts to the stage 1 torque setting **(see illustrations)**.

29 Once all bolts have been tightened to the stage 1 torque, again working in the sequence shown, tighten each bolt through its specified stage 2 angle, using a socket and extension bar. It is recommended that an angle-measuring gauge is used during this stage of tightening, to ensure accuracy. Prior to tightening, use a felt-tip pen or similar to make alignment marks between the radial mark on each bolt head and the cylinder head **(see illustration)**. The second stage torque can then be achieved by tightening each bolt through half-a-turn so that the mark on the bolt head faces away from the corresponding mark on the cylinder head.

30 Finally go around in the specified sequence again and tighten all bolts through the specified stage 3 angle. Each bolt head radial mark should now be realigned with the corresponding mark on the cylinder head again. If any bolt is overtightened beyond the mark on the cylinder head, slacken the bolt by a quarter-turn, then re-tighten until the marks align.

31 Refit the camshaft cover (Section 4).

32 Reconnect the HT lead to the coil/refit the distributor (as applicable - see Chapter 5B).

33 Reconnect the coolant hoses to the cylinder and secure them in position with the retaining clips. Reconnect the coolant temperature sensor wiring connector(s).

34 Refit the inlet manifold (where removed) or reconnect the manifold hoses and wiring as described in Chapter 4A. Ensure all hoses/ wiring are correctly routed and securely reconnected then reconnect and adjust the accelerator cable.

35 Refit the exhaust manifold/reconnect the exhaust front pipe (as applicable) as described in Chapter 4A.

36 Refit the bolts securing the timing belt upper cover to the cylinder head and tighten them to the specified torque.

37 Refit the timing belt tensioner and cam-shaft sprocket(s) as described in Section 8.

38 On 16-valve engines equipped with air conditioning, refit the alternator as described in Chapter 5A.

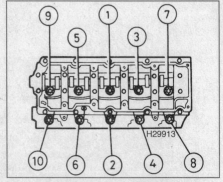

11.28a Cylinder head bolt tightening sequence - 8-valve engine

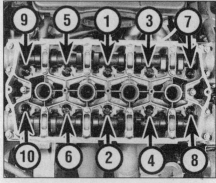

11.28b Cylinder head bolt tightening sequence - 16-valve engine

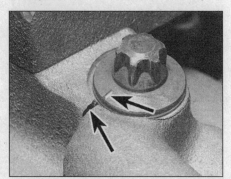

11.29 Make alignment marks between the cylinder head bolt radial marks and the head to check correct bolt tightening

12.5 Removing the flywheel lower cover plate

12.6 Removing the sump

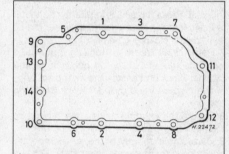

12.10 Ensure the sump gasket pegs are correctly engaged in the locating holes on the sump flange

39 Refit the air cleaner housing as described in Chapter 4A.

40 On completion refill the cooling system as described in Chapter 1A.

12 Sump – removal and refitting

Removal

1 Disconnect the battery negative lead.

2 Drain the engine oil (with reference to Chapter 1A if necessary), then clean and refit the engine oil drain plug, tightening it to the specified torque wrench setting. If the engine is nearing its service interval when the oil and filter are due for renewal, it is recommended that the filter is also removed and a new one fitted. After reassembly, the engine can then be refilled with fresh engine oil.

3 Apply the handbrake, then jack up the front of the vehicle and support it securely on axle stands (see "*Jacking and Vehicle Support*").

4 Remove the exhaust front pipe as described in Chapter 4A.

5 Unscrew the three retaining bolts and remove the flywheel lower cover plate from the base of the transmission housing **(see illustration)**.

6 Progressively slacken and remove the bolts securing the sump to the base of the cylinder block. Break the sump joint by striking the sump with the palm of the hand, then lower the sump away from the engine, along with its gasket **(see illustration)**. Inspect the sump gasket for signs of damage or deterioration and renew if necessary.

7 While the sump is removed, take the opportunity to check the oil pump pick-up/strainer for signs of clogging or splitting. If necessary, unbolt the pick-up/strainer and remove it from the engine along with its sealing ring. The strainer can then be cleaned easily in solvent. Inspect the strainer mesh for signs of clogging or splitting and renew if necessary.

Refitting

8 Clean all traces of gasket from the mating surfaces of the cylinder block/crankcase and

sump, then use a clean rag to wipe out the sump and the engine interior.

9 Where necessary, fit a new sealing ring to oil pump pick-up/strainer groove then carefully refit the pipe, tightening its retaining bolts to the specified torque setting.

10 Fit the gasket to the sump making sure that all its locating pegs are correctly located in the sump holes **(see illustration)**.

11 Offer up the sump to the cylinder block/crankcase then refit the sump retaining bolts, and tighten the bolts finger-tight only.

12 Working in the sequence shown, tighten the sump bolts to the specified torque setting **(see illustration)**.

13 Refit the flywheel lower cover plate and tighten its retaining bolts to the specified torque setting.

14 Refit the exhaust front pipe as described in Chapter 4A.

15 Lower the vehicle to the ground, reconnect the battery negative lead and refill the engine with oil as described in Chapter 1A.

13 Oil pump – removal and refitting

Removal

Note: *New oil pump retaining bolts will be required on refitting. The oil pressure relief valve can be dismantled without removing the oil pump from the vehicle - see Section 14 for details.*

1 Remove the crankshaft sprocket as described in Section 8 and secure the timing belt clear of the working area so that it cannot be contaminated with oil.

2 Drain the engine oil, then clean and refit the engine oil drain plug, tightening it to the specified torque wrench setting. If the engine is nearing its service interval when the oil and filter are due for renewal, it is recommended that the filter is also removed and a new one fitted. After reassembly, the engine can then be refilled with fresh engine oil (see Chapter 1A).

3 Unscrew the two bolts securing the engine wiring harness guide to the oil pump and position the guide clear **(see illustration)**.

12.12 Sump bolt tightening sequence

4 Slacken and remove the oil pump retaining bolts, noting the correct fitted location of the shorter bolt. Discard the bolts; new one must be used on refitting.

5 Free the oil pump from the cylinder block then slide it off the end of the crankshaft. Note the correct fitted locations of the pump locating dowels; if the dowels are loose, remove them and store with the pump for safe-keeping. Remove the gasket and discard it.

Refitting

6 Prior to refitting, carefully lever out the crankshaft oil seal using a flat-bladed screwdriver. Fit the new oil seal, ensuring its sealing lip is facing inwards, and press it squarely into the housing using a tubular drift which bears only on the hard outer edge of

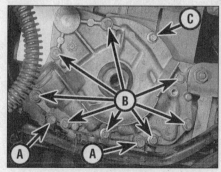

13.3 Oil pump fixings

A Engine wiring harness bolts
B Oil pump retaining bolts (long)
C oil pump retaining bolt (short)

2A

14.5 The oil pump pressure relief valve can be removed with the engine in the vehicle

the seal. Press the seal into position so that it is flush with the housing and lubricate the oil seal lip with clean engine oil.

7 Remove all traces of locking compound from the threads of the oil pump bolts and cylinder block and ensure the mating surfaces of the oil pump and cylinder block are clean and dry.

8 Ensure the locating dowels are in position then fit a new gasket to the cylinder block.

9 Carefully manoeuvre the oil pump into position and engage the inner rotor with the crankshaft end. Locate the pump on the dowels, taking great care not to damage the oil seal lip.

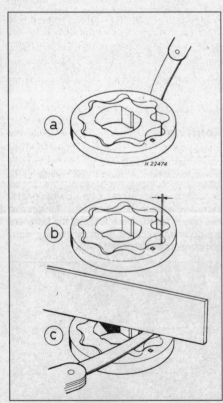

14.7 Oil pump checking measurements

a *Outer rotor-to-pump body clearance*
b *Inner rotor tip-to-outer rotor clearance*
c *Rotor endfloat*

10 If the threads of the new bolts are not pre-coated with locking compound, apply suitable locking compound to them (Rover recommend the use of Loctite 242). Fit the new bolts, ensuring the shorter bolt is fitted in the correct location, and tighten them progressively to the specified torque wrench setting.

11 Secure the engine wiring harness guide to the oil pump and securely tighten its retaining bolts.

12 Refit the crankshaft sprocket as described in Section 8.

13 On completion, refill the engine with oil as described in Chapter 1A.

14 Oil pump –
dismantling, inspection and reassembly

Note: *If oil pump wear is suspected, check the cost and availability of new parts (only available in the form of a repair kit) against the cost of a new pump. Examine the pump as described in this Section and then decide whether renewal or repair is the best course of action.*

Dismantling

1 Remove the oil pump as described in Section 13.

2 Unscrew the retaining screws and remove the pump cover plate and sealing ring.

3 Note the identification marks on the outer rotor then remove both the rotors from the body.

4 The oil pressure relief valve can be dismantled, if required, without disturbing the pump. If this is to be done with the pump in position and the engine still installed in the vehicle, it will first be necessary to jack up the front of the vehicle and remove the right-hand roadwheel to gain access to the valve (see *"Jacking and Vehicle Support"*).

5 To dismantle the valve, slacken and remove the threaded plug and washer then recover the valve spring and plunger **(see illustration)**.

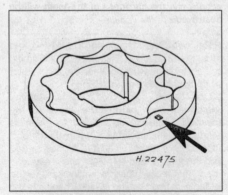

14.12 On reassembly, ensure the identification mark on the outer rotor (arrowed) faces outwards

Inspection

6 Inspect the rotors for obvious signs of wear or damage and renew if necessary. If the pump body or cover plate is scored or damaged, then the complete oil pump assembly must be renewed.

7 Refit the rotors to the body and, using feeler blades of the appropriate thickness, measure the clearance between the outer rotor and the pump body, then between the inner rotor tip and the outer rotor **(see illustration)**.

8 Using feeler blades and a straight-edge placed across the top of the pump body and the rotors, measure the rotor endfloat.

9 If any measurement is outside the specified limits, the complete pump assembly must be renewed.

10 If the pressure relief valve plunger is scored, or if it does not slide freely in the pump body bore, then it must be renewed, using all the components from the repair kit.

11 Thoroughly clean the threads of the pump cover plate securing screws and renew the cover sealing ring and relief valve washer, if damaged.

Reassembly

12 Lubricate the pump rotors with clean engine oil and refit them to the pump body, ensuring that the identification mark on the outer rotor faces outwards (ie, towards the pump cover) **(see illustration)**.

13 Fit the sealing ring to the pump body and refit the cover plate. Apply thread-locking compound (Rover recommend the use of Loctite 222) to the threads of the cover plate screws then refit the screws, tightening them securely.

14 Check that the pump rotates freely, then prime it by injecting oil into its passages and rotating it. If a long time elapses before the pump is refitted to the engine, prime it again before installation.

15 Refit the oil pressure relief valve plunger, ensuring that it is the correct way up, then install the spring **(see illustration)**. Fit the sealing washer to the threaded plug and tighten the plug securely.

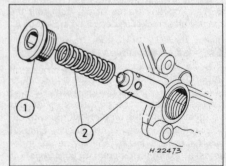

14.15 Oil pump pressure relief valve components

1 *Threaded plug and sealing washer*
2 *Plunger and spring*

15.9 Carefully ease the seal over the crankshaft end, taking care not to damage its sealing lip

15 Crankshaft oil seals – renewal

Right-hand (timing belt end) seal

1 Remove the crankshaft sprocket as described in Section 8, and secure the timing belt clear of the working area so that it cannot be contaminated with oil.

2 Carefully punch or drill two small holes opposite each other in the oil seal. Screw a self-tapping screw into each and pull on the screws with pliers to extract the seal.

Caution: Great care must be taken to avoid damage to the oil pump.

3 Clean the seal housing and polish off any burrs or raised edges which may have caused the seal to fail in the first place.

4 Lubricate the lips of the new seal with clean engine oil and ease it into position on the end of the shaft. Press the seal squarely into position until it is flush with the housing. If necessary, a suitable tubular drift, such as a socket, which bears only on the hard outer edge of the seal can be used to tap the seal into position. Take great care not to damage the seal lips during fitting and ensure that the seal lips face inwards; if a genuine Rover seal is being installed, use the seal protector supplied to protect the seal during fitting and remove the protector once the seal is correctly located.

5 Wash off any traces of oil, then refit the crankshaft sprocket as described in Section 8.

Left-hand (flywheel end) oil seal

6 Remove the flywheel as described in Section 16.

7 Taking care not to mark either the crankshaft or any part of the cylinder block/crankcase, lever the seal evenly out of its housing, using a large flat-bladed screwdriver or similar tool.

8 Clean the seal housing and polish off any burrs or raised edges which may have caused the original seal to fail.

9 Grease the lips of the new seal and the crankshaft shoulder, then offer up the seal to the cylinder block/crankcase **(see illustration)**.

10 Ease the sealing lip of the seal over the crankshaft shoulder, by hand only, then press the seal evenly into its housing until its outer flange seats evenly on the housing lip. If necessary, a soft-faced mallet can be used to tap the seal gently into place.

11 Wash off any oil, then refit the flywheel as described in Section 16.

16 Flywheel – removal, inspection and refitting

Removal

Note: *New flywheel retaining bolts must be used on refitting.*

1 Remove the clutch assembly as described in Chapter 6.

2 As a precaution, unbolt the crankshaft position sensor from the cylinder block (see Chapter 4A) to prevent possible damage as the flywheel is removed.

3 Prevent the flywheel from turning by locking the ring gear teeth with a similar arrangement to that shown in illustration 16.9. Alternatively, bolt a strap between the flywheel and the cylinder block/crankcase. Make alignment marks between the flywheel and crankshaft using paint or a suitable marker pen.

4 Slacken and remove the retaining bolts and remove the flywheel. **Do not** drop it, as it is very heavy. Discard the bolts, they must be renewed whenever they are disturbed.

Inspection

5 If the flywheel clutch mating surface (where applicable) is deeply scored, cracked or otherwise damaged, then the flywheel must be renewed, unless it is possible to have it surface ground. Seek the advice of a Rover dealer or engine reconditioning specialist.

6 If the ring gear is badly worn or has missing teeth, then it must be renewed. This job is best left to a Rover dealer or engine reconditioning specialist. The temperature to which the new ring gear must be heated for installation (350°C - shown by an even light blue colour) is critical and, if not done accurately, the hardness of the teeth will be destroyed.

Refitting

7 Clean the mating surfaces of the flywheel and crankshaft and remove all traces of locking compound from the crankshaft threaded holes.

8 Fit the flywheel to the crankshaft, engaging it with the crankshaft locating dowel, and fit the new retaining bolts **(see illustration)**.

9 Lock the flywheel using the method employed on dismantling then, working in a diagonal sequence, evenly and progressively tighten the retaining bolts to the specified torque wrench setting **(see illustration)**.

10 Refit the crankshaft position sensor and tighten its retaining bolt to the specified torque (see Chapter 4A).

11 Refit the clutch assembly (see Chapter 6).

17 Engine/transmission mountings – inspection and renewal

Inspection

1 If improved access is required, raise the front of the vehicle and support it securely on axle stands (see *"Jacking and Vehicle Support"*). If necessary, undo the retaining screws and fasteners and remove the undercover from beneath the engine/transmission unit.

2 Check the mounting rubber to see if it is cracked, hardened or separated from the metal at any point. Renew the mounting if any such damage or deterioration is evident.

3 Check that all mounting fasteners are securely tightened. Use a torque wrench to check, if possible.

4 Using a large screwdriver or a pry bar, check for wear in the mounting by carefully levering against it to check for free play. Where this is not possible, enlist the aid of an assistant to move the engine/gearbox unit back and forth or from side to side while you watch the mounting. While some free play is to be expected even from new components, excessive wear should be obvious. If excessive free play is found, check first that the fasteners are correctly secured, then renew any worn components as described below.

16.8 Locate the flywheel on its dowel and fit the new retaining bolts

16.9 Lock the flywheel as shown then tighten the retaining bolts to the specified torque

2A

Renewal

Rear mounting

5 Firmly apply the handbrake, then jack up the front of the vehicle and support securely on axle stands (see "*Jacking and Vehicle Support*").

6 Remove the exhaust front pipe as described in Chapter 4A.

7 Referring to Chapter 7, disconnect the wiring connector from the vehicle speed sensor then unclip and remove the gearchange linkage link rods.

8 Slacken and remove the bolt securing the rear mounting support bar to the engine.

9 Unscrew the three bolts securing the rear mounting bracket to the transmission housing.

10 Unscrew the through bolt securing the rear mounting bracket to the mounting, then remove the support bar and manoeuvre the mounting bracket out of position.

11 Slacken and remove the retaining bolts and remove the rear mounting rubber from the top of the subframe.

12 On refitting, fit the mounting to the subframe and tighten its retaining bolts to the specified torque.

13 Refit the mounting bracket and support bar and refit the mounting bolts and through bolt. Securely tighten the bolt securing the support bar to the engine then tighten the bolts securing the mounting bracket to the transmission to the specified torque. Rock the engine to settle the mounting in position, then tighten the mounting through bolt to the specified torque.

14 Reconnect the wiring connector to the speed sensor and clip the link rods back onto the linkage/transmission (see Chapter 7).

15 Refit the exhaust front pipe (see Chapter 4A) then lower the vehicle to the ground.

Right-hand upper mounting

Note: *New mounting retaining nuts will be required on refitting.*

16 Support the weight of the engine/transmission using a trolley jack with a block of wood placed on its head. Position the jack underneath the engine and raise the engine slightly to remove all load from the mounting.

17 Slacken and remove the nuts securing the mounting to the engine bracket **(see illustration)**. Discard both nuts, they must be renewed whenever they are disturbed.

18 Unscrew the through bolt then remove the mounting from the vehicle. Inspect the rubber spacers, which are fitted between the mounting and body, for signs of damage or deterioration and renew, if necessary.

19 On refitting, ensure the rubber spacers are correctly fitted then manoeuvre the mounting into position. Refit the through bolt, tightening it by hand only at this stage.

20 Fit the new mounting retaining nuts and tighten them to the specified torque.

21 Remove the jack then rock the engine to settle the mounting in position before tightening the through bolt to the specified torque.

Left-hand upper mounting

22 Remove the air cleaner housing as described in Chapter 4A.

23 Release the evaporative emission system canister from its bracket and position it clear of the mounting (see Chapter 4C).

24 Support the weight of the engine/transmission using a trolley jack with a block of wood placed on its head. Position the jack underneath the transmission and raise it slightly to remove all load from the mounting.

25 Unscrew the bolts securing the mounting to the transmission **(see illustration)**.

26 Slacken and remove the through bolt and remove the mounting from the engine compartment. Inspect the rubber spacers, which are fitted between the mounting and body, for signs of damage or deterioration and renew, if necessary.

27 On refitting, ensure the rubber spacers are correctly fitted then manoeuvre the mounting into position. Refit the through bolt, tightening it by hand only at this stage.

28 Fit the mounting retaining bolts and tighten them to the specified torque.

29 Remove the jack then rock the engine to settle the mounting in position before tightening the through bolt to the specified torque.

Left- and right-hand lower mountings

30 Firmly apply the handbrake, then jack up the front of the vehicle and support securely on axle stands (see "*Jacking and Vehicle Support*"). Remove the relevant roadwheel

31 Slacken and remove the nut and washer securing the mounting to its bracket.

32 Unscrew the retaining bolts then slide the mounting off the bracket stud and remove it from the vehicle.

33 Refitting is the reverse of removal, ensuring the mounting nut and bolts are securely tightened.

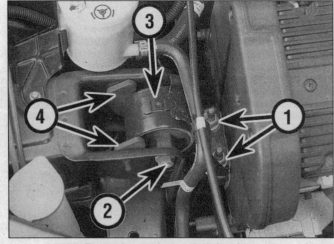

17.17 Engine/transmission right-hand mounting

1	Mounting-to-engine bracket nuts	3	Mounting
2	Through bolt	4	Rubber spacers

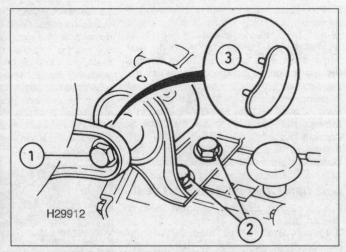

17.25 Engine/transmission right-hand mounting

1	Through bolt
2	Mounting-to-transmission bolts
3	Rubber spacers

Chapter 2 Part B:
2.0 litre petrol engine in-car repair procedures

Contents

Degrees of difficulty

Easy, suitable for novice with little experience	Fairly easy, suitable for beginner with some experience	Fairly difficult, suitable for competent DIY mechanic	Difficult, suitable for experienced DIY mechanic	Very difficult, suitable for expert DIY or professional

2B

Specifications

General

Engine type	Four-cylinder in-line, four-stroke, liquid-cooled
Designation	T16
Bore	84.45 mm
Stroke	89.00 mm
Capacity	1994 cc
Firing order	1-3-4-2 (No 1 cylinder at timing belt end)
Direction of crankshaft rotation	Clockwise (seen from right-hand side of vehicle)
Compression ratio	10:1

Camshaft

Bearing journal running clearance:	
Standard	0.06 to 0.094 mm
Service limit	0.15 mm
Camshaft endfloat	0.06 to 0.25 mm

Lubrication system

Minimum system pressure - at idle	1.0 bar
Pressure relief valve opening pressure	4.1 bar
Low oil pressure warning light comes on	0.3 to 0.5 bar
Oil pump clearances:	
Outer rotor-to-body clearance	0.05 to 0.10 mm
Inner rotor tip-to-outer rotor clearance	0.025 to 0.12 mm
Rotor endfloat	0.03 to 0.08 mm

Torque wrench settings

	Nm	lbf ft
Anti-beaming bracket bolts:		
Bracket-to-transmission bolts	60	44
Bracket-to-cylinder block bolt	45	33
Camshaft bearing carrier bolts	25	18
Camshaft cover bolts	8	6
Camshaft sprocket bolt	65	48
Connecting rod big-end bearing cap nuts	55	41
Crankshaft pulley bolt:		
Centre bolt	85	63
Outer bolts	8	6
Crankshaft rear oil seal housing bolts	8	6
Cylinder head bolts:		
Stage 1	45	33
Stage 2	80	59
Stage 3	Angle-tighten a further 90°	
Engine/transmission mountings:		
Left-hand mounting:		
Mounting-to-body bolts	45	33
Mounting-to-bracket bolts	45	33
Bracket-to-transmission bolts	60	44
Right-hand mounting:		
Steady rod bolts	100	74
Mounting bracket-to-engine bracket bolts	105	78
Mounting bracket-to-mounting nut	80	59
Mounting-to-body bolts	45	33
Rear steady rod bolts	80	59
Flywheel bolts	110	81
Main bearing cap bolts	110	81
Oil pump:		
Retaining bolts:		
M6 bolts	8	6
M10 bolt	45	33
Cover screws	6	4
Oil pump pick-up/strainer bolts	8	6
Roadwheel nuts	110	81
Spark plugs	25	18
Sump bolts	25	18
Sump drain plug	25	18
Timing belt cover bolts:		
Rear cover bolts	10	7
All other bolts	6	4
Timing belt tensioner pulley bolt	25	18
Transmission mounting plate screws	45	33

1 General information and precautions

How to use this Chapter

This Part of the Chapter describes those repair procedures that can reasonably be carried out on the engine whilst it remains in the vehicle. If the engine has been removed from the vehicle and is being dismantled as described in Part D of this Chapter, any preliminary dismantling procedures can be ignored.

Note that whilst it may be possible physically to overhaul items such as the piston/connecting rod assemblies with the engine in the vehicle, such tasks are not usually carried out as separate operations and usually require the execution of several additional procedures (not to mention the cleaning of components and oilways). For this reason, all such tasks are classed as major overhaul procedures and are described in Part D of this Chapter.

Engine description

The 2.0 litre engine is from the Rover T-series engine family, and is a four-cylinder, in-line unit, mounted transversely at the front of the vehicle with the clutch and transmission on the left-hand end.

The cast-iron cylinder block is of the dry-liner type. The crankshaft is supported within the cylinder block on five shell-type main bearings. Thrustwashers are fitted to the centre main bearing to control crankshaft endfloat.

The connecting rods rotate on horizontally-split bearing shells at their big-ends. The pistons are attached to the connecting rods by gudgeon pins which are an interference fit in the connecting rod small-end eyes. The aluminium alloy pistons are fitted with three piston rings, comprising two compression rings and an oil control ring.

The inlet and exhaust valves are each closed by coil springs and operate in guides pressed into the cylinder head. The valve seat inserts are pressed into the cylinder head and can be renewed separately if worn.

The camshafts are driven by a toothed timing belt, and operate the valves via followers. Each follower incorporates a hydraulic self-adjusting valve which automatically adjusts the valve clearance. The camshaft rotates in bearings which are line-bored directly into the cylinder head and the (bolted-on) bearing carrier. This means that the bearing carrier and cylinder head are matched, and cannot be renewed independently.

The coolant pump is driven by the auxiliary drivebelt.

Lubrication is by means of an eccentric-rotor type pump driven directly from the right-hand (timing belt end) of the crankshaft. The pump draws oil through a strainer located in the sump, and then forces it through an externally-mounted full-flow cartridge-type oil filter into galleries in the oil rail and the cylinder block/crankcase, from where it is distributed to the crankshaft (main bearings) and camshaft. The big-end bearings are supplied with oil via internal drillings in the crankshaft, while the camshaft bearings and the followers receive a pressurised supply via drillings in the cylinder head. The camshaft lobes and valves are lubricated by oil splash, as are all other engine components.

Repair operations possible with the engine in the car

The following work can be carried out with the engine in the vehicle:

a) *Compression pressure - testing.*
b) *Camshaft covers - removal and refitting.*
c) *Crankshaft pulley - removal and refitting.*
d) *Timing belt covers - removal and refitting.*
e) *Timing belt - removal and refitting.*
f) *Timing belt tensioner and sprockets - removal and refitting.*
g) *Camshaft oil seals - renewal.*
h) *Camshafts and followers - removal, inspection and refitting.*
i) *Cylinder head - removal and refitting.*
j) *Cylinder head and pistons - decarbonising.*
k) *Sump - removal and refitting.*
l) *Oil pump - removal, overhaul and refitting.*
m) *Crankshaft oil seals - renewal.*
n) *Engine/transmission mountings - inspection and renewal.*
o) *Flywheel - removal, inspection and refitting.*

2 Compression test – description and interpretation

1 Refer to Chapter 2A, Section 2, noting that the ignition system should be disabled by disconnecting the wiring connector from the ignition coil (see Chapter 5B). On completion, ensure the wiring connector is securely reconnected.

3 Engine assembly/valve timing marks – general information and usage

Note: *A suitable pin will be required to lock the crankshaft in position (see paragraph 8).*

1 The camshaft sprockets have timing marks which align when the crankshaft is at 90° BTDC. This positions the pistons half-way up the bores, ensuring there is no danger of the valves contacting the pistons when refitting the cylinder head/timing belt. There is also a mark on the crankshaft pulley which aligns with a mark on the timing belt centre cover; these marks align when Nos 1 and 4 pistons are at TDC and are not used for any specific purpose.
2 Disconnect the battery negative terminal. If necessary, remove all the spark plugs as described in Chapter 1A to enable the engine to be easily turned over.
3 To gain access to the camshaft sprocket timing marks, remove the timing belt upper cover as described in Section 6.
4 Firmly apply the handbrake, then jack up the front of the vehicle and support it securely on axle stands (see "*Jacking and Vehicle Support*"). To gain access to the crankshaft pulley, undo the bolts securing the oil pump/filter cover to the cylinder block and sump and remove the cover from the right-hand end of the engine, noting the correct fitted locations of the spacers. Note that it may be necessary to unbolt the rear steady rod bolts and pivot it away from the sump (see Section 17) in order to gain the clearance necessary to remove the cover.
5 Using a socket and extension bar on the crankshaft pulley centre bolt, turn the crankshaft whilst keeping an eye on the camshaft sprockets.
6 Rotate the crankshaft until the "EXHAUST" mark is at the rear (inlet manifold side) of each sprocket and the "IN" mark is at the front. Position the sprockets so that the inlet camshaft (rear) sprocket "IN" mark and the exhaust camshaft (front) sprocket "EXHAUST" mark are pointing towards each other and are both correctly aligned on the axis of the sprocket retaining bolt centres **(see illustration)**.

3.6 Align the inlet camshaft IN mark and the exhaust camshaft EX mark as described in text

7 With the crankshaft pulley and camshaft sprocket timing marks positioned as described, the engine can be safely dismantled. If necessary, the crankshaft and camshafts can be locked in position as follows.
8 To lock the crankshaft in position, a 6.75 mm diameter pin will be required. Rover technicians use service tool 18G 1523, but an acceptable substitute can be a 6 or 6.5 mm drill or bolt with tape wrapped around it to bring its diameter up to 6.75 mm. Ensure the timing marks are correctly positioned then insert the pin through the hole in the front of the transmission mounting plate, making sure it is correctly located in the hole in the rear of the flywheel **(see illustrations)**.
9 If necessary, the camshafts can also be held in position by locking the camshaft sprockets together. Rover technicians use service tool 18G 1524 which slots in between the sprocket teeth, but an acceptable substitute can be fabricated from a length of steel square-section tube cut to fit as closely as possible around the sprocket spokes **(see illustration)**.

3.8a Rover service tool (18G 1523) for locking the crankshaft in position

3.8b Insert the pin through the mounting plate and locate it in the rear of the flywheel

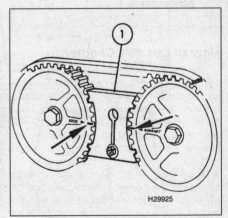

3.9 Rover service tool (1 - No 18G 1524) for locking camshafts in position (timing marks arrowed)

4.9 Ensure the gasket is correctly located in the cover groove

4 Camshaft covers – removal and refitting

Removal

1 Disconnect the battery negative lead.
2 Undo the retaining screws and remove the spark plug cover from between the camshaft covers.

Exhaust camshaft cover

3 Working in the **reverse** of the tightening sequence (**see illustration 4.11**), slacken and remove the cover retaining bolts.
4 Remove the cover from the exhaust camshaft and discard its gasket.

Inlet camshaft cover

5 Release the retaining clips and disconnect the breather hoses from the rear of the cover.
6 Slacken and remove the two bolts securing the support brackets to the inlet manifold.

7 Working in the **reverse** of the tightening sequence (**see illustration 4.14**), slacken and remove the cover retaining bolts along with the manifold support brackets.
8 Remove the cover from the inlet camshaft and discard its gasket.

Refitting

Exhaust camshaft cover

9 Ensure the mating surfaces are clean and dry then fit the new gasket to the cover (**see illustration**).
10 Refit the cover to the cylinder head, ensuring that the gasket remains correctly seated.
11 Refit the cover retaining bolts and tighten them all by hand. Once all bolts are in position, go around in the sequence shown and tighten them to the specified torque setting (**see illustration**).
12 Refit the spark plug cover, tightening its retaining screws securely, and reconnect the battery.

Inlet camshaft cover

13 Refit the cover as described in paragraphs 9 and 10.
14 Refit the cover retaining bolts, ensuring the manifold support brackets are correctly positioned, and tighten them all by hand. Once all bolts are in position, go around in the sequence shown and tighten them to the specified torque setting (**see illustration**).
15 Securely reconnect the breather hoses then refit the spark plug cover, tightening its retaining screws securely. Reconnect the battery.

5 Crankshaft pulley – removal and refitting

Removal

1 Firmly apply the handbrake then jack up the front of the vehicle and support it securely on axle stands (see "*Jacking and Vehicle Support*"). Remove the right-hand front roadwheel.
2 Remove the auxiliary drivebelt as described in Chapter 1A.
3 If further dismantling is to be carried out, align the engine assembly/valve timing marks as described in Section 3.
4 Slacken and remove the four outer bolts securing the crankshaft pulley to the sprocket (**see illustration**).
5 Slacken the crankshaft pulley centre bolt. To prevent crankshaft rotation, have an assistant select top gear and apply the brakes firmly. If the engine is removed from the vehicle it will be necessary to lock the flywheel (see Section 16).
Caution: Do not be tempted to use the crankshaft locking pin (see Section 3) to prevent rotation as the centre bolt is slackened.
6 Unscrew the centre bolt and remove the pulley from the crankshaft.

Refitting

7 Fit the pulley to the crankshaft and screw in the centre bolt.
8 Refit the pulley outer retaining bolts, noting that the bolt holes are offset, and tighten them to the specified torque. Lock the crankshaft

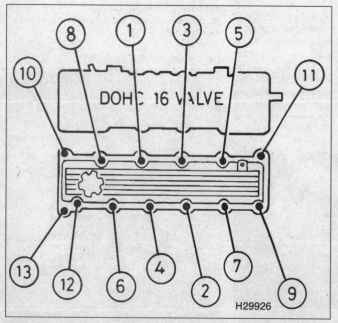

4.11 Exhaust camshaft cover retaining bolt tightening sequence

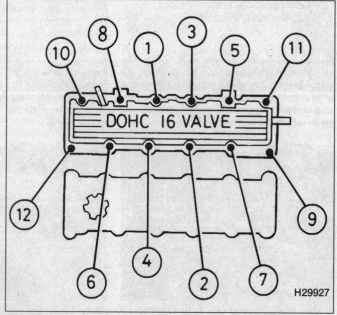

4.14 Inlet camshaft cover retaining bolt tightening sequence

using the method employed on removal and tighten the pulley centre bolt to the specified torque setting **(see illustration)**.
9 Refit the auxiliary drivebelt as described in Chapter 1A.
10 Refit the roadwheel then lower the vehicle to the ground and tighten the wheel nuts to the specified torque.

6 Timing belt covers – removal and refitting
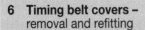

Upper cover

Removal

1 Remove the right-hand engine/transmission mounting as described in Section 17.
2 Unscrew the four retaining bolts and remove the upper cover from the engine **(see illustration)**.

Refitting

3 Refit the cover, ensuring it is correctly located, and tighten its retaining bolts to the specified torque setting. Refit the engine/transmission mounting assembly as described in Section 17.

Centre cover

Removal

4 Remove the upper cover as described in paragraphs 1 to 2.
5 Unclip the engine wiring harness from the cover and position it clear **(see illustration)**.

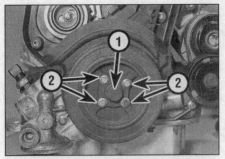

5.4 Crankshaft pulley centre bolt (1) and outer retaining bolts (2)

6 Unscrew the five retaining bolts and remove the centre cover from the engine **(see illustration)**.

Refitting

7 Refit the centre cover, ensuring it is correctly located, and tighten its retaining bolts to the specified torque setting. Refit the upper cover as described in paragraph 3.

Lower cover

Removal

8 Remove the upper and centre covers as described above.
9 Remove the crankshaft pulley as described in Section 5.
10 Unscrew the three retaining bolts and remove the lower cover from the engine **(see illustration)**.

Refitting

11 Refit the cover, tightening its retaining bolts to the specified torque, then refit the

5.8 Lock the crankshaft and tighten the pulley centre bolt to the specified torque

centre and upper covers as described in paragraphs 7 and 3.

Rear upper cover

Removal

12 Remove the camshaft sprockets as described in Section 8.
13 Slacken and remove the five retaining bolts, complete with their spacers **(see illustration)**. Remove the rear upper cover from the engine noting the rubber grommets which are fitted to the retaining bolt holes. Inspect the grommets for signs of damage or deterioration and renew as necessary.

Refitting

14 Ensure the grommets are correctly fitted to the retaining bolts holes then manoeuvre the cover into position. Refit the retaining bolts, complete with spacers, and tighten them to the specified torque **(see illustration)**. Refit the camshaft sprockets as described in Section 8.

2B

6.2 Unscrew the retaining bolts (locations arrowed) and remove the upper cover from the engine

6.5 Unclip the wiring harness from the centre cover . . .

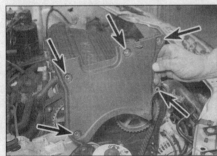

6.6 . . . then undo the retaining bolts (locations arrowed) and remove the cover

6.10 Lower cover retaining bolt locations (arrowed)

6.13 Timing belt rear upper cover retaining bolt locations (arrowed)

6.14 Ensure the spacers are correctly fitted to the grommets then refit the retaining bolts

6.17 Timing belt rear lower cover retaining bolt locations (arrowed)

Rear lower cover

Removal

15 Remove the timing belt as described in Section 7.

16 Remove the timing belt tensioner as described in Section 8.

17 Slacken and remove the retaining bolts, complete with their spacers **(see illustration)**. Remove the rear lower cover from the engine, noting the rubber grommets which are fitted to the retaining bolt holes. Inspect the grommets for signs of damage or deterioration and renew as necessary.

Refitting

18 Ensure the grommets are correctly fitted to the retaining bolts holes then manoeuvre the cover into position. Refit the retaining bolts, complete with spacers, and tighten them to the specified torque **(see illustration)**. Refit the timing belt tensioner and belt as described in Sections 7 and 8.

---

7 Timing belt – removal and refitting

Removal

1 Disconnect the battery negative lead.

2 On models with air conditioning, remove the alternator as described in Chapter 5A.

3 Align the engine assembly/valve timing marks as described in Section 3 and lock the crankshaft in position. If a tool is available, also lock the camshafts in position.

7.6 Unhook the tensioner spring and remove it from the pulley

---

6.18 On refitting ensure the spacers are correctly fitted to the cover grommets

4 Remove the crankshaft pulley as described in Section 5. As a precaution, remove the locking tools whilst the pulley centre bolt is slackened then refit them once the bolt is loose.

Caution: Do not be tempted to use the crankshaft locking pin to prevent rotation as the centre bolt is slackened.

5 Remove the timing belt lower cover as described in Section 6.

6 Carefully unhook the spring from the timing belt tensioner and remove it from the engine **(see illustration)**.

7 Slacken the timing belt tensioner pulley bolt through half a turn. Pivot the pulley fully away from the timing belt and hold it in position by retightening the bolt.

8 Slide the timing belt off from its sprockets and remove it from the engine **(see illustration)**. If the belt is to be re-used, use white paint or similar to mark the direction of rotation on the belt.

Caution: Do not rotate the crankshaft or camshafts until the timing belt has been refitted.

9 Check the timing belt carefully for any signs of uneven wear, splitting or oil contamination, and renew it if there is the slightest doubt about its condition. If the engine is undergoing an overhaul and has covered close to 60 000 miles or it was more than 5 years since the original belt was fitted, renew the belt as a matter of course, regardless of its apparent condition. If signs of oil contamination are found, trace the source of the oil leak and rectify it, then wash down the engine timing belt area and all related components to remove all traces of oil.

7.8 Carefully slip the timing belt off the pulleys and remove it from the engine

---

10 Examine the timing belt tensioner spring for signs of wear or damage and measure its free length. If the spring shows signs of wear, or its free length is longer than 58.5 mm, then it must be renewed. Bearing in mind that the spring condition is critical to ensuring the timing belt is correctly tensioned, we recommend that the spring is renewed whenever a new belt is fitted.

Refitting

11 Thoroughly clean and dry the timing belt sprockets. Check that the camshafts are still positioned with the engine assembly marks correctly aligned and the crankshaft is still locked in position (see Section 3) **(see illustration)**.

12 Hook the lower end of the tensioner spring onto the tensioner backplate and locate the upper end in the stud groove.

13 Fit the timing belt over the crankshaft and camshaft sprockets, ensuring that the belt front run is taut (ie, all slack is on the tensioner side of the belt), then fit the belt over the tensioner pulley. Do not twist the belt sharply while refitting it. Ensure that the belt teeth are correctly seated centrally in the sprockets, and that the timing marks remain in alignment. If a used belt is being refitted, ensure that the arrow mark made on removal points in the normal direction of rotation, as before.

14 Slacken the timing belt tensioner pulley bolt, to release the tensioner and tension the timing belt, then securely tighten the bolt.

15 Check the sprocket timing marks are still correctly aligned. If adjustment is necessary, release the tensioner again then disengage the belt from the sprockets and make any necessary adjustments.

16 Refit the timing belt lower cover to the engine and tighten its retaining bolts to the specified torque.

17 Fit the pulley to the crankshaft and tighten its outer retaining bolts to the specified torque. Refit the centre bolt, tightening it lightly only at this stage.

18 Remove the locking tools from the camshafts and flywheel (as applicable) then, using a socket on the crankshaft pulley centre bolt, rotate the crankshaft smoothly through two complete turns (720°) in the normal direction of rotation to settle the timing belt in position.

7.11 Prior to fitting the belt, ensure the camshaft sprocket timing marks are correctly positioned

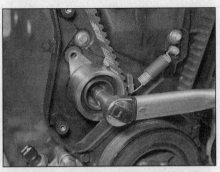

7.19 Settle the timing belt in position then slacken the tensioner pulley bolt before retightening it to the specified torque

19 Check that both camshaft sprocket marks are correctly realigned and the flywheel locking pin can be reinserted. Ensure that the belt front run is taut (ie, all slack is on the tensioner side of the belt), then slacken the tensioner pulley bolt and retighten it to the specified torque setting **(see illustration)**.
20 Remove the locking pin from the flywheel then lock the crankshaft (see Section 5) and tighten the crankshaft pulley centre bolt to the specified torque setting.
21 Refit the centre and upper timing belt covers, tightening their retaining bolts to the specified torque.
22 On models with air conditioning, refit the alternator as described in Chapter 5A.
23 On all models, refit the auxiliary drivebelt as described in Chapter 1A.

24 Refit the roadwheel, and lower the vehicle to the ground, and tighten the wheel nuts to the specified torque. Reconnect the battery negative lead.

8 Timing belt tensioner and sprockets – removal and refitting

Camshaft sprockets

Removal

1 Disconnect the battery negative lead.
2 Align the engine assembly/valve timing marks as described in Section 3 and lock the crankshaft in position.
3 Undo the retaining bolts and remove the timing belt centre cover from the engine.
4 Slacken the timing belt tensioner pulley bolt through half a turn then pivot the tensioner fully away to remove all the tension from the timing belt **(see illustration)**. Secure the tensioner pulley in position by retightening the pulley bolt.
5 Position the timing belt clear of the camshaft sprocket(s), taking care not to twist the belt too sharply; use only your fingers to move the belt.
6 Slacken and remove the camshaft sprocket retaining bolt(s) along with the washer(s). To prevent camshaft rotation, either use the sprocket locking tool (see Section 3) or fabricate a holding tool from two lengths of

steel strip (one long, the other short) and three nuts and bolts. One nut and bolt should form the pivot of a forked tool with the remaining two nuts and bolts at the tips of the forks to engage with the sprocket spokes **(see illustration)**.
7 Remove the sprocket(s) from the camshaft(s) taking care not to lose the sprocket locating pin(s). If a pin is a loose fit in the end of the camshaft, remove it and store it with the sprocket for safe-keeping.
8 Check the sprocket(s) for signs of wear or damage and renew if necessary.

Refitting

9 Prior to refitting, check the oil seal(s) for signs of damage or leakage. If necessary, renew as described in Section 9.
10 Ensure the locating pin(s) is in position in the camshaft end(s). Note that the pin(s) should be fitted with the split facing inwards **(see illustration)**.
11 Both inlet and exhaust camshaft sprockets are the same but each one is equipped with two locating pin cut-outs. If the sprocket is being fitted to the inlet camshaft, engage the locating pin in the "IN" cutout, and if the sprocket is being fitted to the exhaust camshaft, engage the locating pin in the "EX" cutout. Ensure the camshaft locating pin is engaged in the correct sprocket cutout then refit the washer and retaining bolt **(see illustrations)**.

8.4 Slacken the retaining bolt then pivot the tensioner pulley away from the belt before retightening the bolt to hold it in position

8.6 Using a home-made tool to retain the camshaft sprocket whilst the retaining bolt is slackened

8.10 Ensure each sprocket locating pin is securely fitted to the camshaft with its split (arrowed) innermost

8.11a Camshaft sprocket locating pin slots: EX slot (1) for use on the exhaust camshaft and IN slot (2) for use on the Inlet camshaft

8.11b Refit the sprocket ensuring the locating pin (arrowed) is located in the correct cutout (inlet camshaft shown) . . .

8.11c . . . then refit the retaining bolt and washer

2B

8.12 Retain the sprocket and tighten the sprocket bolt to the specified torque

8.21 Removing the crankshaft sprocket

8.23 Ensure the Woodruff key (arrowed) is correctly located in the crankshaft groove

12 Retain the sprocket(s) by the method used on removal, and tighten the pulley retaining bolt(s) to the specified torque setting **(see illustration)**.
13 Ensure the crankshaft is still locked in position and the camshaft sprocket marks are correctly aligned (see Section 3).
14 Ensure that the belt is correctly engaged with the crankshaft sprocket then fit it over the camshaft sprockets, ensuring that the belt front run is taut (ie, all slack is on the tensioner side of the belt). **Do not** twist the belt sharply while refitting it and ensure that the belt teeth are correctly seated centrally in the sprockets, and that the timing marks remain in alignment.
15 Slacken the timing belt tensioner bolt to release the tensioner and tension the timing belt, then securely tighten the bolt. Check the sprocket timing marks are still correctly aligned. If adjustment is necessary, release the tensioner again then disengage the belt from the sprockets and make any necessary adjustments.
16 Remove the locking tool(s) then, using a socket on the crankshaft pulley centre bolt, rotate the crankshaft smoothly through two complete turns (720°) in the normal direction of rotation to settle the timing belt in position.
17 Check that the camshaft sprocket timing marks are correctly realigned and that the crankshaft locking pin can be reinserted into the flywheel (see Section 3). Ensure that the belt front run is taut (ie, all slack is on the tensioner side of the belt), then slacken the

tensioner pulley bolt before retightening it to the specified torque setting.
18 Refit the centre and upper timing belt covers, tightening their retaining bolts to the specified torque.
19 Refit the roadwheel, and lower the vehicle to the ground, and tighten the wheel nuts to the specified torque. Reconnect the battery negative lead.

Crankshaft sprocket

Removal

20 Remove the timing belt as described in Section 7.
21 Slide the sprocket off from the end of the crankshaft, noting which way around it is fitted **(see illustration)**.
22 If the Woodruff key is a loose fit in the crankshaft end, remove it and store it with the sprocket for safe-keeping.

Refitting

23 Ensure the Woodruff key is correctly seated in the crankshaft end **(see illustration)**.
24 Refit the sprocket to the crankshaft, aligning its slot with the Woodruff key.
25 Refit the timing belt as described in Section 7.

Tensioner assembly

Removal

26 Disconnect the battery negative lead.
27 Align the engine assembly/valve timing marks as described in Section 3 and lock the crankshaft in position. If the tool is available, also lock the camshafts in position.
28 Undo the retaining bolts and remove the timing belt centre cover from the engine (see Section 6).
29 Using a pair of pliers, carefully unhook the tensioner spring and remove it from the backplate and locating stud.
30 Unscrew the tensioner pulley bolt then manoeuvre the tensioner assembly away from the engine.
31 Clean the tensioner assembly but do not use any strong solvent which may enter the pulley bearing. Check that the pulley rotates freely on the backplate, with no sign of stiffness or free play. Renew the assembly if there is any doubt about its condition or if

there are any obvious signs of wear or damage. The same applies to the tensioner spring, which should be checked with great care as its condition is critical for the correct tensioning of the timing belt. The condition of the spring can be judged by measuring its free length; if the spring is longer than 58.5 mm it must be renewed.

Refitting

32 Check that the crankshaft is still locked in position and the camshaft sprocket timing marks are still correctly aligned (see Section 3).
33 Ensure that the belt is correctly engaged with the crankshaft and camshaft sprockets and the belt front run is taut (ie, all slack is on the tensioner side of the belt).
34 Hook the tensioner spring onto the tensioner pulley then manoeuvre the tensioner pulley assembly into position, hooking the spring over its locating stud. Engage the backplate pivot pin in the bracket recess, and refit the pulley bolt **(see illustration)**. Pivot the pulley fully away from the belt and lightly tighten the bolt to hold it in position.
35 Carry out the operations described in paragraphs 14 to 19 of this Section.

9	Camshaft oil seals – renewal

Right-hand (timing belt end) seal

Note: *If the oil seal is to be renewed with the timing belt still in place, then check that the belt is free from oil contamination. Renew the belt if signs of oil contamination are found. Cover the belt to protect it from contamination while work is in progress and ensure that all traces of oil are removed from the area before the belt is refitted.*

1 Remove the camshaft sprockets as described in Section 8.
2 Remove the timing belt rear upper cover from the cylinder head (see Section 6 for details).
3 Punch or drill two small holes opposite each other in the oil seal. Screw a self-tapping screw into each hole, and pull on the screws with pliers to extract the seal **(see illustration)**.

8.34 Hook the tensioner spring over the stud then engage the backplate pivot pin in the recess (arrowed) and refit the retaining bolt

9.3 Removing a camshaft oil seal using a self-tapping screw and pliers

9.5a Ensure the new seal is fitted the correct way around . . .

9.5b . . . and tap it into position using a socket which bears on the hard outer edge of the seal

4 Clean the seal housing and polish off any burrs or raised edges which may have caused the seal to fail.

5 Lubricate the lips of the new seal with clean engine oil and drive it fully into position. Use a suitable tubular drift, such as a socket, which bears only on the hard outer edge of the seal. Take care not to damage the seal lips during fitting and note that the seal lips should face inwards **(see illustrations)**.

6 Refit the timing belt cover (Section 6) then refit the camshaft sprockets as described in Section 8.

Left-hand (flywheel end) seal

7 Remove the air cleaner housing as described in Chapter 4A. To improve access to the inlet camshaft sealing cap, remove the throttle housing as described in Chapter 4A.

8 Position an absorbent cloth beneath the left-hand end of the cylinder head to catch any spilt oil.

9 Using a flat-bladed screwdriver, lever the relevant sealing cap out from the end of the cylinder head, taking great care not to damage the cylinder surface **(see illustration)**.

10 Clean the surface of the cylinder head and remove any burrs or raised edges from the head surface.

11 Fit the new sealing cap to the cylinder head and press it squarely into position, using a suitable tubular drift such as a socket, which bears only on the cap outer edge **(see illustration)**.

12 Wipe off all traces of spilt oil then refit the throttle housing (where removed) and air cleaner housing (see Chapter 4A).

10 Camshaft(s) and followers – removal, inspection and refitting

Note: Rover produce a sealant kit which consists of a plastic scraper, gasket removing compound and the recommended sealant for the camshaft carrier joint. It is recommended that this kit is used during the following procedure.

Note: Each camshaft bearing carrier is secured in position by ten bolts of which five

9.9 Carefully lever out the sealing cap from the left-hand end of the camshaft

are self-locking bolts which must be renewed whenever they are disturbed. New camshaft oil seals and sealing caps will also be required.

Removal

Note: Each camshaft can be removed individually without disturbing the other camshaft.

1 Remove the camshaft cover(s) as described in Section 4.

2 Remove the camshaft sprockets as described in Section 8.

3 Slacken and remove the retaining bolts and remove the timing belt rear upper cover from the cylinder head. Each camshaft can then be removed as follows.

4 Working in the **reverse** of the tightening sequence **(see illustration 10.16a)**, slacken the camshaft bearing carrier retaining bolts evenly progressively, by one turn at a time, to gradually release the pressure of the valve springs. Discard the five outer retaining bolts, these must be renewed whenever they are disturbed.

Caution: If the bearing carrier bolts are carelessly slackened, the carrier might break. If the carrier is broken the complete cylinder head assembly must be renewed; the carrier is matched to the head and is not available separately.

5 Lift the camshaft bearing carrier away from the cylinder, noting the correct fitted positions of the locating dowels **(see illustration)**. If the dowels are loose, remove them and store them with the bearing carrier for safe-keeping.

6 Carefully lift the camshaft from the cylinder head. Remove the oil seal from the right-hand

9.11 Tap the new cap squarely into position with a large socket

end of the shaft and the sealing cap from the left-hand end of the cylinder head and discard them; new ones should be used on refitting. If both camshafts are to be removed at the same time, make identification marks (IN and EX) on them to ensure they are correctly positioned on refitting. Both camshafts are identical and have no identification markings but it is important to ensure they are refitted in their original positions so that the rate of camshaft wear is not increased.

7 If necessary, obtain sixteen small, clean plastic containers, and label them for identification. Alternatively, divide a larger container into compartments. Using a sucker or magnet, withdraw each follower in turn, invert it to prevent oil loss and place it in its respective container, which should then be filled with clean engine oil.

10.5 Remove the camshaft bearing carrier noting the correct locations of the dowels (one arrowed)

2B

10.10 Lubricate the followers and refit them in their original locations

10.11a Lubricate the camshaft bearings with clean engine oil . . .

10.11b . . . and refit the camshaft

Caution: Do not interchange the followers, and do not allow the followers to lose oil, as they will take a long time to refill with oil on restarting the engine, which could result in incorrect valve clearances.

Inspection

8 Examine the camshaft bearing surfaces and cam lobes for signs of wear ridges and scoring. Renew the camshaft if any of these conditions are apparent. Examine the condition of the bearing surfaces both on the camshaft journals and in the cylinder head. If the head bearing surfaces are worn excessively, the cylinder head will need to be renewed.

9 Examine the follower bearing surfaces which contact the camshaft lobes for wear ridges and scoring. Check the followers and

10.12 Position the inlet and exhaust camshaft sprocket locating pins (arrowed) as described in text

their bores in the cylinder head for signs of wear or damage. If the engine's valve clearances have sounded noisy, particularly if the noise persists after initial start-up from cold, then there is reason to suspect a faulty follower. If any follower is thought to be faulty or is visibly worn it should be renewed.

Refitting

10 Where removed, lubricate the followers with clean engine oil and carefully insert each one into its original location in the cylinder head **(see illustration)**.

11 Liberally oil the camshaft bearings and followers then refit the camshaft(s) to the cylinder head **(see illustrations)**. If both camshafts have been removed, use the marks made on removal to ensure they are refitted in their original positions.

12 Position the camshafts so that the camshaft sprocket locating pins are positioned as shown **(see illustration)**. When viewed from the right-hand end of the engine, the inlet camshaft sprocket pin should be in the 4 o'clock position and the exhaust camshaft sprocket pin should be in the 8 o'clock position. Each bearing carrier can be refitted as follows.

13 Ensure the mating surfaces of the camshaft bearing carrier and cylinder head are clean and dry and remove all traces of locking compound from the outer retaining bolt threads.

14 Apply a bead of sealant to the mating surfaces of the cylinder head as shown. Spread the sealant to an even film, taking care

not to allow any sealant to enter the oilway grooves **(see illustrations)**.

15 Ensure that the locating dowels are in position and refit the camshaft bearing carrier to the cylinder head. Ensure the carrier is correctly located and screw in the retaining bolts. Fit the five new bolts in the outer positions and refit the five inner bolts, tightening them all by hand only at this stage **(see illustration)**.

16 Working in the specified sequence, evenly and progressively tighten the retaining bolts to draw the bearing carrier squarely down into contact with the cylinder head. Once the carrier is in contact with the head, go around in the specified sequence and tighten the retaining bolts to the specified torque **(see illustrations)**.

Caution: If the bearing carrier bolts are carelessly tightened, the carrier might break. If the carrier is broken then the complete cylinder head assembly must be renewed; the carrier is matched to the head and is not available separately.

17 Fit a new camshaft oil seal and sealing cap as described in Section 9.

18 Where necessary, repeat the operations described in 14 to 17 on the remaining camshaft.

19 Refit the timing belt rear cover to the cylinder head and tighten its retaining bolts to the specified torque.

20 Refit the camshaft sprockets as described in Section 8 then rotate the sprockets around to realign their timing marks (see Section 3) **(see illustration)**.

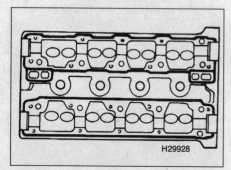

10.14a Apply sealant to the highlighted areas of the cylinder head surface as shown

10.14b Apply sealant to the cylinder head mating surface and spread to an even film

10.15 Refit the camshaft bearing carrier and screw in the retaining bolts. Fit the five new bolts along the outer edge of the carrier

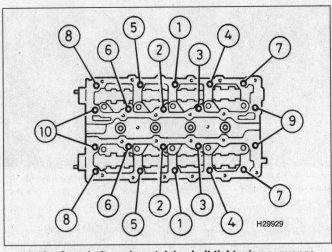

10.16a Camshaft carrier retaining bolt tightening sequence

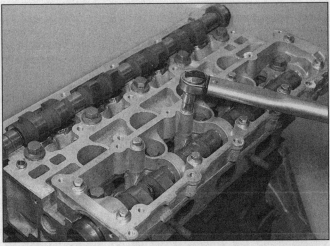

10.16b Carefully tighten the camshaft bearing carrier retaining bolts as described in text

21 Refit the timing belt as described in Section 7.

22 Refit the camshaft cover(s) as described in Section 4.

11 Cylinder head – removal and refitting

Removal

1 Disconnect the battery negative lead.

2 Drain the cooling system, as described in Chapter 1A.

3 Remove the air cleaner housing as described in Chapter 4A.

4 Align the engine assembly/valve timing marks as described in Section 3 and lock the camshaft sprockets and crankshaft in position.

5 Undo the retaining bolts and remove the timing belt centre cover from the engine (see Section 6).

6 Slacken the timing belt tensioner pulley bolt through half a turn then pivot the tensioner fully away to remove all the tension from the timing belt. Secure the tensioner pulley in position by retightening the pulley bolt.

7 Position the timing belt clear of the camshaft sprockets, taking care not to twist the belt too sharply; use only your fingers to move the belt **(see illustration)**.

8 Remove the exhaust manifold as described in Chapter 4A.

9 Remove the inlet manifold as described in Chapter 4A. If no work is to be carried out on the cylinder head, the head can be removed complete with the manifold once the following operations have been carried out (see Chapter 4A).

a) Depressurise the fuel system and disconnect the fuel feed and return hoses from the manifold/fuel rail.

b) Unbolt the throttle housing assembly from the manifold and position it clear; the wiring and accelerator cable can be left attached.

c) Disconnect the various wiring connectors from the manifold components and free all wiring from the manifold.

d) Disconnect the various vacuum, breather and (where necessary) coolant hoses from the manifold, noting each one's correctly fitted location and routing.

e) Unbolt the fuel hose/wiring clips from the rear of the manifold.

10.20 Rotate the camshafts to bring the timing marks (arrowed) back into alignment

10 Slacken the retaining clips and disconnect the coolant hoses from the thermostat housing on the front, right-hand end of the cylinder head. Disconnect the wiring connectors from the coolant temperature sensors which are screwed into the housing **(see illustrations)**.

11 Remove the camshaft covers as described in Section 4.

12 Unclip the HT leads from their retaining clips on the top of the cylinder head then unbolt the HT lead bracket from the left-hand end of the cylinder head **(see illustrations)**.

11.7 Free the timing belt from the camshaft sprockets and position it clear

11.10a Slacken the retaining clips and disconnect the coolant hoses (arrowed) from the thermostat housing

11.10b Disconnect the wiring connectors from the coolant temperature sensors (arrowed) in the thermostat housing

2B

11.12a Unplug the HT leads and free them from the head . . .

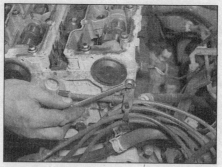

11.12b . . . then undo the retaining bolt and free the lead clip from the left-hand end of the cylinder head

11.13 Undo the retaining bolts (arrowed) and free the power steering pipe from the head

13 Undo the retaining bolts and free the power steering and coolant pipes from the left-hand end of the cylinder head **(see illustration)**.

14 Make a final check to ensure that all relevant hoses, pipes and wires, etc, have been disconnected.

15 Working in the **reverse** of the tightening sequence **(see illustration 11.29a)**, progressively slacken the cylinder head bolts by a third of a turn at a time until all bolts can be unscrewed by hand. Withdraw the bolts, and store them in order, so that they can be refitted in their original locations. The bolts can be stored by pushing them through a clearly-marked cardboard template **(see illustration)**.

16 Lift the cylinder head from the cylinder block **(see illustration)**. If necessary, tap the cylinder head gently with a soft-faced mallet to free it from the block, but **do not** lever at the mating faces.

17 When the joint is broken, lift the cylinder head away then remove the gasket and discard it. Support the cylinder head on wooden blocks or stands – do not rest the lower face of the cylinder head on the work surface. Note the fitted positions of the two locating dowels, and remove them for safe keeping if they are loose.

18 If the cylinder head is to be dismantled, remove the camshafts and followers, as described in Section 10, then refer to the relevant Sections of Part D of this Chapter.

Preparation for refitting

19 The mating faces of the cylinder head and block must be perfectly clean before refitting the head. Use a scraper to remove all traces of gasket and carbon, and also clean the tops of the pistons. Take particular care with the aluminium surfaces, as the soft metal is damaged easily. Also, make sure that debris is not allowed to enter the oil and water channels - this is particularly important for the oil circuit, as carbon could block the oil supply to the camshaft or crankshaft bearings. Using adhesive tape and paper, seal the water, oil and bolt holes in the cylinder block. To prevent carbon entering the gap between the pistons and bores, smear a little grease in the gap. After cleaning the piston, rotate the crankshaft so that the piston moves down the bore, then wipe out the grease and carbon with a cloth rag. Clean the piston crowns in the same way.

20 Check the block and head for nicks, deep scratches and other damage. If slight, they may be removed carefully with a file. More serious damage may be repaired by machining, but this is a specialist job.

21 If warpage of the cylinder head gasket surface is suspected, use a straight-edge to check it for distortion. Refer to Part D of this Chapter if necessary.

22 Ensure that the cylinder head bolt holes in the crankcase are clean and free of oil. Syringe or soak up any oil left in the bolt holes. This is most important in order that the correct bolt tightening torque can be applied and to prevent the possibility of the block being cracked by hydraulic pressure when the bolts are tightened.

23 Check the condition of the cylinder head bolts, particularly their threads. Keeping all bolts in their correct fitted order, wash them and wipe dry. Check each bolt for any sign of visible wear or damage, renewing as necessary. Although Rover do not specify that the bolts must be renewed, as a precaution, we recommend that the bolts are renewed as a complete set, regardless of their apparent condition. **Note:** *The cylinder head bolts fitted to these engines have been modified and it is important to ensure that only the modified bolts are used. If the original bolts are to be re-used, check the marking on the head of each bolt (see illustration).*
Caution: Under no circumstances should bolts with the marking "MSPS" be refitted; these are the old unmodified bolts and must not be used.

Refitting

24 Check that the camshafts and crankshaft are still locked in position with the engine assembly marks correctly aligned (see Section 3).

25 Wipe clean the mating faces of the head and block and ensure that the two locating dowels are in position at each end of the cylinder block/crankcase surface.

11.15 If the cylinder head bolts are to be reused, store them in a cardboard template to ensure correct refitting

11.16 Removing the cylinder head

11.23 Check the cylinder head bolt markings if the bolts are to be re-used. Do not use bolts which are marked MSPS (see text)

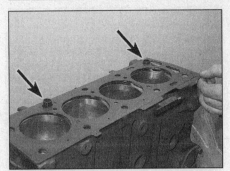

11.26 Ensure the locating dowels (arrowed) are in position then fit the new gasket

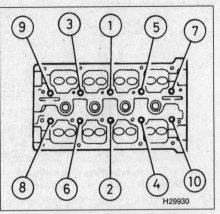

11.29a Cylinder head bolt tightening sequence

11.29b Working in the specified sequence, tighten the head bolts to the specified stage 1 torque setting and then to the stage 2 torque setting

26 Fit the new cylinder head gasket to the block, making sure it is fitted with the correct way up **(see illustration)**.

27 Carefully refit the cylinder head, locating it on the dowels.

28 Keeping all the cylinder head bolts in their correct fitted order, wash them and wipe dry. Lightly oil under the head and on the threads of each bolt, carefully enter it into its original hole and screw it in, by hand only, until finger-tight. **Do not** drop the bolts into their holes.

29 Working progressively and in the sequence shown, first tighten all the cylinder head bolts to the stage 1 torque setting **(see illustrations)**.

30 Once all bolts have been tightened to the stage 1 torque, go around again in the specified sequence and tighten all bolts to the specified stage 2 torque setting **(see illustration 11.29b)**.

31 Finally go around in the specified sequence and tighten each bolt through its specified stage 3 angle, using a socket and extension bar. It is recommended that an angle-measuring gauge is used during this stage of the tightening, to ensure accuracy. Prior to tightening, use paint or a felt-tip pen to make alignment marks between the first radial mark on each bolt head and the cylinder head. The stage 3 torque can then be achieved by tightening each bolt through 90° so that the second mark on the bolt head is now in alignment with the mark on the cylinder head **(see illustrations)**.

32 Refit the retaining bolts securing the pipes to the left-hand end of the cylinder head and tighten securely.

33 Clip the HT leads back into position then refit the camshaft covers as described in Section 4.

34 Securely reconnect the coolant hoses to the thermostat and reconnect the wiring connectors to the temperature sensors.

35 Refit the inlet manifold (where removed) or reconnect the manifold hoses and wiring as described in Chapter 4A. Ensure all hoses/wiring are correctly routed and securely reconnected then reconnect and adjust the accelerator cable.

11.31a Using an angle-tightening gauge to tighten the head bolts through the specified stage 3 angle

36 Refit the exhaust manifold as described in Chapter 4A.

37 Refit the timing belt as described in paragraphs 13 to 20 of Section 7.

38 Refit the air cleaner housing as described in Chapter 4A.

39 On completion refill the cooling system as described in Chapter 1A.

12 Sump – removal and refitting

Removal

1 Disconnect the battery negative lead.

2 Apply the handbrake, then jack up the front of the vehicle and support it securely on axle stands (see *"Jacking and Vehicle Support"*).

3 Drain the engine oil and remove the oil filter as described in Chapter 1A. If the oil filter is damaged on removal (which is likely), then a new filter must be used on refitting and the engine filled with fresh oil.

4 Remove the exhaust front pipe as described in Chapter 4A.

5 Slacken and remove the mounting bolts securing the rear engine/transmission steady rod to the bracket and subframe and remove the rod. Unscrew the retaining bolts and

11.31b If an angle gauge is not available, use the radial marks on the bolt heads as described in text to ensure each bolt is correctly tightened

remove the mounting bracket.

6 Slacken and remove the two bolts securing the anti-beaming bracket to the transmission housing then undo the bolt securing it to the rear of the cylinder block. Remove the bracket from the engine **(see illustration)**.

7 Progressively slacken and remove the bolts securing the sump to the base of the cylinder block, noting the correct fitted location of the longer bolt.

8 Break the sump joint by striking the sump with the palm of the hand, then lower the sump away from the engine. Remove the gasket and discard it, a new one should be used on refitting.

12.6 Unscrew the retaining bolts and remove the anti-beaming bracket

2B

12.9 Undo the retaining bolts (arrowed) and remove the oil pump pick-up/strainer from the base of the cylinder block

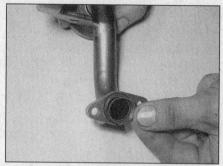

12.11 Fit a new sealing ring to the oil pump pick-up/strainer groove

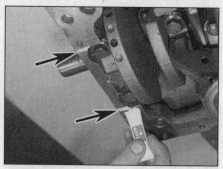

12.12 Apply sealant to the joints between the front main bearing cap and block (arrowed)

9 While the sump is removed, take the opportunity to check the oil pump pick-up/strainer for signs of clogging or splitting. If necessary, unbolt the pick-up/strainer and remove it from the engine along with its sealing ring **(see illustration)**. The strainer can then be cleaned easily in solvent. Inspect the strainer mesh for signs of clogging or splitting and renew if necessary.

Refitting

10 Clean all traces of gasket from the mating surfaces of the cylinder block/crankcase and sump, then use a clean rag to wipe out the sump and the engine interior.

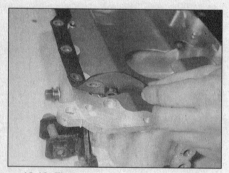

12.13 Fit the new gasket to the sump ensuring its locating lugs are correctly seated

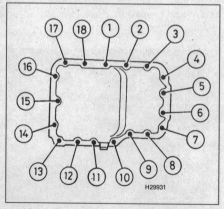

12.14 Sump retaining bolt tightening sequence

11 Where necessary, fit a new sealing ring to the oil pump pick-up/strainer groove then carefully refit the pipe, tightening its retaining bolts to the specified torque setting **(see illustration)**.
12 Apply a bead of suitable sealant (recommended sealant is available from your Rover dealer) to the front main bearing cap joint areas of the cylinder block mating surface **(see illustration)**.
13 Fit the gasket to the sump, locating its lugs in the sump holes, then offer up the sump to the cylinder block/crankcase **(see illustration)**. Refit the sump retaining bolts, and tighten the bolts finger-tight only. Ensure that the longer bolt is refitted in the correct location (bolt 7 in the tightening sequence).
14 Working in the sequence shown, tighten the sump bolts to the specified torque setting **(see illustration)**.
15 Refit the anti-beaming bracket to the engine/transmission unit, tightening its retaining bolts to their specified torque settings.
16 Refit the rear mounting steady rod bracket to the engine and tighten its retaining bolts to the specified torque. Refit the steady rod and tighten both its bolts to the specified torque.
17 Refit the exhaust front pipe as described in Chapter 4A.
18 Fit the oil filter then lower the vehicle to the ground and refill the engine with oil as described in Chapter 1A.

13 Oil pump –
removed and refitting

Removal

Note: *The oil pressure relief valve can be dismantled without removing the oil pump from the vehicle - see Section 14 for details.*
1 Drain the engine oil and remove the oil filter as described in Chapter 1A. If the oil filter is damaged on removal (which is likely), then a new filter must be used on refitting and the engine filled with fresh oil.
2 Remove the crankshaft sprocket and timing belt tensioner assembly as described in

Section 8. Secure the timing belt clear of the working area so that it cannot be contaminated with oil.
3 Remove the timing belt rear lower cover from the cylinder block (see Section 6).
4 Slacken and remove the oil pump retaining bolts, noting the correct fitted location of the larger (M10) bolt.
5 Free the oil pump from the cylinder block then slide it off the end of the crankshaft. Note the correct fitted locations of the pump locating dowels; if the dowels are loose, remove them and store with the pump for safe-keeping. Remove the gasket and discard it.
6 Remove the oil pump drive Woodruff key from the crankshaft and store it with the pump for safe-keeping.

Refitting

7 Prior to refitting, carefully lever out the crankshaft oil seal using a flat-bladed screwdriver **(see illustration)**. Fit the new oil seal, ensuring its sealing lip is facing inwards, and press it squarely into the housing using a tubular drift which bears only on the hard outer edge of the seal. Press the seal into position so that it is flush with the housing and lubricate the oil seal lip with clean engine oil.
8 Remove all traces of locking compound and sealant from the threads of the oil pump bolts and cylinder block and ensure the mating surfaces of the oil pump and cylinder block are clean and dry.

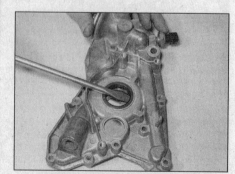

13.7 Prior to refitting the oil pump carefully lever out the old oil seal

13.9 Apply sealant to the joints between the front main bearing cap and the block (arrowed)

13.11 Ensure the locating dowels (arrowed) are in position then fit the gasket

13.12 Fit the pump to the engine engaging the inner rotor slot with the Woodruff key (arrowed)

9 Apply a bead of suitable sealant (recommended sealant is available from your Rover dealer) to the front main bearing cap joint areas of the cylinder block **(see illustration)**.

10 Fit the Woodruff key to the crankshaft slot.

11 Ensure the locating dowels are in position then fit a new gasket to the cylinder block **(see illustration)**.

12 Carefully manoeuvre the oil pump into position, aligning the inner rotor groove with the Woodruff key **(see illustration)**. Locate the pump on the dowels, taking great care not to damage the oil seal lip.

13 Apply a drop of locking compound (Rover recommend the use of Loctite 222) to the threads of the oil pump retaining bolts then screw the bolts into position. Tighten all bolts by hand then go around in the specified sequence and tighten them to their specified torque settings **(see illustration)**.

14 Refit the timing belt cover to the cylinder block and tighten its retaining bolts to the specified torque (see Section 6).

15 Refit the crankshaft sprocket and timing belt tensioner as described in Section 8.

16 Fit the oil filter then lower the vehicle to the ground and refill the engine with oil as described in Chapter 1A.

14 Oil pump – dismantling, inspection and reassembly

Note: *A new pressure relief valve plug will be required. If oil pump wear is suspected, check the cost and availability of new parts (only the pressure relief valve components seem to be available separately) against the cost of a new pump. Examine the pump as described in this Section and then decide whether renewal or repair is the best course of action.*

Dismantling

1 Remove the oil pump as described in Section 13.

2 Make alignment marks between the cover and pump body then unscrew the retaining screws and remove the cover.

3 Make identification marks on the inner and outer rotors with a suitable marker pen to ensure they are fitted the same way around on reassembly. Remove both the rotors from the body **(see illustration)**.

4 The oil pressure relief valve can be dismantled, if required, without disturbing the pump. If this is to be done with the pump in position and the engine still installed in the vehicle, it will first be necessary to remove the auxiliary drivebelt (see Chapter 1A) and unbolt the drivebelt tensioner.

5 To dismantle the valve, slacken and remove the threaded plug and washer then recover the valve spring and plunger. Discard the threaded plug; a new one should be used on reassembly.

Inspection

6 Inspect the rotors for obvious signs of wear or damage and renew if necessary. If the pump body or cover plate is scored or damaged, then the complete oil pump assembly must be renewed.

7 Refit the rotors to the body and, using feeler blades of the appropriate thickness, measure the clearance between the outer rotor and the pump body, then between the inner rotor tip and the outer rotor **(see illustrations)**.

8 Using feeler blades and a straight-edge placed across the top of the pump body and the rotors, measure the rotor endfloat **(see illustration)**.

2B

13.13 Oil pump retaining bolt tightening sequence

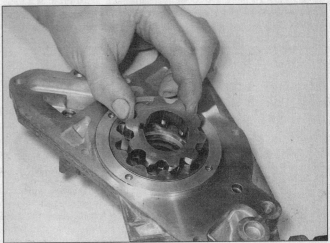

14.3 Remove the inner and outer rotors from the oil pump

14.7a Using feeler blades, check the outer rotor to pump body clearance . . .

14.7b . . . and the inner rotor tip to outer rotor clearance

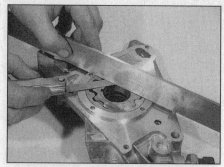

14.8 Using a straight-edge and feeler blade measure the pump rotor endfloat

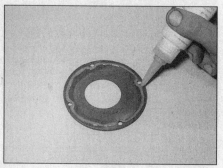

14.13a Apply a bead of sealant to the pump cover . . .

14.13b . . . then refit the cover making sure the TOP mark (arrowed) is uppermost

14.14 Apply locking compound to the oil pump cover screws prior to refitting them

9 If any measurement is outside the specified limits, the complete pump assembly must be renewed.

10 If the pressure relief valve plunger is scored, or if it does not slide freely in the pump body bore, then it must be renewed.

Reassembly

11 Remove all traces of sealant and locking compound from the pump and cover mating surfaces and the threads of the body and cover screws.

12 Lubricate the pump rotors with clean engine oil and refit them to the pump body, using the marks made on dismantling to ensure they are fitted the correct way around. The rotors should be fitted with their square marks facing away from the pump body.

13 Ensure the mating surfaces are clean and dry then apply a bead of sealant (Rover recommend the use of Loctite 573),

approximately 1.0 mm thick, to the outer edge of the pump cover. Refit the cover to the pump body, aligning the marks made on dismantling; the cover upper retaining screw hole is marked "TOP" to avoid the possibility of fitting the cover incorrectly **(see illustrations)**.

14 Ensure the threads of the cover screws are clean and dry and apply a drop of the thread-locking compound (Rover recommend the use of Loctite 222) to each screw **(see illustration)**. Refit the screws and tighten them to the specified torque.

15 Check that the pump rotates freely, then prime it by injecting oil into its passages and rotating it. If a long time elapses before the pump is refitted to the engine, prime it again before installation.

16 Refit the oil pressure relief valve plunger, ensuring that it is the correct way up, then install the spring. Fit the new threaded plug, tightening it securely.

15 Crankshaft oil seals – renewal

Right-hand (timing belt end) seal

1 Remove the crankshaft sprocket as described in Section 8, and secure the timing belt clear of the working area so that it cannot be contaminated with oil.

2 Carefully punch or drill two small holes opposite each other in the oil seal **(see illustration)**. Screw a self-tapping screw into

each and pull on the screws with pliers to extract the seal.

Caution: Great care must be taken to avoid damage to the oil pump.

3 Clean the seal housing and polish off any burrs or raised edges which may have caused the seal to fail in the first place.

4 Lubricate the lips of the new seal with clean engine oil and ease it into position on the end of the shaft. Press the seal squarely into position until it is flush with the housing. If necessary, a suitable tubular drift, such as a socket, which bears only on the hard outer edge of the seal can be used to tap the seal into position. Take great care not to damage the seal lips during fitting and ensure that the seal lips face inwards.

5 Wash off any traces of oil, then refit the crankshaft sprocket as described in Section 8.

Left-hand (flywheel end) oil seal

Caution: The new oil seal is supplied complete with housing and is pre-lubricated with a special coating. The seal must be fitted "dry" and the seal protector must not be removed until the housing assembly is in position on the engine. Under no circumstances must the oil seal lip be touched, or lubricated with oil or grease, as this will destroy the special coating. If the seal coating is damaged there is a risk of oil leakage once the engine is started.

6 Remove the flywheel as described in Section 16.

15.2 Removing the crankshaft right-hand oil seal

15.10a Ease the seal housing into position over the end of the crankshaft . . .

15.10b . . . and seat it on the cylinder block and recover the oil seal protector

15.11 Crankshaft left-hand oil seal housing bolt tightening sequence

7 Remove the sump as described in Section 12.

8 Slacken and remove the retaining bolts and remove the oil seal housing from the end of the crankshaft.

9 Ensure the crankshaft surface and cylinder block mating surface are clean and dry; this is most important to ensure the oil seal coating is not damaged (see Caution at the start of this Section).

10 Carefully ease the new seal housing onto the end of the crankshaft, making sure the sealing lip is not damaged. Slide the housing fully into position, making sure it is correctly seated, then carefully remove the oil seal protector **(see illustrations)**.

11 Refit the housing retaining bolts and tighten them to the specified torque, working in the sequence shown **(see illustration)**.

12 Refit the sump as described in Section 12.

13 Refit the flywheel as described in Section 16.

16 Flywheel – removal, inspection and refitting

Removal

Note: *New flywheel retaining bolts must be used on refitting.*

1 Remove the clutch assembly as described in Chapter 6.

2 As a precaution, unbolt the crankshaft position sensor from the engine mounting plate (see Chapter 4A) to prevent possible damage as the flywheel is removed.

3 Prevent the flywheel from turning by locking the ring gear teeth with a similar arrangement to that shown **(see illustration)**. Alternatively, bolt a strap between the flywheel and the cylinder block/crankcase.

4 Slacken and remove the retaining bolts and remove the flywheel, noting its locating dowel. **Do not** drop it, as it is very heavy. Discard the bolts, they must be renewed whenever they are disturbed.

Inspection

5 If the flywheel clutch mating surface (where applicable) is deeply scored, cracked or

otherwise damaged, then the flywheel must be renewed, unless it is possible to have it surface ground. Seek the advice of a Rover dealer or engine reconditioning specialist.

6 If the ring gear is badly worn or has missing teeth, then it must be renewed. This job is best left to a Rover dealer or engine reconditioning specialist. The temperature to which the new ring gear must be heated for installation (350°C - shown by an even light blue colour) is critical and, if not done accurately, the hardness of the teeth will be destroyed.

Refitting

7 Clean the mating surfaces of the flywheel and crankshaft and remove all traces of locking compound from the crankshaft threaded holes.

8 Fit the flywheel to the crankshaft, engaging it with the crankshaft locating dowel, and fit the new retaining bolts.

9 Lock the flywheel using the method employed on dismantling then, working in a diagonal sequence, evenly and progressively tighten the retaining bolts to the specified torque wrench setting.

10 Refit the crankshaft position sensor and tighten its retaining bolt to the specified torque (see Chapter 4A).

11 Refit the clutch assembly as described in Chapter 6.

16.3 Lock the flywheel (home-made tool arrowed) then slacken and remove the retaining bolts

17 Engine/transmission mountings – inspection and renewal

Inspection

1 If improved access is required, raise the front of the vehicle and support it securely on axle stands (see *"Jacking and Vehicle Support"*). If necessary, undo the retaining screws and fasteners and remove the undercover from beneath the engine/transmission unit.

2 Check the mounting rubber to see if it is cracked, hardened or separated from the metal at any point. Renew the mounting if any such damage or deterioration is evident.

3 Check that all mounting fasteners are securely tightened. Use a torque wrench to check, if possible.

4 Using a large screwdriver or a pry bar, check for wear in the mounting by carefully levering against it to check for free play. Where this is not possible, enlist the aid of an assistant to move the engine/gearbox unit back and forth or from side to side while you watch the mounting. While some free play is to be expected even from new components, excessive wear should be obvious. If excessive free play is found, check first that the fasteners are correctly secured, then renew any worn components as described below.

Renewal

Right-hand mounting

5 Support the weight of the engine/transmission using a trolley jack with a block of wood placed on its head. Position the jack underneath the engine and raise the engine slightly to remove all load from the mounting.

6 Unscrew the power steering fluid reservoir mounting bolts and position the reservoir clear of the mounting **(see illustration)**. Keep the reservoir upright to prevent fluid loss.

7 Unscrew the mounting bolts securing the steady rod to the body and bracket and remove it from the vehicle **(see illustrations)**.

8 Slacken and remove the nut and washer

2B

17.6 Unscrew the retaining bolts (arrowed) and position the power steering fluid reservoir clear of the mounting

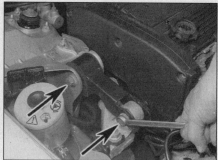

17.7a Unscrew the bolts (arrowed) . . .

17.7b . . . and remove the steady rod from the right-hand mounting assembly

17.8a Slacken and remove the mounting nut and washer . . .

17.8b . . . and remove the special plate

17.9 Undo the mounting bolts and remove the right-hand mounting bracket

securing the mounting bracket to the top of the mounting and remove the special plate **(see illustrations)**.

9 Undo the three bolts securing the mounting bracket to the engine bracket then lift the bracket out of position **(see illustration)**.

10 Undo the two bolts securing the mounting to the body then remove the restraint bar and mounting from the engine compartment **(see illustration)**.

11 Examine all components for signs of wear or damage and renew as necessary.

12 Fit the mounting to the body and refit the mounting bracket. Refit the bolts securing the mounting bracket to the engine bracket and tighten them to the specified torque and refit the mounting nut, tightening it by hand only at this stage.

13 Refit the restraint bar to the mounting then refit the mounting bolts and tighten them to the specified torque.

14 Refit the steady rod and fit its retaining bolts. Remove the jack then rock the engine to settle the mounting in position. Tighten the bolt securing the rod to the engine bracket first then tighten the bolt securing the rod to the body, tightening them both to the specified torque.

15 Tighten the mounting nut to the specified torque.

16 Refit the power steering reservoir, tightening its retaining bolts securely.

Left-hand mounting

17 Remove the air cleaner housing as described in Chapter 4A.

18 Remove the battery and battery tray as described in Chapter 5A.

19 Support the weight of the engine/transmission using a trolley jack with a block of wood placed on its head. Position the jack underneath the transmission and raise it slightly to remove all load from the mounting.

20 Slacken and remove the two bolts securing the mounting to the transmission bracket **(see illustration)**.

21 Lower the transmission unit slightly until it is possible to unscrew the four bolts securing the mounting to the body then remove the mounting from the engine compartment **(see illustration)**.

22 If necessary, slacken and remove the two bolts securing the mounting bracket to the transmission and lift off the bracket, noting the rubber spacers which are fitted to it **(see illustration)**.

17.10 Undo the bolts (arrowed) and remove the mounting and restraint bar from the body

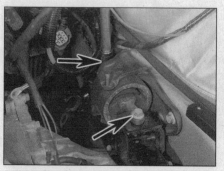

17.20 Slacken and remove the two bolts (arrowed) securing the mounting to the transmission bracket . . .

17.21 . . . then lower the transmission unit and unbolt the mounting from the body

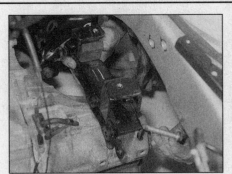

17.22 If necessary, unbolt the mounting bracket and remove it from the top of the transmission unit

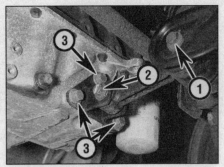

17.29 Slacken the bolts securing the steady rod to the body (1) and engine (2) and remove the rod. If necessary undo the bolts (3) and remove the bracket from the sump

23 Examine all components for signs of wear or damage and renew as necessary.

24 Fit the mounting to the body and tighten its retaining bolts to the specified torque.

25 Refit the mounting bracket (where removed) to the top of the transmission and tighten its retaining bolts to the specified torque. Ensure the rubber spacers are correctly fitted to the transmission bracket.

26 Raise the transmission unit then refit the bolts securing the mounting to the bracket and tighten them to the specified torque.

27 Remove the jack, then refit the battery tray, battery and air cleaner housing as described in Chapters 4A and 5A.

Rear steady rod

28 Firmly apply the handbrake, then jack up the front of the vehicle and support securely on axle stands (see *"Jacking and Vehicle Support"*).

29 Unscrew the steady rod mounting bolts and remove the rod from the rear of the engine. If necessary, unbolt the rod mounting bracket from the engine (see illustration).

30 Inspect the rod and mounting bracket for signs of wear or damage and renew as necessary.

31 Refit the steady rod bracket to the engine and tighten its retaining bolts to the specified torque.

32 Fit the steady rod and refit the mounting bolts. Tighten the bolt securing the rod to the engine to the specified torque then tighten the subframe bolt to the specified torque. Lower the vehicle to the ground.

Chapter 2 Part C:
Diesel engine in-car repair procedures

Contents

Degrees of difficulty

Easy, suitable for novice with little experience 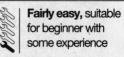	Fairly easy, suitable for beginner with some experience	Fairly difficult, suitable for competent DIY mechanic	Difficult, suitable for experienced DIY mechanic	Very difficult, suitable for expert DIY or professional

2C

Specifications

General

Engine type	Four-cylinder in-line, four-stroke, liquid-cooled
Designation:	
Models with an intercooler	20T2N
Models without an intercooler	20T2R
Bore	84.0 mm
Stroke	89.0 mm
Capacity	1994 cc
Firing order	1-3-4-2 (No 1 cylinder at timing belt end)
Direction of crankshaft rotation	Clockwise (seen from right-hand side of vehicle)
Compression ratio	19.5:1

Camshaft

Bearing journal running clearance	0.043 to 0.094 mm
Camshaft endfloat (service limit)	0.51 mm
Follower outside diameter	34.959 to 34.975 mm

Lubrication system

Minimum system pressure - at idle	0.7 bar
Pressure relief valve opening pressure	4.5 bar
Low oil pressure warning light comes on	0.4 to 0.7 bar
Oil pump clearances:	
Outer rotor-to-body clearance	0.05 to 0.10 mm
Inner rotor tip-to-outer rotor clearance	0.025 to 0.12 mm
Rotor endfloat	0.03 to 0.08 mm

Torque wrench settings	Nm	lbf ft
Camshaft bearing carrier bolts	11	8
Camshaft cover bolts	12	9
Camshaft fuel injection pump belt sprocket:		
Sprocket-to-hub bolts	25	18
Hub centre bolt:		
Stage 1	20	15
Stage 2	Angle-tighten a further 90°	
Camshaft timing belt sprocket bolt:		
Stage 1	20	15
Stage 2	Angle-tighten a further 90°	
Connecting rod big-end bearing cap nuts - early engines	48	35
Connecting rod big-end bearing cap bolts - later engines:		
Stage 1	20	15
Stage 2	Angle-tighten a further 85°	
Crankshaft pulley bolt:		
Stage 1	63	46
Stage 2	Angle-tighten a further 90°	
Crankshaft left-hand oil seal housing bolts	8	6
Cylinder head bolts:		
Stage 1	30	22
Stage 2	65	48
Stage 3	Angle-tighten a further 90°	
Stage 4	Angle-tighten a further 90°	
Engine/transmission mountings:		
Left-hand mounting:		
Mounting-to-body bolts	45	33
Mounting-to-bracket bolts	45	33
Bracket-to-transmission bolts	60	44
Right-hand mounting:		
Steady rod bolts	100	74
Mounting bracket-to-engine bracket bolts	105	78
Mounting bracket-to-mounting nut	80	59
Mounting-to-body bolts	45	33
Engine mounting bracket cover plate:		
Retaining bolts	45	33
Retaining nuts	35	26
Rear steady rod bolts	80	59
Flywheel bolts:		
Stage 1	15	11
Stage 2	Angle-tighten a further 90°	
Fuel injection pump belt cover bolts	8	6
Fuel injection pump belt tensioner bolt	45	33
Main bearing cap bolts	112	83
Oil cooler mounting bolts:		
M8 bolts	25	18
M10 bolts	45	33
Oil cooler pipe union nuts	25	18
Oil filter	17	11
Oil pump:		
Retaining bolts:		
M6 bolts	9	6
M10 bolt	45	33
Oil cooler pipe adaptor	35	26
Pick-up/strainer bolts	8	6
Piston oil jet spray tubes	12	9
Roadwheel nuts	110	81
Sump bolts	25	18
Sump drain plug	25	18
Timing belt cover bolts:		
Rear cover bolts	8	6
All other bolts	5	4
Timing belt idler pulley nut	45	33
Timing belt tensioner:		
Pulley bolt	55	41
Backplate bolt	45	33
Transmission mounting plate	45	33

1 General information and precautions

How to use this Chapter

This Part of the Chapter describes those repair procedures that can reasonably be carried out on the engine whilst it remains in the vehicle. If the engine has been removed from the vehicle and is being dismantled as described in Part D of this Chapter, any preliminary dismantling procedures can be ignored.

Note that whilst it may be possible physically to overhaul items such as the piston/connecting rod assemblies with the engine in the vehicle, such tasks are not usually carried out as separate operations and usually require the execution of several additional procedures (not to mention the cleaning of components and of oilways). For this reason, all such tasks are classed as major overhaul procedures and are described in Part D of this Chapter.

Engine description

The 2.0 litre diesel engine is from the Rover L-series engine family, and is a four-cylinder, in-line unit, mounted transversely at the front of the vehicle with the clutch and transmission on the left-hand end.

The cast-iron cylinder block is of the dry-liner type. The crankshaft is supported within the cylinder block on five shell-type main bearings. Thrustwashers are fitted to the centre main bearing to control crankshaft endfloat.

The connecting rods rotate on horizontally-split bearing shells at their big-ends. The pistons are attached to the connecting rods by gudgeon pins which are secured in position with circlips. The aluminium alloy pistons are fitted with three piston rings, comprising two compression rings and an oil control ring.

The inlet and exhaust valves are each closed by coil springs and operate in guides pressed into the cylinder head. The valve seat inserts are pressed into the cylinder head and can be renewed separately if worn.

The camshaft is driven by a toothed timing belt, and operate the valves via followers. Each follower incorporates a hydraulic self-adjusting valve which automatically adjusts the valve clearance. The camshaft rotates in bearings which are line-bored directly into the cylinder head and the (bolted-on) bearing carrier. This means that the bearing carrier and cylinder head are matched, and cannot be renewed independently.

The fuel injection pump is driven off the left-hand (flywheel) end of the camshaft by a second toothed timing belt and the coolant pump is driven by the auxiliary drivebelt.

Lubrication is by means of an eccentric-rotor type pump driven directly from the right-hand (timing belt end) of the crankshaft. The pump draws oil through a strainer located in the sump, and then forces it through an externally-mounted full-flow cartridge-type oil filter into galleries in the oil rail and the cylinder block/crankcase, from where it is distributed to the crankshaft (main bearings) and camshaft. The big-end bearings are supplied with oil via internal drillings in the crankshaft, while the camshaft bearings and the followers receive a pressurised supply via drillings in the cylinder head. The camshaft lobes and valves are lubricated by oil splash, as are all other engine components. An oil cooler is fitted to keep the oil temperature stable under arduous operating conditions.

Repair operations possible with the engine in the car

The following work can be carried out with the engine in the vehicle:
a) Compression pressure - testing.
b) Camshaft cover - removal and refitting.
c) Crankshaft pulley - removal and refitting.
d) Timing belt covers - removal and refitting.
e) Timing belt - removal and refitting.
f) Fuel injection pump belt - removal and refitting.
g) Timing belt/fuel injection pump belt tensioner and sprockets - removal and refitting.
h) Camshaft oil seals - renewal.
i) Camshafts and followers - removal, inspection and refitting.
j) Cylinder head - removal and refitting.
k) Cylinder head and pistons - decarbonising.
l) Sump - removal and refitting.
m) Oil pump - removal, overhaul and refitting.
n) Oil cooler - removal and refitting.
o) Crankshaft oil seals - renewal.
p) Engine/transmission mountings - inspection and renewal.
q) Flywheel - removal, inspection and refitting.

2 Compression test – description and interpretation

Compression test

Note: *A compression tester specifically designed for diesel engines must be used for this test.*

1 When engine performance is down, or if misfiring occurs which cannot be attributed to the fuel system, a compression test can provide diagnostic clues as to the engine's condition. If the test is performed regularly, it can give warning of trouble before any other symptoms become apparent.

2 A compression tester specifically intended for diesel engines must be used, because of the higher pressures involved. The tester is connected to an adaptor which screws into the glow plug or injector hole. On these models, an adaptor suitable for use in the injector holes will be required, due to there only be glow plugs fitted to Nos 1 to 3 cylinders. It is unlikely to be worthwhile buying such a tester for occasional use, but it may be possible to borrow or hire one - if not, have the test performed by a garage.

3 Unless specific instructions to the contrary are supplied with the tester, observe the following points:
a) *The battery must be in a good state of charge, the air filter must be clean, and the engine should be at normal operating temperature.*
b) *All the injectors should be removed before starting the test (see Chapter 4B).*
c) *Unscrew the retaining nut and disconnect the wiring connector from the fuel injection pump fuel cut-off solenoid (see Chapter 4B) to prevent fuel from being discharged.*

4 There is no need to hold the accelerator pedal down during the test, because the diesel engine air inlet is not throttled.

5 Crank the engine on the starter motor; after one or two revolutions, the compression pressure should build up to a maximum figure, and then stabilise. Record the highest reading obtained.

6 Repeat the test on the remaining cylinders, recording the pressure in each.

7 All cylinders should produce very similar pressures; a difference of more than 2 bars between any two cylinders indicates a fault. Note that the compression should build up quickly in a healthy engine; low compression on the first stroke, followed by gradually-increasing pressure on successive strokes, indicates worn piston rings. A low compression reading on the first stroke, which does not build up during successive strokes, indicates leaking valves or a blown head gasket (a cracked head could also be the cause). Deposits on the undersides of the valve heads can also cause low compression. **Note:** *The cause of poor compression is less easy to establish on a diesel engine than on a petrol one. The effect of introducing oil into the cylinders ("wet" testing) is not conclusive, because there is a risk that the oil will sit in the swirl chamber or in the recess on the piston crown instead of passing to the rings.*

8 Although Rover do not specify exact compression pressures, as a guide, any cylinder pressure of below 20 bar can be considered as less than healthy. Refer to a Rover dealer or other specialist if in doubt as to whether a particular pressure reading is acceptable.

9 On completion of the test, reconnect the injection pump fuel cut-off solenoid wiring connector then refit the injectors as described in Chapter 4B.

Leakdown test

10 A leakdown test measures the rate at which compressed air fed into the cylinder is lost. It is an alternative to a compression test, and in many ways it is better, since the escaping air provides easy identification of where pressure loss is occurring (piston rings, valves or head gasket).

11 The equipment needed for leakdown testing is unlikely to be available to the home mechanic. If poor compression is suspected, have the test performed by a suitably-equipped garage.

2C

3.6 Align the camshaft sprocket timing mark (1) with the mark (2) on the timing belt rear cover

3.8 Lock the crankshaft in position by inserting a 6.75 mm diameter pin through the hole in the rear of the mounting plate and locating it in the flywheel hole

3 Engine assembly/valve timing marks – general information and usage

Note: *A suitable pin will be required to lock the crankshaft in position (see paragraph 8).*

1 The camshaft sprocket has a timing mark which aligns when the crankshaft is at TDC with No1 and 4 pistons (No1 piston is at TDC on its compression stroke).

2 Disconnect the battery negative terminal. If necessary, remove all the injectors as described in Chapter 4B to enable the engine to be easily turned over.

3 To gain access to the camshaft sprocket timing mark, remove the timing belt upper cover as described in Section 6.

4 Firmly apply the handbrake, then jack up the front of the vehicle and support it securely on axle stands (see *"Jacking and Vehicle Support"*). Remove the right-hand front roadwheel then undo the retaining screws and fasteners and remove the engine/transmission undercover to gain access to the crankshaft pulley; on some models it may be possible to access the pulley through a hole in the undercover.

5 Using a socket and extension bar on the crankshaft pulley centre bolt, turn the crankshaft whilst keeping an eye on the camshaft sprocket.

6 Rotate the crankshaft until the timing mark on the sprocket is correctly aligned with the mark on the timing belt rear cover **(see illustration)**.

7 With the camshaft sprocket timing mark positioned as described, the engine can be safely dismantled. If necessary, the crankshaft can be locked in position as follows.

8 To lock the crankshaft in position, a 6.75 mm diameter pin will be required. Rover technicians use service tool 18G 1523, but an acceptable substitute can be a 6 or 6.5 mm drill or bolt with tape wrapped around it to

bring its diameter up to 6.75 mm. Ensure the camshaft sprocket timing mark is correctly positioned then insert the pin in through the hole in the rear of the transmission mounting plate, situated just below the crankshaft sensor, making sure it is correctly located in the hole in the rear of the flywheel **(see illustration)**.

4 Camshaft cover – removal and refitting

Removal

1 Disconnect the battery negative lead.

2 Unscrew the retaining bolts and remove the plastic cover from the top of the engine, taking care not to lose the spacers which are fitted to the cover mounting rubbers **(see illustrations)**.

3 On models with an intercooler, referring to Chapter 4B for further information, carry out the following.
 a) Remove the duct linking the turbocharger to the intercooler.
 b) Remove the inlet manifold intake pipe. Discard the gasket; a new gasket must be used on refitting

4 On all models, release the retaining clip and disconnect the breather hose from the camshaft cover.

5 Undo the retaining bolt and free the braking system vacuum hose from the right-hand end of the cover.

6 Working in the **reverse** of the tightening sequence **(see illustration 4.10)**, slacken and remove the cover retaining bolts.

7 Remove the cover and discard its gasket.

Refitting

8 Ensure the mating surfaces are clean and dry then fit the new gasket to the cover.

9 Refit the cover to the cylinder head, ensuring that the gasket remains correctly seated.

10 Refit the cover retaining bolts and tighten them all by hand. Once all bolts are in position, go around in the sequence shown and tighten them to the specified torque setting **(see illustration)**.

11 Connect the breather hose to the cover and secure it in position with the retaining clip.

12 Secure the vacuum hose to the right-hand end of the cover, tightening its retaining bolt securely.

13 On models with an intercooler, refit the inlet manifold intake pipe and the intake duct (see Chapter 4B).

4.2a Unscrew the retaining bolts . . .

4.2b . . . and remove the plastic cover from the top of the engine

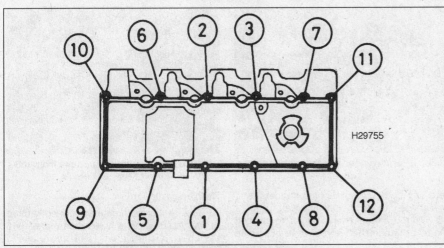

4.10 Camshaft cover bolt tightening sequence

14 On all models, refit the engine cover, ensuring the spacers are correctly fitted to each mounting rubber, and securely tighten its retaining bolts. Reconnect the battery.

5 Crankshaft pulley – removal and refitting

Removal

1 Firmly apply the handbrake then jack up the front of the vehicle and support it securely on axle stands (see *Jacking and Vehicle Support*).

5.5a Slacken and remove the retaining bolt . . .

2 Remove the auxiliary drivebelt as described in Chapter 1B.
3 If further dismantling is to be carried out, align the engine assembly/valve timing marks as described in Section 3.
4 Slacken the crankshaft pulley retaining bolt. To prevent crankshaft rotation, have an assistant select top gear and apply the brakes firmly. If the engine is removed from the vehicle it will be necessary to lock the flywheel (see Section 19).
Caution: Do not be tempted to use the crankshaft locking pin (see Section 3) to prevent rotation as the centre bolt is slackened.
5 Unscrew the retaining bolt and remove the pulley from the crankshaft (see illustrations).

Refitting

6 Fit the pulley to the crankshaft and screw in the retaining bolt.
7 Lock the crankshaft by the method used on removal, and tighten the pulley retaining bolt to the specified stage 1 torque setting then angle-tighten the bolt through the specified stage 2 angle, using a socket and extension bar. It is recommended that an angle-measuring gauge is used during the final stages of the tightening, to ensure accuracy. If

a gauge is not available, use white paint to make alignment marks between the bolt head and pulley prior to tightening; the marks can then be used to check that the bolt has been rotated through the correct angle.
8 Refit the auxiliary drivebelt as described in Chapter 1B.
9 Refit the roadwheel then lower the vehicle to the ground and tighten the wheel nuts to the specified torque.

6 Timing belt covers – removal and refitting

Upper cover

Removal

1 Slacken and remove the four retaining bolts then remove the upper cover from the engine, complete with its sealing strip (see illustrations). Inspect the sealing strip for signs of wear or damage and renew if necessary.

Refitting

2 Ensure the sealing strip is correctly positioned then refit the cover, tightening its bolts to the specified torque.

Lower cover

Removal

3 Remove the crankshaft pulley as described in Section 5.
4 Remove the upper cover as described in paragraph 1.
5 Slacken and remove the six retaining bolts then remove the lower cover from the engine, complete with its sealing strips (see illustrations). Inspect the sealing strips for signs of damage or deterioration and renew if necessary.

Refitting

6 Ensure the sealing strips are correctly positioned then refit the lower cover, tightening its bolts to the specified torque.
7 Refit the upper cover (see paragraph 2) then refit the crankshaft pulley as described in Section 5.

2C

5.5b . . . then remove the crankshaft pulley from the engine

6.1a Undo the retaining bolts . . .

6.1b . . . and remove the timing belt upper cover from the engine

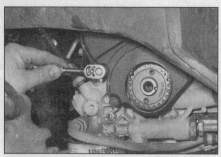

6.5a Unscrew the retaining bolts . . .

6.5b . . . and remove the timing belt lower cover

6.10 Unclip the wiring harness from the top of the rear cover

Rear upper cover

Removal

8 Remove the complete engine/transmission right-hand mounting assembly as described in Section 20.
9 Remove the camshaft sprocket as described in this Section 9.
10 Free the wiring harness from the top of the rear cover **(see illustration)**.
11 Slacken and remove the five retaining bolts, complete with their spacers. Remove the rear upper cover from the engine, complete with the rubber sealing strip, noting the rubber grommets which are fitted to the retaining bolt holes **(see illustrations)**. Inspect the sealing strip and grommets for signs of damage or deterioration and renew as necessary.

Refitting

12 Ensure the grommets are correctly fitted to the retaining bolts holes then manoeuvre the rear upper cover into position. Refit the

retaining bolts, complete with spacers, and tighten them to the specified torque.
13 Clip the wiring harness back into position the refit the camshaft sprocket as described in Section 9.
14 Refit the right-hand mounting assembly as described in Section 20.

Rear lower cover

Removal

15 Remove the timing belt (see Section 7).
16 Remove the timing belt idler pulley as described in Section 9.
17 Slacken and remove the retaining bolts, complete with their spacers. Remove the rear lower cover from the engine, complete with the rubber sealing strip, noting the rubber grommets which are fitted to the retaining bolt holes **(see illustrations)**. Inspect the sealing strip and grommets for signs of damage or deterioration and renew as necessary.

Refitting

18 Ensure the grommets are correctly fitted to the retaining bolts holes then manoeuvre the cover into position. Refit the retaining bolts, complete with spacers, and tighten them to the specified torque.
19 Refit the idler pulley (Section 9) then refit the timing belt (Section 7).

| 7 | Timing belt –
removal and refitting | |

Note: *A long M6 bolt, nut and washer will be helpful for this procedure (see paragraph 7).*

Removal

1 Disconnect the battery negative lead.
2 Align the engine assembly/valve timing marks as described in Section 3 and lock the crankshaft in position.
3 Remove the crankshaft pulley as described in Section 5. As a precaution, remove the crankshaft locking tool whilst the pulley bolt is slackened then refit it once the bolt is loose.
Caution: Do not be tempted to use the crankshaft locking pin to prevent rotation as the pulley bolt is slackened.
4 Remove the timing belt lower cover as described in Section 6.
5 Slacken and remove the retaining nuts and bolts and remove the cover plate from the engine/transmission right-hand mounting bracket **(see illustration)**. **Note:** *This is only necessary if the timing belt is to be completely removed.*

6.11a Undo the retaining bolts (arrowed - shown with engine removed) . . .

6.11b . . . then remove the rear upper cover from the engine

6.17a Slacken and remove the retaining bolts (arrowed) . . .

6.17b . . . then remove the timing belt rear lower cover from the engine

7.5 Undo the retaining nuts and bolts and remove the cover plate from the right-hand mounting bracket

7.6 Remove the rubber plug to gain access to the rear of the tensioner plunger

7.7 Screw the M6 bolt (1) into the rear of the tensioner spring plunger and use the nut (2) to draw the plunger back into the mounting bracket

6 Remove the rubber plug from the rear of the timing belt rear lower cover to gain access to the rear of the tensioner spring plunger **(see illustration)**.

7 Screw the nut onto the M6 bolt and fit the washer. Screw the bolt into the rear of the tensioner spring plunger then draw the plunger back into the bracket by holding the bolt stationary and rotating the nut **(see illustration)**.

8 Slacken the tensioner pulley retaining bolt **(see illustration)**. Pivot the pulley away from the timing belt and hold it in position by lightly tightening the pulley bolt.

9 Slide the timing belt off from its sprockets and remove it from the engine **(see illustration)**. If the belt is to be re-used, use white paint or similar to mark the direction of rotation on the belt. **Do not** rotate the crankshaft or camshafts until the timing belt has been refitted.

10 Check the timing belt carefully for any signs of uneven wear, splitting or oil contamination, and renew it if there is the slightest doubt about its condition. If the engine is undergoing an overhaul and has covered close to 72 000 miles or it was more than 6 years since the original belt was fitted, renew the belt as a matter of course, regardless of its apparent condition. If signs of oil contamination are found, trace the source of the oil leak and rectify it, then wash down the engine timing belt area and all related components to remove all traces of oil. **Note:** *Rover recommend that a timing belt should not be refitted if it has covered more than 36 000 miles.*

Refitting

11 Thoroughly clean and dry the timing belt sprockets. Check that the crankshaft is still locked in position and the camshaft sprocket engine assembly mark is still correctly aligned (see Section 3).

12 Fit the timing belt over the crankshaft and camshaft sprockets, ensuring that the belt

front run is taut (ie, all slack is on the tensioner side of the belt), then fit the belt over the tensioner pulley. **Do not** twist the belt sharply while refitting it. Ensure that the belt teeth are correctly seated centrally in the sprockets, and that the timing mark remains in alignment. If a used belt is being refitted, ensure that the arrow mark made on removal points in the normal direction of rotation, as before.

13 Refit the cover plate to the mounting bracket, tighten its retaining nuts and bolts to their specified torque settings.

14 Slacken the timing belt tensioner pulley bolt then carefully release the tensioner spring plunger. Once the plunger is in contact with the pulley backplate, unscrew the M6 bolt from the rear of the plunger and refit the rubber plug to the timing belt cover.

15 Check the camshaft sprocket timing mark is still correctly aligned then lightly tighten the tensioner pulley bolt. If adjustment is necessary, release the tensioner again then disengage the belt from the sprockets and make any necessary adjustments.

16 Ensure the sealing strips are correctly positioned then refit the timing belt lower cover, tightening its bolts to the specified torque. Remove the rubber plug from the cover to gain access to the tensioner pulley bolt.

17 Fit the pulley to the crankshaft and tighten its retaining bolt, tightening it lightly only at this stage.

18 Remove the locking tool from the flywheel then, using a socket on the crankshaft pulley centre bolt, rotate the crankshaft smoothly through two complete turns (720°) in the normal direction of rotation to settle the timing belt in position.

19 Realign the camshaft sprocket mark then check that the locking tool can be inserted into the rear of the flywheel (see Section 3). Ensure that the belt front run is taut (ie, all slack is on the tensioner side of the belt), then slacken the tensioner pulley bolt. Allow the tensioner spring and plunger to force the pulley into contact with the belt, then tighten the tensioner pulley bolt to the specified torque setting. Refit the rubber plug to the lower cover.

20 Lock the crankshaft (see Section 5) and tighten the crankshaft pulley bolt to the specified stage 1 torque setting and then through the specified stage 2 angle.

21 Refit the upper timing belt cover, ensuring its sealing strip is correctly positioned, and tighten its retaining bolts to the specified torque.

22 Refit the right-hand mounting assembly as described in Section 20.

23 Refit the auxiliary drivebelt as described in Chapter 1B.

2C

7.8 Slacken the tensioner pulley retaining bolt and pivot the pulley away from the belt

7.9 Release the timing belt from the sprockets and remove it from the engine

8.5a Unscrew the retaining bolts . . .

8.5b . . . and remove the fuel injection pump belt cover from the engine

8.6 Lock the injection pump sprocket in position using a 9.5 mm diameter pin or drill

8 Fuel injection pump belt – removal and refitting

Note: *Suitable pins will be required to lock the crankshaft (see Section 3) and injection pump sprocket in position (see paragraph 6).*

Removal

1 Disconnect the battery negative lead.
2 Align the engine assembly/valve timing marks as described in Section 3 and lock the crankshaft in position.
3 Unscrew the retaining bolts and remove the plastic cover from the top of the engine, taking care not to lose the spacers which are fitted to the cover mounting rubbers.
4 Remove the air cleaner housing as described in Chapter 4B.
5 Slacken and remove the retaining bolts,

complete with the spacers, and remove the fuel injection pump belt cover and seal from the left-hand end of the engine **(see illustrations)**. Inspect the seal and grommets which are fitted to the cover bolt holes; these must be renewed if damaged.
6 To lock the injection pump sprocket in position, a 9.5 mm diameter pin will be required. Rover technicians use service tool 18G 1717, but an acceptable substitute can be a 9.5 mm drill. Insert the pin in through the hole in the sprocket, making sure it is correctly located in the pump mounting plate **(see illustration)**.
7 Loosen the four bolts securing the injection pump belt sprocket to the hub just sufficiently to allow the sprocket to be moved. To prevent camshaft rotation, fit a 3/8 drive ratchet or wrench to the square-section cutout in the sprocket and hold the sprocket stationary **(see illustrations)**.

8 Slacken the tensioner pulley retaining bolt then slide the injection pump belt off from its sprockets and remove it from the engine **(see illustrations)**. If the belt is to be re-used, use white paint or similar to mark the direction of rotation on the belt.
9 Check the belt carefully for any signs of uneven wear, splitting or oil contamination, and renew it if there is the slightest doubt about its condition. If the engine is undergoing an overhaul and has covered close to 72 000 miles or it was more than 6 years since the original belt was fitted, renew the belt as a matter of course, regardless of its apparent condition. If signs of oil contamination are found, trace the source of the oil leak and rectify it, then wash down the belt area and all related components to remove all traces of oil.
Note: *Rover recommend that a fuel injection pump belt should not be refitted if it has covered more than 36 000 miles.*

Refitting

10 Thoroughly clean and dry the sprockets. Check that the crankshaft and injection pump sprockets are still locked in position and the camshaft sprocket engine assembly mark is still correctly aligned (see Section 3).
11 Rotate the camshaft sprocket fully clockwise on its hub then fit the timing belt over the injection pump and tensioner pulley **(see illustration)**. Ensure that the belt lower run is taut (ie, all slack is on the tensioner side of the belt), then seat the belt on the camshaft sprocket, rotating the sprocket anti-clockwise on the hub until it engages with the belt teeth. **Do not** twist the belt sharply while refitting it

8.7a Insert a 3/8 drive ratchet or wrench into the square-section hole (arrowed) . . .

8.7b . . . to retain the sprocket then slacken the four bolts securing the sprocket to the hub

8.8a Slacken the tensioner pulley retaining bolt . . .

8.8b . . . then slip the belt off from the sprockets and remove it from the engine

8.11 Rotate the sprocket fully clockwise on the hub then locate the belt on the sprockets

8.12 Apply the specified torque to the tensioner pulley backplate then securely tighten the pulley retaining bolt

and ensure that the belt teeth are correctly seated centrally in the sprockets. If a used belt is being refitted, ensure that the arrow mark made on removal points in the normal direction of rotation, as before.

12 Using a torque wrench and extension bar fitted to the square-section cut-out in the tensioner backplate, tension the timing belt by applying a torque of 6 Nm (4lbf ft) to the tensioner. Hold the tensioner in position and securely tighten its retaining bolt **(see illustration)**.

13 Retain the camshaft timing belt sprocket (see paragraph 7) and securely tighten the camshaft injection pump belt sprocket bolts.

14 Remove the locking pins from the flywheel and injection pump sprocket then, using a socket on the crankshaft pulley centre bolt, rotate the crankshaft smoothly through two complete turns (720°) in the normal direction of rotation to settle the belt in position.

15 Realign the camshaft sprocket mark then check that the locking tool can be inserted into the rear of the flywheel (see Section 3).

16 Refit the locking pin to the injection pump sprocket then slacken the camshaft injection pump belt sprocket bolts and the tensioner pulley bolt.

17 Refit the torque wrench and extension bar to the square-section cut-out in the tensioner backplate. Tension the timing belt by applying a torque of 6 Nm (4lbf ft) to the tensioner then hold the tensioner in position and tighten its retaining bolt to the specified torque.

18 Fit the torque wrench and extension bar to the square-section cut-out on the camshaft sprocket and apply a torque of 25 Nm (18 lbf ft) to the sprocket in an **anti-clockwise** direction. With the correct force applied to the sprocket, tighten the sprocket retaining bolts to the specified torque then remove the torque wrench.

19 Remove the locking pins from the fuel injection pump sprocket and flywheel.

20 Ensure the rubber grommets are correctly fitted to the belt cover holes then locate the seal in the cover groove. Refit the cover then fit the retaining bolts, complete with spacers, and tighten them to the specified torque.

21 Refit the air cleaner housing as described in Chapter 4B.

22 Ensure the sealing strip is correctly positioned then refit the timing belt upper cover, tightening its retaining bolts to the specified torque.

23 Refit the engine cover, ensuring the spacers are correctly fitted to each mounting rubber, and securely tighten its retaining bolts.

24 Reconnect the battery.

9 Timing belt tensioner and sprockets – removal and refitting

Note: *A long M6 bolt, a nut and washer will be required to release the timing belt tensioner spring (see Section 7).*

Camshaft sprocket

Note: *A new sprocket retaining bolt will be required on refitting.*

Removal

1 Disconnect the battery negative lead.

2 Align the engine assembly/valve timing marks as described in Section 3 and lock the crankshaft in position.

3 Remove the rubber plug from the front of the timing belt lower cover to gain access to the tensioner pulley retaining bolt.

4 Remove the rubber plug from the rear of the timing belt rear lower cover to gain access to the rear of the tensioner spring plunger.

5 Screw the nut onto the M6 bolt and fit the washer. Screw the bolt into the rear of the tensioner spring plunger then draw the plunger back into the bracket by holding the bolt stationary and rotating the nut (see Section 7).

6 Slacken the tensioner pulley retaining bolt. Pivot the pulley away from the timing belt and hold it in position by lightly tightening the pulley bolt.

7 Position the timing belt clear of the camshaft sprocket, taking care not to twist the belt too sharply; use only your fingers to move the belt.

8 Slacken and remove the camshaft sprocket retaining bolt. To prevent camshaft rotation, fabricate a holding tool from two lengths of steel strip (one long, the other short) and three nuts and bolts. One nut and bolt should form the pivot of a forked tool with the remaining

9.9a Remove the camshaft sprocket from the engine . . .

9.8 Using a home-made tool to retain the camshaft sprocket whilst the retaining bolt is slackened

two nuts and bolts at the tips of the forks to engage with the sprocket spokes **(see illustration)**. Discard the bolt, a new one must be used on refitting.

9 Remove the sprocket from the camshaft, taking care not to lose the sprocket locating pin. If a pin is a loose fit in the end of the camshaft, remove it and store it with the sprocket for safe-keeping **(see illustrations)**.

10 Check the sprocket for signs of wear or damage and renew if necessary.

Refitting

11 Prior to refitting check the oil seal for signs of damage or leakage. If necessary, renew as described in Section 11.

12 Ensure the locating pin is in position in the camshaft end. Note that the pin should be fitted with the split facing inwards.

13 Fit the sprocket to the camshaft, aligning the sprocket cutout with the locating pin.

14 Lightly oil the threads of the new retaining bolt then screw the bolt into position.

15 Prevent camshaft rotation by the method used on removal, and tighten the sprocket retaining bolt to the specified stage 1 torque setting then angle-tighten the bolt through the specified stage 2 angle, using a socket and extension bar. It is recommended that an angle-measuring gauge is used during the final stage of the tightening, to ensure accuracy. If a gauge is not available, use white paint to make alignment marks between the bolt head and sprocket prior to tightening; the marks can then be used to check that the bolt has been rotated through the correct angle.

2C

9.9b . . . taking care not to lose the locating pin (arrowed)

9.23 Removing the crankshaft sprocket

16 Ensure the crankshaft is still locked in position and the camshaft sprocket mark is correctly aligned (see Section 3).

17 Ensure that the belt is correctly engaged with the crankshaft sprocket then fit it over the camshaft sprocket, ensuring that the belt front run is taut (ie, all slack is on the tensioner side of the belt). **Do not** twist the belt sharply while refitting it and ensure that the belt teeth are correctly seated centrally in the sprockets, and that the timing mark remains in alignment.

18 Slacken the timing belt tensioner pulley bolt then carefully release the tensioner spring plunger. Once the plunger is in contact with the pulley backplate, unscrew the M6 bolt from the rear of the plunger and refit the rubber plug to the timing belt rear cover.

19 Remove the locking tool from the flywheel then, using a socket on the crankshaft pulley centre bolt, rotate the crankshaft smoothly through two complete turns (720°) in the normal direction of rotation to settle the timing belt in position.

20 Realign the camshaft sprocket mark then check that the locking tool can be inserted into the rear of the flywheel (see Section 3). Ensure that the belt front run is taut (ie, all slack is on the tensioner side of the belt), then slacken the tensioner pulley bolt. Allow the tensioner spring and plunger to force the pulley into contact with the belt, then tighten the tensioner pulley bolt to the specified torque setting. Refit the rubber plug to the lower cover.

21 Ensure the sealing strip is correctly positioned then refit the timing belt upper cover, tightening its retaining bolts to the specified torque. Reconnect the battery.

Crankshaft sprocket

Removal

22 Remove the timing belt as described in Section 7.

23 Slide the sprocket off from the end of the crankshaft, noting which way around it is fitted **(see illustration)**.

Refitting

24 Prior to refitting check the oil seal for signs of damage or leakage. If necessary, renew as described in Section 18.

25 Refit the sprocket to the crankshaft, aligning its key with the crankshaft slot.

26 Refit the timing belt as described in Section 7.

Tensioner assembly

Removal

27 Disconnect the battery negative lead.

28 Align the engine assembly/valve timing marks as described in Section 3 and lock the crankshaft in position.

29 Remove the timing belt lower cover as described in Section 6.

30 Remove the rubber plug from the rear of the timing belt rear lower cover to gain access to the rear of the tensioner spring plunger.

31 Screw the nut onto the M6 bolt and fit the washer. Screw the bolt into the rear of the tensioner spring plunger then draw the plunger back into the bracket by holding the bolt stationary and rotating the nut (see Section 7).

32 Slacken and remove the tensioner pulley bolt and the backplate bolt then remove the tensioner pulley from the mounting bracket **(see illustration)**.

33 With the tensioner removed, carefully release the spring plunger then remove the plunger and spring from the mounting bracket **(see illustration)**.

34 Clean the tensioner assembly but **do not** use any strong solvent which may enter the pulley bearing. Check that the pulley rotates freely on the backplate, with no sign of stiffness or free play. Renew the assembly if there is any doubt about its condition or if

there are any obvious signs of wear or damage. The same applies to the tensioner spring, which should be checked with great care as its condition is critical for the correct tensioning of the timing belt. The condition of the spring can be judged by measuring its free length; if the spring is less than 65 mm it must be renewed.

Refitting

35 Check that the camshaft timing marks are still correctly aligned and the crankshaft is still locked in position (see Section 3).

36 Ensure that the belt is correctly engaged with the crankshaft and camshaft sprockets and the belt front run is taut (ie, all slack is on the tensioner side of the belt).

37 Lubricate the plunger with a smear of molybdenum disulphide grease then fit the tensioner spring and plunger to the mounting bracket. Use the nut and bolt to draw the plunger fully into the bracket.

38 Fit the tensioner pulley and screw in the backplate and pulley retaining bolts. Tighten the backplate bolt to the specified torque but do not tighten the pulley bolt yet.

39 Tension the timing belt as described in paragraphs 14 to 23 of Section 7.

Idler pulley

Removal

40 Carry out the operations described in paragraphs 27 to 31 of this Section.

41 Slacken the tensioner pulley bolt then pivot the pulley fully away from the belt and secure it in position by lightly retightening the bolt.

42 Slacken and remove the retaining nut and remove the idler pulley from its mounting stud. If the mounting stud is unscrewed with the pulley, carefully clamp the stud in a vice equipped with soft jaws then remove the retaining nut and separate the pulley and stud.

43 Clean the idler pulley but do not use any strong solvent which may enter the pulley bearing. Check that the pulley rotates freely, with no sign of stiffness or free play. Renew the pulley if there is any doubt about its condition or if there are any obvious signs of wear or damage.

Refitting

44 Remove all traces of locking compound from the threads of the retaining nut and mounting stud.

45 Where the mounting stud has been removed, apply locking compound (Rover recommend the use of Loctite 275) to the stud threads then refit the stud to the engine and tighten it securely.

46 Fit the idler pulley to the mounting stud. Apply locking compound (Rover recommend the used of Loctite 275) to the threads of the pulley retaining nut then refit the nut and tighten it to the specified torque.

47 Tension the timing belt as described in paragraphs 14 to 23 of Section 7.

9.32 Unscrew the pulley and backplate retaining bolts and remove the tensioner pulley from the engine

9.33 Carefully unscrew the bolt and remove the plunger and spring from the mounting bracket

10 Fuel injection pump belt tensioner and sprockets – removal and refitting

Camshaft sprocket

Note: *A new sprocket hub retaining bolt will be required on refitting.*

Removal

1 Remove the injection pump belt as described in Section 8.
2 Unscrew the four sprocket retaining bolts and remove the sprocket from the hub. To remove the hub, proceed as follows.
3 Retain the camshaft timing belt sprocket with the holding tool (see Section 9) then slacken and remove the bolt securing the sprocket hub to the camshaft.
4 Remove the hub from the camshaft, taking care not to lose the locating pin. If a pin is a loose fit in the end of the camshaft, remove it and store it with the hub for safe-keeping.
5 Check the sprocket and hub for signs of wear or damage and renew if necessary.

Refitting

6 Prior to refitting check the oil seal for signs of damage or leakage. If necessary, renew as described in Section 11.
7 Ensure the locating pin is in position in the camshaft end. Note that the pin should be fitted with the split facing inwards.
8 Fit the sprocket hub to the camshaft, aligning its cutout with the locating pin.
9 Lightly oil the threads of the new retaining bolt then screw the bolt into position.
10 Prevent camshaft rotation by the method used on removal, and tighten the hub retaining bolt to the specified stage 1 torque setting then angle-tighten the bolt through the specified stage 2 angle, using a socket and extension bar. It is recommended that an angle-measuring gauge is used during the final stage of the tightening, to ensure accuracy.

 If a gauge is not available, use white paint to make alignment marks between the bolt head and hub prior to tightening; the marks can then be used to check that the bolt has been rotated through the correct angle.

11 Refit the sprocket to the hub, tightening its bolts lightly only at this stage.
12 Refit the fuel injection pump belt as described in Section 8.

Fuel injection pump sprocket

13 This is described as part of the fuel injection pump removal and refitting procedures. Remove the fuel injection pump belt as described in Section 8 then proceed as described in Chapter 4B, Section 10.

Tensioner pulley

Removal

14 Remove the injection pump belt as described in Section 8.
15 Unscrew the retaining bolt and remove the tensioner assembly from the cylinder head.
16 Clean the tensioner pulley but **do not** use any strong solvent which may enter the pulley bearing. Check that the pulley rotates freely, with no sign of stiffness or free play. Renew the tensioner pulley if there is any doubt about its condition or if there are any obvious signs of wear or damage.

Refitting

17 Refit the tensioner pulley, making sure its backplate is correctly located on the pivot pin, and refit the retaining bolt **(see illustration)**.
18 Refit the fuel injection pump belt as described in Section 8.

11 Camshaft oil seals – renewal

Right-hand (timing belt end) seal

Note: *If the seal is to be renewed with the timing belt still in place, then check that the belt is free from oil contamination. Renew the belt if signs of oil contamination are found. Cover the belt to protect it from contamination while work is in progress and ensure that all traces of oil are removed from the area before the belt is refitted.*
1 Remove the timing belt rear upper cover as described in Section 6.
2 Carefully punch or drill two small holes opposite each other in the oil seal. Screw a self-tapping screw into each hole, and pull on the screws with pliers to extract the seal.
3 Clean the seal housing and polish off any burrs or raised edges which may have caused the seal to fail.
4 Lubricate the lips of the new seal with clean engine oil and drive it fully into position. Use a suitable tubular drift, such as a socket, which bears only on the hard outer edge of the seal. Take care not to damage the seal lips during fitting and note that the seal lips should face inwards.
5 Refit the timing belt cover as described in Section 6.

11.8a Unscrew the retaining bolts . . .

10.17 Ensure the tensioner pulley backplate hole is correctly engaged with the pivot pin (arrowed)

Left-hand (flywheel end) seal

6 Renew the fuel injection pump belt as described in Section 8. The belt must be renewed if it has been contaminated with oil.
7 Remove the camshaft sprocket hub and the tensioner pulley as described in Section 10.
8 Slacken and remove the three retaining bolts, noting the correct fitted position of the engine cover bracket, and remove the injection pump belt rear cover from the end of the cylinder head **(see illustrations)**.
9 Renew the oil seal as described in paragraphs 2 to 4.
10 Refit the rear cover to the cylinder head and tighten its retaining bolts to the specified torque, ensuring the engine cover mounting bracket is correctly positioned.
11 Refit the fuel injection pump belt camshaft sprocket and tensioner as described in Section 10 then refit the belt as described in Section 8.

2C

12 Camshaft and followers – removal, inspection and refitting

Note: *Rover produce a sealant kit which consists of a plastic scraper, gasket removing compound and the recommended sealant for the camshaft carrier joint. It is recommended that this kit is used during the following procedure.*

Removal

1 Remove the timing belt rear upper cover as described in Section 6.

11.8b . . . and remove the injection pump belt rear cover from the cylinder head

12.11 Lubricate the followers with clean engine oil and insert them into their original bores

12.12 Lay the camshaft in position in the cylinder head making sure the locating pin (arrowed) is in the 2 o'clock position

2 Remove the fuel injection pump belt camshaft sprocket hub and the tensioner pulley as described in Section 10.

3 Slacken and remove the three retaining bolts, noting the correct fitted position of the engine cover bracket, and remove the injection pump belt rear cover from the end of the cylinder head.

4 Remove the camshaft cover as described in Section 4.

5 Working in the **reverse** of the tightening sequence **(see illustration 12.15)**, slacken the camshaft bearing carrier retaining bolts evenly progressively, by one turn at a time, to gradually release the pressure of the valve springs. Once all bolts are loose, remove them from the cylinder head.

Caution: If the bearing carrier bolts are carelessly slackened, the carrier might break. If the carrier is broken, the complete cylinder head assembly must be renewed; the carrier is matched to the head and is not available separately.

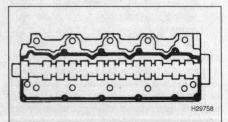

12.13a Apply sealant to the highlighted areas of the cylinder head camshaft bearing carrier as shown

12.13b If the Rover sealant is being used, apply a bead of sealant to the mating surface . . .

6 Lift the camshaft bearing carrier away from the cylinder, noting the correct fitted positions of the locating dowels. If the dowels are loose, remove them and store them with the bearing carrier for safe-keeping.

7 Carefully lift the camshaft from the cylinder head. Remove the oil seal from each end of the shaft and discard them; new ones should be used on refitting.

8 If necessary, obtain eight small, clean plastic containers, and label them for identification. Alternatively, divide a larger container into compartments. Using a sucker or magnet, withdraw each follower in turn, invert it to prevent oil loss and place it in its respective container, which should then be filled with clean engine oil.

Caution: Do not interchange the followers, and do not allow the followers to lose oil, as they will take a long time to refill with oil on restarting the engine, which could result in incorrect valve clearances.

Inspection

9 Examine the camshaft bearing surfaces and cam lobes for signs of wear ridges and scoring. Renew the camshaft if any of these conditions are apparent. Examine the condition of the bearing surfaces both on the camshaft journals and in the cylinder head. If the head bearing surfaces are worn excessively, the cylinder head will need to be renewed.

10 Examine the follower bearing surfaces which contact the camshaft lobes for wear ridges and scoring. Check the followers and their bores in the cylinder head for signs of

12.13c . . . then spread the sealant to an even film using the brush supplied

wear or damage. If the engine's valve clearances have sounded noisy, particularly if the noise persists after initial start-up from cold, then there is reason to suspect a faulty follower. If any follower is thought to be faulty or is visibly worn it should be renewed.

Refitting

11 Where removed, lubricate the followers with clean engine oil and carefully insert each one into its original location in the cylinder head **(see illustration)**.

12 Liberally oil the camshaft bearings and followers then refit the camshaft to the cylinder head. Position the shaft so that the timing belt sprocket locating pin is in the 2 o'clock position when viewed from the right-hand end of the engine **(see illustration)**.

13 Ensure the mating surfaces of the camshaft bearing carrier and cylinder head are clean and dry then apply a bead of sealant to the mating surfaces of the bearing carrier as shown **(see illustrations)**. Spread the sealant to an even film, taking care not to allow any sealant to enter the oilway grooves.

14 Ensure that the locating dowels are in position and refit the camshaft bearing carrier to the cylinder head. Ensure the carrier is correctly located and screw in the retaining bolts, tightening them all by hand only at this stage.

15 Working in the specified sequence, evenly and progressively tighten the retaining bolts to draw the bearing carrier squarely down into contact with the cylinder head. Once the carrier is in contact with the head, go around in the specified sequence and tighten the retaining bolts to the specified torque **(see illustration)**.

Caution: If the bearing carrier bolts are carelessly tightened, the carrier might break. If the carrier is broken then the complete cylinder head assembly must be renewed; the carrier is matched to the head and is not available separately.

16 Refit the camshaft cover as described in Section 4.

17 Fit a new oil seal to either end of the camshaft as described in Section 11.

18 Refit the timing belt rear cover as described in Section 6 and refit the camshaft sprocket as described in Section 9.

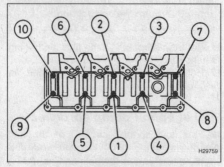

12.15 Camshaft bearing carrier bolt tightening sequence

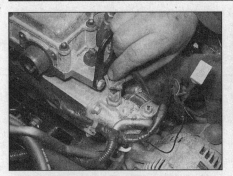

13.9a Disconnect the wiring connector from the coolant temperature sensor . . .

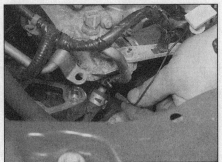

13.9b . . . and the temperature gauge sender wiring connector from the cylinder head coolant elbow

13.10 Slacken and remove the dipstick retaining bolt

19 Refit the fuel injection pump belt rear cover to the cylinder head and tighten its retaining bolts to the specified torque, ensuring the engine cover mounting bracket is correctly positioned.

20 Refit the fuel injection pump belt camshaft sprocket and tensioner as described in Section 10 then refit the belt as described in Section 8.

13 Cylinder head – removal and refitting

Removal

1 Disconnect the battery negative lead.

2 Drain the cooling system, as described in Chapter 1B.

3 Align the engine assembly/valve timing marks as described in Section 3 and lock the crankshaft in position.

4 Remove the fuel injection pump belt as described in Section 8.

5 Remove the fuel injection pump belt tensioner and camshaft sprocket and hub as described in Section 10. Slacken and remove the three retaining bolts, noting the correct fitted position of the engine cover bracket, and remove the injection pump belt rear cover from the end of the cylinder head.

6 Remove the timing belt upper rear cover as described in Section 6.

7 Remove the camshaft cover as described in Section 4.

8 On models equipped with air conditioning, unbolt the alternator from the upper mounting bracket then unbolt the mounting bracket and remove it from the cylinder head.

9 On all models, disconnect the wiring connector from the coolant temperature sensors which are screwed into the coolant elbow on the front of the cylinder head **(see illustrations)**.

10 Release the retaining clip and disconnect the coolant hose from the cylinder head coolant elbow then slacken and remove the bolt securing the engine oil dipstick tube in position **(see illustration)**.

11 Referring to Chapter 4B, carry out the following operations
  a) *Remove the inlet and exhaust manifolds.*
  b) *Remove the injector pipes connecting the injection pump to the injectors.*
  c) *Disconnect the needle lift sensor wiring connector from No 1 injector.*
  d) *If the cylinder head is to be overhauled, remove all the injectors.*

12 Unscrew the retaining nut and disconnect the glow plug feed wiring connector from No 2 glow plug **(see illustration)**. If the cylinder head is to be overhauled, remove the glow plugs as described in Chapter 5C.

13 Slacken the retaining clip securing the braking system servo unit vacuum hose to the pump (which is fitted to the alternator) and position the hose clear of the cylinder head.

14 Make a final check to ensure that all relevant hoses, pipes and wires, etc, have been disconnected.

15 Working in the **reverse** of the tightening sequence **(see illustration 13.36)**, progressively slacken the cylinder head bolts by a third of a turn at a time until all bolts can be unscrewed by hand. Withdraw the bolts, and store them in order, so that they can be refitted in their original locations **(see illustration)**. The bolts can be stored by pushing them through a clearly-marked cardboard template.

16 Lift the cylinder head from the cylinder block **(see illustration)**. If necessary, tap the cylinder head gently with a soft-faced mallet to free it from the block, but **do not** lever at the mating faces.

17 When the joint is broken, lift the cylinder head away then remove the gasket. Note the fitted positions of the two locating dowels, and remove them for safe-keeping if they are loose. Keep the gasket for identification purposes (see paragraph 24).

Caution: Do not lay the head on its lower mating surface; support the head on wooden blocks, ensuring each block only contacts the head mating surface not the glow plugs or injector nozzles. The glow plugs and injector nozzles protrude out the bottom of the head and they will be damaged if the head is placed directly onto a bench.

18 If the cylinder head is to be dismantled, remove the camshaft, as described in Section 12, then refer to the relevant Sections of Part D of this Chapter.

2C

13.12 Unscrew the retaining nut and disconnect the glow plug feed wiring from No 2 glow plug

13.15 Remove the cylinder head bolts. If the bolts are to be re-used, store them in their correct fitted order

13.16 Removing the cylinder head from the engine

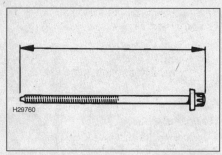

13.23 Measure the length of each cylinder head bolt. If any bolt exceeds the specified limit (see text) all bolts must be renewed as a set

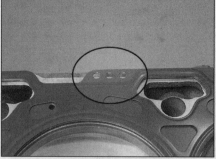

13.24 The cylinder head gasket thickness identification marking can be found at the front of No 2 cylinder

13.26 Measure the protrusion of each piston as described in text to calculate the correct thickness of cylinder head gasket

Preparation for refitting

19 The mating faces of the cylinder head and block must be perfectly clean before refitting the head. Use a scraper to remove all traces of gasket and carbon, and also clean the tops of the pistons. Take particular care with the aluminium surfaces, as the soft metal is damaged easily. Also, make sure that debris is not allowed to enter the oil and water channels - this is particularly important for the oil circuit, as carbon could block the oil supply to the camshaft or crankshaft bearings. Using adhesive tape and paper, seal the water, oil and bolt holes in the cylinder block. To prevent carbon entering the gap between the pistons and bores, smear a little grease in the gap. After cleaning the piston, rotate the crankshaft so that the piston moves down the bore, then wipe out the grease and carbon with a cloth rag. Clean the piston crowns in the same way.
20 Check the block and head for nicks, deep scratches and other damage. If slight, they may be removed carefully with a file. More serious damage may be repaired by machining, but this is a specialist job.
21 If warpage of the cylinder head gasket surface is suspected, use a straight-edge to check it for distortion. Refer to Part D of this Chapter if necessary.
22 Ensure that the cylinder head bolt holes in the crankcase are clean and free of oil. Syringe or soak up any oil left in the bolt holes. This is most important in order that the correct bolt tightening torque can be applied and to prevent the possibility of the block

being cracked by hydraulic pressure when the bolts are tightened.
23 Check the condition of the cylinder head bolts, particularly their threads. Keeping all bolts in their correct fitted order, wash them and wipe dry. Check each bolt for any sign of visible wear or damage and measure the length of each bolt (see illustration). If any bolt shows signs of wear or damage or is longer than 243.41 mm then all the bolts must be renewed as a complete set. If all bolts are in good condition and are less than 243.41 mm in length, then it is permissible to re-use them. However, as a precaution, we recommend that the bolts are renewed as a complete set, regardless of their apparent condition.
24 On this engine, the cylinder head to piston clearance is controlled by fitting different thickness head gaskets. The gasket thickness can be determined by looking at the tab situated directly in front of No 2 cylinder (the tab is visible once the plastic cover has been removed from the top of the engine) (see illustration).

Holes on gasket tab	Gasket thickness
One hole	1.05 mm
Two holes	1.20 to 1.25 mm
Three holes	1.30 to 1.35 mm

The correct thickness of gasket required is selected by measuring the piston protrusions as follows.
25 Remove the locking pin from the flywheel and mount a dial test indicator securely on the block so that its pointer can be easily pivoted between the piston crown and block mating

surface. Temporarily refit the crankshaft pulley bolt to enable the crankshaft to be easily rotated.
26 Ensure the piston is at exactly TDC then zero the dial test indicator on the gasket surface of the cylinder block. Carefully move the indicator over No 1 piston, taking measurements in line with the gudgeon pin axis, measure the protrusion on both the left-hand and right-hand side of the piston (see illustration). Repeat this procedure on No 4 piston.
27 Rotate the crankshaft half-a-turn to bring Nos 2 and 3 pistons to TDC. Ensure the crankshaft is accurately positioned then measure the protrusions of Nos 2 and 3 pistons, taking two measurements for each piston. Once both pistons have been measured, rotate the crankshaft through half-a-turn to bring Nos 1 and 4 pistons back to TDC and lock the crankshaft in position again.
28 Using the largest protrusion measurement of the four pistons, select the correct thickness of gasket required using the following table.

Largest piston protrusion measurement	Gasket required
0.1 to 0.25 mm	One hole in tab
0.25 to 0.4 mm	Two holes in tab
0.4 to 0.55 mm	Three holes in tab

Refitting

29 Remove the locking pin from the rear of the flywheel and turn the crankshaft slightly **backwards** so that pistons 1 and 4 are positioned approximately 25 mm down their bores. This will ensure the valves do not contact the pistons as the head is refitted. **Note:** *Make a note of the approximate angle through which the crankshaft is rotated; this will be useful when refitting the locking pin prior to fitting the timing belt (see paragraph 47).*
30 Wipe clean the mating faces of the head and block and ensure that the two locating dowels are in position at each end of the cylinder block/crankcase surface (see illustration).
31 Check that the oil restrictor is in position on the front, left-hand end of the cylinder block. Ensure the restrictor is unblocked and

13.30 Ensure the locating dowels (arrowed) are in position . . .

13.32 . . . then fit the new gasket making sure it is the correct way up

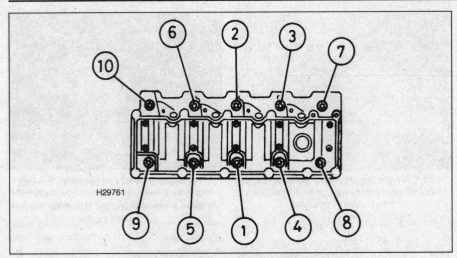

13.36 Cylinder head bolt tightening sequence

does not protrude above the block mating surface.

32 Fit the new cylinder head gasket to the block, making sure it is fitted with the correct way up **(see illustration)**.

33 Prior to refitting the cylinder head, check that the camshaft is still positioned correctly with its timing belt sprocket locating pin in the 2 o'clock position when viewed from the right-hand end of the head **(see illustration 12.12)**.

34 Carefully refit the cylinder head, locating it on the dowels.

35 Keeping all the cylinder head bolts in their correct fitted order, wash them and wipe dry. Lightly oil under the head and on the threads of each bolt, carefully enter it into its original hole and screw it in, by hand only, until finger-tight. *Caution: Do not drop the bolts into their holes.*

36 Working progressively and in the sequence shown, first tighten all the cylinder head bolts to the stage 1 torque setting **(see illustration)**.

37 Once all bolts have been tightened to the stage 1 torque, go around again in the specified sequence and tighten all bolts to the specified stage 2 torque setting.

38 Once all bolts have been tightened to the stage 2 torque, again working in the sequence shown, tighten each bolt through its specified stage 3 angle, using a socket and extension bar. It is recommended that an angle-measuring gauge is used during this stage of the tightening, to ensure accuracy. Prior to tightening, use a felt-tip pen or similar to make alignment marks between the radial mark on each bolt head and the cylinder head.

39 Finally go around in the specified sequence again and tighten all bolts through the specified stage 4 angle. Each bolt head radial mark should now be exactly opposite the corresponding mark made on the cylinder head.

40 Refit the glow plugs (where removed) and connect the glow plug wiring to No 2 glow plug (see Chapter 5C).

41 Referring to Chapter 4B, carry out the following.
 a) *Refit the injectors (where removed)*
 b) *Reconnect the needle lift sensor wiring connector.*
 c) *Refit the injector pipes.*
 d) *Refit the manifolds.*

42 Reconnect the coolant hose to the cylinder head elbow and secure it in position with the retaining clip. Refit the dipstick tube retaining bolt, tighten it securely, and reconnect the coolant temperature sensor wiring connectors.

43 On models equipped with air conditioning, refit the alternator upper mounting bracket tightening its retaining bolts securely.

44 On all models, refit the camshaft cover as described in Section 4.

45 Reconnect the vacuum hose to the braking system vacuum pump.

46 Refit the timing belt upper cover as described in Section 6 then refit the camshaft sprocket as described in Section 9.

47 Ensure the camshaft sprocket timing mark is correctly aligned with the mark on the cover (see Section 3) then carefully rotate the crankshaft in the normal direction of rotation, to bring Nos 1 and 4 pistons back to TDC. Lock the crankshaft in position by inserting pin into the rear of the flywheel.
Caution: Do not rotate the crankshaft any further than is necessary as there is a risk that the pistons will contact and damage the valves.

48 Refit the timing belt as described in Section 7.

49 Refit the fuel injection pump belt rear cover to the cylinder head and tighten its retaining bolts to the specified torque, ensuring the engine cover mounting bracket is correctly positioned.

50 Refit the fuel injection pump belt camshaft sprocket and tensioner as described in Section 10 then refit the belt as described in Section 8.

51 Reconnect the battery and refill the cooling system as described in Chapter 1B.

14 Sump – removal and refitting

Removal

1 Disconnect the battery negative lead.

2 Apply the handbrake, then jack up the front of the vehicle and support it securely on axle stands (see "*Jacking and Vehicle Support*"). Remove the retaining screws and fasteners and remove the undercover from beneath the engine and transmission.

3 Drain the engine oil and remove the oil filter as described in Chapter 1B. If the oil filter is damaged on removal (which is likely), then a new filter must be used on refitting and the engine filled with fresh oil.

4 Slacken and remove the mounting bolts securing the rear engine/transmission steady rod to the bracket and subframe and remove the rod. If necessary, unbolt the rod bracket from the sump.

5 Undo the bolts securing the power steering pipe clips to the sump and position the pipe clear.

6 Undo the retaining bolts and remove the support bracket securing the rear of the sump to the transmission mounting plate.

7 Wipe clean the area around the vacuum pump hose union on the sump then position a container beneath the union **(see illustration)**. Disconnect the hose from the sump and allow any oil to drain into the container.

8 Unscrew the retaining bolts securing the oil cooler pipes to the sump and bracket. Unscrew the union nut and disconnect the front oil cooler pipe from the pump. Position both pipes clear of the sump and remove the sealing ring which is fitted to the pipe end fitting. Discard the sealing ring; a new one should be used on refitting.

9 Working in the **reverse** of the tightening sequence **(see illustration 14.17)**, progressively slacken and remove the bolts securing the sump to the base of the cylinder block.

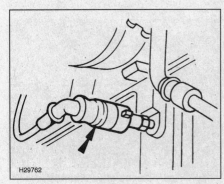

14.7 Disconnect the vacuum pump oil hose union (arrowed) from the sump

2C

14.11 Undo the retaining bolts (arrowed) and remove the oil pump pick-up/strainer

14.13 On refitting, fit a new sealing ring to the oil pump pick-up/strainer groove

14.14 Apply a bead of sealant to the front main bearing cap/cylinder block joints (arrowed) and ensure the cap grooves are filled with sealant

10 Break the sump joint by striking the sump with the palm of the hand, then lower the sump away from the engine. Remove the gasket and discard it, a new one should be used on refitting.

11 While the sump is removed, take the opportunity to check the oil pump pick-up/strainer for signs of clogging or splitting. If necessary, unbolt the pick-up/strainer, noting the correct fitted location of the shorter bolt, and remove it from the engine along with its sealing ring **(see illustration)**. The strainer can then be cleaned easily in solvent. Inspect the strainer mesh for signs of clogging or splitting and renew if necessary. If the pick-up/strainer bolts are damaged they must be renewed.

Refitting

12 Clean all traces of gasket from the mating surfaces of the cylinder block/crankcase and sump, then use a clean rag to wipe out the sump and the engine interior.

13 Where necessary, fit a new sealing ring to the oil pump pick-up/strainer groove then carefully refit the pipe **(see illustration)**. Refit the retaining bolts, making sure the shorter bolt is screwed into the main bearing cap, and tighten them to the specified torque setting.

14 Apply a bead of suitable sealant (recommended sealant is available from your Rover dealer) to the front main bearing cap joint areas of the cylinder block mating surface and ensure the cap grooves are completely filled with sealant **(see illustration)**.

15 Apply a bead of sealant to the joint between the crankshaft left-hand (flywheel) oil seal housing and cylinder block **(see illustration)**.

16 Fit the gasket to the sump then offer up the sump to the cylinder block/crankcase. Refit the sump retaining bolts, and tighten the bolts finger-tight only.

17 Working in the sequence shown, tighten the sump bolts to the specified torque setting **(see illustration)**. Go around again in the specified sequence and recheck the tightness of each bolt.

18 Fit a new sealing ring to the oil cooler pipe union and reconnect the pipe. Refit the pipe retaining clip bolts, tightening them securely, then tighten the union nut to the specified torque.

19 Securely reconnect the vacuum pipe return hose to the sump.

20 Refit the support bracket connecting the sump to the transmission mounting plate, tightening its bolts to their specified torque settings.

21 Ensure the power steering pipe is correctly routed and securely tighten the retaining clip bolts.

22 Refit the engine/transmission rear steady rod and tighten its bolts to the specified torque.

23 Fit the oil filter then refit the engine/transmission undercover. Lower the vehicle to the ground and refill the engine with oil (see Chapter 1B).

15 Oil pump – removal and refitting

Removal

Note: *The oil pressure relief valve can be dismantled without removing the oil pump from the vehicle - see Section 16 for details.*

1 Drain the engine oil and remove the oil filter as described in Chapter 1B. If the oil filter is damaged on removal (which is likely), then a new filter must be used on refitting and the engine filled with fresh oil.

2 Remove the crankshaft sprocket and timing belt idler pulley as described in Section 9. Secure the timing belt clear of the working area so that it cannot be contaminated with oil.

3 Unbolt the timing belt rear lower cover and remove it from the cylinder block (see Section 6).

14.15 Apply a bead of sealant to the joint between the crankshaft oil seal housing and the cylinder block (arrowed)

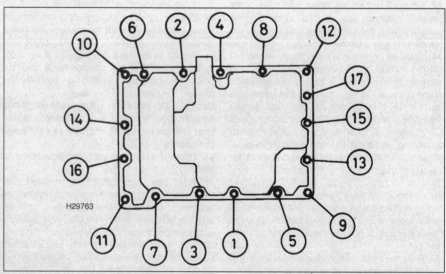

14.17 Sump retaining bolt tightening sequence

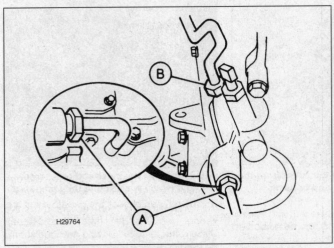

15.4 Oil pump oil cooler pipe unions (A) and turbocharger oil pipe union (B)

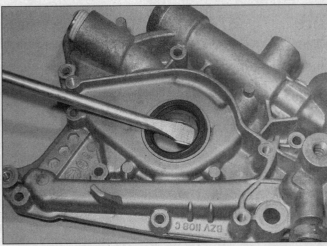

15.8 Prior to refitting the oil pump, renew the crankshaft oil seal

4 Wipe clean the area around the oil cooler pipe unions on the front of the oil pump and the turbocharger oil feed pipe union on the rear of the pump (see illustration). Slacken and remove the pipe retaining clip bolts then unscrew the union nuts and disconnect the pipes from the pump. Remove the sealing rings from the pipe end fittings and discard; new ones must be used on refitting.

5 Working in the reverse of the tightening sequence (see illustration 15.13), progressively slacken and remove the oil pump retaining bolts, noting the correct fitted location of the larger (M10) bolt.

6 Free the oil pump from the cylinder block then slide it off the end of the crankshaft. Note the correct fitted locations of the pump locating dowels; if the dowels are loose, remove them and store with the pump for safe-keeping. Remove the gasket and discard it; if the oil pump bolts are damaged they must also be renewed.

7 Remove the oil pump drive Woodruff key from the crankshaft and store it with the pump for safe-keeping.

Refitting

8 Prior to refitting, carefully lever out the crankshaft oil seal using a flat-bladed screwdriver (see illustration). Fit the new oil seal, ensuring its sealing lip is facing inwards, and press it squarely into the housing using a tubular drift which bears only on the hard outer edge of the seal. Press the seal into position so that it is flush with the housing and lubricate the oil seal lip with clean engine oil.

9 Ensure the mating surfaces of the oil pump and cylinder block are clean and dry then apply a bead of suitable sealant (recommended sealant is available from your Rover dealer) to the front main bearing cap joint areas of the cylinder block (see illustration).

10 Ensure the locating dowels are in position then fit a new gasket to the cylinder block (see illustration).

11 Fit the Woodruff key to the crankshaft slot.

12 Carefully manoeuvre the oil pump into position, aligning the inner rotor slot with the Woodruff key. Locate the pump on the dowels, taking great care not to damage the oil seal lip.

15.9 Apply a bead of sealant to the joints between the front main bearing cap and cylinder block (arrowed)

13 Fit the pump retaining bolts, tightening them all by hand, then go around in the specified sequence and tighten them to their specified torque settings (see illustration).

14 Fit new sealing rings to the oil cooler and turbocharger oil pipe end fittings and reconnect the pipes to the pump. Refit the retaining clip bolts, tightening them securely, then tighten the pipe union nuts to the specified torque.

15.10 Fit a new gasket over the locating dowels

15.13 Oil pump retaining bolt tightening sequence

2C

16.2a Slacken the retaining screws . . .

16.2b . . . and remove the cover from the rear of the oil pump housing

16.3 Remove the inner and outer rotors, noting which way around they are fitted

15 Refit the rear lower timing belt cover (see Section 6) then refit the timing belt idler pulley and crankshaft sprocket (see Section 9).

16 Fit the oil filter then lower the vehicle to the ground and refill the engine with oil as described in Chapter 1B.

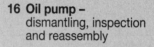

16 Oil pump –
dismantling, inspection
and reassembly

Note: *A new pressure relief valve plug will be required. If oil pump wear is suspected, check the cost and availability of new parts (only the pressure relief valve and thermostatic valve components seem to be available separately) against the cost of a new pump. Examine the pump as described in this Section and then decide whether renewal or repair is the best course of action.*

Dismantling

1 Remove the oil pump as described in Section 15.

2 Make alignment marks between the cover and pump body then unscrew the retaining screws and remove the cover **(see illustrations)**.

3 Make identification marks on the inner and outer rotors with a suitable marker pen to ensure they are fitted the same way around on reassembly. Remove both the rotors from the body **(see illustration)**.

4 The oil pressure relief valve can be dismantled, if required, without disturbing the pump. If this is to be done with the pump in position and the engine still installed in the vehicle, it will first be necessary to remove the auxiliary drivebelt (see Chapter 1B) and unbolt the drivebelt tensioner.

5 To dismantle the valve, slacken and remove

the threaded plug then recover the valve spring and plunger **(see illustrations)**. Discard the threaded plug; a new one should be used on reassembly.

6 To dismantle the thermostatic valve, unscrew the oil cooler pipe adaptor from the front of the pump body then remove the valve and spring, noting each components correct fitted location **(see illustrations)**. Remove the sealing washer from the adaptor and discard it, a new one must be used on refitting.

Inspection

7 Inspect the rotors for obvious signs of wear or damage and renew if necessary. If the pump body or cover plate is scored or damaged, then the complete oil pump assembly must be renewed.

8 Refit the rotors to the body and, using feeler blades of the appropriate thickness, measure the clearance between the outer rotor and the

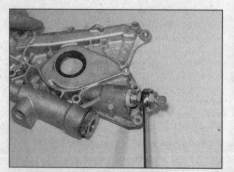

16.5a Unscrew the threaded plug . . .

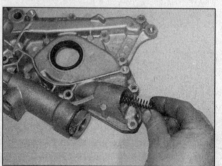

16.5b . . . and withdraw the oil pressure relief valve spring . . .

16.5c . . . and plunger from the pump body

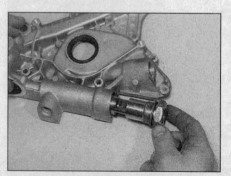

16.6a Unscrew the oil cooler pipe adaptor . . .

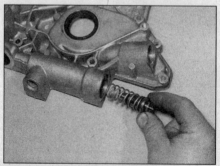

16.6b . . . and withdraw the thermostatic valve and spring from the pump

16.8a Using feeler blades, check the outer rotor to body clearance . . .

16.8b . . . and the inner rotor tip to outer rotor clearance

pump body, then between the inner rotor tip and the outer rotor **(see illustrations)**.

9 Using feeler blades and a straight-edge placed across the top of the pump body and the rotors, measure the rotor endfloat **(see illustration)**.

10 If any measurement is outside the specified limits, the complete pump assembly must be renewed.

11 If the pressure relief valve plunger is scored, or if it does not slide freely in the pump body bore, then it must be renewed. Check the relief valve spring for signs of wear or damage and measure its free length. If the spring shows signs of damage or is less than 38.9 mm in length then it must be renewed **(see illustration)**.

12 Check the thermostatic valve and spring for signs of damage and renew them if there is any doubt about their condition.

Reassembly

13 Remove all traces of sealant and locking compound from the pump and cover mating surfaces and the threads of the body and cover screws. Also clean the adaptor and body threads.

14 Lubricate the pump rotors with clean engine oil and refit them to the pump body, using the marks made on dismantling to ensure they are fitted the correct way around. The rotors should be fitted with their square marks facing away from the pump body **(see illustration)**.

16.9 Measuring the oil pump rotor endfloat

15 Ensure the mating surfaces are clean and dry then apply a bead of sealant (Rover recommend the use of Loctite 573), approximately 1.0 mm thick, to the surface of the pump cover. Refit the cover to the pump body, aligning the marks made on dismantling; the cover upper retaining screw hole is marked "TOP" to avoid the possibility of fitting the cover incorrectly.

16 Ensure the threads of the cover screws are clean and dry and apply a drop of the thread-locking compound (Rover recommend the use of Loctite 222) to each screw. Refit the screws and tighten them securely.

17 Check that the pump rotates freely, then prime it by injecting oil into its passages and rotating it. If a long time elapses before the pump is refitted to the engine, prime it again before installation.

18 Refit the oil pressure relief valve plunger, ensuring that it is the correct way up, then install the spring. Fit the new threaded plug, tightening it securely.

19 Position the pump so that the thermostatic valve bore is vertical. Lubricate the valve and spring with clean engine oil and fit them to the pump body, making sure the valve is positioned centrally in the pump bore. Fit a new sealing washer to the adaptor then apply a smear of sealant (Rover recommend the use of Loctite 577) to the adaptor threads. Carefully refit the adaptor to the pump body, ensuring that it engages correctly with the valve piston, and tighten it to the specified torque.

17 Oil cooler –
removal and refitting

Removal

1 Remove the radiator (see Chapter 3).
2 Wipe clean the area around the oil pipe unions on the base of the oil cooler then undo the retaining bolt and free the pipe retaining clamp from the block **(see illustration)**. Position a container beneath the cooler to catch any spilt oil.
3 Unscrew the union nuts and disconnect both oil pipes from the cooler. Remove the sealing ring from the end of each pipe and discard them, new ones must be used on refitting.
4 Slacken and remove the bolts securing the cooler to the cylinder block.
5 Release the retaining clips then disconnect the coolant hoses and remove the oil cooler from the vehicle.

Refitting

6 Remove all traces of locking compound from the threads of the oil cooler bolts and the cylinder block.
7 Manoeuvre the cooler into position and reconnect the coolant hoses, securing them in position with the retaining clips.
8 Apply a drop of thread locking compound (Rover recommend the use of Loctite 242) to the threads of the oil cooler retaining bolts then refit the bolts and tighten them to the specified torque.
9 Fit new sealing rings to the oil pipe end fittings and seat the pipes in the cooler. Refit the pipe retaining clamp, tightening its retaining bolt securely, then tighten the pipe union nuts to the specified torque.
10 Refit the radiator (see Chapter 3).
11 On completion, check the engine oil level as described in *"Weekly checks"*.

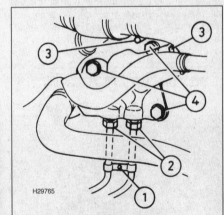

H29765

17.2 Oil cooler and associated components

1 *Oil pipe retaining clamp*
2 *Oil pipe union nuts*
3 *Coolant hose retaining clips*
4 *Retaining bolts*

2C

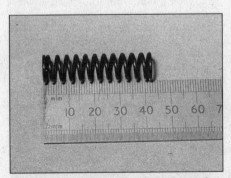

16.11 If the oil pressure relief valve spring is less than 38.9 mm in length it must be renewed

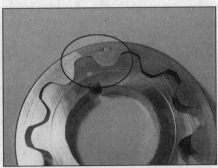

16.14 The oil pump rotors should be fitted with their identification marks facing away from the pump body

18.10 Carefully ease the crankshaft oil seal into position noting that the protector will be displaced as the housing is fitted

18.11 Refit the housing retaining bolts and tighten them to the specified torque in the sequence shown

18 Crankshaft oil seals – renewal

Right-hand (timing belt end) seal

1 Remove the crankshaft sprocket as described in Section 9, and secure the timing belt clear of the working area so that it cannot be contaminated with oil.

2 Carefully punch or drill two small holes opposite each other in the oil seal. Screw a self-tapping screw into each and pull on the screws with pliers to extract the seal.

Caution: Great care must be taken to avoid damage to the oil pump.

3 Clean the seal housing and polish off any burrs or raised edges which may have caused the seal to fail in the first place.

4 Lubricate the lips of the new seal with clean engine oil and ease it into position on the end of the shaft. Press the seal squarely into position until it is flush with the housing. If necessary, a suitable tubular drift, such as a socket, which bears only on the hard outer edge of the seal can be used to tap the seal into position. Take great care not to damage

the seal lips during fitting and ensure that the seal lips face inwards.

5 Wash off any traces of oil, then refit the crankshaft sprocket as described in Section 9.

Left-hand (flywheel end) oil seal

Caution: The new oil seal is supplied complete with housing and is pre-lubricated with a special coating. The seal must be fitted "dry" and the seal protector must not be removed until the housing assembly is in position on the engine. Under no circumstances must the oil seal lip be touched, or lubricated with oil or grease, as this will destroy the special coating. If the seal coating is damaged there is a risk of oil leakage once the engine is started.

6 Remove the flywheel as described in Section 19.

7 Remove the sump as described in Section 14.

8 Slacken and remove the retaining bolts and remove the oil seal housing from the end of the crankshaft.

9 Ensure the crankshaft surface and cylinder block mating surface are clean and dry; this is most important to ensure the oil seal coating

is not damaged (see Caution at the start of this section).

10 Carefully ease the new seal housing onto the end of the crankshaft, making sure the sealing lip is not damaged. Slide the housing fully into position, making sure it is correctly located, and carefully remove the oil seal protector **(see illustration)**.

11 Refit the housing retaining bolts and tighten them to the specified torque, working in the sequence shown **(see illustration)**.

12 Refit the sump as described in Section 14.

13 Refit the flywheel as described in Section 19.

19 Flywheel – removal, inspection and refitting

Removal

Note: New flywheel retaining bolts must be used on refitting.

1 Remove the clutch assembly as described in Chapter 6.

2 As a precaution, unbolt the crankshaft position sensor from the engine mounting plate (see Chapter 4B) to prevent possible damage as the flywheel is removed.

3 Prevent the flywheel from turning by locking the ring gear teeth with a similar arrangement to that shown **(see illustration)**. Alternatively, bolt a strap between the flywheel and the cylinder block/crankcase.

4 Slacken and remove the retaining bolts and remove the flywheel, noting its locating dowel **(see illustration)**. **Do not** drop it, as it is very heavy. Discard the bolts, they must be renewed whenever they are disturbed.

Inspection

5 If the flywheel clutch mating surface (where applicable) is deeply scored, cracked or otherwise damaged, then the flywheel must

19.3 Lock the flywheel with a tool similar to that shown (arrowed) then slacken the retaining bolts

19.4 Remove the flywheel taking care not to drop it

19.8 Fit new retaining bolts on refitting . . .

19.9a . . . tightening them first to the stage 1 torque setting . . .

19.9b . . . and then through the stage 2 angle

be renewed, unless it is possible to have it surface ground. Seek the advice of a Rover dealer or engine reconditioning specialist.

6 If the ring gear is badly worn or has missing teeth, then it must be renewed. This job is best left to a Rover dealer or engine reconditioning specialist. The temperature to which the new ring gear must be heated for installation (350°C - shown by an even light blue colour) is critical and, if not done accurately, the hardness of the teeth will be destroyed.

Refitting

7 Clean the mating surfaces of the flywheel and crankshaft and remove all traces of locking compound from the crankshaft threaded holes.

8 Fit the flywheel to the crankshaft, engaging it with the crankshaft locating dowel, and fit the new retaining bolts **(see illustration)**.

9 Lock the flywheel using the method employed on dismantling then, working in a diagonal sequence, tighten all the retaining bolts to the specified stage 1 torque setting. Go around again in a diagonal sequence and angle-tighten each retaining bolt through the specified stage 2 angle, using a socket and extension bar. It is recommended that an angle-measuring gauge is used during the final stages of the tightening, to ensure accuracy **(see illustrations and Haynes Hint)**.

10 Refit the crankshaft position sensor and tighten its retaining bolt to the specified torque (see Chapter 4B).

HAYNES HINT *If a gauge is not available, use white paint to make alignment marks between the bolt head and pulley prior to tightening; the marks can then be used to check that the bolt has been rotated through the correct angle.*

11 Refit the clutch assembly as described in Chapter 6.

20 Engine/transmission mountings – inspection and renewal

Refer to Chapter 2B, Section 17.

2C

Notes

Chapter 2 Part D:
Engine removal and overhaul procedures

Contents

Degrees of difficulty

Easy, suitable for novice with little experience	**Fairly easy,** suitable for beginner with some experience	**Fairly difficult,** suitable for competent DIY mechanic	**Difficult,** suitable for experienced DIY mechanic	**Very difficult,** suitable for expert DIY or professional

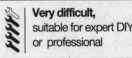

2D

Specifications

1.4 and 1.6 litre engine

Cylinder head

Height	118.95 to 119.05 mm
Reface limit	0.2 mm
Maximum acceptable gasket face distortion	0.05 mm
Valve seat width	1.5 mm

Valves, valve springs and guides

	8-valve engine	16-valve engine
Valve stem diameter:		
Inlet	6.960 to 6.975 mm	5.952 to 5.967 mm
Exhaust	6.952 to 6.967 mm	5.947 to 5.962 mm
Valve stem installed height:		
New	38.95 to 40.81 mm	38.93 to 39.84 mm
Service limit	41.06 mm	40.10 mm
Valve guide inside diameter	7.000 to 7.025 mm	6.000 to 6.025 mm
Valve stem-to-guide clearance:		
Inlet:		
Standard	0.025 to 0.065 mm	0.033 to 0.063 mm
Service limit	0.07 mm	0.07 mm
Exhaust:		
Standard	0.033 to 0.073 mm	0.038 to 0.078 mm
Service limit	0.11 mm	0.11 mm
Valve guide installed height	10.3 mm	6.0 mm
Valve spring free length	46.2 mm	50.0 mm

Cylinder block/liner

	1.4 litre engine	1.6 litre engine
Cylinder liner bore diameter:		
Grade A (Red)	74.970 to 74.985 mm	80.000 to 80.015 mm
Grade B (Blue)	74.986 to 75.000 mm	80.016 to 80.030 mm

Pistons and rings

	1.4 litre engine	1.6 litre engine
Piston diameter:		
Grade A (Red)	74.940 to 74.955 mm	79.975 to 79.990 mm
Grade B (Blue)	74.956 to 74.970 mm	79.991 to 80.005 mm
Piston-to-bore clearance	0.015 to 0.045 mm	0.010 to 0.040 mm
Piston ring fitted end gaps:		
Top compression ring	0.17 to 0.37 mm	0.2 to 0.35 mm
Second compression ring	0.37 to 0.57 mm	0.28 to 0.48 mm
Oil control ring	0.15 to 0.40 mm	0.15 to 0.4 mm
Piston ring-to-groove clearance:		
Top compression ring	0.04 to 0.08 mm	0.04 to 0.072 mm
Second compression ring	0.03 to 0.062 mm	0.03 to 0.062 mm
Oil control ring	0.044 to 0.055 mm	0.01 to 0.18 mm

Crankshaft

Main bearing journal diameter	47.979 to 48.000 mm
Main bearing journal size grades:	
Grade 1	47.993 to 48.000 mm
Grade 2	47.986 to 47.993 mm
Grade 3	47.979 to 47.986 mm
Big-end (crankpin) journal diameter	42.986 to 43.007 mm
Big-end (crankpin) journal size grades:	
Grade A	43.000 to 43.007 mm
Grade B	42.993 to 43.000 mm
Grade C	42.986 to 42.993 mm
Maximum journal ovality	0.01 mm
Main bearing running clearance	0.02 to 0.05 mm
Big-end bearing running clearance	0.021 to 0.049 mm
Crankshaft endfloat:	
Standard	0.1 to 0.3 mm
Service limit	0.4 mm
Thrustwasher thickness	2.61 to 2.65 mm

Torque wrench settings | Refer to Chapter 2A Specifications

2.0 litre petrol engine

Cylinder head

Height	135.0 to 135.1 mm
Maximum acceptable gasket face distortion	0.1 mm
Valve seat width	1.5 to 2.0 mm

Valves, valve springs and guides

Valve stem diameter:	
Inlet	7.09 to 7.10 mm
Exhaust	7.07 to 7.09 mm
Valve head diameter:	
Inlet	31.7 to 31.95 mm
Exhaust	29.2 to 29.43 mm
Valve stem installed height (maximum)	43.4 mm
Valve guide inside diameter	7.137 to 7.162 mm
Valve stem-to-guide clearance:	
Inlet:	
Standard	0.04 to 0.06 mm
Service limit	0.09 mm
Exhaust:	
Standard	0.06 to 0.07 mm
Service limit	0.1 mm
Valve guide installed height	10.3 mm
Valve spring free length	46.25 mm

Cylinder block

Cylinder bore diameter:	
Grade A	84.442 to 84.455 mm
Grade B	84.456 to 84.469 mm

Pistons and rings

Piston diameter:	
Grade A	84.409 to 84.422 mm
Grade B	84.423 to 84.436 mm

Piston-to-bore clearance (maximum)	0.04 mm
Piston ring fitted end gaps:	
Top compression ring	0.25 to 0.35 mm
Second compression ring	0.3 to 0.5 mm
Oil control ring	0.38 to 1.14 mm
Piston ring-to-groove clearance:	
Top compression ring	0.06 to 0.09 mm
Second compression ring	0.05 to 0.07 mm
Oil control ring	0.03 to 0.05 mm

Crankshaft

Main bearing journal diameter	54.005 to 54.026 mm
Big-end (crankpin) journal diameter	47.648 to 47.661 mm
Maximum journal ovality	0.01 mm
Main bearing running clearance	0.03 to 0.07 mm
Big-end bearing running clearance	0.04 to 0.08 mm
Crankshaft endfloat	0.03 to 0.20 mm
Thrustwasher thickness	2.31 to 2.36 mm

Torque wrench settings

Refer to Chapter 2B Specifications

2.0 litre diesel engine

Cylinder head

Maximum acceptable gasket face distortion	0.1 mm

Valves, valve springs and guides

Valve stem diameter:	
Inlet	6.907 to 6.923 mm
Exhaust	6.897 to 6.913 mm
Valve head recess below cylinder head surface (maximum):	
Inlet	1.45 mm
Exhaust	1.35 mm
Valve guide inside diameter	6.950 to 6.963 mm
Valve stem-to-guide clearance:	
Inlet	0.056 mm
Exhaust	0.066 mm
Valve guide installed height	61.1 to 61.7 mm
Valve spring free length	37.0 mm

Cylinder block

Cylinder bore diameter	84.442 to 84.460 mm

Pistons and rings

Piston diameter	84.262 mm
Piston-to-bore clearance	0.18 to 0.20 mm
Piston ring fitted end gaps:	
Top compression ring	0.25 to 0.27 mm
Second compression ring	0.4 to 0.42 mm
Oil control ring	0.3 to 0.32 mm
Piston ring-to-groove clearance:	
Top compression ring	0.115 to 0.135 mm
Second compression ring	0.05 to 0.082 mm
Oil control ring	0.05 to 0.082 mm

Crankshaft

Main bearing journal diameter	60.703 to 60.719 mm
Big-end (crankpin) journal diameter	57.683 to 57.696 mm
Maximum journal ovality	0.01 mm
Main bearing running clearance	0.03 to 0.07 mm*
Big-end bearing running clearance	0.04 to 0.08 mm*
Crankshaft endfloat	0.03 to 0.26 mm
Thrustwasher thickness	2.31 to 2.36 mm

These are suggested figures - no exact figures are quoted by Rover. Seek the advice of a Rover dealer or engine overhaul specialist before condemning components

Torque wrench settings

Refer to Chapter 2C Specifications

2D

1 General information

Included in this Part of Chapter 2 are details of removing the engine/transmission from the car and general overhaul procedures for the cylinder head, cylinder block and all other engine internal components.

The information given ranges from advice concerning preparation for an overhaul and the purchase of replacement parts, to detailed step-by-step procedures covering removal, inspection, renovation and refitting of engine internal components.

After Section 6, all instructions are based on the assumption that the engine has been removed from the car. For information concerning in-car engine repair, as well as the removal and refitting of those external components necessary for full overhaul, refer to the relevant in-car repair procedure section (Chapter 2A to 2C) of this Chapter and to Section 7. Ignore any preliminary dismantling operations described in the relevant in-car repair sections that are no longer relevant once the engine has been removed from the car.

Apart from torque wrench settings, which are given at the beginning of the relevant in-car repair procedure Chapter (2A to 2C), all specifications relating to engine overhaul are at the beginning of this Part of Chapter 2.

2 Engine overhaul - general information

It is not always easy to determine when, or if, an engine should be completely overhauled, as a number of factors must be considered.

High mileage is not necessarily an indication that an overhaul is needed, while low mileage does not preclude the need for an overhaul. Frequency of servicing is probably the most important consideration. An engine which has had regular and frequent oil and filter changes, as well as other required maintenance, should give many thousands of miles of reliable service. Conversely, a neglected engine may require an overhaul very early in its life.

Excessive oil consumption is an indication that piston rings, valve seals and/or valve guides are in need of attention. Make sure that oil leaks are not responsible before deciding that the rings and/or guides are worn. Perform a compression test, as described in the relevant Part of this Chapter, to determine the likely cause of the problem.

Check the oil pressure with a gauge fitted in place of the oil pressure switch, and compare it with that specified. If it is extremely low, the main and big-end bearings, and/or the oil pump, are probably worn out.

Loss of power, rough running, knocking or metallic engine noises, excessive valve gear noise, and high fuel consumption may also point to the need for an overhaul, especially if they are all present at the same time. If a complete service does not remedy the situation, major mechanical work is the only solution.

An engine overhaul involves restoring all internal parts to the specification of a new engine. During an overhaul, the pistons and the piston rings are renewed. New main and big-end bearings are generally fitted; if necessary, the crankshaft may be renewed, to restore the journals. The valves are also serviced as well, since they are usually in less-than-perfect condition at this point. While the engine is being overhauled, other components, such as the starter and alternator, can be overhauled as well. The end result should be an as-new engine that will give many trouble-free miles. **Note:** *Critical cooling system components such as the hoses, thermostat and coolant pump should be renewed when an engine is overhauled. The radiator should be checked carefully, to ensure that it is not clogged or leaking. Also, it is a good idea to renew the oil pump whenever the engine is overhauled.*

Before beginning the engine overhaul, read through the entire procedure, to familiarise yourself with the scope and requirements of the job. Overhauling an engine is not difficult if you follow carefully all of the instructions, have the necessary tools and equipment, and pay close attention to all specifications. It can, however, be time-consuming. Plan on the car being off the road for a minimum of two weeks, especially if parts must be taken to an engineering works for repair or reconditioning. Check on the availability of parts and make sure that any necessary special tools and equipment are obtained in advance. Most work can be done with typical hand tools, although a number of precision measuring tools are required for inspecting parts to determine if they must be renewed. Often the engineering works will handle the inspection of parts and offer advice concerning reconditioning and renewal. **Note:** *Always wait until the engine has been completely dismantled, and until all components (especially the cylinder block and the crankshaft) have been inspected, before deciding what service and repair operations must be performed by an engineering works. The condition of these components will be the major factor to consider when determining whether to overhaul the original engine, or to buy a reconditioned unit. Do not, therefore, purchase parts or have overhaul work done on other components until they have been thoroughly inspected. As a general rule, time is the primary cost of an overhaul, so it does not pay to fit worn or sub-standard parts.*

As a final note, to ensure maximum life and minimum trouble from a reconditioned engine, everything must be assembled with care, in a spotlessly-clean environment.

3 Engine removal - methods and precautions

If you have decided that the engine must be removed for overhaul or major repair work, several preliminary steps should be taken.

Locating a suitable place to work is extremely important. Adequate work space, along with storage space for the car, will be needed. If a workshop or garage is not available, at the very least, a flat, level, clean work surface is required.

Cleaning the engine compartment and engine/transmission before beginning the removal procedure will help keep tools clean and organised.

An engine hoist or A-frame will also be necessary. Make sure the equipment is rated in excess of the combined weight of the engine and transmission. Safety is of primary importance, considering the potential hazards involved in lifting the engine/transmission out of the car.

If this is the first time you have removed an engine, an assistant should ideally be available. Advice and aid from someone more experienced would also be helpful. There are many instances when one person cannot simultaneously perform all of the operations required when lifting the engine out of the vehicle.

Plan the operation ahead of time. Before starting work, arrange for the hire of or obtain all of the tools and equipment you will need. Some of the equipment necessary to perform engine/transmission removal and installation safely and with relative ease (in addition to an engine hoist) is as follows: a heavy duty trolley jack, complete sets of spanners and sockets as described in the front of this manual, wooden blocks, and plenty of rags and cleaning solvent for mopping up spilled oil, coolant and fuel. If the hoist must be hired, make sure that you arrange for it in advance, and perform all of the operations possible without it beforehand. This will save you money and time.

Plan for the car to be out of use for quite a while. An engineering works will be required to perform some of the work which the do-it-yourselfer cannot accomplish without special equipment. These places often have a busy schedule, so it would be a good idea to consult them before removing the engine, in order to accurately estimate the amount of time required to rebuild or repair components that may need work.

Always be extremely careful when removing and refitting the engine/transmission. Serious injury can result from careless actions. Plan ahead and take your time, and a job of this nature, although major, can be accomplished successfully.

4 Petrol engine and transmission unit - removal, separation and refitting

Note: *On models with air conditioning, it will be necessary to disconnect the refrigerant lines in order to remove the engine/transmission unit from the vehicle (see Warnings in Chapter 3). Have the refrigerant discharged by an air conditioning specialist before starting work and have ready some caps and plugs to plug the hose/pipe end fittings whilst the engine is removed. On completion it will be necessary to have the system recharged by an air conditioning specialist.* **Do not** *operate the air conditioning system whilst it is discharged. Note that Rover also recommend that the air conditioning system receiver/drier unit should be renewed whenever the refrigerant lines are disconnected.*

1.4 and 1.6 litre engine

Removal

Note: *The engine can be removed from the car only as a complete unit with the transmission; the two are then separated for overhaul. The engine/transmission unit is lowered out of position, and withdrawn from under the vehicle. Bearing this in mind, ensure the vehicle is raised sufficiently so that there is enough clearance between the front of the vehicle and the floor to allow the engine/transmission unit to be slid out once it has been lowered out of position.*

Note: *New right-hand engine/transmission mounting nuts will be required on refitting. It will also be necessary to fabricate some engine lifting brackets to attach the hoist to (see paragraph 18).*

1 On models with air conditioning, have the refrigerant discharged by an air conditioning specialist.

2 On all models, park the vehicle on firm, level ground then open the bonnet and support it in the upright position.

3 Referring to Chapter 5A, remove the battery, mounting tray and bracket. Disconnect the main supply lead from the starter motor terminal then remove the starter motor bolt securing the earth leads in position.

4 Chock the rear wheels, firmly apply the handbrake then jack up the front of the vehicle (see "Jacking and Vehicle Support"). Securely support it on axle stands, bearing in mind the note at the start of this Section, and remove both front roadwheels.

5 Undo the retaining screws and fasteners and remove the undercover from beneath the engine/transmission unit.

6 If the engine is to be dismantled, working as described in Chapter 1A, first drain the engine oil and remove the oil filter. Also drain the cooling system.

7 Referring to Chapter 4A, carry out the following procedures.

 a) *Remove the air cleaner housing and associated components.*

 b) *Remove the exhaust front pipe.*

 c) *Depressurise the fuel system and disconnect the pipe from the top of the fuel filter. Release the retaining clip and disconnect the return hose from the fuel rail return pipe.*

 d) *Disconnect the accelerator cable and position it clear of the engine.*

 e) *Disconnect the brake servo hose and various vacuum/coolant hoses from the inlet manifold, noting each hose correct fitted location.*

 f) *Remove the electronic control module (ECM) and relay module.*

8 Remove the evaporative emission system charcoal canister as described in Chapter 4C.

9 Slacken the retaining clips then disconnect and remove the radiator top hose. Disconnect the wiring connector from the radiator cooling fan and release the wiring from its retaining clips.

10 On models with air conditioning, trace the refrigerant pipes/hoses back from the compressor to the unions on the top of the radiator cooling fan and bulkhead. Slacken the union nuts and disconnect both pipes/hoses, noting the sealing rings. Work back along the pipes/hoses, releasing their retaining clips, then undo the bolt securing the union to the compressor and remove the pipe/hose assembly from the engine compartment **(see illustration)**. Recover the sealing ring from each union and plug the hose/pipe ends and compressor ports to prevent the entry of dirt and moisture into the air conditioning system. Discard all sealing rings, new ones must be used on refitting. Also disconnect the wiring connectors from the air conditioning system relay module.

11 On all models, referring to Chapter 6, trace the clutch hydraulic pipe back from the master cylinder to its quick-release fitting on the bulkhead. Wipe clean and disconnect the two halves of the fitting. Mop up any spilt fluid and take precautions not to allow any dirt to enter the hydraulic system; the hose fittings are fitted with valves to prevent fluid loss when they are disconnected.

12 Unclip the lid from the engine compartment fusebox then undo the retaining screw and disconnect the positive lead situated at the front of the box.

13 Locate the engine wiring harness connectors in the left-hand, rear corner of the engine compartment. Unclip the wiring harness from the retaining clip then disconnect the wiring connectors so the wiring is free to be removed with the engine.

14 Referring to Chapter 10, disconnect the feed pipe and return hose from the power steering pump and free the pipe and hose clips from the engine. Plug the pipe/hose ends and pump unions to minimise fluid loss and prevent the entry of dirt into the hydraulic system.

15 Referring to Chapter 7, carry out the following procedures:

 a) *Drain the transmission oil or be prepared for oil spillage as the engine/transmission unit is removed.*

 b) *Remove the gearchange linkage link rods from the top of the transmission unit.*

 c) *Remove the vehicle speed sensor from the top of the speedometer drive.*

16 Referring to Chapter 8, disconnect the driveshaft inner ends from the transmission unit. Note that it is not necessary to remove the driveshafts completely, they can be left attached to the hub assemblies and released as the hub is pulled outwards.

Caution: Do not allow the shafts to hang down under their own weight as this could damage the constant velocity joints/ gaiters.

17 Locate the heater matrix coolant hoses on the engine compartment bulkhead. Release the retaining clips and disconnect the hose from the heater temperature control valve and the other hose from the matrix. Also disconnect the coolant hose from the expansion tank and free it from its clips so that it is free to be removed with the engine.

18 Attach suitable engine lifting brackets to the cylinder head. On 8-valve engines, the Rover lifting brackets (tool no 18G 1572/2) are bolted to the threaded holes on the rear, right-hand end of the rear of the cylinder head and the left-hand end of the front of the cylinder head. On 16-valve engines, the Rover lifting brackets (tool nos 18G 1572/1 and 18G

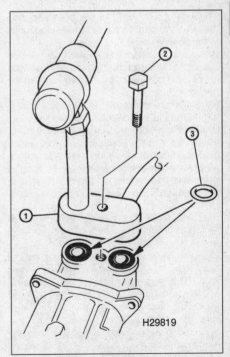

4.10 Air conditioning compressor refrigerant pipe/hose union

1 Union
2 Retaining bolt
3 Sealing rings

2D

4.18a On 8-valve engines the lifting brackets should be mounted onto the threaded hole (arrowed) on the right-hand rear end of the head . . .

4.18b . . . and onto the threaded hole (arrowed) on the left-hand front end of the head

1572/2) are bolted to the threaded hole on the right-hand end of the rear of the cylinder head and into the exhaust camshaft cover plate holes on the left-hand end of the head, once the cover plate bolts have been removed **(see illustrations)**.

19 Manoeuvre the engine hoist into position, and attach it to the lifting brackets bolted onto the engine/transmission (as applicable). Raise the hoist until it is supporting the weight of the engine.

20 Remove the engine/transmission rear mounting bracket as described in Chapter 2A, Section 17.

21 Slacken and remove the bolts securing the left-hand and right-hand lower mountings to the vehicle body.

22 Loose the left-hand engine/transmission mounting through bolt then slacken and remove the bolts securing the mounting to the transmission unit.

23 Slacken and remove the through bolt from the right-hand engine/transmission mounting. Unscrew the nuts securing the mounting to the engine bracket and remove the mounting from the engine compartment. Discard the nuts, new ones must be used on refitting. If the rubber spacers which are fitted between the mounting and body are loose, remove

them and store them with the mounting for safe-keeping.

24 Make a final check that any components which would prevent the removal of the engine/transmission from the car have been removed or disconnected. Ensure that components such as the driveshafts are secured so that they cannot be damaged on removal.

25 If available, a low trolley should be placed under the engine/transmission assembly, to facilitate its easy removal from under the vehicle. Lower the engine/transmission assembly, making sure that nothing is trapped, taking great care not to damage the radiator/cooling fan assembly. Enlist the help of an assistant during this procedure, as it may be necessary to tilt the assembly slightly to clear the body panels.

Caution: Great care must be taken to ensure that no components are trapped and damaged during the removal procedure.

26 Detach the hoist and withdraw the engine/transmission unit from under the vehicle.

Separation

27 With the engine/transmission assembly removed, support the assembly on suitable

blocks of wood, on a workbench (or failing that, on a clean area of the workshop floor).

28 Undo the retaining bolts and remove the flywheel front, rear and lower cover plates.

29 Undo the retaining bolts and remove the starter motor from the transmission (see Chapter 5A).

30 Ensure that both engine and transmission are adequately supported, then slacken and remove the remaining bolts securing the transmission housing to the engine. Note the correct fitted positions of each bolt (and the relevant brackets) as they are removed, to use as a reference on refitting.

31 Carefully withdraw the transmission from the engine, ensuring that the weight of the transmission is not allowed to hang on the input shaft while it is engaged with the clutch friction disc.

32 If they are loose, remove the locating dowels from the engine or transmission, and keep them in a safe place.

Refitting

33 If the engine and transmission have been separated, perform the operations described below in paragraphs 34 to 38. If not, proceed as described from paragraph 39 onwards.

34 Referring to Chapter 6, apply a smear of molybdenum disulphide grease (Rover recommend the use of Molykote BR2 plus, G-n plus or G-Rapid plus) to the clutch release bearing, fork and guide sleeve contact surfaces and check the operation of the clutch release mechanism. Also apply a smear of grease to the transmission input shaft splines; **do not** apply too much grease otherwise the clutch friction plate may be contaminated.

35 Ensure the locating dowels are correctly positioned then carefully offer the transmission to the engine, until the locating dowels are engaged. Ensure that the weight of the transmission is not allowed to hang on the input shaft as it is engaged with the clutch friction disc.

4.18c On 16-valve engines attach the lifting brackets to the threaded hole on the right-hand rear end of the head . . .

4.18d . . . and into the exhaust camshaft cover plate hole(s) on the left-hand end of the head

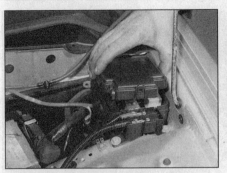

4.51a On 2.0 litre engines, unclip the engine compartment fusebox lid . . .

4.51b . . . then undo the retaining screw (arrowed) and disconnect the engine harness lead

4.52a Release the engine harness wiring connectors (arrowed) from the body . . .

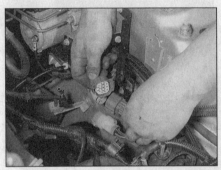

4.52b . . . and disconnect them so the harness is free to be removed with the engine

36 Refit the transmission housing-to-engine bolts, ensuring that all the necessary brackets are correctly positioned, and tighten them to the specified torque setting.

37 Refit the starter motor and tighten its mounting bolts to the specified torque (see Chapter 5A).

38 Refit the flywheel cover plates to the transmission, tightening all the retaining bolts to the specified torque.

39 Slide the engine/transmission unit into position and reconnect the hoist and lifting tackle to the engine lifting brackets.

40 With the aid of an assistant, carefully lift the assembly into position in the engine compartment, manipulating the hoist and lifting tackle as necessary, taking great care not to trap any components.

41 Align the engine with the left-hand mounting bracket and screw in the mounting retaining bolts.

42 Ensure the rubber spacers are correctly fitted to the body then refit the right-hand mounting, tightening its through bolt by hand only at this stage. Fit the new mounting nuts to the engine bracket and tighten them to the specified torque.

43 Tighten the bolts securing the left-hand mounting to the transmission unit to the specified torque then tighten the through bolt by hand only.

44 Refit the bolts securing the left-hand and right-hand lower mountings to the vehicle body, tightening them to the specified torque.

45 Rock the engine to settle it in position then tighten the left- and right-hand mounting through bolts to the specified torque.

46 Refit the rear mounting assembly as described in Chapter 2A, Section 17 then remove the hoist.

47 The remainder of the refitting procedure is a direct reversal of the removal sequence, noting the following points:
a) Ensure that all wiring is correctly routed and retained by all the relevant retaining clips and that all connectors are correctly and securely reconnected.
b) Ensure that all disturbed hoses are correctly reconnected, and securely retained by their retaining clips.
c) Renew the transmission differential oil

seals (see Chapter 7) before refitting the driveshafts.
d) Renew all power steering/air conditioning pipe/hose union sealing rings and tighten the union nuts/bolts to the specified torque.
e) Adjust the accelerator cable as described in the Chapter 4A.
f) Refill the transmission with correct quantity and type of oil, as described in Chapter 7. If the oil was not drained, top-up the level as described in Chapter 1A.
g) Refill the engine with oil as described in Chapter 1A and also refill the cooling system.
h) On models with air conditioning, have the system recharged with refrigerant by an air conditioning specialist.

2.0 litre engine

Removal

Note: The engine can be removed from the car only as a complete unit with the transmission; the two are then separated for overhaul. It will be necessary to fabricate some engine lifting brackets to attach the hoist to (see paragraph 60).

48 Carry out the operations described in paragraphs 1 to 8, ignoring the remark about the earth leads on the starter motor bolt.

49 Remove the radiator cooling fan as described in Chapter 3.

50 Slacken and remove the engine mounting rear steady bar bolts and remove the bar from the rear of the sump.

51 Unclip the lid from the engine compartment fusebox then undo the retaining screw and disconnect the engine harness lead, situated at the front of the box (see illustrations).

52 Locate the engine wiring harness connectors in the left-hand, rear corner of the engine compartment. Unclip the wiring harness from the retaining clip then disconnect the wiring connectors so the wiring is free to be removed with the engine (see illustrations).

53 Release the retaining clips and disconnect the heater matrix coolant hoses from the rear of the coolant pipes on the left-hand end of the cylinder head. Also disconnect the hose from the front of the coolant pipe (see illustrations).

4.53a Release the retaining clips . . .

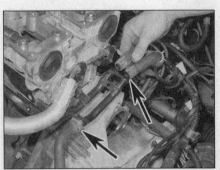

4.53b . . . and disconnect the heater matrix hoses and front hose from the coolant pipe

4.54 Disconnect the top hose and expansion tank hose from the thermostat housing

4.57 Unscrew the union nut (arrowed) and disconnect the power steering feed pipe at the union between the engine and bulkhead

54 Disconnect the radiator top hose and the expansion tank hose from the thermostat housing then disconnect the bottom hose from the engine coolant pump outlet **(see illustration).**

55 On models with air conditioning, remove the refrigerant pipe/hose assembly from the compressor as described in paragraph 10.

56 On all models, referring to Chapter 6, trace the clutch hydraulic pipe back from the master cylinder to its quick-release union situated at the rear of the transmission unit. Wipe clean the union then depress the locking collar and disconnect the two halves of the fitting. Mop up any spilt fluid and take precautions not to allow any dirt to enter the hydraulic system; the hose fittings are fitted with valves to prevent fluid loss when they are disconnected.

57 Referring to Chapter 10, disconnect the feed pipe and return hose from the power steering pump and free the pipe from the engine. Locate the feed pipe union at the rear of the engine then slacken the union nut and separate the pipe and hose so the pipe is free to be removed with the engine **(see illustration).** Plug the pipe/hose ends and pump unions to minimise fluid loss and prevent the entry of dirt into the hydraulic system.

4.64 Removing the engine/transmission unit - 2.0 litre engine

58 Referring to Chapter 7, carry out the following procedures.

a) *Drain the transmission oil or be prepared for oil spillage as the engine/transmission unit is removed.*

b) *Disconnect the gearchange selector and steady rods from the transmission unit.*

c) *Disconnect the wiring connector from the vehicle speed sensor.*

d) *Unbolt the earth lead from the front of the transmission housing.*

59 Referring to Chapter 8, disconnect the driveshaft inner ends from the transmission unit. Note that it is not necessary to remove the driveshafts completely, they can be left attached to the hub assemblies and released as the hub is pulled outwards.

Caution: Do not allow the shafts to hang down under their own weight as this could damage the constant velocity joints/ gaiters.

60 Attach suitable engine lifting brackets to the cylinder head. The Rover lifting bracket (tool no 18G 1644) is bolted to the HT lead clip holes on the top of the cylinder head, once the spark plug cover and the retaining HT lead clips have been removed.

61 Manoeuvre the engine hoist into position, and attach it to the lifting brackets bolted onto the engine/transmission (as applicable). Raise the hoist until it is supporting the weight of the engine.

62 Remove the engine/transmission right-hand and left-hand mounting assemblies as described in Chapter 2B, Section 17.

63 Make a final check that any components which would prevent the removal of the engine/transmission from the car have been removed or disconnected. Ensure that components such as the driveshafts are secured so that they cannot be damaged on removal.

64 Raise the engine/transmission assembly out of position, making sure that nothing is

trapped, taking great care not to damage the radiator. Enlist the help of an assistant during this procedure, as it may be necessary to tilt the assembly slightly to clear the body panels **(see illustration).** Great care must be taken to ensure that no components are trapped and damaged during the removal procedure.

65 Once the engine is high enough, lift it out over the front of the body, and lower the unit to the ground.

Separation

66 With the engine/transmission assembly removed, support the assembly on suitable blocks of wood, on a workbench (or failing that, on a clean area of the workshop floor).

67 Undo the retaining bolts and remove the starter motor from the transmission (see Chapter 5A).

68 Ensure that both engine and transmission are adequately supported, then slacken and remove the remaining bolts securing the transmission housing to the engine mounting plate. Note the correct fitted positions of each bolt (and the relevant brackets) as they are removed, to use as a reference on refitting.

69 Carefully withdraw the transmission from the engine, ensuring that the weight of the transmission is not allowed to hang on the input shaft while it is engaged with the clutch friction disc.

70 If they are loose, remove the locating dowels from the engine or transmission, and keep them in a safe place.

Refitting

71 If the engine and transmission have been separated, perform the operations described below in paragraphs 72 to 75. If not, proceed as described from paragraph 76 onwards.

72 Referring to Chapter 6, apply a smear of molybdenum disulphide grease (Rover recommend the use of Molykote BR2 plus, G-n plus or G-Rapid plus) to the clutch release bearing, fork and guide sleeve contact surfaces and check the operation of the clutch release mechanism. Also apply a smear of grease to the transmission input shaft splines; **do not** apply too much grease otherwise the clutch friction plate may be contaminated.

73 Ensure the locating dowels are correctly positioned then carefully offer the transmission to the engine, until the locating dowels are engaged. Ensure that the weight of the transmission is not allowed to hang on the input shaft as it is engaged with the clutch friction disc.

74 Refit the transmission housing-to-engine bolts, ensuring that all the necessary brackets are correctly positioned, and tighten them to the specified torque setting.

75 Refit the starter motor and tighten its mounting bolts to the specified torque (see Chapter 5A).

76 Reconnect the hoist and lifting tackle to the engine lifting brackets. With the aid of an assistant, lift the assembly over the engine compartment.

77 The assembly should be tilted as necessary to clear the surrounding components, as during removal; lower the assembly into position in the engine compartment, manipulating the hoist and lifting tackle as necessary.

78 Refit the right-hand and left-hand mounting assemblies as described in Chapter 2B, Section 17. Tighten the right-hand mounting steady rod bolts by hand only at this stage; tighten them to the specified torque once the vehicle is resting on its wheels and all other items are correctly reconnected.

79 The remainder of the refitting procedure is a direct reversal of the removal sequence, noting the following points:

a) *Ensure that all wiring is correctly routed and retained by all the relevant retaining clips and that all connectors are correctly and securely reconnected.*

b) *Ensure that all disturbed hoses are correctly reconnected, and securely retained by their retaining clips.*

c) *Renew the transmission differential oil seals (see Chapter 7) before refitting the driveshafts.*

d) *Renew all power steering/air conditioning pipe/hose union sealing rings and tighten the union nuts/bolts to the specified torque.*

e) *Adjust the accelerator cable as described in the Chapter 4A.*

f) *Refill the transmission with correct quantity and type of oil, as described in Chapter 7. If the oil was not drained, top-up the level as described in Chapter 1A.*

g) *Refill the engine with oil as described in Chapter 1A and also refill the cooling system.*

h) *On models with air conditioning, have the system recharged with refrigerant by an air conditioning specialist.*

5 Diesel engine and transmission unit - removal, separation and refitting

Note: *On models with air conditioning, it will be necessary to disconnect the refrigerant lines in order to remove the engine/transmission unit from the vehicle (see Warnings in Chapter 3). Have the refrigerant discharged by an air conditioning specialist before starting work and have ready some caps and plugs to plug the hose/pipe end fittings whilst the engine is removed. On completion it will be necessary to have the system recharged by an air conditioning specialist.* **Do not** *operate the air conditioning system whilst it is discharged. Note that Rover also recommend that the air conditioning system receiver/drier unit should be renewed whenever the refrigerant lines are disconnected.*

Removal

Note: *The engine can be removed from the car only as a complete unit with the transmission.*

1 On models with air conditioning, have the refrigerant discharged by an air conditioning specialist.

2 On all models, park the vehicle on firm, level ground then remove the bonnet as described in Chapter 11.

3 Unscrew the retaining bolts and remove the plastic cover from the top of the engine, taking care not to lose the spacers which are fitted to the cover mounting rubbers.

4 Chock the rear wheels, firmly apply the handbrake then jack up the front of the vehicle (see "*Jacking and Vehicle Support*"). Securely support it on axle stands, bearing in mind the note at the start of this Section, and remove both front roadwheels.

5 Undo the retaining screws and fasteners and remove the undercover from beneath the engine/transmission unit.

6 If the engine is to be dismantled, working as described in Chapter 1B, first drain the engine oil and remove the oil filter. Also drain the cooling system.

7 Referring to Chapter 4B, carry out the following procedures.

a) *Remove the air cleaner housing and intake duct.*

b) *Remove the exhaust front pipe.*

c) *Release the retaining clips and disconnect the fuel feed and return hoses from the pipes on the left-hand end of the rear of the engine. Plug the hose and pipe ends to minimise fuel loss and prevent the entry of dirt into the system. Mop up all spilt fuel.*

d) *Remove the injection system airflow meter and electronic control module (ECM).*

e) *Disconnect the wiring connectors from the injection pump, the fuel injector needle lift sensor (fitted to No 1 injector) and the crankshaft sensor.*

f) *On models not fitted with an intercooler, disconnect the accelerator cable from the injection pump and position it clear of the engine.*

g) *On models with an intercooler, remove the ducts linking the intercooler to the turbocharger and manifold.*

8 Referring to Chapter 5A, carry out the following operations.

a) *Remove the battery, mounting tray and bracket.*

b) *Disconnect the wiring from the starter motor.*

c) *Disconnect the wiring from the alternator.*

9 Slacken and remove the engine mounting rear steady bar bolts and remove the bar from the rear of the sump.

10 Disconnect the wiring connector from the exhaust gas recirculation (EGR) solenoid valve (see Chapter 4C) and the oil pressure switch then unclip the wiring harness from the right-hand end of the engine unit.

11 Disconnect the wiring connectors from the coolant temperature sensors which are screwed into the thermostat housing on the front of the cylinder head. Unclip the wiring harness and position it clear of the engine unit.

12 Unscrew the terminal nut and disconnect the glow plug feed wiring from No 2 glow plug. Refit the nut to the glow plug for safe-keeping.

13 Disconnect the wiring connector from the radiator cooling fan.

14 Referring to Chapter 7, carry out the following procedures.

a) *Drain the transmission oil or be prepared for oil spillage as the engine/transmission unit is removed.*

b) *Disconnect the gearchange selector and steady rods from the transmission unit.*

c) *Disconnect the wiring connector from the vehicle speed sensor and reversing light switch.*

d) *Unbolt the earth lead from the front of the transmission housing.*

15 Unclip the engine wiring harness from the left-hand end of the cylinder head and position it clear of the engine.

16 Release the retaining clip and disconnect the servo unit vacuum hose which is situated at the right-hand end of the camshaft cover. Also disconnect the vacuum hose from the EGR valve.

17 Release the retaining clip and disconnect the radiator top and bottom hoses from the cylinder head and oil cooler. Also disconnect the heater coolant hose from the pipe on the left-hand end of the rear of the cylinder head.

18 Referring to Chapter 6, trace the clutch hydraulic pipe back from the master cylinder to its quick-release fitting on the bulkhead. Wipe clean and disconnect the two halves of the fitting. Mop up any spilt fluid and take precautions not to allow any dirt to enter the hydraulic system; the hose fittings are fitted with valves to prevent fluid loss when they are disconnected.

2D

19 Referring to Chapter 10, disconnect the feed pipe and return hose from the power steering pump and free the pipe from the engine. Locate the feed pipe union at the rear of the engine then slacken the union nut and separate the pipe and hose so the pipe is free to be removed with the engine. Plug the pipe/hose ends and pump unions to minimise fluid loss and prevent the entry of dirt into the hydraulic system.

20 Referring to Chapter 8, disconnect the driveshaft inner ends from the transmission unit. Note that it is not necessary to remove the driveshafts completely, they can be left attached to the hub assemblies and released as the hub is pulled outwards. *Caution: Do not allow the shafts to hang down under their own weight as this could damage the constant velocity joints/ gaiters.*

21 Release the fuel filter from its mounting bracket and position it clear of the engine/transmission unit.

22 On models with air conditioning, trace the refrigerant pipes/hoses back from the compressor to the unions at the front of the engine and bulkhead. Slacken the union nuts and disconnect both pipes/hoses, noting the sealing rings. Free both pipes from any relevant clips/ties so they are free to be removed with the engine unit. Recover the sealing ring from each union and plug the hose/pipe ends to prevent the entry of dirt and moisture into the air conditioning system. Discard all sealing rings, new ones must be used on refitting. Also disconnect the wiring connector from the air conditioning compressor.

23 On all models, manoeuvre the engine hoist into position, and attach it to the lifting brackets bolted onto the cylinder head. Raise the hoist until it is supporting the weight of the engine.

24 Remove the engine/transmission right-hand and left-hand mounting assemblies as described in Chapter 2B, Section 17.

25 Make a final check that any components which would prevent the removal of the engine/transmission from the car have been removed or disconnected. Ensure that components such as the driveshafts are secured so that they cannot be damaged on removal.

26 Raise the engine/transmission assembly out of position, making sure that nothing is trapped, taking great care not to damage the radiator. Enlist the help of an assistant during this procedure, as it may be necessary to tilt the assembly slightly to clear the body panels. Great care must be taken to ensure that no components are trapped and damaged during the removal procedure.

27 Once the engine is high enough, lift it out over the front of the body, and lower the unit to the ground.

Separation

28 With the engine/transmission assembly removed, support the assembly on suitable blocks of wood, on a workbench (or failing that, on a clean area of the workshop floor).

29 Undo the retaining bolts and remove the starter motor from the transmission (see Chapter 5A).

30 Ensure that both engine and transmission are adequately supported, then slacken and remove the remaining bolts securing the transmission housing to the engine mounting plate. Note the correct fitted positions of each bolt (and the relevant brackets) as they are removed, to use as a reference on refitting.

31 Carefully withdraw the transmission from the engine, ensuring that the weight of the transmission is not allowed to hang on the input shaft while it is engaged with the clutch friction disc.

32 If they are loose, remove the locating dowels from the engine or transmission, and keep them in a safe place.

Refitting

33 If the engine and transmission have been separated, perform the operations described below in paragraphs 34 to 37. If not, proceed as described from paragraph 38 onwards.

34 Referring to Chapter 6, apply a smear of molybdenum disulphide grease (Rover recommend the use of Molykote BR2 plus, G-n plus or G-Rapid plus) to the clutch release bearing, fork and guide sleeve contact surfaces and check the operation of the clutch release mechanism. Also apply a smear of grease to the transmission input shaft splines; **do not** apply too much grease otherwise the clutch friction plate may be contaminated.

35 Ensure the locating dowels are correctly positioned then carefully offer the transmission to the engine, until the locating dowels are engaged. Ensure that the weight of the transmission is not allowed to hang on the input shaft as it is engaged with the clutch friction disc.

36 Refit the transmission housing-to-engine bolts, ensuring that all the necessary brackets are correctly positioned, and tighten them to the specified torque setting.

37 Refit the starter motor and tighten its mounting bolts to the specified torque (see Chapter 5A).

38 Reconnect the hoist and lifting tackle to the engine lifting brackets. With the aid of an assistant, lift the assembly over the engine compartment.

39 The assembly should be tilted as necessary to clear the surrounding components, as during removal; lower the assembly into position in the engine compartment, manipulating the hoist and lifting tackle as necessary.

40 Refit the right-hand and left-hand mounting assemblies as described in Chapter 2B, Section 17. Tighten the right-hand mounting steady rod bolts by hand only at this stage; tighten them to the specified torque once the vehicle is resting on its wheels and all other items are correctly reconnected.

41 The remainder of the refitting procedure is a direct reversal of the removal sequence, noting the following points:

a) Ensure that all wiring is correctly routed and retained by all the relevant retaining clips and that all connectors are correctly and securely reconnected.

b) Ensure that all disturbed hoses are correctly reconnected, and securely retained by their retaining clips.

c) Renew the transmission differential oil seals (see Chapter 7) before refitting the driveshafts.

d) Renew all power steering/air conditioning pipe/hose union sealing rings and tighten the union nuts/bolts to the specified torque.

e) Refill the transmission with the correct quantity and type of oil, as described in Chapter 7 and "Lubricants and fluids". If the oil was not drained, top-up the level as described in Chapter 1B.

f) Refill the engine with oil (Chapter 1B) and also refill the cooling system.

g) Prime and bleed the fuel system and adjust the accelerator cable (models not fitted with an intercooler only) as described in Chapter 4B.

h) On models with air conditioning, have the system recharged with refrigerant by an air conditioning specialist.

6 Engine overhaul - dismantling sequence

1 It is much easier to dismantle and work on the engine if it is mounted on a portable engine stand. These stands can often be hired from a tool hire shop. Before the engine is mounted on a stand, the flywheel/driveplate should be removed, so that the stand bolts can be tightened into the end of the cylinder block.

2 If a stand is not available, it is possible to dismantle the engine with it blocked up on a sturdy workbench, or on the floor. Be extra-careful not to tip or drop the engine when working without a stand.

3 If you are going to obtain a reconditioned engine, all the external components must be removed first, to be transferred to the replacement engine (just as they will if you are doing a complete engine overhaul yourself). These components include the following:

a) Inlet and exhaust manifolds (Chapter 4).

b) Alternator/power steering pump/air conditioning compressor bracket(s) (as applicable).

c) Coolant pump (Chapter 3).

d) Fuel system components (Chapter 4).

e) Wiring harness and all electrical switches and sensors.

f) Oil filter (Chapter 1).

g) Flywheel (relevant Part of this Chapter).

h) Coolant pump housing - 2.0 litre engine.

i) Transmission mounting plate - 2.0 litre engine.

Note: *When removing the external components from the engine, pay close attention to details that may be helpful or important during refitting. Note the fitted position of gaskets, seals, spacers, pins, washers, bolts, and other small items.*

4 If you are obtaining a "short" engine (which consists of the engine cylinder block, crankshaft, pistons and connecting rods all assembled), then the cylinder head, sump, oil pump, and timing belt/chains (as applicable) will have to be removed also.

5 If you are planning a complete overhaul, the engine can be dismantled, and the internal components removed, in the order given below, referring to the relevant Part of this Chapter unless otherwise stated.

   a) Inlet and exhaust manifolds (Chapter 4).
   b) Timing belt, sprockets and tensioner.
   c) Fuel injection pump belt, sprockets and tensioner - diesel engine only.
   d) Cylinder head.
   e) Flywheel.
   f) Sump.
   g) Oil pump.
   h) Piston/connecting rod assemblies.
   i) Crankshaft.
   j) Coolant pump housing - 2.0 litre engine.
   k) Transmission mounting plate - 2.0 litre engine

6 Before beginning the dismantling and overhaul procedures, make sure that you have all of the correct tools necessary. Refer to the *"Tools and working facilities"* Section of this manual for further information.

7 Cylinder head - dismantling

Note: *New and reconditioned cylinder heads are available from the manufacturer, and from engine overhaul specialists. Be aware that some specialist tools are required for the dismantling and inspection procedures, and new components may not be readily available. It may therefore be more practical and economical for the home mechanic to purchase a reconditioned head, rather than dismantle, inspect and recondition the original head.*

1 On petrol engines, referring to Part A or B of this Chapter (as applicable), remove the camshaft(s) and followers then remove the cylinder head from the engine. Remove the spark plugs (see Chapter 1A).

2 On diesel engines, remove the glow plugs (Chapter 5C) and injectors (Chapter 4B). Remove the camshaft and followers from the cylinder head then remove the cylinder head from the engine as described in Part C of this Chapter.

3 On all engines, using a valve spring compressor, compress each valve spring in turn until the split collets can be removed. Release the compressor, and lift off the spring retainer and spring. Using a pair of pliers,

7.3a Using a spring compressor to compress a valve spring

carefully extract the valve stem seal (which incorporates the spring seat) from the valve guide **(see illustrations)**.

4 If, when the valve spring compressor is screwed down, the spring retainer refuses to free and expose the split collets, gently tap the top of the tool, directly over the retainer, with a light hammer. This will free the retainer.

5 Withdraw the valve through the combustion chamber. It is essential that each valve is stored together with its collets, retainer and spring. The valves should also be kept in their correct sequence, unless they are so badly worn that they are to be renewed. **(see Haynes Hint).**

8 Cylinder head and valves - cleaning and inspection

1 Thorough cleaning of the cylinder head and valve components, followed by a detailed inspection, will enable you to decide how much valve service work must be carried out during the engine overhaul. **Note:** *If the engine has been severely overheated, it is best to assume that the cylinder head is warped - check carefully for signs of this.*

HAYNES HINT

If the components are to be refitted, place each valve and its associated components in a labelled polythene bag or similar small container, and mark the bag/container with the relevant valve number to ensure that it is refitted in its original location

7.3b Using pliers, carefully remove the valve stem oil seal from the valve guide

Cleaning

2 Scrape away all traces of old gasket material from the cylinder head.

3 Scrape away the carbon from the combustion chambers and ports, then wash the cylinder head thoroughly with paraffin or a suitable solvent.

4 Scrape off any heavy carbon deposits that may have formed on the valves, then use a power-operated wire brush to remove deposits from the valve heads and stems.

Inspection

Note: *Be sure to perform all the following inspection procedures before concluding that the services of a machine shop or engine overhaul specialist are required. Make a list of all items that require attention.*

Cylinder head

5 Inspect the head very carefully for cracks, evidence of coolant leakage, and other damage. If cracks are found, a new cylinder head should be obtained.

6 Use a straight-edge and feeler blade to check that the cylinder head surface is not distorted **(see illustration)**. If it is, it may be possible to resurface it, provided that the cylinder head is not reduced to less than the minimum specified height.

7 Examine the valve seats in each of the combustion chambers. If they are severely pitted, cracked or burned, then they will need to be renewed or recut by an engine overhaul specialist. If they are only slightly pitted, this can be removed by grinding-in the valve heads and seats with fine valve-grinding compound, as described below.

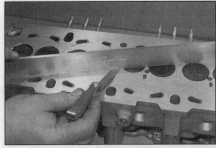

8.6 Using a straight edge and feeler blade to check the cylinder head surface for distortion

2D

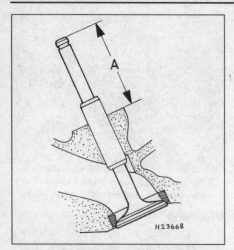

8.8a Valve stem installed height measurement (A) - petrol engine

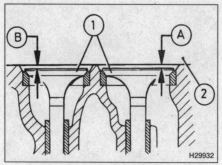

8.8b Valve head recess measurement - diesel engine

1 Valves   A Inlet valve
2 Straight edge   B Exhaust valve

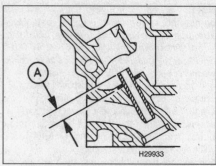

8.10a Valve guide installed height measurement (A) - petrol engine

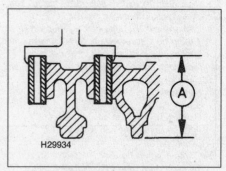

8.10b Valve guide installed height measurement (A) - diesel engine

8 Check valve seat wear by inserting each valve into its relevant guide. On petrol engines, measure the projected height of the valve stem above the cylinder head surface and on diesel engines, using a straight edge and feeler blades, measure the valve head recess from the cylinder head mating surface **(see illustrations)**. If any measurement exceeds the specified limit, repeat the check with a new valve. If the measurement still exceeds the specified limit, then the valve seat is excessively worn and must be renewed.

9 If the valve guides are worn (indicated by a side-to-side motion of the valve, and accompanied by excessive blue smoke in the exhaust when running) new guides must be fitted. Measure the diameter of the existing valve stems (see below) and the bore of the guides, then calculate the clearance and compare the result with the specified value. If the clearance is not within the specified limits, renew the valves and/or guides as necessary.

10 The renewal of valve guides is best carried out by an engine overhaul specialist. If the work is to be carried out at home, however, use a stepped, double-diameter drift to drive out the worn guide towards the combustion chamber. On petrol engines, drive the guide into position until it projects the specified amount above the cylinder head surface and on diesel engines, position the

guide so its upper surface is the specified distance above the cylinder head lower mating surface **(see illustrations)**.

> **HAYNES HiNT** *On fitting the new guide, place it first in a deep-freeze for one hour, then drive it into its cylinder head bore from the camshaft side.*

11 If the valve seats are to be re-cut this must be done only after the guides have been renewed.

Valves

12 Examine the head of each valve for pitting, burning, cracks and general wear, and check the valve stem for scoring and wear ridges. Rotate the valve, and check for any obvious indication that it is bent. Look for pitting and excessive wear on the tip of each valve stem. Renew any valve that shows any such signs of wear or damage.

13 If the valve appears satisfactory at this stage, measure the valve stem diameter at several points using a micrometer **(see illustration)**. Any significant difference in the readings obtained indicates wear of the valve stem. Should any of these conditions be apparent, the valve(s) must be renewed.

14 If the valves are in satisfactory condition, they should be ground (lapped) into their respective seats, to ensure a smooth gas-tight seal. If the seat is only lightly pitted, or if

it has been re-cut, fine grinding compound **only** should be used to produce the required finish. Coarse valve-grinding compound should **not** be used unless a seat is badly burned or deeply pitted; if this is the case, the cylinder head and valves should be inspected by an expert to decide whether seat re-cutting, or even the renewal of the valve or seat insert, is required.

15 Valve grinding is carried out as follows. Place the cylinder head upside-down on a bench.

16 Smear a trace of the appropriate grade of valve-grinding compound on the seat face, and press a suction grinding tool onto the valve head. With a semi-rotary action, grind the valve head to its seat, lifting the valve occasionally to redistribute the grinding compound **(see illustration)**. A light spring placed under the valve head will greatly ease this operation.

17 If coarse grinding compound is being used, work only until a dull, matt even surface is produced on both the valve seat and the valve, then wipe off the used compound and repeat the process with fine compound. When a smooth unbroken ring of light grey matt finish is produced on both the valve and seat, the grinding operation is complete. **Do not** grind in the valves any further than absolutely necessary, or the seat will be prematurely sunk into the cylinder head.

18 When all the valves have been ground-in, carefully wash off all traces of grinding compound using paraffin or a suitable solvent before reassembly of the cylinder head.

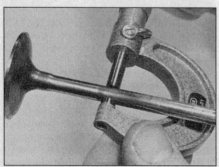

8.13 Using a micrometer to measure a valve stem diameter

8.16 Grinding-in a valve seat

8.19 Measuring valve spring free length

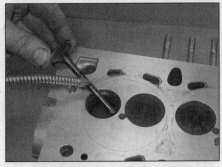

9.1 Lubricate the valve stem with oil and insert it into the correct guide

9.2a Fit the new valve stem seal onto the guide . . .

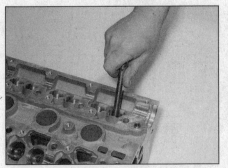

9.2b . . . and press it fully into position using a socket

9.3a Fit the valve spring . . .

9.3b . . . and locate the spring retainer on the top of the valve

Valve components

19 Examine the valve springs for signs of damage and discoloration. The condition of each spring can be judged by measuring its free length **(see illustration)**. Stand each spring on a flat surface, and check it for squareness. If any of the springs are less than the specified free length or are damaged or distorted, obtain a complete new set of springs.

9 Cylinder head - reassembly

1 Lubricate the stems of the valves, and insert them into their original locations **(see illustration)**. If new valves are being fitted, insert them into the locations to which they have been ground.

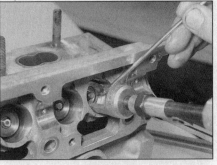

9.4 Compress the valve spring and locate the collets in position

2 Working on the first valve, dip the new valve stem seal in fresh engine oil, then carefully locate it over the valve and onto the guide. Take care not to damage the seal as it is passed over the valve stem. Use a suitable socket or metal tube to press the seal firmly onto the guide **(see illustrations)**.
3 Locate the spring on the seal seat and fit the spring retainer **(see illustrations)**.
4 Compress the valve spring, and locate the split collets in the recess in the valve stem **(see illustration and Haynes Hint)**. Release the compressor, then repeat the procedure on the remaining valves.
5 With all the valves installed, using a hammer and interposed block of wood, lightly tap the end of each valve stem to settle the components.

Use a dab of grease to hold the collets in position on the valve stem whilst the spring compressor is released

6 On petrol engines, working as described in Part A or B, refit the cylinder head to the engine and install the followers and camshaft(s).
7 On diesel engines, working as described in Part C, refit the cylinder head to the engine and install the followers and camshaft. Refit the injectors and glow plugs as described in Chapters 4B and 5C.

10 Piston/connecting rod assembly - removal

1.4 and 1.6 litre engine

Note: *Due to the design of the engine, it will become very difficult, almost impossible, to turn the crankshaft once the cylinder head bolts have been slackened. The manufacturer accordingly states that the crankshaft will be 'tight' and should not be rotated more than absolutely necessary once the head has been removed. If the crankshaft cannot be rotated, then it must be removed for overhaul work to proceed. With this in mind, during any servicing or overhaul work the crankshaft must always be rotated to the desired position before the bolts are disturbed.*
1 Remove the camshaft(s) and followers then remove the sump and oil pump pick-up/strainer as described in Part A of this Chapter.
2 Rotate the crankshaft until Nos 1 and 4 cylinder pistons are at the top of their stroke then remove the cylinder head and clamp the

2D

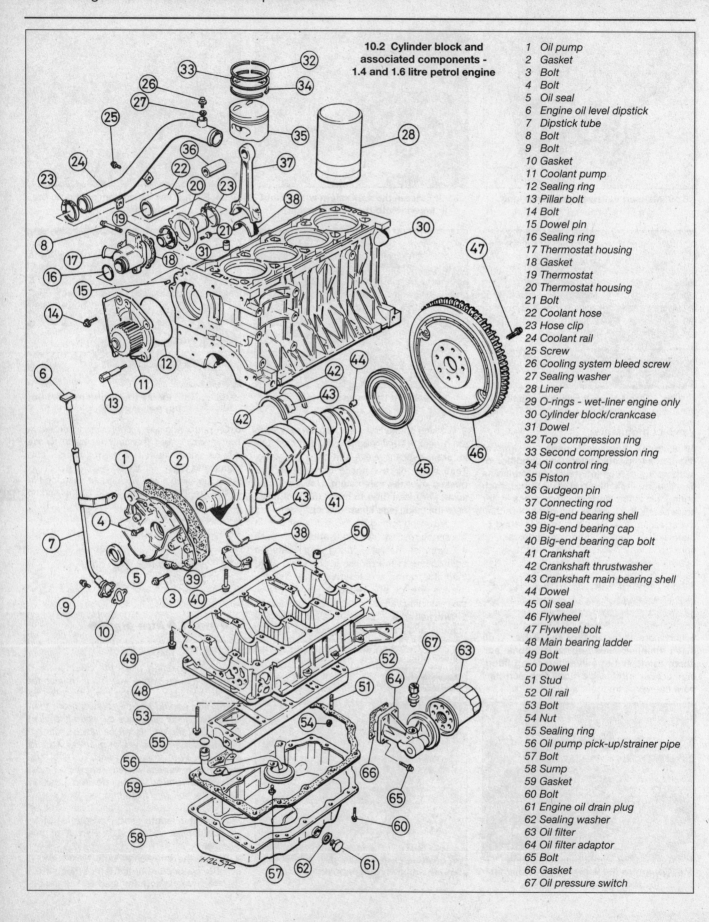

10.2 Cylinder block and associated components - 1.4 and 1.6 litre petrol engine

1 Oil pump
2 Gasket
3 Bolt
4 Bolt
5 Oil seal
6 Engine oil level dipstick
7 Dipstick tube
8 Bolt
9 Bolt
10 Gasket
11 Coolant pump
12 Sealing ring
13 Pillar bolt
14 Bolt
15 Dowel pin
16 Sealing ring
17 Thermostat housing
18 Gasket
19 Thermostat
20 Thermostat housing
21 Bolt
22 Coolant hose
23 Hose clip
24 Coolant rail
25 Screw
26 Cooling system bleed screw
27 Sealing washer
28 Liner
29 O-rings - wet-liner engine only
30 Cylinder block/crankcase
31 Dowel
32 Top compression ring
33 Second compression ring
34 Oil control ring
35 Piston
36 Gudgeon pin
37 Connecting rod
38 Big-end bearing shell
39 Big-end bearing cap
40 Big-end bearing cap bolt
41 Crankshaft
42 Crankshaft thrustwasher
43 Crankshaft main bearing shell
44 Dowel
45 Oil seal
46 Flywheel
47 Flywheel bolt
48 Main bearing ladder
49 Bolt
50 Dowel
51 Stud
52 Oil rail
53 Bolt
54 Nut
55 Sealing ring
56 Oil pump pick-up/strainer pipe
57 Bolt
58 Sump
59 Gasket
60 Bolt
61 Engine oil drain plug
62 Sealing washer
63 Oil filter
64 Oil filter adaptor
65 Bolt
66 Gasket
67 Oil pressure switch

H26575

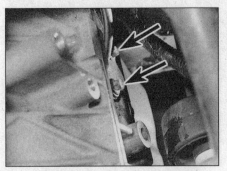

10.3 Dipstick tube retaining bolts (arrowed)

10.4 Removing the oil rail from the main bearing ladder

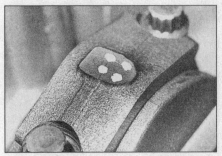

10.5 Mark each big-end bearing cap with its cylinder number prior to removal (No 4 shown)

liners securely in position as described in Part A. The crankshaft should not be rotated once the head has been removed **(see illustration)**.

3 Slacken and remove the dipstick tube retaining bolts and remove the tube from the cylinder block/crankcase **(see illustration)**.

4 Unscrew the two retaining nuts and remove the oil rail from the base of the main bearing ladder **(see illustration)**.

5 Using a hammer and centre punch, paint or similar, mark each connecting rod big-end bearing cap with its respective cylinder number on the flat, machined surface provided **(see illustration)**. If the engine has been dismantled before, note carefully any identifying marks made previously. Note that No 1 cylinder is at the timing belt end of the engine.

6 Unscrew and remove the big-end bearing cap bolts and withdraw the cap, complete with bearing shell, from the connecting rod. If only the bearing shells are being attended to, push the connecting rod up and off the crankpin, ensuring that the connecting rod big-ends do not mark the cylinder bore walls, then remove the upper bearing shell. Keep the cap, bolts and (if they are to be refitted) the bearing shells together in their correct sequence.

7 With Nos 2 and 3 cylinder big-ends disconnected, repeat the procedure (exercising great care to prevent damage to any of the components) to remove Nos 1 and 4 cylinder bearing caps.

8 Remove the ridge of carbon from the top of each cylinder bore. Push each piston/connecting rod assembly up and remove it from the top of the bore, and ensure that the

connecting rod big-ends do not mark the cylinder bore walls.

9 Note that the number stamped by you on each bearing cap should match the cylinder number stamped on the front of each connecting rod (the letter on the rod is the weight code and the number on the front of bearing cap is the big-end bore size code - **see illustration 19.3**). If any connecting rod number does not match its correct cylinder, mark or label it immediately so that each piston/connecting rod assembly can be refitted to its original bore. Fit the bearing cap, shells and bolts to each removed piston/connecting rod assembly, so that they are all kept together as a matched set.

2.0 litre engine

10 Referring to Part B or C of this Chapter (as applicable), remove the cylinder head and sump then unbolt the pick-up/strainer from the base of the cylinder block.

11 If there is a pronounced wear ridge at the top of any bore, it may be necessary to remove it with a scraper or ridge reamer, to avoid piston damage during removal. Such a ridge indicates excessive wear of the cylinder bore.

12 Using a hammer and centre-punch, paint or similar, mark each connecting rod and its bearing cap with its respective cylinder number on the flat machined surface provided; make the marks in such a way that there is no possibility in fitting the caps the wrong way around on refitting **(see illustration)**. If the engine has been dismantled before, note carefully any identifying marks made

previously. Note that No 1 cylinder is at the timing belt end of the engine.

13 Turn the crankshaft to bring pistons 1 and 4 to BDC (bottom dead centre).

14 Unscrew the nuts/bolts (as applicable) from No 1 piston big-end bearing cap. Take off the cap and recover the bottom half bearing shell. If the bearing shells are to be re-used, tape the cap and the shell together.

Caution: On some engines, the connecting rod/bearing cap mating surfaces are not machined flat; the big-end bearing caps are "cracked" (a process known as fracture-split) off from the rod during production and left untouched to ensure the cap and rod mate perfectly. Where this type of connecting rod is fitted, great care must be taken to ensure the mating surfaces of the cap and rod are not marked or damaged in anyway. Any damage to the mating surfaces will adversely affect the strength of the connecting rod and could lead to premature failure.

15 Using a hammer handle, push the piston up through the bore, and remove it from the top of the cylinder block. Recover the bearing shell, and tape it to the connecting rod for safe-keeping.

16 Loosely refit the big-end cap to the connecting rod, and secure with the nuts/bolts - this will help to keep the components in their correct order.

17 Remove No 4 piston assembly in the same way.

18 Turn the crankshaft through 180° to bring pistons 2 and 3 to BDC (bottom dead centre), and remove them in the same way **(see illustrations)**.

2D

10.12 Make identification markings (arrowed) on each connecting rod and bearing cap prior to removal

10.18a Slacken and remove the nuts . . .

10.18b . . . and remove the big-end bearing cap from the connecting rod

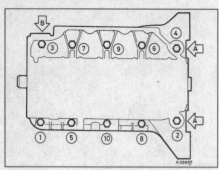

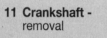

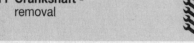

11.4a Main bearing ladder bolt slackening sequence - 1.4 and 1.6 litre petrol engine

A Bolts hidden in ladder flanges
B Location of longer bolt

11.4b Remove the main bearing ladder from the cylinder block noting the correct fitted locations of the dowels (arrowed)

11.5 Removing No 1 cylinder big-end bearing cap and shell

11 Crankshaft - removal

1.4 and 1.6 litre engine

1 Remove the cylinder head, sump, oil pump and flywheel as described in Part A of this Chapter.

2 Slacken and remove the dipstick tube retaining bolts and remove the tube from the cylinder block/crankcase.

3 Unscrew the two retaining nuts and remove the oil rail from the base of the main bearing ladder.

4 Working in the sequence shown, progressively unscrew the main bearing ladder retaining bolts by a turn at a time, then withdraw the ladder. Note the two locating dowels and the main bearing shells, which should be removed from the ladder and stored in their correct fitted order **(see illustrations)**.

5 Remove the piston and connecting rod assemblies as described in Section 10 **(see illustration)**. If no work is to be done on the pistons and connecting rods, unbolt the caps and push the pistons far enough up the bores so that the connecting rods are positioned clear of the crankshaft journals.

6 Check the crankshaft endfloat as described in Section 14, then remove the crankshaft **(see illustration)**.

7 Withdraw the two thrustwashers from the No 3 main bearing upper location. Noting the position of the grooved shells, remove the upper main bearing shells, which must be kept with their correct respective partners from the main bearing ladder so that all shells can be identified and (if necessary) refitted in their original locations.

2.0 litre petrol engine

8 Referring to Part B of this Chapter, remove the oil pump, flywheel and crankshaft left-hand oil seal housing.

9 Remove the piston and connecting rod assemblies as described in Section 10. If no work is to be done on the pistons and connecting rods, the cylinder head can be left in position then unbolt the caps and push the pistons far enough up the bores so that the connecting rods are positioned clear of the crankshaft journals.

10 Check the crankshaft endfloat as described in Section 14, then proceed as follows.

11 The main bearing caps should be numbered 1 to 5 from the timing belt end of the engine and the arrow on each cap should point towards the timing belt end of the engine. If the bearing caps are not marked, using a hammer and punch or a suitable marker pen, number the caps from 1 to 5 from the timing belt end of the engine and mark each cap to indicate its correct fitted direction to avoid confusion on refitting.

Caution: Do not mark the mating surfaces of number 1 and 5 bearing caps.

12 Working in a diagonal sequence, evenly and progressively slacken the ten main bearing cap retaining bolts by half a turn at a time until all bolts are loose. Remove all bolts, keeping them in the correct fitted order.

13 Carefully remove each cap from the cylinder block, noting the locating dowels, ensuring that the lower main bearing shell remains in position in the cap **(see illustration)**. Note the fitted locations of the shells; grooved shells are fitted to Nos 1, 3 and 5 bearings and plain shells to Nos 2 and 4 bearings.

14 Withdraw the two thrustwasher lower halves from the sides of the centre main bearing cap.

15 Carefully lift out the crankshaft, taking care not to displace the upper main bearing shells.

16 Recover the upper bearing shells from the cylinder block and tape them to their respective caps for safe-keeping. Withdraw the two thrustwasher upper halves from the sides of the centre main bearing.

2.0 litre diesel engine

17 Referring to Part C of this Chapter, remove the oil pump, flywheel and crankshaft left-hand oil seal housing.

18 Remove the crankshaft as described in paragraphs 9 to 16, ignoring paragraph 14 (there are no thrustwasher lower halves). Also note that all lower bearing shells are plain and all upper bearing shells are grooved.

12 Cylinder block - cleaning and inspection

Cleaning

1 Remove all external components and electrical switches/sensors from the block. For complete cleaning, the core plugs should ideally be removed. Drill a small hole in the plugs, then insert a self-tapping screw into the hole. Pull out the plugs by pulling on the screw with a pair of grips, or by using a slide hammer.

2 On 1.4 and 1.6 litre engines, remove the liners as described in paragraph 18.

11.6 Removing the crankshaft

11.13 Remove the main bearing caps noting the locating dowels (one arrowed)

3 On diesel engines, undo the retaining bolt and remove each piston oil jet spray tube from inside the cylinder block **(see illustration)**. Discard the retaining bolts, new ones must be used on refitting.

4 On all engines, scrape all traces of gasket from the cylinder block/crankcase, and from the main bearing ladder/caps (as applicable), taking care not to damage the gasket/sealing surfaces.

5 Remove all oil gallery plugs (where fitted). The plugs are usually very tight - they may have to be drilled out, and the holes re-tapped. Use new plugs when the engine is reassembled.

6 If any of the castings are extremely dirty, all should be steam-cleaned.

7 After the castings are returned, clean all oil holes and oil galleries one more time. Flush all internal passages with warm water until the water runs clear. Dry thoroughly, and apply a light film of oil to all mating surfaces, to prevent rusting. Also oil the cylinder bores. If you have access to compressed air, use it to speed up the drying process, and to blow out all the oil holes and galleries.

> **Warning: Wear eye protection when using compressed air!**

8 If the castings are not very dirty, you can do an adequate cleaning job with hot (as hot as you can stand!), soapy water and a stiff brush. Take plenty of time, and do a thorough job. Regardless of the cleaning method used, be sure to clean all oil holes and galleries very thoroughly, and to dry all components well. Protect the cylinder bores as described above, to prevent rusting.

9 All threaded holes must be clean, to ensure accurate torque readings during reassembly. To clean the threads, run the correct-size tap into each of the holes to remove rust, corrosion, thread sealant or sludge, and to restore damaged threads. If possible, use compressed air to clear the holes of debris produced by this operation. A good alternative is to inject aerosol-applied water-dispersant lubricant into each hole, using the long spout usually supplied.

> **Warning: Wear eye protection when cleaning out these holes in this way!**

10 Apply suitable sealant to the new oil gallery plugs, and insert them into the holes in the block. Tighten them securely.

11 On diesel engines, apply a drop of thread-locking compound (Rover recommend the use of Loctite 275) to the threads of the oil jet spray tube new retaining bolts, ensuring that the bolt oil holes are not obstructed. Refit the piston oil jet spray tubes to the cylinder block, then fit the new retaining bolts, tightening them to the specified torque setting **(see illustration)**.

12 If the engine is not going to be reassembled right away, cover it with a large plastic bag to keep it clean; protect all mating

12.3 Unscrew the retaining bolts and remove the piston oil jet spray tubes from the cylinder block

surfaces and the cylinder bores as described above, to prevent rusting.

Inspection

2.0 litre engine

13 Visually check the castings for cracks and corrosion. Look for stripped threads in the threaded holes. If there has been any history of internal water leakage, it may be worthwhile having an engine overhaul specialist check the cylinder block/crankcase with special equipment. If defects are found, have them repaired if possible, or renew the assembly.

14 Check each cylinder bore for scuffing and scoring. Check for signs of a wear ridge at the top of the cylinder, indicating that the bore is excessively worn.

15 If the necessary measuring equipment is available, measure the bore diameter of each cylinder bore. On petrol engines the measurement should be taken 60 mm down from the top of the bore and on diesel engines the measurement should be taken 70 mm down from the top of the bore. Take two measurements, one parallel to the crankshaft axis and the other at right-angles to the crankshaft axis **(see illustration)**. Compare the results with the figures given in the Specifications. On petrol engines, the cylinder bore size group markings are stamped onto the rear, left-hand end of the cylinder block.

16 At the time of writing, it was not clear whether oversize pistons were available. Consult your Rover dealer and/or engine reconditioning specialist for the latest information on piston availability. If oversize pistons are available, then it may be possible to have the cylinder bores rebored and fit the oversize pistons. If oversize pistons are not available, and the bores are worn, renewal of the block seems to be the only option. Seek the advice of a Rover dealer or engine reconditioning specialist on the best course of action.

17 If the bores are in reasonably good condition and not worn to the specified limits, then the piston rings should be renewed. If this is the case, the bores should be honed to allow the new rings to bed in correctly and provide the best possible seal. The conventional type of hone has spring-loaded

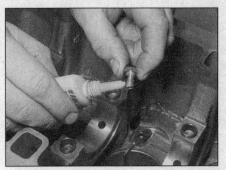

12.11 Apply thread-locking compound (see text) to the threads of the piston oil jet spray tubes prior to installation

stones, and is used with a power drill. You will also need some paraffin (or honing oil) and rags. The hone should be moved up and down the bore to produce a crosshatch pattern, and plenty of honing oil should be used. Ideally, the crosshatch lines should intersect at approximately a 60° angle. Do not take off more material than is necessary to produce the required finish. If new pistons are being fitted, the piston manufacturers may specify a finish with a different angle, so their instructions should be followed. Do not withdraw the hone from the bore while it is still being turned – stop it first. After honing a bore, wipe out all traces of the honing oil. If equipment of this type is not available, or if you are not sure whether you are competent to undertake the task yourself, an engine overhaul specialist will carry out the work at moderate cost.

1.4 and 1.6 litre engine

Note: *There are two different types of liner used in these engines; most engines are fitted with "damp-liners" where the liner-to-block joint is sealed with a bead of sealant whereas some early engines have "wet-liners" where the liner-to-block joint is sealed with two sealing rings.*

18 Remove the liner clamps (where used), then use a hard wood drift to tap out each liner from the inside of the cylinder block. When all the liners are released, tip the cylinder block/crankcase on its side and remove each liner from the top of the block.

12.15 Using an internal micrometer to measure cylinder bore diameter

2D

12.18 On "wet-liner" engines, remove the sealing rings from the base of each cylinder liner

As each liner is removed, stick masking tape on its left-hand (flywheel side) face, and write the cylinder number on the tape. No 1 cylinder is at the timing belt end of the engine. Where "wet-liners" are fitted, remove the sealing rings from the base of each liner, and discard them **(see illustration)**.

19 Check each cylinder liner for scuffing and scoring. Check for signs of a wear ridge at the top of the liner, indicating that the bore is excessively worn.

20 If the necessary measuring equipment is available, measure the bore diameter of each cylinder bore. On "damp-liner" engines the measurement should be taken 65 mm down from the top of the bore and on "wet-liner" engines the measurement should be taken 60 mm down from the top of the bore. Take two measurements, one parallel to the crankshaft axis and the other at right-angles to the crankshaft axis. Compare the results with the figures given in the Specifications.

21 If the liner wear exceeds the permitted tolerances at any point, or if the cylinder liner walls are badly scored or scuffed, then renewal of the relevant liner assembly will be necessary. If there is any doubt about the condition of the cylinder bores, seek the advice of a Rover dealer or engine reconditioning specialist. If the bores are in reasonably good condition and not

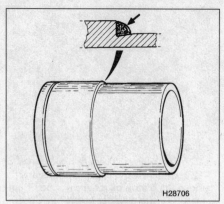

12.25 On "damp-liner" engines, apply a 2 mm bead of sealant to the liner locating shoulder - see text

worn to the specified limits, then the piston rings should be renewed and the bores should be honed (see paragraph 17).

22 If renewal is necessary, new liners, can be purchased from a Rover dealer. New piston/connecting rod assemblies will also be required.

23 To allow for manufacturing tolerances, pistons and liners are separated into two size groups. The size group of each piston is indicated by a letter (A or B) stamped onto its crown, and the size group of each liner is indicated by a paint marking; Red for size group A and Blue for size group B. Ensure that each piston and its respective liner are both of the same size group. It is permissible to have different size group piston and liner assemblies fitted to the same engine, but never fit a piston of one size group to a liner in a different group.

24 Prior to installing the liners, thoroughly clean the liner mating surfaces in the cylinder block, and use fine abrasive paper to polish away any burrs or sharp edges which hinder installation

25 On "damp-liner" engines, ensure the liner and block mating surfaces are clean and dry. Apply a continuous bead of sealant (Rover recommend the use of Hylomar) which is approximately 2.0 mm thick around the locating shoulder on the liner **(see illustration)**.

26 On "wet-liner" engines, fit new sealing rings to the recesses on the base of each liner and lubricated them with clean engine oil to ease installation. Great care must be taken to ensure the sealing rings are not damaged as the liner is located in the block.

27 On all engines, carefully insert the liner squarely into the cylinder block and press it fully into position. If the original liners are being refitted, use the marks made on removal to ensure that each is refitted the correct way round, and is inserted into its original bore. Insert each liner into the cylinder block and press it home as far as possible by hand. Using a hammer and a block of wood, tap each liner lightly but fully onto its locating shoulder **(see illustration)**. Wipe clean, then lightly oil, all exposed liner surfaces, to prevent rusting. If possible, clamp the liners in position.

28 Check the condition of the cylinder head bolts and particularly their threads whenever they are removed. If the cylinder head only is removed, check the bolts as described in Part A of this Chapter. If the cylinder head and the oil rail are removed, check as follows.

29 Keeping all the bolts in their correct fitted order, wash them and wipe dry, then check each for any sign of visible wear or damage. Renew any bolt if necessary. Carefully enter each bolt into its original hole in the oil rail and screw it in, by hand only until finger-tight. If the full length of thread is engaged, the bolt may be re-used. If the full length of thread is not engaged, measure the distance from the oil rail gasket surface to under the bolt head **(see illustration)**.

30 If the distance measured is less than 378 mm, then the bolt may be re-used. If the distance measured is more than 378 mm, the bolt must be renewed. As a precaution, we recommend that the bolts are renewed as a complete set, regardless of their apparent condition. Note that if any of the cylinder head bolt threads in the oil rail are found to be damaged, then the oil rail must be renewed, helicoils (thread inserts) are not an acceptable repair in this instance.

13 Piston/connecting rod assembly - inspection

1 Before the inspection process can begin, the piston/connecting rod assemblies must be cleaned, and the original piston rings removed from the pistons.

2 Carefully expand the old rings over the top of the pistons. The use of two or three old feeler blades will be helpful in preventing the rings dropping into empty grooves **(see illustration)**. Be careful not to scratch the piston with the ends of the ring. The rings are brittle, and will snap if they are spread too far. They're also very sharp - protect your hands and fingers. Note that the third (oil control) ring consists of a spacer and two side rails. Always remove the rings from the top of the piston.

12.27 Ease the liner into the cylinder block and tap it lightly into position to ensure it is correctly seated

12.29 Checking the condition of the cylinder head bolts - see text

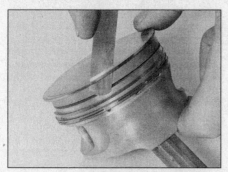

13.2 Using a feeler blade to remove a piston ring

13.10 Measuring a piston diameter - 1.4 and 1.6 litre engine

13.17 Measuring a piston diameter - 2.0 litre petrol engine

Keep each set of rings with its piston if the old rings are to be re-used.

3 Scrape away all traces of carbon from the top of the piston. A hand-held wire brush (or a piece of fine emery cloth) can be used, once the majority of the deposits have been scraped away. The piston identification markings should now be visible.

4 Remove the carbon from the ring grooves in the piston, using an old ring. Break the ring in half to do this (be careful not to cut your fingers - piston rings are sharp). Be careful to remove only the carbon deposits - do not remove any metal, and do not nick or scratch the sides of the ring grooves.

5 Once the deposits have been removed, clean the piston/connecting rod assembly with paraffin or a suitable solvent, and dry thoroughly. Make sure that the oil return holes in the ring grooves are clear.

6 If the cylinder bores are not damaged or worn excessively (see Section 12), check the piston/connecting rods as follows.

1.4 and 1.6 litre engine

7 Carefully inspect each piston for cracks around the skirt, around the gudgeon pin holes, and at the piston ring "lands" (between the ring grooves).

8 Look for scoring and scuffing on the piston skirt, holes in the piston crown, and burned areas at the edge of the crown. If the skirt is scored or scuffed, the engine may have been suffering from overheating, and/or abnormal combustion which caused excessively high operating temperatures. The cooling and lubrication systems should be checked thoroughly. Scorch marks on the sides of the pistons show that blow-by has occurred. A hole in the piston crown, or burned areas at the edge of the piston crown, indicates that abnormal combustion (pre-ignition, knocking, or detonation) has been occurring. If any of the above problems exist, the causes must be investigated and corrected, or the damage will occur again. The causes may include incorrect ignition/injection pump timing (as applicable), or a faulty injector.

9 Corrosion of the piston, in the form of pitting, indicates that coolant has been leaking into the combustion chamber and/or the crankcase. Again, the cause must be corrected, or the problem may persist in the rebuilt engine.

10 Measure the piston diameter at right angles to the gudgeon pin axis, 8 mm up from the base of the piston skirt, and compare the results with the Specifications at the beginning of this Chapter **(see illustration)**. Note that there are two piston size group to allow for manufacturing tolerances; the size group marking is stamped on the piston crown.

11 To measure the piston-to-bore clearance, measure the bore diameter at right-angles to the crankshaft axis, 20 mm up from the base of the bore (see Section 12). Calculate the clearance by subtracting the piston diameter from the bore measurement. Alternatively, insert each piston into its original bore, then select a feeler blade and slip it into the bore along with the piston. The piston must be aligned exactly in its normal attitude, and the feeler blade must be between the piston and bore, on one of the thrust faces, 20 mm from the bottom of the bore. If the clearance is excessive, a new piston will be required. If the piston binds at the lower end of the bore and is loose towards the top, the bore is tapered. If tight spots are encountered as the piston/feeler blade is rotated in the bore, the bore is out-of-round.

12 Repeat this procedure for the remaining pistons and cylinder bores. Any piston which is worn beyond the specified limits must be renewed.

13 Examine each connecting rod carefully for signs of damage, such as cracks around the big-end and small-end bearings. Check that the rod is not bent or distorted. Damage is highly unlikely, unless the engine has been seized or badly overheated. Detailed checking of the connecting rod assembly can only be carried out by a Rover dealer or engine repair specialist with the necessary equipment.

14 The gudgeon pins are an interference fit in the connecting rod small-end bearings and Rover state that they the pistons and connecting rods must not be dismantled. Rover only supply pistons and connecting rods as an assembly; it is not possible to purchase them separately. Therefore, if either the piston or connecting rod is damaged then both must be renewed as an assembly.

15 Inspect the connecting rod big-end cap bolts closely for signs of wear or damage and check that they screw easily into the connecting rods. Renew any bolt which

shows visible signs of damage or does not screw easily into position.

2.0 litre petrol engine

16 Carry out the checks described in paragraphs 7 to 9.

17 Measure the piston diameter at right angles to the gudgeon pin axis, 10 mm up from the base of the piston skirt, and compare the results with the Specifications at the beginning of this Chapter **(see illustration)**. Note that there are two piston size group to allow for manufacturing tolerances; the size group marking is stamped on the piston crown.

18 To measure the piston-to-bore clearance, measure the bore diameter at right-angles to the crankshaft axis, 60 mm down from the top of the bore (see Section 12). Calculate the clearance by subtracting the piston diameter from the bore measurement. Alternatively, invert the piston and fit it into its original bore so that the arrow on the piston crown is facing towards the flywheel end of the engine. Position the piston so that the base of its skirt is 50 mm down from the top of the bore then select a feeler blade and slip it into the bore along with the piston. The piston must be aligned exactly in its normal attitude, and the feeler blade must be between the piston and bore, on one of the thrust faces, approximately 60 mm down from the top of the bore **(see illustration)**. If the clearance is excessive, a new piston will be required. If the

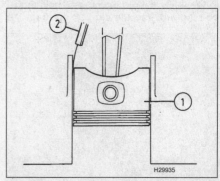

13.18 Position the piston (1) as described in text then check the piston-to-bore clearance by inserting a feeler blade (2) between the piston and bore

13.24 Measure the piston diameter in the circular areas left in the graphite coating (arrowed)

13.28a On diesel engines, remove the circlips . . .

13.28b . . . then press out the gudgeon pin and separate the piston and connecting rod

piston binds at the lower end of the bore and is loose towards the top, the bore is tapered. If tight spots are encountered as the piston/feeler blade is rotated in the bore, the bore is out-of-round.

19 Repeat this procedure for the remaining pistons and cylinder bores. Any piston which is worn beyond the specified limits must be renewed.

20 Examine each connecting rod carefully for signs of damage, such as cracks around the big-end and small-end bearings. Check that the rod is not bent or distorted. Damage is highly unlikely, unless the engine has been seized or badly overheated. Detailed checking of the connecting rod assembly can only be carried out by a Rover dealer or engine repair specialist with the necessary equipment.

21 The gudgeon pins are an interference fit in the connecting rod small-end bearing and Rover state that they the pistons and connecting rods must not be dismantled. Rover only supply pistons and connecting rods as an assembly; it is not possible to purchase them separately. Therefore, if either the piston or connecting rod is damaged then both must be renewed as an assembly.

22 Check the condition of the connecting rod bearing cap nuts and bolts by screwing each nut onto its original bolt. Use only your fingers, make sure that the nuts screw fully onto their respective bolt with no sign of roughness or binding. If there is any damage to the threads, both the nut and bolt should be renewed. Tap the old bolt out from the

connecting rod and install the new ones, making sure the arrow on the bolt head is pointing outwards (away from the connecting rod).

2.0 litre diesel engine

23 Carry out the checks described in paragraphs 7 to 9.

24 Measure the piston diameter at right angles to the gudgeon pin axis, 44 mm up from the base of the piston skirt, and compare the results with the Specifications at the beginning of this Chapter. **Note:** *The piston diameter should be measured in the exposed circular area left in the graphite coating on the front and rear of the piston* **(see illustration)**.

25 To measure the piston-to-bore clearance, measure the bore diameter at right-angles to the crankshaft axis, 70 mm down from the top of the bore (see Section 12). Calculate the clearance by subtracting the piston diameter from the bore measurement. Alternatively, invert the piston and fit it into its original bore so that the arrow on the piston crown is facing towards the flywheel end of the engine. Position the piston so that the base of its skirt is 25 mm down from the top of the bore then select a feeler blade and slip it into the bore along with the piston. The piston must be aligned exactly in its normal attitude, and the feeler blade must be between the piston and bore, on one of the thrust faces, approximately 70 mm down from the top of the bore **(see illustration 13.18)**. If the clearance is excessive, a new piston will be

required. If the piston binds at the lower end of the bore and is loose towards the top, the bore is tapered. If tight spots are encountered as the piston/feeler blade is rotated in the bore, the bore is out-of-round.

26 Repeat this procedure for the remaining pistons and cylinder bores. Any piston which is worn beyond the specified limits must be renewed.

27 Examine each connecting rod carefully for signs of damage, such as cracks around the big-end and small-end bearings. Check that the rod is not bent or distorted. Damage is highly unlikely, unless the engine has been seized or badly overheated. Detailed checking of the connecting rod assembly can only be carried out by a Rover dealer or engine repair specialist with the necessary equipment. The pistons and connecting rods can be separated as follows.

28 Using circlip pliers, remove the circlips from the piston then push out the gudgeon pin **(see illustrations)**. Hand pressure should be sufficient to remove the pin. Identify the piston and rod to ensure correct reassembly. Discard the circlips - new ones *must* be used on refitting.

29 Examine the gudgeon pin and connecting rod small-end bearing for signs of wear or damage. Wear will require the renewal of both the pin and connecting rod.

30 The connecting rods themselves should not be in need of renewal, unless seizure or some other major mechanical failure has occurred. Check the alignment of the connecting rods visually, and if the rods are not straight, take them to an engine overhaul specialist for a more detailed check.

31 Examine all components, and obtain any new parts from your Rover dealer. If new pistons are purchased, they will be supplied complete with gudgeon pins and circlips. Circlips can also be purchased individually.

32 On early engines (where the big-end caps are retained by nuts and bolts), assemble the piston and connecting rod so that the big-end bearing shell locating cut-out on the connecting rod is positioned on the left-hand side of the arrow on the piston crown when the piston is viewed from the left-hand (flywheel) end **(see illustrations)**.

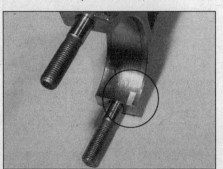

13.32a On early engines position the connecting rod so the bearing shell locating cut-out . . .

13.32b . . . is on the left-hand side of the arrow on the piston crown when the piston is viewed from the left-hand (flywheel) end

14.2 Using a dial gauge to measure crankshaft endfloat (2.0 litre petrol engine shown)

14.3 Using feeler blades to measure crankshaft endfloat (2.0 litre petrol engine shown)

14.10 Measuring a crankshaft main bearing journal diameter

33 On later engines (where the big-end caps are retained by bolts), assemble the piston and connecting rod so that the arrow on the piston crown is pointing towards from the assembly mark/boss which is cast onto one side of the connecting rod.

34 On all engines, apply a smear of clean engine oil to the gudgeon pin. Slide it into the piston and through the connecting rod small-end. Check that the piston pivots freely on the rod, then secure the gudgeon pin in position with two new circlips, ensuring that each circlip is correctly located in its groove in the piston.

35 On early engines, check the condition of the connecting rod big-end cap nuts and bolts as described in paragraph 22, renewing them as necessary.

36 On later engines, check the condition of the connecting rod big-end bearing cap bolts as described in paragraph 15, renewing them as necessary.

14 Crankshaft - inspection

Checking crankshaft endfloat

1 If the crankshaft endfloat is to be checked, this must be done when the crankshaft is still installed in the cylinder block, but is free to move (see Section 11).

2 Check the endfloat using a dial gauge in contact with the end of the crankshaft. Push the crankshaft fully one way, and then zero the gauge. Push the crankshaft fully the other way, and check the endfloat **(see illustration)**. The result can be compared with the specified amount, and will give an indication as to whether new thrustwasher halves are required.

3 If a dial gauge is not available, feeler blades can be used. First push the crankshaft fully towards the flywheel end of the engine, then use feeler blades to measure the gap between the web of the crankpin and the side of thrustwasher **(see illustration)**. On 2.0 litre petrol engines thrustwashers are fitted to the sides of the upper and lower centre (No 3) main bearing shells, whereas on all other engines the thrustwashers are only fitted to the sides of the upper centre (No 3) main bearing shell.

Inspection

4 Clean the crankshaft using paraffin or a suitable solvent, and dry it, preferably with compressed air if available. Be sure to clean the oil holes with a pipe cleaner or similar probe, to ensure that they are not obstructed.

⚠️ **Warning: Wear eye protection when using compressed air.**

5 Check the main and big-end bearing journals for uneven wear, scoring, pitting and cracking.

6 Big-end bearing wear is accompanied by distinct metallic knocking when the engine is running (particularly noticeable when the engine is pulling from low speed) and some loss of oil pressure.

7 Main bearing wear is accompanied by severe engine vibration and rumble - getting progressively worse as engine speed increases - and again by loss of oil pressure.

8 Check the bearing journal for roughness by running a finger lightly over the bearing surface. Any roughness (which will be accompanied by obvious bearing wear) indicates that the crankshaft requires regrinding (where possible) or renewal.

9 Check for burrs around the crankshaft oil holes (the holes are usually chamfered, so burrs should not be a problem unless regrinding has been carried out carelessly). Remove any burrs with a fine file or scraper, and thoroughly clean the oil holes as described previously.

10 Using a micrometer, measure the diameter of the main and big-end bearing journals (see Sections 18 and 19 for size group marking information on 1.4 and 1.6 litre engines), and compare the results with the Specifications **(see illustration)**. By measuring the diameter at a number of points around each journal's circumference, you will be able to determine whether or not the journal is out-of-round. Take the measurement at each end of the journal, near the webs, to determine if the journal is tapered. Compare the results obtained with those given in the Specifications.

11 Check the oil seal contact surfaces at each end of the crankshaft for wear and damage. If the seal has worn a deep groove in the surface of the crankshaft, consult an engine overhaul specialist; repair may be possible, but otherwise a new crankshaft will be required.

12 At the time of writing, it appeared that Rover do not produce undersize bearing shells for any of these engines. Therefore, if the crankshaft has worn beyond the specified limits, it will have to be renewed. Consult your Rover dealer or engine specialist for further information on parts availability.

13 Carefully inspect the main bearing ladder/cap bolts (as applicable) and renew any bolt which shows signs of damage.

15 Main and big-end bearings - inspection

1 Even though the main and big-end bearings should be renewed during the engine overhaul, the old bearings should be retained for close examination, as they may reveal valuable information about the condition of the engine.

2 Bearing failure can occur due to lack of lubrication, the presence of dirt or other foreign particles, overloading the engine, or corrosion **(see illustration)**. Regardless of the

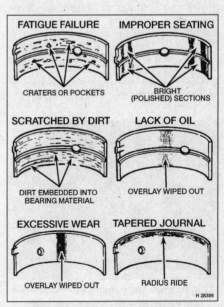

15.2 Typical bearing shell failures

2D

cause of bearing failure, the cause must be corrected (where applicable) before the engine is reassembled, to prevent it from happening again.

3 When examining the bearing shells, remove them from the cylinder block, the main bearing caps, the connecting rods and the connecting rod big-end bearing caps. Lay them out on a clean surface in the same general position as their location in the engine. This will enable you to match any bearing problems with the corresponding crankshaft journal.

4 Dirt and other foreign matter gets into the engine in a variety of ways. It may be left in the engine during assembly, or it may pass through filters or the crankcase ventilation system. It may get into the oil, and from there into the bearings. Metal chips from machining operations and normal engine wear are often present. Abrasives are sometimes left in engine components after reconditioning, especially when parts are not thoroughly cleaned using the proper cleaning methods. Whatever the source, these foreign objects often end up embedded in the soft bearing material, and are easily recognised. Large particles will not embed in the bearing, and will score or gouge the bearing and journal. The best prevention for this cause of bearing failure is to clean all parts thoroughly, and keep everything spotlessly-clean during engine assembly. Frequent and regular engine oil and filter changes are also recommended.

5 Lack of lubrication (or lubrication breakdown) has a number of interrelated causes. Excessive heat (which thins the oil), overloading (which squeezes the oil from the bearing face) and oil leakage (from excessive bearing clearances, worn oil pump or high engine speeds) all contribute to lubrication breakdown. Blocked oil passages, which usually are the result of misaligned oil holes in a bearing shell, will also oil-starve a bearing, and destroy it. When lack of lubrication is the cause of bearing failure, the bearing material is wiped or extruded from the steel backing of the bearing. Temperatures may increase to the point where the steel backing turns blue from overheating.

6 Driving habits can have a definite effect on bearing life. Full-throttle, low-speed operation

(labouring the engine) puts very high loads on bearings, tending to squeeze out the oil film. These loads cause the bearings to flex, which produces fine cracks in the bearing face (fatigue failure). Eventually, the bearing material will loosen in pieces, and tear away from the steel backing.

7 Short-distance driving leads to corrosion of bearings, because insufficient engine heat is produced to drive off the condensed water and corrosive gases. These products collect in the engine oil, forming acid and sludge. As the oil is carried to the engine bearings, the acid attacks and corrodes the bearing material.

8 Incorrect bearing installation during engine assembly will lead to bearing failure as well. Tight-fitting bearings leave insufficient bearing running clearance, and will result in oil starvation. Dirt or foreign particles trapped behind a bearing shell result in high spots on the bearing, which lead to failure.

9 As mentioned at the beginning of this Section, the bearing shells should be renewed as a matter of course during engine overhaul; to do otherwise is false economy.

16 Engine overhaul - reassembly sequence

Note: *Rover produce a sealant kit which consists of a plastic scraper, gasket removing compound and the recommended sealant for the main bearing ladder joint. It is recommended that this kit is used during reassembly.*

1 Before reassembly begins, ensure that all new parts have been obtained, and that all necessary tools are available. Read through the entire procedure to familiarise yourself with the work involved, and to ensure that all items necessary for reassembly of the engine are at hand. In addition to all normal tools and materials, thread-locking compound will be needed. A good quality tube of liquid sealant will also be required for the joint faces that are fitted without gaskets.

2 In order to save time and avoid problems, engine reassembly can be carried out in the following order:
- a) Crankshaft.
- b) Piston/connecting rod assemblies.
- c) Oil pump.
- d) Sump.
- e) Flywheel.
- f) Cylinder head.
- g) Timing belt tensioner and sprockets, and belts.
- h) Inlet and exhaust manifolds (Chapter 4).
- i) Fuel injection pump sprockets, tensioner and belt - diesel engine only.
- j) Engine external components.

3 At this stage, all engine components should be absolutely clean and dry, with all faults repaired. The components should be laid out (or in individual containers) on a completely clean work surface.

17 Piston rings - refitting

1 Before fitting new piston rings, the ring end gaps must be checked as follows.

2 Lay out the piston/connecting rod assemblies and the new piston ring sets, so that the ring sets will be matched with the same piston and cylinder during the end gap measurement and subsequent engine reassembly.

3 Insert the top ring into the first cylinder, and push it down the bore using the top of the piston. This will ensure that the ring remains square with the cylinder walls. Push the ring down into the bore until it is positioned 20 mm down from the top edge of the bore on petrol engines, and 30 mm down from the top of the bore on diesel engines. Withdraw the piston.

4 Measure the end gap using feeler blades, and compare the measurements with the figures given in the Specifications **(see illustration)**.

5 If the gap is too small (unlikely if genuine Rover parts are used), it must be enlarged, or the ring ends may contact each other during engine operation, causing serious damage. Ideally, new piston rings providing the correct end gap should be fitted. As a last resort, the end gap can be increased by filing the ring ends very carefully with a fine file. Mount the file in a vice with soft jaws, slip the ring over the file with the ends contacting the file face, and slowly move the ring to remove material from the ends. Take care, as piston rings are sharp, and are easily broken.

6 With new piston rings, it is unlikely that the end gap will be too large. If the gaps are too large, check that you have the correct rings for your engine and for the particular cylinder bore size.

7 Repeat the checking procedure for each ring in the first cylinder, and then for the rings in the remaining cylinders. Remember to keep rings, pistons and cylinders matched up.

8 Once the ring end gaps have been checked and if necessary corrected, the rings can be fitted to the pistons as follows, using the same technique as for removal.

1.4 and 1.6 litre engine

9 Fit the oil control ring expander first (it will be easier if the end gap is correctly positioned at this point), then fit the ring, making sure its identification ("TOP") marking is uppermost **(see illustration)**. The second and top rings are different and can be identified by their cross-sections. Fit the second and top compression rings ensuring that each ring is fitted the correct way up with its identification ("TOP") mark uppermost. **Note:** *Always follow any instructions supplied with the new piston ring sets - different manufacturers may specify different procedures. Do not mix up the top and second compression rings.*

17.4 Position the pin ring as described in text then measure the end gap using feeler blades

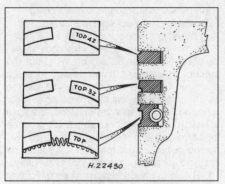

17.9 Piston ring identification - 1.4 and 1.6 litre petrol engine

10 Check that each ring is free to rotate easily in its groove, then measure the ring-to-groove clearance of each ring, using feeler blades. If the clearance is within the specified range, position the ring end gaps as shown **(see illustration)**.

2.0 litre petrol engine

11 Fit the oil control ring spacer first then install both the side rails, noting that both the spacer and side rails can be installed either way up **(see illustrations)**. The second and top compression rings are different and can be identified by their cross-sections.
12 The top ring is square whilst the second

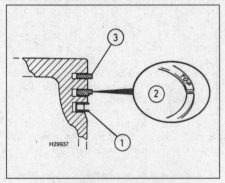

17.12 Piston ring identification - 2.0 litre petrol engine

1 Oil control ring
2 Second compression ring
3 Top compression ring

17.13a Measuring piston ring-to-groove side clearance

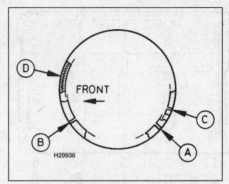

17.10 Piston ring end gap locations - 1.4 and 1.6 litre petrol engine

A Top compression ring
B Second compression ring
C Oil control ring
D Oil control ring expander

ring is stepped **(see illustration)**. Fit the second compression ring to the piston, ensuring it is fitted the correct way up with its identification ("TOP") mark uppermost, then install the top ring; the top ring has no identification marking and can be fitted either way up. **Note:** *Always follow any instructions supplied with the new piston ring sets - different manufacturers may specify different procedures. Do not mix up the top and second compression rings. On some engines the top ring will not have an identification marking and can be fitted either way up.*
13 With the piston rings correctly installed, check that each ring is free to rotate easily in its groove, then measure the ring-to-groove clearance of each ring, using feeler blades. If the clearance is within the specified range, position the ring end gaps as shown **(see illustrations)**.

2.0 litre diesel engine

14 Fit the oil control ring expander first then carefully fit the ring to the piston, the ring has no identification marking and can be fitted either way up.

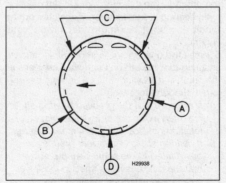

17.13b Piston ring end gap locations - 2.0 litre petrol engine

A Top compression ring
B Second compression ring
C Oil control ring side rails
D Oil control ring spacer

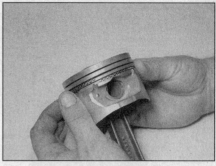

17.11a On 2.0 litre petrol engines, fit the oil control ring spacer . . .

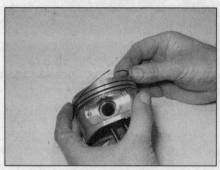

17.11b . . . then install the side rails

15 The second and top rings are different and can be identified by their cross-sections **(see illustration)**. Fit the second and top compression rings ensuring that each ring is fitted the correct way up with its identification ("TOP") mark uppermost. **Note:** *Always follow any instructions supplied with the new piston ring sets - different manufacturers may specify different procedures. Do not mix up the top and second compression rings.*
16 Check that each ring is free to rotate easily in its groove, then measure the ring-to-groove clearance of each ring, using feeler blades. If the clearance is within the specified range, space the ring end gaps at 120° intervals making sure no end gap is in line with the piston thrust (front and rear) faces.

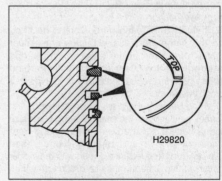

17.15 Piston ring identification - 2.0 litre diesel engine

1 Oil control ring
2 Second compression ring
3 Top compression ring

2D

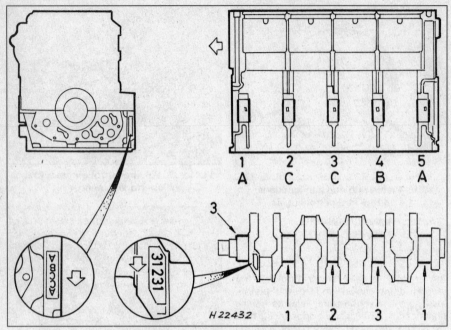

18.3 Crankshaft and cylinder block main bearing size group code locations - 1.4 and 1.6 litre petrol engine

18 Crankshaft -
refitting and main bearing clearance check

Note: *It is recommended that new main bearing shells are fitted regardless of the condition of the original ones.*

1.4 and 1.6 litre engine

Selection of bearing shells

1 The main bearing running clearance is controlled in production by selecting one of three grades of bearing shell. The grades are indicated by a colour-coding marked on the edge of each shell which governs the shell's thickness, as follows:
  a) *Green - Thin.*
  b) *Blue - Intermediate.*
  c) *Red - Thick.*

2 If shells of differing grades are to be fitted to the same journal, the thicker shell must always be fitted in the lower (main bearing ladder) location. Bear this carefully in mind when ordering replacement shells for Nos 2, 3 and 4 bearings.

3 If the bearing shells are to be renewed, first check and record the main bearing bore size group letters stamped on the right-hand front face of the main bearing ladder **(see illustration)**. The letters are read with the ladder inverted, No 1 bearing's size group letter then being at the top and the remainder following in order from the engine's timing belt end.

4 Secondly, check and record the crankshaft journal size group numbers stamped on the crankshaft's right-hand web, No 1 journal's code number being the first.

5 Match the relevant main bearing bore size group letter with its crankshaft journal size group number, and select a new set of bearing shells using the table at the foot of this page. The crankshaft numbers are listed down the left-hand side, and the main bearing bore letters along the top; the required grades are indicated where the two columns intersect.

Main bearing running clearance check

6 Clean the backs of the bearing shells and the bearing locations in both the cylinder block/crankcase and the main bearing ladder.

7 Press the bearing shells into their locations, ensuring that the tab on each shell engages in the notch in the cylinder block/crankcase or main bearing ladder location. Take care not to touch any shell bearing surface with your fingers.

8 Press the bearing shells into their locations, ensuring that the tab on each shell engages in the notch in the cylinder block or main bearing cap, noting the following
  a) *Make sure that the grooved bearing shells are fitted in the upper (cylinder block) locations of Nos 2, 3 and 4 main bearings.*
  b) *If bearing shells of different grades are being fitted to the same bearing, ensure that the thicker shell is fitted in the lower (main bearing ladder) location (see paragraph 1).*

  c) *If the original bearing shells are being used for the check ensure they are refitted in their original locations.*

9 The main bearing running clearance should be checked if there is any doubt about the amount of crankshaft wear that has taken place, or if non-genuine bearing shells are to be fitted. If the original crankshaft or a Rover replacement part is to be installed, the shell selection procedure given above will produce the correct clearances and a further check will not be necessary. If the clearance is to be checked, it can be done in either of two ways.

10 The first method (which will be difficult to achieve without a range of internal micrometers or internal/external expanding calipers) is to refit the main bearing ladder to the cylinder block/crankcase, with bearing shells in place. With the ladder retaining bolts tightened to the specified torque, refit the oil rail and the cylinder head, then measure the internal diameter of each assembled pair of bearing shells. If the diameter of each corresponding crankshaft journal is measured and then subtracted from the bearing internal diameter, the result will be the main bearing running clearance.

11 The second (and more accurate) method is to use product known as Plastigauge. This consists of a fine thread of perfectly round plastic which is compressed between the bearing shell and the journal. When the shell is removed, the plastic is deformed and can be measured with a special card gauge supplied with the kit. The running clearance is determined from this gauge. Plastigauge is sometimes difficult to obtain but enquiries at one of the larger specialist quality motor factors should produce the name of a stockist in your area. The procedure for using Plastigauge is as follows.

12 With the main bearing upper shells in place, carefully lay the crankshaft in position. Do not use any lubricant. The crankshaft journals and bearing shells must be perfectly clean and dry.

13 Cut several lengths of the appropriate size Plastigauge (they should be slightly shorter than the width of the main bearings) and place one length on each crankshaft journal axis **(see illustration)**.

18.13 Lay the length of Plastigauge on the journal to be measured, parallel to the crankshaft centre-line

	Size group A		Size group B		Size group C	
Size group 1	Blue - Blue		Blue - Green		Green - Green	
Size group 2	Red - Blue		Blue - Blue		Blue - Green	
Size group 3	Red - Red		Red - Blue		Blue - Blue	

18.17 Measure the width of the deformed Plastigauge using the scale on the card supplied

18.24a Tighten the big-end bearing cap bolts to the specified stage 1 torque . . .

18.24b . . . and then through the specified stage 2 angle

14 With the main bearing lower shells in position, refit the main bearing ladder (see below) and the oil rail, tightening the fasteners to the specified torque wrench settings. Take care not to disturb the Plastigauge.

15 Referring to Part A of this Chapter, refit the cylinder head (use the original gasket), tightening the bolts to the specified torque and then through the specified angles in the specified sequence. **Do not** rotate the crankshaft at any time during this operation.

16 Remove the cylinder head, the oil rail and the main bearing ladder. Do not disturb the Plastigauge or rotate the crankshaft.

17 Compare the width of the crushed Plastigauge on each journal to the scale printed on the Plastigauge envelope to obtain the main bearing running clearance **(see illustration)**.

18 If the clearance is not as specified, the bearing shells may be the wrong grade (or excessively worn if the original shells are being re-used). Before deciding that different grade shells are needed, make sure that no dirt or oil was trapped between the bearing shells and the ladder or cylinder block/crankcase when the clearance was measured. If the Plastigauge was wider at one end than at the other, the journal may be tapered.

19 Carefully scrape away all traces of the Plastigauge material from the crankshaft and bearing shells using a fingernail or other object which is unlikely to score the shells.

Final crankshaft refitting

20 Carefully lift the crankshaft out of the cylinder block once more.

21 Using a little grease, stick the thrustwashers to each side of the centre (No 3) main bearing upper location. Ensure that the oilway grooves on each thrustwasher face outwards.

22 Place the bearing shells in their locations, as described in paragraphs 6 to 8. If new shells are being fitted, ensure that all traces of the protective grease are cleaned off using paraffin. Wipe dry the shells and connecting rods with a lint-free cloth.

23 Liberally lubricate each bearing shell in the cylinder block/crankcase, then lower the crankshaft into position. Check the crankshaft endfloat as described in Section 14.

24 Refit the piston/connecting rod assemblies to the crankshaft as described in Section 19 and position the crankshaft so the pistons are half-way up the bores **(see illustrations)**.

25 Thoroughly degrease the mating surfaces of the cylinder block and the main bearing ladder. Apply a continuous bead of sealant to the mating surface of the cylinder block/crankcase as shown then spread the sealant to an even film **(see illustration)**. Carefully follow the instructions supplied with the sealant.

26 Ensure the lower bearing shells are correctly fitted to the bearing ladder and lubricate them with clean engine oil.

27 Ensure the locating dowels are in position then refit the main bearing ladder to the cylinder block, taking care to ensure that the shells are not displaced. Once the ladder is correctly located on the dowels, refit the retaining bolts, tightening them all by hand only.

28 Working in the specified sequence, go around and tighten all bolts to the specified stage 1 torque setting then go around again in the specified sequence and tighten them to the specified stage 2 torque setting **(see illustration)**. **Note:** *The crankshaft cannot now be rotated until the cylinder head has been refitted.*

29 Thoroughly degrease the mating surfaces of the oil rail and the main bearing ladder. Apply sealant to the oil rail mating surface as shown **(see illustration)**.

30 Refit the oil rail to the main bearing ladder and tighten its retaining nuts to the specified torque.

31 Refit the dipstick tube, using a new gasket, and securely tighten its retaining bolts.

32 Working as described in Part A of this Chapter, carry out the following procedures in order.

a) *Refit the oil pump, pick-up/strainer and sump.*
b) *Fit a new left-hand oil seal to the crankshaft and refit the flywheel.*
c) *Refit the cylinder head and camshaft(s).*
d) *Refit the timing belt sprockets and belt.*

33 On completion, remove the spark plugs then fit a torque wrench to the crankshaft pulley bolt and rotate the crankshaft in the normal direction of rotation. The crankshaft must rotate smoothly, without any sign of

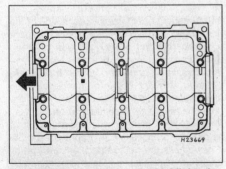

18.25 Apply sealant to the highlighted areas (shown by thick lines) of the cylinder block/bearing ladder mating surface as shown

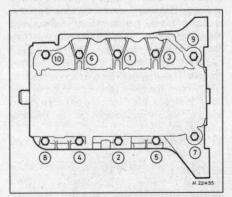

18.28 Crankshaft main bearing ladder bolt tightening sequence

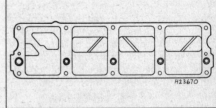

18.29 Apply sealant to the highlighted areas (shown by thick black lines) of the oil rail

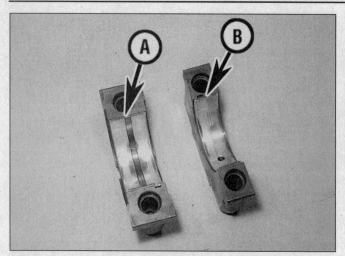

18.36a Ensure the grooved bearing shells (A) are fitted to Nos 1, 3 and 5 bearings and the plain shells (B) to Nos 2 and 4

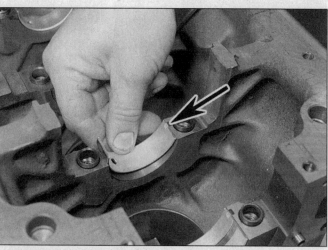

18.36b Fit the bearing shells making sure their locating tabs are correctly located in the slots (arrowed)

binding, and the amount of force required to rotate the crankshaft should not exceed 31 Nm. If the effort required is greater than this, the engine should be dismantled again to trace and rectify the cause. This value takes into account the increased friction of a new engine and is much higher than the actual pressure required to rotate a run-in engine, so do not make allowances for tight components.

2.0 litre petrol engine

Selection of bearing shells

34 On these engines all the bearing shells are of the same thickness. Rover only produce standard size bearing shells; no undersize shells are available for use with a re-ground crankshaft. Consult your Rover dealer or engine specialist for further information on parts availability.

Main bearing running clearance check

35 Clean the backs of the bearing shells and the bearing locations in both the cylinder block and the main bearing caps.
36 Press the bearing shells into their locations, ensuring that the tab on each shell engages in the notch in the cylinder block or main bearing cap. Fit the grooved bearing shells to Nos 1, 3 and 5 bearings and the plain bearing shells to Nos 2 and 4 bearings **(see illustrations)**. If the original bearing shells are being used for the check ensure they are refitted in their original locations. The clearance can be checked in either of two ways.
37 One method (which will be difficult to achieve without a range of internal micrometers or internal/external expanding calipers) is to refit the main bearing caps to the cylinder block, with bearing shells in place. With the cap retaining bolts correctly tightened, measure the internal diameter of each assembled pair of bearing shells. If the diameter of each corresponding crankshaft journal is measured and then subtracted from the bearing internal diameter, the result will be the main bearing running clearance.

38 The second (and more accurate) method is to use a product known as Plastigauge. This consists of a fine thread of perfectly round plastic which is compressed between the bearing shell and the journal. When the shell is removed, the plastic is deformed and can be measured with a special card gauge supplied with the kit. The running clearance is determined from this gauge. Plastigauge is sometimes difficult to obtain but enquiries at one of the larger specialist quality motor factors should produce the name of a stockist in your area. The procedure for using Plastigauge is as follows.
39 With the main bearing upper shells in place, carefully lay the crankshaft in position. Do not use any lubricant; the crankshaft journals and bearing shells must be perfectly clean and dry.
40 Cut several lengths of the appropriate size Plastigauge (they should be slightly shorter than the width of the main bearings) and place one length on each crankshaft journal axis **(see illustration 18.13)**.
41 With the main bearing lower shells in position, ensure the locating dowels are correctly fitted, then refit the main bearing caps. Use the identification marks to ensure each cap is correctly positioned then refit the retaining bolts, tighten them evenly and progressively to the specified torque. Take care not to disturb the Plastigauge and **do not** rotate the crankshaft at any time during this operation. Evenly and progressively slacken and remove the main bearing cap bolts then lift off the caps again taking great care not to disturb the Plastigauge or rotate the crankshaft.
42 Compare the width of the crushed Plastigauge on each journal to the scale printed on the Plastigauge envelope to obtain the main bearing running clearance **(see illustration 18.17)**. Compare the clearance measured with that given in the Specifications at the start of this Chapter.

43 If the clearance is significantly different from that expected, the bearing shells may be the wrong size (if non-genuine shells are fitted), or excessively worn if the original shells are being re-used. Before deciding that the crankshaft is worn, make sure that no dirt or oil was trapped between the bearing shells and the caps or block when the clearance was measured. If the Plastigauge was wider at one end than at the other, the crankshaft journal may be tapered.
44 Before condemning the components concerned, seek the advice of your Rover dealer or suitable engine repair specialist. They will also be able to inform as to the best course of action or whether renewal will be necessary.
45 Where necessary, obtain new bearing shells and repeat the running clearance checking procedure as described above.
46 On completion, carefully scrape away all traces of the Plastigauge material from the crankshaft and bearing shells using a fingernail or other object which is unlikely to score the bearing surfaces.

Final crankshaft refitting

47 Carefully lift the crankshaft out of the cylinder block once more.
48 Using a little grease, stick the thrustwasher upper halves to each side of the centre (No 3) main bearing upper location, ensuring that the oilway grooves on each thrustwasher face outwards. **Note:** *The thrustwasher upper and lower halves are different and are not interchangeable; the lower halves have locating tabs where as the upper halves do not* **(see illustrations)**.
49 Place the bearing shells in their locations as described above in paragraphs 35 and 36. If new shells are being fitted, ensure that all traces of the protective grease are cleaned off using paraffin. Wipe dry the shells and caps with a lint-free cloth. Lubricate the upper shells with clean engine oil then lower the crankshaft into position **(see illustrations)**.

18.48a Smear grease over the rear of each thrustwasher . . .

18.48b . . . and stick the upper halves to the cylinder block making sure the oil grooves (arrowed) are facing outwards

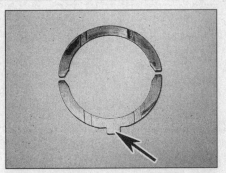

18.48c The upper and lower thrustwasher halves are different; the lower halves have locating tabs (arrowed)

50 Ensure the bearing shells are correctly located in the caps and all locating dowels are in position.

51 Using a little grease, stick the thrustwasher lower halves to each side of the centre (No 3) main bearing cap, ensuring that the oilway grooves on each thrustwasher face outwards. Ensure the locating tab of each thrustwasher is correctly seated in the cap groove **(see illustration)**.

52 Refit the caps to the cylinder block, ensuring each cap is fitted in their original location. No1 cap should be at the at the timing belt end and all caps must be fitted the correct way around so that the arrow on each cap points towards the timing belt end of the engine **(see illustration)**.

53 Apply a smear of clean engine to oil to the threads and underneath the heads of the main bearing cap bolts **(see illustration)**. Fit the bolts tightening them all by hand.

54 Working in a diagonal sequence from the centre outwards, tighten the main bearing cap bolts evenly and progressively to the specified torque setting.

55 Check that the crankshaft is free to rotate smoothly; if excessive pressure is required to turn the crankshaft, investigate the cause before proceeding further.

56 Check the crankshaft endfloat as described in Section 14.

57 Refit/reconnect the piston connecting rod assemblies to the crankshaft as described in Section 19.

18.49a Lubricate the upper bearing shells . . .

58 Referring to Part B, fit a new left-hand oil crankshaft oil seal then refit the flywheel, oil pump, cylinder head, timing belt sprockets and fit a new timing belt.

2.0 litre diesel engine

Selection of bearing shells

59 On these engines all the bearing shells are of the same thickness. Rover only produce standard size bearing shells; no undersize shells are available for use with a re-ground crankshaft. Consult your Rover dealer or engine specialist for further information on parts availability.

Main bearing running clearance check

60 Clean the backs of the bearing shells and the bearing locations in both the cylinder block and the main bearing caps.

18.49b . . . then lower the crankshaft into position

61 Press the bearing shells into their locations, ensuring that the tab on each shell engages in the notch in the cylinder block or main bearing cap; on shells with no locating tab, ensure the shell is positioned centrally. Fit the grooved bearing shells in the upper (cylinder block) locations and fit the plain shells in the lower (bearing cap) locations **(see illustrations)**. If the original bearing shells are being used, ensure they are refitted in their original locations. The clearance can be checked in either of two ways.

62 Check the running clearance as described in paragraphs 37 to 46.

Final crankshaft refitting

63 Carefully lift the crankshaft out of the cylinder block once more.

2D

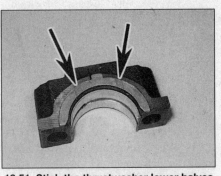

18.51 Stick the thrustwasher lower halves to the centre main bearing cap ensuring the oil grooves are facing outwards

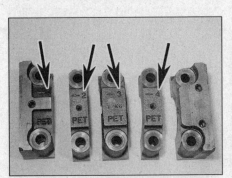

18.52 Use the identification markings on the main bearing caps to ensure they are correctly fitted

18.53 Lubricate the threads and underside of the heads of the main bearing bolts prior to installation

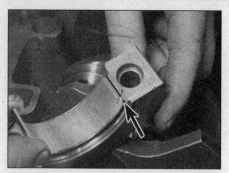

18.61a Fit the plain bearing shells to the bearing caps (locating tab cutout arrowed) . . .

18.61b . . . and the grooved bearing shells to the cylinder block

18.61c Where the bearing shells have no locating tabs, ensure the shells are position centrally in the cap/block

64 Using a little grease, stick the thrustwasher halves to each side of the centre (No 3) main bearing upper location, ensuring that the oilway grooves on each thrustwasher face outwards **(see illustration)**.

65 Place the bearing shells in their locations as described above in paragraphs 60 and 61. If new shells are being fitted, ensure that all traces of the protective grease are cleaned off using paraffin. Wipe dry the shells and caps with a lint-free cloth.

66 Lubricate the upper shells with clean engine oil then lower the crankshaft into position **(see illustration)**.

67 Ensure the bearing shells are correctly located in the caps and all locating dowels are in position. Refit the caps to the cylinder block. Ensure the caps are fitted in their

correct locations, with number 1 cap at the timing belt end, and are fitted the correct way around so that the arrow on each cap points towards the timing belt end of the engine.

68 Apply a smear of clean engine to oil to the threads and underneath the heads of the main bearing cap bolts **(see illustration)**. Fit the bolts tightening them all by hand.

69 Working in a diagonal sequence from the centre outwards, tighten the main bearing cap bolts evenly and progressively to the specified torque setting **(see illustration)**.

70 Check that the crankshaft is free to rotate smoothly; if excessive pressure is required to turn the crankshaft, investigate the cause before proceeding further.

71 Check the crankshaft endfloat as described in Section 14.

72 Refit/reconnect the piston connecting rod assemblies to the crankshaft as described in Section 19.

73 Working as described in Part C of this Chapter, carry out the following procedures in order.

  a) Refit the oil pump.
  b) Oil pump pick-up/strainer and sump. Ensure the grooves of No1 main bearing cap are completely filled with sealant, prior to refitting the sump.
  c) Fit a new left-hand oil seal to the crankshaft and refit the flywheel.
  d) Refit the cylinder head and camshaft.
  e) Refit the timing belt sprockets and belt.

19 Piston/connecting rod assembly - refitting and big-end clearance check

Note: *It is recommended that new piston rings and big-end bearing shells are fitted regardless of the condition of the original ones. On the 2.0 litre diesel engine Rover state that new big-end shells must be used.*

1.4 and 1.6 litre engine

Selection of bearing shells

1 The big-end bearing running clearance is controlled in production by selecting one of three grades of bearing shell. The grades are indicated by a colour-coding marked on the edge of each shell which governs the shell's thickness, as follows:

  a) Yellow - Thin.
  b) Blue - Intermediate.
  c) Red - Thick.

2 If shells of differing grades are to be fitted to the same journal, the thicker shell must always be fitted to the big-end bearing cap location.

3 If the bearing shells are to be renewed, first check and record the size group number stamped on the front face of each big-end bearing cap and connecting rod. The number stamped on the big-end bearing cap is the bearing size group code, the number stamped on the connecting rod is the piston/rod

18.64 Ensure that the thrustwasher halves are fitted with their oil grooves (arrowed) facing outwards

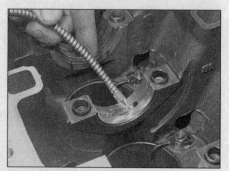

18.66 Lubricate the upper shells with clean engine oil prior to refitting the crankshaft

18.68 Lubricate the threads and underside of the heads of the main bearing cap bolts with a smear of oil prior to refitting

18.69 Tighten the main bearing cap bolts to the specified torque as described in text

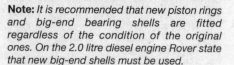

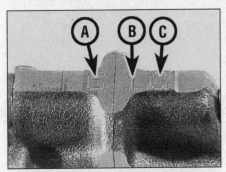

19.3 Connecting rod/bearing cap markings - 1.4 and 1.6 litre petrol engine

A *Big-end bearing size group number*
B *Cylinder number*
C *Connecting rod weight group*

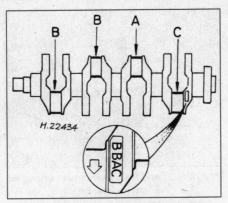

19.4 Crankshaft big-end (crankpin) journal size group letters - 1.4 and 1.6 litre petrol engines

H.22434

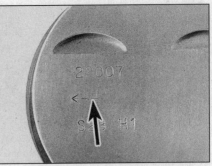

19.15a Arrow (or FRONT marking) (arrowed) on piston crown must point to the timing belt end of the engine

assembly's cylinder number and the letter stamped on the connecting rod is the weight code **(see illustration)**.

4 Secondly, check and record the crankpin/big-end journal size group code letters stamped on the crankshaft's left-hand (flywheel end) web **(see illustration)**, No 1 journal's code letter being the first.

5 Match the relevant connecting rod bore size group number with its crankshaft journal size group letter, and select a new set of bearing shells using the table at the foot of the page. The connecting rod bearing bore numbers are listed down the left-hand side, and the crankshaft journal letters along the top; the required bearing grades are indicated where the two columns intersect.

Big-end bearing running clearance check

6 The big-end bearing running clearance should be checked if there is any doubt about the amount of crankshaft wear that has taken place, or if non-genuine bearing shells are to be fitted. If the original crankshaft or a Rover replacement part is to be installed, the shell selection procedure given above will produce the correct clearances and a further check will not be necessary. If the clearance is to be checked, it can be done in either of two ways.

7 The first method is to refit the big-end bearing cap to the connecting rod, with bearing shells in place. With the cap retaining bolts tightened to the specified torque and then through the specified angle (see paragraph 17), use an internal micrometer or vernier caliper to measure the internal diameter of each assembled pair of bearing shells. If the diameter of each corresponding crankshaft journal is measured and then subtracted from the bearing internal diameter, the result will be the big-end bearing running clearance.

8 The second method is to use Plastigauge (see Section 18). Place a strand of Plastigauge

on each (cleaned) crankpin journal and refit the (clean) piston/connecting rod assemblies, shells and big-end bearing caps, tightening the bolts to the specified torque setting and then through the specified angle (see paragraph 17). Take care not to disturb the Plastigauge. Dismantle the assemblies without rotating the crankshaft and use the scale printed on the Plastigauge envelope to obtain the big-end bearing running clearance. On completion of the measurement, carefully scrape off all traces of Plastigauge from the journal and shells using a fingernail or other object which will not score the components.

9 If the clearance is not as specified, the bearing shells may be the wrong grade (or excessively worn if the original shells are being re-used). Before deciding that different grade shells are needed, make sure that no dirt or oil was trapped between the bearing shells and the ladder or cylinder block/crankcase when the clearance was measured. If the Plastigauge was wider at one end than at the other, the journal may be tapered.

Final piston/connecting rod assembly refitting

10 Note that the following procedure assumes that the cylinder liners have been refitted to the cylinder block/crankcase and that the crankshaft and main bearing ladder are in place. It is of course possible to refit the piston/connecting rod assemblies to the cylinder bores, to refit the crankshaft and to reassemble the piston/connecting rods on the crankshaft before refitting the main bearing ladder (see Section 18).

11 Clean the backs of the bearing shells and the bearing recesses in both the connecting rod and the big-end bearing cap. If new shells are being fitted, ensure that all traces of the protective grease are cleaned off using paraffin. Wipe dry the shells and connecting rods with a lint-free cloth.

12 Press the bearing shells into their locations, ensuring that the tab on each shell engages in the notch in the connecting rod or big-end bearing cap and taking care not to touch any shell's bearing surface with your fingers. Note the following points:

a) If bearing shells of differing grades are to be fitted to the same connecting rod, the thicker shell must always be fitted in the lower (bearing cap) location (see paragraph 1).

b) If the original big-end bearing shells are being re-used, these must be refitted to their original locations in the connecting rod and big-end bearing cap.

13 Lubricate the cylinder bores, the pistons and piston rings, then lay out each piston/connecting rod assembly in its respective position.

14 Starting with assembly No 1, make sure that the piston rings are still correctly spaced (see Section 17) then clamp them in position with a piston ring compressor.

15 Insert the piston/connecting rod assembly into the top of liner No 1, ensuring that the arrow (or FRONT marking) on the piston crown faces the timing belt end of the engine. Note that the stamped marks on the connecting rod and big-end bearing cap should face the front of the engine **(see illustrations)**. Using a block of wood or hammer handle against the piston crown, tap the assembly into the liner until the piston crown is flush with the top of the liner.

16 Ensure that the bearing shell is still correctly installed. Taking care not to mark the

19.15b Using a piston ring compressor to refit a piston/connecting rod assembly

	Size group A			Size group B			Size group C	
Size group 5	Blue - Blue			Red - Blue			Red - Red	
Size group 6	Blue - Yellow			Blue - Blue			Red - Blue	
Size group 7	Yellow - Yellow			Blue - Yellow			Blue - Blue	

2D

19.17a Tighten the big-end bearing cap bolts to the specified stage 1 torque . . .

19.17b . . . and then through the specified stage 2 angle

liner bores, liberally lubricate the crankpin and both bearing shells, then pull the piston/connecting rod assembly down the bore and onto the crankpin. Noting that the faces with the stamped marks must match (which means that the bearing shell locating tabs abut each other), refit the big-end bearing cap, tightening the bolts finger-tight at first.

17 Evenly and progressively tighten the big-end bearing cap bolts to the specified stage 1 torque setting then angle-tighten each bolt through the specified stage 2 angle. It is recommended that an angle-measuring gauge is used during this stage of the tightening, to ensure accuracy (see illustrations).

18 Repeat the procedure for the remaining three piston/connecting rod assemblies, but do not attempt to rotate the crankshaft.

19 Ensure the mating surfaces of the oil rail and the main bearing ladder are clean and dry. Apply sealant to the areas of the oil rail mating surface shown in illustration 18.29.

20 Refit the oil rail to the main bearing ladder and tighten its retaining nuts to the specified torque.

21 Refit the dipstick tube, using a new gasket, and securely tighten its retaining bolts.

22 Working as described in Part A of this Chapter, carry out the following procedures in order.
a) Refit the oil pump pick-up/strainer and sump.
b) Refit the cylinder head and camshaft(s).
c) Refit the timing belt sprockets and belt.

23 On completion, remove the spark plugs then fit a torque wrench to the crankshaft pulley bolt and rotate the crankshaft in the normal direction of rotation. The crankshaft must rotate smoothly, without any sign of binding, and the amount of force required to rotate the crankshaft should not exceed 31 Nm. If the effort required is greater than this, the engine should be dismantled again to trace and rectify the cause. This value takes into account the increased friction of a new engine and is much higher than the actual pressure required to rotate a run-in engine, so do not make allowances for tight components.

2.0 litre engine

Selection of bearing shells

24 On these engines all the bearing shells are of the same thickness. Rover only produce standard size bearing shells; no undersize shells are available for use with a re-ground crankshaft. Consult your Rover dealer or engine specialist for further information on parts availability.

Big-end bearing running clearance check

25 The big-end bearing running clearance should be checked if there is any doubt about the amount of crankshaft wear that has taken place, or if non-genuine bearing shells are to be fitted. The clearance can be checked as described in paragraphs 7 to 9, noting that the big-end bearing cap nuts/bolts should be tightened as described in paragraphs 33 and 34.

Final piston/connecting rod assembly refitting

26 Clean the backs of the bearing shells and the bearing recesses in both the connecting rod and the big-end bearing cap. If new shells are being fitted, ensure that all traces of the protective grease are cleaned off using paraffin. Wipe dry the shells and connecting rods with a lint-free cloth.

27 Press the bearing shells into their locations, ensuring that the tab on each shell engages in the notch in the connecting rod or big-end bearing cap; on shells with no locating tab, ensure the shell is positioned centrally (see illustrations). If the original big-end bearing shells are being re-used, these must be refitted to their original locations in the connecting rod and big-end bearing cap.

28 Lubricate the bores, the pistons and piston rings then lay out each piston/connecting rod assembly in its respective position (see illustration).

29 Starting with assembly No 1, make sure that the piston rings are still spaced as described in Section 17, then clamp them in position with a piston ring compressor (see illustration).

19.27a If the bearing shells are equipped with locating tabs, ensure the tabs are correctly engaged with the cutouts in the cap/rod (arrowed)

19.27b Where the bearing shells have no locating tabs, ensure the shell is positioned centrally in the cap/rod

19.28 Lubricate the piston rings with clean engine oil

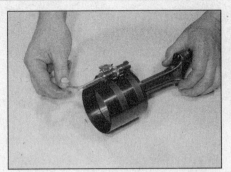

19.29 Ensure the ring gaps are correctly spaced then clamp them in position with the ring compressor

19.30 Ensure the arrow (arrowed) on the piston crown points towards the timing belt end of the engine

30 Insert the piston/connecting rod assembly into the top of cylinder No 1, ensuring that the arrow marking on the piston crown is pointing towards the timing belt end of the engine (see illustration). On diesel engines, the cut-out on the piston skirt should then be aligned with the oil spray jet in the cylinder block.

31 Using a block of wood or hammer handle against the piston crown, tap the assembly into the cylinder until the piston crown is flush with the top of the cylinder (see illustration).

32 Taking care not to mark the cylinder bore, liberally lubricate the crankpin and both bearing shells, then pull the piston/connecting rod assembly down the bore and onto the crankpin (see illustration). Refit the big-end bearing cap using the markings made prior to removal to ensure it is fitted the correct way around; the connecting rod and bearing cap shell locating notches (where fitted) should abut each other.

33 Where the bearing caps are secured by nuts and bolts, lubricate the threads of the bolts with clean engine oil then screw on the nuts. Tighten both nuts by hand only then evenly and progressively tighten them to the specified torque setting (see illustration).

34 Where the bearing caps are secured by bolts only, lubricate the threads of the bolts with clean engine oil then screw them into position in the connecting rod, tightening them both by hand. Evenly and progressively tighten the bolts to the specified stage 1

torque setting then angle-tighten each bolt through the specified stage 2 angle. It is recommended that an angle-measuring gauge is used during this stage of the tightening, to ensure accuracy.

35 Refit the remaining three piston and connecting rod assemblies in the same way.

36 Rotate the crankshaft, and check that it turns freely, with no signs of binding or tight spots.

37 On all engines, refit the oil pump strainer, sump and the cylinder head as described in Part B or C (as applicable) of this Chapter.

20 Engine -
initial start-up after overhaul

With the engine refitted in the vehicle, double-check the engine oil and coolant levels (see "Weekly checks"). Make a final check that everything has been reconnected, and that there are no tools or rags left in the engine compartment.

On 1.4 and 1.6 litre petrol engine models, disable the ignition system by disconnect the ignition coil HT lead from the distributor and securely connecting it to a good earth point, then remove the spark plugs. Turn the engine on the starter until the oil pressure warning light goes out then stop and reconnect the HT lead and refit the spark plugs.

On 2.0 litre petrol engine models, disable the ignition system by disconnecting the wiring connector ignition HT coil (see Chapter 5B), then remove the spark plugs. Turn the engine on the starter until the oil pressure warning light goes out then stop and reconnect the wiring connector and refit the spark plugs.

On diesel engine models, switch on the ignition and immediately turn the engine on the starter (without allowing the glow plugs to heat up) until the oil pressure warning light goes out.

On all models, start the engine as normal noting that this may take a little longer than usual, due to the fuel system components having been disturbed.

While the engine is idling, check for fuel, water and oil leaks. Don't be alarmed if there are some odd smells and smoke from parts getting hot and burning off oil deposits.

Assuming all is well, keep the engine idling until hot water is felt circulating through the top hose, then switch off the engine.

Allow the engine to cool then recheck the oil and coolant levels as described in "Weekly checks", and top-up as necessary.

If new pistons, rings or crankshaft bearings have been fitted, the engine must be treated as new, and run-in for the first 500 miles (800 km). Do not operate the engine at full-throttle, or allow it to labour at low engine speeds in any gear. It is recommended that the oil and filter be changed at the end of this period.

2D

19.31 Insert the piston/connecting rod and tap it gently into position using a hammer handle

19.32 Lubricate the big-end journal . . .

19.33 . . . then refit the bearing cap and tighten the nuts evenly and progressively to the specified torque

Chapter 3
Cooling, heating and ventilation systems

Contents

Degrees of difficulty

| **Easy,** suitable for novice with little experience | **Fairly easy,** suitable for beginner with some experience | **Fairly difficult,** suitable for competent DIY mechanic | **Difficult,** suitable for experienced DIY mechanic | **Very difficult,** suitable for expert DIY or professional 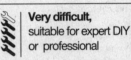 |

Specifications

System
Type .... Pressurised, pump-assisted with front mounted radiator and thermostatically-controlled electric cooling fan

Thermostat
Type .... Wax

Operating temperatures:	**Starts to open**	**Fully open**
1.4 and 1.6 litre petrol engines	86°C to 90°C	98°C to 102°C
2.0 litre petrol engines	82°C to 86°C	88°C
2.0 litre diesel engines	Not available	77°C to 87°C

Expansion tank
Cap pressure:
1.4 and 1.6 litre petrol engines ... 0.9 to 1.2 bar
2.0 litre petrol engines ... 0.9 to 1.0 bar
2.0 litre diesel engines ... 0.9 bar

Cooling fan

1.4 and 1.6 litre petrol engines:	**On**	**Off**
Models without air conditioning	104°C	98°C
Models with air conditioning:		
Slow speed	104°C	98°C
Fast speed	112°C	106°C

2.0 litre petrol engines
Switch on temperature .... 96°C to 100°C

2.0 litre diesel engines without intercooler:	**On**	**Off**
Models without air conditioning	104°C	94°C
Models with air conditioning:		
Slow speed	98°C	94°C
Fast speed	112°C	104°C

2.0 litre diesel engines with intercooler:		
Models without air conditioning	105°C	94°C
Models with air conditioning:		
Slow speed	105°C	94°C
Fast speed	112°C	103°C

3

Torque wrench settings

	Nm	lbf ft
Cooling system		
1.4 and 1.6 litre petrol engines		
Expansion tank	9	7
Thermostat housing cover	9	7
Thermostat housing to block	9	7
Coolant rail to block	9	7
Thermostatic switch	25	19
Coolant pump	10	7
Temperature gauge sensor	10	7
2.0 litre petrol engines		
Cooling fan to radiator	9	7
Thermostat housing cover	25	19
Coolant pump cover	45	33
Coolant rail to cylinder head	25	19
2.0 litre diesel engines		
Outlet elbow to cylinder head	25	19
Coolant pump	10	7
Cooling fan to housing	9	7
Cooling fan housing to radiator	9	7
Expansion tank	9	7
Radiator to crossmember	9	7
Temperature gauge sensor	5	4
Heating system		
Heater unit:		
6 mm nuts	10	7
8 mm nuts	22	16
Air conditioning system		
1.4 and 1.6 litre petrol engines		
Compressor to bracket	45	33
Pipe union to compressor	45	33
Cooling fan to housing	9	7
Pipe bracket to condenser	5	4
Condenser to fan housing	9	7
Condenser pipe to compressor	25	19
Trinary switch	12	9
Receiver/drier to body	9	7
2.0 litre petrol engines		
Compressor	45	33
Condenser cooling fan	9	7
Pipe to compressor	45	33
Cooling fan to housing	9	7
Cooling fan housing to condenser	9	7
Pipe to condenser	5	4
Condenser pipe union to compressor	25	19
Pressure switch to receiver/drier	12	9
2.0 litre diesel engines		
Compressor	45	33
Condenser cooling fan to housing	9	7
Cooling fan housing to condenser	9	7
Pipe to condenser	5	4
Pipe to compressor	45	33
Pressure switch to receiver/drier	12	9
Receiver/drier to body	9	7

1 General information and precautions

General information

The cooling system is of pressurised type, comprising a front-mounted radiator, an expansion tank mounted in the rear right-hand corner of the engine compartment, a thermostatically-controlled electric cooling fan mounted on the rear of the radiator, a thermostat and a centrifugal coolant pump **(see illustration)**. The thermostat is located in the coolant pump inlet on the rear right-hand side of the cylinder block on 1.4 and 1.6 litre petrol engines, in the outlet on the front right-hand side of the cylinder head on 2.0 litre petrol engines, and in the outlet on the front of the cylinder block, just above the oil cooler on 2.0 litre diesel engines. On 1.4 and 1.6 litre petrol engines the coolant pump is located on the right-hand rear end of the cylinder block and is driven by the timing belt. On 2.0 litre petrol and diesel engines the coolant pump is located on a bracket attached to the front right-hand end of the cylinder block, and is driven by the power steering pump which is driven from the crankshaft pulley by the auxiliary drivebelt.

The system functions as follows. With the engine cold, the thermostat is closed and circulation is restricted to the cylinder block, cylinder head and heater matrix; there is no circulation through the radiator. When the coolant reaches a predetermined temperature, the thermostat opens and the coolant is allowed to flow freely through the top hose to the radiator. As the coolant circulates through the radiator, it is cooled by the inrush of air when the vehicle is in forward motion. Airflow is supplemented by the action of the electric cooling fan when necessary. Upon reaching the bottom of the radiator, the coolant is now cooled and the cycle is repeated.

With the engine at normal operating temperature, the coolant expands and some of it is displaced into the expansion tank. This coolant collects in the tank and is returned to the radiator when the system cools.

The electric cooling fan mounted behind the radiator is controlled by a thermostatic switch located in the radiator side tank. At a predetermined coolant temperature the switch contacts close, thus actuating the fan.

Precautions

Cooling system

Do not attempt to remove the expansion tank filler cap or to disturb any part of the cooling system with the engine hot, as there is a risk of scalding. If the expansion tank filler cap must be removed before the engine and radiator have fully cooled down (even though this is not recommended) the pressure in the cooling system must first be released. Cover the cap with a thick layer of cloth, to avoid scalding, and slowly unscrew the filler cap until a hissing sound can be heard. When the hissing has stopped, showing that the pressure is released, slowly unscrew the filler cap until it can be removed. If more hissing sounds are heard, wait until they have stopped before unscrewing the cap completely. At all times keep well away from the filler opening.

Do not allow antifreeze to come in contact with your skin or painted surfaces of the vehicle. Rinse off spills immediately with plenty of water. Never leave antifreeze lying around; it is fatal if ingested.

If the engine is hot, the electric cooling fan may start rotating even if the engine is not running, so be careful to keep hands, hair and loose clothing well clear when working in the engine compartment.

Air conditioning system

On models equipped with an air conditioning system, it is necessary to observe special precautions whenever dealing with any part of the system, its associated components and any items which necessitate disconnection of the system. If for any reason the system must be disconnected, entrust this task to your Rover dealer or a refrigeration engineer.

Refrigerant must not be allowed to come in contact with a naked flame, otherwise a poisonous gas will be created. **Do not** allow the fluid to come in contact with the skin or eyes.

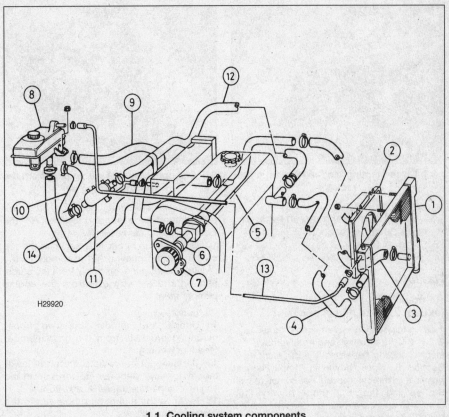

1.1 Cooling system components

1 Radiator	6 Thermostat housing	11 Heater temperature
2 Electric cooling fan and	7 Coolant pump	control valve
cowling	8 Expansion tank	12 Bleed screw
3 Bottom hose	9 Heater matrix return	13 Air purge hose to
4 Top hose	hose	expansion tank
5 Hose to thermostat	10 Heater matrix feed hose	14 Expansion tank feed hose

2 Cooling system hoses - disconnection and renewal

Warning: Never work on the cooling system when it is hot. Release any pressure from the system by loosening the expansion tank cap, having first covered it with a cloth to avoid any possibility of scalding.

1 If inspection of the cooling system reveals a faulty hose, then it must be renewed as follows.

2 First drain the cooling system (see Chapter 1). If the coolant is not due for renewal, it may be re-used if collected in a clean container.

3 To disconnect any hose, use a screwdriver to slacken the clips then move them along the hose clear of the outlet. Carefully work the hose off its outlets.

Caution: Do not attempt to disconnect any part of the system when still hot.

4 Note that the radiator hose outlets are fragile. **Do not** use excessive force when attempting to remove the hoses. If a hose proves stubborn, try to release it by rotating it on its outlets before attempting to work it off.

HAYNES HINT *If all else fails, cut the hose with a sharp knife then slit it so that it can be peeled off in two pieces. While expensive, this is preferable to buying a new radiator.*

5 When refitting a hose, first slide the clips onto the hose then work the hose onto its outlets. If the hose is stiff, use washing-up liquid as a lubricant.

6 Work each hose end fully onto its outlet, check that the hose is settled correctly and is properly routed, then slide each clip along the hose until it is behind the outlet flared end before tightening it securely.

7 Refill the system with coolant (see Chapter 1).

8 Check carefully for leaks as soon as possible after disturbing any part of the cooling system.

3

3.4 Disconnecting the top hose from the radiator

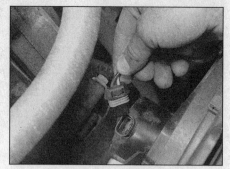

3.5 Disconnecting the wiring plug from the electric cooling fan

3 Radiator and expansion tank - removal, inspection and refitting

Radiator

Removal
(except 2.0 litre diesel engines)

1 Drain the cooling system (see Chapter 1).
2 On 2.0 litre petrol engines, remove the electric cooling fan assembly as described in Section 6. Note, however, that it is just possible to remove the radiator complete with the cooling fan, but there is very little clearance and care must be taken to prevent damage to the radiator fins.
3 At the top right-hand side of the radiator, loosen the clip and disconnect the expansion tank hose from the outlet stub.
4 Loosen the clip and disconnect the top hose from the top right-hand side of the radiator **(see illustration)**.
5 Disconnect the wiring plug from the electric cooling fan on the rear of the radiator **(see illustration)**.

Models with air conditioning

6 Loosen the clip and disconnect the top hose from the outlet elbow. Remove the hose. To ensure correct refitting, mark the hose and elbow in relation to each other.
7 Disconnect the wiring plug from the coolant temperature sensor on the outlet elbow.
8 Unscrew the lower nuts securing the bottom of the electric cooling fan assembly to the radiator.

9 Unscrew the nut securing the air conditioning pipe support bracket to the electric cooling fan assembly.
10 Unscrew the upper nuts securing the top of the electric cooling fan assembly to the radiator, release the assembly from the studs, and withdraw it upwards from the engine compartment

All models

11 Unbolt and remove the two upper mounting brackets from the crossmember **(see illustration)**.
12 Carefully lift the radiator from the lower mountings and withdraw upwards from the engine compartment **(see illustration)**.
13 Remove the mounting rubbers from the bottom of the radiator.
14 If necessary, on 1.4 and 1.6 litre petrol engines without air conditioning, the electric cooling fan assembly can be removed from the radiator by unscrewing the mounting nuts.

Removal (2.0 litre diesel engines)

15 Drain the cooling system as described in Chapter 1.
16 On models without air conditioning, remove the electric cooling fan as described in Section 6, then loosen the clips and remove the top hose.
17 On models with air conditioning, unclip the accelerator cable from the engine compartment front crosspanel and position to one side, then unbolt and remove the panel. Loosen the clips and disconnect the expansion tank hose and top hose from the radiator; position the hoses to one side.
18 Unbolt and remove the radiator top

3.11 Removing the radiator upper mounting brackets

3.12 Removing the radiator from the engine compartment

mounting brackets, then carefully lift the radiator from the lower mountings and withdraw upwards from the engine compartment.
19 Remove the mounting rubbers from the bottom of the radiator.

Inspection

20 If the radiator was removed because of clogging (causing overheating) then try reverse flushing or, in severe cases, use a radiator cleanser strictly in accordance with the manufacturer's instructions. Refer to Chapter 1 for further information
21 Use a soft brush and an air line or garden hose to clear the radiator matrix of leaves, insects etc.

> **HAYNES HiNT**
> *Minor leaks from the radiator can be cured using a suitable sealant with the radiator in situ.*

22 Major leaks or extensive damage should be repaired by a specialist, or the radiator should be renewed or exchanged for a reconditioned unit.
23 Examine the mounting rubbers for signs of damage or deterioration and renew if necessary.

Refitting

24 Refitting is a reversal of removal, but tighten all nuts and bolts to the specified torque where given in the Specifications. On completion, refill the cooling system as described in Chapter 1.

Expansion tank

Removal

25 With the engine cold, unscrew and remove the filler cap from the expansion tank.
26 Place a suitable container near the expansion tank to collect the drained coolant.
27 Loosen the clip and disconnect the air purge hose from the top of the expansion tank.
28 Unscrew the mounting bolts and release the expansion tank from the rubber grommet, then loosen the clip and disconnect the coolant feed hose from the bottom of the tank. Drain the coolant into the container.
29 Withdraw the expansion tank from the engine compartment.

Inspection

30 Empty any remaining coolant from the tank and flush it with fresh water to clean it. If the tank is leaking it must be renewed.
31 The expansion tank cap should be cleaned and checked whenever it is removed. Check that its sealing surfaces and threads are clean and undamaged.
32 The cap's performance can only be checked by using a cap pressure-tester (cooling system tester) with a suitable adaptor. On applying pressure, the cap's pressure relief valve should hold until the specified pressure is reached, at which point the valve should open.

4.10a The top hose has a white line to indicate the correct fitted position

4.10b Disconnecting the purge hose

4.10c Disconnecting the top hose from the thermostat housing cover - note the white lines to assist refitting

4.10d Disconnecting the by-pass hose

33 If there is any doubt about the cap's performance, then it must be renewed. Ensure that the replacement is of the correct type and rating.

Refitting

34 Refitting is a reversal of removal, but tighten the expansion tank mounting bolts to the specified torque and top up the cooling system with reference to "Weekly checks".

4 Thermostat -
removal, testing and refitting

Removal

1 Disconnect the battery negative (earth) lead (see Chapter 5A).
2 Drain the cooling system (see Chapter 1).

4.11a Unscrew the bolts . . .

1.4 and 1.6 litre petrol engines

3 The thermostat is located on the rear right-hand side of the cylinder block, and access to it is best gained from underneath the engine by jacking up the front of the vehicle (see "Jacking and Vehicle Support").
4 Loosen the clip and disconnect the heater hose from the thermostat housing located on the rear of the cylinder block.
5 Unscrew the bolts securing the coolant rail to the cylinder block, then ease the rail from the thermostat housing using a twisting action.
6 Unscrew the bolt securing the thermostat housing to the cylinder block. Ease the thermostat housing from the coolant pump with a twisting action and withdraw.
7 Remove the O-ring seals from the grooves in the housing inlet and outlet stubs using a small screwdriver.
8 Unscrew the bolts and separate the cover from the thermostat housing.
9 Remove the thermostat from the housing noting which way round it is fitted, then remove the rubber seal from the periphery of the thermostat.

2.0 litre petrol engines without air conditioning

10 Loosen the clips and disconnect the purge, top and by-pass hoses from the thermostat housing cover located on the front right-hand side of the cylinder head. Note that the top hose has a white line to indicate the correct refitting position **(see illustrations)**.

11 Unscrew the bolts and lift the cover from the thermostat housing. Note the location of the support bracket on the outer bolt **(see illustrations)**.
12 Remove the gasket followed by the thermostat **(see illustrations)**.

2.0 litre petrol engines with air conditioning

13 Loosen the clip and disconnect the radiator top hose from the outlet housing located on the front right-hand side of the cylinder head.
14 Loosen and remove the clip securing the thermostat inside the top hose.
15 Smear the inside of the hose with washing-up liquid to aid removal of the thermostat, then carefully ease out the thermostat

3

4.11b . . . and lift the cover from the thermostat housing

4.12a Remove the gasket . . .

4.12b . . . followed by the thermostat

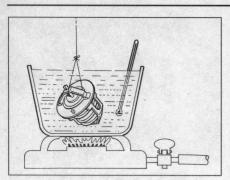

4.20 Testing the thermostat

4.21 The thermostat opening temperature is normally stamped on its end

2.0 litre diesel engines

16 The thermostat is located on the front of the cylinder block, just above the oil cooler. Improved access may be gained from underneath the engine by jacking up the front of the vehicle (see *"Jacking and Vehicle Support"*).

17 Loosen the clips and disconnect the three hoses from the thermostat housing; the front right-hand hose is from the coolant pump, the rear right-hand hose is to the top of the radiator, and the left-hand hose is to the cylinder block.

18 Withdraw the thermostat from the engine.

Testing

19 If the thermostat remains in the open position at room temperature, then it is faulty and must be renewed.

20 To test it fully, suspend the (closed) thermostat on a length of string in a container

of cold water, with a thermometer beside it **(see illustration)**.

21 Heat the water and check the temperature at which the thermostat begins to open. Compare this value with that specified. Continue to heat the water until the thermostat is fully open. The temperature at which this should happen is usually stamped in the unit's end **(see illustration)**. Allow the thermostat to cool down and check that it closes fully.

22 If the thermostat does not open and close as described, if it sticks in either position, or if it does not open at the specified temperature, then it must be renewed.

Refitting

23 Refitting is a reversal of removal, but note the following additional points:

a) *Clean all mating surfaces thoroughly before reassembly.*

b) *Renew all seals and gaskets, and smear O-rings with a little rubber grease to aid seating.*

c) *On 2.0 litre petrol engines without air conditioning, make sure that the thermostat lower support legs are located clear of the heater outlet pipe hole.*

d) *Tighten all bolts to their specified torque wrench settings (where given).*

e) *Ensure the coolant hose clips are positioned so that they do not foul any other component, then tighten them securely.*

f) *Refill the cooling system (see Chapter 1).*

5 Coolant pump - removal and refitting

Note: *On 2.0 litre petrol models with air conditioning, the air conditioning system must be discharged, requiring the services of a qualified refrigeration engineer.*

Removal

1 Coolant pump failure is usually indicated by coolant leaking from the gland behind the pump bearing, or by rough and noisy operation, usually accompanied by excessive pump spindle play. If the pump shows any of these symptoms then it must be renewed as follows.

2 Drain the cooling system (see Chapter 1).

1.4 and 1.6 litre petrol engine

3 The coolant pump is located on the right-hand rear end of the cylinder block.

4 Remove the timing belt as described in Chapter 2A.

Caution: Do not rotate the engine with the timing belt removed.

5 Unscrew and remove the single rear bolt securing the coolant pump to the cylinder block flange.

6 Note the location of the pillar bolt for the timing cover, then unscrew and remove all the retaining bolts.

7 Withdraw the coolant pump from the cylinder block, then prise out the O-ring seal from the groove in the rear mating face. Discard the seal and obtain a new one. Note the location dowel on the cylinder block.

2.0 litre petrol engines without air conditioning

8 The coolant pump is located on the front right-hand end of the cylinder block, and is driven by the power steering pump which is driven from the crankshaft pulley by the auxiliary drivebelt **(see illustration)**.

9 Loosen the clip and disconnect the coolant return hose from the bottom of the coolant pump rear cover **(see illustration)**. Plug or tape over the hose to prevent any items dropping into the cooling system.

10 Unscrew the pump/cover bolts then carefully prise the cover from the rear of the pump **(see illustrations)**.

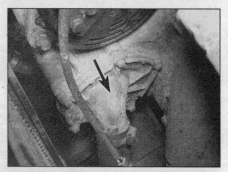

5.8 The coolant pump is located on the front right-hand end of the cylinder block (2.0 litre petrol engine)

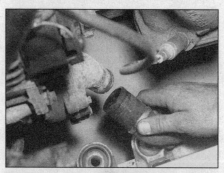

5.9 Disconnecting the coolant return hose (bottom hose extension) from the coolant pump rear cover

5.10a Unscrew the bolts . . .

5.10b . . . and remove the coolant pump cover

11 Remove the O-ring seal from the groove in the water pump flange. Discard the seal and obtain a new one.

12 Remove the coolant pump from the bracket/housing and prise out the O-ring seal. Discard the seal and obtain a new one (see illustration).

2.0 litre petrol engines with air conditioning

 Warning: The following procedure includes work on the air conditioning system which must only be carried out by a qualified refrigeration engineer. Do not attempt to open the system, as the refrigerant is dangerous to handle and highly toxic in certain conditions. Refer to the precautions given in Section 10 of this Chapter. Note also that Rover recommend the receiver/drier is renewed every time the system is opened.

13 The coolant pump is located on a bracket attached to the front right-hand end of the cylinder block, and is driven by the power steering pump which is driven from the crankshaft pulley by the auxiliary drivebelt. The bracket incorporates an internal channel connected to the cylinder block.

14 Loosen the clip and disconnect the coolant rail hose from the coolant pump. Plug or tape over the hose to prevent any items dropping into the cooling system.

15 Unscrew the bolt securing the air conditioning pipe clip to the coolant rail.

16 Taking the necessary safety precautions (ie wearing gloves and glasses), unscrew the bolt securing the air conditioning pipes to the compressor. Move the pipes to one side and recover the O-ring seals. Obtain new seals for the refitting procedure. Plug or tape over the pipes and compressor apertures to prevent entry of dust, dirt and moisture.

17 Unscrew the pump mounting bolts.

18 Remove the pump rear cover and prise the O-ring seal from the groove in the water pump flange. Discard the seal and obtain a new one.

19 Remove the coolant pump from the bracket and prise out the O-ring seals. Discard the seals and obtain new ones.

2.0 litre diesel engines

20 The coolant pump is located on a bracket attached to the front right-hand end of the cylinder block, and is driven by the power steering pump which is driven from the crankshaft pulley by the auxiliary drivebelt. The bracket incorporates an internal channel connected to the cylinder block.

21 Remove the alternator (see Chapter 5A).

22 Loosen the clips and disconnect the top hose from the radiator, thermostat and engine outlet. Withdraw the hose from the engine compartment.

23 On models with air conditioning, unscrew the air conditioning compressor mounting bolts and pivot the compressor forwards for access to the coolant pump.

5.12 Removing the coolant pump from the bracket/housing

24 Loosen the clip and disconnect the hose from the coolant pump.

25 Unscrew the pump mounting bolts.

26 Remove the pump rear cover and prise the O-ring seal from the groove in the water pump flange. Discard the seal and obtain a new one.

27 Remove the coolant pump from the bracket and prise out the O-ring seals. Discard the seals and obtain new ones.

Refitting

28 Refitting is a reversal of removal, but note the following additional points:

a) Clean all mating surfaces thoroughly before reassembly.

b) Renew all seals and gaskets, and, except on the air conditioning compressor (where applicable), smear O-rings with a little rubber grease (Rover recommend Locktite 405) to aid seating. On the compressor, the O-rings must be smeared with a little refrigerant oil.

c) Tighten all bolts to their specified torque wrench settings (where given).

d) Ensure the coolant hose clips are positioned so that they do not foul any other component, then tighten them securely.

e) Refill the cooling system as described in Chapter 1.

f) On 2.0 litre petrol engines with air conditioning, renew the receiver/drier and have the system re-charged by a refrigeration engineer.

6 Electric cooling fan assembly - testing, removal and refitting

Testing

1 The cooling fan motor is supplied with current via the ignition switch, a fuse and the cooling fan relay. The relay is energised by the radiator-mounted thermostatic switch.

2 If the fan does not appear to work, first check that the fuse is in good condition and not blown (see Chapter 12). Run the engine until normal operating temperature is reached, then allow it to idle. If the fan does not cut in within a few minutes, switch off the ignition

and disconnect the two wires from the thermostatic switch. Bridge these two wires with a length of spare wire and switch on the ignition. If the fan now operates, the thermostatic switch is probably faulty and must be tested further as described in Section 7.

3 If the fan still fails to operate, check that full battery voltage is available at the switch. If not, check the feed for a blown fuse or other fault such as a broken wire. If the feed is good, check the cooling fan relay (see Chapter 12). If the relay operates correctly, check for continuity between the fan motor earth wire terminal and a good earth point on the body. If not, then the earth connection is faulty and must be remade.

4 If the switch and wiring are in good condition, the fault must be in the motor itself. This can be checked by disconnecting it from the wiring loom and connecting a 12 volt supply directly to it. If the motor does not work then it must be renewed.

Removal

5 Disconnect the battery negative (earth) lead (see Chapter 5A).

1.4 and 1.6 litre petrol engines without air conditioning

6 Disconnect the wiring multiplug from the electric cooling fan motor.

7 Move the top hose from the clip on the cooling fan assembly.

8 Unscrew the lower mounting nuts securing the bottom of the assembly to the radiator.

9 Unscrew the upper mounting nuts, then withdraw the assembly from the mounting studs and withdraw it upwards while guiding it around the top hose.

10 To dismantle the assembly, first remove the heatshield where applicable (2 screws). Unscrew the fan retaining circlip, then lift the fan off the motor spindle. Unscrew the bolts and remove the motor from the cowling.

1.4 and 1.6 litre petrol engines with air conditioning

11 Remove the air cleaner as described in Chapter 4A.

12 Disconnect the wiring multiplug from the electric cooling fan motor.

13 Position a suitable container beneath the radiator top hose to catch spilt coolant, then loosen the clips and disconnect the hose from the radiator and outlet elbow. Place the hose to one side.

14 Disconnect the wiring from the coolant temperature sensor.

15 Unscrew the lower mounting nuts securing the bottom of the assembly to the radiator.

16 Unscrew the nut and remove the air conditioning pipe support from the cooling fan assembly.

17 Unscrew the upper mounting nuts, then withdraw the assembly from the mounting studs and withdraw it upwards while guiding it around the air conditioning pipe.

3

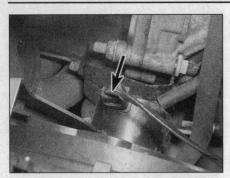

6.19 Electric cooling fan wiring multiplug

18 To dismantle the assembly, first remove the heatshield where applicable (2 screws). Unscrew the fan retaining circlip, then lift the fan off the motor spindle. Unscrew the bolts and remove the motor from the cowling.

2.0 litre petrol engines

19 Disconnect the wiring multiplug and release the wiring from the support on the electric cooling fan motor **(see illustration)**.
20 On models with air conditioning, remove the screw securing the air conditioning pipe support to the cowling.
21 Unscrew the mounting nuts and withdraw the assembly from the lower studs.
22 To dismantle the assembly, first remove the heatshield where applicable (2 screws). Unscrew the fan retaining circlip, then lift the fan off the motor spindle. Unscrew the bolts and remove the motor from the cowling.

2.0 litre diesel engines without air conditioning

23 Disconnect the wiring multiplug from the electric cooling fan motor.
24 Unscrew the upper nuts then release the assembly from the stud and withdraw the assembly upwards from the radiator while guiding it around the top hose.

25 To dismantle the assembly, first remove the heatshield where applicable (2 screws). Unscrew the fan retaining circlip, then lift the fan off the motor spindle. Unscrew the bolts and remove the motor from the cowling.

2.0 litre diesel engines with air conditioning

 Warning: The following procedure includes work on the air conditioning system which must only be carried out by a qualified refrigeration engineer. Do not attempt to open the system, as the refrigerant is dangerous to handle and highly toxic in certain conditions. Refer to the precautions given in Section 10 of this Chapter. Note also that Rover recommend the receiver/drier is renewed every time the system is opened.

26 Remove the condenser with reference to Section 11.
27 Remove the front bumper as described in Chapter 11.
28 Disconnect the wiring multiplug from the electric cooling fan motor and release the wiring from the clip.
29 Unscrew the mounting nuts and withdraw the fan motor and fan from the housing.

Refitting

30 Refitting is a reversal of removal, but on completion refill the cooling system as described in Chapter 1. On 2.0 litre diesel engines with air conditioning, renew the receiver/drier and have the air conditioning system recharged by a qualified refrigeration engineer.

---

7 Cooling system electrical switches - testing, removal and refitting

Cooling fan thermostatic switch (2.0 litre diesel engines only)

Testing

Note: *On 1.4, 1.6 and 2.0 litre petrol engines the electric cooling fan is controlled by the Engine Control Module (ECM). Refer to Chapter 4A for more details.*

1 Refer to Section 6 for details of a quick test which should eliminate most faulty switches. If the switch is to be renewed, or to be tested thoroughly, it must be removed.
2 To carry out a thorough test of the switch, use two spare wires to connect to it either a multimeter (set to the resistance function) or a battery and bulb test circuit. Suspend the switch in a pan of water which is being heated. Measure the temperature of the water with a thermometer. **Do not** let either the switch or the thermometer touch the pan itself **(see illustration)**.
3 The switch contacts should close to the ON position (ie: continuity should exist) when the water reaches the temperature specified. Stop heating the water and allow it to cool down. The switch contacts should open.
4 If the switch's performance is significantly different from that specified, or if it does not work at all, then it must be renewed.

Removal

5 With the engine and radiator cold, either drain the cooling system (see Chapter 1B) down to the level of the sender unit, or unscrew the expansion tank filler cap to release any remaining pressure and have a suitable plug ready that can be used to stop the escape of coolant while the switch is removed.
6 Disconnect the battery negative (earth) lead (see Chapter 5A).
7 Disconnect the wiring connectors from the switch then rotate the locking ring anti-clockwise to release it. Withdraw the switch and sealing ring from the radiator **(see illustration)**.

Refitting

8 Refitting is a reversal of removal, but renew the sealing ring if it is worn or compressed and carefully clean the radiator seat before pressing in the sealing ring and switch. Refit the locking ring and rotate it clockwise to tighten it. Reconnect the switch wiring and the battery negative lead, then top up the cooling system with reference to "Weekly checks" **(see illustration)**.

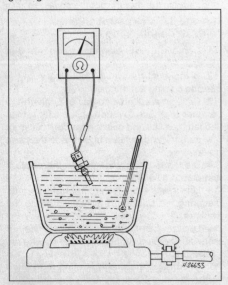

7.2 Testing the cooling fan thermostatic switch

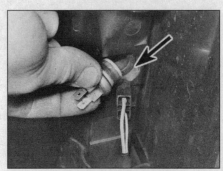

7.7 Removing the cooling fan thermostatic switch and sealing ring (2.0 litre diesel engine)

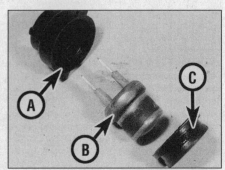

7.8 Cooling fan switch locking ring (A) thermostatic switch (B) and sealing ring (C)

Coolant temperature gauge sender unit

Testing

9 The coolant temperature gauge mounted in the instrument panel is fed with a stabilised 10 volt supply from the instrument panel feed (via the ignition switch and a fuse), its earth being controlled by the sender unit.

10 On 1.4 and 1.6 litre petrol engines, the sender unit is screwed into the coolant outlet elbow mounted on the front left-hand end of the cylinder head. On 2.0 litre petrol engines, it is located beneath the coolant outlet elbow on the front right-hand end of the cylinder head and where two units are fitted it is the lower one. On 2.0 litre diesel engines, it is located beneath the coolant outlet elbow on the front right-hand end of the cylinder head. The sender unit contains a thermistor, which is an element whose electrical resistance decreases at a predetermined rate as its temperature rises. Thus, when the coolant is cold, the sender's resistance is high, current flow through the gauge is reduced and the gauge needle points to the cold end of the scale.

11 If the gauge develops a fault, check first the other instruments. If they do not work at all, check the instrument panel feed. If the readings are erratic, there may be a fault in the voltage stabiliser which will necessitate the renewal of the gauge unit or printed circuit. If the fault is in the temperature gauge alone, check it as follows.

12 If the gauge needle remains at the cold end of the scale, disconnect the sender unit wire and earth it to the cylinder head. If the needle then deflects when the ignition is switched on, then the sender unit is proven faulty and must be renewed. If the needle still does not move, remove the instrument panel and check the continuity of the wire between the gauge and the sender unit and the feed to the gauge unit. If continuity is shown and the fault still exists, then the gauge is faulty and the gauge unit must be renewed.

13 If the gauge needle remains at the hot end of the scale, disconnect the sender unit wire. If the needle then returns to the cold end of the scale when the ignition is switched on, then the sender unit is proven faulty and must be renewed. If the needle still does not move, check the remainder of the circuit.

Removal

14 With the engine and radiator cold, either drain the cooling system down to the level of the switch (see Chapter 1), or unscrew the expansion tank filler cap to release any remaining pressure and have a suitable plug ready that can be used to stop the escape of coolant while the unit is removed.

15 Disconnect the battery negative (earth) lead (see Chapter 5A).

16 Disconnect the wiring and unscrew the sender unit from the coolant outlet elbow (see illustration).

Refitting

17 Refitting is a reversal of removal, but apply suitable sealant to the unit threads and tighten it securely. Top up the cooling system with reference to "*Weekly checks*".

Coolant temperature sensor

Testing

18 On 1.4 and 1.6 litre petrol engines, the sensor is screwed into the coolant outlet elbow mounted on the front left-hand end of the cylinder head. On 2.0 litre petrol engines it is located on the coolant outlet elbow on the front right-hand end of the cylinder head and is the upper of the two units. On 2.0 litre diesel engines it is located beneath the coolant outlet elbow on the front right-hand end of the cylinder head. The sensor is a thermistor, and is supplied with approximately 5 volts by the engine management system ECU. The ECU also controls the sensor's earth path and, by measuring the amount of current in the sensor circuit, determines the engine's temperature. This information is used, in conjunction with other inputs, to control idle speed, injector opening time duration and ignition timing. On diesel engines the information is also used to determine how long the glow plugs remain energised.

19 If the sensor circuit should fail to provide adequate information, the ECU's back-up facility assumes a value corresponding to 60°C. The sensor itself can be tested only by having a Rover dealer check the complete system using the correct diagnostic equipment. **Do not** attempt to test the circuit using any other equipment, or the ECU will be damaged.

Removal

20 With the engine and radiator cold, either drain the cooling system down to the level of the switch (see Chapter 1), or unscrew the expansion tank filler cap to release any remaining pressure and have a suitable plug ready that can be used to stop the escape of coolant while the unit is removed.

21 Disconnect the wiring and unscrew the sender unit from the coolant outlet elbow.

7.16 Disconnecting the wiring from the coolant temperature gauge sender unit on the outlet elbow (2.0 litre petrol engine)

Refitting

22 Refitting is a reversal of removal, but apply suitable sealant to the unit threads and tighten it to the specified torque wrench setting. Top up the cooling system with reference to "*Weekly checks*".

8 Heating and ventilation system - general information

The heating/ventilation system consists of a blower motor (housed beneath the left-hand side of the facia), face level vents in the centre and at each end of the facia, and air ducts to the front and rear footwells.

The control unit is located in the centre of the facia, and the controls operate flap valves to deflect and mix the air flowing through the various parts of the heating/ventilation system. The flap valves are contained in the air distribution housing, which acts as a central distribution unit, passing air to the various ducts and vents.

Cold air enters the system through the grille at the rear of the engine compartment. If required, the airflow is boosted by the blower fan, and then flows through the various ducts, according to the settings of the controls. Stale air is expelled through ducts at the rear of the vehicle. If warm air is required, the cold air is passed over the heater matrix, which is heated by the engine coolant.

On models fitted with air conditioning, a recirculation switch enables the outside air supply to be closed off, while the air inside the vehicle is recirculated. This can be useful to prevent unpleasant odours entering from outside the vehicle, but should only be used briefly, as the recirculated air inside the vehicle will soon become stale.

9 Heating and ventilation system components - removal and refitting

Heater unit

Removal

1 Drain the cooling system as described in Chapter 1, or alternatively clamp the heater hoses at the bulkhead in the engine compartment using purpose-made hose clamps.

2 Where necessary, for improved access to the heater hoses on the bulkhead, remove the engine management ECU and bracket with reference to Chapter 4 (see illustrations).

3 In the engine compartment on the lower bulkhead, disconnect the cable from the heater control valve by releasing the clip securing the outer cable, then disconnecting the inner cable from the lever (see illustration).

3

9.2a To remove the engine management ECU, disconnect the vacuum hose . . .

9.2b . . . disconnect the wiring multi-plug . . .

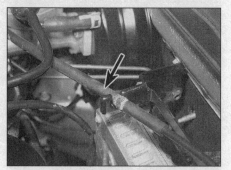

9.2c . . . release the accelerator cable (arrowed) from the bracket . . .

9.2d . . . unscrew the mounting nuts . . .

9.2e . . . and remove the ECU . . .

9.2f . . . and bracket

4 Release the clips and disconnect the hoses from the heater matrix tubes on the bulkhead. If the original spring-type clips are fitted, use a pair of grips to release them as they are very tight (see illustration).

5 Unscrew and remove the heater mounting nut on the bulkhead. It is the nut located above and to the left of the heater hoses.
6 Working inside the vehicle, remove the facia panel as described in Chapter 11.

7 Where fitted, disconnect the wiring plug from the air duct on the left-hand side of the heater unit (see illustration).
8 Unscrew the bolts securing the air duct to the heater unit and blower and remove the duct (see illustrations).
9 Unscrew the bolts and position the inertia switch and relay bracket away from the steering column support beam.
10 Unbolt and remove the steering column support beam.
11 Release the clips supporting the airbag/SRS wiring on the heater unit (see illustration).
12 Remove the clips securing the radio aerial cable to the heater mounting studs.
13 Unscrew the stud securing the heater unit to the tunnel duct.
14 Unscrew the nuts securing the heater unit to the bulkhead (see illustration).

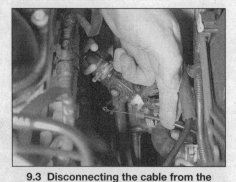

9.3 Disconnecting the cable from the heater control valve

9.4 Disconnecting the hoses from the heater matrix tubes on the bulkhead

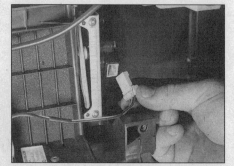

9.7 Disconnecting the wiring plug from the air duct

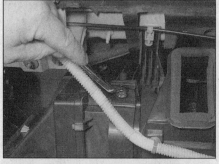

9.8a Unscrew the mounting bolts . . .

9.8b . . . and remove the air duct

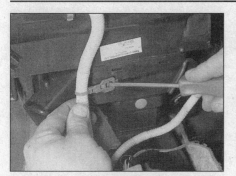

9.11 Releasing the airbag/SRS wiring from the heater unit

9.14 Unscrew the mounting nuts . . .

9.15 . . . and remove the heater unit

15 Withdraw the heater unit from the tunnel duct and remove the unit from inside the vehicle **(see illustration)**.

Refitting

16 Refitting is a reverse of the removal procedure, but tighten all nuts and bolts to the specified torque and on completion refill the cooling system as described in Chapter 1. When reconnecting the control cable, set the controls and heater lever to their cold positions then secure the outer cable with the clip.

Heater matrix

Removal

17 Remove the heater unit as described previously in this Section.

18 With the heater unit on the bench, remove the rubber grommet from the matrix tubes **(see illustration)**.
19 Remove the screw and remove the pipe retaining clamp.
20 Remove the screws and lift off the matrix cover **(see illustration)**.
21 Slide the matrix from the heater housing **(see illustration)**.
22 If the matrix is leaking, it is best to obtain a new or reconditioned unit as home repairs are seldom successful. If it is blocked, it can sometimes be cleared by reverse flushing using a garden hose. Use a proprietary radiator cleaning product if absolutely necessary.

Refitting

23 Refitting is a reversal of removal.

Heater blower motor

Removal

24 Remove the mounting screws and lower the blower motor from its housing under the left-hand side of the facia **(see illustration)**.
25 Disconnect the wiring and remove the blower motor **(see illustration)**.

Refitting

26 Refitting is a reversal of removal.

Heater blower motor resistor

Removal

27 Remove the glovebox as described in Chapter 11.
28 Disconnect the wiring, then remove the screws and lift the resistor from the motor housing **(see illustrations)**.

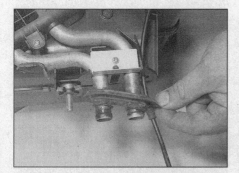

9.18 Removing the rubber grommet from the matrix tubes

9.20 Removing the cover from the matrix

9.21 Sliding the matrix from the heater housing

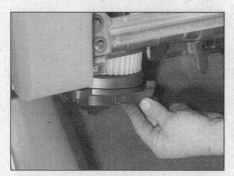

9.24 Lowering the heater blower motor from the facia

9.25 Disconnecting the wiring from the blower motor

9.28a Disconnect the wiring . . .

3

9.28b . . . then remove the screws and lift the resistor from the motor housing

9.37a Undo the mounting screws . . .

9.37b . . . and withdraw the heater control panel

Refitting

29 Refitting is a reversal of removal.

Heater valve

Removal

30 Working in the engine compartment, disconnect the inner cable from the heater valve lever and free the outer cable from the retaining clip.
31 Either drain the cooling system (see Chapter 1) or clamp the coolant hoses on each side of the coolant valve to minimise the loss of coolant.
32 Release the clips and disconnect the coolant hoses from the valve.
33 Unscrew the bracket mounting nut and remove the heater valve from the bulkhead.

Refitting

34 Refitting is a reversal of removal. When reconnecting the control cable, set the controls and heater lever to their cold positions then secure the outer cable with the clip. Top up the cooling system with reference to "Weekly checks".

Heater control panel

Removal

35 Remove the centre console as described in Chapter 11.
36 Note the position of the outer control cables in their clips as a guide for refitting, then disconnect them.
37 Undo the mounting screws and withdraw the heater control panel from the facia (see illustrations).

38 Disconnect the wiring multiplugs and withdraw the control panel (see illustrations).
39 If necessary, pull off the control knobs, remove the Torx screws and disconnect the cables. The base and control shaft can be removed after removal of the screws.

Refitting

40 Refitting is a reversal of removal, but position the cables to their original settings.

---

10 Air conditioning system -
general information and
precautions

General information

1 An air conditioning system is available as an option on all models. The system enables the temperature of incoming air to be lowered, and it also dehumidifies the air, which makes for rapid demisting and increased comfort.
2 The cooling side of the system works in the same way as a domestic refrigerator. Refrigerant gas is drawn into a belt-driven compressor, and passes into a condenser mounted on the front of the radiator, where it loses heat and becomes liquid. The liquid passes through an expansion valve to an evaporator, where it changes from liquid under high pressure to gas under low pressure. This change is accompanied by a drop in temperature, which cools the evaporator. The refrigerant returns to the compressor, and the cycle begins again (see illustration opposite).

3 Air blown through the evaporator passes to the air distribution unit and then into the passenger compartment.
4 The heating side of the system works in the same way as on models without air conditioning.
5 The system is electronically-controlled. Any problems with the system should be referred to a Rover dealer.

Precautions

6 With an air conditioning system, it is necessary to observe special precautions whenever dealing with any part of the system, or its associated components. If for any reason the system must be disconnected, entrust this task to your Rover dealer or a refrigeration engineer.

 Warning: The refrigeration circuit contains a liquid refrigerant which is potentially dangerous, and should only be handled by qualified persons. If it is splashed onto the skin, it can cause frostbite. It is not itself poisonous, but in the presence of a naked flame (including a cigarette), it forms a poisonous gas. Uncontrolled discharging of the refrigerant is dangerous, and potentially damaging to the environment. For all these reasons, it is dangerous to disconnect any part of the system without specialised knowledge and equipment. Note that Rover recommend the receiver/drier is renewed every time the air conditioning system is opened.
7 Do not operate the air conditioning system if it is known to be short of refrigerant, as this may damage the compressor.

9.38a Disconnect the illumination wiring . . .

9.38b . . . and blower motor control wiring

11 Air conditioning system components - removal and refitting

⚠ *Warning: The air conditioning system must be professionally discharged before carrying out any of the following work. Cap or plug the pipe lines as soon as they are disconnected to prevent the entry of moisture. Note also that Rover recommend the receiver/drier is renewed every time the system is opened.*

Compressor

Removal

1 Have the air conditioning system discharged by a qualified refrigeration engineer.
2 Disconnect the battery negative (earth) lead (see Chapter 5A).
3 Apply the handbrake, then jack up the front of the vehicle and support it on axle stands (see *"Jacking and Vehicle Support"*).
4 Remove the alternator as described in Chapter 5A.
5 Disconnect the wiring plug from the compressor located in the right-hand corner of the engine compartment.
6 Unscrew the bolt and detach the air conditioning pipe union from the compressor. Tape over or plug the refrigerant apertures.
7 Remove the seal and discard. A new one must be fitted on refitting.
8 Support the compressor, then unscrew and remove the mounting bolts and lower the unit from under the engine compartment.

Refitting

9 Refitting is a reversal of removal, but renew the receiver/drier and tighten all bolts to the specified torque. Before fitting the new seal, smear a little refrigerant oil on each side. On completion, have the air conditioning system recharged by a refrigeration specialist or suitably-equipped Rover dealer.

Condenser

Removal

10 Have the air conditioning system discharged by a qualified refrigeration engineer.
11 Remove the radiator as described in Section 3.
12 Unscrew the bolt and detach the air conditioning pipe connector from the receiver/drier. Tape over or plug the refrigerant apertures. Remove the seal and discard. A new one must be fitted on refitting.
13 Using two spanners, slacken the union and disconnect the condenser pipe from the compressor pipe. Remove the seal and discard. A new one must be fitted on refitting. Tape over or plug the refrigerant apertures.
14 Unscrew the upper bolts securing the condenser to the housing, then release the

bottom mountings and withdraw the condenser upwards from the front of the vehicle.
15 Unscrew the bolts and remove the air conditioning pipes from the condenser. Remove the O-ring seals and discard. New ones must be fitted on refitting.

Refitting

16 Refitting is a reversal of removal, but renew the receiver/drier and tighten all bolts to the specified torque. Before fitting the new seals, smear a little refrigerant oil on them. On completion, have the air conditioning system recharged by a refrigeration specialist or suitably-equipped Rover dealer.

Condenser cooling fan

Removal

17 Remove the condenser as described previously in this Section.
18 Remove the front bumper as described in Chapter 11.
19 Disconnect the wiring, then unscrew the nuts and remove the cooling fan.

Refitting

20 Refitting is a reversal of removal, but renew the receiver/drier and tighten the mounting nuts to the specified torque. On completion, have the air conditioning system recharged by a refrigeration specialist or suitably-equipped Rover dealer.

Evaporator

Removal

21 Have the air conditioning system discharged by a qualified refrigeration engineer.
22 On left-hand drive models, unscrew the two bolts and release the evaporator pipes from the support brackets at the left-hand rear of the engine compartment.
23 Using a socket and extension, unscrew the bolt securing the air conditioning pipe connector to the evaporator.
24 Working inside the vehicle, remove the glovebox as described in Chapter 11.
25 At the bottom of the glovebox aperture, remove the screws and detach the lower rail from the facia.
26 Disconnect the wiring from the evaporator thermostat.
27 Unscrew the lower screws securing the evaporator housing brackets to the heater and body.
28 Unscrew the evaporator housing upper screws and nut from the heater housing and body.
29 With the help of an assistant, detach the air conditioning pipe connector from the evaporator then carefully withdraw the unit from between the heater housings while pulling the drain tube from the body panel.

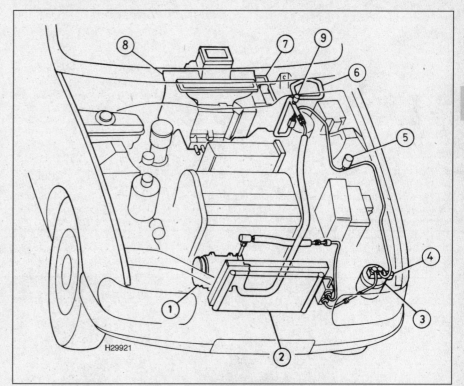

10.2 Air conditioning system layout

1	Compressor	5	High pressure service
2	Condenser		connection
3	Receiver/drier	6	Blower unit
4	Trinary pressure switch	7	Evaporator
		8	Heater housing
		9	Low pressure service connection

3

30 Remove the O-ring seals from the pipe flange and discard them. New seals must be fitted on refitting.

Refitting

31 Refitting is a reversal of removal, but renew the receiver/drier and tighten the bolts to the specified torque where given. Before fitting the new seals, smear a little refrigerant oil on each side. On completion, have the air conditioning system recharged by a refrigeration specialist or suitably-equipped Rover dealer.

Receiver/drier

Removal

32 Have the air conditioning system discharged by a qualified refrigeration engineer.

33 Remove the air cleaner as described in Chapter 4.

34 Unscrew the support bolt and detach the air intake hose from the battery tray.

35 Unscrew the bolts and detach the air conditioning pipe connectors from the receiver/drier. Remove the O-ring seals and discard them; new ones must be fitted on refitting. Tape over or plug the refrigerant apertures.

36 Using an Allen key unscrew the mounting screws, then turn the receiver/drier 45° and disconnect the trinary pressure switch wiring plug.

37 Withdraw the receiver/drier. If necessary, unscrew the trinary switch and discard the O-ring seal. A new seal must be fitted on refitting.

Refitting

38 Refitting is a reversal of removal, but tighten the mounting bolts to the specified torque where given. Before fitting the new seals, smear a little refrigerant oil on each side. On completion, have the air conditioning system recharged by a refrigeration specialist or suitably-equipped Rover dealer.

Trinary pressure switch

Removal and refitting

39 Since the receiver/drier must be renewed whenever the air conditioning system is opened, the removal and refitting procedure for the trinary pressure switch is identical to that given for the receiver/drier. Refer to the previous paragraphs.

Chapter 4 Part A:
Fuel and exhaust systems - petrol engines

Contents

Degrees of difficulty

Easy, suitable for novice with little experience	**Fairly easy,** suitable for beginner with some experience	**Fairly difficult,** suitable for competent DIY mechanic	**Difficult,** suitable for experienced DIY mechanic	**Very difficult,** suitable for expert DIY or professional

Specifications

System type . . . . Rover/Motorola multi-point injection Modular Engine Management system (MEMS-Mpi)*

See Section 6 for further information

Fuel system data

Fuel pump type . . . . Electric, immersed in tank
Fuel pump pressure (approximate):
   Maximum . . . . 4.1 bar
   Constant regulated pressure . . . . 3.0 ± 0.2 bar
Specified idle speed*:
   1.4 and 1.6 litre engine . . . . 875 ± 50 rpm
   2.0 litre engine . . . . 850 ± 25 rpm
Idle mixture CO content* . . . . Less than 0.5%
Not adjustable - controlled by ECM

Recommended fuel

Minimum octane rating . . . . 95 RON unleaded (UK unleaded premium).
Leaded fuel must **not** be used

Torque wrench settings

	Nm	lbf ft
Coolant temperature sensor	15	11
Crankshaft sensor bolt	6	4
Electronic Control Module (ECM) nuts	9	6
Exhaust manifold nuts/bolts	45	33
Exhaust system fasteners:		
1.4 litre 8-valve engines:		
Front pipe-to-manifold nuts	45	33
All other nuts	50	37
All other engines:		
Front pipe-to-manifold nuts	45	33
Front pipe-to-catalytic converter nuts	22	16
Front pipe mounting nuts	25	18
Intermediate pipe-to-catalytic converter nuts	34	25
Intermediate pipe-to-tailpipe nuts	45	33
Fuel breather valve retaining nut	9	6
Fuel feed pipe union bolts	10	7
Fuel filter pipe union nuts	30	22
Fuel pump housing-to-tank nuts	9	6
Fuel rail bolts - 1.4 and 1.6 litre engine	10	7
Fuel rail/support bracket bolts - 2.0 litre engine	10	7
Fuel temperature sensor - 2.0 litre engine	15	11
Idle air control valve screws	1.5	1
Inlet manifold nuts/bolts:		
1.4 litre 8-valve engine:		
Lower section nuts and bolts	25	18
Support bracket bolts	25	18
Upper section bolts	25	18
1.4 litre 16-valve and 1.6 litre engine	25	18
2.0 litre engine:		
Lower section nuts and bolts	25	18
Upper section bolts	10	7
Upper section support bracket bolts	6	4
Intake air temperature sensor	7	5
Knock sensor - 2.0 litre engine	12	9
Throttle housing:		
Retaining bolts - 1.4 and 1.6 litre engine	7	5
Retaining nuts - 2.0 litre engine	8	6
Throttle position sensor screws	1.5	1

1 General information and precautions

The fuel system consists of a fuel tank (which is mounted under the rear of the car, with an electric fuel pump immersed in it), a fuel filter and the fuel feed and return lines. The fuel pump supplies fuel to the fuel rail, which acts as a reservoir for the four fuel injectors which inject fuel into the inlet tracts. In addition, there is an Electronic Control Module (ECM) and various sensors, electrical components and related wiring.

Refer to Section 6 for further information on the operation of each fuel injection system, and to Section 16 for information on the exhaust system.

 Warning: Many of the procedures in this Chapter require the removal of fuel lines and connections, which may result in some fuel spillage. Before carrying out any operation on the fuel system, refer to the precautions given in "Safety first!" at the beginning of this manual, and follow them implicitly. Petrol is a highly-dangerous and volatile liquid, and the precautions necessary when handling it cannot be overstressed.

2.2 Slacken the retaining clip and disconnect the air cleaner duct from the throttle body (2.0 litre engine shown)

Note: Residual pressure will remain in the fuel lines long after the vehicle was last used. Before disconnecting any fuel line, first depressurise the fuel system as described in Section 7.

2 Air cleaner assembly and intake ducts - removal and refitting

Removal

1 Remove the battery as described in Chapter 5A.

2 Release the retaining clip and detach the air cleaner duct from the throttle housing (see illustration).

3 Slacken and remove the bolts securing the air cleaner housing to the battery tray. Detach the housing from its intake duct and lift the assembly out from the engine compartment (see illustrations).

2.3a Slacken and remove the retaining bolts (arrowed) . . .

4 If necessary, remove the intake duct retaining bolt and fasteners and remove the duct from the engine compartment.

Refitting

5 Refitting is the reverse of removal making sure all the ducts are securely reconnected.

3 Accelerator cable - removal, refitting and adjustment

Removal

1 On right-hand drive models, to improve access, slacken and remove the coolant expansion tank retaining bolts and position the tank clear of the accelerator cable.
2 On all models, unclip the accelerator cable adjustment nut from the mounting bracket then detach the inner cable from the throttle cam **(see illustration)**.
3 Work back along the length of the cable, free it from any retaining clips or ties, noting its correct routing. Free the cable sealing grommet from the engine compartment bulkhead.
4 From inside the vehicle, remove the retaining clips then unclip the undercover from the driver's side of the facia to gain access to the accelerator pedal.
5 Reaching up behind the facia, unclip the accelerator inner cable from the top of the accelerator pedal **(see illustration)**.

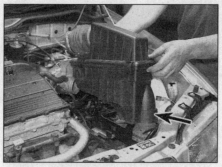

2.3b . . . then lift the air cleaner housing out of position, freeing it from the intake duct (location arrowed)

6 Return to the engine compartment then remove the cable and bulkhead sealing grommet from the vehicle.
7 Examine the cable for signs of wear or damage and renew if necessary. Check the rubber grommet for signs of damage or deterioration and renew it if necessary.

Refitting

8 Feed the cable into position from the engine compartment and seat the outer cable grommet in the bulkhead.
9 From inside the vehicle, clip the inner cable into position in the pedal end and check to make sure the grommet is correctly located in the bulkhead. Check that the cable is securely retained, then refit the undercover to the facia.
10 From within the engine compartment, ensure the outer cable is correctly seated in the bulkhead, then work along the cable, securing it in position with the retaining clips and ties, and ensuring that the cable is correctly routed.
11 Connect the inner cable to the throttle cam and clip the cable adjusting nut into its mounting bracket and adjust the cable as described below. On right-hand drive models refit the coolant expansion tank retaining bolts and tighten securely.

Adjustment

12 On 2.0 litre engines, switch on the ignition and wait for 5 seconds before switching it back off. This will ensure that the throttle

housing stepper motor is set to the correct position to allow for cable adjustment.
13 On all engines, slide the cable adjustment nut out from the mounting bracket and position the cable so that the adjustment nut is resting against the upper surface of the bracket **(see illustration)**.
14 Slacken the adjustment nut until the throttle cam is fully against its stop then slowly tighten the nut until the point is found where all freeplay is removed from the cable but the cam is still against its stop.
15 Clip the adjustment nut correctly back into position then have an assistant depress the accelerator pedal. Check that the throttle cam opens fully and returns smoothly to its stop, readjusting the cable if necessary.

4 Accelerator pedal - removal and refitting

1.4 and 1.6 litre engine

Removal

1 From inside the vehicle, remove the retaining clips then unclip the undercover from the driver's side of the facia to gain access to the accelerator pedal.
2 Reaching up behind the facia, unclip the accelerator inner cable from the top of the accelerator pedal.
3 Unbolt the pedal assembly and remove it from the vehicle.
4 Inspect the pedal assembly for signs of wear, paying particular attention to the pedal pivot. If the assembly shows signs of wear or damage, it must be renewed.

Refitting

5 Refitting is the reverse of removal, adjusting the accelerator cable as described in Section 3.

2.0 litre engine

6 The accelerator pedal is an integral part of the brake pedal bracket assembly and is not available separately. Refer to Chapter 9 for removal and refitting details.

4A

3.2 Unclip the accelerator outer cable from the mounting bracket and free the inner cable from the throttle cam

3.5 Unclip the accelerator inner cable (arrowed) from the upper end of the pedal

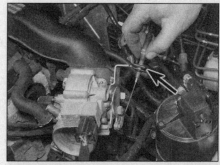

3.13 Unclip the accelerator outer cable from its mounting bracket and adjust as described in text by rotating the nut (arrowed)

5 Unleaded petrol -
general information and usage

Note: *The information given in this Chapter is correct at the time of writing. If updated information is thought to be required, check with a Rover dealer. If travelling abroad, consult one of the motoring organisations (or a similar authority) for advice on the fuel available.*

The fuel recommended by Rover is given in the Specifications Section of this Chapter, followed by the equivalent petrol currently on sale in the UK.

All petrol models are designed to run on fuel with a minimum octane rating of 95 (RON) and all models have a catalytic converter, and so must be run on unleaded fuel only. Under no circumstances should leaded fuel (UK "4-star") be used, as this may damage the converter.

Super unleaded petrol (98 octane) can also be used in all models if wished, though there is no advantage in doing so.

6 Fuel injection system -
general information

All petrol engines are equipped with a multi-point Rover/Motorola modular engine management (fuel injection/ignition) system (MEMS-Mpi). The system incorporates a closed-loop catalytic converter and an evaporative emission control system, and complies with the latest emission control standards. The fuel injection side of the system operates as follows; refer to Chapter 5B for information on the ignition system.

The fuel pump, immersed in the fuel tank, pumps fuel from the fuel tank to the fuel rail, via a filter which is located in the engine compartment. Fuel supply pressure is controlled by the pressure regulator which allows excess fuel to be returned to the tank.

The electrical control system consists of the electronic control module (ECM), along with the following sensors.

a) *Throttle position sensor - informs the*

7.3 Depressurising the fuel system

ECM of the throttle position, and the rate of throttle opening or closing.

b) *Coolant temperature sensor - informs the ECM of engine temperature.*

c) *Intake air temperature sensor - informs the ECM of the temperature of the air passing through the inlet manifold.*

d) *Oxygen sensor - informs the ECM of the oxygen content of the exhaust gases (explained in greater detail in Part C of this Chapter).*

e) *Crankshaft sensor - informs the ECM of engine speed and crankshaft position.*

f) *Manifold absolute pressure (MAP) sensor (contained within the ECM) - informs the ECM of the engine load by monitoring the pressure in the inlet manifold.*

g) *Vehicle speed sensor - informs the ECM of vehicle speed.*

h) *Knock sensor (2.0 litre engine only) - informs the ECM when pre-ignition ("pinking") is occurring.*

All the above information is analysed by the ECM and, based on this, the ECM determines the appropriate ignition and fuelling requirements for the engine. The ECM controls the fuel injector by varying its pulse width - the length of time the injector is held open - to provide a richer or weaker mixture, as appropriate. The mixture is constantly varied by the ECM, to provide the best setting for cranking, starting (with either a hot or cold engine), warm-up, idle, cruising, and acceleration.

The ECM also has full control over the engine idle speed. On 1.4 and 1.6 litre engines the idle speed is controlled via the idle air control valve; the valve controls the opening of an air passage which bypasses the throttle valve. When the throttle valve is closed, the ECM controls the opening of the valve, which in turn regulates the amount of air entering the manifold, and so controls the idle speed. On 2.0 litre engines, the idle speed is controlled by the ECM via a stepper motor fitted to the throttle housing. The motor has a pushrod controlling the opening of the throttle valve when the valve is closed (accelerator pedal released); this regulates the amount of air which flows through the throttle housing passage, so controlling the idle speed.

The ECM also controls the exhaust and evaporative emission control systems, which are described in detail in Part C of this Chapter.

If there is an abnormality in any of the readings obtained from any sensor, the ECM enters its back-up mode. In this event, the ECM ignores the abnormal sensor signal, and assumes a pre-programmed value which will allow the engine to continue running (albeit at reduced efficiency). If the ECM enters this back-up mode, the warning light on the instrument panel will come on, and the relevant fault code will be stored in the ECM memory.

If the warning light comes on, the vehicle should be taken to a Rover dealer at the earliest opportunity. A complete test of the engine management system can then be carried out, using a special electronic diagnostic test unit which is simply plugged into the system's diagnostic connector. The connector is located behind the driver's side of the facia; to gain access to the connector unclip the storage pocket and reach in through the facia aperture.

An inertia switch is incorporated into the fuel system to cut off the fuel supply in the event of an accident. The switch is located behind the front of the centre console, on the driver's side, and can be reset by depressing the button on the top of the switch.

7 Fuel injection system -
depressurisation

⚠ *Warning: Refer to the warning note in Section 1 before proceeding. The following procedure will merely relieve the pressure in the fuel system - remember that fuel will still be present in the system components, and take precautions accordingly before disconnecting any of them.*

1 The fuel system referred to in this Section is defined as the tank-mounted fuel pump, the fuel filter, the fuel injector(s) and the pressure regulator, and the metal pipes and flexible hoses of the fuel lines between these components. All these contain fuel which will be under pressure while the engine is running, and/or while the ignition is switched on. The pressure will remain for some time after the ignition has been switched off, and it must be relieved in a controlled fashion when any of these components are disturbed for servicing work.

2 The fuel system is depressurised by slackening the fuel filter outlet union nut.

3 Ensure the ignition is switched off and position wads of rag around the filter and union nut to catch the spilled fuel. Retain the filter union with a spanner and slowly slacken the union nut to relieve the pressure in the fuel system **(see illustration)**.

4 Ensure all fuel pressure has been released, then tighten the union nut to the specified torque.

8 Fuel pump -
removal and refitting

⚠ *Warning: Refer to the warning note in Section 1 before proceeding.*
Note: *A new fuel pump cover sealing ring will be required on refitting.*

Removal

1 Remove the fuel tank as described in Section 10.

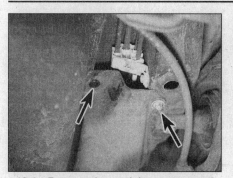

10.4a Remove the retaining screws and fasteners (front ones arrowed) . . .

2 Release the fuel pump wiring from its clip on the side of the fuel tank.

3 Release the retaining clips and disconnect the fuel feed and return pipes from the pump unions; the feed hose is fitted with a quick-release fitting, depress the collar to release the fitting.

4 Undo the breather valve retaining nut and position it clear of the fuel pump.

5 Slacken and remove the fuel pump retaining nuts then carefully manoeuvre the pump assembly out of position, taking great care not to damage the fuel gauge float. Recover the pump seal and discard it; a new one must be used on refitting.

6 The pump assembly must be treated as a sealed unit with no spares being available individually.

Refitting

7 Fit a new sealing ring to the tank then manoeuvre the fuel pump assembly into position.

8 Ensure the pump unit is correctly seated then refit the retaining nuts and tighten them to the specified torque.

9 Refit the breather valve and tighten its retaining nut to the specified torque.

10 Reconnect the feed and return hoses to the pump and route the pump wiring through the clip on the side of the tank.

11 Refit the fuel tank as described in Section 10.

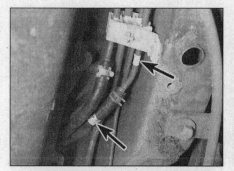

10.7 Disconnect the fuel return and breather hoses from the pipes. Identification marks (arrowed) to avoid reconnecting the hoses incorrectly

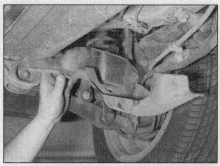

10.4b . . . and remove the protective cover from the left-hand side of the fuel tank

9 Fuel gauge sender unit - removal and refitting

The fuel gauge sender unit is an integral part of the fuel pump assembly. Refer to Section 8 for removal and refitting details.

10 Fuel tank - removal and refitting

⚠ **Warning: Refer to the warning note in Section 1 before proceeding.**

Removal

1 Disconnect the battery negative terminal then depressurise the fuel system as described in Section 7.

2 Before removing the fuel tank, all fuel must be drained from the tank. Since a fuel tank drain plug is not provided, it is therefore preferable to carry out the removal operation when the tank is nearly empty. The remaining fuel can then be siphoned or hand-pumped from the tank.

3 Chock the front wheels then jack up the rear of the vehicle and support it securely on axle stands (see *"Jacking and Vehicle Support"*). Remove the left-hand rear roadwheel.

4 Slacken and remove the retaining screws and fasteners and remove the protective cover from the left-hand side of the fuel tank

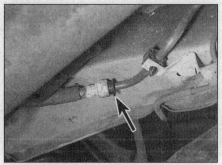

10.8 Depress the collar (arrowed) and disconnect the fuel feed hose

to gain access to the fuel pipes and pump wiring connector **(see illustrations)**.

5 Free the fuel pump wiring connector from its retaining clip and separate the two halves of the connector.

6 Release the retaining clips and disconnect the main filler and breather hoses from the filler neck.

7 Release the retaining clips and disconnect the fuel return and breather hoses from their unions on the side of the tank **(see illustration)**.

8 Depress the collar and disconnect the fuel feed hose from its union at the side of the fuel tank **(see illustration)**.

9 Place a trolley jack with an interposed block of wood beneath the tank, then raise the jack until it is supporting the weight of the tank.

10 Loosen the locknuts which are located above the fuel tank retaining straps. Unscrew the two strap retaining nuts and unhook the straps from beneath the fuel tank **(see illustration)**.

11 Slowly lower the fuel tank out of position and remove the tank from underneath the vehicle.

12 If the tank is contaminated with sediment or water, remove the fuel pump (Section 8), and swill the tank out with clean fuel. The tank is injection-moulded from a synthetic material - if seriously damaged, it should be renewed. However, in certain cases, it may be possible to have small leaks or minor damage repaired. Seek the advice of a specialist before attempting to repair the fuel tank.

Refitting

13 Refitting is the reverse of the removal procedure, noting the following points:

a) *When lifting the tank back into position, take care to ensure that none of the hoses or the fuel pump wiring become trapped between the tank and vehicle body. Refit the retaining straps, securely tighten the strap nuts then secure them in position by tightening the locknuts.*

b) *Ensure all pipes and hoses are correctly routed and all hoses unions are securely joined.*

c) *On completion, refill the tank with a small amount of fuel, and check for signs of leakage prior to taking the vehicle out on the road.*

4A

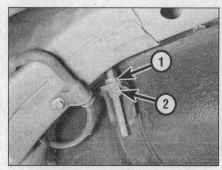

10.10 Slacken the locknut (1) then unscrew the retaining nut (2) and free the fuel tank strap from its mounting

11.9a On 2.0 litre engines, disconnect the wiring connector from the throttle position sensor . . .

11.9b . . . and disconnect the breather hose from the throttle housing

11.10 Disconnect the wiring connector from the idle speed control motor

11 Throttle housing - removal and refitting

Removal

1.4 and 1.6 litre engine

1 Disconnect the battery negative lead.
2 Release the retaining clip and disconnect the intake duct from the throttle housing.
3 Disconnect the wiring connector from the throttle position sensor.
4 Release the retaining clip and disconnect the breather hose from the throttle housing.
5 Unclip the accelerator cable adjustment nut from its bracket then detach the inner cable from the throttle cam.
6 Disconnect the idle air control valve hose from the throttle housing.
7 Slacken and remove the four retaining bolts then remove the throttle housing from the manifold. Recover the sealing ring which is fitted between the housing and manifold and renew it if it is damaged.

2.0 litre engine

8 Remove the air cleaner housing as described in Section 2.
9 Carry out the operations described in paragraphs 1 to 5 **(see illustrations)**.
10 Disconnect the wiring connector from the idle speed control motor **(see illustration)**.
11 On models with cruise control, working as described in Chapter 12, remove the actuator from the throttle housing.
12 Slacken and remove the four retaining nuts and remove the throttle housing from the manifold **(see illustration)**.
13 With the housing removed, check the insulating spacer which is fitted between the housing and manifold. If the spacer shows signs of damage or deterioration it must be renewed; the spacer is retained by three bolts **(see illustration)**.

Refitting

14 Refitting is the reverse of removal, bearing in mind the following points:
 a) On 1.4 and 1.6 litre engines, ensure the sealing ring is in position then refit the

throttle housing to the manifold and tighten the retaining bolts to the specified torque.
 b) On 2.0 litre engines, ensure the housing and spacer surfaces are clean and dry then refit the housing and tighten its retaining nuts to the specified torque.
 c) Ensure all hoses and wiring connectors are correctly and securely reconnected.
 d) Reconnect and adjust the accelerator cable as described in Section 3.

12 Fuel injection system - testing and adjustment

Testing

1 If a fault appears in the fuel injection system, first ensure that all the system wiring connectors are securely connected and free of corrosion. Ensure that the fault is not due to poor maintenance; ie, check that the air cleaner filter element is clean, the spark plugs are in good condition and correctly gapped, the cylinder compression pressures are correct, and that the engine breather hoses are clear and undamaged, referring to Chapters 1A, 2A and 5 for further information (as applicable).
2 If these checks fail to reveal the cause of the problem, the vehicle should be taken to a suitably-equipped Rover dealer for testing. A wiring block connector is incorporated in the engine management circuit, into which a

special electronic diagnostic tester can be plugged (see Section 6). The tester will locate the fault quickly and simply, alleviating the need to test all the system components individually, which is a time-consuming operation that carries a risk of damaging the ECM.

Adjustment

3 Experienced home mechanics with a considerable amount of skill and equipment (including a tachometer and an accurately calibrated exhaust gas analyser) may be able to check the exhaust CO level and the idle speed. However, if these are found to be in need of adjustment, the car will have to be taken to a suitably-equipped Rover dealer who has access to the necessary diagnostic equipment required to test and (where possible) adjust the settings.

13 Fuel injection system components - removal and refitting

Fuel rail and injectors

⚠️ **Warning: Refer to the warning note in Section 1 before proceeding.**

Note: *If a faulty injector is suspected, before condemning the injector, it is worth trying the effect of one of the proprietary injector-cleaning treatments.*

11.12 Unscrew the retaining nuts and remove the throttle housing from the manifold

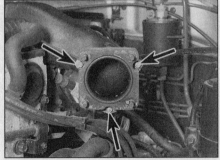

11.13 Throttle housing insulating spacer is retained by three bolts (arrowed)

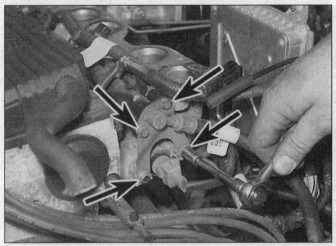

13.19 Slacken and remove the four retaining bolts (arrowed) . . .

13.20 . . . remove the support bracket and free the fuel feed pipe union from the end of the fuel rail (sealing ring arrowed)

1.4 litre 8-valve engine

1 Disconnect the battery negative terminal then depressurise the fuel system as described in Section 7.

2 Remove the upper section of the inlet manifold as described in Section 14.

3 Release the retaining clip and disconnect the vacuum hose from the fuel pressure regulator.

4 Release the retaining clip and disconnect the fuel return hose from the right-hand end of the fuel rail then undo the retaining bolts and disconnect the fuel feed pipe union from the left-hand end of the fuel rail. Recover the sealing ring from the feed hose union and discard it; a new one must be used on refitting.

5 Slide out the four injector retaining clips then slacken and remove the bolts securing the fuel rail to the manifold. Carefully ease the fuel rail off from the top of the injectors and remove it from the manifold. Remove the upper sealing rings from the injectors and discard them; they must be renewed whenever they are disturbed.

6 Disconnect the wiring connector(s) then ease the injector(s) out of position and remove from the manifold. Remove the lower sealing ring from each removed injector and discard; all disturbed sealing rings must be renewed.

7 Refitting is a reversal of the removal procedure, noting the following points:

 a) Renew all disturbed sealing rings and apply a smear of engine oil to them to aid installation.

 b) Ease the injector(s) into the manifold, ensuring that the sealing ring(s) remain correctly seated.

 c) Refit the fuel rail, ensuring that all sealing rings remain in position. Once the fuel rail is correctly seated, refit the injector retaining clips then refit the rail retaining bolts and tighten them to the specified torque.

 d) Fit a new sealing ring to the fuel feed pipe union and tighten its retaining bolts to the specified torque.

 e) On completion start the engine and check for fuel leaks.

1.4 litre 16-valve and 1.6 litre engine

8 Disconnect the battery negative terminal then depressurise the fuel system as described in Section 7.

9 Release the retaining clip(s) and disconnect the breather hose(s) from the camshaft cover.

10 Disconnect the wiring connector from the idle air control valve.

11 Release the retaining clip and disconnect the vacuum pipe from the fuel pressure regulator.

12 Release the retaining clip and disconnect the fuel return hose from the right-hand end of the fuel rail then undo the retaining bolts and disconnect the fuel feed pipe union from the left-hand end of the fuel rail. Recover the sealing ring from the feed hose union and discard it; a new one must be used on refitting.

13 Undo the retaining bolt then free the injector wiring bracket from the fuel rail and disconnect the wiring connector.

14 Remove the engine oil dipstick then slacken and remove the bolts securing the fuel rail to the manifold. Carefully ease the fuel rail and injector assembly out of position and remove it from the manifold. Remove the lower sealing rings from the injectors and discard them; they must be renewed whenever they are disturbed.

15 Disconnect the wiring connector from the relevant injector then slide off the retaining clip and withdraw the injector from the fuel rail. Remove the upper sealing ring from the injector and discard it; all disturbed sealing rings must be renewed.

16 Refitting is a reversal of the removal procedure, noting the following points:

 a) Renew all disturbed sealing rings and apply a smear of engine oil to them to aid installation.

 b) Ease the injector(s) into the fuel rail, ensuring that the sealing ring(s) remain correctly seated. Secure in position with the retaining clips and reconnect the wiring connectors.

 c) On refitting the fuel rail, take care not to damage the injectors and ensure that all sealing rings remain in position. Once the fuel rail is correctly seated, tighten its retaining bolts to the specified torque.

 d) Fit a new sealing ring to the fuel feed pipe union and tighten its bolts to the specified torque.

 e) On completion start the engine and check for fuel leaks.

2.0 litre engine

17 Disconnect the battery negative terminal then depressurise the fuel system as described in Section 7.

18 Remove the inlet manifold upper section as described in Section 14.

19 Position a wad of rag beneath the left-hand end of the fuel rail then slacken and remove the retaining bolts securing the support bracket to the fuel rail/manifold (see illustration).

20 Ease the fuel feed pipe union out from the fuel rail, noting its sealing ring, and remove the support bracket (see illustration). Discard the sealing ring, a new one must be used on refitting.

21 Disconnect the wiring connectors from the four injectors and position the wiring harness clear of the manifold (see illustration).

22 Release the retaining clip and disconnect the fuel return hose from the right-hand end of the fuel rail (see illustration).

23 Slacken and remove the bolts securing the fuel rail to the manifold. Carefully ease the fuel

4A

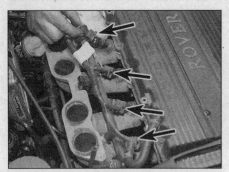

13.21 Disconnect the wiring connectors from the injectors (arrowed)

13.22 Release the retaining clip and detach the fuel return hose from the rail

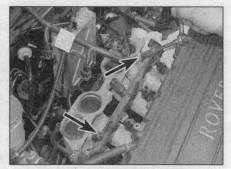

13.23a Undo the retaining bolts (arrowed) . . .

13.23b . . . then ease the fuel rail and injector assembly out from the manifold and remove it from the engine

13.24a Slide off the retaining clip . . .

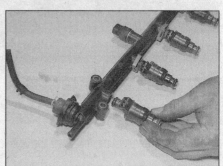

13.24b . . . then ease the injector out from the fuel rail

rail and injector assembly out of position and remove it from the manifold **(see illustrations)**. Remove the lower sealing rings from the injectors and discard them; they must be renewed whenever they are disturbed.

24 Slide off the retaining clip and withdraw the relevant injector from the fuel rail **(see illustrations)**. Remove the upper sealing ring from the injector and discard it; all disturbed sealing rings must be renewed.

25 Refitting is a reversal of the removal procedure, noting the following points:

a) Renew all disturbed sealing rings and apply a smear of engine oil to them to aid installation **(see illustration)**.

b) Ease the injector(s) into the fuel rail, ensuring that the sealing ring(s) remain correctly seated, and secure them in position with the retaining clips.

c) On refitting the fuel rail, take care not to damage the injectors and ensure that all sealing rings remain in position. Once the fuel rail is correctly seated, tighten its retaining bolts to the specified torque.

d) Fit a new sealing ring to the fuel feed pipe union then refit the support bracket and tighten its bolts to the specified torque.

e) On completion start the engine and check for fuel leaks.

Fuel pressure regulator

26 The regulator is an integral part of the fuel rail and cannot be renewed separately. If the regulator is faulty, renew the fuel rail as described earlier in this Section.

Throttle position sensor

Note: *New retaining screws must be used on refitting.*

1.4 and 1.6 litre engine

27 Ensure the ignition is switched off then disconnect the wiring connector from the sensor which is fitted to the side of the throttle housing **(see illustration)**.

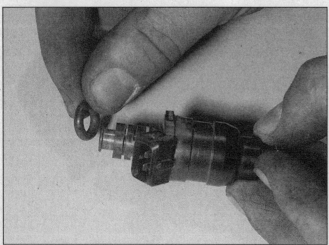

13.25 On refitting renew all injector sealing rings

13.27 Disconnect the wiring connector (1), undo the screws (2) and remove the retaining plate and throttle position sensor (1.6 litre engine shown)

13.37 Idle air control valve wiring connector (1) and upper retaining screw (2)

13.41 Coolant temperature sensor location on 1.4 and 1.6 litre engines (16-valve engine shown)

13.45 Crankshaft sensor retaining bolts (arrowed) - 2.0 litre engine

28 Undo the two retaining screws and remove the retaining plate and sensor. Discard the screws, new ones should be used on refitting **(see illustration 13.27).**

29 On refitting, carefully align the throttle valve spindle with the sensor slot and seat the sensor on the housing.

30 Fit the retaining plate and new retaining screws, tightening them to the specified torque, and reconnect the wiring connector. *Caution: Do not overtighten the retaining screws as the sensor is easily damaged.*

2.0 litre engine

31 Removal and refitting is as described in paragraphs 20 to 22, noting that access to the sensor is poor with the housing in position. If necessary, to improve access, remove the throttle housing as described in Section 11.

Intake air temperature sensor

32 The sensor is screwed into the left-hand end of the inlet manifold.

33 Ensure the ignition is switched off then disconnect the wiring connector from the sensor.

34 Unscrew the sensor and remove it from the manifold along with its sealing washer (where fitted).

35 On refitting, ensure the manifold and sensor threads are clean and dry. If the sensor was originally fitted with a sealing washer, use a new sealing washer. Where no sealing washer was fitted, clean the threads and apply a smear of sealant to them.

36 Refit the sensor to the manifold, tightening it to the specified torque, and reconnect the wiring connector.

Idle air control valve - 1.4 and 1.6 litre engine

37 Ensure the ignition is switched off then disconnect the wiring connector from the valve which is fitted to the top of the inlet manifold **(see illustration)**.

38 Undo the two retaining screws **(see illustration 13.37)** then carefully remove the motor from its mounting bracket and lift it away from the engine. Recover the sealing ring and discard it, a new one should be used on refitting.

39 On refitting, ensure the mating surfaces are clean and dry. Fit a new sealing ring then ease the motor into position and tighten its retaining screws to the specified torque. Reconnect the wiring connector.

Idle speed control stepper motor - 2.0 litre engine

40 The motor is an integral part of the throttle housing and cannot be renewed separately. If the motor is faulty, the complete throttle housing assembly must be renewed as described in Section 11.

Coolant temperature sensor

41 The sensor is screwed into the coolant outlet union on the front, left-hand end of the engine on 1.4 and 1.6 litre engines, and into the thermostat housing on 2.0 litre engines **(see illustration)**. Refer to Chapter 3 for removal and refitting details.

Manifold absolute pressure (MAP) sensor

42 The sensor is an integral part of the ECM and cannot be renewed separately. See below for details.

Crankshaft sensor

43 Firmly apply the handbrake then jack up the front of the vehicle and support it on axle stands (see *"Jacking and Vehicle Support"*). The sensor is mounted onto the rear of the transmission mounting plate and is accessible from underneath the vehicle.

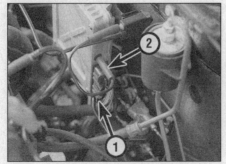

13.49 Disconnect the wiring connector (1) and vacuum hose (2) . . .

44 Ensure the ignition is switched off then disconnect the wiring connector from the sensor.

45 Unscrew the retaining bolt(s) and remove the sensor from the engine **(see illustration)**.

46 Refitting is the reverse of removal, tightening the retaining bolt(s) to the specified torque.

Vehicle speed sensor

47 The sensor is driven by the speedometer drive on the transmission unit. Refer to Chapter 7, Section 6 for removal and refitting details.

Electronic control module (ECM)

Note: *If a new ECM is to be fitted, it will be necessary to entrust the task to a Rover dealer. After fitting, it will be necessary to programme the anti-theft system code into the ECM to enable it function correctly. This can only be done using the special Rover equipment which is plugged into the diagnostic connector (see Section 6).*

48 The ECM is mounted onto the engine compartment bulkhead. Prior to removal, first disconnect the battery negative terminal.

49 Disconnect the wiring connector and vacuum hose from the ECM **(see illustration)**.

50 Undo the retaining nut(s) then free the ECM from its lower mounting and remove it from the engine compartment **(see illustration)**.

4A

13.50 . . . then unscrew the retaining nuts and remove the ECM from the engine compartment

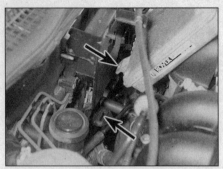

13.51 On refitting ensure the ECM lug is correctly located in the mounting bracket (arrowed)

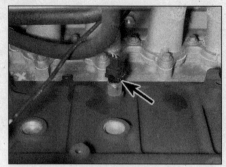

13.53 Knock sensor location - 2.0 litre engine (viewed from below)

13.56 Disconnect the fuel temperature sensor wiring connector - 2.0 litre engine

51 Refitting is the reverse of removal ensuring the wiring connector and vacuum hose are securely reconnected **(see illustration)**. Tighten the module nut(s) to the specified torque setting.

Knock sensor - 2.0 litre engine

52 Firmly apply the handbrake then jack up the front of the vehicle and support it on axle stands (see "*Jacking and Vehicle Support*"). The sensor is mounted onto the rear of the cylinder block.
53 Disconnect the wiring connector then unscrew the sensor and remove it from the engine **(see illustration)**.
54 On refitting, ensure the sensor and block are clean and dry. Screw the sensor into position, tightening it to the specified torque, and reconnect the wiring connector. Lower the vehicle to the ground.

13.58 Unclip the relay module from the ECM mounting bracket . . .

13.59 . . . then disconnect the wiring connectors and remove the module

Fuel temperature sensor - 2.0 litre engine

⚠ **Warning: Refer to the warning note in Section 1 before proceeding.**

55 Depressurise the fuel system as described in Section 7.
56 Disconnect the wiring connector then unscrew the sensor from the fuel rail **(see illustration)**. Remove the sealing washer and discard it, a new one must be used on refitting.
57 On refitting, fit the sensor using a new sealing washer. Tighten the sensor to the specified torque then reconnect the wiring connector.

Relay module

58 Unclip the relay module from the rear of the ECM mounting bracket and manoeuvre it out of position **(see illustration)**.
59 Disconnect the wiring connectors and remove the relay module from the engine compartment **(see illustration)**.
60 Refitting is the reverse of removal.

Fuel cut-off inertia switch

61 The fuel cut-off inertia switch is located behind the front of the centre console, on the driver's side.
62 Ensure the ignition is switched off then reach in behind the console and disconnect the wiring connector from the switch.

13.63 Disconnect the wiring connector, undo the screws and remove the switch from the facia bracket (centre console removed)

63 Undo the retaining screws and remove the switch **(see illustration)**.
64 Refitting is the reverse of removal, ensuring the switch is fitted the correct way up. On completion, reset the switch by depressing the button on the top of the switch.

---

14 Inlet manifold - removal and refitting

1.4 litre 8-valve engine

Upper manifold section - removal and refitting

1 Disconnect the battery negative terminal.
2 Release the retaining clip and disconnect the intake duct from the manifold.
3 Disconnect the wiring connector from the throttle position sensor and the idle air control valve.
4 Release the retaining clips and disconnect the various vacuum and breather hoses from the throttle housing and manifold. The vacuum servo unit hose is fitted with a quick release fitting; depress the locking collar with a screwdriver to release the hose.
5 Unclip the accelerator cable adjustment nut from its bracket then detach the inner cable from the throttle cam.
6 Unclip the HT lead and injector wiring connector from the base of the manifold upper section.
7 Slacken and remove the retaining bolts then lift the manifold upper section away from the lower section. Recover the gasket and discard it.
8 Refitting is the reverse of removal noting the following:
   a) Ensure the mating surfaces are clean and dry and fit the new gasket. Refit the upper section and tighten the retaining bolts evenly and progressively to the specified torque.
   b) Ensure that all relevant hoses are reconnected to their original positions, and are securely held (where necessary) by their retaining clips.
   c) Reconnect and adjust the accelerator cable as described in Section 3.

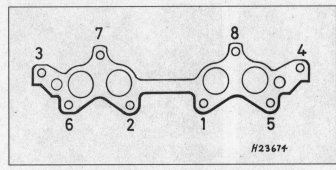

14.18 Inlet manifold nut and bolt tightening sequence - 1.4 litre 8-valve engine

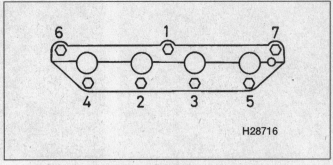

14.29 Inlet manifold nut and bolt tightening sequence - 1.4 litre 16-valve engine and 1.6 litre engine

Complete manifold - removal and refitting

9 Disconnect the battery negative terminal then depressurise the fuel system as described in Section 7.

10 Drain the cooling system as described in Chapter 1A.

11 Carry out the operations described in paragraphs 2 to 6.

12 Disconnect the injector harness wiring connector and disconnect the connector from the intake air temperature sensor.

13 Release the retaining clip and disconnect the fuel return hose from the pipe at the rear of the manifold then undo the retaining bolts and disconnect the fuel feed pipe union from the left-hand end of the fuel rail. Recover the sealing ring from the feed hose union and discard it; a new one must be used on refitting.

14 Slacken the retaining clip and disconnect the coolant hose from the right-hand end of the manifold.

15 Slacken and remove the bolt securing the support bracket to the right-hand end of the manifold.

16 Check that all the necessary vacuum/breather hoses have been disconnected then evenly and progressively slacken and remove the manifold retaining bolts and nuts.

17 Remove the manifold from the engine and recover the manifold gasket, noting which way around it is fitted.

18 Refitting is the reverse of refitting, noting the following:

a) Prior to refitting, check the manifold studs and renew any that are worn or damaged.

b) Ensure the manifold and cylinder mating surfaces are clean and dry and fit the new gasket. Refit the manifold and tighten the retaining bolts and nuts to the specified torque in the sequence shown **(see illustration)**.

c) Ensure that all relevant hoses are reconnected to their original positions, and are securely held (where necessary) by their retaining clips.

d) Fit a new sealing ring to the fuel feed pipe union and tighten its bolts to the specified torque.

e) Reconnect and adjust the accelerator cable as described in Section 3.

f) On completion refill the cooling system as described in Chapter 1A.

1.4 litre 16-valve and 1.6 litre engine

Removal

19 Disconnect the battery negative terminal then depressurise the fuel system as described in Section 7.

20 Drain the cooling system as described in Chapter 1A.

21 Remove the throttle housing as described in Section 11.

22 Release the retaining clips and disconnect the various vacuum and breather hoses from the manifold. The vacuum servo unit hose is fitted with a quick release fitting; depress the locking collar with a screwdriver to release the hose.

23 Release the retaining clip and disconnect the fuel return hose from the right-hand end of the fuel rail then undo the retaining bolts and disconnect the fuel feed pipe union from the left-hand end of the fuel rail. Recover the sealing ring from the feed hose union and discard it; a new one must be used on refitting.

24 Disconnect the wiring connectors from the idle air control valve and the intake air temperature sensor.

25 Free the injector wiring harness connector from the left-hand side of the manifold and disconnect the connector. Unclip the HT lead from the manifold.

26 Slacken the retaining clip and disconnect the coolant hose from the right-hand end of the manifold.

27 Check that all the necessary vacuum/breather hoses have been disconnected then evenly and progressively slacken and remove the manifold retaining bolts and nuts.

28 Remove the manifold from the engine and remove the gasket from the manifold recess.

Refitting

29 Refitting is the reverse of refitting, noting the following:

a) Prior to refitting, check the manifold studs and renew any that are worn or damaged.

b) Ensure the manifold and cylinder mating surfaces are clean and dry and fit the new gasket to the manifold recess. Refit the manifold and tighten the retaining bolts and nuts to the specified torque in the sequence shown **(see illustration)**.

c) Ensure that all relevant hoses are reconnected to their original positions, and are securely held (where necessary) by their retaining clips.

d) Fit a new sealing ring to the fuel feed pipe union and tighten its bolts to the specified torque.

e) Reconnect and adjust the accelerator cable as described in Section 3.

f) On completion refill the cooling system as described in Chapter 1A.

2.0 litre engine

Removal

30 Disconnect the battery negative terminal.

31 Remove the throttle housing as described in Section 11.

32 Release the retaining clips and disconnect the various vacuum and breather hoses from the manifold upper section. The vacuum servo unit hose is fitted with a quick release fitting; depress the locking collar with a screwdriver to release the hose **(see illustrations)**.

33 Unscrew the retaining bolts and remove the support bracket from the front of the manifold upper section **(see illustrations)**.

4A

14.32a On 2.0 litre engines, disconnect the vacuum hoses (arrowed) from the left-hand . . .

14.32b ... and right-hand ends of the manifold upper section ...

14.32c ... then depress the locking collar with a screwdriver and disconnect the servo unit hose

14.33a Unscrew the retaining bolts securing the support brackets (arrowed) in position ...

14.33b ... and remove both brackets from the engine

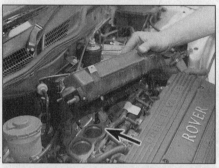

14.35 Remove the manifold upper section and recover the gasket (arrowed)

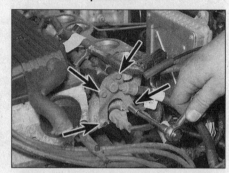

14.37 Slacken and remove the retaining bolts (arrowed) ...

34 Disconnect the wiring connector from the fuel temperature switch.

14.38 ... then remove the support bracket and free the fuel feed pipe union from the fuel rail

35 Slacken and remove the retaining bolts then lift the manifold upper section away from the lower section (**see illustration**). Recover the gasket and discard it. If the lower section of the manifold is also to be removed, continue as follows.
36 Depressurise the fuel system as described in Section 7.
37 Slacken and remove the retaining bolts and remove the support bracket from the left-hand end of the fuel rail/manifold (**see illustration**).
38 Free the fuel feed pipe union from the end of the fuel rail noting its sealing ring (**see illustration**). Discard the sealing ring, a new one must be used on refitting.
39 Disconnect the wiring connectors from the four injectors and position the wiring harness clear of the manifold. Also disconnect

the connector from the intake air temperature sensor (**see illustrations**).
40 Release the retaining clip and disconnect the fuel return hose from the right-hand end of the fuel rail.
41 Undo the retaining bolts and free the pipe/wiring mounting brackets from the rear of the manifold lower section (**see illustration**).
42 Evenly and progressively slacken and remove the manifold retaining bolts and nuts then remove the manifold lower section from the engine. Remove the manifold gasket and discard it (**see illustration**).

Refitting

43 Refitting is the reverse of refitting, noting the following.
 a) Prior to refitting, check the manifold studs

14.39a Disconnect the wiring connectors from the four injectors ...

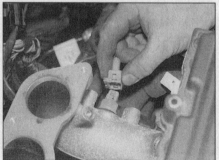

14.39b ... and the intake air temperature sensor

14.41 Undo the retaining bolts and free the pipe/wiring brackets from the rear of the manifold lower section

14.42 Removing the inlet manifold lower section

14.43 Inlet manifold lower section nut and bolt tightening sequence - 2.0 litre engine

and renew any that are worn or damaged.

b) *Ensure the manifold lower section and cylinder mating surfaces are clean and dry and fit the new gasket. Refit the manifold and tighten the retaining bolts and nuts to the specified torque in the sequence shown (see illustration).*

c) *Ensure that all relevant hoses are reconnected to their original positions, and are securely held (where necessary) by their retaining clips.*

d) *Fit a new sealing ring to the fuel feed pipe union then refit the support bracket and tighten its bolts to the specified torque.*

e) *Ensure the manifold mating surfaces are clean and dry then fit a new gasket. Tighten the upper section bolts to the specified torque.*

f) *Reconnect and adjust the accelerator cable as described in Section 3.*

15 Exhaust manifold - removal and refitting

1.4 and 1.6 litre engine

Removal

1 Trace the wiring back from the oxygen sensor then free the wiring connector from its retaining clip and disconnect it.

2 On models with air conditioning, remove the alternator as described in Chapter 5A then unbolt the alternator mounting bracket from the cylinder head. Undo the retaining bolts and remove the heatshield from the side of the exhaust manifold.

3 On all models, slacken and remove the nuts securing the front pipe to the manifold. Undo the two retaining bolts and remove the manifold support bracket (where fitted then free the front pipe from the manifold and recover the gasket. **Note:** *On some 16-valve engines, it may be necessary to raise the front of the vehicle (see "Jacking and Vehicle Support") and undo the nuts securing the front pipe to its mounting bracket to enable the front pipe and manifold to be separated.*

4 Undo the retaining nuts securing the manifold to the head. Manoeuvre the manifold out of the engine compartment, complete with the gasket.

Refitting

5 Examine all the exhaust manifold studs for signs of damage and corrosion; remove all traces of corrosion, and repair or renew any damaged studs.

6 Ensure that the manifold and cylinder head sealing faces are clean and flat, and fit the new gasket.

7 Refit the manifold then refit the retaining nuts and tighten them to the specified torque in the sequence shown **(see illustration)**.

8 Fit a new gasket and reconnect the front pipe to the manifold. Refit the manifold support bracket (where fitted) then tighten the front pipe retaining nuts to the specified torque. Where necessary, refit the front pipe mounting bracket nuts, tightening them to the specified torque, and securely tighten the manifold support bracket bolts (as applicable).

9 On models with air conditioning, refit the heatshield to the manifold and tighten its retaining bolts to the specified torque. Refit the mounting bracket to the cylinder head then refit the alternator as described in Chapter 5A.

10 On all models, ensure the oxygen sensor wiring is correctly routed then reconnect the connector and clip it back onto its bracket.

2.0 litre engine - models not equipped with air conditioning

Removal

11 Trace the wiring back from the oxygen sensor then free the wiring connector from its retaining clip. Disconnect the connector so that the oxygen sensor is free to be removed with the manifold **(see illustration)**.

12 Slacken and remove the nuts securing the front pipe joint to the manifold then free the pipe from the manifold and recover the gasket.

13 Slacken and remove the bolt securing the power steering pipe to the coolant pipe on the front of the cylinder head **(see illustration)**.

14 Undo the bolt securing the coolant pipes to the left-hand end of the cylinder head **(see illustration)**.

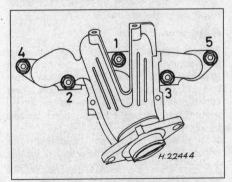

15.7 Exhaust manifold nut tightening sequence - 1.4 and 1.6 litre engine

15.11 On 2.0 litre engines, disconnect the oxygen sensor wiring connector and free it from its retaining clip

15.13 Unscrew the bolt securing the power steering pipe to the coolant pipe at the front of the cylinder head

4A

15.14 Unscrew the bolt securing the coolant pipes to the left-hand end of the cylinder head

15.15a Remove the dipstick then unscrew the retaining bolt . . .

15.15b . . . and remove the dipstick tube from the engine

15 Remove the engine oil dipstick then unscrew the retaining bolt and carefully remove the dipstick tube from the engine **(see illustrations)**.

16 Slacken and remove the retaining nuts and bolts then manoeuvre the manifold out of position. Remove the manifold gasket.

Refitting

17 Examine the exhaust manifold studs for signs of damage and corrosion; remove all traces of corrosion, and repair or renew any damaged studs.

18 Ensure that the manifold and cylinder head sealing faces are clean and flat, and fit the new gasket. Refit the manifold and fit the retaining nuts, tightening them by hand only at this stage.

19 Remove all traces of sealant from the end of the dipstick tube and apply a smear of fresh sealant (Rover recommend the use of Loctite 601) to it. Ease the dipstick tube back into position then tighten its retaining bolt securely and refit the dipstick.

20 Refit the power steering pipe and coolant pipe retaining bolts and tighten securely.

21 Align the coolant pipe with the manifold

then refit the manifold retaining bolts. Tighten the manifold retaining nuts and bolts to the specified torque in the sequence shown **(see illustration)**.

22 Fit a new gasket then reconnect the front pipe to the manifold, tighten its retaining nuts to the specified torque.

23 Ensure the oxygen sensor wiring is correctly routed then reconnect the connector and clip it back onto its bracket.

2.0 litre engine - models with air conditioning

Removal

24 Remove the air cleaner as described in Section 2.

25 Remove the radiator cooling fan as described in Chapter 3.

26 Remove the alternator as described in Chapter 5A.

27 Wipe clean the area around the high-pressure pipe union on the power steering pump. Slacken and remove the union bolt and sealing washers and disconnect the pipe from the pump. Plug the pipe end and the pump union to minimise fluid loss and prevent the

entry of dirt into the system then undo the bolts securing the power steering pipe to the cylinder head. Discard the pipe sealing washers; new ones must be used on refitting.

28 Remove the manifold as described in paragraphs 11 to 16, noting that it will also be necessary to unbolt the air conditioning pipe from the coolant rail on the front of the cylinder head.

Refitting

29 Refit the manifold as described in paragraphs 17 to 23. The remainder of refitting is a direct reversal of the removal procedure, noting the following:

a) *Position a new sealing washer on each side of the power steering pipe union and tighten the union bolt to the specified torque (see Chapter 10).*

b) *On completion, bleed the power steering hydraulic system (see Chapter 10).*

---

16 Exhaust system -
general information,
removal and refitting

General information

1 The exhaust system consists of four sections: the front pipe, the catalytic converter, the intermediate pipe, the tailpipe and main silencer box.

2 All exhaust sections are joined by flanged joints, which are secured by nuts, and the system is suspended throughout its entire length by rubber mountings.

Removal

3 Each exhaust section can be removed individually, or alternatively, the complete system can be removed as a unit. Even if only one part of the system needs attention, it can sometimes be easier to remove the whole system and separate the sections on the bench.

4 To remove the system or part of the system, first jack up the front or rear of the car and support it securely on axle stands (see *"Jacking and Vehicle Support"*). Alternatively, position the car over an inspection pit or on car ramps.

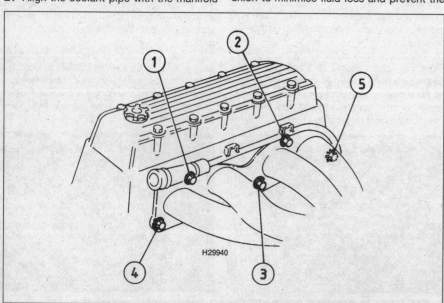

H29940

15.21 Exhaust manifold nut and bolt tightening sequence - 2.0 litre engine

Front pipe

5 On 1.4 litre 8-valve engines, trace the wiring back from the oxygen sensor then free the wiring connector from its retaining clip. Disconnect the connector so that the oxygen sensor is free to be removed with the front pipe.

6 On all engines, slacken and remove the nuts securing the front pipe flange joints to the manifold and catalytic converter. Where necessary, unbolt the manifold support bracket from the block and remove it from the manifold studs.

7 Where necessary, undo the retaining nuts securing the front pipe to its mounting bracket.

8 Unhook the front pipe from its mounting rubber then free the pipe from its joints and remove it from underneath the vehicle. Recover the gasket from each joint and discard them.

Catalytic converter

9 Slacken and remove the nuts securing the catalytic converter to the front pipe and intermediate pipe joints.

10 Free the catalytic converter from the flange joints and remove it from underneath the vehicle. Recover the gasket from each joint and discard them.

11 If necessary, undo the retaining bolts and remove the heatshields from the converter.

Intermediate pipe

12 Slacken and remove the nuts securing the intermediate pipe to the catalytic converter and tailpipe joints.

13 Free the intermediate pipe from its mounting rubbers then detach the pipe from the flange joints and remove it from underneath the vehicle. Recover the gasket from each joint and discard them.

14 If necessary, undo the retaining bolts and remove the heatshields from the pipe.

Tailpipe

15 Slacken and remove the nuts securing the tailpipe joint to the intermediate pipe.

16 Free the tailpipe from its mounting rubbers and remove it along with its gasket.

Complete system

17 On 1.4 litre 8-valve engines, trace the wiring back from the oxygen sensor then free the wiring connector from its retaining clip. Disconnect the connector so that the oxygen sensor is free to be removed with the front pipe.

18 On all engines, undo the nuts securing the front pipe flange joint to the manifold. Where necessary, also undo the nuts securing the front pipe to its mounting bracket and unbolt the manifold support bracket (as applicable).

19 Working with the aid of an assistant, free the system from all its mounting rubbers and lower it from under the vehicle. Recover the gasket from the front pipe joint.

Heat shield(s)

20 Heatshields are fitted to the catalytic converter and intermediate pipe. Each shield can be removed once its retaining bolts have been undone.

Refitting

21 Each section is refitted by reversing the removal sequence, noting the following points:

  a) *Ensure that all traces of corrosion have been removed from the flanges and renew all gaskets.*
  b) *Inspect the rubber mountings for signs of damage or deterioration, and renew as necessary.*
  c) *If the catalytic converter or intermediate pipe are being renewed, ensure that the heatshields are transferred onto the new components before fitting.*
  d) *Prior to tightening the exhaust system fasteners to the specified torque, ensure that all rubber mountings are correctly located, and that there is adequate clearance between the exhaust system and vehicle underbody.*

4A

Chapter 4 Part B:
Fuel and exhaust systems – diesel engines

Contents

Degrees of difficulty

Easy, suitable for novice with little experience	**Fairly easy,** suitable for beginner with some experience	**Fairly difficult,** suitable for competent DIY mechanic 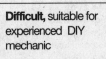	**Difficult,** suitable for experienced DIY mechanic	**Very difficult,** suitable for expert DIY or professional

Specifications

General

System type:
  Models without intercooler . . . . Indirect injection with Rover Electronic Diesel Control (EDC) system
  Models with intercooler . . . . Indirect injection with Bosch Electronic Diesel Control (EDC) system
Idle speed*:
  Models without intercooler . . . . 850 ± 50 rpm
  Models with intercooler . . . . 805 ± 50 rpm
*Not adjustable - controlled by engine control module (ECM)

Torque wrench settings

	Nm	lbf ft
Coolant temperature sensor	15	11
Crankshaft sensor bolt	6	4
Exhaust gas recirculation (EGR) valve/pipe bolts:		
M6 bolts	10	7
M8 bolts	25	18
Engine control module (ECM) nuts/bolts	9	6
Exhaust system fasteners:		
Front pipe-to-manifold nuts	45	33
Front pipe-to-catalytic converter nuts	22	16
Intermediate pipe-to-catalytic converter nuts	34	25
Intermediate pipe-to-tailpipe nuts	45	33
Fuel cut-off solenoid	20	15
Fuel hose union bolt	25	18
Fuel injection pump:		
Front mounting nuts	25	18
Support bracket bolts	25	18
Sprocket retaining nut	60	44
Vacuum pipe union bolt	10	7
Fuel injector retaining plate bolt	25	18
Injector pipe union nuts	20	15
Intake air temperature sensor	12	9
Manifold absolute pressure (MAP) sensor bolt	9	7
Manifold fasteners:		
Retaining nuts and bolts	25	18
Intake/turbocharger pipe-to-manifold bolts	9	6
Turbocharger fasteners:		
Retaining nuts	25	18
Exhaust flange nuts	25	18
Oil feed hose union bolt	20	15
Oil return hose union bolts	10	7

4B

1 General information and precautions

General information

The operation of the fuel injection system is described in more detail in Section 6.

Fuel is supplied from a tank mounted under the rear of the vehicle, and then passes through a filter, to the fuel injection pump, which delivers the fuel to the injectors. The injection pump is controlled by an engine control module (ECM) on the basis of information provided by various sensors.

The inducted air passes through an air cleaner, which incorporates a paper filter element to filter out potentially-harmful particles (serious internal engine damage can be caused if foreign particles enter through the air intake system).

The engine control module (ECM) controls both the fuel injection pump and the pre-heating system, integrating the two into a complete engine management system. Refer to Chapter 5C for details of the pre-heating side of the system.

The exhaust system incorporates a catalytic converter to reduce exhaust gas emissions. Further details can be found in Chapter 4C, along with details of the other emission control systems and components.

Precautions

When working on fuel system components, scrupulous cleanliness must be observed, and care must be taken not to introduce any foreign matter into fuel lines or components.

After carrying out any work involving disconnection of fuel lines, it is advisable to check the connections for leaks; pressurise the system by cranking the engine several times.

Electronic control units are very sensitive components, and certain precautions must be taken to avoid damage to these units as follows.

When carrying out welding operations on the vehicle using electric welding equipment, the battery and alternator should be disconnected.

2.3 Release the retaining clips securing the airflow meter to the air cleaner housing

Although the underbonnet-mounted modules will tolerate normal underbonnet conditions, they can be adversely affected by excess heat or moisture. If using welding equipment or pressure-washing equipment in the vicinity of an electronic module, take care not to direct heat, or jets of water or steam, at the module. If this cannot be avoided, remove the module from the vehicle, and protect its wiring plug with a plastic bag.

Before disconnecting any wiring, or removing components, always ensure that the ignition is switched off.

Do not attempt to improvise fault diagnosis procedures using a test lamp or multi-meter, as irreparable damage could be caused to the module.

After working on fuel injection/engine management system components, ensure that all wiring is correctly reconnected before reconnecting the battery or switching on the ignition.

2 Air cleaner assembly – removal and refitting

Removal

1 Remove the battery as described in Chapter 5A.
2 Unclip the accelerator cable from the side of the air cleaner housing.
3 Release the two retaining clips securing the airflow meter to the air cleaner housing **(see illustration)**. Ease the airflow meter out from the housing and recover the sealing ring; the sealing ring must be renewed if it shows signs of damage or deterioration.
4 Slacken and remove the two bolts securing the air cleaner assembly to the battery tray.
5 Detach the intake duct from the base of the air cleaner housing then remove the housing assembly from the engine compartment.
6 The various intake duct(s) can be removed once the engine cover has been unbolted and removed.

Refitting

7 Refitting is a reversal of removal. **Do not** forget to fit the sealing ring to the airflow meter and make sure the meter and intake duct are clipped securely into position.

3 Fuel tank – removal and refitting

1 Refer to Chapter 4A, Section 10, noting the following points.
a) There is no need to depressurise the fuel system.
b) The wiring connector is for the fuel gauge sender unit, not the fuel pump.

4 Accelerator cable – removal, refitting and adjustment

Models without intercooler

Removal

1 Unscrew the retaining bolts and remove the plastic cover from the top of the engine, taking care not to lose the spacers which are fitted to the cover mounting rubbers.
2 On right-hand drive models, to improve access, slacken and remove the coolant expansion tank retaining bolts and position the tank clear of the accelerator cable.
3 Working at the injection pump end of the cable, free the inner cable from the accelerator lever then slacken the locknut and adjuster nut and free the outer cable from its mounting bracket.
4 Work back along the length of the cable, free it from any retaining clips or ties, noting its correct routing. Free the cable sealing grommet from the engine compartment bulkhead.
5 From inside the vehicle, remove the retaining clips then unclip the undercover from the driver's side of the facia to gain access to the accelerator pedal.
6 Reaching up behind the facia, unclip the accelerator inner cable from the top of the accelerator pedal.
7 Return to the engine compartment then free the cable sealing grommet from the bulkhead and remove the cable and grommet from the vehicle.
8 Examine the cable for signs of wear or damage and renew if necessary. Check the rubber grommet for signs of damage or deterioration and renew it if necessary.

Refitting

9 Feed the cable into position from the engine compartment and seat the outer cable grommet in the bulkhead.
10 From inside the vehicle, clip the inner cable into position in the pedal end and check to make sure the grommet is correctly located in the bulkhead. Check that the cable is securely retained, then refit the undercover to the facia.
11 From within the engine compartment, ensure the outer cable is correctly seated in the bulkhead, then work along the cable, securing it in position with the retaining clips and ties, ensuring that the cable is correctly routed.
12 Seat the outer cable in its mounting bracket and reconnect the inner cable to the injection pump accelerator lever. Adjust the cable as described below.
13 Refit the engine cover, ensuring the spacers are correctly fitted to each mounting rubber, and securely tighten its retaining bolts. On right-hand drive models refit the coolant expansion tank retaining bolts and tighten securely.

Adjustment

14 With the accelerator lever on the fuel injection pump resting against its stop screw, and the accelerator pedal in the at-rest position, there should be approximately 4 mm of freeplay. Check this by moving the inner cable gently up and down whilst measuring the cable movement.

15 If adjustment is necessary, working at the injection pump end of the cable, slacken the locknut then rotate the adjuster nut until the specified freeplay is obtained. Once the cable is correctly adjusted retain the adjuster nut and securely tighten the locknut.

16 Have an assistant fully depress the accelerator pedal, and check that the accelerator lever contact the maximum speed stop screw on the fuel injection pump. Release the pedal and check that the accelerator lever returns fully against its stop.

Models with intercooler

Removal

17 On right-hand drive models, to improve access, slacken and remove the coolant expansion tank retaining bolts and position the tank clear of the accelerator cable.

18 Unscrew the retaining bolts and remove the plastic cover from the top of the engine, taking care not to lose the spacers which are fitted to the cover mounting rubbers.

19 Slacken and remove the retaining nuts securing the EGR valve solenoid mounting bracket to the right-hand suspension strut turret. Position the valve assembly clear of the throttle position sensor assembly.

20 Slacken and remove the retaining nuts then unclip the heatshield from the throttle position sensor.

21 Unclip the adjustment nut and free the accelerator outer cable from the bracket then detach the inner cable from the throttle position sensor cam.

22 Remove the cable as described in paragraphs 4 to 8.

Refitting

23 Refit the cable as described in paragraphs 9 to 11.

24 Connect the inner cable to the throttle position sensor cam and seat the outer cable in its mounting bracket. Adjust the cable as described below.

25 Refit the heatshield to the throttle position sensor. Ensure the heatshield is clipped correctly in position and securely tighten its retaining nuts.

26 Refit the EGR valve bracket to the strut turret and securely tighten its retaining nuts.

27 Refit the engine cover, ensuring the spacers are correctly fitted to each mounting rubber, and securely tighten its retaining bolts. On right-hand drive models refit the coolant expansion tank retaining bolts and tighten securely.

Adjustment

28 Remove the heatshield from the throttle

position sensor as described in paragraphs 18 to 20.

29 Slide the cable adjustment nut out from the mounting bracket and position the cable so that the adjustment nut is resting against the upper surface of the bracket.

30 Slacken the adjustment nut until the throttle position sensor cam is fully against its stop then slowly tighten the nut until the point is found where all freeplay is removed from the cable but the cam is still against its stop.

31 Clip the adjustment nut correctly back into position then have an assistant depress the accelerator pedal. Check that the throttle position sensor cam opens fully and returns smoothly to its stop, readjusting the cable if necessary.

32 Once the cable is correctly adjusted, refit the heatshield and associated components.

---

5 Accelerator pedal – removal and refitting

The accelerator pedal is an integral part of the brake pedal bracket assembly and is not available separately. Refer to Chapter 9 for removal and refitting details.

---

6 Fuel injection system – general information

The system is under the overall control of the Electronic Diesel Control (EDC) system, which also controls the pre-heating system (see Chapter 5C).

Fuel is supplied from the rear-mounted fuel tank, via a fuel filter, to the fuel injection pump. The fuel injection pump supplies the exact amount of fuel required by the engine, according to the prevailing engine operating conditions.

The engine is fitted with various sensors, which monitor the engine operating conditions, and transmit data to the engine control module (ECM). The control module processes the data from the various sensors, and determines the optimum amount of fuel required, and the injection timing for the prevailing running conditions. Additionally, the control module activates the fuel injection pump stop solenoid, the pre-heating system, and the exhaust gas recirculation (EGR) system (see Chapter 4C).

The system uses the following sensors.

a) *Crankshaft sensor – informs the ECM of the crankshaft speed and position.*

b) *Coolant temperature sensor – informs the ECM of engine temperature.*

c) *Fuel temperature sensor – informs the ECM of fuel temperature (in the injection pump).*

d) *Airflow meter – informs the ECM of the mass of air entering the intake tract.*

e) *Fuel injector needle lift sensor – informs*

the ECM of the start of the injection sequence.

f) *Vehicle speed sensor – informs the ECM of the vehicle speed.*

g) *Fuel quantity servo position sensor – informs the ECM of the quantity of fuel supplied to the injectors by the fuel injection pump.*

On models with an intercooler, a "drive-by-wire" throttle control system is used. The accelerator pedal is not physically connected to the fuel injection pump, but instead is connected by a cable to a throttle position sensor, mounted in the engine compartment, which provides the engine control module (ECM) with a signal relating to accelerator pedal movement. As well as all the sensors listed in paragraph 4, models with an intercooler are fitted with the following additional sensors.

a) *Throttle position sensor - informs the ECM of throttle position, and the rate of throttle opening/closing.*

b) *Manifold absolute pressure (MAP) sensor - informs the ECM of the pressure of air entering the intake tract (used in conjunction with the intake air temperature sensor to calculate the volume of oxygen in the air entering the engine).*

c) *Intake air temperature sensor - informs the ECM of the temperature of air entering the engine.*

d) *Stop-light switch – informs the ECM when the brakes are being applied.*

The signals from the various sensors are processed by the ECM, and the optimum fuel quantity and injection timing settings are selected for the prevailing engine operating conditions.

A catalytic converter and an exhaust gas recirculation (EGR) system is fitted, to reduce harmful exhaust gas emissions. Details of this and other emissions control system equipment are given in Chapter 4C.

If there is an abnormality in any of the readings obtained from any sensor, the ECM enters its back-up mode. In this event, the ECM ignores the abnormal sensor signal, and assumes a pre-programmed value which will allow the engine to continue running (albeit at reduced efficiency). If the ECM enters this back-up mode, the warning light on the instrument panel will come on, and the relevant fault code will be stored in the ECM memory.

If the warning light comes on, the vehicle should be taken to a Rover dealer at the earliest opportunity. A complete test of the Electronic Diesel Control (EDC) system can then be carried out, using a special electronic test unit which is simply plugged into the system's diagnostic connector. The connector is located behind the driver's side of the facia; to gain access to the connector unclip the storage pocket and reach in through the facia aperture.

4B

7 Fuel system – priming and bleeding

1 After any operation which requires the disconnection of any fuel hose, it is necessary to prime and bleed the fuel system; the priming pump is located in the left-hand rear corner of the engine compartment, where it is fitted to the fuel filter inlet pipe.

2 Position wads of absorbent rag around the fuel filter then slacken the bleed screw which is fitted to the top of the fuel filter (see illustration). Gently squeeze and release the pump until fuel which is free of air bubbles is flowing out of the filter. Once all traces of air have been removed, squeeze and hold the pump then securely tighten the bleed screw before releasing the pump. Remove the rag from around the filter and mop up any spilt fuel.

3 Turn on the ignition switch and gently squeeze and release the pump until resistance is felt. Once the lines are full of fuel (indicated by the resistance felt when the pump is squeezed), stop pumping and turn off the ignition.

4 Depress the accelerator pedal to the floor then start the engine as normal (this may take longer than usual, especially if the fuel system has been allowed to run dry - operate the starter in ten second bursts with 5 seconds rest in between each operation). Run the engine at a fast idle speed for a minute or so to purge any remaining trapped air from the fuel lines. After this time the engine should idle smoothly at a constant speed.

5 If the engine idles roughly, then there is still some air trapped in the fuel system. Increase the engine speed again for another minute or so then recheck the idle speed. Repeat this procedure as necessary until the engine is idling smoothly.

8 Fuel gauge sender unit – removal and refitting

Removal

1 The fuel gauge sender unit is mounted in the top of the fuel tank, and cannot be accessed with the tank in place.

2 Remove the fuel tank as described in Section 3.

3 Disconnect the wiring connector from the sender unit which is fitted on the right-hand side of the tank; the assembly on the left is the fuel pick-up pipe unit.

4 Unscrew the locking ring and remove it from the tank. In the absence of the special Rover ring spanner (tool number 18G 1595), a pair of slip-jointed pliers can be used to slacken the ring or the ring may be tapped around using a large flat-bladed screwdriver against one of the ring tabs.

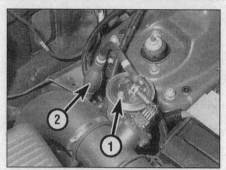

7.2 Fuel filter bleed screw (1) and priming pump (2)

5 Carefully lift the sender unit out from the fuel tank, taking care not to damage the sender unit float. Recover the sealing ring and discard it; a new one must be used on refitting.

Refitting

6 Ensure the tank and sender unit faces are clean and dry then fit the new sealing ring to the tank.

7 Carefully ease the sender unit into position, taking care not to bend the float arm, and seat it in the tank. Ensure the sender unit tag is correctly engaged with the tank cutout then secure it in position with the locking ring.

8 Reconnect the wiring connector to the sender unit.

9 Refit the fuel tank as described in Section 3.

9 Fuel injection system – testing and adjustment

Testing

1 If a fault appears in the fuel injection system, first ensure that all the system wiring connectors are securely connected and free from corrosion. Ensure that the fault is not due to poor maintenance; ie, check that the air cleaner filter element is clean, that the cylinder compression pressures are correct (see Chapter 2C), and that the engine breather hoses are clear and undamaged (see Chapter 4C).

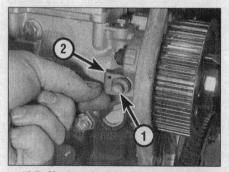

10.7 Slacken the injection pump shaft clamp bolt (1) and slide out the spacer plate (2)

2 If the engine will not start, check the condition of the glow plugs (see Chapter 5C).

3 If these checks fail to reveal the cause of the problem, the vehicle should be taken to a Rover dealer for testing using special electronic equipment which is plugged into the diagnostic connector (see Section 6). The tester should locate the fault quickly and simply, avoiding the need to test all the system components individually, which is time-consuming, and also carries a risk of damaging the ECM.

Adjustment

4 The engine idle speed, maximum speed and fuel injection pump timing are all controlled by the ECM. Whilst in theory it is possible to check the settings, if they are found to be in need of adjustment, the car will have to be taken to a suitably-equipped Rover dealer. They will have access to the necessary diagnostic equipment required to test and (where possible) adjust the settings.

10 Fuel injection pump – removal and refitting

Caution: Be careful not to allow dirt into the injection pump or injector pipes during this procedure.

Models without intercooler

Note: *Renew all sealing washers disturbed on removal.*

Removal

1 Disconnect the battery negative lead.

2 Unscrew the retaining bolts and remove the plastic cover from the top of the engine, taking care not to lose the spacers which are fitted to the cover mounting rubbers.

3 Drain the cooling system as described in Chapter 1B.

4 Remove the fuel injection pump timing belt as described in Chapter 2C.

5 Detach the accelerator inner cable from the injection pump lever then slacken the locknut and free the outer cable from the mounting bracket.

6 To improve access to the pump, release the retaining clips and remove the radiator top hose. If necessary, also disconnect the coolant hose from the rear of the coolant pump.

7 Working at the front of the fuel injection pump, slacken the pump shaft clamp bolt and remove the spacer plate from the bolt (see illustration). With the spacer plate removed, tighten the bolt to 31 Nm (22 lbf ft). Take care not to lose the spacer plate.

Caution: Do not exceed the specified torque when tightening the pump shaft clamp bolt, as this could damage the pump shaft. If the pump shaft is damaged, the injection pump will have to be renewed.

8 Ensure that the locking pin is correctly fitted to the fuel injection pump sprocket, then slacken and remove the sprocket retaining nut and washer.

9 Remove the locking pin from the sprocket and remove the sprocket from the injection pump shaft. The sprocket is a tight-fit on the shaft and a puller will be needed to remove it. In the absence of the special Rover puller (tool number 18G 1512B), the sprocket can be removed using a two M8 bolts and a length of bar with two holes drilled in it. Fit the bar and screw the bolts into the sprocket, tightening them evenly and progressively until the sprocket is freed from the pump shaft.

Caution: The pump shaft clamp screw must not be slackened until after the sprocket has been refitted and its retaining nut tightened to the specified torque. Failure to heed this warning will lead to the injection pump timing setting being lost. If the injection pump timing is lost, the vehicle will have to be taken to a Rover dealer to have the pump timing reset.

10 Unscrew the retaining nut and disconnect the glow plug feed wiring from the No 2 cylinder glow plug.

11 Release the fuel injection pump wiring connector(s) from the pump mounting bracket and separate the two halves of each connector. Detach the engine wiring harness from the pump.

12 Place a wad of absorbent cloth around the injection pump to catch any spilt fuel.

13 Slacken and remove the union bolt securing the fuel feed pipe union to the pump. Recover and discard the sealing washers. Plug or cover the open ends of the pipe and the pump to prevent dirt entry.

14 Unscrew the cap nut and disconnect the fuel return pipe/hose union from the injection pump. Recover and discard the sealing washers. Release the retaining clip and disconnect the fuel return hose from the union then position the union clear of the pump. Plug or cover the open ends of the pump and the hose to prevent dirt entry.

15 Remove the injector pipe clamp which is situated at the rear of the injection pump.

16 Unscrew the union bolt securing the vacuum pipe to the top of the injection pump. Recover the sealing washers which are fitted on each side of the pipe union and discard them.

17 Place a wad of absorbent cloth around the fuel feed pipe unions on Nos 1 and 2 cylinder fuel injectors, then working on each of the two injectors in turn, slacken the union nut (counterhold the union on the injector using a second spanner), and disconnect the fuel pipe from the injector. Plug or cover the open ends of the pipes and fuel injectors to prevent dirt entry.

18 Repeat the procedure to disconnect Nos 1 and 2 cylinder fuel injector pipes from the pump, then remove the pipe assembly **(see illustrations)**.

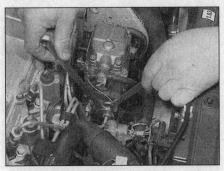

10.18a Slacken the injector pipe union nuts . . .

19 Repeat the procedure given in paragraphs 17 and 18 and remove Nos 3 and 4 cylinder fuel injector pipes.

20 Unscrew the four bolts securing the injection pump support bracket to the engine. Slacken and remove the two nuts and bolts securing the bracket to the pump and remove the bracket **(see illustrations)**.

21 Slacken and remove the three nuts securing the pump to the engine/transmission mounting plate, then lift the pump away from the engine **(see illustrations)**.

Refitting

22 Thoroughly clean the mating faces of the injection pump and the engine/transmission mounting plate.

23 Manoeuvre the injection pump into position then refit the pump retaining nuts, tightening them to the specified torque.

24 Refit the support bracket to the pump and

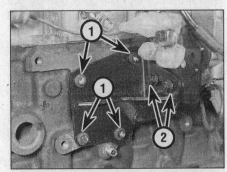

10.20a Slacken and remove the bolts (1) and the nuts and bolts (2) . . .

10.21a Unscrew the pump mounting nuts (two arrowed) . . .

10.18b . . . and remove the pipes from the engine

refit its retaining nuts and bolts, tighten them all by hand only. Tighten the bolts securing the bracket to the pump to the specified torque first, then tighten the bolts securing the bracket to the cylinder block to the specified torque.

25 Ensure the unions are clean and dry then refit Nos 3 and 4 injector pipes, tightening their union nuts to the specified torque. Refit the Nos 1 and 2 pipes, tightening their union nuts to the specified torque then refit the clamp to the pipes.

26 Reconnect all the fuel/vacuum pipes to the injection pump. Position a new sealing washer on each side of all hose unions and tighten the union bolts/cap nut (as applicable) to the specified torque. Reconnect the leak-off pipe to the injector.

27 Reconnect the injection pump wiring connector(s) and clip the connector onto the bracket. Also clip the engine wiring harness into position on the bracket.

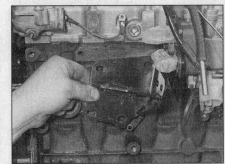

10.20b . . . then remove the pump support bracket from the engine

10.21b . . . and remove the pump from the engine unit

4B

10.39a On models with an intercooler, unscrew the EGR pipe bolts (arrowed) . . .

10.39b . . . then undo the bolts securing the intake pipe to the manifold . . .

10.39c . . . and cylinder head cover and remove the pipe from the engine

28 Reconnect the glow plug feed wiring to No 2 cylinder glow plug, and securely tighten the retaining nut.

29 Ensure the pump shaft and sprocket are clean and dry then fit the sprocket, washer and retaining nut to the pump. Insert the locking pin then tighten the sprocket retaining nut to the specified torque.

30 Slacken the pump shaft clamp bolt, then refit the spacer plate under the bolt head, and tighten the clamp bolt to 10 Nm (7 lbf ft).

31 Refit the fuel injection pump timing belt as described in Chapter 2C.

32 Reconnect the hose to the coolant pump and refit the radiator top hose, ensure the retaining clips are securely refitted.

33 Reconnect the accelerator cable to the pump and adjust as described in Section 4.

34 Refill the cooling system as described in Chapter 1B.

35 Refit the cover to the engine, ensuring the

spacers are correctly fitted to the mounting rubbers, and securely tighten its retaining bolts.

36 Reconnect the battery negative lead then prime the fuel system (see Section 7).

Models with intercooler

Note: *Renew all sealing washers disturbed on removal. A new inlet manifold intake pipe gasket will also be required.*

Removal

37 Proceed as described in paragraphs 1 to 4.

38 Release the retaining clip and disconnect the intercooler duct from the inlet manifold intake pipe.

39 Slacken and remove the two bolts securing the exhaust gas recirculation (EGR) pipe to the rear of the inlet manifold intake pipe then unscrew the bolts securing the pipe to the manifold. Undo the bolt securing the pipe to the cylinder head cover then remove the pipe from the engine, along with its gasket **(see illustrations)**. Recover and discard the gasket.

40 Remove the pump as described in paragraphs 6 to 21, ignoring the remark about disconnecting the vacuum pipe (paragraph 16).

Refitting

41 Proceed as described in paragraphs 22 to 32.

42 Refit the intake pipe to the manifold, using a new gasket, and reconnect the EGR pipe. Tighten all the intake pipe bolts to the specified torque setting.

43 Refill the cooling system as described in Chapter 1B.

44 Refit the cover to the engine, ensuring the spacers are correctly fitted to the mounting rubbers, and securely tighten its retaining bolts.

45 Reconnect the battery negative lead then prime the fuel system (see Section 7).

11 Fuel injectors – removal and refitting

Caution: Be careful not to allow dirt into the injection pump or injector pipes during this procedure.

Removal

Note: *Renew all sealing washers disturbed on removal.*

1 Disconnect the battery negative lead.

2 Unscrew the retaining bolts and remove the plastic cover from the top of the engine, taking care not to lose the spacers which are fitted to the cover mounting rubbers.

3 On models with an intercooler, referring to Section 16, disconnect the intercooler duct from the intake pipe then unbolt the pipe and remove it from the inlet manifold. Discard the gasket, a new one should be used on refitting. **Note:** *If Nos 2 and 3 injectors are not to be disturbed then the intake pipe can be left in position.*

4 Wipe clean the area around each injector then remove the injector pipe clamp which is situated at the rear of the injection pump. Each injector can then be removed as follows.

5 Position a wad of absorbent cloth around the fuel feed pipe union on the injector, then slowly unscrew the union nut, and disconnect the pipe from the injector (counterhold the union on the injector using a second spanner) **(see illustration)**. Slacken the union on the rear of the injection pump then pivot the pipe away from the injector. Plug or cover the open ends of the injector and pipe to prevent dirt entry.

6 Slacken and remove the union bolt securing the return hose union to the injector **(see illustration)**. Recover the sealing washer fitted to each side of the union and discard them; new ones must be used on refitting.

7 Slacken and remove the retaining bolt and slide the retaining plate out from the injector **(see illustration)**.

11.5 Retain the injector and unscrew the injector pipe union nut

11.6 Unscrew the union bolt and detach the return hose union from the injector

11.7 Undo the retaining bolt and slide out the injector retaining plate . . .

11.8a . . . then remove the injector (No1 shown) from the cylinder head . . .

8 Withdraw the injector from the cylinder head along with its sealing washer; discard the washer, a new one must be used on refitting **(see illustrations)**. Note that if No 1 cylinder injector is being removed, it will be necessary to disconnect the needle lift sensor wiring connector (the sensor is an integral part of the injector).

Refitting

9 Thoroughly clean the injector, and the injector seat in the cylinder head.
10 Fit a new sealing washer to the injector making sure the domed surface of the washer is facing the top of the injector.
11 Fit the retaining plate to the injector and carefully refit the injector to the cylinder head, aligning the retaining plate bolt hole with the threaded hole in the cylinder head. Ensure the injector is correctly seated then refit the retaining bolt and tighten to the specified torque.
12 Position a new sealing washer on each side of the return hose union then refit the union bolt, tightening it to the specified torque.
13 If No 1 cylinder injector has been removed, ensure the needle lift sensor wiring is correctly routed then securely reconnect the connector.
14 Reconnect the injector pipe to the injector and pump, tightening its union nuts to the specified torque. Ensure all pipe union nuts are correctly tightened then refit the clamp to the injection pump end of the pipes.

11.8b . . . complete with its sealing washer

15 On models with an intercooler, referring to Section 16, refit the intake pipe (where removed) to the manifold and securely reconnect the intercooler duct.
16 Refit the cover to the engine, ensuring the spacers are correctly fitted to the mounting rubbers, and securely tighten its retaining bolts.
17 Reconnect the battery negative lead then prime the fuel system (see Section 7).

---

12 Electronic Diesel Control (EDC) system components –
removed and refitting

Crankshaft sensor

1 The sensor is located at the rear of the engine where it is mounted onto the engine/transmission mounting plate, at the rear of the flywheel. To gain access to the sensor, slacken the retaining clips and remove the intake duct linking the airflow meter to the manifold.
2 Ensure the ignition is switched off, then disconnect the wiring connector from the sensor.
3 Slacken and remove the retaining bolt and carefully remove the sensor from the engine **(see illustration)**.
4 Refitting is the reverse of removal, tightening the retaining bolt to the specified torque.

Airflow meter

5 Ensure the ignition is switched off then release the retaining clip and disconnect the wiring connector from the airflow meter **(see illustration)**.
6 Slacken the retaining clip and detach the intake duct from the airflow meter.
7 Release the retaining clips then remove the airflow meter from the air cleaner housing, along with its sealing ring.
8 Refitting is the reverse of removal, using a new sealing ring. Make sure the meter is clipped securely in position and the intake duct is securely retained by its clip.

Fuel injector needle lift sensor

9 The fuel injector needle lift sensor is an integral part of No 1 cylinder fuel injector and cannot be renewed separately. Refer to Section 11 for injector removal and refitting details.

Coolant temperature sensor

10 The sensor is screwed into the coolant outlet union on the front, right-hand end of the cylinder head **(see illustration)**. Refer to Chapter 3 for removal and refitting details.

Fuel temperature sensor

11 The sensor is an integral part of the fuel injection pump, and cannot be renewed separately (see Section 10).

Vehicle speed sensor

12 The sensor is driven by the speedometer drive on the transmission unit. Refer to Chapter 7, Section 6 for removal and refitting details.

Fuel quantity servo position sensor

13 The sensor is integral with the fuel injection pump, and cannot be renewed separately (see Section 10).

Throttle position sensor - models with intercooler

14 Working as described in Section 4, disconnect the accelerator cable from the throttle position sensor.

4B

12.3 Crankshaft sensor retaining bolt (arrowed)

12.5 Disconnecting the airflow meter wiring connector

12.10 The coolant temperature sensor (arrowed) is screwed into the cylinder head outlet union

12.23 The intake air temperature sensor (arrowed) is screwed into the right-hand end of the inlet manifold

15 Unclip the wiring connector from the side of the sensor mounting bracket then separate the two halves of the connector.

16 Unscrew the retaining bolts then remove the sensor and mounting bracket from the engine compartment. Undo the retaining nuts and bolts and separate the sensor and bracket.

17 Refitting is the reverse of removal, adjusting the accelerator cable as described in Section 4.

Manifold absolute pressure (MAP) sensor - models with intercooler

18 The sensor is mounted onto the engine compartment bulkhead, where it is located on the left-hand side of the engine control module (ECM), below the relays.

19 Ensure the ignition is switched off then disconnect the wiring connector and vacuum hose from the sensor.

20 Slacken and remove the retaining bolt and remove the MAP sensor from the vehicle.

21 Refitting is the reverse of removal, tightening the sensor retaining bolt to the specified torque.

Intake air temperature sensor - models with intercooler

22 Unscrew the retaining bolts and remove the plastic cover from the top of the engine, taking care not to lose the spacers which are fitted to the cover mounting rubbers.

23 Ensure the ignition is switched off then disconnect the wiring connector from the intake air temperature sensor which is screwed into the right-hand end of the inlet manifold **(see illustration)**.

24 Unscrew the sensor and remove it from the manifold.

25 On refitting, remove all traces of sealant from the sensor and manifold threads and apply a smear of fresh sealant (Rover recommend the use of Loctite 577) to the sensor threads. Refit the sensor, tightening it to the specified torque, and reconnect the wiring connector. Refit the cover to the engine.

Stop-light switch - models with intercooler

26 The engine control module receives a signal from the stop-light switch which indicates when the brakes are being applied. Stop-light switch removal and refitting details can be found in Chapter 9.

Fuel cut-off solenoid

Caution: Be careful not to allow dirt into the injection pump during this procedure.

27 The fuel cut-off solenoid is fitted to the top of the fuel injection pump.

28 Unscrew the retaining bolts and remove the plastic cover from the top of the engine, taking care not to lose the spacers which are fitted to the cover mounting rubbers. On models with an intercooler, slacken the retaining clip and disconnect the intercooler duct from the manifold to improve access to the pump.

29 Ensure the ignition is switched off then unscrew the retaining nut and disconnect the wire from the solenoid terminal **(see illustration)**.

30 Wipe clean the area around the solenoid and position a wad of absorbent cloth around the pump to absorb escaping fuel.

31 Slacken and remove the solenoid from the injection pump and recover the solenoid plunger and spring, noting each components correct fitted location. Remove the sealing ring and discard it; a new one must be used on refitting.

32 Refitting is the reverse of removal using a new sealing ring. Ensure the plunger and spring are fitted the correct way around and tighten the solenoid to the specified torque.

Engine control module (ECM)

Note: *If a new ECM is to be fitted, it will be necessary to entrust the task to a Rover dealer. After fitting, it will be necessary to programme the anti-theft system code into the ECM to enable it function correctly. This can only be done using the special Rover equipment which is plugged into the diagnostic connector (see Section 6).*

33 The electronic control module (ECM) is mounted onto the engine compartment bulkhead. Prior to removal, first disconnect the battery negative terminal.

Models without intercooler

34 Disconnect the wiring connector then undo the retaining nut(s) then free the ECM from its lower mounting pin and remove it from the engine compartment

35 Refitting is the reverse of removal ensuring the wiring connector is securely reconnected. Tighten the ECM retaining nut(s) to the specified torque setting.

Models with intercooler

36 Unscrew the retaining bolts and remove the heatshield from around the ECM **(see illustration)**.

12.29 Fuel injection pump fuel cut-off solenoid location (arrowed)

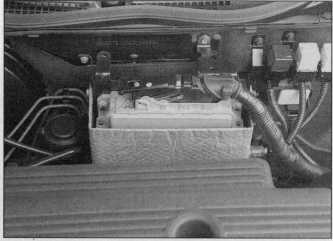

12.36 Engine control module (ECM) location - models with intercooler

37 Slacken and remove the retaining bolts and free the ECM from its mounting bracket.

38 Unscrew the wiring connector retaining screw then carefully lift the retaining clip and disconnect the wiring connector. The ECM can then be removed from the vehicle.

39 Refitting is the reverse of removal ensuring the wiring connector is securely reconnected. Tighten the ECM retaining bolts to the specified torque setting.

Relays

Models without intercooler

40 On theses models, a relay module (containing the injection pump relay, starter relay and pump cut-off relays) is fitted; the module is clipped onto the rear of the ECM mounting bracket. A separate relay which operates the glow plugs is also fitted and is located just to the left of the ECM. Prior to removal, ensure the ignition is switched off.

41 To remove the relay module, unclip the module from the rear of the ECM mounting bracket and remove it from the engine compartment, disconnecting the wiring connectors as they become accessible.

42 To remove a relay, unclip it from the bulkhead then pull the relay out of the wiring connector.

43 Refitting is the reverse of removal.

Models with intercooler

44 On these models, the main (fuel injection pump) relay and the glow plug relay are mounted onto the engine compartment bulkhead, on the left-hand side of the ECM; the glow plug relay is the one nearest the ECM and the main relay is situated next to the glow plug relay **(see illustration)**.

45 Each relay is a push-fit in its wiring connector. Ensure the ignition is switched off prior to removing/refitting the relay.

---

13 Turbocharger –
description and precautions

Description

A turbocharger is fitted to all diesel engines. It increases engine efficiency by raising the pressure in the inlet manifold above atmospheric pressure. Instead of the air simply being sucked into the cylinders, it is forced in. Additional fuel is supplied by the injection pump in proportion to the increased air intake.

Energy for the operation of the turbocharger comes from the exhaust gas. The gas flows through a specially-shaped housing (the turbine housing) and in so doing, spins the turbine wheel. The turbine wheel is attached to a shaft, at the end of which is another vaned wheel known as the compressor wheel. The compressor wheel spins in its own housing and compresses the inducted air on the way to the inlet manifold.

12.44 The glow plug relay (1) and main relay (2) are located to the left of the ECM

On certain models, the compressed air passes through an intercooler. This is an air-to-air heat exchanger, mounted with the radiator at the front of the vehicle. The purpose of the intercooler is to remove from the inducted air some of the heat gained in being compressed. Because cooler air is denser, removal of this heat further increases engine efficiency.

Boost pressure (the pressure in the inlet manifold) is limited by a wastegate, which diverts the exhaust gas away from the turbine wheel in response to a pressure-sensitive actuator.

The turbo shaft is pressure-lubricated by an oil feed pipe from the main oil gallery. The shaft "floats" on a cushion of oil. A drain pipe returns the oil to the sump.

Precautions

The turbocharger operates at extremely high speeds and temperatures. Certain precautions must be observed to avoid premature failure of the turbo or injury to the operator.

Do not operate the turbo with any parts exposed. Foreign objects falling onto the rotating vanes could cause excessive damage and (if ejected) personal injury.

Do not race the engine immediately after start-up, especially if it is cold. Give the oil a few seconds to circulate.

Always allow the engine to return to idle speed before switching it off - do not blip the throttle and switch off, as this will leave the turbo spinning without lubrication.

Allow the engine to idle for several minutes before switching off after a high-speed run.

14.9 Unscrew the bolts (arrowed) securing the turbocharger to the mounting bracket

Observe the recommended intervals for oil and filter changing, and use a reputable oil of the specified quality (see "*Lubricants and fluids*"). Neglect of oil changing, or use of inferior oil, can cause carbon formation on the turbo shaft and subsequent failure.

14 Turbocharger –
removal and refitting

Removal

Note: *A new oil return pipe union gasket, and exhaust front pipe gasket will be required on refitting, as will new oil feed pipe union sealing washers.*

1 Disconnect the battery negative lead.

2 Firmly apply the handbrake, then jack up the front of the vehicle and support securely on axle stands (see "*Jacking and Vehicle Support*"). Slacken and remove the retaining screws and fasteners and remove the undercover from beneath the engine/transmission unit.

3 Unscrew the retaining bolts and remove the plastic cover from the top of the engine, taking care not to lose the spacers which are fitted to the cover mounting rubbers.

4 Unscrew the retaining nuts then detach the exhaust front pipe from the turbocharger flange and recover the gasket.

5 On models not fitted with an intercooler, slacken the retaining clips and disconnect the air intake duct and the inlet manifold pipe adaptor from the turbocharger.

6 On models with an intercooler, slacken the retaining clips and disconnect the air intake duct and the intercooler duct adaptor from the turbocharger.

7 On all models, disconnect the pipe from the turbocharger wastegate actuator.

8 Remove all traces of dirt from around the turbocharger oil feed pipe and return hose unions. Undo the union bolt securing the turbocharger oil feed pipe to the cylinder block and recover the sealing washers then undo the retaining bolts and disconnect the oil return hose union. Mop up any spilt oil and remove the return hose union gasket.

9 Unscrew the two bolts securing the turbocharger flange to its mounting bracket **(see illustration)**.

10 Slacken and remove the three nuts securing the turbocharger to the exhaust manifold and remove the turbocharger assembly from the engine compartment.

11 If necessary, the exhaust flange can be removed from the turbocharger after unscrewing the four retaining nuts.

Refitting

12 Remove all traces of dirt from the manifold and turbocharger mating surfaces.

13 Fit the exhaust flange (where removed), using a new gasket, and tighten its retaining nuts to the specified torque.

4B

14 Fit a new gasket to the turbocharger flange then manoeuvre the assembly into position. Refit the retaining nuts and tighten them evenly and progressively to the specified torque.

15 Refit the bolts securing the support bracket to the exhaust flange and tighten them securely.

16 Ensure the oil return hose union and turbocharger mating surfaces are clean and dry then fit a new gasket. Refit the union retaining bolts and tighten them to the specified torque.

17 Position a new sealing washer on each side of the oil feed pipe union then refit the union bolt and tighten it to the specified torque.

18 Reconnect the pipe to the wastegate actuator.

19 Reconnect the intake duct and adaptor to the turbocharger, making sure both are correctly seated, and securely tighten the retaining clips.

20 Fit a new gasket to the exhaust front pipe then reconnect the pipe to the flange and tighten its retaining nuts to the specified torque.

21 Refit the undercover then lower the vehicle to the ground.

22 Check and, if necessary, top-up the oil level as described in "Weekly checks".

23 Before refitting the engine cover, disconnect the wiring from the injection pump fuel cut-off solenoid (see Section 12) then turn the engine over on the starter until the oil pressure warning light goes out; this will allow oil to be circulated around the turbocharger bearings before the engine is started. Reconnect the solenoid then refit the engine cover and start the engine as normal.

15 Turbocharger –
examination and overhaul

With the turbocharger removed, inspect the housing for cracks or other visible damage.

Spin the turbine or the compressor wheel to verify that the shaft is intact and to feel for excessive shake or roughness. Some play is normal since in use the shaft is 'floating' on a film of oil. Check that the wheel vanes are undamaged.

The wastegate and actuator are integral with the turbocharger, and cannot be checked or renewed separately. Consult a Rover dealer or other specialist if it is thought that the wastegate may be faulty.

If the exhaust or induction passages are oil-contaminated, the turbo shaft oil seals have probably failed. (On the induction side, this will also have contaminated the intercooler, where applicable, which if necessary should be flushed with a suitable solvent.)

No DIY repair of the turbo is possible. A new unit may be available on an exchange basis.

16 Intercooler –
removal and refitting

Removal

1 Remove the air cleaner assembly as described in Section 2.

2 Undo the retaining screws and remove the protective panel from above the radiator.

3 Slacken the retaining clip and disconnect the upper duct from the intercooler.

4 Firmly apply the handbrake, then jack up the front of the vehicle and support securely on axle stands (see "Jacking and Vehicle Support"). Slacken and remove the retaining screws and fasteners and remove the undercover from beneath the engine/transmission unit.

5 Slacken and remove the upper and lower retaining nuts and bolts then free the intercooler from the radiator and remove it from the vehicle.

Refitting

6 Refitting is the reverse of removal.

17 Manifolds –
removal and refitting

Note: *Although the inlet and exhaust manifolds are separate, they are retained by the same nuts and bolts and share the same gasket. Therefore, in order to renew the gasket both manifolds must be removed at the same time.*

Removal

Note: *Renew all gaskets disturbed on removal. New turbocharger oil feed pipe union sealing washers will also be required..*

1 Carry out the operations described in paragraphs 1 to 9 of Section 14.

2 Slacken the retaining clip securing the intake duct to the airflow meter and remove the duct from the engine compartment, disconnecting the breather hose from the camshaft cover.

3 Disconnect the vacuum pipe from the exhaust gas recirculation (EGR) valve. Slacken and remove the bolts securing the EGR valve joint and the connecting pipe joint to the manifolds then remove the EGR valve and pipe assembly from the engine. Recover the gasket(s) and discard.

4 On models not fitted with an intercooler, unscrew the retaining bolts then remove the turbocharger pipe from the rear of the inlet manifold. Recover the gasket and discard it.

5 On models fitted with an intercooler, slacken the retaining clip and disconnect the intercooler duct from the inlet manifold intake pipe. Slacken and remove the retaining bolts securing the pipe to the manifold then undo

the bolt securing the pipe to the camshaft cover. Remove the pipe from the engine and discard its gasket.

6 On all models, evenly and progressively slacken and remove the manifold retaining nuts and bolts.

7 Remove the exhaust manifold and turbocharger assembly from the cylinder head then lift off the inlet manifold. Remove the gasket from the manifold studs and discard it.

Refitting

8 Examine all the manifold studs for signs of damage and corrosion; remove all traces of corrosion, and repair or renew any damaged studs.

9 Ensure that the manifold and cylinder head sealing faces are clean and flat, and fit the new gasket.

10 Refit the inlet manifold followed by the exhaust manifold and refit the retaining nuts and bolts. Tighten all nuts and bolts by hand only then evenly and progressively tighten them to the specified torque setting.

11 On models with an intercooler, fit a new gasket to the front of the inlet manifold then refit the intake pipe retaining bolts, tightening them to the specified torque. Reconnect the intercooler duct to the pipe and securely tighten its retaining clip.

12 On models not fitted with an intercooler, fit a new gasket to the rear of the manifold then refit the turbocharger pipe, tightening its retaining bolts to the specified torque.

13 Refit the EGR valve and pipe assembly, using new gasket(s), and tighten the retaining bolts to their specified torque settings. Reconnect the vacuum hose to the manifold.

14 Refit the intake duct then carry out the operations described in paragraphs 15 to 23 of Section 14.

18 Exhaust system –
general information and component renewal

General information

1 The exhaust system consists of four sections: the front pipe, the catalytic converter, the intermediate pipe, the tailpipe and main silencer box.

2 All exhaust sections are joined by flanged joints, which are secured by nuts, and the system is suspended throughout its entire length by rubber mountings.

Removal

3 Each exhaust section can be removed individually, or alternatively, the complete system can be removed as a unit. Even if only one part of the system needs attention, it can sometimes be easier to remove the whole system and separate the sections on the bench.

4 To remove the system or part of the system, first jack up the front or rear of the car and support it securely on axle stands (see "*Jacking and Vehicle Support*"). Alternatively, position the car over an inspection pit or on car ramps.

Front pipe

5 Slacken and remove the nuts securing the front pipe flange joints to the turbocharger flange and catalytic converter.

6 Unhook the front pipe from its mounting rubber then free the pipe from its joints and remove it from underneath the vehicle. Recover the gasket from each joint and discard them.

Catalytic converter

7 Slacken and remove the nuts securing the catalytic converter to the front pipe and intermediate pipe joints.

8 Free the catalytic converter from the flange joints and remove it from underneath the vehicle. Recover the gasket from each joint and discard them.

Intermediate pipe

9 Slacken and remove the nuts securing the intermediate pipe to the catalytic converter and tailpipe joints.

10 Free the intermediate pipe from its mounting rubbers then detach the pipe from the flange joints and remove it from underneath the vehicle. Recover the gasket from each joint and discard them.

Tailpipe

11 Slacken and remove the nuts securing the tailpipe joint to the intermediate pipe.

12 Free the tailpipe from its mounting rubbers and remove it along with its gasket.

Complete system

13 Undo the nuts securing the front pipe flange joint to the turbocharger flange.

14 Working with the aid of an assistant, free the system from all its mounting rubbers and lower it from under the vehicle. Recover the gasket from the front pipe joint.

Heat shield

15 Heatshield(s) are fitted to the underside of the vehicle body. Each shield can be removed once its retaining bolts have been undone.

Refitting

16 Each section is refitted by reversing the removal sequence, noting the following points:

a) *Ensure that all traces of corrosion have been removed from the flanges and renew all gaskets.*

b) *Inspect the rubber mountings for signs of damage or deterioration, and renew as necessary.*

c) *Prior to tightening the exhaust system fasteners to the specified torque, ensure that all rubber mountings are correctly located, and that there is adequate clearance between the exhaust system and vehicle underbody.*

4B

Chapter 4 Part C:
Emission control systems

Contents

Degrees of difficulty

Easy, suitable for novice with little experience	**Fairly easy,** suitable for beginner with some experience	**Fairly difficult,** suitable for competent DIY mechanic	**Difficult,** suitable for experienced DIY mechanic	**Very difficult,** suitable for expert DIY or professional

4C

Specifications

Torque wrench settings	Nm	lbf ft
Exhaust gas recirculation (EGR) valve/pipe bolts - diesel engines:		
M6 bolts	10	7
M8 bolts	25	18
Oxygen sensor - petrol engines	55	41

1 General information

All petrol engine models use unleaded petrol and also have various other features built into the fuel system to help minimise harmful emissions. All models are equipped with a crankcase emission-control system, a catalytic converter and an evaporative emission control system to keep fuel vapour/exhaust gas emissions down to a minimum.

All diesel engine models are also designed to meet strict emission requirements. All models are fitted with a crankcase emission control system, a catalytic converter and an exhaust gas recirculation (EGR) system to keep exhaust emissions down to a minimum.

The emission control systems function as follows.

Petrol models

Crankcase emission control

To reduce the emission of unburned hydrocarbons from the crankcase into the atmosphere, the engine is sealed and the blow-by gases and oil vapour are drawn from inside the crankcase, through a wire mesh oil separator, into the inlet tract to be burned by the engine during normal combustion.

Under conditions of high manifold depression (idling, deceleration) the gases will be sucked positively out of the crankcase. Under conditions of low manifold depression (acceleration, full-throttle running) the gases are forced out of the crankcase by the (relatively) higher crankcase pressure; if the engine is worn, the raised crankcase pressure (due to increased blow-by) will cause some of the flow to return under all manifold conditions.

2.4 Disconnect the charcoal canister outlet hose from the manifold (2.0 litre engine shown) . . .

2.5 . . . and the inlet hose from the fuel vapour pipe

2.7 Disconnect the wiring connector from the purge valve . . .

Exhaust emission control

To minimise the amount of pollutants which escape into the atmosphere, all models are fitted with a catalytic converter in the exhaust system. The system is of the closed-loop type, in which a oxygen sensor in the exhaust system provides the fuel-injection/ignition system ECM with constant feedback, enabling the ECM to adjust the mixture to provide the best possible conditions for the converter to operate. The oxygen sensor has a built-in heating element which is controlled by the ECM; the heating element is used to warm the sensor when the engine is cold to bring it quickly up to an efficient operating temperature.

The oxygen sensor's tip is sensitive to oxygen and sends the ECM a varying voltage depending on the amount of oxygen in the exhaust gases; if the intake air/fuel mixture is too rich, the exhaust gases are low in oxygen so the sensor sends a low-voltage signal, the voltage rising as the mixture weakens and the amount of oxygen rises in the exhaust gases. Peak conversion efficiency of all major pollutants occurs if the intake air/fuel mixture is maintained at the chemically-correct ratio for the complete combustion of petrol of 14.7 parts (by weight) of air to 1 part of fuel (the 'stoichiometric' ratio). The sensor output voltage alters in a large step at this point, the ECM using the signal change as a reference point and correcting the intake air/fuel mixture accordingly by altering the fuel injector pulse width.

Evaporative emission control

To minimise the escape into the atmosphere of unburned hydrocarbons, an evaporative emissions control system is also fitted to all models. The fuel tank filler cap is sealed and a charcoal canister is mounted in the engine compartment. The canister collects the petrol vapours generated in the tank when the car is parked and stores them until they can be cleared from the canister (under the control of the fuel-injection/ignition system ECM) via the purge valve into the inlet tract to be burned by the engine during normal combustion.

To ensure that the engine runs correctly when it is cold and/or idling and to protect the catalytic converter from the effects of an over-rich mixture, the purge control valve is not opened by the ECM until the engine has warmed up, and the engine is under load; the valve solenoid is then modulated on and off to allow the stored vapour to pass into the inlet tract.

Diesel models

Crankcase emission control

To reduce the emission of unburned hydrocarbons from the crankcase into the atmosphere, the engine is sealed and the blow-by gases and oil vapour are drawn from inside the crankcase, through a wire mesh oil separator, into the inlet tract to be burned by the engine during normal combustion.

Exhaust emission control

To minimise the level of exhaust pollutants released into the atmosphere, a catalytic converter is fitted in the exhaust system of some models.

The catalytic converter consists of a canister containing a fine mesh impregnated with a catalyst material, over which the hot exhaust gases pass. The catalyst speeds up the oxidation of harmful carbon monoxide, unburned hydrocarbons and soot, effectively reducing the quantity of harmful products released into the atmosphere via the exhaust gases.

Exhaust gas recirculation (EGR) system

This system is designed to recirculate small quantities of exhaust gas into the inlet tract, and therefore into the combustion process. This process reduces the level of unburnt hydrocarbons present in the exhaust gas before it reaches the catalytic converter. The system is controlled by the injection system ECM, using the information from its various sensors, via the EGR valve which is fitted to the metal pipe connecting the inlet and exhaust manifolds. The EGR valve is vacuum operated and is switched on and off by an electrical solenoid valve.

2 Petrol engine emission control systems - testing and component renewal

Crankcase emission control

1 The components of this system require no attention other than to check that the hose(s) are clear and undamaged at regular intervals.

Evaporative emission control system

Testing

2 If the system is thought to be faulty, disconnect the hoses from the charcoal canister and purge control valve and check that they are clear by blowing through them. Full testing of the system can only be carried out using specialist electronic equipment which is connected to the engine management system diagnostic wiring connector (see Chapter 4A). If the purge control valve or charcoal canister are thought to be faulty, they must be renewed.

Charcoal canister - renewal

3 The charcoal canister is located on the left-hand side of the engine compartment.
4 Trace the outlet hose back from the canister to the inlet manifold. Release the retaining clip and disconnect the hose from the manifold (see illustration).
5 Trace the inlet hose back from the canister then release the retaining clip and disconnect it from the fuel vapour pipe (see illustration).
6 Release the breather hose from its retaining clips so that it is free to be removed with the canister.
7 Disconnect the wiring connector from the canister purge valve (see illustration).
8 Unclip the canister mounting bracket from the body and remove the assembly from the engine compartment. If necessary, slacken the clamp bolt and separate the canister and bracket (see illustration).
9 Refitting is a reverse of the removal procedure ensuring the hoses are correctly and securely reconnected.

Purge valve - renewal

Note: *On some models the purge valve is an integral part of the canister and cannot be renewed individually. If this is the case and the valve is faulty, the complete canister assembly must be renewed.*

10 The purge valve is mounted onto the top of the charcoal canister, which is located on the left-hand side of the engine compartment.

11 To renew the valve, ensure the ignition is switched off then disconnect the wiring connector from the valve.

12 Release the retaining clip and disconnect the hose from the valve.

13 Release the retaining clips and remove the purge valve from the top of the canister. Recover the sealing ring from the valve union and discard it; a new one must be used on refitting.

14 Refitting is the reverse of removal, using a new sealing ring. Ensure the valve and the hose are securely held by the retaining clips.

Evaporative emission system 2-way valve - renewal

15 The 2-way valve is mounted onto the top of the fuel tank. To gain access, remove the fuel tank as described in Chapter 4A.

16 Release the retaining clips then disconnect the hoses from the valve, noting each hose's correct fitted position.

17 Unscrew the retaining nut and remove the valve from the tank.

18 Refitting is the reverse of removal ensuring the hoses are correctly and securely reconnected.

Exhaust emission control

Testing

19 The performance of the catalytic converter can be checked only by measuring the exhaust gases using a good-quality, carefully-calibrated exhaust gas analyser.

20 If the CO level at the tailpipe is too high, the vehicle should be taken to a Rover dealer so that the complete fuel-injection and ignition systems, including the oxygen sensor, can be thoroughly checked using the special diagnostic equipment. Once these have been checked and are known to be free from faults, the fault must be in the catalytic converter, which must be renewed.

Catalytic converter - renewal

21 Refer to Chapter 4A.

Oxygen sensor - renewal

Note: *The oxygen sensor is delicate and will not work if it is dropped or knocked, if its power supply is disrupted, or if any cleaning materials are used on it.*

22 The sensor is screwed into the top of the exhaust front pipe on 1.4 litre 8-valve engines and into the exhaust manifold on all other engines.

2.8 . . . then unclip the canister mounting bracket from the body (clamp bolt arrowed)

23 Ensure the ignition is switched off then trace the wiring back from the oxygen sensor. Free the connector from its retaining clip and disconnect the two halves of the connector.

24 Unscrew the sensor and remove it from the manifold/front pipe (as applicable). Recover the sensor sealing washer and discard it; a new one must be used on refitting.

25 Refitting is a reverse of the removal procedure, using a new sealing washer. Tighten the sensor to the specified torque and ensure that the wiring is correctly routed and in no danger of contacting either the exhaust manifold or the engine.

---

3 Diesel engine emission control systems - testing and component renewal

---

Crankcase emission control

Testing

1 The components of this system require no attention other than to check that the hose(s) are clear and undamaged at regular intervals. If the system is thought to be faulty, renew the crankcase pressure limiting valve as follows.

Crankcase pressure limiting valve - renewal

2 Slacken the retaining clip and disconnect the breather hose then ease the valve out from the intake duct and remove it from the engine compartment.

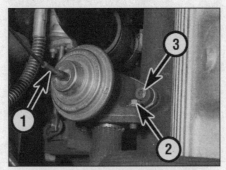

3.9 EGR valve vacuum hose (1), valve-to-connecting pipe bolts (2) and valve-to-manifold bolts (3) - models with intercooler

3 Refitting is the reverse of removal ensuring that the valve is positioned the correct way around with the outlet marked "F" fitted to the intake duct.

Exhaust emission control

Testing

4 The performance of the catalytic converter can be checked only by measuring the exhaust gases using a good-quality, carefully-calibrated exhaust gas analyser.

5 Before assuming that the catalytic converter is faulty, it is worth checking whether the problem is not due to a faulty injector(s). Refer to your Rover dealer for further information.

Catalytic converter - renewal

6 Refer to Chapter 4B for removal and refitting details.

Exhaust gas recirculation (EGR) system

Testing

7 Comprehensive testing of the system can only be carried out using specialist electronic equipment which is connected to the injection system diagnostic wiring connector (see Chapter 4B). If the EGR valve or solenoid valve are thought to be faulty, they must be renewed as follows.

Exhaust gas recirculation (EGR) valve - renewal

8 Unscrew the retaining bolts and remove the plastic cover from the top of the engine unit, taking care not to lose the spacers from the engine cover mounting rubbers. The EGR valve is fitted to the metal pipe linking the inlet and exhaust manifolds.

9 Disconnect the vacuum hose from the EGR valve **(see illustration)**.

10 Slacken and remove the bolts securing the valve to the manifold and connecting pipe and remove it from the engine. Recover the gaskets and discard them; new ones must be used on refitting. If necessary, the connecting pipe can then be unbolted and removed from the other manifold.

11 Refitting is the reverse of the removal, using new gaskets and tightening the valve retaining bolts to the specified torque.

Exhaust gas recirculation (EGR) solenoid valve - renewal

12 Slacken and remove the retaining bolts and remove the cover from the top of the engine unit. The EGR solenoid valve is located on the right-hand side of the engine compartment where it is mounted onto the front suspension strut turret.

13 Disconnect the wiring connector and vacuum hoses from the valve then undo the retaining screws and remove the valve from its mounting bracket.

14 Refitting is the reverse of removal.

4C

4 Catalytic converter - general information and precautions

1 The catalytic converter is a reliable and simple device which needs no maintenance in itself, but there are some facts of which an owner should be aware if the converter is to function properly for its full service life.

Petrol engine

a) DO NOT use leaded petrol in a car equipped with a catalytic converter - the lead will coat the precious metals, reducing their converting efficiency and will eventually destroy the converter.

b) Always keep the ignition and fuel systems well-maintained in accordance with the manufacturer's schedule.

c) If the engine develops a misfire, do not drive the car at all (or at least as little as possible) until the fault is cured.

d) DO NOT push- or tow-start the car - this will soak the catalytic converter in unburned fuel, causing it to overheat when the engine does start.

e) DO NOT switch off the ignition at high engine speeds.

f) DO NOT use fuel or engine oil additives - these may contain substances harmful to the catalytic converter.

g) DO NOT continue to use the car if the engine burns oil to the extent of leaving a visible trail of blue smoke.

h) Remember that the catalytic converter operates at very high temperatures. DO NOT, therefore, park the car in dry undergrowth, over long grass or piles of dead leaves after a long run.

i) Remember that the catalytic converter is FRAGILE - do not strike it with tools during servicing work.

j) In some cases a sulphurous smell (like that of rotten eggs) may be noticed from the exhaust. This is common to many catalytic converter-equipped cars and once the car has covered a few thousand miles the problem should disappear.

k) The catalytic converter, used on a well-maintained and well-driven car, should last for between 50 000 and 100 000 miles - if the converter is no longer effective it must be renewed.

Diesel engine

2 Refer to the information given in parts f, g, h and i of the petrol engine information given above.

Chapter 5 Part A:
Starting and charging systems

Contents

Degrees of difficulty

Easy, suitable for novice with little experience	Fairly easy, suitable for beginner with some experience	Fairly difficult, suitable for competent DIY mechanic	Difficult, suitable for experienced DIY mechanic	Very difficult, suitable for expert DIY or professional

Specifications

System type .... 12-volt, negative earth

Battery
Charge condition:
  Poor .... 12.5 volts
  Normal .... 12.6 volts
  Good .... 12.7 volts

Torque wrench settings	Nm	lbf ft
Alternator fixings:		
1.4 and 1.6 litre engine:		
Mounting bolts	45	33
Upper mounting bracket nut/bolt	25	18
2.0 litre petrol engine:		
Mounting bolts	25	18
2.0 litre diesel engine:		
Upper mounting bolt	25	18
Lower mounting bolt	45	33
Oil pressure switch	12	9
Starter motor bolts:		
1.4 and 1.6 litre engine:		
Mounting bolts	45	33
Support bracket nuts/bolt	25	18
2.0 litre engine:		
Mounting bolts	85	63

1 General information and precautions

General information

The engine electrical system consists mainly of the charging and starting systems. Because of their engine-related functions, these components are covered separately from the body electrical devices such as the lights, instruments, etc (which are covered in Chapter 12). On petrol engine models refer to Part B for information on the ignition system, and on diesel models refer to Part C for information on the pre-heating system.

The electrical system is of the 12-volt negative earth type.

The battery is of the low maintenance or "maintenance-free" (sealed for life) type and is charged by the alternator, which is belt-driven from the crankshaft pulley.

The starter motor is of the pre-engaged type incorporating an integral solenoid. On starting, the solenoid moves the drive pinion into engagement with the flywheel ring gear before the starter motor is energised. Once the engine has started, a one-way clutch prevents the motor armature being driven by the engine until the pinion disengages from the flywheel.

Precautions

Further details of the various systems are given in the relevant Sections of this Chapter. While some repair procedures are given, the usual course of action is to renew the component concerned. The owner whose interest extends beyond mere component renewal should obtain a copy of the *"Automobile Electrical & Electronic Systems Manual"*, available from the publishers of this manual.

It is necessary to take extra care when working on the electrical system to avoid damage to semi-conductor devices (diodes and transistors), and to avoid the risk of personal injury. In addition to the precautions given in *"Safety first!"* at the beginning of this manual, observe the following when working on the system:

Always remove rings, watches, etc before working on the electrical system. Even with the battery disconnected, capacitive discharge could occur if a component's live terminal is earthed through a metal object. This could cause a shock or nasty burn.

Do not reverse the battery connections. Components such as the alternator, electronic control units, or any other components having semi-conductor circuitry could be irreparably damaged.

If the engine is being started using jump leads and a slave battery, connect the batteries *positive-to-positive* and *negative-to-negative* (see *"Jump starting"*). This also applies when connecting a battery charger.

Never disconnect the battery terminals, the alternator, any electrical wiring or any test instruments when the engine is running.

Do not allow the engine to turn the alternator when the alternator is not connected.

Never "test" for alternator output by "flashing" the output lead to earth.

Never use an ohmmeter of the type incorporating a hand-cranked generator for circuit or continuity testing.

Always ensure that the battery negative lead is disconnected when working on the electrical system.

Before using electric-arc welding equipment on the car, disconnect the battery, alternator and components such as the fuel injection/ignition electronic control unit to protect them from the risk of damage.

The radio/cassette unit fitted as standard equipment by Rover is equipped with a built-in security code to deter thieves. If the power source to the unit is cut, the anti-theft system will activate. Even if the power source is immediately reconnected, the radio/cassette unit will not function until the correct security code has been entered. Therefore, if you do not know the correct security code for the radio/cassette unit do not disconnect the battery negative terminal of the battery or remove the radio/cassette unit from the vehicle. Refer to *"Radio/cassette unit anti-theft system precaution"* Section for further information.

2 Electrical fault finding - general information

Refer to Chapter 12.

3 Battery - testing and charging

Standard and low maintenance battery - testing

1 If the vehicle covers a small annual mileage, it is worthwhile checking the specific gravity of the electrolyte every three months to determine the state of charge of the battery. Use a hydrometer to make the check and compare the results with the following table. Note that the specific gravity readings assume an electrolyte temperature of 15°C (60°F); for every 10°C (18°F) below 15°C (60°F) subtract 0.007. For every 10°C (18°F) above 15°C (60°F) add 0.007.

| | Ambient temperature: | |
	above 25°C (77°F)	below 25°C (77°F)
Fully-charged	1.210 to 1.230	1.270 to 1.290
70% charged	1.170 to 1.190	1.230 to 1.250
discharged	1.050 to 1.070	1.110 to 1.130

2 If the battery condition is suspect, first check the specific gravity of electrolyte in each cell. A variation of 0.040 or more between any cells indicates loss of electrolyte or deterioration of the internal plates.

3 If the specific gravity variation is 0.040 or more, the battery should be renewed. If the cell variation is satisfactory but the battery is discharged, it should be charged as described later in this Section.

Maintenance-free battery - testing

4 In cases where a "sealed for life" maintenance-free battery is fitted, topping-up and testing of the electrolyte in each cell is not possible. The condition of the battery can therefore only be tested using a battery condition indicator or a voltmeter.

5 Certain models may be fitted with a "Delco" type maintenance-free battery, with a built-in charge condition indicator. The indicator is located in the top of the battery casing, and indicates the condition of the battery from its colour. If the indicator shows green, then the battery is in a good state of charge. If the indicator turns darker, eventually to black, then the battery requires charging, as described later in this Section. If the indicator shows clear/yellow, then the electrolyte level in the battery is too low to allow further use, and the battery should be renewed. **Do not** attempt to charge, load or jump start a battery when the indicator shows clear/yellow.

6 If testing the battery using a voltmeter, connect the voltmeter across the battery and compare the result with those given in the Specifications under "charge condition". The test is only accurate if the battery has not been subjected to any kind of charge for the previous six hours. If this is not the case, switch on the headlights for 30 seconds, then wait four to five minutes before testing the battery after switching off the headlights. All other electrical circuits must be switched off, so check that the doors and tailgate are fully shut when making the test.

7 If the voltage reading is less than 12.2 volts, then the battery is discharged, whilst a reading of 12.2 to 12.4 volts indicates a partially discharged condition.

8 If the battery is to be charged, remove it from the vehicle (Section 4) and charge it as described later in this Section.

Standard and low maintenance battery - charging

Note: *The following is intended as a guide only. Always refer to the manufacturer's recommendations (often printed on a label attached to the battery) before charging a battery.*

9 Charge the battery at a rate of 3.5 to 4 amps and continue to charge the battery at this rate until no further rise in specific gravity is noted over a four hour period.

10 Alternatively, a trickle charger charging at the rate of 1.5 amps can safely be used overnight.

11 Specially rapid "boost" charges which are claimed to restore the power of the battery in 1 to 2 hours are not recommended, as they can cause serious damage to the battery plates through overheating.

12 While charging the battery, note that the temperature of the electrolyte should never exceed 37.8°C (100°F).

Maintenance-free battery - charging

Note: *The following is intended as a guide only. Always refer to the manufacturer's recommendations (often printed on a label attached to the battery) before charging a battery.*

13 This battery type takes considerably longer to fully recharge than the standard type, the time taken being dependent on the extent of discharge, but it can take anything up to three days.

14 A constant voltage type charger is required, to be set, when connected, to 13.9 to 14.9 volts with a charger current below 25 amps. Using this method, the battery should be usable within three hours, giving a voltage reading of 12.5 volts, but this is for a partially discharged battery and, as mentioned, full charging can take considerably longer.

15 If the battery is to be charged from a fully discharged state (condition reading less than 12.2 volts), have it recharged by your Rover dealer or local automotive electrician, as the charge rate is higher and constant supervision during charging is necessary.

4 Battery - removal and refitting

Note: *If a Rover radio/cassette unit is fitted, refer to "Radio/cassette unit anti-theft system - precaution".*

Removal

1 The battery is located on the left-hand side of the engine compartment.

2 Slacken the clamp nut and disconnect the clamp from the battery negative (earth) terminal **(see illustration)**.

3 Lift the insulation cover and disconnect the positive terminal lead in the same way.

4 Unscrew the bolt and remove the battery retaining clamp then lift the battery out of the engine compartment **(see illustrations)**.

5 To remove the battery tray, undo the bolts securing the battery tray to the air cleaner housing and mounting brackets then remove the tray from the engine compartment. The tray mounting brackets can then be unbolted and removed, once the wiring/hoses have been unclipped. On UK models it will be necessary to disconnect the wiring connector from the "dim-dip" lighting resistor which is mounted onto the bracket; on 2.0 litre models with cruise control it will also be necessary to disconnect the wiring connector and hose from the vacuum control unit.

Refitting

6 Refitting is a reversal of removal, but smear petroleum jelly on the terminals when reconnecting the leads, and always reconnect the positive lead first, and the negative lead last.

5 Charging system - testing

Note: *Refer to the warnings given in "Safety first!" and in Section 1 of this Chapter before starting work.*

1 If the ignition warning light fails to illuminate when the ignition is switched on, first check the alternator wiring connections for security. If satisfactory, check that the warning light bulb has not blown, and that the bulbholder is secure in its location in the instrument panel. If the light still fails to illuminate, check the continuity of the warning light feed wire from the alternator to the bulbholder. If all is satisfactory, the alternator is at fault and should be renewed or taken to an auto-electrician for testing and repair.

2 If the ignition warning light illuminates when the engine is running, stop the engine and check that the drivebelt is correctly tensioned (see Chapter 1) and that the alternator connections are secure. If all is so far satisfactory, have the alternator checked by an auto-electrician for testing and repair.

3 If the alternator output is suspect even though the warning light functions correctly, the regulated voltage may be checked as follows.

4 Connect a voltmeter across the battery terminals and start the engine.

5 Increase the engine speed until the voltmeter reading remains steady; the reading should be approximately 12 to 13 volts, and no more than 14 volts.

6 Switch on as many electrical accessories (eg, the headlights, heated rear window and heater blower) as possible, and check that the alternator maintains the regulated voltage at around 13 to 14 volts.

7 If the regulated voltage is not as stated, the fault may be due to worn brushes, weak brush

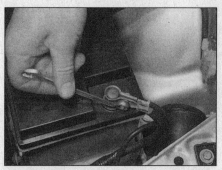

4.2 Slacken the clamp nut and disconnect the negative (earth) lead from the battery

springs, a faulty voltage regulator, a faulty diode, a severed phase winding or worn or damaged slip rings. The alternator should be renewed or taken to an auto-electrician for testing and repair.

6 Alternator drivebelt - removal, refitting and tensioning

Refer to the procedure given for the auxiliary drivebelt(s) in Chapter 1.

7 Alternator - removal and refitting

Removal

1 Firmly apply the handbrake then jack up the front of the vehicle and support it securely on axle stands (see *"Jacking and Vehicle Support"*). Where necessary, undo the retaining bolts and remove the undercover from beneath the engine/transmission unit. Disconnect the battery negative lead and proceed as described under the relevant sub-heading.

1.4 and 1.6 litre engine - models without air conditioning

2 Release the auxiliary drivebelt as described in Chapter 1A and disengage it from the alternator pulley.

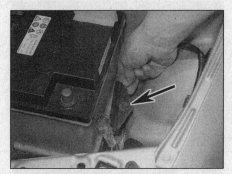

4.4a Unscrew the retaining bolt (arrowed) and remove the clamp . . .

4.4b . . . then lift the battery out from the engine compartment

5A

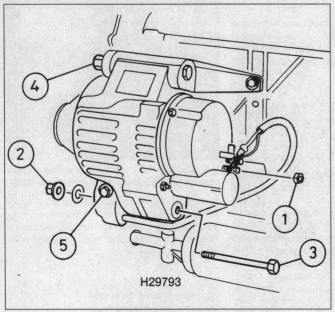

7.3 Alternator fixings -
1.4 and 1.6 litre engines without air conditioning

1 Wiring retaining nut	4 Upper mounting bolt
2 Lower mounting nut	5 Adjuster bolt
3 Lower mounting bolt	

7.6 Alternator fixings -
1.4 and 1.6 litre engines with air conditioning

1 Drivebelt tensioner	3 Upper mounting bracket bolts
2 Lower mounting bolt	4 Upper mounting bracket

3 Remove the rubber covers (where fitted) from the alternator terminals, then unscrew the retaining nuts and disconnect the wiring from the rear of the alternator (**see illustration**).

4 Unscrew the nuts and remove the alternator upper and lower mounting bolts

1.4 and 1.6 litre engine - models with air conditioning

5 Release the auxiliary drivebelt as described in Chapter 1A and disengage it from the alternator pulley.

6 Slacken and remove the alternator upper and lower mounting nuts and bolts and free the alternator from its mountings (**see illustration**).

7 Unscrew the upper mounting bracket retaining bolt then slacken the nut and pivot the upper mounting bracket away from the alternator.

8 Remove the rubber covers (where fitted) from the alternator terminals, then unscrew the retaining nuts. Disconnect the wiring from the rear of the alternator and remove the alternator from the engine compartment.

2.0 litre petrol engine - models without air conditioning

9 Release the auxiliary drivebelt as described in Chapter 1A and disengage it from the alternator pulley.

10 Remove the insulating cover from the rear of the alternator, then unscrew the retaining nuts and disconnect the wiring from the alternator.

11 Disconnect the oxygen sensor wiring connector, which is situated directly above the alternator, then undo the bolt securing the power steering pipe to the front of the cylinder head.

12 Slacken and remove the alternator front and rear mounting bolts and manoeuvre the alternator out of position. Note that on some models it may be necessary to unbolt the radiator upper mounting brackets and tilt the radiator slightly (see Chapter 3) to gain the necessary clearance required to remove the alternator.

2.0 litre petrol engine - models with air conditioning

13 The alternator can be removed as described in paragraphs 9 to 12 noting that it will probably be necessary to drain the cooling system (see Chapter 1A) and disconnect the coolant hoses from the thermostat housing to gain the clearance required to remove the alternator.

2.0 litre diesel engine

14 Undo the retaining screws and remove the cover from the top of the engine, noting the spacers which are fitted to the cover mounting rubbers.

15 Release the auxiliary drivebelt as described in Chapter 1B and disengage it from the alternator pulley.

16 Peel back the rubber cover from the alternator terminal, then unscrew the retaining nut and disconnect the wiring. Also disconnect the wiring connector from the rear of the alternator (**see illustration**).

17 Release the retaining clip and disconnect the pipe from the braking system vacuum pump which is fitted to the front of the alternator (**see illustration**).

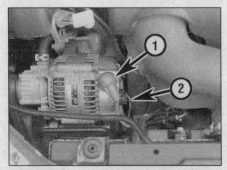

7.16 Peel back the rubber cover (1), undo the nut, disconnect the wiring then unplug the connector (2) from the alternator

7.17 Release the retaining clip and disconnect the pipe (arrowed) from the braking system vacuum pump

18 Wipe clean the area around the vacuum pump oil feed and return pipes unions on the cylinder block. Position a container beneath the unions then unscrew the feed pipe union nut and disconnect the return pipe union and allow any oil to drain into the container.

19 Slacken and remove the mounting bolts and free the alternator from its mountings. Unscrew the oil feed pipe union nut from the vacuum pump then remove the alternator assembly from the vehicle.

20 If necessary, referring to Chapter 9, remove the vacuum pump from the alternator.

Refitting

21 Refitting is the reverse of removal tightening all mounting bolts to their specified torque settings (where given). Ensure the drivebelt is correctly refitted and tensioned as described in Chapter 1A or 1B (as applicable).

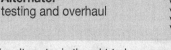

8 Alternator -
testing and overhaul

If the alternator is thought to be suspect, it should be removed from the vehicle and taken to an auto-electrician for testing. Most auto-electricians will be able to supply and fit brushes at a reasonable cost. However, check on the cost of repairs before proceeding as it may prove more economical to obtain a new or exchange alternator.

9 Starting system -
testing

Note: *Refer to the precautions given in "Safety first!" and in Section 1 of this Chapter before starting work.*

1 If the starter motor fails to operate when the ignition key is turned to the appropriate position, the following possible causes may be to blame:
 a) *The battery is faulty.*
 b) *The electrical connections between the switch, solenoid, battery and starter motor are somewhere failing to pass the necessary current from the battery through the starter to earth.*
 c) *The solenoid is faulty.*
 d) *The starter motor is mechanically or electrically defective.*

2 To check the battery, switch on the headlights. If they dim after a few seconds, this indicates that the battery is discharged - recharge (see Section 3) or renew the battery. If the headlights glow brightly, operate the ignition switch and observe the lights. If they dim, then this indicates that current is reaching the starter motor, therefore the fault must lie in the starter motor. If the lights continue to glow brightly (and no clicking sound can be heard from the starter motor solenoid), this indicates that there is a fault in

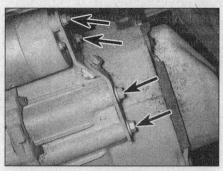

10.4 Undo the nuts and bolts (arrowed) and remove the support bracket from the rear of the starter motor

the circuit or solenoid - see following paragraphs. If the starter motor turns slowly when operated, but the battery is in good condition, then this indicates that either the starter motor is faulty, or there is considerable resistance somewhere in the circuit.

3 If a fault in the circuit is suspected, disconnect the battery leads (including the earth connection to the body), the starter/solenoid wiring and the engine/transmission earth strap. Thoroughly clean the connections, and reconnect the leads and wiring, then use a voltmeter or test lamp to check that full battery voltage is available at the battery positive lead connection to the solenoid, and that the earth is sound. Smear petroleum jelly around the battery terminals to prevent corrosion - corroded connections are amongst the most frequent causes of electrical system faults.

4 If the battery and all connections are in good condition, check the circuit by disconnecting the wire from the solenoid blade terminal. Connect a voltmeter or test lamp between the wire end and a good earth (such as the battery negative terminal), and check that the wire is live when the ignition switch is turned to the 'start' position. If it is, then the circuit is sound - if not the circuit wiring can be checked as described in Chapter 12.

5 The solenoid contacts can be checked by connecting a voltmeter or test lamp between the battery positive feed connection on the starter side of the solenoid, and earth. When the ignition switch is turned to the "start" position, there should be a reading or lighted bulb, as applicable. If there is no reading or

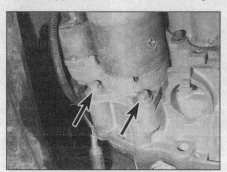

10.5 Starter motor lower mounting bolts - 1.4 and 1.6 litre engine

lighted bulb, the solenoid is faulty and should be renewed.

6 If the circuit and solenoid are proved sound, the fault must lie in the starter motor. In this event, it may be possible to have the starter motor overhauled by a specialist, but check on the cost of spares before proceeding, as it may prove more economical to obtain a new or exchange motor.

10 Starter motor -
removal and refitting

Removal

1 Disconnect the battery negative lead, firmly apply the handbrake then jack up the front of the vehicle and support it on axle stands (see *"Jacking and Vehicle Support"*). Where necessary, undo the retaining bolts and remove the undercover from beneath the engine/transmission unit. Proceed as described under the relevant sub-heading.

1.4 and 1.6 litre engine

2 Remove the air cleaner housing assembly as described in Chapter 4A.

3 Remove the rubber cover then unscrew the retaining nut and disconnect the main supply lead from the solenoid. Disconnect the wiring connector from the solenoid terminal.

4 Slacken and remove the retaining nuts and bolts and remove the support bracket from the rear of the starter motor **(see illustration)**.

5 Slacken and remove the starter motor mounting bolts, noting the correct fitted location of the earth leads, then manoeuvre the starter motor out of position and remove it from the vehicle **(see illustration)**.

2.0 litre engine

6 Remove the air cleaner housing assembly as described in Chapter 4A. On petrol engines, unclip the charcoal canister (see Chapter 4C) from its bracket and position it clear of the starter to improve access.

7 Remove the rubber cover then unscrew the retaining nut and disconnect the main supply lead from the solenoid. Disconnect the wiring connector from the solenoid terminal **(see illustrations)**.

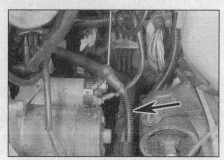

10.7a On 2.0 litre engines, undo the nut and disconnect the main lead from the starter motor . . .

5A

10.7b . . . then disconnect the wiring connector from the solenoid terminal

10.8a Slacken the retaining bolts (upper bolt arrowed) . . .

10.8b . . . and remove the starter motor from the engine

8 Remove the starter motor mounting bolts then manoeuvre the motor out of position and remove it from the vehicle **(see illustrations)**.

Refitting

9 Refitting is a reversal of removal tightening the mounting bolts to the specified torque. Ensure all wiring is correctly routed and its retaining nuts are securely tightened.

11 Starter motor -
testing and overhaul

If the starter motor is thought to be suspect, it should be removed from the vehicle and taken to an auto-electrician for testing. Most auto-electricians will be able to supply and fit brushes at a reasonable cost. However, check on the cost of repairs before proceeding as it may prove more economical to obtain a new or exchange motor.

12 Ignition switch -
removal and refitting

The ignition switch is integral with the

steering column lock and can be removed as described in Chapter 10.

13 Oil pressure warning
light switch -
removal and refitting

Removal

1 On 1.4 and 1.6 litre engines, the switch is screwed into the oil filter housing which is mounted onto the front of the cylinder block, and on 2.0 litre engines the switch is screwed into the rear of the oil pump housing which is mounted onto the right-hand end of the cylinder block **(see illustrations)**.
2 To improve access to the switch, firmly apply the handbrake then jack up the front of the vehicle and support it on axle stands (see "*Jacking and Vehicle Support*").
3 Where necessary, undo the retaining bolts and remove the undercover from beneath the engine/transmission unit. On 2.0 litre petrol engines, to gain access to the switch, undo the bolts securing the oil pump/filter cover to the cylinder block and sump and remove the cover from the right-hand end of the engine, noting the correct fitted locations of the spacers. Note that it may be necessary to

unbolt the rear steady rod bolts and pivot it away from the sump (see Chapter 2B) in order to gain the clearance necessary to remove the cover.
4 Disconnect the wiring connector then unscrew the switch and remove it form the engine. Be prepared for oil spillage, and if the switch is to be left removed from the engine for any length of time, plug the switch aperture.

Refitting

5 Ensure the switch threads are clean and dry. Apply a smear of sealant to the switch threads then refit the switch to the housing and tighten it to the specified torque.
6 Reconnect the wiring connector then (where removed) refit the undercover to the vehicle.
7 On 2.0 litre petrol engines, refit the oil pump/filter cover to the engine, ensuring the washers and spacers are correctly positioned, and securely tighten its retaining bolts. Where necessary, refit the engine steady bar and tighten its retaining bolts to their specified torque settings (see Chapter 2B).
8 Lower the vehicle to the ground then check and, if necessary, top up the engine oil as described in "*Weekly checks*".

13.1a Oil pressure switch location - 1.4 and 1.6 litre engine

13.1b Oil pressure switch location - 2.0 litre engine (diesel shown)

Chapter 5 Part B:
Ignition system - petrol engine models

Contents

Degrees of difficulty

Easy, suitable for novice with little experience	**Fairly easy,** suitable for beginner with some experience	**Fairly difficult,** suitable for competent DIY mechanic 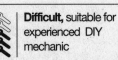	**Difficult,** suitable for experienced DIY mechanic	**Very difficult,** suitable for expert DIY or professional

Specifications

System type .... Rover/Motorola Modular Engine Management System (MEMS) controlled by ECM (see Chapter 4A for further information)

Firing order .... 1-3-4-2 (No 1 cylinder at timing belt end)

Ignition timing
At idle speed*:
1.4 and 1.6 litre engine .... $10 \pm 5°$ BTDC
2.0 litre engine .... $12 \pm 5°$ BTDC

*Ignition timing is being constantly altered by the ECM and cannot be checked without special equipment

Torque wrench settings	Nm	lbf ft
Ignition coil retaining bolts:		
1.4 and 1.6 litre engine:		
M6 bolt	9	6
M10 bolts	25	18
2.0 litre engine	9	6
Rotor arm screw - 1.4 and 1.6 litre engine	8	5

1 Ignition system - general information

The ignition system is integrated with the fuel injection system to form a combined engine management system under the control of one ECM (See Chapter 4A for further information).

On 1.4 and 1.6 litre engines the ignition side of the system incorporates an ignition coil and a distributor, which is driven off the end of the inlet camshaft. The ECM uses its inputs from the various sensors to calculate the required ignition advance setting and coil charging time. This causes a high voltage to be induced in the coil secondary (HT) windings which then travels down the HT lead to the distributor and onto the relevant spark plug.

On 2.0 litre engines, the ignition system is off the distributorless type, incorporating a four-output ignition coil and a knock sensor. The ignition coil actually consists of two separate HT coils which supply two cylinders each (one coil supplies cylinders 1 and 4, and the other cylinders 2 and 3). Under the control of the ECM, the coil operates on the "wasted spark" principle, ie. each spark plug sparks twice for every cycle of the engine, once on the compression stroke and once on the exhaust stroke. The ECM uses its inputs from the various sensors to calculate the required ignition advance setting and coil charging time. The knock sensor is mounted onto the cylinder block and informs the ECM when the engine is "pinking" under load. The sensor is sensitive to vibration and detects the knocking which occurs when the engine starts to "pink" (pre-ignite). The knock sensor sends an electrical signal to the ECM which in turn retards the ignition advance setting until the "pinking" ceases.

⚠️ Warning: Voltages produced by an electronic ignition system are considerably higher than those produced by conventional ignition systems. Extreme care must be taken when working on the system with the ignition switched on. Persons with surgically-implanted cardiac pacemaker devices should keep well clear of the ignition circuits, components and test equipment.

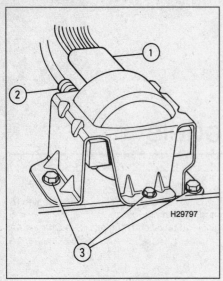

**3.2 Ignition HT coil fixings -
1.4 and 1.6 litre engine**

1	Wiring	2	HT lead
	connector	3	Retaining bolts

2 Ignition system - testing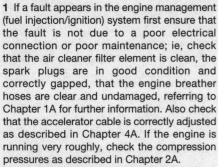

1 If a fault appears in the engine management (fuel injection/ignition) system first ensure that the fault is not due to a poor electrical connection or poor maintenance; ie, check that the air cleaner filter element is clean, the spark plugs are in good condition and correctly gapped, that the engine breather hoses are clear and undamaged, referring to Chapter 1A for further information. Also check that the accelerator cable is correctly adjusted as described in Chapter 4A. If the engine is running very roughly, check the compression pressures as described in Chapter 2A.

2 If these checks fail to reveal the cause of the problem the vehicle should be taken to a suitably equipped Rover dealer for testing. A wiring block connector is incorporated in the engine management circuit into which a special electronic diagnostic tester can be plugged. The tester will locate the fault quickly and simply alleviating the need to test all the system components individually which is a time consuming operation that carries a high risk of damaging the ECM.

3 The only ignition system checks which can be carried out by the home mechanic are those described in Chapter 1A, relating to the spark plugs, HT leads and (where fitted) distributor cap and rotor arm. If necessary, the system wiring and wiring connectors can be checked as described in Chapter 12 ensuring that the ECM wiring connector(s) have first been disconnected.

3 Ignition HT coil - removal and refitting

Removal

1.4 and 1.6 litre engine

1 Disconnect the battery negative terminal. The ignition coil is mounted onto the rear of the cylinder block; to improve access to the coil, firmly apply the handbrake then jack up the front of the vehicle and support it on axle stands (see "Jacking and Vehicle Support").

2 Disconnect the wiring connector and HT lead from the coil (see illustration).

3 Slacken and remove the retaining bolts and remove the coil from the engine.

2.0 litre engine

4 Disconnect the battery negative terminal. To improve access to the coil, unclip the charcoal canister from its mounting bracket and position it clear of the coil.

5 Disconnect the wiring connector from the coil.

6 Disconnect the HT leads from the coil terminals. If the coil terminals and the HT leads are not numbered with their respective cylinder numbers, make identification markings to avoid confusion on refitting.

7 Undo the retaining nuts and bolts and remove the coil from its bracket on the rear of the cylinder block.

Refitting

8 Refitting is the reverse of removal, tightening the coil retaining bolts to the specified torque. Ensure the HT lead(s) and wiring connector are correctly and securely reconnected.

4 Distributor (1.4 and 1.6 litre engine) - removal and refitting

Removal

Note: A new rotor arm retaining screw will be needed on refitting.

1 Ensure the ignition is switched off. To improve access, unclip and remove the air cleaner housing lid.

2 Slacken the distributor cap retaining screws then release the cap from the cylinder head and position it clear of the rotor arm (see illustrations).

3 Slacken the retaining screw then remove the rotor arm from the end of the camshaft (see illustration). Slide the oil splash shield off from the camshaft, noting which way around it is fitted.

4 Examine all components for signs of wear or damage as described in Chapter 1A and renew as necessary.

Refitting

5 Refitting is the reverse of removal, using a new rotor arm retaining screw and tightening it to the specified torque.

5 Ignition timing - checking and adjustment

The timing is constantly being monitored and adjusted by the engine management ECM. The values given in the Specifications just show the operating range of the ECM and are of no real use for the home mechanic.

The only way in which the ignition timing can be checked and (where possible) adjusted is by using special electronic test equipment, connected to the engine management system diagnostic connector (refer to Chapter 4A for further information). Refer to your Rover dealer for further information.

4.2a On 1.4 and 1.6 litre engines, slacken the retaining screws . . .

4.2b . . . then free the distributor cap from the cylinder head (8-valve engine shown)

4.3 Slacken the retaining screw (arrowed) and remove the rotor arm from the camshaft

Chapter 5 Part C:
Pre-heating system – diesel engine models

Contents

Degrees of difficulty

Easy, suitable for novice with little experience	**Fairly easy,** suitable for beginner with some experience	**Fairly difficult,** suitable for competent DIY mechanic	**Difficult,** suitable for experienced DIY mechanic	**Very difficult,** suitable for expert DIY or professional 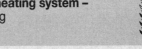

Specifications

Torque wrench settings

	Nm	lbf ft
Coolant outlet elbow bolts	25	18
Glow plugs	20	15
Inlet manifold intake pipe bolts	9	6

1 General information

To assist cold starting, diesel engine models are fitted with a pre-heating system, which comprises a relay, three glow plugs (fitted to Nos 1, 2 and 3 cylinders). The system is controlled by the Electronic Diesel Control (EDC) system, using information provided by the coolant temperature sensor (see Chapter 4B).

The glow plugs are miniature electric heating elements, encapsulated in a metal case with a probe at one end, and an electrical connection at the other. The combustion chambers of cylinders No 1 to 3 each have a glow plug threaded into it. When the glow plug is energised, it heats up rapidly causing the temperature of the air charge drawn into each of the combustion chambers to rise. Each glow plug probe is positioned directly in line with the incoming spray of fuel from the injector. Hence the fuel passing over the glow plug probe is also heated, allowing its optimum combustion temperature to be achieved more readily. In addition, small particles of the fuel passing over the glow plugs are ignited and this helps to trigger the combustion process.

The duration of the pre-heating period is governed by the Electronic Diesel Control (EDC) system control module (ECM), using information provided by the coolant temperature sensor (see Chapter 4B). The ECM alters the pre-heating time (the length for which the glow plugs are supplied with current) to suit the prevailing conditions.

A warning light informs the driver that pre-heating is taking place. The lamp extinguishes when sufficient pre-heating has taken place to allow the engine to be started, but power will still be supplied to the glow plugs for a further period until the engine is started. If no attempt is made to start the engine, the power supply to the glow plugs is switched off to prevent battery drain and glow plug burn-out.

2 Pre-heating system – testing

1 Full testing of the system can only be carried out using specialist diagnostic equipment which is connected to the engine management system diagnostic wiring connector (see Chapter 4B). If the pre-heating system is thought to be faulty, some preliminary checks of the glow plug operation may be made as described in the following paragraphs.

2 Connect a voltmeter or 12-volt test lamp between the glow plug supply cable, and a good earth point on the engine.

Caution: Make sure that the live connection is kept well clear of the engine and bodywork.

3 Have an assistant activate the pre-heating system by turning the ignition key to the second position, and check that battery voltage is applied to the glow plug electrical connection. **Note:** *The supply voltage will be less than battery voltage initially, but will rise and settle as the glow plug heats up. It will then drop to zero when the pre-heating period ends and the safety cut-out operates.*

4 If no supply voltage can be detected at the glow plug, then the glow plug relay or the supply cable may be faulty.

5 To locate a faulty glow plug, first operate the pre-heating system to allow the glow plugs to reach working temperature, then disconnect the battery negative cable and position it away from the battery terminal.

6 Refer to Section 3, and remove the supply cable from No 2 glow plug terminal. Measure the electrical resistance between the glow plug terminal and the engine earth. A reading of anything more than a few Ohms indicates that the glow plug is defective.

7 As a final check, remove the glow plugs and inspect them visually, as described in Section 3.

8 If no problems are found, take the vehicle to a Rover dealer for testing using the appropriate diagnostic equipment.

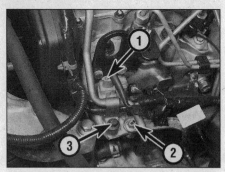

3.6 Disconnect the wiring connector from the coolant temperature sensor (1) then undo the vacuum pipe bolt (3) and dipstick tube bolt (2)

3 Glow plugs – removal, inspection and refitting

Removal

1 Disconnect the battery negative lead.
2 Unscrew the retaining bolts and remove the plastic cover from the top of the engine, taking care not to lose the spacers which are fitted to the cover mounting rubbers.

No 1 cylinder glow plug

3 Drain the cooling system as described in Chapter 1B.
4 On models with air conditioning, remove the alternator, as described in Part A of this Chapter.
5 Disconnect the wiring connectors from the coolant temperature sensor and sender which are screwed into the coolant outlet elbow on the front, right-hand of the cylinder head (see illustration 3.6).
6 Unscrew the retaining bolts securing the dipstick tube and vacuum pipe to the coolant outlet (see illustration).
7 Slacken the retaining clip and disconnect the coolant hose then unscrew the retaining bolts and remove the coolant outlet from the front of the cylinder head. Discard the outlet seal, a new one should be used on refitting.
8 Unscrew the terminal nut securing the feed wiring to the glow plugs, then disconnect the wiring, and move it to one side.

9 Unscrew the glow plug and remove it from the cylinder head.

Nos 2 and 3 cylinder glow plugs

10 To improve access on models with an intercooler, slacken the retaining clip and disconnect the intercooler duct from the inlet manifold intake pipe. Slacken and remove the two bolts securing the exhaust gas recirculation (EGR) pipe to the rear of the intake pipe then unscrew the bolts securing the pipe to the manifold. Undo the bolt securing the pipe to the cylinder head cover then remove the pipe from the engine, along with its gasket. Recover and discard the gasket.
11 Remove the glow plug(s) as described in paragraphs 8 and 9 (see illustrations).

Inspection

12 Inspect the glow plugs for signs of damage. Burt or eroded glow plug tips can be caused by a bad injector spray pattern. Have the injectors checked if this sort of damage is found.
13 If the glow plugs are in good condition, check them electrically, as described in Section 2.
14 The glow plugs can be energised by applying 12 volts to them to verify that they heat up evenly and in the required time. Observe the following precautions:
   a) Support the glow plug by clamping it carefully in a vice or self-locking pliers. Remember it will be red hot.
   b) Make sure that the power supply or test lead incorporates a fuse or overload trip to protect against damage from a short-circuit.
   c) After testing, allow the glow plug to cool for several minutes before attempting to handle it.
15 A glow plug in good condition will start to glow red at the tip after drawing current for 5 seconds or so. Any plug which takes much longer to start glowing, or which starts glowing in the middle instead of at the tip, is defective.

Refitting

No 1 cylinder glow plug

16 Thoroughly clean the glow plugs, and the glow plug seating areas in the cylinder head.

17 Apply a smear of anti-seize compound to the glow plug threads, then refit the glow plug and tighten it to the specified torque.
18 Reconnect the wiring to the glow plug and securely tighten the terminal nut.
19 Ensure the coolant outlet and cylinder head surfaces are clean and dry. Fit a new gasket to the cylinder head then refit the outlet, tightening its retaining bolts to the specified torque.
20 Reconnect the coolant hose, tightening its retaining clip securely, then refit the vacuum pipe and dipstick tube bolts, tightening them securely.
21 Reconnect the coolant temperature sensor/sender wiring connectors.
22 On models with air conditioning refit the alternator as described in Part A.
23 Refill the cooling system as described in Chapter 1B then refit the cover to the engine.

Nos 2 and 3 cylinder glow plugs

24 Refit the glow plug(s) as described in paragraphs 16 to 18, ensuring that the main feed wire is connected to No 2 glow plug.
25 Where necessary, fit a new gasket to the inlet manifold then refit the intake pipe. Tighten all the bolts to the specified torque and securely reconnect the intercooler duct.

4 Glow plug relay – removal and refitting

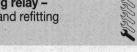

Removal

1 The relay is mounted onto the engine compartment bulkhead, where it is situated just to the left of the engine control module (ECM). On models without an intercooler there is only one relay and on models with an intercooler the glow plug relay is the one nearest the ECM.
2 Ensure the ignition is switched off then unclip the relay from the bulkhead and pull it out of the wiring connector (see illustration).

Refitting

3 Refitting is a reversal of removal.

3.11a Unscrew the retaining nut and disconnect the wiring connector ...

3.11b ... then unscrew the glow plug from the cylinder head

4.2 On models with an intercooler the glow plug relay (arrowed) is the one next to the ECM

Chapter 6
Clutch

Contents

Degrees of difficulty

| **Easy,** suitable for novice with little experience | | **Fairly easy,** suitable for beginner with some experience | | **Fairly difficult,** suitable for competent DIY mechanic | | **Difficult,** suitable for experienced DIY mechanic | | **Very difficult,** suitable for expert DIY or professional | |

Specifications

Type . . . .   Single dry plate with diaphragm spring, hydraulically-operated

Friction plate
Diameter:
  Petrol engines:
    1.4 litre engine . . . .   190 mm
    1.6 litre engine . . . .   200 mm
    2.0 litre engine . . . .   215 mm
  Diesel engines . . . .   228 mm
Friction material-to-rivet head depth:
  New (approximate) . . . .   1.0 mm
  Service limit . . . .   0.2 mm
Runout:
  Standard . . . .   Less than 0.8 mm
  Service limit . . . .   1.0 mm

Pressure plate
Maximum diaphragm spring finger height difference . . . .   1.0 mm
Maximum warpage or machined surface . . . .   0.18 mm

Torque wrench settings

	Nm	lbf ft
Pressure plate retaining bolts:		
1.4 and 1.6 litre engines	18	11
2.0 litre engine	26	19
Release fork retaining bolt - 2.0 litre engine	29	21

6

1 General information

The clutch consists of a friction plate, a pressure plate assembly, a release bearing and the release mechanism; all of these components are contained in the large cast-aluminium alloy bellhousing, sandwiched between the engine and the transmission. The clutch release mechanism is hydraulically operated.

The friction plate is fitted between the engine flywheel and the clutch pressure plate, and is allowed to slide on the transmission input shaft splines.

The pressure plate assembly is bolted to the engine flywheel. When the engine is running, drive is transmitted from the crankshaft, via the flywheel, to the friction plate (these components being clamped securely together by the pressure plate assembly) and from the friction plate to the transmission input shaft.

To interrupt the drive, the spring pressure must be relaxed. Depressing the pedal pushes on the master cylinder pushrod. This hydraulically forces the slave cylinder piston which is connected to the end of the clutch release fork lever. The release fork acts on its pivot and presses the release bearing against the pressure plate spring fingers. This causes the springs to deform and releases the clamping force on the pressure plate. The hydraulic clutch is self-adjusting and requires no manual adjustment.

2 Clutch pedal - removal and refitting

Removal

1 Remove the retaining clips then unclip the undercover from the driver's side of the facia.
2 Remove the retaining clip and withdraw the clevis pin securing the clutch pedal to the master cylinder pushrod. Discard the retaining clip; a new one should be used on refitting.

4.4 Slide out the retaining clip and remove the slave cylinder from its mounting bracket (2.0 litre engine shown)

On some models the clevis may be secured in position with a roll pin, where this is the case tap out the pin and discard it; a new one must be used on refitting.
3 Slacken and remove the nuts and bolt securing the pedal assembly to the bulkhead then manoeuvre the assembly out from underneath the facia. Do not attempt to dismantle the pedal assembly, if it is worn or damaged the complete assembly must be renewed; no individual components are available.

Refitting

4 Manoeuvre the pedal assembly into position, ensuring it is correctly engaged with the pushrod clevis. Refit the bracket mounting nuts and bolt and tighten them securely.
5 Insert the clevis pin and secure it in position with the new retaining clip. Where a roll pin is fitted, tap the new pin into position making sure it is securely located.
6 Check the operation of the clutch pedal then refit the facia panel (where removed) and undercover.

3 Clutch master cylinder - removal and refitting

Removal

1 Disconnect the battery negative terminal then remove the fuel system electronic control module (ECM) as described in Chapter 4.
2 Working inside the vehicle, carry out the operations described in paragraphs 1 and 2 of Section 2.
3 Working back from the master cylinder, release the clutch pipe from all the necessary retaining clips until you come to the quick-release fitting. Position a suitable container beneath the fitting then wipe it clean and separate the two sections of the pipe; the fitting is released by depressing the plastic collar. Mop up any spilt fluid and take precautions not to allow any dirt to enter the hydraulic system; the hose fittings are fitted with valves to prevent fluid loss when they are disconnected.
4 Rotate the master cylinder 45° in a clockwise direction to release it from its mounting plate then manoeuvre the assembly out of position. **Do not** attempt to dismantle the master cylinder/pipe assembly; if it is faulty the complete assembly must be renewed, no individual components are available.

Refitting

5 Ensure the cylinder and bulkhead mating surfaces are clean and dry then manoeuvre the master cylinder into position.
6 Position the cylinder reservoir 45° clockwise from the vertical position then seat the cylinder firmly in the bulkhead and secure it in position by rotating it 45° anti-clockwise.
7 From inside the vehicle, ensure that the pushrod clevis is correctly engaged with the

pedal then insert the clevis pin and secure it in position with the new retaining clip. Where a roll pin is fitted, tap the new pin into position making sure it is securely located.
8 Return to the engine compartment and wipe clean both halves of the clutch pipe end fitting. Ensure the master cylinder pipe is correctly routed and retained by all the necessary clips then reconnect both halves of the pipe. Check that the pipe is securely joined by gently pulling on the end fittings.
9 Check the operation of the clutch pedal (the clutch hydraulic system is sealed and does not need bleeding) then refit the facia panel (where removed) and undercover.
10 On completion, refit the fuel system electronic control module (ECM) as described in Chapter 4.

4 Clutch slave cylinder - removal and refitting

Removal

1 On 1.4 and 1.6 litre engines, to gain access to the slave cylinder, remove the air cleaner housing as described in Chapter 4.
2 On 2.0 litre engines, firmly apply the handbrake then jack up the front of the vehicle and support it on axle stands (see *"Jacking and Vehicle Support"*). Remove the retaining bolts and fasteners and remove the undercover to gain access to the slave cylinder on the front of the transmission unit.
3 On all engines, working back from the slave cylinder, release the clutch pipe from all the necessary retaining clips until you come to the quick-release fitting. Position a suitable container beneath the fitting then wipe it clean and separate the two sections of pipe; the fitting is released by depressing the plastic collar. Mop up any spilt fluid and take precautions not to allow any dirt to enter the hydraulic system; the hose fittings are fitted with valves to prevent fluid loss when they are disconnected.
4 Slide out the retaining clip then free the slave cylinder from the mounting bracket release lever and remove it from the transmission unit **(see illustration)**. **Do not** attempt to dismantle the slave cylinder/pipe assembly; if it is faulty the complete assembly must be renewed, no individual components are available.

Refitting

5 Manoeuvre the cylinder into position and locate it in the mounting bracket. Ensure the pushrod is correctly engaged with the release lever then secure the slave cylinder in position with the retaining clip.
6 Wipe clean both halves of the clutch pipe end fitting. Ensure the slave cylinder pipe is correctly routed and retained by all the necessary clips then reconnect both halves of the pipe. Check that the pipe is securely joined by gently pulling on the end fittings.

7 Check the operation of the clutch pedal (the clutch hydraulic system is sealed and does not need bleeding) then refit the air cleaner housing (see Chapter 4) or refit the undercover and lower the vehicle to the ground (as applicable).

5 Clutch hydraulic system - bleeding

The clutch hydraulic system is a sealed system and never requires topping-up or bleeding, even after the hydraulic pipe has been disconnected. If a problem develops then either the master cylinder or slave cylinder is faulty and renewal is the only option.

6 Clutch assembly - removal, inspection and refitting

⚠️ *Warning: Dust created by clutch wear and deposited on the clutch components may contain asbestos, which is a health hazard. DO NOT blow it out with compressed air, or inhale any of it. DO NOT use petrol or petroleum-based solvents to clean off the dust. Brake system cleaner or methylated spirit should be used to flush the dust into a suitable receptacle. After the clutch components are wiped clean with rags, dispose of the contaminated rags and cleaner in a sealed, marked container.*

Note: *Although some friction materials may no longer contain asbestos, it is safest to assume that they do, and to take precautions accordingly.*

Removal

1 Unless the complete engine/transmission unit is to be removed from the car and separated for major overhaul (see Chapter 2), the clutch can be reached by removing the transmission as described in Chapter 7.
2 Before disturbing the clutch, use chalk or a marker pen to mark the relationship of the pressure plate assembly to the flywheel.
3 Working in a diagonal sequence, slacken the pressure plate bolts by half a turn at a time, until spring pressure is released and the bolts can be unscrewed by hand.
4 Prise the pressure plate assembly off its locating dowels, and collect the friction plate, noting which way round the friction plate is fitted (see illustration).

Inspection

Note: *Due to the amount of work necessary to remove and refit clutch components, it is usually considered good practice to renew the clutch friction plate, pressure plate assembly and release bearing as a matched set, even if only one of these is actually worn enough to*

require renewal. It is also worth considering the renewal of the clutch components on a preventive basis if the engine and/or transmission have been removed for some other reason.
5 Remove the clutch assembly.
6 When cleaning clutch components, read first the warning at the beginning of this Section; remove dust using a clean, dry cloth, and working in a well-ventilated atmosphere.
7 Check the friction plate facings for signs of wear, damage or oil contamination. If the friction material is cracked, burnt, scored or damaged, or if it is contaminated with oil or grease (shown by shiny black patches), the friction plate must be renewed. Measure the friction plate thickness and check the depth of the rivets below the friction material surface (see illustration). If the friction plate thickness or the depth of any rivet is equal to, or less than, the service limit given in the Specifications, then the friction plate must be renewed.
8 If the friction material is still serviceable, check that the centre boss splines are unworn, that the torsion springs are in good condition and securely fastened, and that all the rivets are tight. If any wear or damage is found, the friction plate must be renewed.
9 If the friction material is fouled with oil, this must be due to an oil leak from the crankshaft left-hand oil seal, from the sump-to-cylinder block joint, or from the transmission input shaft. Renew the seal or repair the joint, as appropriate, as described in Chapter 2 or 7, before installing the new friction plate.
10 Check the pressure plate assembly for obvious signs of wear or damage; shake it to check for loose rivets or worn or damaged fulcrum rings, and check that the drive straps securing the pressure plate to the cover do not show signs (such as a deep yellow or blue discoloration) of overheating. Check the diaphragm spring fingers for signs of wear or damage and check that the height of each finger above the pressure plate machined face. If the finger height exceeds the specified service limit or the diaphragm spring is worn or damaged, or if its pressure is in any way suspect, the pressure plate assembly should be renewed.

6.4 Remove the clutch pressure plate and friction plate from the flywheel

11 Examine the machined bearing surfaces of the pressure plate and of the flywheel; they should be clean, completely flat, and free from scratches or scoring. If either is discoloured from excessive heat, or shows signs of cracks, it should be renewed - although minor damage of this nature can sometimes be polished away using emery paper. Using a straight edge and feeler blades check the pressure plate surface for warpage at several points around its diameter, if the warpage exceeds the specified limit the plate must be renewed.
12 Check that the release bearing contact surface rotates smoothly and easily, with no sign of noise or roughness. Also check that the surface itself is smooth and unworn, with no signs of cracks, pitting or scoring. If there is any doubt about its condition, the bearing must be renewed.

Refitting

13 On reassembly, ensure that the bearing surfaces of the flywheel and pressure plate are completely clean, smooth, and free from oil or grease. Use solvent to remove any protective grease from new components.
14 Fit the friction plate so that its spring hub assembly faces away from the flywheel; there may also be a marking showing which way round the plate is to be refitted. On genuine Rover clutches the friction plate should be fitted with the "FLYWHEEL SIDE" marking facing towards the flywheel (see illustration).

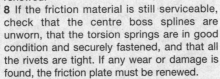

6.7 Using a vernier to measure friction plate rivet head depth below the friction material

6.14 Ensure the friction plate is fitted with the FLYWHEEL SIDE marking facing towards the flywheel

6

6.17 A typical clutch-aligning tool

6.18 Ensure the friction plate is centralised then progressively tighten the pressure plate bolts to the specified torque

15 Refit the pressure plate assembly, aligning the marks made on dismantling (if the original pressure plate is re-used), and locating the pressure plate on its locating dowels. Fit the pressure plate bolts, but tighten them only finger-tight, so that the friction plate can still be moved.

16 The friction plate must now be centralised, so that when the transmission is refitted, its input shaft will pass through the splines at the centre of the friction plate.

17 Centralisation can be achieved by passing a screwdriver or other long bar through the friction plate and into the hole in the crankshaft; the friction plate can then be moved around until it is centred on the crankshaft hole. Alternatively, a clutch-aligning tool can be used to eliminate the guesswork; these can be obtained from most accessory shops **(see illustration)**.

TOOL TIP

A home-made aligning tool can be fabricated from a length of metal rod or wooden dowel which fits closely inside the crankshaft hole, and has insulating tape wrap around it to match the diameter of the friction plate splined hole.

18 When the friction plate is centralised, tighten the pressure plate bolts evenly and in a diagonal sequence to the specified torque setting **(see illustration)**. Ensure the pressure plate is drawn squarely onto the flywheel, to prevent the pressure plate being distorted.

19 Refit the transmission as described in Chapter 7.

7 Clutch release mechanism -
removal, inspection and refitting

Note: *Refer to the warning concerning the dangers of asbestos dust at the beginning of Section 6.*

Removal

1 Unless the complete engine/transmission unit is to be removed from the car and separated for major overhaul (see Chapter 2), the clutch release mechanism can be reached by removing the transmission only, as described in Chapter 7.

2 Slide the release bearing off from the transmission shaft guide sleeve and disengage it from the release fork **(see illustration)**.

1.4 and 1.6 litre engine

3 Tap out the retaining pin securing the release lever to the top of the release fork shaft and lift off the lever **(see illustration)**. Discard the pin, a new one should be used on refitting.

4 Release the release fork upper bush from the transmission housing and slide it off the lever shaft. Disengage the release fork from the lower bush and remove it from the transmission unit **(see illustrations)**. The lower bush can then be removed from the transmission housing.

7.2 Free the release bearing from the fork and remove it from the transmission

7.3 On 1.4 and 1.6 litre engines, tap out the roll pin and remove the release lever

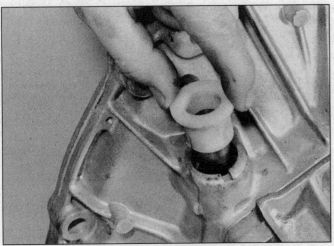

7.4a Remove the release fork upper bush . . .

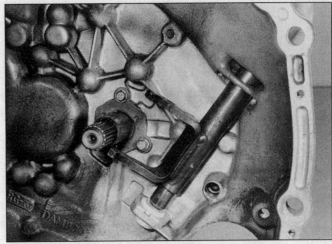

7.4b . . . then manoeuvre the release fork out of position

2.0 litre engine

5 Slacken and remove the retaining bolt and washer securing the release fork to the lever shaft (see illustration).
6 Withdraw the lever from the transmission housing and remove the fork, noting which way around the fork is fitted (see illustration).

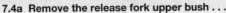

7.5 On 2.0 litre engines, slacken and remove the release fork bolt . . .

Inspection

7 Check the release mechanism, renewing any component which is worn or damaged. Carefully check all bearing surfaces and points of contact.
8 When checking the release bearing itself, note that it is often considered worthwhile to renew it as a matter of course. Check that the contact surface rotates smoothly and easily, with no sign of noise or roughness, and that the surface itself is smooth and unworn, with no signs of cracks, pitting or scoring. If there is any doubt about its condition, the bearing must be renewed.

Refitting

1.4 and 1.6 litre engine

9 Ensure all components are clean and dry then apply molybdenum disulphide grease (Rover recommend the use of Molykote BR2 plus, G-n plus or G-Rapid plus) to the contact areas of the pivot bushes, release fork and release bearing.

10 Clip the lower bush into position ensuring its tab is correctly located in the housing cutout (see illustration).
11 Manoeuvre the fork into position and seat it in the lower bush. Slide the upper bush down the fork and clip it into the transmission housing, aligning its locating tab with the cutout.
12 Refit the release lever to the top of the fork and fit the new retaining pin, tapping it firmly into position.
13 Slide the release bearing onto the transmission shaft guide sleeve and engage it with the release fork.
14 Check the operation of the release mechanism then refit the transmission as described in Chapter 7.

2.0 litre models

15 Ensure all components are clean and dry then apply molybdenum disulphide grease to the contact areas of the release lever shaft, release fork and release bearing.

7.6 . . . then withdraw the release lever and remove the fork, noting which way around it is fitted

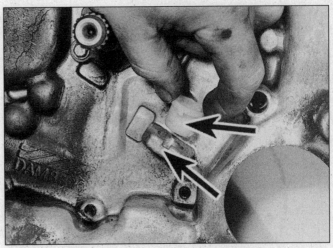

7.10 Ensure the bush locating tabs are correctly aligned with the bellhousing slots (arrowed)

6

7.16 On 2.0 litre engines tighten the release fork bolt to the specified torque

16 Position the release fork in the transmission housing, making sure it is fitted the correct way around, then insert the release lever. Align the fork with the shaft hole then refit the retaining bolt and washer, tighten it to the specified torque **(see illustration)**.

17 Slide the release bearing onto the transmission shaft guide sleeve and engage it with the release fork.

18 Check the operation of the release mechanism then refit the transmission as described in Chapter 7.

Chapter 7
Manual transmission

Contents

Degrees of difficulty

Easy, suitable for novice with little experience		Fairly easy, suitable for beginner with some experience		Fairly difficult, suitable for competent DIY mechanic		Difficult, suitable for experienced DIY mechanic		Very difficult, suitable for expert DIY or professional	

Specifications

General

Type .... Manual, five forward speeds and reverse.
Synchromesh on all forward speeds

Lubrication

Recommended oil .... See "Lubricants and fluids"
Capacity:
  1.4 and 1.6 litre engine:
    From dry .... 2.0 litres
    Drain and refill .... 1.8 litres
  2.0 litre engine:
    From dry .... 2.2 litres
    Drain and refill .... 2.0 litres

Torque wrench settings

	Nm	lbf ft
1.4 and 1.6 litre engines		
Drain plug	25	18
Engine/transmission mountings:		
Lower left-hand mounting bolts	45	33
Upper left-hand mounting:		
Mounting-to-transmission bolts	80	59
Through bolt	75	55
Rear mounting bracket bolts	100	74
Filler/level plug	25	18
Flywheel cover plate bolts	9	6
Gearchange selector rod rear mounting nuts	22	16
Reversing light switch	25	18
Transmission-to-engine bolts	85	63

7

Torque wrench settings (continued)

	Nm	lbf ft
2.0 litre engine		
Anti-beaming bracket bolts - petrol engine:		
Bracket-to-transmission bolts	60	44
Bracket-to-cylinder block bolt	45	33
Drain plug	45	33
Engine/transmission mountings:		
Left-hand mounting:		
Mounting-to-transmission bolts	60	44
Mounting-to-mounting bracket bolts	45	33
Filler/level plug	40	29
Gearchange steady rod-to-transmission bolt	10	7
Reversing light switch	25	18
Transmission-to-engine bolts:*		
Petrol engine	83	61
Diesel engine	70	51

*This setting is for the bolts which secure only the transmission housing to the engine. Those which also secure the starter motor and anti-beaming bracket (petrol engine only) have different torque settings (see Chapter 5A for starter motor bolt torque).

1 General information

The transmission is contained in a cast-aluminium alloy casing bolted to the engine's left-hand end, and consists of the gearbox and final drive differential - often called a transaxle.

Drive is transmitted from the crankshaft via the clutch to the input shaft, which has a splined extension to accept the clutch friction plate, and rotates in sealed ball-bearings. From the input shaft, drive is transmitted to the output shaft, which rotates in a roller bearing at its right-hand end, and a sealed ball-bearing at its left-hand end. From the output shaft, the drive is transmitted to the differential crownwheel, which rotates with the differential case and planetary gears, thus driving the sun gears and driveshafts. The rotation of the planetary gears on their shaft allows the inner roadwheel to rotate at a slower speed than the outer roadwheel when the car is cornering.

The input and output shafts are arranged side by side, parallel to the crankshaft and driveshafts, so that their gear pinion teeth are in constant mesh. In the neutral position, the output shaft gear pinions rotate freely, so that drive cannot be transmitted to the crownwheel.

Gear selection is via a floor-mounted lever and selector rod mechanism. The selector rod causes the appropriate selector fork to move its respective synchro-sleeve along the shaft, to lock the gear pinion to the synchro-hub. Since the synchro-hubs are splined to the output shaft, this locks the pinion to the shaft, so that drive can be transmitted. To ensure that gear-changing can be made quickly and quietly, a synchro-mesh system is fitted to all forward gears, consisting of baulk rings and spring-loaded fingers, as well as the gear pinions and synchro-hubs. The synchro-mesh cones are formed on the mating faces of the baulk rings and gear pinions.

2 Transmission oil - draining and refilling

1 This operation is much quicker and more efficient if the car is first taken on a journey of sufficient length to warm the engine/transmission up to normal operating temperature.

2 Park the car on level ground, switch off the ignition and apply the handbrake firmly. For improved access, jack up the front of the car and support it securely on axle stands (see "Jacking and Vehicle Support"). Note that the car must be lowered to the ground and level, to ensure accuracy, when refilling and checking the oil level. Where necessary, undo the retaining screws and fasteners then remove the engine/transmission undercover from the vehicle to gain access to the filler/level and drain plugs (see illustrations).

3 Remove all traces of dirt from around the filler/level plug which is located on the left-hand side of the transmission, where it is situated behind the driveshaft inner joint. Unscrew the plug and recover the sealing washer.

4 Position a suitable container under the drain plug which is also situated on the left-hand side of the transmission housing.

5 Unscrew the drain plug and allow the oil to drain completely into the container (see illustration). If the oil is hot, take precautions against scalding. Clean both the filler/level and the drain plugs, being especially careful to wipe any metallic particles off the magnetic inserts. Discard the original sealing washers; they should be renewed whenever they are disturbed.

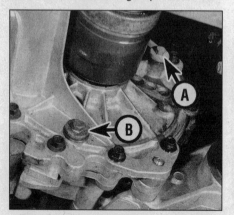

2.2a Transmission oil filler/level plug (A) and drain plug (B) - 1.4 and 1.6 litre engines

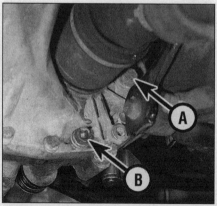

2.2b Transmission oil filler/level plug (A) and drain plug (B) - 2.0 litre engine

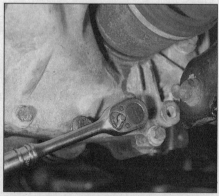

2.5 On 2.0 litre engines, the transmission drain plug can be unscrewed using a 3/8 drive ratchet

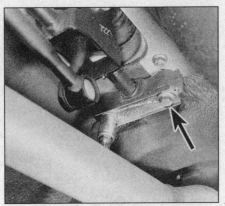

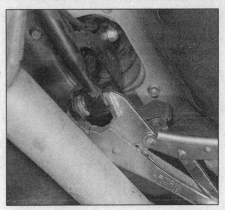

3.4 On 1.4 and 1.6 litre engines, unclip the selector rod balljoint from the base of the gearchange lever

3.7 Undo the retaining nuts securing the control rod rear mounting to the body (remaining one arrowed)

3.11 Ensure that all gearchange linkage balljoints are pressed firmly together

6 When the oil has finished draining, clean the drain plug threads and those of the transmission casing, fit a new sealing washer and refit the drain plug, tightening it to the specified torque. It the car was raised for the draining operation, now lower it to the ground.

7 Refilling the transmission is an extremely awkward operation. Above all, allow plenty of time for the oil level to settle properly before checking it. Note that the car must be parked on flat level ground when checking the oil level.

8 Refill the transmission with the exact amount of the specified type of oil (see "Lubricants and fluids") then check the oil level as described in Chapter 1. When the level is correct, refit the filler/level plug with a new sealing washer and tighten it to the specified torque. Refit the undercover (where removed).

If the correct amount was poured into the transmission and a large amount flows out on checking the level, refit the filler/level plug and take the car on a short journey so that the new oil is distributed fully around the transmission components, then check the level again on your return.

3 Gearchange linkage - removal and refitting

1 Park the vehicle on level ground, switch off the ignition, and apply the handbrake firmly. Jack up the front of the vehicle and support it securely on axle stands (see "Jacking and Vehicle Support"). Proceed as described under the relevant sub-heading.

1.4 and 1.6 litre engines

Removal

2 Although not strictly necessary, access to the gearchange linkage is greatly improved if the exhaust front pipe is first removed (see Chapter 4A).

3 Using a suitable flat-bladed screwdriver, carefully lever the link rod balljoints off the transmission levers. Make a note of each link rods correct fitted location and which way around they are fitted then detach them from the bellcrank assembly and remove them from the vehicle.

4 Unclip the selector rod from its balljoints on the gearchange lever and bellcrank assembly and manoeuvre it out from underneath the vehicle (see illustration).

5 Working inside the vehicle, remove the centre console as described in Chapter 11.

6 With the console removed, carefully peel the rubber cover off the base of the gearchange lever and slide the cover off the lever to gain access to the control rod pivot bolt. Slacken the nut and remove the pivot bolt and thrustwashers.

7 From underneath the vehicle, unscrew the nut securing the front of the control rod to the bellcrank pivot. Undo the two nuts and remove the retaining plate securing the control rod rear mounting to the body (see illustration). Remove the mounting assembly, taking care not to lose its spacers, then manoeuvre the control rod out from underneath the vehicle.

8 If necessary, slacken and remove the three mounting bolts and remove the bellcrank from the subframe.

9 If necessary, slacken and remove the gearchange lever housing retaining nuts and

remove the seal, mounting plate and lever assembly from the vehicle.

10 Thoroughly clean all components and check them for wear or damage, renewing all worn or faulty items.

Refitting

11 Refitting is the reverse of the removal procedure, applying a smear of the specified grease to all linkage pivot points and balljoints (see "Lubricants and fluids"). Ensure all nuts and bolts are securely tightened and that all gearchange linkage balljoints are pressed firmly together (see illustration).

2.0 litre engine

Removal

12 Working at the transmission end of the selector shaft, slide the gaiter towards the transmission then remove the roll pin retaining clip from the selector rod. Tap the roll pin out of position and disconnect the selector rod from the transmission (see illustrations).

13 Slacken and remove the nut and pivot bolt securing the selector rod to the base of the gearchange lever and remove the rod from the vehicle.

14 Working inside the vehicle, remove the centre console as described in Chapter 11. Release the gearchange lever rubber gaiter from the housing and slide it off the top of the lever.

3.12a On 2.0 litre engines, peel back the gaiter then remove the retaining clip from the selector rod . . .

3.12b . . . and tap out the roll pin using a hammer and punch (steady rod disconnected for clarity)

7

3.16 Remove the retaining bolt and washer and disconnect the steady rod from the transmission

15 From underneath the vehicle, slacken and remove the bolts and retaining plate securing the steady rod rear mounting to the body. Remove the mounting rubber from the steady rod, taking care not to lose its spacers.

16 Remove the bolt securing the gearchange steady rod to the transmission unit and recover the washers and mounting rubber **(see illustration)**. Manoeuvre the steady rod and gearchange lever assembly out from underneath the vehicle; if necessary, the two can then be separated.

17 If necessary, slacken and remove the retaining nuts and remove the gearchange lever plate assembly and seal.

18 Thoroughly clean all components and check them for wear or damage, renewing all worn or faulty items.

Refitting

19 Refitting is the reverse of the removal procedure, applying a smear of the specified grease to all linkage pivot points (see *"Lubricants and fluids"*). Ensure all nuts and bolts are securely tightened.

---

4 Oil seals - renewal

Driveshaft oil seals

1 Chock the rear wheels, apply the handbrake, then jack up the front of the car and support it

4.5 ... and press the new seal into position with a tubular drift which bears only on the outer edge of the seal (1.4 litre engine shown)

4.4 Prise the driveshaft oil seal out from the transmission using a large flat-bladed screwdriver ...

on axle stands (see *"Jacking and Vehicle Support"*). Remove the appropriate front roadwheel.

2 Drain the transmission oil as described in Section 2 or be prepared for some fluid loss as the driveshaft is removed.

3 Working as described in Chapter 8, free the inner end of the driveshaft from the transmission, and place it clear of the seal, noting that there is no need to unscrew the driveshaft retaining nut; the driveshaft can be left secured to the hub. Support the driveshaft, to avoid placing any strain on the driveshaft joints or gaiters.

4 Carefully prise the oil seal out of the transmission using a large flat-bladed screwdriver **(see illustration)**.

5 Remove all traces of dirt from the area around the oil seal aperture, then apply a smear of grease to the outer lip of the new oil seal. Ensure the seal is correctly positioned, with its sealing lip facing inwards, and drive it squarely into position, using a suitable tubular drift (such as a socket) which bears only on the hard outer edge of the seal **(see illustration)**.

6 Ensure the seal is correctly located in the transmission housing then refit the driveshaft as described in Chapter 8.

7 Refill/top-up the transmission with the specified type of oil (see *"Lubricants and fluids"*) and check the oil level as described in Chapter 1.

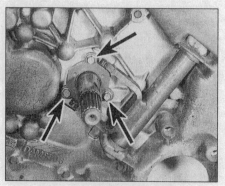

4.9 Clutch release bearing guide sleeve retaining bolts (arrowed) - 1.4 and 1.6 litre engines

Input shaft oil seal

1.4 and 1.6 litre engines

Note: *New release bearing guide sleeve retaining bolts will be required.*

8 Remove the transmission unit from the vehicle and slide off the clutch release bearing (see Chapter 6).

9 Undo the three bolts securing the clutch release bearing guide sleeve in position and slide the guide off the input shaft **(see illustration)**. Discard the bolts as they must be renewed whenever they are disturbed.

10 Carefully lever the oil seal out of the guide by using a suitable flat-bladed screwdriver.

11 Before fitting a new seal, check the input shaft's seal rubbing surface for signs of burrs, scratches or other damage which may have caused the seal to fail in the first place. It may be possible to polish away minor faults of this sort using fine abrasive paper, however, more serious defects will require the renewal of the input shaft.

12 Remove all traces of thread locking compound from the guide sleeve bolt holes (Rover recommend the use of Loctite Chisel and a suitable tap) then degrease thoroughly. Ensure that the input shaft is clean and greased to protect the seal lips on refitting.

13 Dip the new seal in clean oil and fit it to the rear of the guide sleeve, making sure its sealing lip is facing outwards.

14 Carefully slide the guide sleeve into position, taking care not to damage the oil seal lips on the input shaft splines. Fit the new retaining bolts and tighten them to the specified torque wrench setting (see Chapter 6).

15 Lubricate the release bearing, fork and guide sleeve contact surfaces with molybdenum disulphide grease. Slide the release bearing into position and engage it with the release fork fingers.

16 Check the operation of the release mechanism, then wipe off any surplus of oil or grease and refit the transmission to the vehicle.

2.0 litre models

17 To renew the input shaft oil seal, the transmission must be dismantled. This task should therefore be entrusted to a Rover dealer or transmission specialist.

Gearchange selector shaft oil seal

1.4 and 1.6 litre engine

Note: *A new roll pin will be required on refitting.*

18 Access to the selector shaft is very poor with the transmission in position but can only be significantly improved by removing the transmission unit from the vehicle (see Section 7).

19 Tap out the roll pin and detach the selector lever from the transmission shaft.

20 Carefully lever the seal out of position, taking great care not to damage the shaft or casing.

4.27a On 2.0 litre engines, slide off the rubber gaiter . . .

4.27b . . . then prise out the selector shaft oil seal

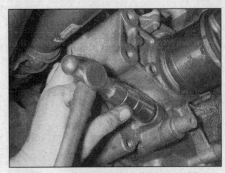

4.29 Tap the new oil seal into position using a socket which bears on the outer edge of the seal

21 Before fitting a new seal, check the selector shaft's seal rubbing surface for signs of burrs, scratches or other damage which may have caused the seal to fail in the first place. It may be possible to polish away minor faults of this sort using fine abrasive paper, however, more serious defects will require the renewal of the shaft.

22 Lubricate the new seal with a smear of transmission oil then ease the seal into position. Press the seal squarely into position, ensuring its sealing lip is facing inwards, using a socket which bears only on the hard outer edge of the seal.

23 Refit the selector lever to the transmission shaft and secure it in position with the new roll pin.

2.0 litre engine

24 Firmly apply the handbrake then jack up the front of the vehicle and support it on axle stands (see "Jacking and Vehicle Support"). Drain the transmission oil as described in Section 2 or be prepared for fluid loss as the seal is removed.

25 To improve access to the selector shaft, undo the retaining bolt securing the gearchange steady rod to the transmission. Free the rod from the transmission and recover the washers and mounting rubber.

26 Slide the selector shaft gaiter towards the transmission then remove the roll pin retaining clip from the selector rod. Tap the roll pin out of position and disconnect the selector rod from the transmission.

27 Remove the gaiter from the transmission then carefully prise out the selector shaft oil seal **(see illustrations)**.

28 Before fitting a new seal, check the selector shaft's seal rubbing surface for signs of burrs, scratches or other damage which may have caused the seal to fail in the first place. It may be possible to polish away minor faults of this sort using fine abrasive paper, however, more serious defects will require the renewal of the shaft.

29 Lubricate the new seal with clean transmission oil and ease it over the end of the selector shaft. Press the seal squarely into the transmission housing using a socket which bears only on the hard outer edge of the seal **(see illustration)**.

30 Refit the gaiter ensuring it is correctly engaged with the seal.

31 Reconnect the selector rod to the transmission shaft and refit the roll pin. Secure the roll pin in position with the retaining clip and seat the gaiter correctly on the shaft.

32 Ensure the mounting rubber is correctly fitted then position the washers on each side of the steady rod end fitting. Reconnect the rod to the transmission housing and tighten its retaining bolt to the specified torque.

33 Refill/top-up the transmission with the specified type of oil (see "Lubricants and fluids") and check the oil level as described in Chapter 1.

---

5 Reversing light switch -
testing, removal and refitting

Testing

1 The reversing light circuit is controlled by a plunger-type switch that is screwed into the transmission casing, on 1.4 and 1.6 litre engines the switch is screwed into the top of the casing and on 2.0 litre engines it is screwed into the bottom of the casing. If a fault develops in the circuit, first ensure that the circuit fuse has not blown (see Chapter 12).

2 To test the switch, disconnect the wiring connector. Use a multimeter (set to the resistance function) or a battery-and-bulb test circuit to check that there is continuity between the switch terminals only when reverse gear is selected. If this is not the case, and there are no obvious breaks or other damage to the wires, the switch is faulty and must be renewed.

Removal

Note: A new sealing washer will be required on refitting.

1.4 and 1.6 litre engines

3 To improve access to the switch, remove the air cleaner housing (see Chapter 4A).

4 Disconnect the wiring connector, then unscrew the switch and remove it from the top of the transmission casing along with its sealing washer.

2.0 litre engine

5 Firmly apply the handbrake then jack up the front of the vehicle and support it on axle stands (see "Jacking and Vehicle Support"). Where necessary, remove the retaining screws and fasteners and remove the undercover to gain access to the switch.

6 Trace the wiring back from the switch, freeing it from any relevant retaining clips, and disconnect it at the wiring connector.

7 Be prepared for oil loss when the switch is removed and have ready a suitable plug to plug the transmission aperture whilst the switch is removed.

8 Wipe clean the area around the switch then unscrew it and remove it from the transmission unit along with its sealing washer **(see illustration)**. Plug the switch aperture to minimise oil loss.

Refitting

1.4 and 1.6 litre engines

9 Fit a new sealing washer to the switch, then screw it back into position in the top of the transmission housing and tighten it to the specified torque. Reconnect the wiring connector, test the operation of the switch then refit the air cleaner housing as described in Chapter 4A.

2.0 litre engine

10 Fit a new sealing washer to the switch then remove the plug from the transmission and quickly screw in the switch. Tighten the switch to the specified torque.

7

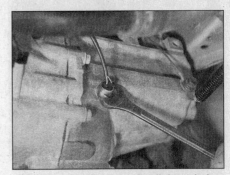

5.8 Removing the reversing light switch - 2.0 litre engine

11 Work back along the switch wiring, securing it in position with all the relevant clips and ties, and reconnect the wiring connector.
12 Refit the undercover (where removed) then lower the vehicle to the ground and check the transmission oil level as described in Chapter 1.

6 Speedometer drive - removal and refitting

Removal

1 All models are fitted with an electrically-operated speedometer which is operated by the vehicle speed sensor which is mounted on the top of the speedometer drive. The speedometer drive is situated on the top of the transmission housing, next to the inner end of the right-hand driveshaft. Access to the drive is poor from above, to gain access from below, firmly apply the handbrake then jack up the front of the vehicle and support it on axle stands (see "*Jacking and Vehicle Support*").
2 Disconnect the wiring connector from the vehicle speed sensor then unscrew the sensor and remove it from the top of the speedometer drive.
3 Slacken and remove the retaining bolt and withdraw the speedometer drive assembly from the transmission housing, along with its sealing ring.

Refitting

4 Fit a new sealing ring to the speedometer housing and lubricate it with a smear of oil to ease installation.
5 Ease the speedometer drive into position in the transmission, ensuring that the drive and driven pinions are correctly engaged, and securely tighten the retaining bolt.
6 Fit the speed sensor to the top of the drive, ensuring its drive pin is correctly engaged with the pinion, and securely tighten its retaining nut.
7 Reconnect the wiring connector to the speed sensor then lower the vehicle to the ground.

7 Transmission - removal and refitting

Removal

1.4 and 1.6 litre engines

1 Chock the rear wheels, then firmly apply the handbrake. Jack up the front of the vehicle, and securely support it on axle stands (see "*Jacking and Vehicle Support*"). Remove both front roadwheels then undo the retaining screws and fasteners and remove the undercover from beneath the engine/transmission unit.
2 Drain the transmission oil as described in Section 2 then refit the drain and filler/level plugs, and tighten them to their specified torque settings.
3 Remove the air cleaner housing as described in Chapter 4A.
4 Remove the battery, battery tray and mounting brackets and the starter motor (see Chapter 5A).
5 Slide off the retaining clip from the clutch slave cylinder then free the cylinder from its mounting bracket and position it clear of the transmission.

Caution: Whilst the cylinder is removed from the transmission, do not depress the clutch pedal.

6 Disconnect the wiring connector from the reversing light switch.
7 Carefully lever the gearchange linkage link rods off from the transmission unit balljoints. Position the gearchange lever so that both link rods are clear of the transmission unit and will not be damaged on removal.
8 Unscrew the retaining bolts and remove the flywheel lower cover plate from the base of the transmission housing.
9 Free the starter motor wiring from the flywheel front cover plate then undo the retaining bolts and remove the cover from the transmission.
10 Disconnect the wiring connector from the vehicle speed sensor which is fitted to the top of the speedometer drive (see Section 6).

11 Referring to Chapter 8, disconnect both driveshafts from the transmission unit. Note that it is not necessary to remove the driveshafts completely, they can be left attached to the hub assemblies and released from the transmission as the hub is pulled outwards.
Caution: Do not allow the shafts to hang down under their own weight as this could damage the constant velocity joints/gaiters.
12 Slacken and remove the three bolts securing the rear engine mounting bracket to the transmission unit.
13 Undo the retaining bolts and remove the flywheel rear cover plate from the transmission housing.
14 Place a jack with a block of wood beneath the engine, to take the weight of the engine. Alternatively, attach a couple of lifting eyes to the engine, and fit a hoist or support bar to take the engine weight. Also place a jack and block of wood beneath the transmission, and raise the jack to take the weight of the transmission.
15 Unclip the evaporative emission system charcoal canister and position it clear of the engine/transmission left-hand upper mounting.
16 Slacken the through bolt securing the left-hand upper mounting to the body then undo the two bolts securing the mounting to the transmission.
17 Slacken and remove the bolts securing the left-hand lower mounting to the body.
18 With the jack positioned beneath the transmission taking the weight, slacken and remove the remaining bolts securing the transmission housing to the engine. Note the correct fitted positions of each bolt, and the necessary brackets, as they are removed, to use as a reference on refitting. Make a final check that all components have been disconnected, and are positioned clear of the transmission so that they will not hinder the removal procedure.
19 With the bolts removed, move the trolley jack and transmission to the left, to free it from its locating dowels. Once the transmission is free, lower the jack and manoeuvre the unit out from under the car. Remove the locating dowels from the transmission or engine if they are loose, and keep them in a safe place.

2.0 litre petrol engine

20 Carry out the operations described in paragraphs 1 to 6 of this Section.
21 Remove the exhaust front pipe as described in Chapter 4A.
22 Disconnect the wiring connector from the vehicle speed sensor then unscrew the retaining bolt and disconnect the earth lead from the front of the transmission housing (see illustration).
23 Undo the bolt securing the coolant pipe assembly to the left-hand end of the cylinder head and free the hose from the left-hand mounting assembly (see illustration).

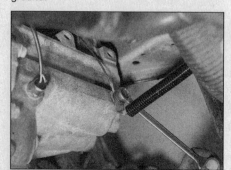

7.22 On 2.0 litre petrol engines unscrew the bolt and disconnect the earth lead from the transmission housing

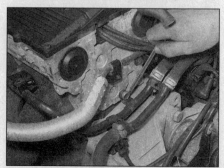

7.23 Remove the bolt securing the coolant pipe to the left-hand end of the cylinder head

24 Slacken and remove the bolts securing the coolant pipe to the front of the cylinder head.

25 Undo the retaining bolts and remove the anti-beaming bracket which connects the transmission housing to the rear of the cylinder block **(see illustration)**.

26 Referring to Section 3, disconnect the selector rod and steady rod from the transmission unit **(see illustrations)**.

27 Referring to Chapter 8, disconnect both driveshafts from the transmission unit. Note that it is not necessary to remove the driveshafts completely, they can be left attached to the hub assemblies and released from the transmission as the hub is pulled outwards.

Caution: Do not allow the shafts to hang down under their own weight as this could damage the constant velocity joints/gaiters.

28 Place a jack with a block of wood beneath the engine, to take the weight of the engine. Alternatively, attach a couple of lifting eyes to the engine, and fit a hoist or support bar to take the engine weight. Also place a jack and block of wood beneath the transmission, and raise the jack to take the weight of the transmission.

29 Slacken and remove the retaining nuts and bolts and remove the clutch slave cylinder mounting bracket from the transmission.

30 Slacken and remove the two bolts securing the left-hand mounting to the top of the transmission unit. Lower the transmission unit slightly then unbolt the mounting bracket and remove it from the top of the transmission housing.

31 Slacken and remove the remaining bolts securing the transmission housing to the engine. Note the correct fitted positions of each bolt, and the necessary brackets, as they are removed, to use as a reference on refitting. Make a final check that all components have been disconnected, and are positioned clear of the transmission so that they will not hinder the removal procedure.

32 With the bolts removed, move the trolley jack and transmission to the left, to free it from its locating dowels. Once the transmission is free, lower the jack and manoeuvre the unit out from under the car. Remove the locating dowels from the transmission or engine if they are loose, and keep them in a safe place.

2.0 litre diesel engine

33 Carry out the operations described in paragraphs 1 to 6 of this Section.

34 Disconnect the wiring connector from the vehicle speed sensor then unscrew the retaining bolt and disconnect the earth lead from the front of the transmission housing.

35 On models with air conditioning, unscrew the retaining bolt securing the air conditioning pipe to the bracket on the front of the transmission housing.

36 On all models, undo the retaining nut then free the coolant pipe from the bracket on the front transmission unit and position the pipe clear.

37 Referring to Section 3, disconnect the selector rod and steady rod from the transmission unit.

38 Referring to Chapter 8, disconnect both driveshafts from the transmission unit. Note that it is not necessary to remove the driveshafts completely, they can be left attached to the hub assemblies and released from the transmission as the hub is pulled outwards.

Caution: Do not allow the shafts to hang down under their own weight as this could damage the constant velocity joints/gaiters.

39 Release the fuel filter from its bracket and position it clear of the transmission unit.

40 Place a jack with a block of wood beneath the engine, to take the weight of the engine. Alternatively, attach a couple of lifting eyes to the engine, and fit a hoist or support bar to take the engine weight. Also place a jack and block of wood beneath the transmission, and raise the jack to take the weight of the transmission.

41 Slacken and remove the two bolts securing the left-hand mounting to the top of the transmission unit. Lower the transmission unit slightly then unbolt the mounting bracket and remove it from the top of the transmission housing.

42 Slacken and remove the bolts securing the clutch slave cylinder mounting bracket in position and remove the bracket.

43 Slacken and remove the remaining bolts securing the transmission housing to the engine. Note the correct fitted positions of each bolt, and the necessary brackets, as they are removed, to use as a reference on refitting. Make a final check that all components have been disconnected, and are positioned clear of the transmission so that they will not hinder the removal procedure.

44 With the bolts removed, move the trolley jack and transmission to the left, to free it from its locating dowels. Once the transmission is free, lower the jack and manoeuvre the unit out from under the car. Remove the locating dowels from the transmission or engine if they are loose, and keep them in a safe place.

7.25 On 2.0 litre petrol engines undo the retaining bolts and remove the anti-beaming bracket

Refitting

45 The transmission is refitted by a reversal of the removal procedure, bearing in mind the following points:

a) *Apply a smear of molybdenum disulphide grease (Rover recommend the use of Molykote BR2 plus, G-n plus or G-Rapid plus) to the clutch release bearing, fork and guide sleeve contact surfaces and check the operation of the clutch release mechanism (see Chapter 6). Also apply a smear of grease to the transmission input shaft splines; do not apply too much grease otherwise the clutch friction plate may be contaminated.*

b) *Ensure the locating dowels are correctly positioned prior to installation.*

c) *Tighten all nuts and bolts to the specified torque (where given). On 1.4 and 1.6 litre engines, apply locking compound (Rover recommend the use of Loctite 243) to the threads of the two transmission unit-to-engine upper bolts prior to refitting.*

d) *Renew the driveshaft oil seals (see Section 4) then refit the driveshafts as described in Chapter 8, renewing the inner joint circlips prior to refitting.*

e) *On completion, refill the transmission with the specified type and quantity of lubricant (see "Lubricants and fluids") then check the oil level as described in Chapter 1.*

7

7.26a Disconnect the gearchange steady rod . . .

7.26b . . . and selector rod and position them clear of the transmission

8 Transmission overhaul - general information

Overhauling a manual transmission unit is a difficult and involved job for the DIY home mechanic. In addition to dismantling and reassembling many small parts, clearances must be precisely measured and, if necessary, changed by selecting shims and spacers. Internal transmission components are also often difficult to obtain, and in many instances, extremely expensive. Because of this, if the transmission develops a fault or becomes noisy, the best course of action is to have the unit overhauled by a specialist repairer, or to obtain an exchange reconditioned unit.

Nevertheless, it is not impossible for the more experienced mechanic to overhaul the transmission, provided the special tools are available, and the job is done in a deliberate step-by-step manner, so that nothing is overlooked.

The tools necessary for an overhaul include internal and external circlip pliers, bearing pullers, a slide hammer, a set of pin punches, a dial test indicator, and possibly a hydraulic press. In addition, a large, sturdy workbench and a vice will be required.

During dismantling of the transmission, make careful notes of how each component is fitted, to make reassembly easier and more accurate.

Before dismantling the transmission, it will help if you have some idea what area is malfunctioning. Certain problems can be closely related to specific areas in the transmission, which can make component examination and replacement easier. Refer to the "Fault finding" Section of this manual for more information.

Chapter 8
Driveshafts

Contents

Degrees of difficulty

Easy, suitable for novice with little experience	**Fairly easy,** suitable for beginner with some experience	**Fairly difficult,** suitable for competent DIY mechanic	**Difficult,** suitable for experienced DIY mechanic	**Very difficult,** suitable for expert DIY or professional

Specifications

General

Type	Unequal-length solid steel shafts, splined to inner and outer constant velocity joints, dynamic damper on both shafts
Lubricant:	
Type/specification	Special grease supplied in sachets with gaiter kits

Torque wrench settings

	Nm	lbf ft
Driveshaft retaining nut	185	137
Roadwheel nuts	110	81

1 General information

Drive is transmitted from the differential to the front wheels by means of two, unequal-length driveshafts.

Each driveshaft is fitted with an inner and outer constant velocity (CV) joint **(see illustration)**. Each outer joint is splined to engage with the wheel hub, and is retained by a large nut. The inner joint is also splined to engage with the differential sunwheel and is held in place by an internal circlip.

The inner joints are of tripode type consisting of a central spider and three supporting roller bearings. The outer joints are of ball and socket type.

The outer joints can be separated from the driveshaft and renewed if necessary. The inner joints form part of the driveshaft and cannot be separated.

Both driveshafts are fitted with a dynamic damper to reduce harmonic vibrations and resonance.

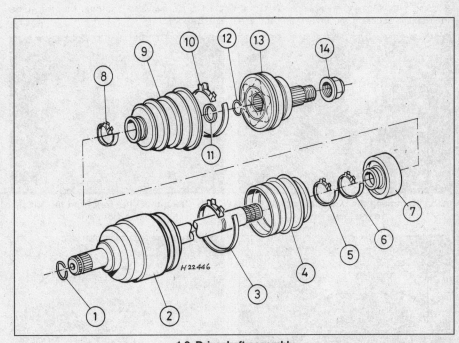

1.2 Driveshaft assembly

1 Circlip
2 Inner joint and shaft assembly
3 Large gaiter retaining clip
4 Gaiter
5 Small gaiter retaining clip
6 Damper clip
7 Dynamic damper
8 Small gaiter retaining clip
9 Gaiter
10 Large gaiter retaining clip
11 Stopper ring
12 Circlip
13 Outer joint assembly
14 Driveshaft retaining nut

8

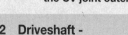

2.2 Tap up the staking securing the driveshaft retaining nut to the groove in the CV joint outer stub

2.3 Removing the driveshaft retaining nut

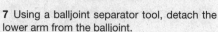

2.4 Removing the clamp bolt securing the fork to the bottom of the front shock absorber

2 Driveshaft - removal and refitting

Removal

Note: *A new front hub nut and inner joint circlip will be required on refitting.*

1 Apply the handbrake, then jack up the front of the vehicle and support it on axle stands (see *"Jacking and Vehicle Support"*). Remove the roadwheel. It is an advantage to only jack up one side of the vehicle as this will prevent loss of oil from the transmission when the driveshaft is withdrawn. If both sides are jacked up, position a suitable container beneath the inner end of the driveshaft to collect the oil.

2 Using a hammer and suitable punch, tap up the staking securing the driveshaft retaining

nut to the groove in the CV joint outer stub **(see illustration)**. Note that a new driveshaft retaining nut must be obtained for reassembly.

3 Have an assistant firmly depress the brake pedal to prevent the front hub from rotating, then using a socket and extension bar, slacken and remove the driveshaft retaining nut **(see illustration)**. Discard the nut.

4 Unscrew and remove the clamp bolt securing the fork to the bottom of the front shock absorber **(see illustration)**.

5 Unscrew and remove the nut and bolt securing the fork to the lower arm. Note that the head of the bolt faces forwards. Lever the fork from the lower arm and ease it from the bottom of the shock absorber **(see illustrations)**.

6 Extract the split pin from the castellated nut securing the lower balljoint to the lower arm, then unscrew and remove the nut **(see illustration)**.

7 Using a balljoint separator tool, detach the lower arm from the balljoint.

Caution: Take care not to damage the rubber boot of the balljoint.

8 Carefully pull the swivel hub assembly outwards and withdraw the driveshaft outer CV joint from the hub assembly. If necessary, the shaft can be tapped out of the hub using a soft-faced mallet.

9 To release the inner CV joint, insert a suitable flat bar in between the joint and transmission housing, then carefully lever the joint out of position, whilst taking care not to damage the driveshaft oil seal **(see illustration)**.

10 Support the inner CV joint whilst withdrawing it from the transmission to ensure the oil seal is not damaged, then remove the driveshaft from the vehicle.

11 Using a small screwdriver, remove the circlip from the inner end of the driveshaft. Discard the circlip and obtain a new one.

12 Whilst the driveshaft is removed, plug or tape over the differential aperture to prevent dirt entry.

Caution: Do not allow the vehicle to rest on its wheels with one or both driveshafts removed, as damage to the wheel bearings(s) may result. If the vehicle must be moved on its wheels, clamp the wheel bearings using spacers and a long threaded rod to take the place of the driveshaft. Note that if you intend to temporarily refit the roadwheel, the fork must first be refitted to the shock absorber and lower arm.

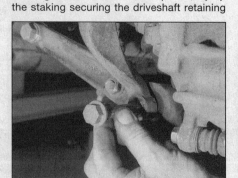

2.5a Removing the bolt securing the fork to the lower arm

2.5b Disconnect the fork from the shock absorber . . .

2.5c . . . then remove the fork

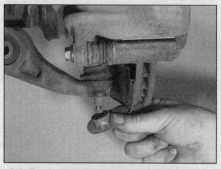

2.6 Removing the nut securing the lower balljoint to the lower arm

2.9 Carefully lever the driveshaft inner CV joint out of the transmission housing

Refitting

13 Before fitting the driveshaft, examine the transmission housing driveshaft oil seal for signs of damage or deterioration and, if necessary, renew it. Similarly, inspect the oil seal which is fitted to the outer CV joint for damage or deterioration and renew if necessary. Regardless of its apparent condition, renew the circlip which is fitted to the groove on the inner CV joint splines as a matter of course **(see illustrations)**.

14 On models with the anti-lock braking ABS 5 system, make sure that the driveshaft has a reluctor ring fitted with 43 teeth.

15 On 2.0 litre petrol engine models with the PG1 transmission, note that the transmission oil seal has been modified on later models. The transmission on later models is machined to accept the later oil seal, and the later oil seal must not be fitted to early transmissions without the machined faces. The inner driveshaft joint is also modified and can be identified by the groove on its perimeter which indicated that an additional groove has been cut on the inner face of the joint. The modified joints can be used with the early or later seals, however do not fit the modified oil seal with an early driveshaft as it will not be possible to insert the driveshaft sufficiently to engage the circlip **(see illustrations)**.

16 Thoroughly clean the driveshaft splines and the apertures in the transmission and hub assembly. Apply a thin film of grease to the oil seal lips and to the driveshaft splines and

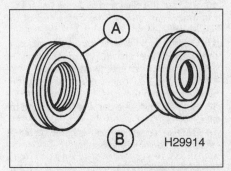

2.15a Original oil seal (A) and modified oil seal (B) on 2.0 litre petrol models with the PG1 transmission

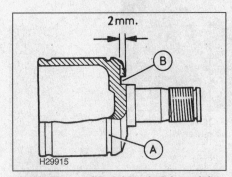

2.15b The modified driveshaft inner joint can be identified by the groove (A) and additional groove (B)

2.13a Inspect the outer CV joint oil seal (arrowed)

shoulders. Check that all gaiter clips are securely fastened.

17 Ensure that the circlip fitted to the inner CV joint is located securely in its groove, then engage the joint splines with those of the differential sun gear, taking care not to damage the oil seal. Push the joint fully into the transmission **(see illustration)**. Check that the joint is securely retained by the circlip by attempting to pull the shaft outwards.

18 Engage the outer CV joint splines with those of the swivel hub and slide the hub onto the shaft. Screw on the new driveshaft retaining nut loosely at this stage.

19 Push the lower arm downwards, then engage the balljoint with the arm and screw on the castellated nut. Tighten the nut to the specified torque (see Chapter 10 Specifications) and align the castellations with the hole in the stub. If necessary, tighten the nut further to the next alignment but no further. Fit a new split pin and bend over the legs to secure.

20 Locate the fork on the shock absorber and on the lower arm. Insert the clamp bolt and tighten to the specified torque (see Chapter 10 Specifications). Insert the bolt through the fork and arm and screw on the nut loosely at this stage. Make sure that the head of the bolt faces forwards.

21 While an assistant firmly depresses the brake pedal, tighten the new driveshaft retaining nut to the specified torque. Stake the nut firmly into the groove on the CV joint using a suitable punch **(see illustration)**.

2.17 Engage the driveshaft inner CV joint with the differential sun gear, taking care not to damage the oil seal

2.13b The inner CV joint circlip (arrowed) must be renewed

22 Refit the roadwheel then lower the vehicle to the ground. Tighten the wheel nuts to the specified torque.

23 With the weight of the vehicle on the suspension, tighten the bolt securing the fork to the lower arm to the specified torque (see Chapter 10 Specifications).

24 If necessary, top-up the transmission with the specified grade of oil with reference to Chapter 1.

3 Driveshaft joint - checking and renewal

Checking

1 Road test the vehicle, and listen for a metallic clicking noise from the front as the vehicle is driven slowly in a circle on full-lock. If evident, this indicates wear in the outer constant velocity joint which must be renewed.

2 To check for wear on the inner joint, apply the handbrake then jack up the front of the vehicle and support it on axle stands (see *"Jacking and Vehicle Support"*). Attempt to move the inner end of the driveshaft up and down, then hold the joint with one hand and attempt to rotate the driveshaft with the other. If excessive wear is evident the inner joint must be renewed together with the driveshaft, since it is not possible to renew the inner joint separately.

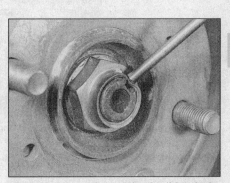

2.21 Use a punch to stake the driveshaft retaining nut

8

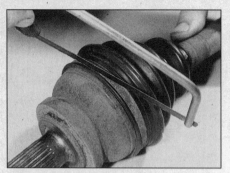

3.4 Using a hack saw, cut free the gaiter clips

3.5 Driving the outer CV joint from the driveshaft

3.7 Make sure that the stopper ring and new circlip are correctly located before fitting the outer CV joint

Renewal

Note: *The following procedure is the same for renewal of the outer joint or the inner joint and driveshaft.*

3 Remove the driveshaft as described in Section 2, then mount it in a vice.

4 If the original clips are fitted, cut them free taking care not to damage the gaiter seating **(see illustration)**. If screw-type clips are fitted, loosen them and remove.

5 Slide the gaiter inwards from the joint, then use a soft metal drift against the inner part of the joint to drive the joint from the end of the driveshaft **(see illustration)**.

6 Check the condition of the rubber gaiter at this stage, and if necessary renew it with reference to Section 4.

7 It is recommended that the joint retaining circlip in the outer end of the driveshaft is renewed. Prise out the old circlip with a screwdriver then fit the new one. If damaged or worn excessively, also renew the stopper ring located in the groove in the splines **(see illustration)**.

8 Wipe clean the splines of the driveshaft, then apply the grease supplied with the new joint to the splines on the driveshaft and in the joint.

9 Slide the joint onto the splines until the retaining circlip engages.

10 Pack the joint with the remainder of the grease, then refit the gaiter, referring to Section 4, if necessary.

11 Refit the driveshaft to the vehicle, as described in Section 2.

4 Driveshaft joint gaiters - renewal

Outer joint gaiter

1 With the driveshaft removed as described in Section 2, remove the outer joint as described in Section 3.

2 Slide the gaiter from the end of the driveshaft.

3 Clean the old grease from the joint, then re-pack the joint with the grease supplied with the new gaiter.

4 Slide the new gaiter and new inner securing clip onto the driveshaft.

5 Slide the outer joint onto the splines until the retaining circlip engages.

6 Locate the gaiter and outer securing clip on the outer joint. Check that the gaiter is not

twisted or stretched, then tighten the securing clips. Rover technicians use a special tool to tighten the original type clips, however it may be possible to tighten the clips sufficiently by gripping them in a vice while the securing tabs are bent over. Alternatively, fit screw-type clips and tighten them securely.

7 Wipe clean any excess grease and refit the driveshaft with reference to Section 2.

Inner joint gaiter

8 Remove the outer joint gaiter as described earlier in this Section.

9 Note the position of the dynamic damper, then release the retaining clip and slide the damper from the outer end of the driveshaft **(see illustration)**.

10 Release the clips and slide the gaiter from the inner joint and off the outer end of the driveshaft.

11 Clean the old grease from the inner joint, then re-pack the joint with the grease supplied with the new gaiter **(see illustration)**.

12 Slide the new gaiter onto the inner joint and secure with the clips.

13 Refit the dynamic damper and tighten the clip.

14 Refit or renew the outer joint gaiter as described earlier in this Section.

4.9 Dynamic damper on the driveshaft

4.11 Pack the inner CV joint with grease supplied in the gaiter kit

Chapter 9
Braking system

Contents

Degrees of difficulty

Easy, suitable for novice with little experience		Fairly easy, suitable for beginner with some experience		Fairly difficult, suitable for competent DIY mechanic		Difficult, suitable for experienced DIY mechanic		Very difficult, suitable for expert DIY or professional

Specifications

Brake system
Type . . . . Dual hydraulic circuit, split diagonally on all models. Disc front brakes. Drum rear brakes except on models with ABS which have rear disc brakes. Vacuum servo-assistance on all models. Cable-operated handbrake on rear brakes

Front brakes
Type . . . . Disc, with single piston sliding caliper
Disc diameter . . . . 262 mm
Disc thickness (new):
  Solid disc . . . . 12.9 to 13.1 mm
  Ventilated disc . . . . 20.9 to 21.1 mm
Disc thickness (minimum):
  Solid disc . . . . 11.0 mm
  Ventilated disc . . . . 19.0 mm
Maximum disc run-out . . . . 0.04 mm
Brake pad friction material minimum thickness . . . . 3.0 mm

Rear brakes

ABS

Type	Disc, with single piston sliding caliper
Disc diameter	239 mm
Disc thickness:	
New	9.9 to 10.1 mm
Minimum	8.0 mm
Maximum disc run-out	0.1 mm
Brake pad friction material minimum thickness	3.0 mm

Non-ABS

Type	Single leading shoe drum
Drum diameter:	
New	203.20 to 203.33 mm
Maximum diameter after machining	204 mm
Maximum drum ovality	0.012 mm
Brake shoe friction material minimum thickness	2.0 mm

Torque wrench settings

	Nm	lbf ft
ABS ECU pipe unions	14	10
ABS ECU to modulator	8	6
ABS wheel sensor	6	4
Brake pipe union nuts to master cylinder	19	14
Brake proportioning valve:		
Bracket nuts	10	7
Pipe unions	19	14
Front brake caliper mounting bracket	108	80
Front caliper guide pin bolts	27	20
Front/rear brake backplate	10	7
Front/rear brake hose to caliper banjo union	34	25
Front/rear disc	10	7
Handbrake cable bracket	22	16
Handbrake cable retainer to backplate	22	16
Handbrake lever	22	16
Master cylinder to servo unit	15	11
Modulator:		
Mounting nut	10	7
Spigot	15	11
Rear backplate to trailing arm	64	47
Rear brake drum to hub	7	5
Rear caliper guide pin bolts	27	20
Rear wheel cylinder:		
Mounting bolt	8	6
Union nut	19	14
Roadwheel nuts	110	81
Vacuum pipe to pump (diesel engine)	10	7
Vacuum pump to alternator (diesel engine)	8	6
Vacuum servo to bulkhead	13	10

1 General information and precautions

General information

The braking system is of servo-assisted, dual circuit hydraulic type. The arrangement of the hydraulic system is such that each circuit operates one front and one rear brake from a tandem master cylinder. Under normal circumstances both circuits operate in unison. However, in the event of hydraulic failure in one circuit, full braking force will still be available in the remaining circuit on one front wheel and the diagonally opposite rear wheel.

A pressure regulating valve is incorporated in the hydraulic circuit to regulate the pressure applied to the rear brakes and reduce the possibility of the rear wheels locking under heavy braking. On non-ABS models the front brake circuit is also connected through the valve body but this is for distribution purposes only; the valve still controls the rear brake circuit. On ABS models the valve is only connected to the rear brake circuit.

All models are fitted with front disc brakes. Models equipped with ABS are fitted with ventilated discs, whereas non-ABS models are fitted with solid discs. The disc brakes are actuated by single piston sliding type calipers which ensure that equal pressure is applied to each disc pad. The front (and rear where applicable) inner brake pads are fitted with audible warning wear indicators which emit a high pitched 'scraping' sound when the linings are worn to the minimum thickness.

Non-ABS models are fitted with rear drum brakes, incorporating leading and trailing shoes which are actuated by twin piston wheel cylinders. A self-adjust mechanism is incorporated to automatically compensate for brake shoe wear. As the brake shoe linings wear, the footbrake operation automatically operates the adjuster mechanism quadrant which effectively lengthens the shoe strut and repositions the brake shoes to reduce the lining-to-drum clearance.

ABS models are equipped with rear disc brakes. The disc brakes are actuated by a single piston sliding caliper which incorporates a mechanical handbrake mechanism.

On all models, the handbrake provides an independent mechanical means of rear brake application.

ABS is available as an option on 416 models, and is fitted as standard on some 420 models. The system comprises a modulator block which contains an ABS Electronic Control Unit (ECU), hydraulic solenoid valves and accumulators, and an electrically-driven return pump **(see illustration)**. One sensor is fitted to each roadwheel. The purpose of this system is to prevent wheel locking during heavy braking. This is achieved by automatic release of the brake on the relevant wheel, followed by reapplication of the brake.

The solenoids are controlled by the ECU which receives signals from the four roadwheel sensors, which monitor the speed of rotation of each wheel. By comparing the speed signals from the four wheels, the ECU can determine when a wheel is about to lock; the ABS system then automatically prevents increased pressurisation of the hydraulic fluid to that wheel. If the wheel still attempts to lock, the system will reduce the hydraulic pressure until the wheel is prevented from locking. This cycle can be carried out at up to 10 times a second. During normal operation, the system functions in the same way as a non-ABS braking system.

The action of the solenoid valves and return pump creates pulses in the hydraulic circuit. When the ABS system is functioning, these pulses can be felt through the brake pedal.

Operation of the ABS system is entirely dependent on electrical signals. To prevent the system responding to any inaccurate signals, a built-in safety circuit monitors all signals received by the ECU. If an inaccurate signal or low battery voltage is detected, the ABS system is automatically shut down and the warning lamp on the instrument panel is illuminated to inform the driver that the ABS system is not operational.

If a fault does develop in the ABS system the vehicle must be taken to a Rover dealer for fault diagnosis and repair.

On diesel engine models, since there is no throttling of the inlet manifold, the manifold is not a suitable source of vacuum to operate the vacuum servo unit. The servo unit is therefore connected to a separate vacuum pump on the engine.

Precautions

 Warning: When servicing any part of the system, work carefully and methodically; also observe scrupulous cleanliness when overhauling any part of the hydraulic system. Always renew components (in axle sets, where applicable) if in doubt about their condition, and use only genuine Rover replacement parts, or at least those of known good quality. Note the warnings given in "Safety first" and at relevant points in this Chapter concerning the dangers of asbestos dust and hydraulic fluid.

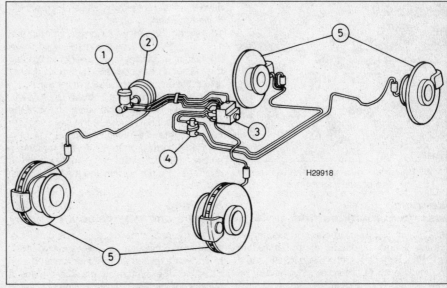

1.7 Anti-lock braking system (ABS) components

1	Master cylinder	4	Brake pressure proportioning valve
2	Vacuum servo unit	5	Reluctor ring and wheel sensor
3	Modulator block and ECU		

2 Hydraulic system - bleeding

 Warning: Hydraulic fluid is poisonous; wash off immediately and thoroughly in the case of skin contact, and seek immediate medical advice if any fluid is swallowed or gets into the eyes.

General

1 The correct operation of any hydraulic system is only possible after removing all air from the components and circuit; this is achieved by bleeding the system.
2 During the bleeding procedure, add only clean, unused hydraulic fluid of the recommended type; never re-use fluid that has already been bled from the system. Ensure that sufficient fluid is available before starting work.
3 If there is any possibility of incorrect fluid being already in the system, the brake components and circuit must be flushed completely with uncontaminated, correct fluid, and new seals should be fitted to the various components.
4 If hydraulic fluid has been lost from the system, or air has entered because of a leak, ensure that the fault is cured before proceeding further.
5 Park the vehicle over an inspection pit or on car ramps. Alternatively, apply the handbrake then jack up the front and rear of the vehicle and support it on axle stands (see "Jacking and Vehicle Support"). For improved access with the vehicle jacked up, remove the roadwheels.
6 Check that all pipes and hoses are secure, unions tight and bleed screws closed. Clean

any dirt from around the bleed screws.
7 Unscrew the master cylinder reservoir cap, and top the master cylinder reservoir up to the "MAX" level line; remember to maintain the fluid level at least above the "MIN" level line throughout the procedure, otherwise there is a risk of further air entering the system.
8 There are a number of one-man, do-it-yourself brake bleeding kits currently available from motor accessory shops. It is recommended that one of these kits is used whenever possible, as they greatly simplify the bleeding operation, and also reduce the risk of expelled air and fluid being drawn back into the system. If such a kit is not available, the basic (two-man) method must be used, which is described in detail below.
9 If a kit is to be used, prepare the vehicle as described previously, and follow the kit manufacturer's instructions, as the procedure may vary slightly according to the type being used; generally, they are as outlined below in the relevant sub-section.
10 Whichever method is used, the same sequence must be followed (paragraphs 11 and 12) to ensure the removal of all air from the system.

Bleeding sequence

11 If the system has been only partially disconnected, and suitable precautions were taken to minimise fluid loss, it should be necessary only to bleed that part of the system (ie the primary or secondary circuit).
12 If the complete system is to be bled, then it should be done working in the following sequence:
a) Left-hand front brake.
b) Right-hand rear brake.
c) Right-hand front brake.
d) Left-hand rear brake.

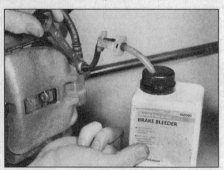

2.22 Using a one-way valve kit to bleed the braking system

Bleeding - basic (two-man) method

13 Collect together a clean glass jar, a suitable length of plastic or rubber tubing which is a tight fit over the bleed screw, and a ring spanner to fit the screw. The help of an assistant will also be required.

14 Remove the dust cap from the first bleed screw in the sequence. Fit the spanner and tube to the screw, place the other end of the tube in the jar, and pour in sufficient fluid to cover the end of the tube.

15 Ensure that the master cylinder reservoir fluid level is maintained at least above the "MIN" level mark throughout the procedure.

16 Have the assistant fully depress and release the brake pedal several times to build up initial pressure in the system.

17 Unscrew the bleed screw approximately half a turn then have the assistant slowly depress the brake pedal down to the floor and hold it there. Tighten the bleed screw and

3.1 Using a brake hose clamp to minimise fluid loss

have the assistant slowly release the pedal to its rest position.

18 Repeat the procedure given in paragraph 17 until the fluid emerging from the bleed screw is free from air bubbles. After every two or three depressions of the pedal, check the level of fluid in the reservoir and top up if necessary.

19 When no more air bubbles appear, securely tighten the bleed screw, remove the tube and spanner, and refit the dust cap. Do not overtighten the bleed screw.

20 Repeat the procedure on the remaining screws in the sequence, until all air is removed from the system and the brake pedal feels firm again.

Bleeding - using a one-way valve kit

21 As the name implies, these kits consist of a length of tubing with a one-way valve fitted, to prevent expelled air and fluid being drawn back into the system; some kits include a translucent container, which can be positioned so that the air bubbles can be more easily seen flowing from the end of the tube.

22 The kit is connected to the bleed screw, which is then opened **(see illustration)**. The user returns to the driver's seat, depresses the brake pedal with a smooth, steady stroke, and slowly releases it; this is repeated until the expelled fluid is clear of air bubbles.

23 Note that these kits simplify work so much that it is easy to forget the master cylinder reservoir fluid level; ensure that this is maintained at least above the "MIN" level line at all times.

Bleeding - using a pressure-bleeding kit

24 These kits are usually operated by a reservoir of pressurised air contained in the spare tyre. However, note that it will probably be necessary to reduce the pressure to a lower level than normal; refer to the instructions supplied with the kit.

25 By connecting a pressurised, fluid-filled container to the master cylinder reservoir, bleeding can be carried out simply by opening each screw in turn (in the specified sequence), and allowing the fluid to flow out until no more air bubbles can be seen in the expelled fluid.

26 This method has the advantage that the large reservoir of fluid provides an additional

safeguard against air being drawn into the system during bleeding.

27 Pressure-bleeding is particularly effective when bleeding "difficult" systems, or when bleeding the complete system at the time of routine fluid renewal.

All methods

28 When bleeding is complete, and firm pedal feel is restored, wipe off any spilt fluid, securely tighten the bleed screws, and refit the dust caps.

29 Check the hydraulic fluid level in the master cylinder reservoir, and top-up if necessary (see *"Weekly checks"*).

30 Discard any hydraulic fluid that has been bled from the system; it will not be fit for re-use.

31 Check the feel of the brake pedal. If it feels at all spongy, air must still be present in the system, and further bleeding is required. Failure to bleed satisfactorily after a reasonable repetition of the bleeding procedure may be due to worn master cylinder seals.

---

3   Hydraulic pipes and hoses - renewal

Note: *Before starting work, refer to the note at the beginning of Section 2 concerning the dangers of hydraulic fluid.*

1 If any pipe or hose is to be renewed, minimise fluid loss by first removing the master cylinder reservoir cap, then tightening it down onto a piece of polythene to obtain an airtight seal. Alternatively, hose clamps can be fitted to flexible hoses to isolate sections of the circuit; metal brake pipe unions can be plugged (if care is taken not to allow dirt into the system) or capped immediately they are disconnected **(see illustration)**. Place a wad of rag under any union that is to be disconnected, to catch any spilt fluid.

2 If a flexible hose is to be disconnected, unscrew the brake pipe union nut before removing the spring clip which secures the hose to its mounting bracket. Where applicable, unscrew the banjo union bolt securing the hose to the caliper and recover the copper washers. When removing the front flexible hose, pull out the spring clip and disconnect it from the strut **(see illustrations)**.

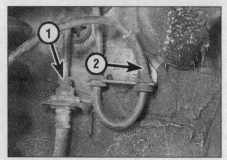

3.2a Brake pipe union nut (1) and ABS sensor wiring (2) under the front wheel arch

3.2b Flexible hose and brake pipe connection under the rear wheel arch

3.2c Flexible hose support bracket on the rear suspension trailing arm

3.3 Using a split brake pipe spanner to unscrew a union nut

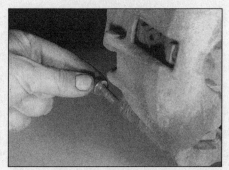

4.2a Remove the lower caliper guide pin bolt . . .

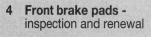

4 Front brake pads - inspection and renewal

3 To unscrew union nuts, it is preferable to obtain a split brake pipe spanner of the correct size; these are available from most motor accessory shops **(see illustration)**. Failing this, a close-fitting open-ended spanner will be required, though if the nuts are tight or corroded, their flats may be rounded-off if the spanner slips. In such a case, a self-locking wrench is often the only way to unscrew a stubborn union, but it follows that the pipe and the damaged nuts must be renewed on reassembly. Always clean a union and surrounding area before disconnecting it. If disconnecting a component with more than one union, make a careful note of the connections before disturbing any of them.

4 If a brake pipe is to be renewed, it can be obtained, cut to length and with the union nuts and end flares in place, from Rover dealers. All that is then necessary is to bend it to shape, following the line of the original, before fitting it

to the car. Alternatively, most motor accessory shops can make up brake pipes from kits, but this requires very careful measurement of the original, to ensure that the replacement is of the correct length. The safest answer is usually to take the original to the shop as a pattern.

5 On refitting, do not overtighten the union nuts.

6 When refitting hoses to the calipers, always use new copper washers and tighten the banjo union bolts to the specified torque. Make sure that the hoses are positioned so that they will not touch surrounding bodywork or the roadwheels.

7 Ensure that the pipes and hoses are correctly routed, with no kinks, and that they are secured in the clips or brackets provided. After fitting, remove the polythene from the reservoir, and bleed the hydraulic system as described in Section 2. Wipe away any spilt fluid, and check carefully for fluid leaks.

> ⚠ **Warning: Renew both sets of front brake pads at the same time. Never renew the pads on only one wheel as uneven braking may result. The dust created by pad wear may contain asbestos, which is a health hazard. Never blow it with compressed air or inhale it. DO NOT use petroleum-based solvents to clean brake parts. Use brake cleaner or methylated spirit only.**

Removal and inspection

1 Apply the handbrake, then jack up the front of the vehicle and support it on axle stands (see *"Jacking and Vehicle Support"*). Remove both front roadwheels.

2 Unscrew and remove the lower caliper guide pin bolt; the guide pin is prevented from turning by the machined shoulders. Pivot the caliper upwards from the disc to gain access to the brake pads and tie it to the suspension strut using a piece of wire **(see illustrations)**.

3 Remove the circular shim which is fitted to the caliper piston **(see illustration)**.

4 Remove the brake pads from the caliper mounting bracket whilst noting the correct position of the pad retainer springs and pad shims **(see illustrations)**.

5 Measure the thickness of friction material remaining on each brake pad **(see illustration)**.

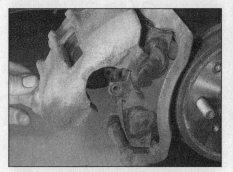

4.2b . . . and pivot the caliper up from the disc and pads

4.3 Removing the circular shim from the caliper piston

4.4a Remove the front brake outer pad . . .

4.4b . . . and inner pad . . .

4.4c . . . then remove the pad shims

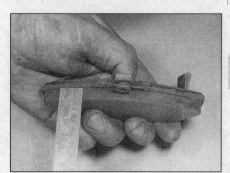

4.5 Measuring the thickness of the brake pad friction material

9

4.8 A special tool being used to push the piston into the caliper

4.9 Check the condition of the guide pins and gaiters before refitting the pads

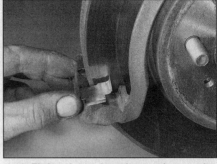

4.10 Fitting the pad retainer springs to the caliper bracket

If either pad is worn at any point to the specified minimum thickness or less, all four pads must be renewed. Also, the pads should be renewed if any are fouled with oil or grease as there is no satisfactory way of degreasing friction material once contaminated. If any of the brake pads are worn unevenly or fouled with oil or grease, trace and rectify the cause before reassembly. New brake pad kits are available from Rover dealers and include new shims and pad retainer springs.

6 If the brake pads are still serviceable, carefully clean them using a clean, fine wire brush or similar, paying particular attention to the sides and back of the metal backing. Carefully clean the pad retainer springs and the pad locations in the caliper body and mounting bracket.

7 Scrape any rust from the periphery of the brake disc.

8 If new brake pads are to be fitted, the caliper piston must be pushed back into the cylinder to make room for them. Either use a G-clamp or similar tool, or use suitable pieces of wood as levers **(see illustration)**. Provided that the master cylinder reservoir has not been overfilled with hydraulic fluid, there should be no spillage, but keep a careful watch on the fluid level while retracting the piston. If the fluid level rises above the "MAX" level line at any time, the surplus should be syphoned off or drained from the bleed screw.

 Warning: Do not syphon the fluid by mouth, as it is poisonous; use a syringe or an old poultry baster.

9 Check that the caliper guide pins are free to slide easily in the caliper bracket and check that the rubber guide pin gaiters are undamaged **(see illustration)**. Inspect the dust seal around the piston for damage and the piston for evidence of fluid leaks, corrosion or damage. Renew as necessary.

Refitting

10 Commence refitting by fitting the pad retainer springs to the caliper mounting bracket **(see illustration)**.

11 Apply a thin smear of high-temperature copper brake grease or anti-seize compound to the sides and back of each pad's metal backing and to the pad contact surfaces on the caliper body and mounting bracket. Fit the shims to the back of both pads **(see illustration)**.

12 Install the brake pads in the caliper mounting bracket, ensuring that the friction material is against the disc. The pad with the wear indicator must be fitted on the inside.

13 Apply a little high temperature grease to the circular shim and fit the shim to the caliper piston. Pivot the caliper body down over the brake pads then refit the bottom guide pin bolt and tighten it to the specified torque wrench setting. Make sure that the guide pin flats locate with the lugs on the caliper body.

14 Check that the caliper body slides smoothly in the mounting bracket, then depress the brake pedal repeatedly until the pads are pressed into firm contact with the brake disc and normal pedal pressure is restored.

15 Repeat the above procedure on the remaining front brake caliper.

16 Refit the roadwheels, then lower the vehicle to the ground and tighten the roadwheel nuts to the specified torque setting.

17 On completion, check and if necessary top up the hydraulic fluid level as described in "Weekly checks".

5 Rear brake pads - inspection and renewal

⚠ **Warning: Renew BOTH sets of rear brake pads at the same time - NEVER renew the pads on only one wheel, as uneven braking may result. Note that the dust created by wear of the pads may contain asbestos, which is a health hazard. Never blow it out with compressed air, and do not inhale any of it. DO NOT use petroleum-based solvents to clean brake parts - use brake cleaner or methylated spirit only.**

Removal and inspection

1 Chock the front wheels, then jack up the rear of the vehicle and support on axle stands (see "Jacking and Vehicle Support"). Remove both rear wheels.

2 Undo the two bolts securing the caliper shield in position and remove the shield from the rear of the caliper **(see illustrations)**.

4.11 Smear high-temperature copper grease on the back of each brake pad

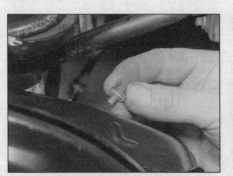

5.2a Unscrew the bolts . . .

5.2b . . . and remove the shield from the rear disc brake

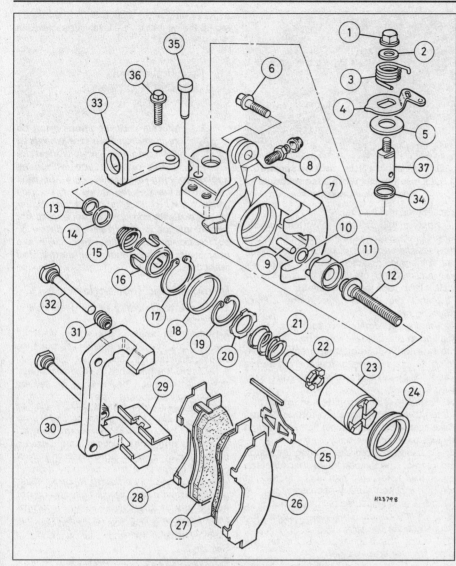

5.3a Rear brake caliper components

1 Handbrake lever retaining nut	13 Bearing	27 Brake pads
2 Washer	14 Spring seat	28 Outer pad shim
3 Return spring	15 Spring	29 Pad spring
4 Handbrake operating lever	16 Spring cover	30 Caliper mounting bracket
5 Dust seal	17 Circlip	31 Gaiter
6 Guide pin bolt	18 Piston seal	32 Guide pin
7 Caliper body	19 Circlip	33 Handbrake cable mounting bracket
8 Bleed screw	20 Thrustwasher	34 Cam washer
9 Pushrod	21 Spring	35 Pin
10 O-ring	22 Adjuster nut	36 Bolt
11 Adjusting bolt piston	23 Piston	37 Handbrake mechanism cam
12 Adjusting bolt	24 Dust seal	
	25 Pad spring	
	26 Inner pad shim	

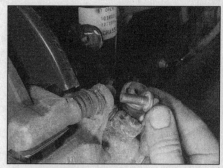

5.3b Unscrew the guide pin bolts . . .

5.3c . . . and lift the caliper from the disc

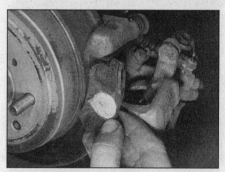

5.4a Remove the outer pad . . .

5.4b . . . and inner pad from the rear disc brake . . .

3 Unscrew and remove both caliper guide pin bolts; the guide pins are prevented from turning by the machined shoulders. Lift the caliper away from the disc, noting the upper pad spring which is fitted to the roof of the caliper. Tie the caliper to the suspension strut using a piece of wire to avoid straining the hydraulic hose **(see illustrations)**.

4 Remove the brake pads from the caliper mounting bracket noting their correct fitted positions and the position of the pad retainer springs and pad shims **(see illustrations)**.
5 Measure the thickness of friction material remaining on each brake pad. If either pad is worn at any point to the specified minimum thickness or less, all four pads must be

renewed. Also, the pads should be renewed if any are fouled with oil or grease as there is no satisfactory way of degreasing friction material once contaminated. If any of the brake pads are worn unevenly or fouled with oil or grease, trace and rectify the cause before reassembly. New brake pad kits are available from Rover dealers and include new shims and pad retainer springs.

9

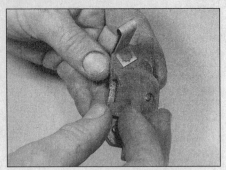

5.4c . . . and remove the pad shims

6 If the brake pads are still serviceable, clean them using a clean, fine wire brush or similar, paying particular attention to the sides and back of the metal backing. Clean the pad locations in the caliper body and mounting bracket.

7 Scrape any rust from the periphery of the brake disc.

8 If new brake pads are to be fitted, the caliper piston must be screwed back into the cylinder to make room for them. Rover technicians use a special tool which engages with the slots in the piston, however a wide-bladed screwdriver will achieve the same result **(see illustration)**. Provided that the master cylinder reservoir has not been overfilled with hydraulic fluid, there should be no spillage, but keep a careful watch on the fluid level while retracting the piston. If the fluid level rises above the "MAX" level line at any time, the surplus should be syphoned off or drained from the bleed screw.

 Warning: Do not syphon the fluid by mouth, as it is poisonous; use a syringe or an old poultry baster.

9 Check that the caliper guide pins are free to slide easily in the caliper bracket and check that the rubber guide pin gaiters are undamaged. Inspect the dust seal around the piston for damage and the piston for evidence of fluid leaks, corrosion or damage. Renew as necessary.

Refitting

10 Commence refitting by fitting the pad retainer springs to the caliper mounting

5.10 Fitting the pad retainer springs to the caliper mounting bracket

5.8 The caliper piston must be screwed back into the caliper to accommodate new pads

bracket **(see illustration)**.

11 Apply a thin smear of high-temperature copper brake grease or anti-seize compound to the sides and back of each pad's metal backing and to the pad contact surfaces on the caliper body and mounting bracket. Fit the shims to the back of both pads **(see illustration)**.

12 Install the brake pads in the caliper mounting bracket.

13 Ensure the upper pad spring is still in position in the caliper then slide the caliper into position in its mounting bracket. When fitting the caliper, ensure that the lug on the rear of the piston side pad is located in one of the piston slots.

14 Refit the caliper guide pin bolts and tighten them to the specified torque setting. Make sure that the guide pin flats locate with the lugs on the caliper body.

15 Depress the footbrake to bring the piston into contact with the pads then check that the lug on the piston side pad is still located in one of the piston slots. If necessary, remove the caliper and adjust the piston position.

16 Refit the caliper shield and tighten the mounting bolts securely.

17 Repeat the above procedure on the remaining rear brake caliper.

18 Once both calipers have been done, repeatedly depress the brake pedal until normal pedal operation returns.

19 Check the operation of the handbrake and, if necessary, adjust the cable as described in Chapter 1.

20 Refit the roadwheels, then lower the vehicle to the ground and tighten the road-wheel nuts to the specified torque setting.

5.11 Smear some copper brake grease on the back of each pad

21 On completion, check and if necessary top up the hydraulic fluid level as described in *"Weekly checks"*.

6 Rear brake shoes - inspection and renewal

 Warning: Brake shoes must be renewed on both rear wheels at the same time - never renew the shoes on only one wheel, as uneven braking may result. Also, the dust created by wear of the shoes may contain asbestos, which is a health hazard. Never blow it out with compressed air, and do not inhale any of it. DO NOT use petrol or petroleum-based solvents to clean brake parts; use brake cleaner or methylated spirit only.

Removal and inspection

1 Remove the brake drum as described in Section 8.

2 Remove all traces of brake dust from the brake drum, backplate and shoes but take care not to inhale the dust.

3 Measure the thickness of friction material remaining on each brake shoe at several points. If either shoe is worn at any point to the specified minimum thickness or less, **all four** shoes must be renewed as a set. Also, the shoes should be renewed if any are fouled with oil or grease as there is no satisfactory way of degreasing friction material once contaminated.

4 If any of the brake shoes are worn unevenly or fouled with oil or grease, trace and rectify the cause before reassembly. If the shoes are to be renewed proceed as described below. If all is well refit the drum as described in Section 8.

5 To remove the brake shoes, first remove the shoe retainer springs and pins, using a pair of pliers to press in each retainer clip until it can be rotated through 90° and released. Ease the shoes out one at a time from the lower pivot point to release the tension of the return spring, then disconnect the lower return spring from both shoes. Ease the upper end of both shoes out from their wheel cylinder locations, taking care not to damage the wheel cylinder seals, and disconnect the handbrake cable from the trailing shoe. The brake shoe and adjuster strut assembly can now be manoeuvred out of position and away from the backplate **(see illustrations)**.

6 Do not depress the brake pedal until the brakes are reassembled. Wrap a strong elastic band around the wheel cylinder pistons to retain them.

7 With the brake shoe assembly on the bench, make a note of the fitted positions of the adjuster strut and springs to use as a guide on reassembly **(see illustration)**. Carefully ease the adjuster strut from its slot in the trailing shoe and remove the short spring

6.5b Remove the brake shoe retainer springs . . .

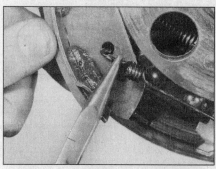

6.5c . . . unhook the lower return spring . . .

6.5d . . . and manoeuvre the shoe and adjuster strut assembly away from the backplate

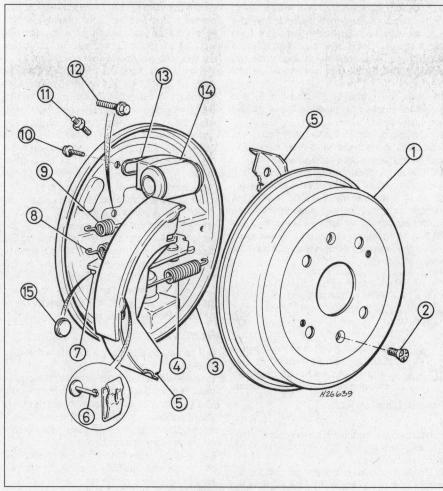

6.5a Rear drum brake assembly

1 Brake drum	6 Retainer pin and spring	11 Bleed screw
2 Drum retaining screw	7 Adjuster strut	12 Backplate mounting
3 Backplate	8 Strut spring	bolt
4 Lower return spring	9 Upper return spring	13 Seal
5 Brake shoe	10 Wheel cylinder retaining	14 Wheel cylinder
	bolt	15 Grommet

which secures the two components together. Detach the upper return spring and separate the shoes and strut.

8 Examine the adjuster strut assembly for signs of wear or damage, paying particular attention to the adjuster quadrant and knurled wheel. If damaged, the strut assembly must be renewed. Renew all the brake shoe return springs if necessary.

9 Peel back the rubber protective caps and check the wheel cylinder for fluid leaks or other damage. Check that both cylinder pistons are free to move easily.

Refitting

10 Prior to fitting, clean the backplate and apply a little high-temperature copper grease to all the shoe contact surfaces on the backplate, adjuster and wheel cylinder pistons. Do not allow the grease to foul the friction material.

11 Ensure the handbrake stop lever on the trailing shoe is correctly engaged with the lever and is pressed tight against the brake shoe (see illustration).

12 Fully extend the adjuster strut quadrant and fit the leading brake shoe into the adjuster

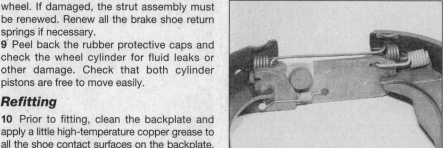

6.7 Correct fitted positions of the adjuster strut and springs

strut slot, ensuring that the strut spring and knurled wheel are situated on the underside of the strut assembly. Using a screwdriver, move the quadrant away from the knurled wheel and set it in the minimum adjustment position.

6.11 Ensure the handbrake stop lever is correctly located

9

6.15 Reset the adjuster strut prior to refitting the drum

13 Fit the upper return spring to its respective location on the leading shoe. Fit the trailing shoe to the upper return spring and carefully ease the shoe into position in the adjuster strut slot. Once in position, fit the small spring which secures the trailing shoe to the strut assembly.

14 Remove the elastic band fitted to the wheel cylinder and manoeuvre the shoe and strut assembly into position on the backplate. Locate the upper end of both shoes with the wheel cylinder pistons and fit the handbrake cable to the trailing shoe operating lever. Fit the lower return spring to both shoes and ease the shoes into position on the lower pivot point.

15 Tap the shoes to centralise them with the backplate, then refit the shoe retainer pins and springs and secure them in position with the retainer clips. Check that the adjuster quadrant is still in the minimum adjuster

7.3 Using a micrometer to measure the brake disc thickness

position and if necessary, reset it by levering the leading shoe away from the wheel cylinder then moving the adjustment cam back **(see illustration)**. Once the adjuster strut is correctly set, ease the leading shoe back into position and check that the shoes are still central.

16 Refit the brake drum (Section 8) and repeat the above operations on the remaining rear brake assembly.

17 On completion, apply the footbrake repeatedly to set the shoe-to-drum clearance, until normal brake pedal operation returns.

18 Check handbrake cable operation and, if necessary, adjust as described in Chapter 1.

19 Refit the roadwheels then lower the vehicle to the ground and tighten the roadwheel nuts to the specified torque.

20 On completion, check and if necessary top up the hydraulic fluid level as described in *"Weekly checks"*.

7 Front/rear brake disc - inspection, removal and refitting

> ⚠ *Warning: Front and rear brake discs must be renewed in axle pairs at the same time, otherwise uneven braking may result.*

Inspection

1 Jack up the front or rear of the vehicle (as applicable) and support it on axle stands (see *"Jacking and Vehicle Support"*). Remove the appropriate wheel.

2 Slowly rotate the brake disc so that the full area of both sides can be checked. Remove the brake pads if better access is required to the inboard surface. Light scoring is normal in the area swept by the brake pads but if heavy scoring is found, then the disc must be renewed. The only alternative to this is to have the disc surface-ground until it is flat again, but this must not reduce the disc to less than the minimum thickness specified.

3 It is normal to find a lip of rust and brake dust around the disc's perimeter. This can be scraped off if required. If, however, a lip has formed due to excessive wear of the brake pad swept area, then the disc's thickness must be measured by using a micrometer

(see illustration). Take measurements at four places around the disc at the inside and outside of the pad swept area. If the disc has worn at any point to the specified minimum thickness or less, then it must be renewed.

4 If the disc is thought to be warped, it can be checked for run-out (at a point 5.0 mm in from the disc's outer edge) by either using a dial gauge mounted on any convenient fixed point, while the disc is slowly rotated, or by using feeler blades to measure (at several points all around the disc) the clearance between the disc and a fixed point, such as the caliper mounting bracket **(see illustration)**. If the measurements obtained exceed the specified maximum, the disc is excessively warped and must be renewed. However, it is worth checking first that the hub bearing is in good condition. Also, try the effect of removing the disc and turning it through 90° at a time to reposition it on the hub. If run-out is still excessive the disc must be renewed.

5 Check the disc for cracks, especially around the stud holes, and any other wear or damage. Renew it if any of these are found.

Removal

6 If removing the rear disc, unbolt the disc shield.

7 Unscrew the two bolts securing the caliper mounting bracket to the swivel hub/stub axle and slide the caliper assembly off the disc. Using a piece of wire or string, tie the caliper to one side to avoid placing any strain on the hydraulic brake hose.

8 Use chalk or paint to mark the relationship of the disc to the hub, then undo the two screws and remove the disc. If the disc is a tight fit on the hub it can be drawn off by screwing two bolts into the holes provided **(see illustrations)**.

Refitting

9 Refitting is the reverse of the removal procedure, noting the following:
a) Ensure that the mating surfaces of the disc and hub are clean and flat.
b) Align the marks made on removal (if applicable).
c) If a new disc is being fitted, there is no need to remove the silver protective coating from the friction surface.

7.4 Using a dial gauge to check the brake disc run-out

7.8a Disc retaining screw

7.8b Drawing off a disc using 8 mm bolts

d) Tighten the disc retaining screws, caliper bracket bolts and roadwheel nuts to their specified torque wrench settings.

8 Rear brake drum - removal, inspection and refitting

⚠️ *Warning: The rear brake drums must be renewed as an axle set at the same time, otherwise uneven braking may result.*

Removal

1 Chock the front wheels, then jack up the rear of the vehicle and support on axle stands (see *"Jacking and Vehicle Support"*). Remove the appropriate rear wheel.

2 Use chalk or paint to mark the relationship of the drum to the hub.

3 With the handbrake firmly applied to prevent drum rotation, unscrew the drum retaining screws **(see illustration)**. Fully release the handbrake cable and withdraw the drum.

4 If the drum will not pull away, first check that the handbrake is fully released. If the drum will still not come away, remove the grommet from the rear of the backplate and, using a small screwdriver, disengage the handbrake lever stop from behind the lever to increase the shoe to drum clearance. If the drum is tight or rusted on the hub, use two bolts in the special holes to force it off **(see illustrations)**.

Inspection

5 Remove all traces of brake dust from the drum, but avoid inhaling the dust as it is injurious to health.

6 Clean the outside of the drum and check it for obvious signs of wear or damage such as cracks around the wheel stud holes. Renew the drum if necessary.

7 Examine carefully the inside of the drum. Light scoring of the friction surface is normal but if heavy scoring is found, the drum must be renewed. It is usual to find a rusty lip on the drum's inboard edge, and this can be scraped away to leave a smooth surface.

8 If the drum is thought to be excessively worn or oval, its internal diameter must be measured at several points by using an internal micrometer. Take measurements in pairs, the second at right angles to the first, and compare the two to check for signs of ovality. Provided that it does not enlarge the drum to beyond the specified maximum diameter, it may be possible to have the drum refinished by skimming or grinding but if this is not possible, the drums on both sides must be renewed.

Refitting

9 Refitting is the reverse of the removal procedure, noting the following:

a) On fitting a new brake drum, use a suitable solvent to remove any

8.3 Removing the brake drum retaining screws (jacking holes arrowed)

preservative coating that may have been applied to its interior.

b) Remove all traces of dirt, brake dust and corrosion from the mating surfaces of the drum and the hub flange.

c) Align (if applicable) the marks made on removal.

d) Tighten the drum retaining screws and the roadwheel nuts to their specified torque wrench settings.

9 Front brake caliper - removal, overhaul and refitting

Removal

1 Apply the handbrake, then jack up the front of the vehicle and support it on axle stands (see *"Jacking and Vehicle Support"*). Remove the appropriate front roadwheel.

2 Minimise fluid loss either by removing the master cylinder reservoir cap and then tightening it down onto a piece of polythene to obtain an airtight seal (taking care not to damage the sender unit), or by using a brake hose clamp to clamp the flexible hose.

3 Clean the area around the union, then unscrew the brake hose union bolt and disconnect the hose from the caliper. Plug or tape over the end of the hose and the aperture in the caliper to prevent dirt entering the hydraulic system. Discard the union sealing washers as they must be renewed.

4 Unscrew the two caliper guide pin bolts.

5 Carefully lift the caliper assembly off the brake pads and remove the circular shim from the caliper piston. Note that the brake pads need not be disturbed and can be left in position in the caliper mounting bracket **(see illustration overleaf)**.

Overhaul

6 With the caliper on the bench, wipe away all traces of dust and dirt.

 ⚠️ *Warning: Avoid inhaling the dust as it is injurious to health.*

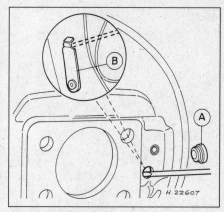

8.4a Releasing the handbrake mechanism stop lever

Remove the rubber grommet (A) and use a small screwdriver to depress the handbrake lever stop (B)

7 Withdraw the piston from the caliper body and remove the dust seal. The piston can be withdrawn by hand or if necessary, pushed out by applying compressed air to the union bolt hole. Only low pressure should be required such as is generated by a foot pump.

8 Using a small screwdriver, extract the piston hydraulic seal taking care not to damage the caliper bore.

9 Withdraw the guide pins from the caliper mounting bracket and remove the guide pin gaiters.

10 Thoroughly clean all components using only methylated spirit or clean hydraulic fluid as a cleaning medium. Never use mineral-based solvents such as petrol or paraffin which will attack the hydraulic system's rubber components. Dry the components using compressed air or a clean, lint-free cloth. Use compressed air to blow clear the fluid passages.

11 Check all components and renew any that are worn or damaged. Check particularly the cylinder bore and piston; if these are scratched, worn or corroded in any way, renew the complete body assembly. Similarly, check the condition of the guide pins and their bores in the mounting bracket. Both guide

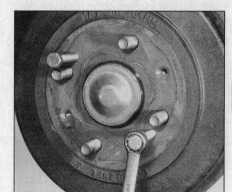

8.4b The brake drum can be drawn off the hub by using two 8 mm bolts

9

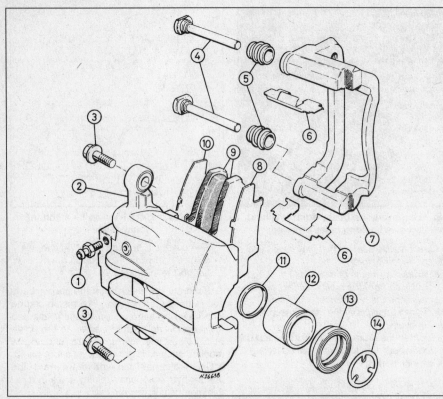

9.5 Front brake caliper components

1 Bleed screw	6 Pad retainer spring	10 Outer pad shim
2 Caliper body	7 Caliper mounting	11 Piston seal
3 Guide pin bolt	bracket	12 Piston
4 Guide pin	8 Inner pad shim	13 Dust seal
5 Gaiter	9 Brake pads	14 Circular shim

pins should be undamaged and a reasonably tight sliding fit in the mounting bracket bores. If there is any doubt about the condition of any component, renew it.

12 If the assembly is fit for further use, obtain the appropriate repair kit. Components are available from Rover dealers.

13 Renew the rubber seals, dust covers and caps, and the copper sealing washers.

14 On reassembly, ensure that all components are absolutely clean and dry.

15 Dip the piston and new seal in clean hydraulic fluid. Smear clean fluid on the cylinder bore surface.

16 Fit the new seal using only the fingers to manipulate it into the cylinder bore groove. Fit the new dust seal to the piston and refit it to the cylinder bore using a twisting motion, ensuring that the piston enters squarely into the bore. Press the piston fully into the bore, then secure the dust seal to the caliper body.

17 Apply the grease supplied in the repair kit, or a good quality high-temperature brake grease, to the guide pins and fit the new gaiters. Fit the guide pins to the caliper mounting bracket, ensuring that the gaiters are correctly located in the grooves on both the guide pin and mounting bracket.

10.3 Spring clip and clevis pin (arrowed) securing the handbrake cable to the caliper handbrake lever

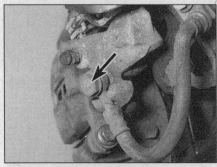

10.5 Flexible brake hose union on the rear brake caliper

Refitting

18 Refit the circular shim to the piston and carefully slide the caliper into position over the brake pads. Refit the caliper guide pin bolts and tighten them to the specified torque setting.

19 Position a new copper sealing washer on each side of the hose union and refit the brake hose union bolt. Ensure that the brake hose union is correctly positioned between the lugs on the caliper then tighten the union bolt to the specified torque setting.

20 Remove the brake hose clamp, where fitted, and bleed the hydraulic system (see Section 2). Providing the precautions described were taken to minimise brake fluid loss, it should only be necessary to bleed the relevant front brake.

21 Refit the roadwheel then lower the vehicle to the ground and tighten the roadwheel nuts to the specified torque.

---

10 Rear brake caliper - removal, overhaul and refitting

Removal

1 Chock the front wheels, then jack up the rear of the vehicle and support on axle stands (see "Jacking and Vehicle Support"). Remove the relevant rear wheel.

2 Undo the two bolts securing the caliper shield in position and remove the shield from the rear of the caliper.

3 Extract the spring clip and clevis pin securing the handbrake cable to the caliper handbrake lever, then remove the clip securing the outer cable to its mounting bracket and detach the handbrake cable from the caliper **(see illustration)**.

4 Minimise fluid loss by removing the master cylinder reservoir cap and then tightening it down onto a piece of polythene to obtain an airtight seal (taking care not to damage the sender unit), or by using a brake hose clamp to clamp the flexible hose.

5 Clean the area around the hose union, then undo the brake hose union bolt and disconnect the hose from the caliper **(see illustration)**. Plug or tape over the end of the hose and the caliper aperture to prevent dirt entering the hydraulic system. Discard the copper sealing washers as they must be renewed whenever disturbed.

6 Remove both the caliper guide pin bolts, then lift the caliper away from the disc, noting the upper pad spring which is fitted to the roof of the caliper **(see illustration)**. Note that the brake pads need not be disturbed and can be left in position in the caliper mounting bracket.

Overhaul

7 With the caliper on the bench, wipe away all traces of dust and dirt.

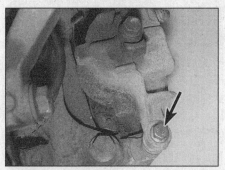

10.6 Rear brake caliper lower guide pin bolt

 Warning: Avoid inhaling the dust as it is injurious to health.

8 Using a small screwdriver, carefully prise out the dust seal from the caliper bore.

9 Remove the piston from the caliper bore by rotating it in an anti-clockwise direction. This can be achieved using a suitable pair of circlip pliers as a peg spanner or by fabricating a peg spanner for the task. Once the piston turns freely but does not come out any further, then it can be withdrawn by hand, or if necessary, pushed out by applying compressed air to the union bolt hole. Only low pressure should be required such as is generated by a foot pump.

10 With the piston removed, extract the circlip from inside the piston and withdraw the thrustwasher, spring and adjuster nut.

11 Remove the piston seal whilst taking great care not to scratch the caliper bore.

12 Extract the circlip from the caliper bore and withdraw the spring cover, spring, spring seat, bearing and adjusting bolt. Then remove the adjusting bolt piston, noting the O-ring fitted to the rear of the piston, and withdraw the small pushrod.

13 Slacken and remove the handbrake lever retaining nut and washer and remove the return spring, lever and dust seal. Withdraw the handbrake mechanism cam from the caliper and remove the cam washer.

14 Withdraw the guide pins from the caliper mounting bracket and remove the guide pin gaiters.

15 Inspect all the caliper components as described for the front brake caliper and renew as necessary.

16 On reassembly ensure that all components are absolutely clean and dry.

17 Apply high-temperature copper-based grease to the handbrake mechanism cam and refit the cam washer and cam to the caliper. Fit the dust seal, lever, return spring and washer and tighten the handbrake lever retaining nut securely.

18 Fit a new O-ring to the adjusting bolt piston then insert the small pushrod into the rear of the piston and install the adjusting bolt piston assembly in the caliper bore. Operate the handbrake lever and check that the piston is free to move smoothly then refit the adjusting bolt, followed by the bearing and

spring seat. Fit the spring, so that its tapered end is innermost, then install the spring cover. Secure all the above components in position with the circlip, ensuring that it is correctly seated in the groove in the caliper bore.

19 Locate the adjusting nut with the cutout on the inside of the caliper piston and refit the spring, thrustwasher and circlip. Ensure the circlip is correctly located in its groove.

20 Dip the piston and the new piston (fluid) seal in clean hydraulic fluid. Smear clean fluid on the cylinder bore surface.

21 Fit the new piston (fluid) seal using only the fingers to manipulate it into the cylinder bore groove and refit the piston assembly. Turn the piston in a clockwise direction, using the method employed on dismantling, until it is fully retracted into the caliper bore.

22 Fit the dust seal to the caliper ensuring that it is correctly located in the caliper and also the groove on the piston.

23 Apply the grease supplied in the repair kit, or high-temperature copper-based grease, to the guide pins and fit the new gaiters. Fit the guide pins to the caliper mounting bracket, ensuring that the gaiters are correctly located in the grooves on both the guide pin and mounting bracket.

Refitting

24 Ensure the upper pad spring is still in position in the caliper then slide the caliper into position in its mounting bracket. When fitting the caliper, ensure that the lug on the rear of the piston side pad is located in the centre of the caliper piston at the point where the two piston slots cross. Refit the caliper guide pin bolts and tighten them to the specified torque setting.

25 Position a new copper sealing washer on each side of the hose union and refit the brake hose union bolt. Ensure that the brake hose union is correctly positioned between the lugs on the caliper then tighten the union bolt to the specified torque setting.

26 Remove the brake hose clamp, where fitted, and bleed the hydraulic system (see Section 2). Providing the precautions described were taken to minimise brake fluid loss, it should only be necessary to bleed the relevant rear brake.

27 Refit the outer handbrake cable to its mounting bracket and secure it in position with the retaining clip. Ensure the return spring is located in the groove in the operating lever then refit the handbrake cable to lever clevis pin and secure it in position with the spring clip.

28 Depress the brake pedal several times until normal operation returns then check and, if necessary, adjust the handbrake cable as described in Chapter 1.

29 Refit the shield to the rear of the caliper and tighten its retaining bolts securely.

30 Refit the roadwheel, then lower the vehicle to the ground and tighten the roadwheel nuts to the specified torque.

11 Rear wheel cylinder - removal, overhaul and refitting

Removal

1 Remove the brake shoes as described in Section 6.

2 Minimise fluid loss by removing the master cylinder reservoir cap and then tightening it down onto a piece of polythene to obtain an airtight seal (taking care not to damage the sender unit), or by using a brake hose clamp to clamp the flexible hose.

3 Wipe away all traces of dirt around the brake pipe union at the rear of the wheel cylinder and unscrew the union nut. Carefully ease the pipe out of the wheel cylinder and plug or tape over its end to prevent dirt entry (see illustration).

4 Unscrew the two wheel cylinder retaining bolts from the rear of the backplate and remove the cylinder, noting the rubber sealing ring which is fitted between the cylinder and backplate.

Overhaul

5 Remove the wheel cylinder from the vehicle and clean it thoroughly.

6 Mount the wheel cylinder in a soft-jawed vice and remove the rubber protective caps. Extract the piston assemblies.

7 Thoroughly clean all components using only methylated spirit or clean hydraulic fluid as a cleaning medium.

Caution: Never use mineral-based solvents such as petrol or paraffin which will attack the hydraulic system's rubber components. Dry the components immediately using compressed air or a clean, lint-free cloth.

8 Check all components and renew any that are worn or damaged. Check particularly the cylinder bore and pistons. The complete assembly must be renewed if these are scratched, worn or corroded. If there is any doubt about the condition of the assembly or of any of its components, renew it. Remove the bleed screw and check that the fluid entry port and bleed screw passages are clear.

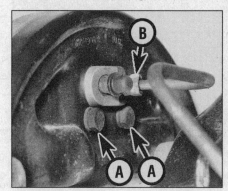

11.3 Wheel cylinder retaining bolts (A) and brake pipe union nut (B)

9 If the assembly is fit for further use, obtain a repair kit. Renew the rubber protective caps, dust caps and seals removed on dismantling; these should never be re-used. Renew also any other items included in the repair kit.

10 On reassembly, dip the pistons and the new seals in clean hydraulic fluid. Smear clean fluid on the cylinder bore surface.

11 Fit the new seals to their pistons using only the fingers to manipulate them into the grooves. Ensure that all components are refitted in the correct order and the right way round.

12 Insert the pistons into the bore using a twisting motion to avoid trapping the seal lips. Apply a smear of rubber lubricant to each piston before fitting the new rubber protective caps.

Refitting

13 Fit a new sealing ring to the rear of the wheel cylinder and place the cylinder in position on the backplate.

14 Refit the wheel cylinder retaining bolts and tighten them to the specified torque.

15 Tighten the brake pipe union nut to the specified torque. Remove the clamp from the brake hose if fitted.

16 Refit the brake shoes as described in Section 6.

17 Bleed the hydraulic braking system (see Section 2). If precautions were taken to minimise fluid loss, it should only be necessary to bleed the relevant rear brake. On completion, check that both footbrake and handbrake function correctly before taking the vehicle on the road.

12 Master cylinder - removal, overhaul and refitting

Removal

1 Remove the master cylinder reservoir cap, having disconnected the sender unit wiring connector, and syphon all hydraulic fluid from the reservoir.

 Warning: Do not syphon the fluid by mouth as it is poisonous but use a syringe or an old poultry baster. Alternatively, open any convenient bleed screw in the system and gently pump the brake pedal to expel the fluid through a plastic tube connected to the screw.

2 Wipe clean the area around the brake pipe unions on the side of the master cylinder and place cloth rags beneath them to catch any

12.2 A brake pipe union nut on the master cylinder

surplus fluid. Unscrew the two union nuts and carefully withdraw the pipes **(see illustration)**. Plug or tape over the pipe ends and master cylinder orifices to minimise loss of brake fluid and to prevent the entry of dirt into the system. Wash off any spilt fluid immediately with warm water.

3 Unscrew and remove the two nuts and washers securing the master cylinder to the vacuum servo unit then withdraw the master cylinder from the engine compartment. On diesel models also unscrew the support bracket mounting bolt and remove the bracket. Remove the O-ring from the rear of the master cylinder and discard it.

Overhaul

4 Clean the master cylinder thoroughly. Check on the availability of parts before dismantling the master cylinder.

5 On models up to VIN 074464, loosen the clip and remove the reservoir from the master cylinder **(see illustration)**.

6 On models from VIN 074465, extract the centre roll pin retaining the reservoir to the master cylinder, then prise the reservoir from the master cylinder body and remove the two mounting seals **(see illustration)**.

7 Using a wooden dowel, press the primary piston in as far as possible and extract the secondary piston stop pin from the reservoir inlet port, then remove the retaining circlip.

8 Noting the order of removal and the direction of fitting of each component, withdraw the piston assemblies with their springs and seals, tapping the body onto a clean wooden surface to dislodge them. If necessary, clamp the master cylinder body in a vice (fitted with soft jaw covers) and use compressed air of low pressure (applied through the secondary circuit fluid port) to assist the removal of the secondary piston assembly.

9 Thoroughly clean all components using only methylated spirit or clean hydraulic fluid as a cleaning medium.

Caution: Never use mineral-based solvents such as petrol or paraffin which will attack the hydraulic system's rubber components. Dry the components immediately using compressed air or a clean, lint-free cloth.

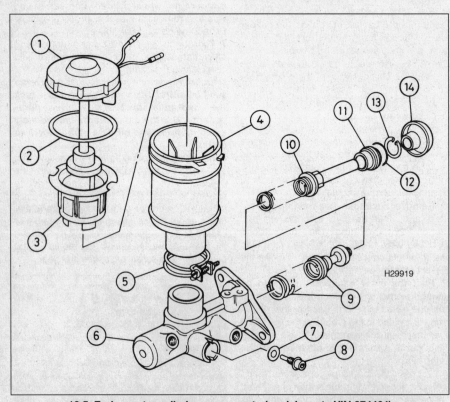

H29919

12.5 Early master cylinder components (models up to VIN 074464)

1 Filler cap	6 Master cylinder body	10 Primary piston assembly
2 Seal	7 Washer	11 Piston guide
3 Filter	8 Stopper bolt	12 O-ring
4 Brake fluid reservoir	9 Secondary piston	13 Circlip
5 Clip	assembly	14 Seal

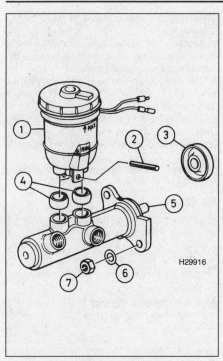

12.6 Later master cylinder components (models from VIN 074465)

1 Fluid reservoir and cap	5 Master cylinder body
2 Roll pin	6 Washer
3 Seal	7 Nut
4 Reservoir seals	

10 Check all components and renew any that are worn or damaged. Check particularly the cylinder bores and pistons. The complete assembly should be renewed if these are scratched, worn or corroded. If there is any doubt about the condition of the assembly or of any of its components, renew it.

11 If the assembly is fit for further use, obtain a repair kit. Renew all seals and O-rings disturbed on dismantling. Renew also any other items included in the repair kit.

12 On reassembly, dip the pistons and new seals in clean hydraulic fluid. Smear clean fluid on the cylinder bore.

13 Fit the new seals to their pistons, using only the fingers to manipulate them into the grooves.

14 Insert the pistons into the bore by using a twisting motion to avoid trapping the seal lips. Ensure that all components are refitted in the correct order and the right way round.

15 Press the secondary piston assembly fully up into the bore using a clean wooden dowel, then refit the stop pin.

16 Refit the primary piston assembly, then secure it in position with a new circlip.

17 On later models, press the new mounting seals into the master cylinder body and carefully refit the reservoir ensuring that it is pressed fully into position. Insert the centre roll pin.

18 On early models, refit the reservoir and tighten the clip.

Refitting

19 Clean the master cylinder and servo unit mating surfaces, then fit a new O-ring to the groove on the master cylinder body.

20 Fit the master cylinder to the servo unit, ensuring that the servo unit pushrod enters the master cylinder bore centrally. Refit the master cylinder washers and mounting nuts and tighten them to the specified torque. On diesel models, make sure the support bracket is refitted and tighten the mounting bolt securely.

21 Wipe clean the brake pipe unions then refit them to the master cylinder ports and tighten them to the specified torque setting.

22 Refill the master cylinder reservoir with new fluid and bleed the hydraulic system with reference to Section 2.

13 Brake proportioning valve - removal and refitting

Removal

1 The brake proportioning valve is located on the bulkhead in the engine compartment **(see illustration)**.

2 Position a container or cloth rags beneath the valve. To prevent excessive loss of hydraulic fluid, either syphon the fluid from the reservoir or temporarily tighten the reservoir filler cap onto a piece of polythene.

3 Note the location of the brake pipes on the valve, then unscrew the union nuts and disconnect the pipes. Tape over or plug the pipe ends and apertures in the valve. Note that on non-ABS models the valve has six pipes, whereas on ABS models it has four pipes.

4 Unscrew the mounting nuts or bolts (as applicable) and remove the valve from the bulkhead. Where applicable, **do not** undo the screws securing the bracket to the valve.

Refitting

5 Refitting is a reversal of removal, but tighten the mounting and union nuts to the specified torque and on completion bleed the hydraulic system as described in Section 2.

13.1 The brake proportioning valve is located on the bulkhead

14 Brake pedal - removal and refitting

Removal

1 Working inside the vehicle, remove the driver's storage pocket from the bottom of the facia.

2 Undo the three screws and remove the lower facia panel from under the steering wheel.

3 Extract the clip and clevis pin securing the servo unit pushrod to the brake pedal.

4 Using pliers, carefully unhook the brake pedal return spring from the pedal.

5 Unscrew and remove the nut then withdraw the pivot bolt and remove the brake pedal and return spring.

6 Examine all brake pedal components for signs of wear, paying particular attention to the pedal bushes, pivot bolt and return spring, renewing them as necessary.

Refitting

7 Refitting is a reverse of the removal procedure. Lubricate the bushes, pivot bolt and clevis pin with multi-purpose grease. Check and if necessary adjust the stop-light switch as described in Section 19.

8 On completion, check the operation of the pedal and ensure that it returns smoothly to its at rest position under the pressure of the return spring.

15 Handbrake - adjustment

1 It is only necessary to adjust the handbrake after renewing or dismantling the rear brake shoes, or renewing the drum/disc.

Rear drum brake models

2 Chock the front wheels, then jack up the rear of the vehicle and support on axle stands (see *"Jacking and Vehicle Support"*).

3 Depress the brake pedal firmly several times to set the self-adjusting rear brake shoe mechanism.

4 Lift out the ashtray from the rear of the centre console to gain access to the handbrake adjusting nut.

5 Apply the handbrake lever and check that the equalizer and cables move freely and smoothly, then set the lever on the first notch of the ratchet mechanism. With the lever in this position, turn the handbrake lever adjusting nut clockwise until only a slight drag can be felt when the rear wheels are turned. Fully release the handbrake lever and check that the wheels rotate freely. Check the adjustment by applying the handbrake lever one notch at a time until both rear wheels are locked. The rear wheels must be locked with the lever applied between 6 and 10 notches.

9

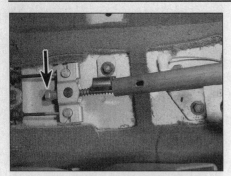

16.4 The handbrake adjustment nut is located behind the equaliser

6 Refit the ashtray and lower the vehicle to the ground.

Rear disc brake models

7 Chock the front wheels, then jack up the rear of the vehicle and support on axle stands (see *"Jacking and Vehicle Support"*). Remove both rear wheels.

8 Unbolt and remove the brake caliper shields from both rear calipers, then check that the handbrake operating arm on each caliper contacts the rest pin. If not, the handbrake cables may be seized or partially seized.

9 Refit the shields and rear wheels.

10 Lift out the ashtray from the rear of the centre console to gain access to the handbrake adjusting nut.

11 Apply the handbrake lever and check that the equalizer and cables move freely and smoothly, then set the lever on the first notch of the ratchet mechanism. With the lever in this position, turn the handbrake lever adjusting nut clockwise until only a slight drag can be felt when the rear wheels are turned. Fully release the handbrake lever and check that the wheels rotate freely. Check the adjustment by applying the handbrake lever one notch at a time until both rear wheels are locked. The rear wheels must be locked with the lever applied between 6 and 10 notches.

12 Refit the ashtray and lower the vehicle to the ground.

16 Handbrake lever -
removal and refitting

Removal

1 With the vehicle parked on level ground, chock the roadwheels so that the vehicle cannot move.

2 Remove the rear console as described in Chapter 11.

3 Remove the rubber gaiter from the lever, then disconnect the wiring from the handbrake warning light switch.

4 Unscrew and remove the handbrake adjustment nut from the equaliser **(see illustration)**.

5 Unscrew the handbrake lever mounting bolts, then withdraw the lever at the same time releasing the adjustment rod from the equaliser.

6 Remove the spring from the adjustment rod.

Refitting

7 Refitting is a reverse of the removal procedure, referring to Chapter 11 for the rear console and tighten the lever mounting bolts to the specified torque. Finally, adjust the handbrake as described in Section 15.

17 Handbrake cables -
removal and refitting

Removal

1 The handbrake cable consists of two sections (right and left-hand), which are linked to the lever assembly by an equalizer plate. Each section can be removed individually.

2 Chock the front wheels, then jack up the rear of the vehicle and support on axle stands (see *"Jacking and Vehicle Support"*). Remove both rear wheels.

3 Remove the rear console as described in Chapter 11.

4 Unscrew and remove the handbrake cable adjusting nut from the rear of the lever and disconnect the equalizer plate, noting the spring which is fitted to the lever adjustment rod **(see illustration)**.

5 Undo the two bolts securing the outer cable retaining plate to the floor pan **(see illustration)**. Remove the retaining plate then detach the relevant inner cable from the equalizer plate and release the cable grommet from the floorpan.

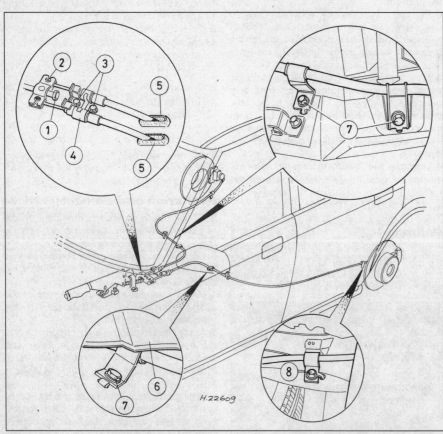

H.22609

17.4 Handbrake mechanism layout

1 *Handbrake cable adjuster nut*	3 *Bolts*	6 *Exhaust heatshield*
	4 *Cable retaining plate*	7 *Bolts - cable to body*
2 *Equalizer plate*	5 *Grommet*	8 *Bolts - cable to trailing arm*

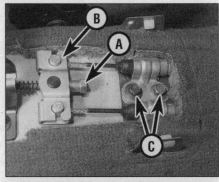

17.5 Handbrake cable adjusting nut (A), equalizer plate (B) and outer cable retaining plate bolts (C)

6 On non-ABS models, remove the relevant rear brake drum as described in Section 8. Remove the trailing shoe retainer spring and pin, using a pair of pliers to press in the retainer clip until it can be rotated through 90° and released. Ease the trailing shoe out of the lower pivot point to release the tension of the return spring, then disconnect the lower return spring from both shoes. Disconnect the handbrake cable from the trailing shoe then use a 12 mm spanner to compress the handbrake cable retaining tangs and withdraw the cable from the rear of the backplate **(see illustration)**.

7 On models equipped with ABS (discs all round), working from underneath the vehicle, remove the two brake caliper shield retaining bolts and remove the shield from the caliper. Extract the spring clip and clevis pin securing the handbrake cable to the caliper handbrake lever then remove the clip securing the outer cable to its mounting bracket and detach the handbrake cable from the caliper.

8 On all models, release the main silencer from its three rubber mountings and carefully lower the tailpipe section to gain access to the fuel tank heat shield. Undo the three heat shield retaining bolts and remove the shield from the vehicle underbody.

9 Work along the length of the cable section and remove all bolts securing the outer cable to the vehicle underbody and trailing arm. Once free, withdraw the cable from underneath the vehicle and, if necessary, repeat the procedure for the remaining cable section **(see illustration)**.

Refitting

10 Refitting is a reversal of the removal procedure noting the following:

a) *Lubricate all exposed linkages and cable pivots with a good quality multi-purpose grease.*

b) *Ensure the cable outer grommet is correctly located in the floorpan and that all retaining bolts are tightened to the specified torque.*

c) *On non-ABS models, refit the trailing shoe and refit the brake drum.*

d) *Prior to refitting the rear console, adjust the handbrake cable as described in Section 15.*

---

18 Handbrake "on" warning light switch -
removal and refitting

Removal

1 Remove the rear console as described in Chapter 11.

2 Remove the rubber gaiter from the handbrake lever.

3 Undo the securing screw and withdraw the switch from the handbrake.

4 Disconnect the wiring from the switch.

17.6 Using a 12 mm spanner to compress the outer cable retaining tangs

Refitting

5 Refitting is a reversal of removal.

---

19 Stop-light switch -
removal, refitting and adjustment

Removal

1 Working inside the vehicle, remove the driver's storage pocket from the bottom of the facia.

2 Undo the three screws and remove the lower facia panel from under the steering wheel.

3 Disconnect the wiring from the stop-light switch **(see illustration)**.

4 Loosen the locknut, then unscrew the switch from the pedal bracket **(see illustration 19.3)**.

Refitting and adjustment

5 Screw the switch a few threads into the pedal bracket, and fully back off the locknut.

6 Connect an ohmmeter across the switch terminals.

7 With the brake pedal released, screw in the switch to the point where the meter reads infinity indicating an open circuit condition. From this point, screw in the switch a further one turn and tighten the locknut.

Caution: Do not screw in the switch more than this otherwise there is the possibility that the switch will prevent the brake pedal fully returning to its rest position.

8 Disconnect the ohmmeter and reconnect the wiring to the switch.

9 Refit the lower facia panel and tighten the screws.

10 Refit the driver's storage pocket.

---

20 Vacuum servo unit -
testing, removal and refitting

Testing

1 To test the operation of the servo unit, depress the footbrake pedal several times to

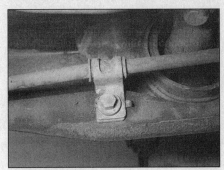
17.9 Handbrake cable support bracket on the trailing arm

exhaust the vacuum, then start the engine whilst keeping the pedal firmly depressed. As the engine starts, there should be a noticeable 'give' in the brake pedal as the vacuum builds up. Allow the engine to run for at least two minutes then switch it off. If the brake pedal is now depressed it should feel normal, but further applications should result in the pedal feeling firmer, with the pedal stroke decreasing with each application.

2 If the servo does not operate as described, inspect the servo unit check valve with reference to Section 21.

3 If the servo unit still fails to operate satisfactorily, the fault lies within the unit itself and it should be renewed.

Removal

4 Remove the master cylinder as described in Section 12.

5 On right-hand drive models, unscrew the bolts securing the cooling system expansion tank to the right-hand rear corner of the engine compartment. Release the spigot from the rubber grommet, and position the expansion tank to one side.

6 Working inside the vehicle, remove the driver's storage pocket from the bottom of the facia.

7 Undo the three screws and remove the lower facia panel from under the steering wheel.

8 Pull back the carpet and remove the two studs from the steering column universal joint cover. Pull off the upper clips and remove the cover.

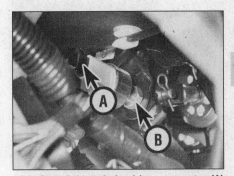
19.3 Stop-light switch wiring connector (A) and locknut (B)

20.9 Spring clip and clevis pin securing the brake pedal to the servo pushrod

20.11 Vacuum hose on the servo unit

Refitting

5 Refitting is a reversal of removal. On completion, start the engine and check the vacuum hose connections for signs of air leaks.

22 Anti-lock braking (ABS) system components - removal and refitting

Note: *After removing any of the ABS components, it is important to have the system tested for correct operation by a Rover dealer.*

Modulator block

Removal

9 Extract the spring clip and remove the clevis pin securing the brake pedal to the servo pushrod **(see illustration)**. Discard the clip and obtain a new one.
10 Unscrew the servo mounting nuts/bolts.
11 In the engine compartment, loosen the clip and disconnect the vacuum hose from the servo unit **(see illustration)**.
12 Withdraw the servo unit from the bulkhead and recover the gasket.
Caution: Do not attempt to adjust the domed nut on the end of the servo unit push rod as this is set in the factory and must not be altered.

Refitting

13 Prior to refitting, check the servo unit to vacuum hose sealing grommet for signs of damage or deterioration and renew if necessary.
14 Fit a new gasket to the rear of the servo unit and locate the unit on the bulkhead. **Note:** *Only fit a genuine gasket as it also acts as a spacer.* Make sure that the vacuum hose stub is uppermost on the servo unit, then fit the nuts and tighten to the specified torque.
15 Reconnect the vacuum hose and tighten the clip.
16 Inside the vehicle, reconnect the servo pushrod to the brake pedal, then apply a little grease to the clevis pin and insert it through the pedal. Secure with the new clip.
17 Refit the steering column universal joint cover and secure with the clips and studs.
18 Refit the lower facia panel and tighten the screws.
19 Refit the driver's storage pocket.

20 Refit the cooling system expansion tank and tighten the mounting bolts to the specified torque.
21 Refit the master cylinder with reference to Section 12.

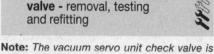

21 Vacuum servo unit check valve - removal, testing and refitting

Note: *The vacuum servo unit check valve is only available as part of the vacuum hose assembly. Do not try to remove the valve from the hose.*

Removal

1 Ease the hose connection from the vacuum servo unit taking care not to damage the sealing grommet.
2 Loosen the clip and disconnect the vacuum hose from the inlet manifold then withdraw the hose assembly from the engine compartment.

Testing

3 Examine the hose for damage, splits, cracks or general deterioration. Make sure that the check valve is working correctly by blowing through the hose from the servo unit connection end. Air should flow in this direction but not when blown through from the inlet manifold union. Renew the hose and check valve assembly if at all suspect.
4 Examine the servo unit sealing grommet for signs of damage or deterioration and renew if necessary.

1 Disconnect the battery negative (earth) lead (see Chapter 5A).
2 Apply the handbrake, then jack up the front of the vehicle and support it on axle stands (see *"Jacking and Vehicle Support"*). Remove both front wheels.
3 On left-hand drive models, unscrew the bolts securing the cooling system expansion tank to the right-hand rear corner of the engine compartment. Release the spigot from the rubber grommet, and position the expansion tank to one side.
4 On models manufactured from May 1997 onwards, connect a bleed tube to the right-hand front brake caliper and pump the brake pedal to drain the hydraulic fluid from the reservoir. Repeat the procedure on the left-hand front brake caliper. On earlier models place a piece of polythene over the fluid reservoir filler neck and tighten the cap onto it. This will minimise the loss of fluid from the brake pipes. As an added precaution, place absorbent rags beneath the modulator brake pipe unions.
5 Disconnect the wiring multiplug from the modulator block by first lifting the locking clip **(see illustrations)**.
6 On early models, unscrew the nut and disconnect the earth lead.
7 Wipe clean the area around the brake pipe unions then make a note of how the pipes are arranged for reference when refitting. Unscrew the union nuts and carefully withdraw the pipes **(see illustration)**. Plug or

22.5a Lift the locking clip . . .

22.5b . . . then unhook the wiring multiplug from the ABS modulator block

22.7 ABS modulator block and brake pipe unions

tape over the pipe ends and valve orifices to minimise the loss of brake fluid and to prevent the entry of dirt into the system. Wash off any spilt fluid immediately with warm water.

8 Unscrew the modulator mounting nuts and withdraw the unit from the mounting bracket. Note that on later models it is only necessary to loosen the mounting nuts and withdraw the modulator upwards from the location slots. Remove the mounting rubbers and renew them if necessary.

Caution: Do not attempt to dismantle the modulator block assembly.

Refitting

9 Refitting is a reversal of removal, but tighten the mounting nuts and brake pipe union nuts to the specified torque. On completion top up and bleed the hydraulic system as described in Section 2 and *"Weekly checks"*.

Front wheel sensor

Removal

10 Apply the handbrake, then jack up the front of the vehicle and support it on axle stands (see *"Jacking and Vehicle Support"*). Remove the relevant front wheel.

11 From inside the engine compartment, disconnect the relevant sensor wiring connector located beneath the ABS modulator bracket or under the servo unit.

12 Disconnect the wiring multiplug, then release the wiring from the grommets in the inner wing panel and on the front suspension strut.

13 Using a Torx key, undo the sensor mounting screws and remove it from the hub carrier.

14 Check the rubber grommets for wear and damage and renew them if necessary.

Refitting

15 Refitting is a reversal of removal, but clean the sensor and hub mating surfaces and tighten the mounting screws to the specified torque.

Rear wheel sensor

Removal

16 Chock the front wheels, then jack up the rear of the vehicle and support on axle stands (see *"Jacking and Vehicle Support"*). Remove the appropriate wheel.

17 Trace the wiring back from the sensor to the wiring connector then free the connector from its retaining clips and disconnect it.

18 Unscrew and remove the bolts from the sensor wiring supports.

19 Unscrew the bolt securing the sensor wiring bracket to the sensor cover, then unbolt and remove the cover **(see illustration)**.

20 Using a Torx key, unscrew the sensor mounting screws and remove the sensor from the hub adaptor.

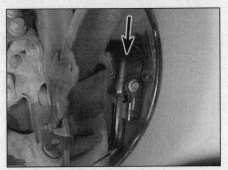

22.19 ABS sensor and cover on a rear brake

Refitting

21 Refitting is a reversal of removal, but clean the sensor and hub adaptor mating surfaces and tighten the mounting screws to the specified torque.

Reluctor rings

22 The reluctor rings are not available as separate items. The front rings are an integral part of the outer constant velocity joint assembly and the rear rings are an integral part of the rear hub.

23 The front reluctor rings are situated on the outer constant velocity joint and the rear reluctor rings are part of the stub axle assembly. Examine the rings for signs of damage such as chipped or missing teeth and renew as necessary.

ABS ECU

Removal

24 The ECU is attached to the modulator. First remove the modulator as described earlier in this Section.

25 Remove the rubber mounting from the spigot, then unscrew the spigot using a Torx key.

26 Unscrew the small screws, again using a Torx key, then separate the ECU from the modulator and disconnect the multiplugs.

27 With the ECU removed, cover the modulator aperture with clean lint-free cloth to prevent entry of any foreign matter.

Refitting

28 Connect the multiplugs and locate the ECU on the modulator.

29 Screw in the spigot but **do not** tighten it at this stage.

30 Insert the small screws and tighten them to the specified torque using the Torx key.

31 Tighten the spigot to the specified torque.

32 Locate the mounting rubber on the spigot.

33 Refit the ECU as described earlier in this Section.

Relays

34 Both the solenoid relay and return pump relay are located in the modulator block

assembly. To gain access to them, undo the relay cover retaining screw and lift off the cover. Either relay can then be simply pulled out of position. Refer to Chapter 12 for further information on relays.

---

23 Vacuum pump (diesel engine models) - removal and refitting

Removal

1 The brake vacuum pump for diesel engines is located on the rear of the alternator **(see illustration)**. First remove the alternator as described in Chapter 5A.

2 With the alternator on the bench, loosen the clip and disconnect the oil return hose from the vacuum pump.

3 Unscrew the union nut and disconnect the oil feed pipe from the vacuum pump.

4 Unscrew the mounting bolts, and withdraw the vacuum pump from the alternator.

Refitting

5 Wipe clean the mating faces of the alternator and vacuum pump.

6 Locate the pump on the alternator then insert the mounting bolts and tighten to the specified torque.

7 Fit the oil feed pipe and hand-tighten the union nut. **Do not** fully tighten the nut until the pipe has been positioned when refitting the alternator.

8 Reconnect the oil return hose and tighten the clip.

9 Refit the alternator with reference to Chapter 5A.

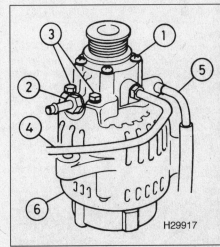

H29917

23.1 On diesel engine models the brake vacuum pump is located on the rear of the alternator

1 Vacuum pump
2 Vacuum stub to servo unit
3 Vacuum pump mounting bolts
4 Oil feed pipe
5 Oil return hose
6 Alternator

9

24 Vacuum pump (diesel engine models) - testing and overhaul

Note: *A vacuum gauge will be required for this check.*

1 The operation of the braking system vacuum pump can be checked using a vacuum gauge.

2 Disconnect the vacuum pipe from the pump, and connect the gauge to the pump union using a suitable length of hose.

3 Start the engine and allow it to idle, then measure the vacuum created by the pump. As a guide, after one minute, a minimum of approximately 500 mm Hg should be recorded. If the vacuum registered is significantly less than this, it is likely that the pump is faulty.

4 Overhaul of the vacuum pump is not possible, since no components are available separately for it. If faulty, the complete pump assembly must be renewed.

Chapter 10
Suspension and steering

Contents

Degrees of difficulty

Easy, suitable for novice with little experience	Fairly easy, suitable for beginner with some experience	Fairly difficult, suitable for competent DIY mechanic	Difficult, suitable for experienced DIY mechanic	Very difficult, suitable for expert DIY or professional

Specifications

Front suspension

Type .... Fully independent, double wishbone with upper and lower control arms. Gas-filled shock absorber and coil spring assembly located on fork to lower control arm. Anti-roll bar fitted to all models.

Rear suspension

Type .... Fully independent, by trailing arms with transverse lateral links, suspension struts with coil springs and integral shock absorbers

Wheel bearings

Endfloat at hub (front and rear) .... 0.0 to 0.05 mm

Steering

Type .... Rack and pinion, power-assisted steering standard on all models
Turns lock-to-lock 3.48

Wheel alignment and steering angles

All measurements are with vehicle at kerb weight
Toe setting:
  Front .... 0° ± 0° 8'
  Rear .... 0° 6' ± 0° 12' toe-in each side
Camber angle:
  Front .... 0° ± 1°
  Rear .... 0° 55' ± 1° positive
Castor angle:
  Front .... 1° 28' ± 1° positive
Steering axis inclination (SAI) or kingpin inclination (KPI) .... 10° 41' ± 1°
Outer wheel toe setting with inner wheel at 20° .... 18° 33'

Tyres

Type .... Tubeless, steel-braced radial

Size:	Standard	Option
1.4 litre petrol	175/65 - R14T	N/A
1.6 litre petrol	185/60 - R14V	185/55 - R15V
2.0 litre petrol	195/55 - R15H	N/A
2.0 litre Diesel	185/65 - R14T	195/55 - R15H

Pressures .... *See Page 0•18*

Roadwheels

	Steel	Alloy
Type . . . . Steel (standard) or alloy (optional)		
Size:		
All models except 2.0 litre petrol	5 x 14	5½ x 15
2.0 litre petrol	5½ x 15	5½ x 15

Torque wrench settings

	Nm	lbf ft
Front suspension		
Anti-roll bar clamp bolts	22	16
Anti-roll bar link nuts	22	16
Brake hose bracket	10	7
Fork to shock absorber	45	33
Hub carrier to lower arm	49	36
Lower arm front pivot bolt	65	48
Lower arm rear pivot bolt	85	63
Lower balljoint nut	49	36
Shock absorber/coil spring assembly fork to lower arm	65	48
Shock absorber/coil spring assembly upper mounting nut	40	30
Shock absorber/coil spring assembly self-locking piston nut	30	22
Upper arm bracket to body nuts	65	48
Upper balljoint nut	39	29
Rear suspension		
Anti-roll bar left-hand link to anti-roll bar	14	10
Anti-roll bar mounting clamp bolt	14	10
Anti-roll bar right-hand link to lower arm	45	33
Compensator arm to trailing arm	45	33
Handbrake cable to trailing arm	22	16
Hub nut	181	134
Lower arm to body	47	35
Lower arm to trailing arm	47	35
Shock absorber mounting plate	38	28
Shock absorber to mounting plate	29	21
Trailing arm compensator bolt	45	33
Trailing arm to body	78	58
Upper arm to trailing arm	47	35
Upper arm to body	78	58
Steering		
Power steering pump:		
Adjuster clamp bolt (1.4 and 1.6 litre petrol)	25	19
Gearchange linkage to rear beam (1.4 and 1.6 litre petrol)	24	18
Mounting bracket bolts (1.4 and 1.6 litre petrol)	25	19
Outlet hose union (1.4 and 1.6 litre petrol)	55	41
Pulley bolts (1.4 and 1.6 litre petrol)	9	7
High pressure hose to PAS pump (2.0 litre diesel)	55	41
PAS pump to coolant pump bolts (2.0 litre diesel)	25	19
Pulley (2.0 litre diesel)	9	7
Hose to gear (2.0 litre petrol)	37	27
Pipe bracket to coolant rail (2.0 litre petrol)	8	6
Pump banjo union bolt (2.0 litre petrol):		
With air conditioning	20	15
Without air conditioning	25	19
Pump pipe brackets to cylinder head (2.0 litre petrol)	25	19
Steering column lower clamp bolts	22	16
Steering column universal joint bolts	28	21
Steering column upper bracket nuts	16	12
Steering gear clamp bolts	38	28
Steering gear feed pipe union	37	27
Steering gear pinion flange bolts	58	43
Steering gear return pipe union	28	21
Steering pipe clip	9	7
Steering wheel nut	49	36
Track rod end:		
Retaining nut	39	29
Locknut	45	33
Roadwheels		
Roadwheel nuts	110	81

1 General information and precautions

General information

The front suspension is of fully independent design with upper and lower control arms, shock absorber/coil spring assemblies and an anti-roll bar **(see illustration)**.

The fully independent rear suspension is of double wishbone type, utilising pressed steel trailing arms which have the roadwheel stub axles bolted into their rear ends **(see illustration)**. These are located longitudinally on the vehicle underbody via a large rubber bush which is situated towards the centre of each arm. Each trailing arm assembly is located transversely by three lateral links, which utilise rubber mounting bushes at both their inner and outer ends. The rear suspension struts incorporate coil springs and integral telescopic shock absorbers and are mounted onto the rear lower lateral link via a rubber mounting bush.

All models are fitted with a power-assisted rack-and-pinion steering gear. The hydraulic system is powered by a belt-driven pump, which is driven from the crankshaft pulley. The hydraulic fluid is cooled by passing it through a single bore cooling tube located in front of the radiator. The power steering is speed-sensitive with more assistance at low speeds, and reduced assistance at higher speeds to give a positive feel for cruising. This system uses a hydraulic control valve incorporated in the vehicle speed sensor on the transmission.

An airbag is fitted as standard and is mounted in the centre of the steering wheel. See Chapter 12 for full details.

The steering column has a universal joint fitted towards the lower end of its length and its bottom end is clamped to a second universal joint, which is in turn clamped to the steering gear pinion.

The steering gear is mounted onto the engine compartment bulkhead and is connected by two track rods, with balljoints at their outer ends, to the steering arms projecting rearwards from the hub carriers. The track rod ends are threaded to facilitate adjustment.

Precautions

The driveshaft hub and stub axle nuts are very tight - ensure the car is securely supported when loosening and tightening them.

A number of precautions must be observed when working on the steering components of vehicles equipped with airbags, and these are listed in Chapter 12.

2 Front hub carrier - removal, overhaul and refitting

Note: *This Section includes renewal of the front suspension lower balljoint.*

Removal

1 Apply the handbrake, then loosen the wheel nuts on the relevant wheel and jack up the front of the vehicle. Support the vehicle on axle stands (see *"Jacking and Vehicle Support"*). Remove the roadwheel.

2 Have an assistant apply the footbrake. Using a socket and extension bar, loosen only the driveshaft nut. Unscrew and remove the nut. If the nut is damaged, obtain a new one for refitting.

Caution: Be careful! the nut is very tight.

3 Unbolt the brake hose bracket from the hub carrier **(see illustration)**, then unbolt the brake caliper bracket from the hub carrier and suspend the caliper (with pads) and bracket to one side with a length of wire attached to the coil spring. If preferred, the caliper and pads can be removed as described in Chapter 9, then the bracket unbolted.

4 Remove the brake disc as described in Chapter 9.

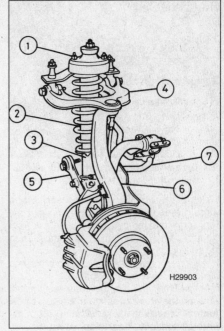

1.1 Front suspension components

1	Strut upper mounting	4	Upper control arm
2	Coil spring	5	Lower control arm
3	Shock absorber	6	Hub carrier
		7	Anti-roll bar

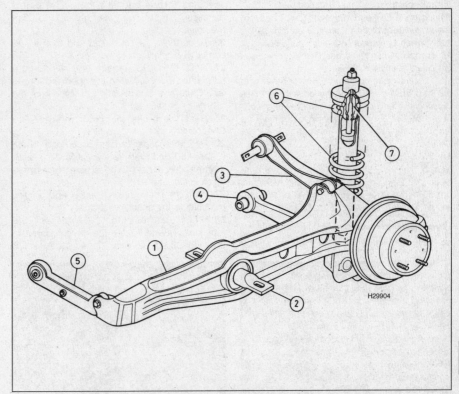

1.2 Rear suspension components

1	Trailing arm	4	Rear lower link	6	Coil spring and shock absorber
2	Compliance bush	5	Front (compensator) link	
3	Rear upper link			7	Bump stop

10

2.3 Brake hose bracket on the hub carrier

5 Unbolt the ABS wheel sensor wiring support **(see illustration)**, then unscrew the Torx screw and remove the wheel sensor from the hub carrier leaving the wiring attached to the sensor.
6 Disconnect the track rod end from the hub carrier with reference to Section 21.
7 Extract the split pin, then unscrew the nut securing the upper control arm balljoint to the hub carrier until it is flush with the end of the balljoint stud **(see illustration)**.
8 Using a balljoint removal tool, separate the upper control arm from the top of the hub carrier.
9 Extract the split pin, then unscrew the nut securing the lower control arm to the hub carrier until it is flush with the end of the balljoint stud.
10 Using a balljoint removal tool, separate the lower control arm from the bottom of the hub carrier. Unscrew and remove the nut.
11 Support the hub carrier, then unscrew and remove the driveshaft nut.
12 Carefully pull the hub carrier together with the hub from the end of the driveshaft, while tapping the end of the driveshaft with a soft-faced mallet. Support the driveshaft with a length of wire to prevent damage to the inner CV joint.
13 With the hub carrier assembly on the bench, remove the hub with reference to Section 3 then undo the screws and withdraw the splash guard. **Note:** *Removal of the hub will necessitate renewal of the bearings.*

Overhaul

14 Check the lower balljoint for excessive

wear. If evident, it can be renewed, however special tools are required and the work should be carried out by a Rover dealer or suitably-equipped garage.
15 Check the balljoint rubber dust cover for damage and splits. If evident, the cover can be renewed separately. Prise off the circlips and remove the old dust cover, then clean the seating and fit the new cover. Secure with the new circlips.

Refitting

16 Before reassembly, clean all the components and examine them for damage.
17 Locate the splash guard on the hub carrier making sure that the location peg engages with the hole, then tighten the screws securely.
18 Refit the hub with reference to Section 3.
19 Apply a little grease to the splines on the driveshaft, then locate the hub carrier together with the hub on the driveshaft splines.
20 Locate the lower end of the hub carrier on the balljoint stud on the lower arm and screw on the nut. Tighten the nut to the specified torque then align the split pin holes and fit a new split pin. If necessary the nut may be tightened to align the holes.
21 Locate the upper end of the hub carrier on the balljoint stud on the upper arm and screw on the nut loosely.
22 Tighten the upper balljoint nut to the specified torque and fit a new split pin. If necessary, the nut may be tightened to align the holes.
23 Reconnect the track rod end to the hub carrier with reference to Section 21.
24 Refit the ABS sensor and wiring and tighten the Torx screw to the specified torque (see Chapter 9 Specifications). Make sure the wiring is not twisted.
25 Refit the brake disc with reference to Chapter 9.
26 Refit the caliper bracket together with the caliper and pads with reference to Chapter 9. Tighten the bolts to the specified torques given in Chapter 9.
27 Refit the brake hose bracket and tighten the bolts to the specified torque.
28 While an assistant depresses the footbrake, fit and tighten the driveshaft nut to the specified torque (see Chapter 8

Specifications). Stake the nut collar into the groove in the driveshaft.
29 Refit the roadwheel, lower the vehicle to the ground then tighten the nuts to the specified torque.

3 Front hub bearings - checking and renewal

Checking

1 Apply the handbrake, then jack up the front of the vehicle and support it on axle stands (see *"Jacking and Vehicle Support"*).
2 Spin the wheel by hand and check for noise and roughness in the wheel bearings indicating excessive wear.
3 For a more thorough check, remove the brake disc as described in Chapter 9, then measure the amount of side play in the bearing. To do this, a dial gauge should be fixed so that its probe is in contact with the wheel contact face of the hub. Attempt to move the hub in and out, and check that the play is within the limits given in the Specifications. Excessive play indicates wear in the bearing, and it must be renewed.

Renewal

Note: *Removal of the bearing renders it unserviceable for further use.*
4 Remove the front hub carrier as described in Section 2.
5 Using a screwdriver, prise out the protector ring from the rear of the hub carrier.
6 The hub must now be pressed from the hub carrier before pressing out the bearing. To successfully carry out this work it will be necessary to support the bearing housing while the hub and bearing are being removed. If the necessary equipment is not available, have the work carried out by a Rover dealer or engineering works. Note also that the outer bearing race will have to be removed from the hub before fitting the hub to the new bearings.
7 With the hub removed, undo the screws and remove the splash shield from the hub carrier.
8 Using circlip pliers, extract the circlip from the groove in the hub carrier.
9 Support the hub and press out the bearing. **Note:** *The bearing will be damaged during this process and must not be re-used.*
10 Before installing the new bearing, thoroughly clean the hub and hub carrier.
11 Support the hub carrier with the circlip groove uppermost, then press the new bearing fully into position using a metal tube or adaptor on the outer race. Fit the circlip making sure that it is fully engaged with the groove.
12 Fit the splash shield and tighten the screws.
13 Support the hub with the wheel studs facing downwards, then locate the new bearing and hub carrier on the hub making sure it is the correct way round.
14 Using a suitable metal tube located only

2.5 ABS wheel sensor wiring support on the hub carrier

2.7 Upper control arm balljoint and nut

on the inner race, press the bearing housing fully onto the hub.

15 Press the protector ring into the rear of the hub carrier.

16 Refit the hub carrier (Section 2).

4 Front shock absorber/ coil spring assembly - removal, overhaul and refitting

Removal

1 Apply the handbrake, then loosen the wheel nuts on the relevant wheel and jack up the front of the vehicle. Support the vehicle on axle stands (see *"Jacking and Vehicle Support"*). Remove the roadwheel.

2 Unbolt the brake hose bracket from the base of the shock absorber.

3 Disconnect the front anti-roll bar from the lower control arm with reference to Section 6.

4 Position a trolley jack under the lower control arm to support it when the shock absorber assembly is removed.

5 Unscrew and remove the pinch bolt securing the fork to the bottom of the shock absorber assembly **(see illustration)**.

6 Unscrew and remove the bolt securing the fork to the lower control arm noting which way round it is fitted, then withdraw the fork **(see illustration)**. If the fork is tight on the shock absorber, tap it free with a hammer. **Note:** *The forks are 'handed' on each side of the vehicle. The left-hand fork is marked VL and the right-hand fork is marked VR.*

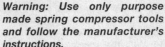

4.5 Pinch bolt securing the fork to the bottom of the shock absorber assembly

7 Open the bonnet. Support the shock absorber assembly from under the front wheel arch, then unscrew the upper mounting nuts from inside the engine compartment and withdraw the unit from under the wheel arch **(see illustrations)**.

> ⚠ *Warning: Do not unscrew the centre nut from the top of the shock absorber.*

Overhaul

Note: *Suitable coil spring compressor tools will be required for this operation.*

8 With the assembly on the bench, check the shock absorber for leaking fluid, dents, cracks or other obvious damage. Check the coil spring for chips or cracks which could cause premature failure and inspect the spring seats for hardness or general deterioration.

9 Clamp the lower end of the shock absorber assembly in a vice fitted with jaw protectors.

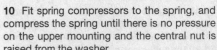

4.6 Bolt securing the fork to the lower control arm

10 Fit spring compressors to the spring, and compress the spring until there is no pressure on the upper mounting and the central nut is raised from the washer.

> ⚠ *Warning: Use only purpose made spring compressor tools and follow the manufacturer's instructions.*

11 Mark the relationship of the shock absorber assembly components to ensure correct reassembly. As the components are removed, lay them out in order to ensure correct refitting **(see illustration)**.

12 Unscrew the self-locking central nut from the top of the shock absorber assembly while holding the shaft stationary with a 5.0 mm Allen key **(see illustrations)**.

13 Remove the washer, upper mounting, collar, mounting plate, lower mounting rubber and upper spring seat **(see illustrations)**.

4.7a Unscrew the upper mounting nuts . . .

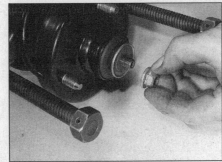

4.7b . . . and withdraw the shock absorber/coil spring assembly from under the wheel arch

4.11 Mark the spring and mounting in relation to each other

4.12a Unscrewing the central nut while holding the shaft stationary with an Allen key

4.12b Removing the central nut

4.13a Remove the washer . . .

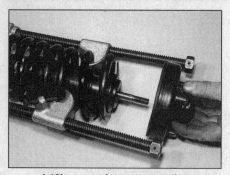

4.13b . . . and upper mounting

14 Remove the coil spring (with compressors fitted), followed by the dust cover, stop plate and bump stop (note which way round it is fitted) **(see illustrations)**. If the compressors are to be left in position on the coil spring, put the spring in a safe place away from the work area as a precaution.

15 With the shock absorber assembly now dismantled, examine all the components for wear and damage. Check the rubber components for deterioration. Examine the shock absorber for damage and signs of fluid leakage, and check the piston rod for pitting along its entire length. While holding it in an upright position, test the operation of the shock absorber by moving the rod through a full stroke, and then through short strokes of 50 to 100 mm. In both cases, the resistance felt should be smooth and continuous. If the resistance is jerky, or uneven, or if there is any visible sign of wear or damage to the shock absorber, renewal is necessary.

16 Renew the coil spring if it is damaged or distorted.

17 To reassemble the shock absorber, first extend the piston rod as far as it will go.

18 Fit the bump stop, stop plate and dust cover onto the piston rod, making sure that the bump stop is the correct way round (ie largest diameter uppermost).

19 Ensure that the coil spring is compressed sufficiently to enable the upper mounting components to be fitted, then fit the spring over the piston rod, ensuring that the lower end of the spring is correctly located on the lower spring seat **(see illustration)**.

20 Locate the upper spring seat on the coil spring, followed by the lower mounting rubber, mounting plate, collar, upper mounting rubber, washer and nut. Before tightening the nut position the components with the previously made marks aligned. Where new components are being fitted, transfer the marks from the old components.

21 Tighten the self-locking nut to the specified torque while holding the piston rod with an Allen key.

22 Release the compressors while guiding the spring ends onto the seats.

23 Remove the assembly from the vice.

Refitting

24 Manoeuvre the shock absorber assembly into position under the wheel arch, passing the mounting studs through the holes in the body turret. Refit the upper mounting nuts loosely, but do not fully tighten them at this stage.

25 Fit the fork to the bottom of the shock absorber, making sure that the alignment tab enters the slot in the fork. Insert the pinch bolt and screw on the nut loosely. **Note:** *The forks are 'handed' on each side of the vehicle. The left-hand fork is marked VL and the right-hand fork is marked VR.*

26 Locate the fork on the lower control arm, and insert the bolt with its head facing forwards. Screw on the nut loosely.

27 Using a trolley jack under the lower control arm, raise the front suspension until the weight of the vehicle is just supported.

28 Tighten the fork-to-shock absorber pinch bolt, upper mounting nuts and fork-to-lower control arm bolt to the specified torques.

29 Reconnect the front anti-roll bar to the lower control arm with reference to Section 6.

30 Refit the brake hose bracket to the base of the shock absorber and tighten the bolts.

31 Refit the roadwheel, lower the vehicle to the ground and tighten the bolts to the specified torque setting.

4.14a Remove the coil spring (with compressors fitted) . . .

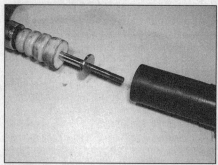

4.14b . . . followed by the dust cover . . .

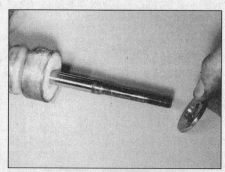

4.14c . . . stop plate . . .

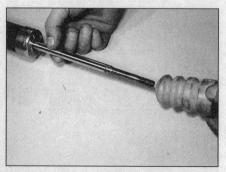

4.14d . . . and bump stop

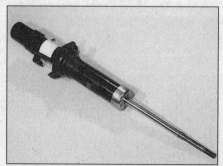

4.14e Front suspension shock absorber/coil spring assembly removed from the vehicle

4.19 Ensure that the lower end of the spring is correctly located on the lower spring seat

5 Front suspension upper and lower control arms - removal, overhaul and refitting

Upper control arm

Note: *The following paragraphs include the renewal of the front suspension upper balljoint.*

Removal

1 Remove the relevant front shock absorber/coil spring assembly as described in Section 4.

2 Position a trolley jack under the lower control arm to support the hub carrier when it is disconnected from the upper control arm.

3 Extract the split pin, then unscrew the nut securing the upper control arm to the hub carrier until it is flush with the end of the balljoint stud.

4 Using a balljoint removal tool, separate the upper control arm from the top of the hub carrier. Support the hub carrier, then unscrew and remove the nut.

5 From the top of the suspension turret inside the engine compartment, unscrew the upper control arm anchor nuts and withdraw the upper control arm and anchor assembly **(see illustration)** from under the wheel arch. Unscrew the nuts and remove the inner pivot bolts from the upper control arm. Note which way round the bolts are fitted; the head of the front bolt faces to the front and the head of the rear bolt faces to the rear.

Overhaul

6 If the inner pivot bushes are worn, remove the anchor from the body by unscrewing the nuts located in the engine compartment. Press the old bushes from the anchor, then press in the new bushes.

7 Check the upper balljoint for excessive wear. If evident, the complete upper control arm must be renewed.

8 Check the rubber dust cover for damage and splits. If evident, the cover can be renewed separately. Prise off the circlip and remove the old dust cover, then clean the seating and fit the new cover. Secure with the new circlip.

Refitting

9 Refitting is a reversal of removal, but tighten the nuts and bolts to the specified torque and delay fully tightening the fork-to-lower arm bolt and the upper arm inner pivot bolts until the weight of the vehicle is on the front suspension. Make sure that the pivot bolts are located with their heads facing away from each other. Fit a new split pin to the balljoint nut. Where necessary, tighten the nut further until the split pin hole is aligned with the serrations on the nut. **Note:** *The left- and right-hand upper control arms are different and must not be interchanged.* Have the front wheel alignment checked and adjusted at the earliest opportunity.

5.5 Front suspension upper control arm and anchor assembly

Lower control arm

Removal

10 Apply the handbrake, then loosen the wheel nuts on the relevant wheel and jack up the front of the vehicle. Support the vehicle on axle stands (see *"Jacking and Vehicle Support"*). Remove the roadwheel.

11 Unscrew the nut and disconnect the front anti-roll bar link from the lower control arm. Recover the rubber bush and washer **(see illustration).**

12 Unscrew and remove the bolt securing the shock absorber lower fork to the lower control arm, noting that its head is facing the front of the vehicle.

13 Extract the split pin, then unscrew the nut securing the lower control arm to the hub carrier until it is flush with the end of the balljoint stud.

14 Using a balljoint removal tool, separate the lower control arm from the bottom of the hub carrier. Unscrew and remove the nut.

15 Unscrew and remove the two bolts securing the anti-roll bar mounting to the subframe.

16 Unscrew the nut and remove the washer from the lower arm rear pivot. Discard the nut and obtain a new one **(see illustration).**

17 Unscrew and remove the front pivot bolt, then loosen the rear pivot bush bracket bolts sufficiently to allow the front bush to clear the subframe **(see illustration).**

18 Withdraw the lower control arm from under the wheel arch and recover the washer from the rear pivot. Note that the front face of the washer is marked FR.

Caution: The lower control arm is in two

5.16 Front suspension lower arm rear pivot nut

5.11 Nut securing the front anti-roll bar link to the lower control arm

sections bolted together. DO NOT attempt to separate the two sections.

Overhaul

19 Check the inner pivot and shock absorber fork rubber bushes for excessive wear including the bush in the rear bracket. The bushes may be renewed separately, however a press is required and the work should be carried out by a Rover dealer or suitably-equipped garage. After installation in the lower arm, the edges of the bush outer casing must be flush with the arm.

Refitting

20 Refitting is a reversal of the removal procedure but renew the inner pivot nut and make sure that the rear pivot washer is positioned with the face marked FR facing the front. Tighten all nuts and bolts to the specified torque, however delay fully tightening the inner pivot bolt and nut and the fork-to-lower arm bolt until the weight of the vehicle is on the suspension. Smear rubber grease to the face of the anti-roll bar washer before refitting it. Have the front wheel alignment checked and adjusted at the earliest opportunity.

6 Front suspension anti-roll bar - removal and refitting

Removal

1 Apply the handbrake, then loosen the wheel nuts on both front wheels and jack up the front of the vehicle. Support the vehicle on axle stands (see *"Jacking and Vehicle Support"*).

5.17 Front suspension lower arm front pivot bolt

10

6.3 Nut securing the anti-roll bar to the link on the lower control arm

Remove both front roadwheels.

2 Mark the anti-roll bar for position as an aid to refitting it.

3 Working on each side at a time, unscrew the nut from the top of the links on the lower arms while holding the links stationary with a spanner on the flats provided. Remove the nuts, cupped washers and rubber bushes noting that the cupped washers are located with their convex sides in contact with the bushes **(see illustration)**.

4 Raise the anti-roll bar from the links, then unscrew the lower nuts and remove the links from the lower arms. Recover the cupped washers and rubber bushes.

5 Detach the exhaust front downpipe from the exhaust manifold with reference to Chapter 4.

6 Beneath the vehicle, unhook the rubber mounting then lower the downpipe to the ground.

7 Prise the gearchange linkage balljoints from the levers on the transmission with reference to Chapter 7.

8 Unbolt the gearchange linkage bracket and lower it onto the exhaust downpipe.

9 Unscrew the bolts from the anti-roll bar mounting clamps on the subframe and remove the clamps. Note that the clamps are marked with an arrow facing the front of the vehicle **(see illustration)**.

10 Manoeuvre the anti-roll bar over the gearchange linkage and withdraw from the vehicle.

11 Note the positions of the mounting rubbers then pull them from the anti-roll bar.

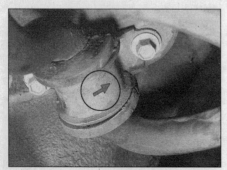

6.9 The front anti-roll bar clamps are marked with front-facing arrows for correct positioning

12 Check the anti-roll bar and mounting components for damage and wear and renew as necessary.

Refitting

13 Smear the bores of the mounting rubbers with rubber grease or similar lubricant, then fit them in their previously noted positions on the anti-roll bar. Make sure that the split ends of the rubbers will face the front of the vehicle when the anti-roll bar is fitted.

14 Refit the links to the lower arms together with the rubber bushes and cupped washers making sure that the convex side of the washers contact the bushes. Tighten the lower nuts to the specified torque. Refit the lower washers and rubber bushes to the links.

15 Manoeuvre the anti-roll bar in position and engage it with the links, then refit the upper washers and rubber bushes. Refit the nuts and tighten to the specified torque.

16 Refit the clamps on the anti-roll bar making sure the arrows point to the front of the vehicle. Insert the bolts and tighten to the specified torque.

17 Refit the gearchange linkage bracket and tighten the mounting bolts to the specified torque (see Chapter 7 Specifications).

18 Lightly grease the gearchange balljoints then press them onto the transmission levers.

19 Refit the exhaust downpipe to the manifold with reference to Chapter 4, and reconnect the rubber mounting.

20 Refit the wheels and lower the vehicle; tighten the nuts to the specified torque.

7 Rear hub and bearings - checking, removal and refitting

Note: *The bearing is a sealed, pre-adjusted and pre-lubricated, double-row tapered-roller type and is intended to last the vehicle's entire service life without maintenance or attention. The bearing is an integral part of the hub and cannot be purchased separately. If renewal of the bearing is necessary, the complete hub assembly must be renewed as a unit.*

Checking

1 Chock the front wheels, then jack up the rear of the vehicle and support on axle stands (see *"Jacking and Vehicle Support"*). Release the handbrake.

2 Spin the wheel by hand and check for noise and roughness in the wheel bearings indicating excessive wear.

3 For a more thorough check, remove the brake drum or disc (as applicable) as described in Chapter 9, then measure the amount of side play in the bearing. To do this, a dial gauge should be fixed so that its probe is in contact with the wheel contact face of the hub. Attempt to move the hub in and out, and check that the play is within the limits given in the Specifications. Excessive play indicates wear in the bearing, and the rear hub must be renewed complete.

Removal

4 Chock the front wheels, then jack up the rear of the vehicle and support it on axle stands. Remove the appropriate rear roadwheel.

5 Remove the rear brake drum or disc (as applicable) with reference to Chapter 9.

6 Prise out the cap from the centre of the hub assembly, then tap up the staking securing the hub retaining nut to the groove in the stub axle using a screwdriver or small cold chisel.

7 Unscrew and remove the hub nut. Note that the nut is tightened to a high torque; make sure the vehicle is adequately supported while loosening the nut.

8 Pull the hub assembly from the stub axle and recover the toothed washer. Discard the hub nut and obtain a new one.

Refitting

9 Prior to refitting the hub, inspect the stub axle for signs of wear or scoring and, if necessary, renew it.

10 Apply a thin smear of grease to the hub bearing seal and refit the hub assembly. Refit the toothed washer, ensuring that its tooth locates with the groove in the stub axle.

11 Screw on the new hub nut and tighten it to the specified torque, then stake the nut into the stub axle groove.

12 Tap the hub centre cap into the hub.

13 Refit the brake drum or disc (as applicable) with reference to Chapter 9.

14 Refit the roadwheel, then lower the vehicle to the ground and tighten the roadwheel nuts to the specified torque.

15 Apply the footbrake firmly several times, then check the handbrake operation and adjustment with reference to Chapter 9.

8 Rear stub axle - removal and refitting

Removal

1 Remove the rear hub assembly (see Section 7).

2 On models fitted with rear drum brakes remove the rear brake shoes and disconnect the handbrake cable from the trailing shoe with reference to Chapter 9. Undo the bolts securing the handbrake cable and brake hose brackets to the trailing arm, then use a 12 mm ring spanner to compress the handbrake cable retaining clip and withdraw the cable from the backplate. Remove the four bolts securing the backplate to the trailing arm and carefully ease the backplate assembly outwards and off the end of the stub axle. Position the backplate assembly out of the way of the stub axle and tie it to the rear suspension unit coil spring using a piece of wire. Place a strong elastic band over the wheel cylinder pistons to prevent them coming out.

3 On models fitted with rear disc brakes, undo the four disc shield retaining bolts and remove the shield from the trailing arm.

4 On all models, using a socket and extension bar, undo the large stub axle retaining nut from the rear of the trailing arm assembly **(see illustration)**.

5 Unscrew and remove the four Torx bolts securing the stub axle mounting plate to the trailing arm assembly, then withdraw the stub axle and remove it from the vehicle.

6 Examine the stub axle spindle and mounting plate for signs of wear or damage such as scoring or cracking. If damaged, the stub axle must be renewed.

Refitting

7 Refitting is a reverse of the removal procedure, tightening all nuts and bolts to the specified torque settings.

9 Rear suspension strut - removal, overhaul and refitting

Removal

1 Remove the rear seat backrest as described in Chapter 11.

2 On Hatchback models, open the tailgate, release the straps and lift out the parcel tray, then remove the parcel tray support panel from the relevant side by undoing the screw and releasing the clips.

3 Remove the luggage compartment side trim with reference to Chapter 11.

4 Chock the front wheels, then jack up the rear of the vehicle and support on axle stands (see "Jacking and Vehicle Support"). Remove the relevant rear wheel.

5 Support the weight of the rear lower lateral link and trailing arm with a trolley jack.

6 Inside the vehicle, remove the rubber cover from the top of the rear suspension strut, then unscrew the two upper mounting nuts **(see illustration)**.

7 Unscrew the bolt securing the rear lower lateral link to the trailing arm.

8 Unscrew the bolt securing the rear suspension strut to the rear lower lateral link, then release the strut from the link and manoeuvre it out from under the rear wheel arch **(see illustration)**.

Overhaul

Note: Suitable coil spring compressor tools will be required for this operation.

9 With the assembly on the bench, clean it thoroughly then check the shock absorber for leaking fluid, dents, cracks or other obvious damage. Check the coil spring and seats for damage or general deterioration.

10 Clamp the lower end of the strut assembly in a vice fitted with jaw protectors.

11 Fit spring compressors to the spring, and compress the spring until there is no pressure on the upper mounting and the central nut is raised from the washer.

 Warning: Use only purpose made spring compressor tools and follow the manufacturer's instructions.

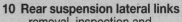

8.4 Large nut retaining the rear stub axle to the trailing arm

12 Note the relationship of the shock absorber assembly components to ensure correct reassembly. As the components are removed, lay them out in order to ensure correct refitting.

13 Unscrew the upper mounting retaining nut whilst retaining the strut piston with an Allen key.

14 Remove the nut and washer followed by the mounting plate assembly, noting the correct fitted positions of the mounting rubbers and spacer, and the upper spring rubber damper. Remove the coil spring then lift the dust seal and cover off the damper and slide the damper stop plate and rubber stop off the strut piston.

15 With the shock absorber assembly now dismantled, examine all the components for wear and damage. Check the rubber components for deterioration. Examine the shock absorber for damage and signs of fluid leakage, and check the piston rod for pitting along its entire length. While holding it in an upright position, test the operation of the shock absorber by moving the rod through a full stroke, and then through short strokes of 50 to 100 mm. In both cases, the resistance felt should be smooth and continuous. If the resistance is jerky, or uneven, or if there is any visible sign of wear or damage to the shock absorber, renewal is necessary.

16 Renew the coil spring if it is damaged or distorted.

17 Reassembly is a reversal of the removal procedure. Ensure that the spring ends are correctly located in the upper and lower seats and that the upper mounting plate retaining nut is tightened to the specified torque setting.

9.6 Removing the rubber cover from the top of the rear suspension strut

Refitting

18 Prior to refitting, examine the rear lower lateral link mounting bushes and renew any which are worn or damaged.

19 Ensure the rubber seal is in position on the upper mounting plate then refit the suspension strut, and screw on the upper mounting nuts hand-tight at this stage.

20 With the nut on the bottom of the strut facing forwards, offer up the lower lateral link and refit the strut mounting bolt followed by the lower lateral link bolts. Tighten the bolts loosely at this stage.

21 Raise the trolley jack so that the rear suspension is supporting weight of the vehicle, then tighten the upper mounting nuts and lower bolts to the specified torque setting. Refit the rubber cover to the upper mounting and remove the trolley jack from under the trailing arm.

22 Refit the roadwheel, then lower the vehicle to the ground and tighten the roadwheel nuts to the specified torque.

23 Refit the luggage compartment side trim and rear seat backrest with reference to Chapter 11.

24 On Hatchback models, refit the parcel tray.

10 Rear suspension lateral links - removal, inspection and refitting

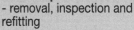

Removal

1 Chock the front wheels, then jack up the rear of the vehicle and support on axle stands (see "Jacking and Vehicle Support"). Remove the relevant rear roadwheel.

Front (compensator) link

2 Mark the position of the lateral link body pivot bolt in relation to the body. This mark can then be used as a guide on refitting and will ensure correct rear wheel alignment **(see illustrations)**.

3 Unscrew and remove both the pivot bolts securing the front lateral link to the body and trailing arm and remove the link from the vehicle. Note that the link has an arrow and the word UP marked on it **(see illustration)**.

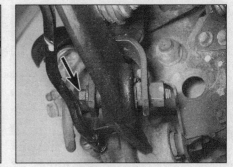

9.8 Bolt securing the rear suspension strut to the rear lower lateral link

10

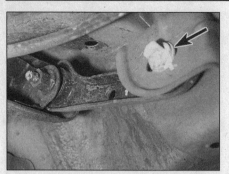

10.2a Front (compensator) link showing elongated hole (arrowed) for adjustment of rear wheel alignment

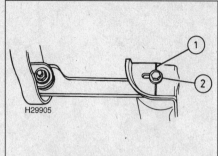

10.2b Mark a centre line (1) before removing the bolt (2)

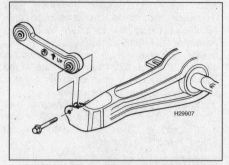

10.3 Front (compensator) link is marked with an arrow and the word UP for correct positioning

Rear upper link

4 Use a trolley jack to support the weight of the trailing arm.
5 Unscrew and remove the pivot bolt securing the rear upper lateral link to the trailing arm assembly **(see illustration)**.
6 Undo the two bolts securing the inner mounting to the vehicle body and remove the link from the vehicle **(see illustration)**.

Rear lower link

7 Use a trolley jack to support the weight of the trailing arm.
8 On models equipped with ABS, undo the bolts securing the wheel sensor wiring lead bracket to the lower arm and release the wiring.
9 On models with a rear anti-roll bar, unscrew the bolt and disconnect the anti-roll bar.

10 Unscrew and remove the pivot bolts securing the lower rear lateral link to the crossmember, strut and trailing arm **(see illustrations)**. Withdraw the link from under the vehicle. Note that the rear faces of the link is marked with an L or R to indicate the left- or right-hand side.

Inspection

11 Examine the link and bushes for damage and wear and renew if necessary.
12 The bushes are a press fit in the link and can be pressed out and in using a vice and two suitable-sized tubular drifts, such as sockets (one bearing on the hard outer edge of the bush and another bearing against the edge of the link).
13 When renewing the inner bush on the rear

upper lateral link, mark the position of the bush mounting plate in relation to the lateral link before removing the worn bush. Fit the new bush so that the mounting plate is in the same position in relation to the lateral link **(see illustration)**.
14 When renewing the bushes of the rear lower link, make sure that the movement cut-outs are positioned as shown **(see illustration)**.

Refitting

15 Refitting is the reverse of removal, but delay fully tightening the pivot bolts until the weight of the vehicle is on the rear suspension. Have the rear wheel alignment checked and adjusted by a Rover dealer or tyre specialist.

10.5 Bolt securing the rear suspension upper link to the trailing arm

10.6 Rear suspension upper link inner mounting

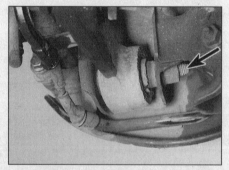

10.10a Bolt securing the rear suspension lower link to the trailing arm

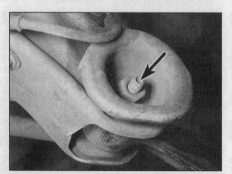

10.10b Bolt securing the rear suspension lower link to the crossmember

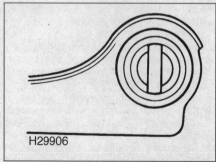

10.13 The rear suspension upper link inner bush must be positioned as shown

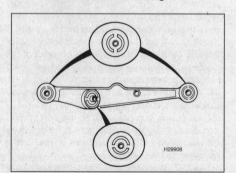

10.14 The rear suspension lower link bushes must be positioned as shown

11 Rear suspension trailing arm - removal and refitting

Removal

1 Chock the front wheels, then jack up the rear of the vehicle and support on axle stands (see *"Jacking and Vehicle Support"*). Remove the relevant rear wheel.
2 Remove the rear hub as described in Section 7.

Non-ABS models

3 Undo the bolts and remove the clips securing the handbrake cable and brake hose brackets to the trailing arm. Remove the four bolts securing the backplate to the trailing arm and carefully ease the backplate assembly outwards and off the end of the stub axle. Position the backplate out of the way of the stub axle and tie it to the rear suspension unit coil spring using a piece of wire.

ABS models

4 Remove the two brake caliper shield retaining screws and remove the shield from the caliper.
5 Slacken and remove the bolts securing the handbrake cable and brake hose retaining clamps to the trailing arm. Undo the two bolts securing the caliper mounting bracket to the trailing arm and slide the caliper off the disc. Tie the caliper to the rear suspension strut coil spring to avoid placing any strain on the hydraulic hose or handbrake cable.
6 Remove the ABS rear wheel sensor with reference to Chapter 9.

All models

7 Unscrew and remove the three pivot bolts securing the front lateral link, rear lower lateral link and rear upper lateral link to the trailing arm.
8 Remove the two bolts securing the trailing arm mounting bracket to the vehicle body, then manoeuvre the trailing arm assembly out of position and away from the vehicle.
9 Inspect the trailing arm and centre bush for wear and damage and renew as necessary. The bush is a press-fit in the arm and can be pressed out and in using a vice and two suitable-sized tubular drifts, such as sockets. The arm must be positioned with the outer face down when pressing out the old bush, and with the inner face down when pressing in the new bush. Make sure that the short mounting stub is located on the outside of the arm, and the arrow and LWR markings pointing downwards; the mounting stubs must be in line with the horizontal position of the arm.

Refitting

10 Refitting is the reverse of removal, but delay fully tightening the link pivot bolts until the weight of the vehicle is on the rear suspension. The trailing arm mounting bolts can be fully

12.2 Rear anti-roll bar and link on the rear lower lateral link

tightened after locating the arm on the body. Refit the rear hub with reference to Section 7. Have the rear wheel alignment checked and adjusted by a Rover dealer or tyre specialist.

12 Rear suspension anti-roll bar - removal and refitting

Removal

1 Chock the front wheels, then jack up the rear of the vehicle and support on axle stands (see *"Jacking and Vehicle Support"*). Remove both rear wheels.
2 Working on each side at a time, unscrew and remove the bolts securing the anti-roll bar links to the mountings on the rear lower lateral links **(see illustration)**.
3 Unscrew and remove the anti-roll bar mounting clamp bolts, then manoeuvre the bar from under the rear of the vehicle **(see illustration)**.
4 Unscrew the bolts at each end of the anti-roll bar and remove the side links and rubber bushes.
5 Note the positions of the mounting rubbers then pull them from the anti-roll bar.
6 Check the anti-roll bar and mounting components for damage and wear and renew as necessary.

Refitting

7 Smear the bores of the mounting rubbers with rubber grease or similar lubricant, then fit them in their previously noted positions on the anti-roll bar. Make sure that the split ends of the rubbers will face the rear of the vehicle (ie towards the mounting brackets) when the anti-roll bar is fitted.
8 Refit the side links and rubber bushes and tighten the bolts.
9 Refit the anti-roll bar to the underbody and locate the mounting rubbers in the brackets with their split ends facing rearwards.
10 Refit the side links to the rear lower lateral links, insert the bolts and tighten to the specified torque.
11 Refit the rear wheels, then lower the vehicle to the ground and tighten the roadwheel nuts to the specified torque setting.

12.3 Rear anti-roll bar mounting clamp

13 Steering wheel - removal and refitting

Removal

⚠️ *Warning: Before starting this procedure, refer to the airbag precautions given in Chapter 12.*

1 Set the front wheels in the straight-ahead position. The steering wheel spokes should be horizontal.
2 Remove the ignition key then disconnect the negative (earth) lead from the battery followed by the positive lead. Wait ten minutes to allow the SRS system backup circuit to fully discharge.
3 Where applicable, remove the cruise control set/ resume switch as described in Chapter 12.
4 Using a Torx key, unscrew the airbag module retaining screws from each side of the steering wheel.
5 Withdraw the airbag module from the steering wheel taking care not to allow it to hang on the wiring. Disconnect the wiring and remove the airbag from inside the vehicle. Store it in a safe place (see Precautions in Chapter 12).
6 Disconnect the horn wiring multiplug from the rotary coupler. The wire is located just above the steering wheel retaining nut **(see illustration)**.
7 Hold the steering wheel stationary, then loosen the retaining nut and unscrew two complete turns.

13.6 Disconnecting the horn wiring multiplug from the rotary coupler

10

13.8a After marking the steering wheel for position, unscrew the nut . . .

8 Mark the steering wheel and steering column in relation to each other, then rock the steering wheel from side to side until it is released from the splines. Remove the nut and steering wheel **(see illustrations)**.

9 To prevent the rotary coupler from loosing its central setting, use adhesive tape to secure the upper part to the base.

10 On models only fitted with a driver's airbag, remove the airbag control and diagnostic unit from the steering wheel as described in Chapter 12.

Refitting

11 Refitting is a reversal of removal, but tighten the retaining nut to the specified torque and refer to Chapter 12 when refitting the airbag module.

13.8b . . . then remove the steering wheel from the column

14 Steering column - removal and refitting

Removal

 Warning: Before starting this procedure, refer to the airbag precautions given in Chapter 12.

1 Remove the steering wheel as described in Section 13.

2 Remove the driver's pocket from the lower facia panel below the steering wheel, then undo the screws and remove the lower facia panel.

3 Undo the screws and remove the steering column upper and lower shrouds.

4 Disconnect the wiring multiplugs from the lighting and wiper switches.

5 Disconnect the two starter switch multiplugs from the fusebox located to the right-hand side of the steering wheel.

6 Release the clips and studs securing the cover to the bottom of the steering column, and remove the cover **(see illustrations)**.

7 Unscrew and remove the clamp bolt securing the universal joint to the bottom of the steering column **(see illustration)**.

8 Unscrew and remove the bolts from the column lower mounting clamp and remove the clamp **(see illustrations)**.

9 At the upper end of the column, unscrew and remove the upper mounting nuts **(see illustration)**.

10 Lower the steering column from its mounting bracket, release the column from the universal joint splines, and withdraw it from inside the vehicle.

11 Undo the screws and remove the rotary coupler from the top of the column.

12 Remove the indicator cancellation cam.

13 Undo the screws and withdraw the combined lighting and wiper switches.

14 If necessary, remove the steering lock/ignition switch as described in Section 15, but note that the shear bolts must be renewed. It is not possible to obtain individual components of the steering column, therefore if excessive wear is evident the column must be renewed complete.

14.6a Removing the clips . . .

14.6b . . . and studs securing the cover to the bottom of the steering column

14.7 Universal joint and clamp at the bottom of the steering column

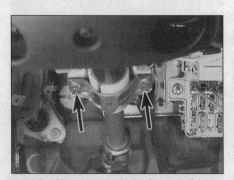

14.8a Unscrew the bolts (arrowed) . . .

14.8b . . . and remove the mounting clamp

14.9 Unscrewing the steering column upper mounting nuts

Refitting

15 Refit the steering lock/ignition switch with reference to Section 16 and tighten the shear bolts until their heads break off.

16 Refit the combined lighting and wiper switches and tighten the screws.

17 Refit the indicator cancellation cam, making sure that the engagement tangs are horizontal.

18 Refit the rotary coupler to the top of the column.

19 Engage the bottom of the column with the universal joint splines making sure that the bolt hole is aligned with the cut-out on the column. Insert the bolt but do not tighten it at this stage.

20 Locate the column on the upper mounting bracket and refit the nuts loosely.

21 Refit the lower clamp and tighten the bolts to the specified torque.

22 Tighten the upper mounting nuts to the specified torque.

23 Tighten the universal joint bolt to the specified torque.

24 Refit the cover to the bottom of the steering column, and secure with the clips and studs.

25 Reconnect the starter switch multiplugs in the fusebox.

26 Reconnect the wiring multiplugs to the lighting and wiper switches.

27 Refit the upper and lower column shrouds.

28 Refit the lower facia panel and the driver's pocket.

29 Refit the steering wheel with reference to Section 13.

15 Steering lock/ignition switch - removal and refitting

Warning: Before starting this procedure, refer to the airbag precautions given in Chapter 12.

Removal

1 Set the front wheels in the straight-ahead position. The steering wheel spokes should be horizontal.

2 Remove the ignition key then disconnect the negative (earth) lead from the battery followed by the positive lead. Wait ten minutes to allow the SRS system backup circuit to fully discharge.

3 Remove the driver's pocket from the lower facia panel below the steering wheel, then undo the screws and remove the lower facia panel.

4 Undo the screws and remove the steering column upper and lower shrouds.

5 Disconnect the two starter switch multiplugs from the fusebox located to the right-hand side of the steering wheel.

6 Detach the ignition switch wiring from the supports by unscrewing the studs. Also release the cable tie.

7 Undo the screws and remove the ignition switch from the lock housing.

8 To remove the lock housing, unscrew and remove the bolts from the column lower mounting clamp and remove the clamp. At the upper end of the column, unscrew and remove the upper mounting nuts.

9 Lower the steering column together with the steering wheel from its mounting bracket and rest it on the floor.

10 The steering lock housing is secured with shear bolts which must be drilled out. Centre punch the bolts and drill them out with a 5 mm drill bit then unscrew the remains of the shear bolts by using a self-locking wrench or similar on the exposed ends. Remove the lock from the steering column.

Refitting

11 Locate the lock housing on the steering column and hand-tighten the new bolts.

12 Insert the ignition key and check that the steering lock operates correctly. If all is well, tighten the shear bolts evenly until their heads shear off.

13 Locate the steering column on the upper mounting bracket and fit the nuts loosely.

14 Refit the lower clamp and tighten the bolts to the specified torque.

15 Tighten the upper mounting nuts to the specified torque.

16 Refit the switch to the housing and tighten the screws.

17 Reconnect the wiring and secure with the cable tie and supports.

18 Refit the steering column upper and lower shrouds.

19 Refit the lower facia panel and the driver's pocket.

20 Reconnect the battery positive then negative leads.

16 Steering gear rubber gaiters - renewal

1 Remove the track rod end as described in Section 21, then unscrew the locknut from the track rod. Note the number of turns necessary to remove the track rod end in order to maintain the toe-in setting.

2 Remove the clips then slide the gaiter off the end of the track rod **(see illustration)**.

3 Thoroughly clean the track rod and the steering gear housing. Repair kits which consist of new gaiters and retaining clips are available from Rover dealers or motor factors.

4 Fit the new rubber gaiter and clips, ensuring that it is correctly seated in the grooves in the steering gear housing and track rod. Check that the gaiter is not twisted then tighten the clips.

5 Refit the locknut and track rod end with reference to Section 21.

6 Have the front wheel alignment checked and adjusted by a Rover dealer or suitably equipped garage at the earliest opportunity.

17 Steering gear - removal, overhaul and refitting

Removal

1 Set the front wheels in the straight-ahead position and remove the ignition key to lock the steering. The steering wheel spokes should be horizontal.

2 Apply the handbrake, then jack up the front of the vehicle and support it on axle stands (see *"Jacking and Vehicle Support"*). Remove both front wheels.

3 Working inside the vehicle, pull back the driver's footwell carpet then release the clips and studs securing the cover to the bottom of the steering column. Remove the cover.

4 Mark the relative positions of the steering gear pinion and joint to use as a guide when refitting, then unscrew and remove the two universal joint pinch-bolts. Slide the universal joint up the steering column shaft splines until it is free from the steering gear pinion.

5 Unscrew and remove the rear engine mounting through bolt.

6 Unscrew and remove the engine steady rod from the cylinder block. Push the rod to one side then unscrew the bolt from the PAS pipe clip.

7 Position a suitable container beneath the steering gear, then unscrew the union nut and disconnect the feed pipe. Loosen the clip and disconnect the return hose from the steering gear housing. Tape over or plug the pipe, hose and apertures in the housing.

8 Remove the track rod ends from each side of the steering gear as described in Section 21, noting the exact number of turns necessary to remove them.

9 Extend the steering rack fully to the passenger's side of the vehicle to enable the assembly to be removed. The pinion is already disconnected from the steering column, so if it is not possible to pull the track rod out, it will be necessary to turn the pinion.

10 Under the vehicle, unscrew the nuts securing the exhaust front pipe to the support bracket on the transmission, then unscrew the nuts and release the downpipe from the exhaust manifold. Recover the gasket and tie the downpipe to one side.

16.2 Clip securing the steering gear rubber gaiter to the track rod

10

17.13 Steering gear mounting clamp

11 Using a wide-bladed screwdriver, disconnect the gearchange balljoints from the levers on the transmission.
12 Unbolt the gearchange linkage from the rear beam and lower it as far as possible.
13 Unscrew the bolts and remove the mounting clamp from the steering gear (see illustration).
14 Unscrew and remove the bolts and washers securing the steering gear to the front beam (see illustration).
15 Carefully lower the steering gear until the pinion is free of the aperture in the underbody. Recover the pinion shaft seal.
16 Move the steering gear to the passenger side of the vehicle, then lower the assembly and rotate it so that the pinion is facing the engine, and withdraw the steering gear from the driver's side.
17 Remove the clamp rubber, the collars, and the mounting bushes from the old steering gear for fitting to the new unit.

Overhaul

18 Examine the steering gear assembly for signs of wear or damage and check that the rack moves freely throughout the full length of its travel with no signs of roughness or excessive free play between the steering gear pinion and rack. The steering gear is available only as a complete assembly with no individual components, the exception being the track rod ends and rubber gaiters. Therefore, if worn, the complete assembly must be renewed.
19 Inspect the steering gear mounting bushes and the pinion shaft seal for signs of damage or deterioration and renew as necessary.

17.14 Steering gear mounting bolt

Refitting

20 Extend the steering rack fully to the passenger's side of the housing, then position the steering gear in the vehicle and fit the pinion shaft seal. Make sure the seal slot is engaged with the tab on the pinion housing.
21 Lift the steering gear and locate the pinion in the aperture, then insert the bolts and washers loosely to secure the assembly on the front beam.
22 Refit the clamp and rubber and tighten the bolts to the specified torque.
23 Fully tighten the mounting bolts to the specified torque.
24 Refit the gearchange linkage and tighten the bolts to the specified torque, then reconnect the balljoints to the levers.
25 Refit the downpipe to the exhaust manifold together with a new gasket and tighten the nuts to the specified torque. Refit the support bracket nuts and tighten to the specified torque.
26 Refit the track rod ends to the track rods with reference to Section 21.
27 Centralise the steering rack.
28 Reconnect the feed pipe and tighten the union nut to the specified torque.
29 Reconnect the return hose and tighten the clip.
30 Refit and tighten the PAS pipe clip, then refit and tighten the engine steady rod to the cylinder block.
31 Refit and tighten the rear engine mounting through bolt.
32 Refit the roadwheels, tightening their nuts to the specified torque setting and position them straight-ahead.
33 Slide the universal joint on the steering gear pinion and refit the pinch-bolts. Make sure the bolts are located correctly then tighten them to the specified torque.
34 Refit the cover to the bottom of the steering column and secure with the clips and studs.
35 Lower the vehicle to the ground.
36 Bleed the power steering hydraulic system as described in Section 20.
37 Have the front wheel alignment checked and adjusted by a Rover dealer or suitably equipped garage at the earliest opportunity.

18 Power steering pump - removal and refitting

1.4 and 1.6 litre petrol models

Removal

1 Apply the handbrake, then jack up the front of the vehicle and support it on axle stands (see "Jacking and Vehicle Support").
2 Loosen only the power steering pump pulley bolts; this will prevent having to hold the pulley stationary later.
3 Remove the power steering pump drivebelt as described in Chapter 1A.
4 Position a suitable container beneath the power steering pump to catch the spilled fluid.

5 Loosen the clip and disconnect the fluid inlet hose from the power steering pump. Tape over or plug the hose and aperture.
6 Unscrew the bolt securing the fluid outlet pipe clamp to the bracket.
7 Using two spanners, one to hold the adaptor stationary, unscrew the union nut and disconnect the outlet pipe from the power steering pump. Note the location of the O-ring. Tape over or plug the pipe and aperture.
8 Hold the drive pulley stationary with an old drivebelt or oil filter strap, then unscrew the bolts and remove the pulley from the drive flange.
9 Unbolt the power steering pump from its mounting bracket.
10 The power steering pump is a sealed unit and cannot be repaired. If faulty, the pump assembly must be renewed.

Refitting

11 Refitting is a reversal of removal, but tighten all nuts and bolts to the specified torques. Fit a new O-ring to the pump outlet pipe union and lubricate it with hydraulic fluid before tightening the union nut. Refit the power steering drivebelt as described in Chapter 1A. On completion bleed the hydraulic system as described in Section 20.

2.0 litre petrol models

Removal

12 Loosen only the power steering pump pulley bolts. This is easier to do at this stage, rather than after the drivebelt has been removed.
13 Remove the alternator as described in Chapter 5A.
14 Fully unscrew the bolts and remove the pulley from the drive flange.
15 Position a suitable container beneath the power steering pump to catch the spilled fluid.
16 Detach the outlet pipe from the power steering pump. To do this on models not fitted with air conditioning, use two spanners, one to hold the adaptor stationary, one to unscrew the union nut and disconnect the outlet pipe from the power steering pump. Note the location of the O-ring. On models with air conditioning unscrew the union bolt and recover the copper washers. Tape over or plug the pipe and aperture.
17 On models with air conditioning, unscrew the bolt securing the PAS pipe clip to the coolant rail.
18 Loosen the clip and disconnect the feed hose from the fluid reservoir. Tape over or plug the hose and apertures.
19 Noting their locations, unscrew the support bracket and pump mounting bolts and remove the bracket from the power steering pump. Note that the short bolt retains the bracket to the pump; if preferred, this bolt and the bracket may remain in position on the pump. Recover the spacer(s), noting their positions.
20 Remove the power steering pump from the coolant pump housing, then loosen the clip and remove the hose.

21 The power steering pump is a sealed unit and cannot be repaired. If faulty, the pump assembly must be renewed.

Refitting

22 Clean the mating surfaces of the power steering pump and coolant pump.
23 Fit the hose to the new pump and tighten the clip.
24 Locate the power steering pump on the coolant pump making sure that the drive lugs are correctly aligned with each other.
25 Where removed, refit the bracket, then insert the bolts together with their spacers and tighten to the specified torque.
26 Reconnect the feed hose to the fluid reservoir and tighten the clip.
27 On models without air conditioning, fit a new O-ring to the outlet pipe union and lubricate it with a little hydraulic fluid. Reconnect the union to the power steering pump and tighten to the specified torque using two spanners, one to hold the adaptor.
28 On models with air conditioning, refit the union bolt together with new copper washers and reconnect the outlet pipe to the power steering pump.
29 Refit the pulley to the drive flange and tighten the bolts to the specified torque. If preferred, delay fully tightening the bolts until the alternator and drivebelt have been refitted.
30 Refit the alternator with reference to Chapter 5A.
31 Top up the hydraulic fluid reservoir and bleed the system as described in Section 20.

2.0 litre diesel models

Removal

32 Loosen only the power steering pump pulley bolts using a Torx key; this will prevent having to hold the pulley stationary later when the drivebelt has been removed.
33 Remove the auxiliary drivebelt as described in Chapter 1B.
34 On models with air conditioning, remove the right-hand engine mounting as described in Chapter 2C, and unscrew the bolt securing the high pressure pipe to the air conditioning compressor.
35 Fully unscrew the bolts and remove the pulley from the drive flange.
36 Position a suitable container beneath the power steering pump to catch the spilled fluid.
37 Using two spanners, one to hold the adaptor stationary, unscrew the union nut and disconnect the outlet pipe from the power steering pump. Note the location of the O-ring.
38 Loosen the clip and disconnect the feed hose from the fluid reservoir. Tape over or plug the hose and apertures.
39 Unscrew the three short bolts securing the support bracket to the power steering pump and coolant pump housing, then unscrew the two long bolts securing the power steering pump to the coolant pump.
40 Remove the power steering pump then loosen the clip and remove the hose.

Refitting

41 Clean the mating surfaces of the power steering pump and coolant pump.
42 Fit the hose to the new pump and tighten the clip.
43 Locate the power steering pump on the coolant pump making sure that the drive lugs are correctly aligned with each other. Insert the bolts together with their spacers and tighten to the specified torque.
44 Insert and hand-tighten the two long bolts securing the power steering pump to the coolant pump.
45 Insert the three short bolts, then progressively tighten all the bolts to the specified torque.
46 Fit a new O-ring to the outlet pipe union and lubricate it with a little hydraulic fluid. Reconnect the union to the power steering pump and tighten to the specified torque using two spanners, one to hold the adaptor.
47 Reconnect the feed hose to the fluid reservoir and tighten the clip.
48 Refit the pulley to the drive flange and tighten the bolts to the specified torque. If preferred, hand-tighten the bolts at this stage and fully tighten them after the drivebelt has been refitted.
49 On models with air conditioning, refit and tighten the bolt securing the high pressure pipe to the air conditioning compressor. Also refit the right-hand engine mounting with reference to Chapter 2C.
50 Refit the auxiliary drivebelt with reference to Chapter 1B.
51 Top up the hydraulic fluid reservoir and bleed the system as described in Section 20.

19 Power steering oil cooler - removal and refitting

Note: *The power steering oil cooler is only fitted to diesel models.*

Removal

1 The oil cooler is located in front of the radiator. First apply the handbrake, then jack up the front of the vehicle and support it on axle stands (see *"Jacking and Vehicle Support"*).
2 Remove the splash guard from under the radiator.
3 Remove the front bumper (see Chapter 11).
4 Unscrew the two bolts securing the oil cooler clips to the front valance **(see illustration)**.
5 Unscrew the mounting bolts securing the oil cooler to the valance and front panel.
6 Remove the clamp plates and the rubber grommets.
7 Loosen the clip and disconnect the hydraulic fluid return hose from the top of the fluid reservoir. Tape over or plug the apertures.
8 Working beneath the vehicle, loosen the clips and disconnect the hoses from the oil cooler.
9 Remove the oil cooler from the vehicle.

Refitting

10 Refitting is the reverse of the removal procedure. On completion, bleed the system as described in Section 20.

20 Power steering system - bleeding

Caution: Do not hold the steering at full lock for more than 10 seconds during the following procedure. Failure to do so could lead to overheating, and possible damage, of the power steering pump and steering gear.

1 Remove the cap from the power steering fluid reservoir and top up the reservoir with the specified fluid (see *"Lubricants and fluids"*) until the level is at the upper mark on the outside of the reservoir.
2 The system must be bled by cranking the engine at starter speed. To prevent the engine starting on petrol engines, disconnect the ignition coil low tension wiring and remove the spark plugs (see Chapter 1A) to prevent unburnt fuel from entering the catalytic converter. On diesel engine models, unscrew the nut and disconnect the wiring from the fuel cut-off solenoid (see Chapter 4B), then wrap some insulation tape around the bare end of the wiring.
3 Initially prime the power steering pump by cranking the engine for 5 seconds on the ignition key.
4 Top up the reservoir, then turn the steering on full right-hand lock and crank the engine for 5 seconds.
5 Top up the reservoir, then turn the steering on full left-hand lock and crank the engine for 5 seconds.
6 Top up the reservoir, then reconnect the coil HT lead to the distributor and refit the spark plugs (see Chapter 1A) on petrol engines, or reconnect the wiring to the fuel cut-off solenoid on diesel engines.
7 Start the engine and allow it to run for 2 minutes.
8 With the engine idling, turn the steering to the full left-hand then full right-hand lock, noting the caution given at the beginning of this Section.

19.4 Bolt securing the oil cooler to the front valance

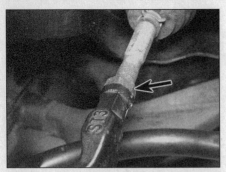

21.2 Track rod end adjustment locknut

9 Stop the engine and top up the fluid level to the upper mark on the reservoir. If any air bubbles are noticed in the fluid, wait until these have dispersed before topping up the level.

10 Refit and tighten the cap to the reservoir. Recheck the level with the engine cold and top up if necessary.

21 Track rod end - removal and refitting

Removal

1 Apply the handbrake, then jack up the front of the vehicle and support it on axle stands (see "Jacking and Vehicle Support"). Remove the relevant roadwheel.

2 Loosen the track rod end locknut by one quarter of a turn only (see illustration). The track rod end will rotate to the end of the balljoint movement, so reposition it to the centre of its movement arc again.

3 Extract the split pin and undo the nut securing the track rod end balljoint to the arm on the hub carrier. Release the balljoint shank by using a suitable balljoint separator tool whilst taking care not to damage the balljoint rubber boot (see illustrations).

4 Unscrew the track rod end from the track rod, counting the exact number of turns necessary to do so. If the locknut is to be removed, mark its position on the track rod and count the number of turns required to remove it so that it can be returned exactly to its original position on reassembly.

5 Clean the track rod end and the threads.

21.3a Nut and split pin securing the track rod end to the arm on the hub carrier

Renew it if the balljoint movement is sloppy or too stiff, or if it is damaged in any way. Check the stud taper and threads and the rubber boot.

Refitting

6 If necessary, screw the locknut onto the track rod by the number of turns noted on removal.

7 Screw the track rod end onto the track rod by the number of turns noted on removal. This should bring it to within a quarter of a turn from the locknut, with the balljoint stud facing downwards.

8 Refit the balljoint stud to the hub carrier arm and tighten the retaining nut to the specified torque setting. Use a new split pin to secure the retaining nut, if necessary tightening it as necessary to align the split pin holes.

9 Hold the track rod end horizontal at the mid point of its movement arc, then tighten the locknut.

10 Refit the roadwheel, then lower the vehicle to the ground and tighten the roadwheel nuts to the specified torque setting.

11 Check and, if necessary, adjust front wheel alignment.

22 Wheel alignment and steering angles

1 A vehicle's steering and suspension geometry is defined in five basic settings. All angles are expressed in degrees and the steering axis is defined as an imaginary line drawn through the centres of the front suspension upper and lower balljoints, extended where necessary to contact the ground.

Camber

2 Camber is the angle between each roadwheel and a vertical line drawn through its centre and tyre contact patch when viewed from the front or rear of the vehicle. Positive camber is when the roadwheels are tilted outwards from the vertical at the top. Negative camber is when they are tilted inwards.

3 Camber is not adjustable and given for reference only. While it can be checked using a camber checking gauge, if the figure obtained is significantly different from that specified, then the vehicle must be taken for

21.3b Using a balljoint separator tool to release the track rod end balljoint from the steering arm

careful checking by a professional, as the fault can only be caused by wear or damage to the body or suspension components.

Castor

4 Castor is the angle between the steering axis and a vertical line drawn through each roadwheel's centre and tyre contact patch when viewed from the side of the vehicle. Positive castor is when the steering axis is tilted so that it contacts the ground ahead of the vertical.

5 Castor is not adjustable and is given for reference only. While it can be checked using a castor checking gauge, if the figure obtained is significantly different from that specified, then the vehicle must be taken for careful checking by a professional, as the fault can only be caused by wear or damage to the body or suspension components.

Steering axis inclination/SAI

6 Also known as kingpin inclination/KPI, this is the angle between the steering axis and a vertical line drawn through each roadwheel's centre and tyre contact patch when viewed from the front or rear of the vehicle.

7 SAI/KPI is not adjustable and is given for reference only.

Toe

8 Toe is the difference, viewed from above, between lines drawn through the roadwheel centres and the vehicle's centre-line. Toe-in is when the roadwheels point inwards, towards each other at the front. Toe-out is when they splay outwards from each other at the front.

9 At the front, toe setting is adjusted by screwing the track rods in or out of the track rod ends to alter the effective length of the track rod assemblies.

10 At the rear, toe setting is adjusted by slackening the front lateral link-to-body pivot bolt and repositioning the bolt in its mounting slot, thereby altering the position of the trailing arm assembly.

Toe-out on turns

11 Also known as turning angles, this is the difference, viewed from above, between the angles of rotation of the inside and outside front roadwheels when they have been turned through a given angle.

12 Toe-out on turns is set in production and is not adjustable as such, but can be disturbed by altering the length of the track rods unequally. It is essential, therefore, to ensure that the track rod lengths are exactly the same on each side and that they are turned by the same amount whenever the toe setting is altered.

Checking and adjustment

13 Due to the special measuring equipment necessary to check wheel alignment and the skill required to use it properly, checking and adjustment of the settings is best left to a Rover dealer or similar expert. Note that most tyre-fitting shops now possess sophisticated checking equipment.

Chapter 11
Bodywork and fittings

Contents

Degrees of difficulty

| Easy, suitable for novice with little experience | | Fairly easy, suitable for beginner with some experience | 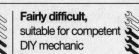 | Fairly difficult, suitable for competent DIY mechanic | 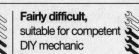 | Difficult, suitable for experienced DIY mechanic | 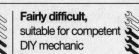 | Very difficult, suitable for expert DIY or professional | |

Specifications

Torque wrench settings	Nm	lbf ft
Bonnet hinge bolt	9	7
Boot lid hinge bolts	22	16
Boot lid lock	6	4
Boot lid striker	9	7
Door glass regulator:		
To door	9	7
To motor	7	5
Roller guide	8	6
Door lock	6	4
Door lock striker	18	13
Exterior handle	9	7
Exterior mirror	4	3
Facia	9	7
Front bumper to valance	9	7
Front door glass rear channel bolt	8	6
Front seat runner to floor	34	25
Rear door glass rear channel nut	4	3
Rear door glass rear channel bolt	8	6
Rear door lock and cover	7	5
Rear seat hinge	10	7
Seat belt anchor bolt	32	24
Seat belt reel	9	7
Seat belt stalk	35	26
Tailgate hinges	22	16
Tailgate lock striker	9	7

1 General information

The bodyshell is made of pressed-steel sections, and is available as a four-door Saloon or five-door Hatchback. Most components are welded together, but some use is made of structural adhesives. The front wings are bolted to the main body.

The front and rear body sections incorporate crumple zones and the doors are fitted with side bars. The lower areas of the body and doors are coated with an anti-stone chipping protective material.

Extensive use is made of plastic materials, mainly in the interior, but also in exterior components. Plastic components such as wheel arch liners and splash guards are fitted to the underside of the vehicle, to improve the body's resistance to corrosion.

2 Maintenance - bodywork and underframe

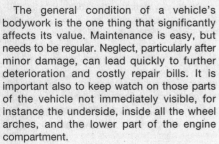

The general condition of a vehicle's bodywork is the one thing that significantly affects its value. Maintenance is easy, but needs to be regular. Neglect, particularly after minor damage, can lead quickly to further deterioration and costly repair bills. It is important also to keep watch on those parts of the vehicle not immediately visible, for instance the underside, inside all the wheel arches, and the lower part of the engine compartment.

The basic maintenance routine for the bodywork is washing - preferably with a lot of water, from a hose. This will remove all the loose solids which may have stuck to the vehicle. It is important to flush these off in such a way as to prevent grit from scratching the finish. The wheel arches and underframe need washing in the same way, to remove any accumulated mud, which will retain moisture and tend to encourage rust. Paradoxically enough, the best time to clean the underframe and wheel arches is in wet weather, when the mud is thoroughly wet and soft. In very wet weather, the underframe is usually cleaned of large accumulations automatically, and this is a good time for inspection.

Periodically, except on vehicles with a wax-based underbody protective coating, it is a good idea to have the whole of the underframe of the vehicle steam-cleaned, engine compartment included, so that a thorough inspection can be carried out to see what minor repairs and renovations are necessary. Steam-cleaning is available at many garages, and is necessary for the removal of the accumulation of oily grime, which sometimes is allowed to become thick in certain areas. If steam-cleaning facilities are not available, there are some excellent grease solvents available which can be brush-applied; the dirt can then be simply hosed off. Note that these methods should not be used on vehicles with wax-based underbody protective coating, or the coating will be removed. Such vehicles should be inspected annually, preferably just prior to Winter, when the underbody should be washed down, and any damage to the wax coating repaired. Ideally, a completely fresh coat should be applied. It would also be worth considering the use of such wax-based protection for injection into door panels, sills, box sections, etc, as an additional safeguard against rust damage, where such protection is not provided by the vehicle manufacturer.

After washing paintwork, wipe off with a chamois leather to give an unspotted clear finish. A coat of clear protective wax polish will give added protection against chemical pollutants in the air. If the paintwork sheen has dulled or oxidised, use a cleaner/polisher combination to restore the brilliance of the shine. This requires a little effort, but such dulling is usually caused because regular washing has been neglected. Care needs to be taken with metallic paintwork, as special non-abrasive cleaner/polisher is required to avoid damage to the finish. Always check that the door and ventilator opening drain holes and pipes are completely clear, so that water can be drained out. Brightwork should be treated in the same way as paintwork. Windscreens and windows can be kept clear of the smeary film which often appears, by the use of proprietary glass cleaner. Never use any form of wax or other body or chromium polish on glass.

3 Maintenance - upholstery and carpets

Mats and carpets should be brushed or vacuum-cleaned regularly, to keep them free of grit. If they are badly stained, remove them from the vehicle for scrubbing or sponging, and make quite sure they are dry before refitting. Seats and interior trim panels can be kept clean by wiping with a damp cloth. If they do become stained (which can be more apparent on light-coloured upholstery), use a little liquid detergent and a soft nail brush to scour the grime out of the grain of the material. Do not forget to keep the headlining clean in the same way as the upholstery. When using liquid cleaners inside the vehicle, do not over-wet the surfaces being cleaned. Excessive damp could get into the seams and padded interior, causing stains, offensive odours or even rot.
Caution: If the inside of the vehicle gets wet accidentally, it is worthwhile taking some trouble to dry it out properly, particularly where carpets are involved. Do not leave oil or electric heaters inside the vehicle for this purpose.

4 Minor body damage - repair

Repairs of minor scratches in bodywork

If the scratch is very superficial, and does not penetrate to the metal of the bodywork, repair is very simple. Lightly rub the area of the scratch with a paintwork renovator, or a very fine cutting paste, to remove loose paint from the scratch, and to clear the surrounding bodywork of wax polish. Rinse the area with clean water.

Apply touch-up paint to the scratch using a fine paint brush; continue to apply fine layers of paint until the surface of the paint in the scratch is level with the surrounding paintwork. Allow the new paint at least two weeks to harden, then blend it into the surrounding paintwork by rubbing the scratch area with a paintwork renovator or a very fine cutting paste. Finally, apply wax polish.

Where the scratch has penetrated right through to the metal of the bodywork, causing the metal to rust, a different repair technique is required. Remove any loose rust from the bottom of the scratch with a penknife, then apply rust-inhibiting paint to prevent the formation of rust in the future. Using a rubber or nylon applicator, fill the scratch with bodystopper paste. If required, this paste can be mixed with cellulose thinners to provide a very thin paste which is ideal for filling narrow scratches. Before the stopper-paste in the scratch hardens, wrap a piece of smooth cotton rag around the top of a finger. Dip the finger in cellulose thinners, and quickly sweep it across the surface of the stopper-paste in the scratch; this will ensure that the surface of the stopper-paste is slightly hollowed. The scratch can now be painted over as described earlier in this Section.

Repairs of dents in bodywork

When deep denting of the vehicle's bodywork has taken place, the first task is to pull the dent out, until the affected bodywork almost attains its original shape. There is little point in trying to restore the original shape completely, as the metal in the damaged area will have stretched on impact, and cannot be reshaped fully to its original contour. It is better to bring the level of the dent up to a point which is about 3 mm below the level of the surrounding bodywork. In cases where the dent is very shallow anyway, it is not worth trying to pull it out at all. If the underside of the dent is accessible, it can be hammered out gently from behind, using a mallet with a wooden or plastic head. Whilst doing this, hold a suitable block of wood firmly against the outside of the panel, to absorb the impact from the hammer blows and thus prevent a large area of the bodywork from being "belled-out".

Should the dent be in a section of the bodywork which has a double skin, or some other factor making it inaccessible from behind, a different technique is called for. Drill several small holes through the metal inside the area - particularly in the deeper section. Then screw long self-tapping screws into the holes, just sufficiently for them to gain a good purchase in the metal. Now the dent can be pulled out by pulling on the protruding heads of the screws with a pair of pliers.

The next stage of the repair is the removal of the paint from the damaged area, and from an inch or so of the surrounding "sound" bodywork. This is accomplished most easily by using a wire brush or abrasive pad on a power drill, although it can be done just as effectively by hand, using sheets of abrasive paper. To complete the preparation for filling, score the surface of the bare metal with a screwdriver or the tang of a file, or alternatively, drill small holes in the affected area. This will provide a really good "key" for the filler paste.

To complete the repair, see the Section on filling and respraying.

Repairs of rust holes or gashes in bodywork

Remove all paint from the affected area, and from an inch or so of the surrounding "sound" bodywork, using an abrasive pad or a wire brush on a power drill. If these are not available, a few sheets of abrasive paper will do the job most effectively. With the paint removed, you will be able to judge the severity of the corrosion, and therefore decide whether to renew the whole panel (if this is possible) or to repair the affected area. New body panels are not as expensive as most people think, and it is often quicker and more satisfactory to fit a new panel than to attempt to repair large areas of corrosion.

Remove all fittings from the affected area, except those which will act as a guide to the original shape of the damaged bodywork (eg headlight shells etc). Then, using tin snips or a hacksaw blade, remove all loose metal and any other metal badly affected by corrosion. Hammer the edges of the hole inwards, in order to create a slight depression for the filler paste.

Wire-brush the affected area to remove the powdery rust from the surface of the remaining metal. Paint the affected area with rust-inhibiting paint, if the back of the rusted area is accessible, treat this also.

Before filling can take place, it will be necessary to block the hole in some way. This can be achieved by the use of aluminium or plastic mesh, or aluminium tape.

Aluminium or plastic mesh, or glass-fibre matting, is probably the best material to use for a large hole. Cut a piece to the approximate size and shape of the hole to be filled, then position it in the hole so that its edges are below the level of the surrounding bodywork. It can be retained in position by several blobs of filler paste around its periphery.

Aluminium tape should be used for small or very narrow holes. Pull a piece off the roll, trim it to the approximate size and shape required, then pull off the backing paper (if used) and stick the tape over the hole; it can be overlapped if the thickness of one piece is insufficient. Burnish down the edges of the tape with the handle of a screwdriver or similar, to ensure that the tape is securely attached to the metal underneath.

Bodywork repairs - filling and respraying

Before using this Section, see the Sections on dent, deep scratch, rust holes and gash repairs.

Many types of bodyfiller are available, but generally speaking, those proprietary kits which contain a tin of filler paste and a tube of resin hardener are best for this type of repair. A wide, flexible plastic or nylon applicator will be found invaluable for imparting a smooth and well-contoured finish to the surface of the filler.

Mix up a little filler on a clean piece of card or board - measure the hardener carefully (follow the maker's instructions on the pack), otherwise the filler will set too rapidly or too slowly. Using the applicator, apply the filler paste to the prepared area; draw the applicator across the surface of the filler to achieve the correct contour and to level the surface. As soon as a contour that approximates to the correct one is achieved, stop working the paste - if you carry on too long, the paste will become sticky and begin to "pick-up" on the applicator. Continue to add thin layers of filler paste at 20-minute intervals, until the level of the filler is just proud of the surrounding bodywork.

Once the filler has hardened, the excess can be removed using a metal plane or file. From then on, progressively-finer grades of abrasive paper should be used, starting with a 40-grade production paper, and finishing with a 400-grade wet-and-dry paper. Always wrap the abrasive paper around a flat rubber, cork, or wooden block - otherwise the surface of the filler will not be completely flat. During the smoothing of the filler surface, the wet-and-dry paper should be periodically rinsed in water. This will ensure that a very smooth finish is imparted to the filler at the final stage.

At this stage, the "dent" should be surrounded by a ring of bare metal, which in turn should be encircled by the finely "feathered" edge of the good paintwork. Rinse the repair area with clean water, until all of the dust produced by the rubbing-down operation has gone.

Spray the whole area with a light coat of primer - this will show up any imperfections in the surface of the filler. Repair these imperfections with fresh filler paste or bodystopper, and once more smooth the surface with abrasive paper. Repeat this spray-and-repair procedure until you are satisfied that the surface of the filler, and the

feathered edge of the paintwork, are perfect. Clean the repair area with clean water, and allow to dry fully.

 If bodystopper is used, it can be mixed with cellulose thinners to form a really thin paste which is ideal for filling small holes.

The repair area is now ready for final spraying. Paint spraying must be carried out in a warm, dry, windless and dust-free atmosphere. This condition can be created artificially if you have access to a large indoor working area, but if you are forced to work in the open, you will have to pick your day very carefully. If you are working indoors, dousing the floor in the work area with water will help to settle the dust which would otherwise be in the atmosphere. If the repair area is confined to one body panel, mask off the surrounding panels; this will help to minimise the effects of a slight mis-match in paint colours. Bodywork fittings (eg chrome strips, door handles etc) will also need to be masked off. Use genuine masking tape, and several thicknesses of newspaper, for the masking operations.

Before commencing to spray, agitate the aerosol can thoroughly, then spray a test area (an old tin, or similar) until the technique is mastered. Cover the repair area with a thick coat of primer; the thickness should be built up using several thin layers of paint, rather than one thick one. Using 400-grade wet-and-dry paper, rub down the surface of the primer until it is really smooth. While doing this, the work area should be thoroughly doused with water, and the wet-and-dry paper periodically rinsed in water. Allow to dry before spraying on more paint.

Spray on the top coat, again building up the thickness by using several thin layers of paint. Start spraying at one edge of the repair area, and then, using a side-to-side motion, work until the whole repair area and about 2 inches of the surrounding original paintwork is covered. Remove all masking material 10 to 15 minutes after spraying on the final coat of paint.

Allow the new paint at least two weeks to harden, then, using a paintwork renovator, or a very fine cutting paste, blend the edges of the paint into the existing paintwork. Finally, apply wax polish.

Plastic components

With the use of more and more plastic body components by the vehicle manufacturers (eg bumpers. spoilers, and in some cases major body panels), rectification of more serious damage to such items has become a matter of either entrusting repair work to a specialist in this field, or renewing complete components. Repair of such damage by the DIY owner is not really feasible, owing to the cost of the equipment and materials required for effecting such repairs. The basic technique involves making a groove along the line of the

11

6.4 Front bumper lower mounting screws

6.6 Disconnecting the wiring from the foglights when removing the front bumper

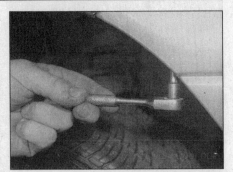

6.10 Unscrewing the rear bumper side mounting screws

crack in the plastic, using a rotary burr in a power drill. The damaged part is then welded back together, using a hot-air gun to heat up and fuse a plastic filler rod into the groove. Any excess plastic is then removed, and the area rubbed down to a smooth finish. It is important that a filler rod of the correct plastic is used, as body components can be made of a variety of different types (eg polycarbonate, ABS, polypropylene).

Damage of a less serious nature (abrasions, minor cracks etc) can be repaired by the DIY owner using a two-part epoxy filler repair material. Once mixed in equal proportions, this is used in similar fashion to the bodywork filler used on metal panels. The filler is usually cured in twenty to thirty minutes, ready for sanding and painting.

If the owner is renewing a complete component himself, or if he has repaired it with epoxy filler, he will be left with the problem of finding a suitable paint for finishing which is compatible with the type of plastic used. At one time, the use of a universal paint was not possible, owing to the complex range of plastics encountered in body component applications. Standard paints, generally speaking, will not bond to plastic or rubber satisfactorily. However, it is now possible to obtain a plastic body parts finishing kit which consists of a pre-primer treatment, a primer and coloured top coat. Full instructions are normally supplied with a kit, but basically, the method of use is to first apply the pre-primer to the component concerned, and allow it to dry for up to 30 minutes. Then the primer is applied, and left to dry for about an hour before finally applying the special-coloured top coat. The result is a correctly-coloured component, where the paint will flex with the plastic or rubber, a property that standard paint does not normally possess.

5 Major body damage - repair

Where serious damage has occurred, or large areas need renewal due to neglect, it means that complete new panels will need welding-in, and this is best left to professionals. If the damage is due to impact, it will also be necessary to check completely the alignment of the bodyshell, and this can only be carried out accurately by a Rover dealer using special jigs. If the body is left misaligned, it is primarily dangerous, as the car will not handle properly, and secondly, uneven stresses will be imposed on the steering, suspension and possibly transmission, causing abnormal wear, or complete failure, particularly to such items as the tyres.

6 Bumpers - removal and refitting

Front bumper

Removal

1 Apply the handbrake, then jack up the front of the vehicle and support it on axle stands (see *"Jacking and Vehicle Support"*).

2 Working beneath the front wheel arches, unscrew and remove the fasteners securing the bottom front of each wheel arch liner to the front wings for access to the bumper upper mounting bolts. Pull back the liners and unscrew the bolts.

3 Undo the screws securing the front of the wheel arch liners to the bottom of the front bumper.

4 Undo the mounting screws from the bottom of the front bumper **(see illustration)**.

5 Undo the screws securing the top of the bumper to the front valance and crossmember.

6 With the help of an assistant, withdraw the bumper from the front of the vehicle and disconnect the wiring for the front foglights **(see illustration)**.

7 If necessary, remove the radiator grille with reference to Section 7. The lower intake grille can also be removed by first undoing the retaining screws, and the foglights can be removed with reference to Chapter 12.

Refitting

8 Refitting is a reversal of removal.

Rear bumper

Removal

9 Open the tailgate or bootlid.

10 Working under each rear wheel arch, undo the screws securing the rear bumper to the body using a cross-head screwdriver **(see illustration)**.

11 Under the rear of the bumper, unscrew and remove the fasteners securing the bumper to the underbody **(see illustration)**.

12 Undo and remove the fasteners along the top edge of the rear bumper **(see illustration)**.

13 With the help of an assistant, withdraw the rear bumper from the vehicle.

Refitting

14 Refitting is a reversal of removal, but make sure that the bumper engages correctly with the side clips and hooks. Tighten all fasteners and screws and make sure that the clips are fully engaged.

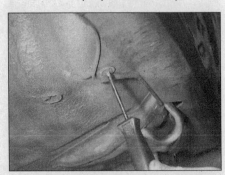

6.11 Unscrewing the fasteners securing the rear bumper to the underbody

6.12 Unscrewing the rear bumper upper fasteners

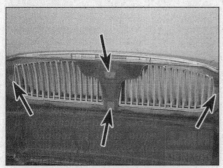

7.2 Location of screws securing the radiator grille to the front bumper

8.2 Disconnecting the windscreen washer fluid supply hose

8.3 Bolts securing the hinges to the bonnet

7 Radiator grille - removal and refitting

Removal

1 The radiator grille is incorporated in the front bumper. Remove the front bumper as described in Section 6.
2 Undo the screws and withdraw the radiator grille from the rear of the bumper **(see illustration)**.
3 If necessary, remove the badge from the front bumper by undoing the two screws.

Refitting

4 Refitting is a reversal of removal with reference to Section 6.

8 Bonnet and hinges - removal, refitting and adjustment

Removal

1 Open the bonnet and have an assistant support it. Using a pencil or felt tip pen, mark the outline of each bonnet hinge relative to the bonnet, to use as a guide on refitting.
2 Disconnect the windscreen washer fluid supply hose from the connector under the bonnet **(see illustration)**.
3 Unscrew the bolts securing the bonnet to the hinges and, with the help of an assistant, carefully lift the bonnet clear. Store the bonnet out of the way in a safe place **(see illustration)**.
4 Inspect the bonnet hinges for signs of wear and free play at the pivots, and if necessary renew them by unscrewing the bolts on the inner wing panel **(see illustration)**. Mark the positions of the hinges before removing them to ensure correct refitting.

Refitting

5 With the aid of an assistant, offer up the bonnet, and loosely fit the retaining bolts. Align the hinges with the marks made on removal, then tighten the retaining bolts securely.

6 Reconnect the windscreen washer fluid supply hose.
7 Adjust the alignment of the bonnet as follows.

Adjustment

8 Close the bonnet, and check for alignment with the adjacent panels. If necessary, slacken the hinge bolts and re-align the bonnet to suit. Once the bonnet is correctly aligned, tighten the hinge bolts to the specified torque setting.
9 Once the bonnet is correctly aligned, check that the bonnet fastens and releases in a satisfactory manner. If adjustment is necessary, slacken the bonnet lock retaining bolts, and adjust the position of the lock to suit. Once the lock is operating correctly, securely tighten its retaining bolts. Make sure that the bonnet striker enters the lock centrally.
10 If necessary, align the front edge of the bonnet with the wing panels by turning the support rubbers screwed into the body front panel, to raise or lower the front edge as required.

9 Bonnet release cable - removal and refitting

Removal

1 Open and support the bonnet.

2 Remove the bonnet lock from the engine compartment front crossmember as described in Section 10.
3 Apply the handbrake, then jack up the front of the vehicle and support it on axle stands (see *"Jacking and Vehicle Support"*). Remove the right-hand front roadwheel.
4 Remove the right-hand front wheel arch liner as described in Section 25.
5 Prise the support clip from the crossmember then remove the clip from the cable **(see illustration)**.
6 Working under the front wing, release the cable from the clips, then pull the cable through from the crossmember.
7 Open the driver's door, then undo the screws and remove the sill finisher from the door aperture.
8 Remove the trim panel from the right-hand side of the driver's footwell. To do this, remove the fastener and unclip the panel.
9 Unhook the inner cable end fitting from the release lever, then carefully push out the rubber grommet from the panel beneath the front wing and pull the cable through into the passenger compartment.
10 If necessary the lever can be unbolted from the side panel.

Refitting

11 Refitting is a reversal of removal, but refer to Section 25 and 10 when refitting the wheel arch liner and bonnet lock and check the bonnet release mechanism for correct operation on completion.

8.4 The bonnet hinges are bolted to the inner wing panel

9.5 Removing the bonnet release cable support from the crossmember

10.2 Bonnet lock security wiring connector

10.3 Bonnet lock showing mounting bolts

10.4 Unhooking the end of the release cable from the bonnet lock

10 Bonnet lock - removal and refitting

Removal

1 Open and support the bonnet. For ease of access, remove the front bumper as described in Section 6.
2 Disconnect the security wiring at the connector **(see illustration)**.
3 Unscrew the securing bolts, and remove the lock assembly from the cross panel **(see illustration)**.
4 Unhook the end of the bonnet release cable from the lock lever, and withdraw the assembly from the vehicle **(see illustration)**.

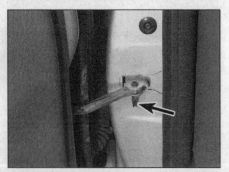

11.2 Door check arm roll pin

Refitting

5 Refitting is a reversal of removal but check that the bonnet is correctly aligned with the front wings. If adjustment is necessary, refer to Section 8.

11 Door - removal, refitting and adjustment

Removal

1 Disconnect the battery negative (earth) lead (see Chapter 5A).
2 Drive out the roll pin securing the door check arm to its body bracket **(see illustration)**.
3 Pull back the rubber boot then disconnect the wiring multiplug between the door and A-pillar.
4 Extract the E-clip from the top of each door hinge pin **(see illustration)**.
5 Support the door on blocks of wood or alternatively have an assistant support the door.
6 Using a soft-metal drift, carefully drive out the hinge pins. Withdraw the door from the body.
7 If necessary, the hinge sections may be unbolted from the A- or B-pillars and doors, however mark their positions before removing them as an aid to refitting **(see illustration)**.

Refitting

8 Refitting is a reversal of removal, but lightly grease the hinge pins before inserting them and make sure that the door fits correctly in its aperture with equal gaps at all points between it and the surrounding bodywork. The door must also be flush with the surrounding bodywork. If necessary, position the vehicle on a firm level surface and adjust the door as follows.

Adjustment

9 To adjust the front edge of the door so that it is flush with the surrounding bodywork, loosen the hinge bolts on the door itself. Move the door in or out, then tighten the bolts. Check that the bottom edge of the door is parallel with the sill, and that the waistline is aligned with the wing and other door. If necessary, a shim may be located between one of the hinges and the door.
10 To adjust the door backwards or forwards, or up and down within the body aperture, loosen the hinge bolts on the body. Move the door as necessary then tighten the bolts.
11 The striker alignment should be checked after either the door or the lock has been disturbed. To adjust a striker, slacken its screws, re-position it then securely tighten the screws **(see illustration)**.

11.4 E-clip securing the door hinge pin

11.7 The door hinges are bolted to the A- and B-pillars

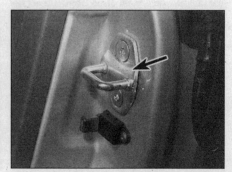

11.11 Door striker

12.3 Undo the screw securing the interior door handle to the door inner panel . . .

12.4a . . . slide the interior door handle forwards . . .

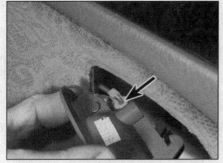

12.4b . . . then disconnect the operating rod

12 Door inner trim panel - removal and refitting

Front door

Removal

1 Ensure the ignition and all accessories are switched off.
2 On models equipped with manually-operated windows, remove the window regulator handle spring clip by hooking it out with a screwdriver or bent piece of wire, then pull the handle off the spindle and remove the escutcheon.
3 Undo the screw securing the interior door handle to the door inner panel **(see illustration)**.
4 Slide the interior door handle forwards and pull it outwards until the operating rod can be disconnected by prising out the plastic clip. Remove the interior door handle **(see illustrations)**.
5 Unscrew and remove the screw from the front upper corner of the inner trim panel **(see illustration)**.
6 Undo the screws from the door grip **(see illustration)**.
7 Using a wide-blade screwdriver, carefully prise out the trim panel clips and lift the panel from the upper shoulder and locking knob. As the panel is being removed, disconnect the wiring for the electric windows (where fitted) and security indicator. Withdraw the trim panel from the door **(see illustrations)**.
8 If necessary the door pocket, grab handle, window lift switch (where fitted), and lock indicator may be removed from the panel by undoing the screws.

9 To remove the plastic membrane, where fitted remove the electric window control unit by undoing the screws and disconnecting the multiplugs. Disconnect the tweeter and door mirror wiring multiplugs and release the wiring clips. Extract the plastic dowels and remove the membrane while feeding the wiring through the hole.

Refitting

10 Refitting is a reversal of removal.

Rear door

Removal

11 On models equipped with manually-operated windows, remove the window regulator handle spring clip by hooking it out with a screwdriver or bent piece of wire, then pull the handle off the spindle and remove the escutcheon.
12 Undo the screw securing the interior door handle to the door inner panel **(see illustration)**.
13 Slide the interior door handle forwards and pull it outwards until the operating rod can be disconnected by prising up the plastic clip **(see illustrations)**.
14 Where necessary, disconnect the wiring from the electric window lift switch. Withdraw the interior door handle **(see illustration)**.
15 Undo the screws from the door grip **(see illustration)**.
16 Using a wide-blade screwdriver, carefully prise out the trim panel clips and lift the panel from the upper shoulder and locking knob.

12.5 Unscrewing the front upper corner screw from the inner trim panel

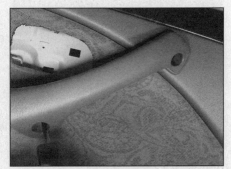

12.6 Removing the door grip

12.7a Using a special tool to prise away the inner trim panel - a wide-bladed screwdriver will do just as well

12.7b Disconnecting the wiring from the security indicator

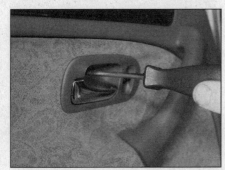

12.12 Removing the screw from the rear door interior door handle

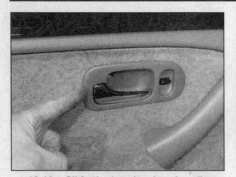

12.13a Slide the interior door handle forwards . . .

12.13b . . . and disconnect the operating rod

12.14 Disconnecting the wiring from the electric window lift switch

12.15 Door grip lower retaining screw

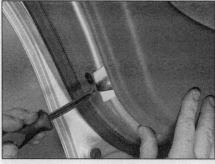

12.16 Prising the inner trim panel from the rear door

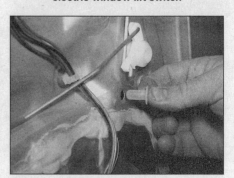

12.18a Remove the plastic dowels . . .

Withdraw the trim panel from the door (see illustration).

17 If necessary, the door protector, door grip, and locking knob guide may be removed from the trim panel by undoing the screws.

12.18b . . . and carefully peel away the membrane

18 To remove the plastic membrane, extract the plastic dowels and detach the wiring harness clips (see illustrations).

Refitting

19 Refitting is a reversal of removal.

---

13 Door handles and lock components - removal and refitting

Interior door handle (front and rear doors)

Removal

1 Undo the screw securing the interior door handle to the door inner panel.

2 Slide the interior door handle forwards and pull it outwards until the operating rod can be disconnected by prising out the plastic clip.

3 On the rear door, disconnect the wiring from the electric window lift switch.

4 Remove the interior door handle.

Refitting

5 Refitting is a reversal of removal.

Exterior door handle (front door)

Removal

6 If necessary as a precaution, protect the paintwork around the exterior handle using adhesive tape.

7 Fully raise the window glass, then remove the door inner trim panel and membrane as described in Section 12.

8 Disconnect the private lock wiring multiplug and release the wiring from the support clips. Alternatively the wiring and micro-switch can be disconnected from the exterior door handle as it is being removed.

13.9 Unscrew the mounting bolts . . .

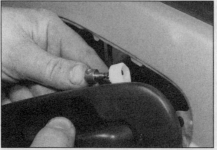

13.10a . . . then disconnect the operating rod and private lock rod from the door handle

13.10b Detach the clip . . .

9 Unscrew the bolts securing the exterior door handle to the door. Access to the bolts is gained through the apertures in the door inner panel **(see illustration)**.

10 Carefully withdraw the handle from the outside of the door, then disconnect the operating rod and private lock rod using a screwdriver. Do not disturb the setting of the threaded operating rod. Where applicable, detach the clip and disconnect the micro-switch from the handle **(see illustrations)**.

11 If necessary, the private lock may be removed from the handle assembly by pulling out the retaining clip.

Refitting

12 Refitting is a reversal of removal, but check the operation of the exterior handle before refitting the door inner trim panel. Remove the protective tape on completion.

Exterior door handle (rear door)

Removal

13 Protect the paintwork around the exterior handle using adhesive tape.

14 Fully raise the window glass, then remove the door inner trim panel and membrane as described in Section 12.

15 Undo the screws and remove the lock rod guide and protector **(see illustration)**.

16 Undo the screw and remove the locking knob crank from the door **(see illustration)**.

17 Release the lock control rods from the guides on the inner door panel. Undo the screws securing the lock to the rear edge of

13.10c . . . and disconnect the micro-switch from the handle

the door, then lower the lock inside the door to allow access to the exterior door handle mounting bolts **(see illustration)**.

18 Unscrew the bolts securing the exterior door handle to the door and carefully withdraw the handle from the outside as far as possible to reveal the operating rods **(see illustrations)**.

19 Disconnect the operating rod using a screwdriver and carefully withdraw the handle from the door **(see illustration)**. Do not disturb the setting of the threaded operating rod.

Refitting

20 Refitting is a reversal of removal, but check the operation of the exterior handle before refitting the door inner trim panel. Remove the protective tape on completion.

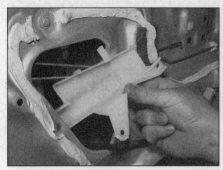

13.15 Removing the rear door lock rod guide and protector

Front door lock

Removal

21 Remove the exterior door handle as described previously in this Section.

22 Reach inside the door and disconnect the interior handle operating rod from the lock by lifting the plastic clip. Alternatively, the rod may be disconnected from the interior handle (removed) and released from the guide **(see illustration)**.

23 Disconnect the central locking wiring at the connector and release the wiring from the clips.

24 Unscrew the bolt securing the bottom of the rear window guide channel to the door.

25 Unscrew the door lock mounting screws on the rear edge of the door **(see illustration)**.

26 Move the rear window guide channel forwards and withdraw the lock from inside

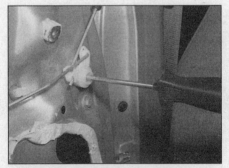

13.16 Removing the locking knob crank from the door

13.17 Undoing the screws securing the lock to the rear edge of the rear door

13.18a Unscrew the bolts . . .

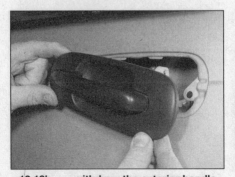

13.18b . . . withdraw the exterior handle from the door . . .

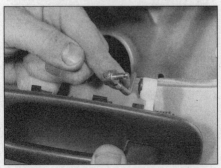

13.19 . . . then disconnect the operating rod

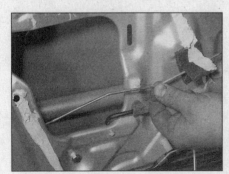

13.22 Releasing the front door lock operating rod from the guide

13.25 Unscrewing the front door lock mounting screws

13.26 Removing the front door lock from the door

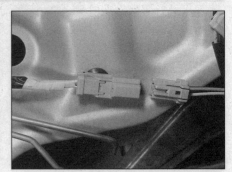

13.32 Disconnecting the central locking wiring for the rear door lock

the door. At the same time, release the operating rod from the felt **(see illustration)**.

27 Undo the screws and remove the cover from the lock.

28 If necessary, separate the mechanism from the lock by undoing the screws. Do not disturb the setting of the threaded operating rod.

Refitting

29 Refitting is a reversal of removal, but check the operation of the door lock before refitting the door inner trim panel.

Rear door lock

Removal

30 Remove the exterior door handle as described previously in this Section.

31 Reach inside the door and disconnect the inner handle and locking knob operating rods

from the lock by lifting the plastic clips. Do not disturb the setting of the threaded operating rod.

32 Disconnect the central locking wiring at the connector and release the wiring from the clips **(see illustration)**.

33 Withdraw the lock from inside the door **(see illustration)**.

34 If necessary, separate the mechanism from the lock by undoing the screws.

Refitting

35 Refitting is a reversal of removal, but check the operation of the door lock before refitting the door inner trim panel.

Front door lock switch

Removal

36 Remove the front door inner trim panel and plastic membrane as described in Section 12.

37 Reach through the aperture and disconnect the wiring leading to the lock switch. Also release the wiring from the clips.

38 Using a suitable instrument, hook out the retaining spring clip from the private lock and withdraw the switch.

Refitting

39 Refitting is a reversal of removal.

---

14 Door window regulator and glass - removal and refitting

Front door window glass and regulator

Removal

1 Remove the door inner trim panel and membrane as described in Section 12.

2 Move the window so that the bolts securing the glass to the regulator are visible through the holes in the inner door panel. To do this on manually-operated windows, temporarily refit the handle to the regulator. On electrically-operated windows, temporarily switch on the ignition and operate the switch on the centre console.

3 Loosen the bolts (do not completely remove them), then position the large holes in the regulator over the bolt heads and release the regulator from the glass **(see illustrations)**.

4 Tilt the glass forwards then withdraw it from the top of the door **(see illustration)**.

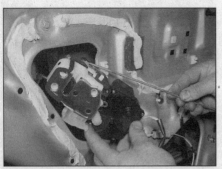

13.33 Removing the rear door lock from the door

14.3a Loosening the rear bolt securing the window glass to the regulator

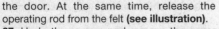

14.3b Loosening the front bolt securing the window glass to the regulator

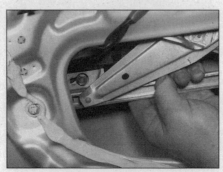

14.3c Releasing the window glass from the regulator

14.4 Removing the window glass from the front door

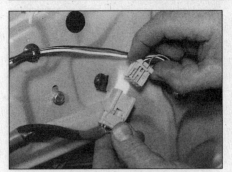

14.5a Disconnect the wiring . . .

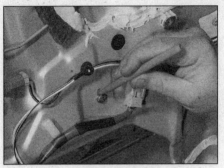

14.5b . . . mark the position of the mounting bolts . . .

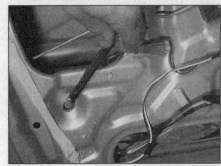

14.6a . . . then unscrew the bolts . . .

5 To remove the regulator, where applicable disconnect the wiring multiplug from the motor and release the wiring from the clip. Mark the position of the regulator mounting bolts using a marker pen or pencil **(see illustrations)**.

6 Unscrew and remove the bolts and withdraw the regulator through the aperture in the door inner panel **(see illustrations)**.

7 To remove the motor (where fitted) from the regulator, first mark the position of the sector gear with a marker pen. Using a Torx key, unscrew the bolts and remove the motor.

Refitting

8 Refitting is a reversal of removal, but apply a little grease to the sliding surfaces of the regulator. Tighten the mounting bolts to the specified torque. Check the operation of the window before refitting the door inner trim panel. When fully raised, the upper edge of

the glass must be aligned with the upper channel in the door. If necessary, adjust the window regulator position then tighten the bolts.

Rear door window glass and regulator

Removal

9 Remove the door inner trim panel and membrane as described in Section 12.

10 Move the window so that the bolts securing the glass to the regulator are visible through the holes in the inner door panel. To do this on manually-operated windows, temporarily refit the handle to the regulator. On electrically-operated windows, temporarily reconnect the wiring to the electric window operating switch.

11 Unscrew and remove the bolts securing the glass to the regulator, and lower the glass

to the bottom of the door **(see illustration)**.

12 Pull the rubber weatherstrip upwards from the rear glass channel **(see illustration)**. Leave the remaining weatherstrip in position.

13 Remove the rear glass channel as follows. Unscrew the upper mounting nut and the two lower mounting bolts, then twist the channel clockwise through 90° while carefully lifting the channel from the door. It will be necessary to carefully pull the top opening slightly apart when easing out the channel bracket **(see illustrations)**.

14 Withdraw the glass from the top of the door without tilting it **(see illustration)**.

15 To remove the regulator, where applicable disconnect the wiring multiplug from the motor and release the wiring from the clip. Mark the position of the regulator mounting bolts using a marker pen or pencil **(see illustrations)**.

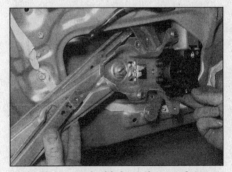

14.6b . . . and withdraw the regulator

14.11 Unscrewing the bolts securing the rear window glass to the regulator

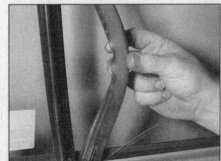

14.12 Removing the rubber weatherstrip from the rear glass channel

14.13a Rear glass channel upper mounting nut

14.13b Remove the rear glass channel from the slotted upper mounting . . .

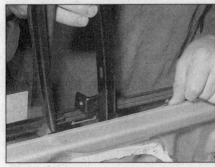

14.13c . . . then twist the channel through 90° and lift from the door

11

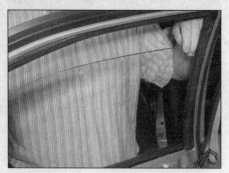

14.14 Removing the rear door glass

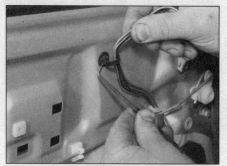

14.15a Releasing the wiring from the clip

14.15b Marking the position of the regulator mounting bolts

16 Unscrew and remove the bolts and withdraw the regulator through the aperture in the door inner panel **(see illustrations)**.

17 To remove the motor (where fitted) from the regulator, first mark the position of the sector gear with a marker pen. Using a Torx key, unscrew the bolts and remove the motor **(see illustration)**.

Refitting

18 Refitting is a reversal of removal, but apply a little grease to the sliding surfaces of the regulator. Delay tightening the rear glass channel mounting bolts and nut to the specified torque until the glass has been wound up and down several times to align the channel. Check the operation of the window before refitting the door inner trim panel. When fully raised, the upper edge of the glass must be aligned with the upper channel in the door. If necessary, adjust the window regulator position then tighten the bolts to the specified torque setting.

---

15 Boot lid - removal, refitting and adjustment

Removal

1 Remove the boot lid lock as described in Section 16.

2 Release the boot lid release cable from the clips on the right-hand hinge arm.

3 Withdraw the release cable from the boot

lid. As an aid to refitting the cable, tie a length of string to it before removing it and leave the string in position in the boot lid.

4 Remove both number plate lights from the boot lid as described in Chapter 12.

5 Remove the private lock access cover from inside the boot lid.

6 Disconnect the wiring multiplug leading to the private lock and release the wiring from the clip.

7 Release the wiring harness from the clips on the boot lid and right-hand hinge arm, then withdraw the harness from the boot lid. As an aid to refitting the wiring, tie a length of string to it before removing it and leave the string in position in the boot lid.

8 Mark the positions of the hinge mounting bolts on the boot lid.

9 With the help of an assistant, unscrew the four hinge retaining bolts and lift the boot lid away from the vehicle.

Refitting and adjustment

10 Offer up the boot lid, and fit the hinge bolts loosely. Align the bolts with the marks made on dismantling, and tighten them securely.

11 Tie the string to the number plate light connectors on the wiring harness, then carefully draw the wiring into the boot lid and secure with the clips in the boot lid and right-hand hinge arm. Untie the string.

12 Refit both number plate lights with reference to Chapter 12.

13 Reconnect the wiring to the private lock and secure in the clip. Refit the access cover.

14 Tie the string to the release cable and draw it into position and secure in the clips on the right-hand hinge arm. Untie the string.

15 Refit the boot lid lock with reference to Section 16.

16 Close the boot lid and check that it is correctly aligned with all surrounding bodywork, with an equal clearance all around. If necessary, adjustment can be made by slackening the hinge bolts and repositioning the boot lid. Once correctly positioned, tighten the hinge bolts to the specified torque. Check that the boot lid closes correctly and that the lock engages centrally with the striker. If not, loosen the striker retaining bolts and reposition the striker. Tighten the striker retaining bolts securely on completion.

---

16 Boot lid lock and lock cylinder - removal and refitting

Boot lid lock

Removal

1 Open the boot lid and unclip the cover from the lock on the bottom edge of the boot lid.

2 Release the clip and disconnect the operating rod from the lock.

3 Unscrew the two bolts and release the lock from the boot lid.

4 Disconnect the wiring, then unhook the release cable and withdraw the lock from the vehicle.

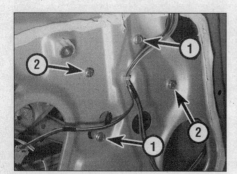

14.16a Loosen bolts 1 and unscrew completely bolts 2

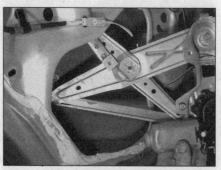

14.16b Removing the regulator from the rear door

14.17 Motor mounting screws on the regulator

17.3 Pull off the control knobs . . .

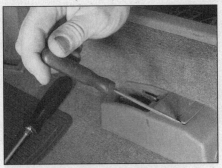

17.4a . . . then prise out the cover . . .

17.4b . . . remove the screw . . .

17.4c . . . prise out the stud . . .

17.4d . . . and remove the cover

17.4e Lever assembly on the floor bracket

Refitting

5 Refitting is a reversal of removal. Tighten the lock retaining bolts to the specified torque. On completion, check that the boot lid closes correctly and that the striker enters the lock centrally. If necessary, adjust the position of the striker by loosening the retaining bolts. Retighten the bolts on completion.

Boot lid lock cylinder

Removal

6 Open the boot lid and remove the lock cylinder access cover.
7 Disconnect the wiring plug and release the wiring from the clip.
8 Lift the plastic clip and disconnect the operating rod from the lock cylinder.
9 Undo the single retaining screw and withdraw the lock cylinder from the boot lid. Recover the chrome ring.

Refitting

10 Refitting is a reversal of removal.

17 Boot lid/tailgate and fuel filler flap release cables - removal and refitting

Removal

1 Remove the rear seat as described in Section 26. Also remove the luggage compartment left-hand side trim panels and rear valance panel with reference to Section 28.

2 Remove the door sill finishers from the rear door apertures and front driver's door aperture.
3 Carefully pull the control knobs from the front cable levers **(see illustration)**.
4 Prise out the cover and remove the screw, then prise out the stud. Undo the screw, and remove the control knob cover **(see illustrations)**.
5 Unscrew the lower anchor bolt for the driver's seat belt.
6 Prise out the studs securing the rear edge of the carpet to the floor, release it from the driver's side and fold it forwards for access to the release cables.
7 At the rear of the vehicle, unclip the cable and disconnect it from the boot lid/tailgate lock **(see illustration)**.
8 Release the cable from the clips in the luggage compartment and pull the rear section through the body.
9 Fold back the carpet from the inner sill and release the cable from the sill clips.
10 Unscrew the front cable control bracket bolts and disconnect the cables.
11 Disconnect the cable from the fuel flap and release it from the clips.
12 Withdraw both cables from inside the vehicle.

Refitting

13 Refitting is a reversal of removal but tighten the seat belt anchor bolt to the specified torque.

18 Tailgate and support struts - removal, refitting and adjustment

Tailgate

Removal

1 Remove the rear seat as described in Section 26. Also remove the luggage compartment side trim panels with reference to Section 28.
2 Working on each side at a time, carefully pull the weatherstrip from the D-pillar. Unscrew the rear seat belt lower anchor bolt, then unclip the D-pillar trim panel and feed the seat belt through it.
3 Unclip and remove the side finishers from each side of the tailgate window.

17.7 Tailgate lock release cable

11

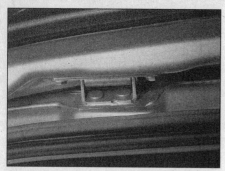

18.10 Tailgate hinge at the rear of the roof

18.18 Using a screwdriver to prise out the upper retaining spring clip from the tailgate strut

4 Undo the screw and remove the grip from the tailgate.

5 Unscrew the centre pins from the retaining clips, then use a wide-bladed screwdriver to prise off the trim panel.

6 Release the wiring harness from the clips on the rear of the body and disconnect the multiplugs located on the right-hand side of the luggage compartment.

7 Remove the wiring harness rubber boot from the top right-hand corner of the tailgate, then pull the harness through onto the tailgate.

8 Have an assistant support the tailgate then disconnect the support struts from the balljoints by carefully prising out the spring clips with a screwdriver. Carefully lower the struts onto the body.

9 Remove the trim from the headlining and carefully pull down the rear edge for access to the tailgate hinges.

10 Unscrew the hinge nuts and lift the tailgate from the rear of the vehicle (**see illustration**).

11 Clean away the sealant from the hinges and roof.

Refitting and adjustment

12 Apply suitable sealant to the faces of the hinges which contact the roof, then with the help of an assistant offer the tailgate onto the body and locate the hinge studs in their holes. Screw on the retaining nuts hand-tight at this stage.

13 Locate the support struts onto the balljoints and press in the spring clips.

14 Carefully close the tailgate and check that it is aligned with the surrounding bodywork. Reposition as necessary then tighten the hinge nuts to the specified torque.

15 Check that the tailgate is flush with the surrounding bodywork, and if necessary screw the support rubbers on each side in or out as required.

16 The remaining procedure is a reversal of removal, but if necessary adjust the tailgate striker as described in Section 19.

Support struts

Removal

17 Support the tailgate in the open position by using a stout piece of wood, or with the help of an assistant.

18 Carefully prise out the upper retaining spring clip from the strut using a screwdriver, and disconnect the strut from the tailgate (**see illustration**).

19 Repeat the procedure for the strut-to-body mounting and remove the strut from the vehicle. Note that the cylinder end of the strut is located on the body.

20 If necessary the ball studs can be unscrewed for renewal.

Refitting

21 Refitting is a reversal of removal, but ensure that the strut is pressed firmly onto each of its balljoints.

19 Tailgate lock - removal, refitting and adjustment

Tailgate lock

Removal

1 Open the tailgate then undo the single screw and remove the hand grip from the trim (**see illustrations**).

2 Loosen the screws and remove the special clips from the lower edge of the trim panel (**see illustrations**).

3 Using a wide-bladed screwdriver, carefully prise off the upper trim strips from each side of the tailgate window (**see illustrations**).

4 Prise off the trim panel.

5 Unscrew the lock mounting bolts (**see illustration**).

6 Withdraw the lock then release the plastic clip and disconnect the operating rod and central locking wiring (**see illustrations**).

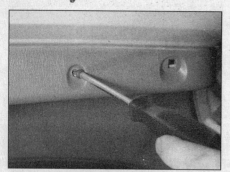

19.1a Undo the screw . . .

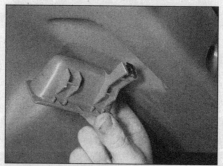

19.1b . . . and remove the hand grip from the tailgate trim

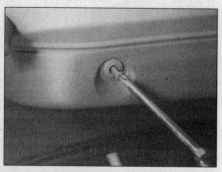

19.2a Loosen the screws . . .

19.2b . . . and remove the clips from the lower edge of the tailgate trim panel

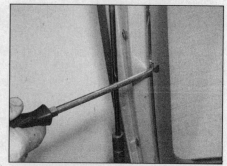

19.3a Carefully prise away the upper trim strips . . .

19.3b . . . and release them from their clips

19.5 Unscrew the tailgate lock mounting bolts . . .

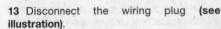

19.6a . . . then release the clip . . .

Refitting

7 Refitting is a reversal of removal. On completion, check that the tailgate closes easily and does not rattle when closed. If adjustment is necessary, slacken the tailgate striker retaining screws and reposition the striker as necessary (see illustration). Once the tailgate operation is satisfactory, tighten the striker retaining bolts to the specified torque.

Tailgate lock cylinder

Removal

8 Open the tailgate then undo the single screw and remove the hand grip from the trim.
9 Loosen the screws and remove the special clips from the lower edge of the trim panel.
10 Using a wide-bladed screwdriver, carefully prise off the upper trim strips from each side of the tailgate window.
11 Prise off the trim panel.
12 The tailgate lock cylinder is accessible through the aperture in the tailgate inner panel (see illustration).

13 Disconnect the wiring plug (see illustration).
14 Prise up the plastic clip and disconnect the operating rod from the lock cylinder (see illustration).
15 Unscrew the mounting bolt and remove the lock cylinder from the tailgate (see illustration).

Refitting

16 Refitting is a reversal of removal.

20 Central locking components - general information

The central locking system is controlled by an ECU located beneath the centre of the facia. The system automatically locks all doors with the exception of the tailgate when the driver's door is locked.

19.6b . . . and disconnect the operating rod

19.6c Disconnecting the central locking wiring from the tailgate lock

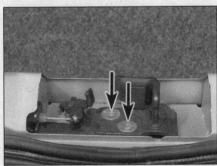

19.7 Tailgate striker retaining screws

19.12 Tailgate lock cylinder accessible through the aperture in the tailgate inner panel

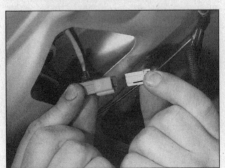

19.13 Disconnecting the wiring plug from the tailgate lock cylinder

19.14 Disconnecting the operating rod from the lock cylinder

19.15 Removing the tailgate lock cylinder

11

22.2a Insert the screwdrivers as described in the text . . .

The driver's door lock incorporates a micro switch which completes an earth circuit in the ECU which then operates the door lock motors on the doors. When the driver's door is unlocked, the earth circuit is completed again and the ECU then unlocks the doors.

The door lock motors are removed when removing the door locks as described in Section 13.

The ECU is removed by first removing the centre console as described in Section 29. Undo the screws securing the ashtray assembly to the facia, then disconnect the wiring for the cigar lighter and withdraw the ashtray assembly. The ECU can now be removed by undoing the screws and disconnecting the wiring multiplugs. Refitting is a reversal of removal.

21 Electric window components - removal and refitting

Window master switch

Removal

1 Remove the rear console as described in Section 29.
2 Invert the rear console, then undo the screws and remove the master switch and housing from the console.
3 Release the cable strap then undo the screws and remove the switches from the housing.

22.6a Use a screwdriver and cloth . . .

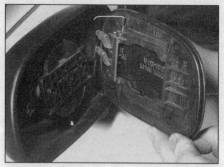

22.2b . . . and release the mirror from its base

Refitting

4 Refitting is a reversal of removal.

Driver's window switch

Removal

5 Remove the driver's door inner trim panel as described in Section 12.
6 Detach the wiring multiplug from the bracket and disconnect.
7 Undo the screws and withdraw the switch.

Refitting

8 Refitting is a reversal of removal.

Front and rear door window switch

9 The procedure is the same as that described in paragraphs 1 to 4.

Window regulator motor

10 The procedure is described in Section 14.

Electronic control unit

Removal

11 Remove the front door inner trim panel as described in Section 12.
12 Pull back the upper corner of the plastic membrane for access to the control unit.
13 Undo the screws and withdraw the unit from the door, then disconnect the two multiplugs.

Refitting

14 Refitting is a reversal of removal.

22.6b . . . to prise away the triangular panel at the front of the window aperture

Electric window relay

Removal

15 The electric window relay is located on the fusebox beneath the facia on the driver's side. To gain access to the relay, remove the driver's pocket from the lower facia panel below the steering wheel, then undo the screws and remove the lower facia panel. Pull the relay out from its socket.

Refitting

16 Refitting is a reversal of removal.

22 Exterior mirror and glass - removal and refitting

Mirror glass

Removal

 Warning: It is recommended that gloves are worn during the following procedure.

1 On models equipped with manually-operated mirrors, heat the mirror glass with a hairdryer to soften the adhesive used to stick the glass to its mounting plate. Once warm, the mirror glass can be levered out of position.
2 On models equipped with electrically-operated mirrors, adjust the position of the mirror glass fully inwards. Two screwdrivers are now required to remove the glass. Insert one screwdriver downwards behind the centre of the mirror in between the glass frame and the plastic base, then insert the other screwdriver behind the outer edge of the mirror and press on the end of the base. **Do not** exert excessive pressure otherwise the base will come away from the mirror housing. With the mirror released, disconnect the wiring from the two terminals **(see illustrations)**.

Refitting

3 On models equipped with manually-operated mirrors, first ensure that all traces of old adhesive are removed from the mounting plate. Remove the backing from the new mirror, then press the glass firmly into place and adjust to the required position.
4 On models equipped with electrically-operated mirrors, connect the wiring connectors to the heating element terminals then locate the flange on the retainer and press the mirror into position using a wad of cloth.

Mirror assembly

Removal

5 Remove the door inner trim panel as described in Section 12.
6 Carefully prise off the triangular panel at the front of the window aperture, then disconnect the mirror and tweeter wiring at the plug and release the wiring from the clips **(see illustrations)**.

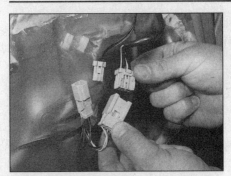

22.6c Disconnecting the electric mirror wiring

22.7a Undo the Torx screws . . .

22.7b . . . and withdraw the mirror from the outside of the door

7 Support the mirror, then undo the Torx screws and withdraw the mirror from the outside of the door **(see illustrations)**.

Refitting

8 Refitting is a reversal of removal.

23 Windscreen and rear window glass - general information

The windscreen and rear window are bonded in position with special adhesive. Renewal of these windows is a difficult, messy and time-consuming task, which is beyond the scope of the home mechanic. It is difficult, unless one has plenty of practice, to obtain a secure, waterproof fit. Furthermore, the task carries a high risk of breakage. In view of this, owners are strongly advised to have this work carried out by one of the many specialist windscreen fitters.

24 Sunroof components - general information

1 A sunroof is available on all models, both electrically-operated and manually-operated. Due to the complexity of the sunroof mechanism, considerable expertise is needed to repair or replace sunroof components successfully. Removal of the sunroof requires the headlining to be removed, which is a complex and tedious operation and not a task to be undertaken lightly. Any problems with the sunroof should therefore be referred to a Rover dealer.

2 On models equipped with an electrically-operated sunroof, if the sunroof motor fails to operate, first check the relevant fuse. If the fault cannot be traced and rectified, then the sunroof can be opened and closed manually by using the cranked key in the vehicle tool kit or a suitable Torx key. Use a screwdriver or coin to remove the round plug in the centre of the headlining, then insert the cranked key and turn it until the roof is fully closed **(see illustrations)**.

25 Body exterior fittings - removal and refitting

Wheel arch liner

Removal

1 Jack up the front or rear of the vehicle and support on axle stands (see *"Jacking and Vehicle Support"*). Remove the roadwheel.

2 The wheel arch liner is retained by screws and bolts together with some fasteners, and with these removed the liner can be withdrawn from under the wheel arch.

Refitting

3 Refitting is a reversal of removal.

Boot lid motif

Removal

4 Open the boot lid then remove the rear number plate.

5 Working through the apertures in the inner panel, unscrew the nuts and screws then remove the motif from the outside of the boot lid.

Refitting

6 Refitting is a reversal of removal.

Engine compartment front splash guard

Removal

7 Apply the handbrake, then jack up the front

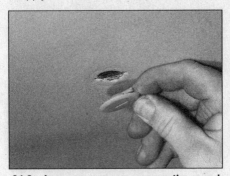

24.2a In an emergency, remove the round plug from the headlining . . .

of the vehicle and support it on axle stands (see *"Jacking and Vehicle Support"*).

8 The guard is retained with bolts and fasteners, and with these removed the guard can be lowered from the front of the vehicle.

Refitting

9 Refitting is a reversal of removal.

Engine compartment main splash guard (diesel engine models)

Removal

10 Apply the handbrake, then jack up the front of the vehicle and support it on axle stands (see *"Jacking and Vehicle Support"*).

11 Unscrew the bolts and fasteners and lower the guard from under the engine compartment.

12 If necessary, the access panel can be removed by turning the fasteners.

Refitting

13 Refitting is a reversal of removal.

26 Seats - removal and refitting

Front seat

Removal

1 Slide the seat fully forwards then unclip the cover from the rear of the inner seat runner **(see illustration)**.

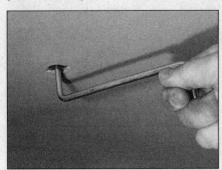

24.2b . . . then use the cranked key from the tool kit to close the roof

11

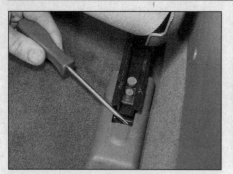

26.1 Unclip the cover from the rear of the front seat inner seat runner . . .

26.2 . . . then unscrew the rear bolts

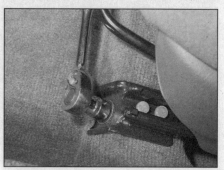

26.3 Unscrewing the front seat runner front mounting bolts

2 Unscrew and remove the bolts from the rear of both seat runners (see illustration).
3 Slide the seat fully rearwards and unscrew the bolts from the front of the seat runners (see illustration).
4 Remove the seat from inside the vehicle.

Refitting
5 Refitting is a reversal of removal, tightening the seat runner bolts to the specified torque.

Rear seat cushion (Saloon models)

Removal
6 Using a socket, unscrew and remove the bolt from the centre rear of the cushion.
7 Lift the rear of the cushion from beneath the backrest taking care to guide the seat belt buckles through the holes in the cushion.
8 Unhook the front of the cushion from the brackets.

26.10a Unclip the cover . . .

26.10b . . . then unscrew the bolts from the rear seat cushion hinges (Hatchback models)

Refitting
9 Refitting is a reversal of removal.

Rear seat cushion (Hatchback models)

Removal
10 Unclip the cover then unscrew the bolts from the front hinges and lift the cushion out from inside the car (see illustrations).

Refitting
11 Refitting is a reversal of removal.

Rear seat backrest (Hatchback models)

Removal
12 Fold the backrest forwards then unclip the cover from the centre hinge (see illustration).
13 Unscrew and remove the bolts securing the centre hinge to the floor.
14 Move the backrest inwards from the hinge pin and remove it from inside the vehicle (see illustration).

Refitting
15 Refitting is a reversal of removal.

Rear seat armrest (Saloon models)

Removal
16 Lower the rear seat armrest, then slide out the backing panel.
17 Undo the crosshead screws securing the armrest to the seat base, then withdraw the armrest.

26.12 Remove the cover for access to the rear seat backrest centre hinges (Hatchback models)

Refitting
18 Refitting is a reversal of removal.

27 Seat belt components - removal and refitting

Note: *Note the positions of any washers and spacers on the seat belt anchors, and ensure that they are refitted in their original positions.*

Front seat belt and stalk

 Warning: On 1998-on models, the front seat belt reel incorporates a pre-tensioner which is activated together with the airbag. Observe the safety precautions given in Chapter 12. When handling the pre-tensioner reel, do not knock or tap it.

Removal
1 Disconnect the battery negative then positive leads, and **wait 10 minutes** (this is a safety requirement of the airbag/SRS system).
2 Remove the lower trim panel from the B-pillar with reference to Section 28.
3 On 1998-on models, the SRS sensor must now be set to its locked position. To do this, swivel out the sensor and turn it clockwise 90°.
4 Prise the cover from the belt upper mounting, and unscrew the bolt (see illustrations).
5 Remove the clip which secures the upper trim panel to the B-pillar, and release the seat belt from the trim.

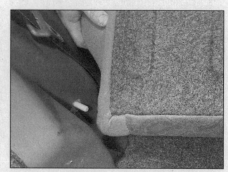

26.14 Removing the rear seat backrest from the hinge pin (Hatchback models)

27.4a Carefully prise away the cover . . .

27.4b . . . for access to the front seat belt upper mounting bolt

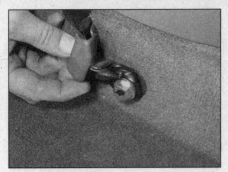

27.6 Front seat belt lower mounting bolt on the inner sill panel

6 Prise the cover from the belt lower mounting, and unscrew the bolt **(see illustration)**.
7 Unscrew the bolts and remove the reel from the bottom of the B-pillar **(see illustrations)**.
8 Remove the seat belt from inside the vehicle.
9 To remove the stalk, first remove the seat as described in Section 26.
10 Unscrew the bolt and remove the stalk from the seat.

Refitting

11 Refitting is a reversal of removal, but tighten the mounting bolts to the specified torque. On 1998-on models, set the SRS sensor to its unlocked position by turning it anticlockwise 90° and swivelling it inward. After resetting the sensor, **do not** knock or tap the reel.

Centre rear seat belt (Hatchback models)

Removal

12 Fold the rear seat cushion forwards and remove the belt and buckles from the clips in the backrest.
13 Unscrew the mounting bolts and remove the buckles and belt **(see illustration)**.

Refitting

14 Refitting is a reversal of removal, but tighten the mounting bolts to the specified torque.

Centre rear seat belt (Saloon models)

Removal

15 Remove both rear loudspeakers as described in Chapter 12.

16 Remove the rear seat cushion as described in Section 26.
17 Remove the upper trim panels from the D-pillars with reference to Section 28.
18 Note the fitted position of the centre seat belt. Unscrew the bolts securing the centre seat belt and buckle to the floor.
19 Undo the screws securing the rear parcel shelf to the body.
20 Prise out the centre guide and remove it from the belt.
21 Remove the parcel shelf for access to the seat belt reel.
22 Unscrew the mounting bolt and remove the reel from the body panel.

Refitting

23 Refitting is a reversal of removal, but tighten the mounting bolts to the specified torque.

Side rear seat belt

Removal

24 Remove the lower trim panel from the D-pillar, then pull out the weatherstrip from the front of the upper trim panel. On Hatchback models, open the tailgate and pull out the weatherstrip from the rear of the upper trim panel, also remove the rear door sill panel and side trim panel **(see illustrations)**.
25 Unscrew and remove the seat belt lower mounting bolt **(see illustration)**.
26 Using a wide-bladed screwdriver, prise out the upper trim panel and feed the seat belt through the hole.

27.7a Unscrewing the front seat belt reel upper mounting bolt . . .

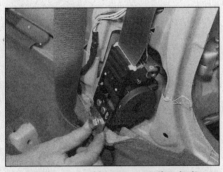

27.7b . . . and lower mounting bolt

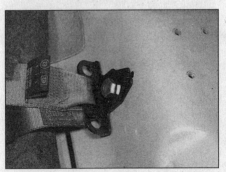

27.13 Centre rear seat belt mounting bolt

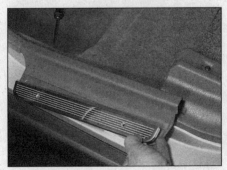

27.24a Removing the rear door sill panel . . .

27.24b . . . and side trim panel . . .

11

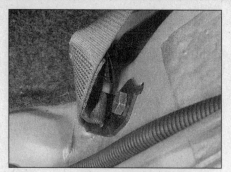

27.25 . . . for access to the rear seat belt lower mounting bolt (Hatchback models)

27.28 Rear seat belt upper mounting bolt (Hatchback models)

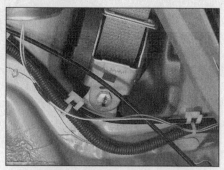

27.29 Rear seat belt reel and mounting bolt (Hatchback models)

27 Remove the side trim/carpet by undoing the screws and depressing the centre pins of the fasteners.

28 Unscrew and remove the seat belt upper mounting bolt **(see illustration)**.

29 Unscrew and remove the mounting bolts and remove the reel from the body **(see illustration)**.

30 Unscrew and remove the mounting bolt and remove the seat belt buckle from the floor.

Refitting

31 Refitting is a reversal of removal, but tighten the mounting bolts to the specified torque.

Side rear seat belt (Saloon models)

Removal

32 Remove the upper and lower trim panels

from the D-pillar (see Section 28), then remove the rear loudspeakers as described in Chapter 12.

33 Note the fitted position of the seat belt buckle then unbolt it.

34 Undo the screws securing the rear parcel shelf to the body and move the shelf for access to the seat belt reel.

35 Unscrew the bolt and remove the reel.

Refitting

36 Refitting is a reversal of removal but tighten the mounting bolts to the specified torque.

28 Interior trim panels - general information

Interior trim panels

1 The interior trim panels are secured either by screws or by various types of trim fasteners, usually studs or clips **(see illustrations)**.

2 Check that there are no other panels overlapping the one to be removed. Usually there is a sequence that has to be followed that will become obvious on close inspection.

3 Remove all obvious fasteners, such as screws. If the panel will not come free then it is held by hidden clips or fasteners. These are usually situated around the edge of the panel and can be prised up to release them. Note, however, that they can break quite easily so replacements should be available. The best

way of releasing such clips in the absence of the correct type of tool, is to use a large flat-bladed screwdriver positioned directly beneath the clip. Note that in many cases the adjacent sealing strip must be prised back to release a panel.

4 When removing a panel, never use excessive force or the panel may be damaged. Always check carefully that all fasteners have been removed or released before attempting to withdraw a panel.

5 Refitting is the reverse of the removal procedure. Secure the fasteners by pressing them firmly into place and ensure that all disturbed components are correctly secured to prevent rattles. Use a suitable trim adhesive (a Rover dealer should be able to recommend a proprietary product) on reassembly.

> **HAYNES HiNT** *If adhesives were found at any point on removal, use white spirit to remove all traces of old adhesive, then wash off all traces of spirit using soapy water.*

Carpets

6 The passenger compartment floor carpet is in one piece and is secured at its edges by screws or clips, usually the same fasteners used to secure the various adjoining trim panels.

7 Carpet removal and refitting is reasonably straightforward but very time-consuming due to the fact that all adjoining trim panels must

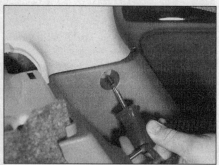

28.1a Screw fixing of a side trim panel

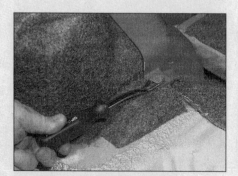

28.1b Removing a stud fixing

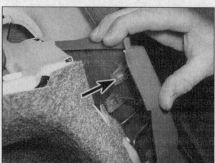

28.1c The clip fixings are very tight and require careful removal to avoid breakage

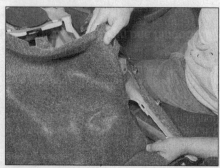

28.1d Removing a side trim panel from the luggage compartment

be removed first, as must components such as the seats, the centre console and seat belt lower anchorages.

Headlining

8 The headlining is clipped to the roof and can be withdrawn once all fittings such as the front seat headrests, grab handles, sun visors, sunroof (if fitted), windscreen and related trim panels have been removed and the door, tailgate and sunroof aperture sealing strips have been pulled clear.

9 Note that headlining removal requires considerable skill and experience if it is to be carried out without damage and is therefore best entrusted to an expert. In particular the headlining must not be bent otherwise it will be permanently creased.

29 Centre and rear consoles - removal and refitting

Rear console

Removal

1 Adjust both front seats fully forward.
2 Using a screwdriver carefully prise the cover from the front end of the rear console **(see illustration)**.
3 Unscrew the two cross-head screws securing the front of the console to the floor **(see illustration)**.

29.2 Prise out the cover . . .

29.3 . . . and unscrew the rear console front mounting screws

4 At the rear lower corners of the console, unscrew and remove the cross-head screws. **Do not** remove the screws from the sides of the console **(see illustration)**.
5 Lift the console slightly and disconnect the wiring multiplugs for the electric windows. Withdraw the console from inside the vehicle **(see illustration)**.
6 If necessary, the console components may be dismantled by undoing the screws/nuts. Remove the ashtray lid first.

Refitting

7 Refitting is a reversal of removal. When reconnecting the electric window wiring multiplugs, connect the brown multiplug to the right-hand side.

Centre console

Removal

8 Remove the rear console as described earlier in this Section.
9 Adjust the front seats fully to the rear.
10 Remove the radio as described in Chapter 12.
11 Carefully prise the gear selector surround panel from the console. If preferred, unscrew the gear knob and leave the surround panel in the console **(see illustration)**.
12 Use a screwdriver to prise out the plastic retaining tabs, then remove the radio mounting box and push out the hazard and heated rear window switches from the console. Disconnect the wiring and remove the switches **(see illustrations)**.

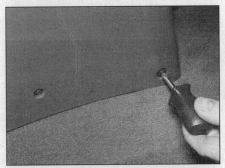

29.4 Removing the rear console rear mounting screws

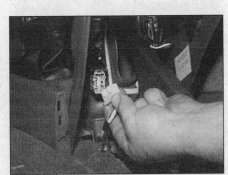

29.5 Disconnecting the electric window wiring multiplugs

29.11 Removing the gear knob

29.12a Prise up the plastic retaining tabs . . .

29.12b . . . and remove the radio mounting box

29.12c Push out the hazard switch . . .

29.12d . . . and disconnect the wiring

29.12e Disconnecting the wiring from the heated rear window switch

29.13a Unscrew the side screws . . .

29.13b . . . centre screw . . .

29.13c . . . and upper screws

29.14 . . . then withdraw the console and disconnect the wiring from the digital clock

13 Undo the five screws securing the front of the console to the facia panel **(see illustrations)**.

14 Withdraw the console from inside the vehicle and disconnect the wiring from the digital clock **(see illustration)**.

Refitting

15 Refitting is a reversal of removal.

30 Glovebox -
removal and refitting

Removal

1 Unscrew the mounting screws from the bottom of the glovebox **(see illustration)**.

2 Withdraw the glovebox from inside the car **(see illustration)**.

Refitting

3 Refitting is a reversal of removal.

31 Facia panel -
removal and refitting

⚠️ **Warning: Make sure that the safety recommendations given in Chapter 12 are followed, particularly where a passenger airbag is fitted, in order to prevent personal injury. Refer also to Chapter 10 when working on the steering column.**

Removal

1 Switch off the ignition and remove the ignition key, then disconnect the battery negative then positive leads, and **wait 10 minutes** (this is a safety requirement of the airbag system).

2 Remove the centre console as described in Section 29.

3 Remove the passenger side airbag module as described in Chapter 12.

4 Remove the driver's storage compartment from the lower trim panel beneath the steering column. To do this lift out the bottom edge and unhook the top **(see illustration)**.

5 Undo the screws and remove the lower and bottom trim panels from under the steering column and facia **(see illustrations)**.

6 Undo the screws securing the ashtray assembly to the facia, then disconnect the wiring for the cigar lighter and withdraw the ashtray assembly **(see illustrations)**.

7 Unhook the heater control cables from the levers on the right-hand side of the heater assembly **(see illustration)**.

8 Undo the screws securing the heater control panel to the facia, then withdraw the panel and disconnect the wiring from the switches.

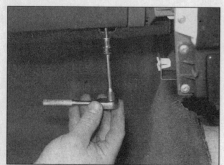

30.1 Unscrew the bottom mounting screws . . .

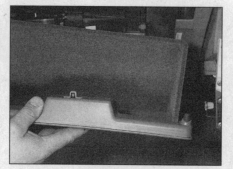

30.2 . . . and withdraw the glovebox from the facia

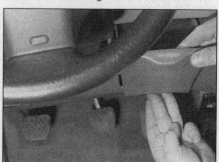

31.4 Removing the driver's storage compartment

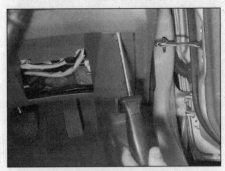

31.5a Undo the outer screw . . .

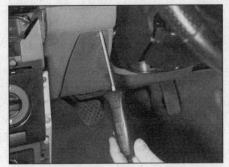

31.5b . . . and inner screw, and remove the lower trim panel from under the steering column

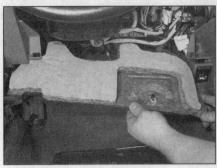

31.5c Removing the bottom trim panel from under the facia

9 Disconnect the facia centre vent cable from the heater assembly. It is located beneath the centre of the facia **(see illustration).**

31.6a Undo the outer screws . . .

10 Remove the glovebox and the lower cover from the passenger side of the facia **(see illustration).**
11 Disconnect the alarm ECU wiring multiplugs and, where applicable, the multiplug for the starter relay. Note on some models the starter relay is located in the engine compartment.
12 Unclip the wiring from the facia support panel.
13 Remove the steering column lower cover by releasing the clips and extracting the studs.
14 At the top of the steering column, remove the wiring harness clip from the stud.
15 Unscrew and remove the steering column upper mounting nuts and lower mounting bolts, then lower the steering column to the floor. There is no need to remove the steering

wheel or to disconnect the steering column from the steering gear. Release the clamps as necessary to prevent straining the wiring harness.
16 Disconnect the multiplugs connecting the facia wiring to the body loom and fusebox. Note carefully the positions of the multiplugs as two of them are of identical type and can be refitted in the wrong positions **(see illustration).**
17 Disconnect the earth wire from the terminal beneath the instrument panel. Also detach the radio aerial lead from the clips on the facia.
18 Carefully prise up the rear edge of the centre upper air vent using a screwdriver and cloth to prevent damage to the facia. Remove the vent and unscrew the facia mounting bolt **(see illustrations).**

31.6b . . . and lower screw . . .

31.6c . . . then remove the ashtray assembly and disconnect the wiring for the cigar lighter

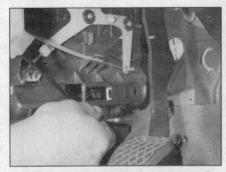

31.7 Disconnecting the heater control cables from the right-hand side of the heater assembly

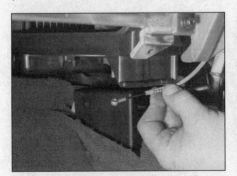

31.9 Disconnecting the facia centre vent cable from the heater assembly

31.10 Removing the lower cover from under the passenger side of the facia

31.16 Disconnecting the facia wiring multiplugs from the fusebox

11

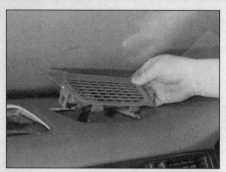

31.18a Removing the centre upper air vent

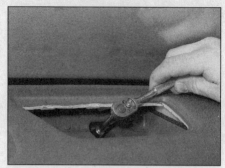

31.18b Unscrewing the facia upper centre mounting bolt

31.19 Carefully prise out the side covers for access to the facia side mounting bolts

19 Prise out the side access covers for access to the facia side mounting bolts. Unscrew and remove the bolts **(see illustration)**.

20 Unscrew and remove the remaining bolts securing the facia to the bulkhead. They are located at the centre bottom and in the

glovebox aperture **(see illustrations)**.

21 Cover the gear lever with a cloth or card to prevent damage to the facia. Alternatively, temporarily refit the gear knob.

22 With the help of an assistant, withdraw the facia from the bulkhead

Refitting

23 Refitting is a reversal of removal, tightening the facia mounting bolts to the specified torque setting.

31.20a Unscrewing the facia lower centre mounting bolt

31.20b The facia mounting bolt located in the glovebox aperture

Chapter 12
Body electrical systems

Contents

Degrees of difficulty

Easy, suitable for novice with little experience		Fairly easy, suitable for beginner with some experience		Fairly difficult, suitable for competent DIY mechanic		Difficult, suitable for experienced DIY mechanic		Very difficult, suitable for expert DIY or professional	

Specifications

System

Type .... 12 volt, negative earth

Fuses

Fusebox inside passenger compartment

Fuse	Rating (amps)	Circuit(s) protected
1	30	Sunroof
2	20	Heated seats
3	7.5	Interior light
4	20	Rear right-hand electric window
5	20	Front right-hand electric window
6	20	Central locking, anti-theft alarm
7	20	Rear left-hand electric window
8	20	Front left-hand electric window
9	10	Right-hand headlight main beam
10	10	Left-hand headlight main beam
11	15	Front foglights
12	Not used	Not used
13	7.5	Exterior mirrors, heater blower, electric cooling fan
14	20	Wipers, washers, electric windows, sunroof
15	10	Indicators, anti-theft alarm, reversing lights
16	10	ABS system
17	10	Rear left-hand tail light
18	7.5	Starting signal
19	10	Rear right-hand tail light, number plate lights, instrument illumination
20	7.5	Rear foglights
21	10	Right-hand headlight low beam
22	10	Left-hand headlight low beam
23	15	Digital clock, radio/cassette, cigar lighter
24	15	Engine management
25	10	SRS and airbag system
26	Not used	Not used

Fusebox at left-hand rear of the engine compartment

Note: *Rover advise owners against removal of the fuses and relays in positions 1 to 3 and A to F as marked on the lid.*

Fuse	Rating (amps)	Circuit(s) protected
G	30	Air conditioning fan
H	15	Engine management system
J	7.5	Digital clock, radio/cassette
K	30 or 15	Electric cooling fan (rating depends on model)
L	30	Heated rear window
M	20	Horn, stop lights
N	10	Hazard warning lights

Additional fuses on left-hand side of the engine compartment

Fuse	Rating (amps)	Circuit(s) protected
1	10	ABS system
2	50	Glow plugs

Note: *On diesel models with ABS, the fuses are in one block.*

Fuse colours

Brown	7.5 amps
Red	10 amps
Blue	15 amps
Yellow	20 amps
Green	30 amps

Bulbs

	Wattage
Headlamps:	
Dipped beam	55
Main bead	55
Front fog light	55
Side light	5
Direction indicator	21
Side repeater	5
Rear tail light	5
Stop light	21
Reversing light	21
Rear fog light	21
Number plate light	5
Glovebox light	5
Interior light	5
Luggage compartment light	5

Torque wrench settings

	Nm	lbf ft
Airbag control unit to steering wheel	3	2.2
Airbag harness earth wire Torx screw	10	7
Driver's airbag module Torx screws	9	7
Horn	22	16
Passenger's airbag module upper nuts	4	3
Passenger's airbag module lower nuts	9	7
SRS impact sensor to front valance	22	16
Tailgate wiper arm	14	10
Tailgate wiper motor	8	6
Tailgate wiper spindle	2	1.5
Windscreen wiper arm	18	13
Windscreen wiper motor linkage	8	6
Windscreen wiper motor	9	7

1 General information and precautions

General information

The electrical system is of the 12-volt negative earth type and comprises a 12-volt battery, an alternator with integral voltage regulator, a starter motor and related electrical accessories, components and wiring. The battery is of the maintenance-free type and is charged by the alternator, which is belt-driven from a crankshaft-mounted pulley.

While some repair procedures are given, the usual course of action is to renew a defective component. The owner whose interest extends beyond mere component renewal should obtain a copy of the *Automobile Electrical & Electronic Systems Manual*, available from the publishers of this Manual.

Precautions

It is necessary to take extra care when working on the electrical system to avoid damage to semi-conductor devices (diodes and transistors) and to avoid the risk of personal injury. Certain procedures must be followed when removing the SRS components. In addition to the precautions given in *"Safety first!"* at the beginning of this Manual, observe the following when working on the system:

a) Always remove rings, watches, etc. before working on the electrical system. Even with the battery disconnected, capacitive discharge could occur if a component's live terminal is earthed through a metal object. This could cause a shock or nasty burn.

b) Do not reverse the battery connections. Components such as the alternator, fuel injection/ignition system ECU, or any other having semi-conductor circuitry could be irreparably damaged.

c) If the engine is being started using jump leads and a slave battery, connect the batteries positive-to-positive and negative-to-negative.

d) Never disconnect the battery terminals, the alternator, any electrical wiring or any test instruments when the engine is running.

e) Do not allow the engine to turn the alternator when the alternator is not connected.

f) Always ensure that the battery negative lead is disconnected when working on the electrical system.

g) Before using electric-arc welding equipment on the vehicle, disconnect the battery, alternator and components such as the fuel injection/ignition system ECU to protect them.

A number of additional precautions must be observed when working on vehicles equipped with airbags (SRS), they are as follows:

a) Before working on any part of the SRS system, switch off the ignition and disconnect the negative then positive battery leads, then **wait at least ten minutes** to allow the system backup circuit to fully discharge.

b) Do not use ohmmeters or any other device capable of supplying current on any of the SRS components, as this may cause accidental detonation.

c) Always use new replacement parts. Never fit parts that are from another vehicle or show signs of damage through being dropped or improperly handled

d) Airbags are classed as pyrotechnical devices and must be stored and handled according to the relevant laws in the country concerned. Place a disconnected airbag unit with the pad surface facing upwards and never rest anything on the pad. Store it on a secure flat surface, away from flammable materials, high heat sources, oils, grease, detergents or water, and never leave it unattended.

e) The SRS indicator light should extinguish 3 seconds after the ignition switch is turned to position "II". If this is not the case, have the system checked by a Rover dealer.

f) No attempt should be made to carry out repairs to the airbag components.

g) Renew the airbag unit and slip ring every ten years, regardless of condition.

h) Return an unwanted airbag unit to your dealer for safe disposal. Do not endanger others by careless disposal of a unit.

2 Electrical fault finding - general information

A typical electrical circuit consists of an electrical component, any switches, relays, motors, fuses, fusible links or circuit breakers related to that component and the wiring and connectors that link the component to both the battery and the chassis. To help you pinpoint an electrical circuit problem, wiring diagrams are included at the end of this Chapter.

Before tackling any troublesome electrical circuit, first study the appropriate wiring diagrams to get a complete understanding of what components are included in that individual circuit. Trouble spots, for instance, can be narrowed down by noting if other components related to the circuit are operating properly. If several components or circuits fail at one time, then the problem is probably in a fuse or earth connection, because several circuits are often routed through the same fuse and earth connections.

Electrical problems usually stem from simple causes, such as loose or corroded connections, a blown fuse, a melted fusible link or a faulty relay. Inspect the condition of all fuses, wires and connections in a problem circuit before testing the components. Use the diagrams to note which terminal connections will need to be checked in order to pinpoint the trouble spot.

The basic tools needed for electrical fault finding include a circuit tester or voltmeter (a 12-volt bulb with a set of test leads can also be used), a continuity tester, a battery and set of test leads, and a jumper wire, preferably with a circuit breaker incorporated, which can be used to bypass electrical components. Before attempting to locate a problem with test instruments, use the wiring diagram to decide where to make the connections.

Voltage checks

Voltage checks should be performed if a circuit is not functioning properly. Connect one lead of a circuit tester to either the negative battery terminal or a known good earth. Connect the other lead to a connector in the circuit being tested, preferably nearest to the battery or fuse. If the bulb of the tester lights then voltage is present, which means that the part of the circuit between the connector and the battery is problem free. Continue checking the rest of the circuit in the same fashion. When you reach a point at which no voltage is present, the problem lies between that point and the last test point with voltage. Most problems can be traced to a loose connection. Bear in mind that some circuits are only live when the ignition switch is switched to a particular position.

Finding a short circuit

One method of finding a short circuit is to remove the fuse and connect a test light or voltmeter to the fuse terminals with all the relevant electrical components switched off. There should be no voltage present in the circuit. Move the wiring from side to side while watching the test light. If the bulb lights up, there is a short to earth somewhere in that area, probably where the insulation has rubbed through. The same test can be performed on each component in the circuit, even a switch.

Earth check

Perform an earth test to check whether a component is properly earthed. Disconnect the battery and connect one lead of a self-powered test light, known as a continuity tester, to a known good earth point. Connect the other lead to the wire or earth connection being tested. If the bulb lights up, the earth is good. If not, the earth is faulty.

If an earth connection is thought to be faulty, dismantle the connection and clean back to bare metal both the bodyshell and the wire terminal or the component's earth connection mating surface. Be careful to remove all traces of dirt and corrosion, then use a knife to trim away any paint, so that a clean metal-to-metal joint is made. On reassembly, tighten the joint fasteners securely; if a wire terminal is being refitted, use serrated washers between the terminal and the bodyshell to ensure a clean and secure connection. When the connection is remade, prevent the onset of corrosion in the future by applying a coat of petroleum jelly or silicone-based grease or by spraying on a proprietary ignition sealer or a water dispersant lubricant at regular intervals.

The vehicle's wiring harness has several multiple-earth connections; refer to the wiring diagrams for further information.

Continuity check

A continuity check is necessary to determine if there are any breaks in a circuit. With the circuit off (ie: no power in the circuit), a self-powered continuity tester can be used to check the circuit. Connect the test leads to both ends of the circuit, or to the positive end and a good earth. If the test light comes on, the circuit is passing current properly. If the light does not come on, there is a break somewhere in the circuit. The same procedure can be used to test a switch, by connecting the continuity tester to the switch terminals. With the switch turned on, the test light should come on.

Finding an open circuit

When checking for possible open circuits, it is often difficult to locate them by sight because oxidation or terminal misalignment are hidden by the connectors. Merely moving a connector on a sensor or in the wiring harness may correct the open circuit condition. Remember this when an open circuit is indicated when fault finding in a circuit. Intermittent problems may also be caused by oxidised or loose connections.

12

3.1 The main fusebox (shown with trim panels removed)

General

Electrical fault finding is simple if you keep in mind that all electrical circuits are basically electricity flowing from the battery, through the wires, switches, relays, fuses and fusible links to each electrical component (light bulb, motor, etc.) and to earth, from which it is passed back to the battery. Any electrical problem is an interruption in the flow of electricity from the battery.

3 Fuses, fusible links and relays - location and renewal

Fuses

1 The main fusebox is located behind the driver's storage compartment located in the facia beneath the steering wheel **(see illustration)**. A further fusebox is located in the rear left-hand corner of the engine compartment for engine related fuses. On models with ABS and/or diesel engine models, additional fuses for the ABS and glowplugs are located on the left-hand side of the engine compartment.

2 To access the fusebox located beneath the steering wheel, first open the storage compartment then push it upwards against the spring tension and release it from the lower pivots. Pull the compartment outwards away from the facia; the fusebox can then be viewed behind the facia.

3 To access the engine compartment

fusebox, open the bonnet then depress the catch and unhook the lid. Further details on fuse ratings and circuits protected are given in the Specifications.

4 To remove a fuse, first switch off the circuit concerned (or the ignition), then fit the tweezers and pull the fuse out of its terminals. Slide the fuse sideways from the tweezers. The wire within the fuse is clearly visible. If the fuse is blown, the wire will be broken or melted.

5 Always renew a fuse with one of an identical rating. Never use a fuse with a different rating from the original or substitute anything else. The fuse rating is stamped on top of the fuse. Fuses are also colour-coded for easy recognition (see Specifications).

6 If a new fuse blows immediately, find the cause before renewing it again. A short to earth as a result of faulty insulation is the most likely cause. Where a fuse protects more than one circuit, try to isolate the defect by switching on each circuit in turn (if possible) until the fuse blows again.

7 If any of the spare fuses are used, always replace them so that a spare of each rating is available.

Fusible links

8 The fusible links are located in the engine compartment fusebox, situated on the left-hand rear side of the engine compartment. Unclip the lid to gain access to them.

9 All links are numbered on the rear of the fusebox lid.

10 To remove a fusible link, first ensure that the circuit concerned is switched off then prise off the plastic cover. Slacken the two link retaining screws then lift the fusible link out of the fusebox. The wire within the fusible link is clearly visible. If the fuse is blown, it will be broken or melted. A blown fusible link indicates a serious wiring or system fault which must be diagnosed before the link is renewed.

11 Always renew a fusible link with one of an identical rating. Never use a link with a different rating from the original or substitute anything else. On refitting, tighten the link retaining screws securely and refit the link cover.

Relays

12 Refer to the relevant wiring diagram for the details of the various relays. The main relays are located in the engine compartment fusebox.

13 If a circuit or system controlled by a relay develops a fault and the relay is suspect, operate the system. If the relay is functioning, it should be possible to hear it click as it is energised. If this is the case, the fault lies with the components or wiring of the system. If the relay is not being energised, then either the relay is not receiving a main supply or a switching voltage, or the relay itself is faulty. Testing is by the substitution of a known good unit but be careful as some relays are identical in appearance, but perform different functions.

14 To renew a relay, ensure that the ignition switch is off, then simply pull direct from the socket and press in the new relay.

4 Switches - removal and refitting

1 Disconnect the battery negative lead before removing any switch and after refitting the switch, reconnect the lead.

Wiper/lighting switches on steering column

Removal

2 Undo the screws and remove the steering column upper and lower shrouds **(see illustrations)**.

3 Disconnect the wiring multiplugs from the lighting and wiper switches **(see illustration)**.

4 With the ignition key inserted, turn the steering wheel to give access to the switch retaining screws. Undo the screws then depress the tab and slide the switch from the base **(see illustrations)**.

5 If it is required to remove the switch base, remove the steering wheel as described in Chapter 10 then undo the screws and remove the rotary coupler from the top of the column. Remove the indicator cancellation cam, then undo the screws and withdraw the base **(see illustrations)**.

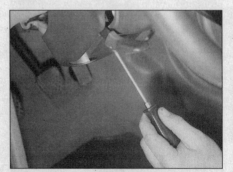

4.2a Undo the screws . . .

4.2b . . . and remove the steering column lower . . .

4.2c . . . and upper shrouds

4.3 Disconnecting the wiring multiplugs from the wiper/lighting switches

4.4a Undo the switch mounting screws . . .

4.4b . . . then depress the tab . . .

4.4c . . . and withdraw the switch from the base

4.5a Removing the indicator cancellation cam . . .

4.5b . . . and switch base

Refitting

6 Refitting is a reversal of removal.

4.7a Using a screwdriver, prise out the hazard switch . . .

Facia switches

Removal

7 Check that the relevant switch is in the off position, then taking care not to scratch or damage the switch or its surround, prise it out using a suitable flat-bladed screwdriver. Withdraw the switch until the connector plug appears then disconnect the wiring connector and remove the switch **(see illustrations)**. Where applicable, tie a piece of string to the wiring connector to prevent it from falling behind the facia panel.

Refitting

8 On refitting, connect the wiring connector to the switch and press the switch into position until the retaining clips click into place.

Exterior mirror switch

Removal

9 Where blanks are fitted next to the switch, prise out one of them and press out the switch from behind **(see illustrations)**.
10 Where there are no blanks, remove the driver's storage compartment from the lower trim panel beneath the steering column then undo the screws and remove the lower trim panel from the facia. Reach up behind the facia and press out the exterior mirror switch.
11 Disconnect the wiring multiplug from the rear of the switch **(see illustration)**.

Refitting

12 Refitting is a reversal of removal.

4.7b . . . then disconnect the wiring multiplug

4.7c Using a screwdriver, prise out the foglight switch . . .

4.7d . . . then disconnect the wiring multiplug

4.9a Use a screwdriver . . .

4.9b . . . to prise out the blank . . .

4.9c . . . then push out the exterior mirror switch . . .

Horn push switch

Removal

13 Remove the driver's airbag as described in Section 16.
14 Disconnect the earth wiring from the base of the steering wheel.
15 Disconnect the wiring leading to the rotary coupler.
16 Using a screwdriver, carefully prise the switch from the steering wheel taking care not to damage the covering.
17 Disconnect the spade connectors and remove the switch.

Refitting

18 Refitting is a reversal of removal.

Courtesy lamp switches

Removal

19 With the door open, undo the screw securing the courtesy lamp to the body. Pull out the switch and tie a piece of string to the wiring to prevent it dropping into the body **(see illustration)**.
20 Disconnect the wiring and remove the switch from the vehicle.

Refitting

21 Refitting is a reverse of removal.

Handbrake warning lamp switch

Removal

22 Remove the rear console as described in Chapter 11.
23 Disconnect the wiring from the switch located on the left-hand side of the handbrake lever **(see illustration)**.
24 Undo the screw and remove the switch.

Refitting

25 Refitting is a reversal of removal.

Glovebox illumination switch

Removal

26 Remove the glovebox (see Chapter 11).
27 Reach up behind the upper lip of the facia and disconnect the wiring from the switch **(see illustration)**.
28 Undo the screws and remove the switch.

Refitting

29 Refitting is a reversal of removal.

Ignition switch

Removal

30 Remove the ignition key then disconnect the negative (earth) lead from the battery followed by the positive lead. Wait ten minutes to allow the SRS system backup circuit to fully discharge.
31 Remove the driver's pocket from the lower facia panel below the steering wheel,

4.11 . . . and disconnect the wiring multiplug

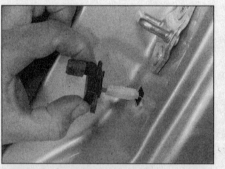

4.19 Removing a courtesy lamp switch

4.23 Handbrake warning lamp switch

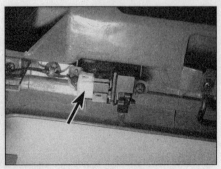

4.27 Wiring plug on the glovebox illumination switch

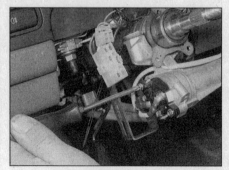

4.35a Undo the screws . . .

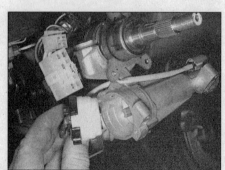

4.35b . . . and remove the ignition switch from the lock housing

4.42a Undo the screws . . .

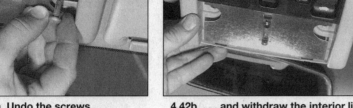

4.42b . . . and withdraw the interior light assembly

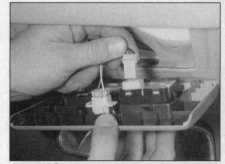

4.43a Disconnect the wiring . . .

then undo the screws and remove the lower facia panel.

32 Undo the screws and remove the steering column upper and lower shrouds.

33 Disconnect the two starter switch multiplugs from the fusebox located to the right-hand side of the steering wheel.

34 Detach the ignition switch wiring from the supports by unscrewing the studs. Also release the cable tie.

35 Undo the screws and remove the ignition switch from the lock housing **(see illustrations)**.

Refitting

36 Refit the switch and tighten the screws.

37 Reconnect the wiring and secure with the cable tie and supports.

38 Refit the steering column upper and lower shrouds.

39 Refit the lower facia panel and the driver's pocket.

5.2 Remove the rubber cover . . .

40 Reconnect the battery positive then negative leads.

Sunroof control switch

Removal

41 Prise the lens from the interior light located at the front of the headlining.

42 Unscrew and remove the screws and withdraw the light assembly **(see illustrations)**.

43 Disconnect the wiring from the rear of the switch and press the switch from the housing **(see illustrations)**.

Refitting

44 Refitting is a reversal of removal.

---

5 Bulbs (exterior lamps) - renewal

General

1 Whenever a bulb is renewed, note the following:

  a) Remember that if the lamp has just been in use, the bulb may be extremely hot.

  b) Always check the bulb contacts and holder, ensuring that there is clean metal-to-metal contact between the bulb and its live contacts and earth. Clean off any corrosion or dirt before fitting a new bulb.

  c) Always ensure that the new bulb is of the correct rating and that the glass envelope is completely clean before fitting. This applies particularly to headlamp bulbs. If necessary clean the glass with methylated spirit.

4.43b . . . and remove the sunroof control switch from the light assembly

Outer (main and dip) headlamp

2 Working in the engine compartment, remove the rubber cover from the rear of the headlamp unit **(see illustration)**.

3 Unplug the wiring connector, then unhook the ears of the bulb retaining clips and swivel them away from the bulb **(see illustrations)**.

4 Withdraw the bulb **(see illustration)**.

5 When handling a new bulb, use a tissue or clean cloth to avoid touching the glass with the fingers. Moisture and grease from the skin can cause blackening and rapid failure of this type of bulb.

> **HAYNES HINT** *If the glass of a headlamp bulb is accidentally touched, wipe it clean using methylated spirit.*

5.3a . . . unplug the wiring connector . . .

5.3b . . . unhook the ears of the retaining clips . . .

5.4 . . . then remove the outer headlamp bulb

5.7 Remove the rubber cover . . .

6 Refitting is the reverse of the removal procedure. Ensure that the metal tab on the bulb base is located in the cut-out at the top of the headlamp.

5.9a . . . disconnect the wiring . . .

5.9b . . . and remove the inner headlamp bulb

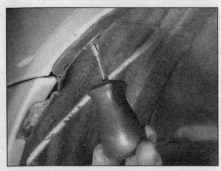

5.16 Undo the screw and pull back the wheel arch liner . . .

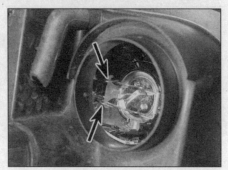

5.8 . . . unhook the ears of the retaining clips . . .

Inner (main) headlamp

7 Working in the engine compartment, remove the rubber cover from the rear of the headlamp unit **(see illustration)**.
8 Unhook the ears of the bulb retaining clips and swivel them away from the bulb **(see illustration)**.
9 Disconnect the wiring, then withdraw the bulb **(see illustrations)**. Observe the precautions given in paragraph 5.
10 Refitting is the reverse of the removal procedure. Ensure that the metal base of the bulb is located correctly in the rear of the headlamp.

Front sidelamp

11 Working in the engine compartment, remove the rubber cover from the rear of the headlamp unit.
12 Pull the bulbholder from the headlamp reflector **(see illustration)**.

5.12 Remove the front sidelamp bulbholder . . .

5.17 . . . then withdraw the bulbholder . . .

13 Pull the capless (push fit) bulb out of its socket **(see illustration)**.
14 Refitting is the reverse of the removal procedure.

Front direction indicator

15 If working on the right-hand indicator turn the front wheels on full left lock, and vice versa.
16 Undo the screw from the fastener securing the wheel arch liner to the front wing behind the front direction indicator, then fold back the liner along its crease line for access to the rear of the light **(see illustration)**.
17 Twist the front direction indicator bulbholder anti-clockwise and remove it from the rear of the indicator light **(see illustration)**. There is no need to disconnect the wiring.
18 Depress and twist the bulb to remove it from the bulbholder **(see illustration)**.
19 Refitting is a reversal of removal.

Front direction indicator side repeater

20 Carefully press the side repeater light towards the front of the vehicle and withdraw it from the wing **(see illustration)**.
21 Twist the bulbholder anti-clockwise and remove it from the light, then pull the capless (push fit) bulb out of its socket **(see illustrations)**.
22 Refitting is a reversal of removal.

Front foglamp/driving lamp

23 Using a cross-head screwdriver, undo the screw and remove the cover from the lamp.
24 Undo the mounting screws and withdraw the lamp from the front bumper.

5.13 . . . then pull the capless bulb out of its socket

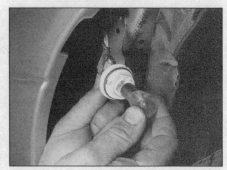

5.18 . . . and remove the front direction indicator bulb

Body electrical systems 12•9

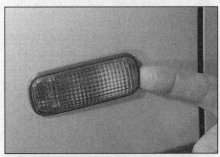

5.20 Press the front direction indicator side repeater light forwards to remove it from the wing

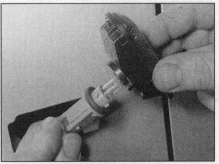

5.21a Twist the bulbholder from the light . . .

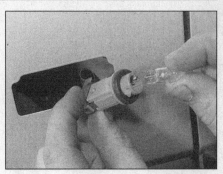

5.21b . . . and pull out the capless bulb

25 Twist the bulbholder anti-clockwise from the rear of the foglamp, then withdraw the bulb **(see illustrations)**.

26 Refitting is a reversal of removal.

Rear light cluster

27 Open the tailgate or bootlid and unclip the covering from the rear of the luggage compartment for access to the rear light. To

release the clip, depress its centre pin slightly using a screwdriver **(see illustrations)**.

28 Depress the clip and disconnect the wiring multiplug from the rear of the light unit **(see illustration)**.

29 On Hatchback models, squeeze together the two tabs then withdraw the bulbholder **(see illustration)**.

30 On Saloon models, move the lever inwards while supporting the rear of the light cluster, then withdraw the unit from the rear.

31 Depress and twist the bulb to remove it from the bulbholder **(see illustration)**. If a bulb has blown, it will be blackened. If necessary, temporarily reconnect the wiring to the cluster and compare the functions of each bulb with its counterpart on the other side of the vehicle.

32 Refitting is a reversal of removal. To refit the luggage compartment covering clips, push the centre pins out before refitting them, then press in the pins flush **(see illustration)**.

5.25a Twist the bulbholder from the rear of the front foglamp . . .

5.25b . . . then withdraw the bulb

5.27a Slightly depress the clip centre pin . . .

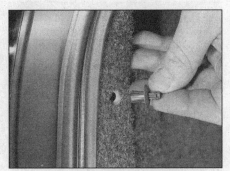

5.27b . . . then remove it

5.28 Disconnecting the wiring from the rear light cluster

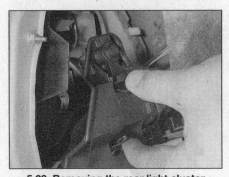

5.29 Removing the rear light cluster bulbholder (Hatchback models)

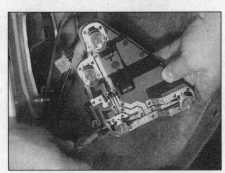

5.31 Removing a rear light cluster bulb

5.32 Press in the clip pins until flush

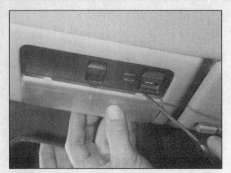

6.2a Use a screwdriver to prise off the interior light lens . . .

6.2b . . . then remove the festoon bulb from its spring contacts

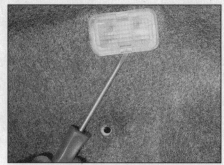

6.4a Prise off the lens . . .

Number plate lamps

33 Open the tailgate/boot lid for access to the number plate lamps.

34 Undo the screws and withdraw the light unit.

35 On Hatchback models, depress the tab and unclip the lens. Recover the gasket. The bulb is of the capless (push fit) type and can be pulled out of the lamp unit.

36 On Saloon models, remove the festoon-type bulb from the spring contacts.

37 Refitting is a reverse of the removal procedure. On Saloon models, check the tension of the spring contacts and if necessary, bend them so that they firmly contact the bulb end caps.

6 Bulbs (interior lamps) - renewal

General

1 Refer to Section 5.

Interior lamps

2 Using a small screwdriver, carefully prise the lens off the lamp unit then remove the festoon bulb from its spring contacts (see illustrations).

3 Fit the new bulb using a reversal of the removal procedure. Check the tension of the spring contacts and if necessary, bend them so that they firmly contact the bulb end caps.

Luggage compartment lamp (Hatchback models)

4 Using a small screwdriver, carefully prise the lens off the lamp unit then remove the festoon bulb from its spring contacts (see illustrations).

5 Fit the new bulb using a reversal of the removal procedure. Check the tension of the spring contacts and if necessary, bend them so that they firmly contact the bulb end caps.

Luggage compartment lamp (Saloon models)

6 Using a small screwdriver, carefully prise the lamp from under the rear shelf.

7 Depress and twist the bulb to remove it.

8 Fit the new bulb using a reversal of the removal procedure.

6.4b . . . then remove the festoon bulb from the luggage compartment lamp

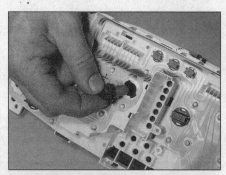

6.11a Removing a main panel illumination bulbholder . . .

6.11b . . . and bulb

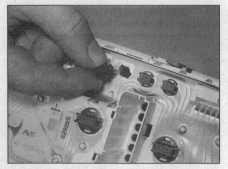

6.11c Removing a warning lamp bulbholder . . .

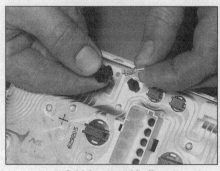

6.11d . . . and bulb

6.11e Removing the SRS warning lamp bulbholder and wiring . . .

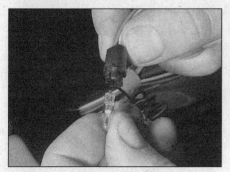

6.11f . . . and bulb

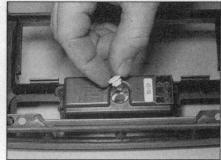

6.14a Remove the bulbholder . . .

6.14b . . . and pull out the digital clock illumination bulb

Instrument panel illumination and warning lamps

9 Remove the instrument panel as described in Section 11.
10 Twist the relevant bulbholder anti-clockwise and withdraw it from the rear of the panel.
11 Most of the main panel illumination bulbs are integral with their holders, however the main panel illumination bulbs (with a red envelope over the glass) and some lower warning bulbs are of the capless (push fit) type **(see illustrations)**.
12 Fit the new bulb/bulbholder using a reversal of the removal procedure.

Digital clock illumination

13 Remove the centre console as described in Chapter 11.

14 Unscrew and remove the bulbholder, then pull out the wedge-type bulb **(see illustrations)**.
15 Fit the new bulb/bulbholder using a reversal of the removal procedure.

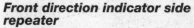

7 Exterior lamp units - removal and refitting

Headlamp and front direction indicator lamp

1 Remove the front bumper as described in Chapter 11.
2 Unscrew the bolts securing the bracket to the front valance just below the headlamp, and remove it **(see illustrations)**.
3 Unscrew the headlamp mounting bolts and nut **(see illustrations)**.

4 Twist the indicator bulbholder anti-clockwise and remove from the rear of the indicator light.
5 Disconnect the headlamp wiring multiplug **(see illustration)**. On later models also disconnect the wiring from the headlamp levelling motor.
6 Withdraw the headlamp from the front of the vehicle.
7 Refitting is a reversal of removal, but tighten the bracket bolts to the specified torque and on completion check and if necessary adjust the headlamp beam setting (see Section 8).

Front direction indicator side repeater

8 Carefully press the side repeater light towards the front of the vehicle and withdraw it from the wing.

7.2a Unscrew the bolts . . .

7.2b . . . and remove the bracket from the front valance

7.3a Headlamp upper mounting bolts . . .

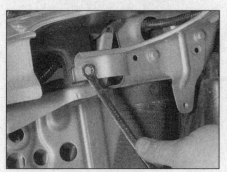

7.3b . . . side bolt . . .

7.3c . . . and lower nut

7.5 Disconnecting the headlamp wiring multiplug

12

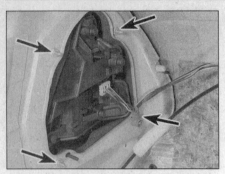

7.13 Rear lamp cluster mounting nuts (Hatchback models)

7.24a Undo the screw . . .

7.24b . . . and remove the cover from the front foglamp

9 Twist the bulbholder anti-clockwise and remove it from the light, then withdraw the side repeater.
10 Refitting is a reversal of removal.

Rear lamp cluster

11 Open the tailgate or bootlid and unclip the covering from the rear of the luggage compartment for access to the rear light. To release the clip, depress its centre pin slightly using a screwdriver.
12 Depress the clip and disconnect the wiring multiplug from the rear of the light unit.
13 On Hatchback models, unscrew the mounting nuts and withdraw the unit from the rear **(see illustration)**.
14 On Saloon models, move the lever inwards while supporting the rear of the light cluster, then withdraw the unit from the rear.
15 Remove the rubber seal.
16 Refitting is a reversal of removal. The rubber seal must be renewed if damaged.

Number plate lamps

17 Open the tailgate/boot lid for access to the number plate lamps.
18 Undo the screws and withdraw the light unit.
19 Disconnect the wiring.
20 Refitting is a reverse of the removal procedure.

High level stop lamp

21 Using a Torx key undo the screws and remove the trim from the high level stop lamp.
22 Unscrew the mounting nuts, withdraw the

stop lamp, and disconnect the wiring.
23 Refitting is a reversal of removal.

Front foglamp/driving lamp

24 Using a cross-head screwdriver, undo the screw and remove the cover from the lamp **(see illustrations)**.
25 Undo the mounting screws and withdraw the lamp from the front bumper **(see illustration)**.
26 Twist the bulbholder anti-clockwise from the rear of the foglight.
27 Refitting is a reversal of removal. If necessary, the foglight beam may be adjusted by removing the clips and turning the knobs on the rear of the lamp **(see illustrations)**.

8 Headlamp beams - alignment

If the headlamps are thought to be out of alignment, then accurate adjustment of their beams is only possible using optical beam setting equipment, and this work should therefore be carried out by a Rover dealer or workshop with the necessary facilities.

For reference, the headlamps can be adjusted by using a suitably-sized crosshead screwdriver to rotate the two adjuster assemblies fitted to the rear of each lamp. The outer adjuster controls the horizontal setting and the inner adjuster controls the vertical setting.

9 Dim-dip headlamp system - operation

This system comprises the dim-dip resistor which is riveted to the underside of the battery tray. The air cleaner and battery tray must be removed for access to the resistor.

The dim-dip unit is supplied with current from the sidelamp circuit and energised by a feed from the ignition switch. When energised, the unit allows battery voltage to pass through the resistor to the headlamp dipped-beam circuits. This energises the headlamps with approximately one-sixth of their normal power so that the vehicle cannot be driven using sidelamps alone.

10 Integrated control unit - removal and refitting

Removal

1 The integrated control unit functions as a central control for the following circuits:
a) *Front and rear wipers*
b) *Courtesy lamp delay*
c) *Heated rear window*
d) *Horn*
e) *Lights-on alarm*
f) *Dim-dip*
g) *Rear fog lights*

7.25 Removing the front foglamp from the bumper

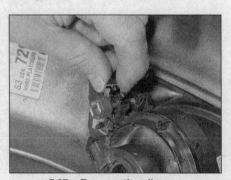

7.27a Remove the clips . . .

7.27b . . . and adjust the front foglamp beam

11.4a Undo the instrument panel surround lower mounting screws . . .

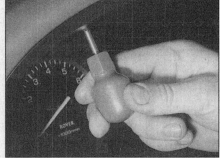

11.4b . . . and upper mounting screws . . .

11.4c . . . and remove the surround

h) *Engine immobiliser*
i) *Catalyst overheat warning*
j) *Seat belt warning*

2 Disconnect the battery negative lead followed by the positive lead.
3 Remove the driver's storage compartment from the lower trim panel beneath the steering column.
4 Undo the screws and remove the lower trim panel from the facia.
5 Disconnect the two multiplugs from the top of the fusebox.
6 Unscrew the fusebox mounting bolts and detach it from the studs.
7 Disconnect the wiring multiplugs from the integrated control unit, and release the unit from the back of the fusebox.
8 Withdraw the unit from inside the vehicle.

Refitting

9 Refitting is a reversal of removal.

11 Instrument panel - removal and refitting

Removal

1 Adjust the steering column to its lowest position.
2 Using a screwdriver, carefully prise out the fog lamp switch from the instrument panel surround and disconnect the wiring multiplug.
3 Similarly, prise out the blank from the other

side of the surround.
4 Using a cross-head screwdriver, undo the screws and withdraw the surround. The retaining screws are located at the lower corners and under the upper edge of the surround **(see illustrations)**.
5 Undo the instrument panel retaining screws and withdraw the panel for access to the wiring. The upper edge of the panel should be tilted down **(see illustrations)**.
6 Disconnect the wiring, where necessary remove the SRS warning bulb holder, and release the wiring from the clip **(see illustration)**.
7 Withdraw the instrument panel from behind the steering wheel.

Refitting

8 Refitting is a reversal of removal. On completion, check the operation of all panel warning lamps and instrument surround switches to ensure that they are functioning correctly.

12 Instrument panel components - removal and refitting

Removal

1 The procedure for removing the following instruments is identical.
a) *Speedometer*
b) *Tachometer*

c) *Coolant temperature gauge*
d) *Fuel gauge*

2 Remove the instrument panel as described in Section 11.
3 Disconnect the illumination bulb and lead from the housing.
4 Undo the screw and remove the support bracket from the housing.
5 Carefully release the clips and remove the front cover from the housing.
6 Undo the screws and remove the appropriate instrument.

Refitting

7 Refitting is a reversal of removal.

13 Cigar lighter - removal and refitting

Removal

1 Remove the centre console as described in Chapter 11.
2 Undo the screws securing the ashtray assembly to the facia, then disconnect the wiring for the cigar lighter and withdraw the ashtray assembly.
3 Remove the cigar lighter element, then unscrew the central screw and remove the cigar lighter components from the assembly.

Refitting

4 Refitting is a reversal of removal.

11.5a Removing the instrument panel lower mounting screws . . .

11.5b . . . and upper mounting screws

11.6 Disconnecting the wiring from the rear of the instrument panel

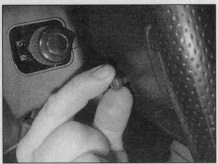

16.2 Removing the Torx-headed screw securing the airbag module to the steering wheel

14 Clock -
removal and refitting

Removal

1 Remove the centre console as described in Chapter 11.
2 Undo the screws and remove the clock from the console.

Refitting

3 Refitting is a reversal of removal.

15 Supplementary Restraint System (SRS) -
operation

At vehicle start-up, a warning light located in the steering wheel centre pad (single airbag system) or instrument panel (twin airbag system) will illuminate when the system electrical circuits are activated by turning the ignition switch to position "II" and will stay illuminated for 3 seconds whilst the system performs a self-diagnosis test. If this test is satisfactory, the light will extinguish. If the test is unsatisfactory, the light will remain on or fail to illuminate at all, denoting that the system must be serviced as soon as possible. System operation is as follows:

Upon the vehicle suffering a frontal impact over a specified force, a sensor inside the airbag control unit, which is located on the

16.3 Disconnecting the wiring from the airbag module

steering wheel (single driver's airbag system) or beneath the front centre console (twin airbag system), activates the system. A safing sensor (fitted to discriminate between actual impact and driving on rough road surfaces, etc.) is also activated and power is supplied to the airbag ignitor from the battery or a backup circuit, causing the airbag to inflate within 30 milliseconds.

As the driver of the vehicle is thrown forward into the inflated airbag it immediately discharges its contents through a vent, thereby providing a progressive deceleration and reducing the risk of injury from contact with the steering wheel, facia or windscreen. The total time taken from the start of airbag inflation to its complete deflation is approximately 0.1 seconds.

A severe frontal impact will also activate the front seat belt pretensioners in order to take up any slack.

16 Supplementary Restraint System (SRS) - component
removal and refitting

> ⚠ **Warning: Under no circumstances, attempt to diagnose problems with SRS components using standard workshop equipment.**

Note: *All SRS system wiring can be identified by its yellow protective covering. The information in this Section is limited to those components which must be removed to gain access to other components on the vehicle. Read carefully the precautions given in Section 1 of this Chapter before commencing work on any part of the system.*

Driver's airbag module

Removal

1 With the ignition switched off, disconnect the battery negative then positive leads and **wait at least 10 minutes** to allow the SRS backup system to completely discharge. With the front wheels in the straight-ahead position, remove the ignition key.
2 Using a Torx key, unscrew the bolts from each side of the steering wheel and release the airbag module from the steering wheel. Do not allow the airbag module to hang on its wiring **(see illustration)**.
3 Disconnect the wiring from the centre rear of the module **(see illustration)**.
4 Remove the module from the steering wheel and place it in safe storage.
5 If the module is to be renewed, record its bar code and obtain the new unit from a Rover dealer.

Refitting

6 Refit the airbag module by reversing the removal procedure, noting the following:
 a) *The cable wiring connector must face upwards when refitted to the rear of the module.*

 b) *Observe the specified torque wrench setting when tightening the airbag retaining screws (TX30 Torx type) and take care not to cross-thread them.*
 c) *Reconnect both battery leads, negative lead last, and turn the ignition switch to the "II" position. Check the condition of the system by observing the SRS warning light located in the steering wheel centre pad. The light should stay illuminated for 3 seconds whilst the system performs a self-diagnosis test. If the test is satisfactory, the light will extinguish. If the test is unsatisfactory, the light will remain on or fail to illuminate at all, denoting that the system must be serviced as soon as possible.*

Driver's airbag control unit

Removal

7 Remove the driver's airbag module as described earlier in this Section.
8 Disconnect the control unit multiplug from the rotary coupler terminal.
9 Carefully prise out the horn switches from the steering wheel using a screwdriver, then disconnect the wiring and remove the switches. Remove the switch wires from their sockets.
10 Disconnect the earth wire from the terminal on the steering wheel.
11 Detach the SRS warning light and its wiring from the recesses in the steering wheel.
12 Using a Torx key, undo the screws and remove the control unit from the steering wheel.

Refitting

13 Refit the control unit by reversing the removal procedure, noting the following:
 a) *If the control unit is to be renewed, then the bar code on the new item must be recorded by your Rover dealer.*
 b) *Take care to ensure that wiring is not trapped.*
 c) *Observe the specified torque wrench setting when tightening the control unit retaining screws (TX20 Torx type).*
 d) *On completion, carry out a system check as described in paragraph 6.*

Passenger airbag module

Removal

14 With the ignition switched off, disconnect the battery negative then positive leads and **wait at least 10 minutes** to allow the SRS backup system to completely discharge.
15 Remove the glovebox as described in Chapter 11.
16 Working from under the facia, identify the two wires on the airbag module for position, then disconnect them **(see illustration)**.
17 Unscrew and remove the six nuts securing the airbag module to the facia, then remove the module and place it in safe storage **(see illustration)**.

16.16 Passenger airbag module viewed from under the facia

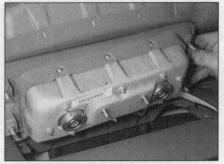

16.17 Removing the passenger airbag module from the top of the facia

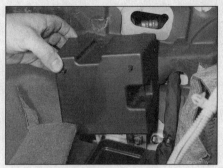

16.22 Remove the cover . . .

18 If the module is to be renewed, record its bar code and obtain the new unit from a Rover dealer.

Refitting

19 Refit the airbag module by reversing the removal procedure, noting the following:

a) *The module lower retaining nuts **must** be renewed. Tighten the nuts progressively to the specified torque noting that the upper nuts are tightened to 4 Nm and the lower nuts are tightened to 9 Nm.*

b) *Reconnect both battery leads, negative lead last, and turn the ignition switch to the "II" position. Check the condition of the system by observing the SRS warning light located in the steering wheel centre pad. The light should stay illuminated for 3 seconds whilst the system performs a self-diagnosis test. If the test is satisfactory, the light will extinguish. If the*

test is unsatisfactory, the light will remain on or fail to illuminate at all, denoting that the system must be serviced as soon as possible.

Twin airbag control unit

Removal

20 With the ignition key removed, disconnect the battery negative then positive leads, then **wait at least 10 minutes** to allow the SRS backup system to completely discharge.

21 Unbolt and remove the driver's footrest.

22 Pull back the carpet then unscrew the studs from the control unit cover and withdraw the cover from the right-hand side **(see illustration)**.

23 Disconnect the wiring multiplug then unscrew the mounting bolts using a Torx key and withdraw the control unit from inside the vehicle **(see illustration)**.

Refitting

24 Refitting is a reversal of removal, noting the following:

a) *If the control unit is to be renewed, then the bar code on the new item must be recorded by your Rover dealer.*

b) *Take care to ensure that wiring is not trapped.*

c) *Observe the specified torque wrench setting when tightening the control unit retaining bolts.*

d) *On completion, carry out a system check as described in paragraph 6.*

Rotary coupler

Removal

25 Remove the steering wheel as described in Chapter 10. To prevent the rotary coupler from loosing its central setting, use adhesive tape to secure the upper part to the base.

26 Undo the screws and remove the steering column lower and upper shrouds **(see illustrations)**.

27 Disconnect the wiring multiplugs from the rotary coupler **(see illustrations)**.

28 Undo the screws and remove the rotary coupler from the wiper/lighting switch base **(see illustrations)**.

Refitting

29 Offer up the rotary coupler to the switch base and align the slots with the projections on the cancelling sleeve. Insert the screws and tighten securely.

16.23 . . . for access to the twin airbag control unit

16.26a Removing the steering column lower shroud . . .

16.26b . . . and upper shroud

16.27a Disconnecting the SRS multiplug . . .

16.27b . . . and horn multiplug from the rear of the rotary coupler

12

16.28a Undo the screws . . .

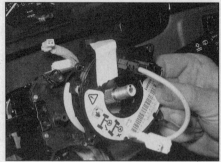

16.28b . . . and remove the rotary coupler from the wiper/lighting switch base

16.45 Removing the inertia switch

30 Remove the adhesive tape from the rotary coupler and reconnect the wiring multiplugs.

31 Refit the steering column upper and lower shrouds.

32 Refit the steering wheel as described in Chapter 10.

Airbag harness

Removal

Note: *The following paragraphs describe the removal and refitting procedure for models fitted with a driver's and passenger's airbag.*

33 With the ignition key removed, disconnect the battery negative then positive leads, then **wait at least 10 minutes** to allow the SRS backup system to completely discharge.

34 Remove the driver's pocket from the lower facia panel below the steering wheel, then undo the screws and remove the lower facia panel.

35 Undo the screws and remove the steering column upper and lower shrouds **(see illustrations 16.26a and b).**

36 Remove the glovebox as described in Chapter 11.

37 Remove the front console as described in Chapter 11.

38 Unbolt and remove the driver's footrest.

39 Pull back the carpet then unscrew the studs from the control unit cover and withdraw the cover from the right-hand side.

40 Using a Torx key, undo the airbag harness earth screw from the control unit bracket.

41 Disconnect the wiring multiplug from the control unit.

42 Disconnect the wiring multiplug from the passenger's airbag.

43 Disconnect the wiring multiplug from the rotary coupler at the top of the steering column.

44 Disconnect the wiring multiplugs from the fusebox.

45 Unscrew the bolts and move the inertia switch and relay bracket clear of the airbag wiring harness clip **(see illustration).**

46 Release the wiring harness from the clips and withdraw from inside the vehicle **(see illustration).**

Refitting

47 Refitting is a reversal of removal, tightening the airbag harness earth screw to the specified torque. On completion turn the ignition switch to the "II" position and check that the SRS warning light illuminates for 3 seconds whilst the system performs a self-diagnosis test. If the test is satisfactory, the light will extinguish. If the test is unsatisfactory, the light will remain on or fail to illuminate at all.

17 Vehicle speed sensor - removal and refitting

Refer to Chapter 7, Section 6.

18 Horn - removal and refitting

Removal

1 Disconnect the battery negative terminal.

2 Remove the front bumper.

3 Disconnect the wiring multiplug and unbolt the horn from the bracket **(see illustration).**

Refitting

4 Refitting is a reversal of the removal procedure.

19 Wiper arm - removal and refitting

Windscreen wiper arm

Removal

1 Operate the wiper motor, then switch it off so that the wiper arm returns to the "parked" position.

2 Stick a piece of tape on the windscreen, along the edge of the wiper blade, to use as an alignment aid on refitting.

3 Unscrew and remove the spindle nut, then lift the blade off the glass and pull the wiper arm off its spindle **(see illustration).** If

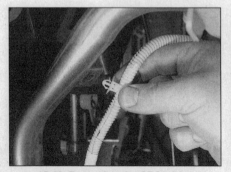

16.46 Removing the SRS wiring

18.3 Horn location behind the front bumper

19.3 Unscrewing the spindle nut from the windscreen wiper arm

necessary, the arm can be levered off the spindle using a suitable flat-bladed screwdriver. If both windscreen wiper arms are removed, note their locations, as different arms are fitted to the driver's and passenger's sides.

Refitting

4 Refitting is a reversal of removal, but ensure that the wiper arm and spindle splines are clean and dry and align the blades with the tape fitted before tightening the spindle nut.

Tailgate wiper arm

Removal

5 Operate the tailgate wiper motor, then switch it off so that the wiper arm returns to the "parked" position.
6 Stick a piece of tape on the windscreen, along the edge of the wiper blade, to use as an alignment aid on refitting.
7 Lift and unclip the plastic cover, then unscrew the spindle nut **(see illustration)**.
8 Lift the blade off the glass and pull the wiper arm off its spindle **(see illustration)**. If necessary, the arm can be levered off the spindle using a suitable flat-bladed screwdriver.

Refitting

9 Refitting is a reversal of removal, but ensure that the wiper arm and spindle splines are clean and dry and align the blade with the tape fitted before tightening the spindle nut to the specified torque.

19.7 Undo the spindle nut . . .

20 Windscreen wiper motor and linkage - removal and refitting

Removal

1 Remove both wiper arms as described in Section 19. For improved access, temporarily unbolt the cooling system expansion tank and position it away from the bulkhead - **do not** disconnect the hoses from it **(see illustration)**.
2 With the bonnet open, remove the fasteners securing the scuttle cover in front of the windscreen. The rear fasteners are removed by prising up their centre discs then lifting them out. To remove the front fasteners use a

19.8 . . . and remove the tailgate wiper arm

pair of pliers to squeeze the bottom tabs, then push them up through the holes. If necessary, release the weatherstrip from the fasteners **(see illustrations)**.
3 Release the outer ends of the scuttle cover from the bonnet hinges on each side, and withdraw it from the car **(see illustration)**. To aid releasing the scuttle cover end rubbers, have an assistant temporarily hold the bonnet semi-closed.
4 Disconnect the wiring multiplug from the wiper motor **(see illustration)**.
5 Unscrew the mounting bolts and withdraw the wiper motor and linkage from the bulkhead **(see illustrations)**.
6 Release the multiplug from the linkage, then unbolt and remove the motor **(see illustration)**.

20.1 Temporarily unbolt the cooling system expansion tank and position it away from the bulkhead

20.2a Removing the scuttle cover rear fasteners

20.2b The scuttle cover front fasteners are removed by squeezing the bottom tabs

20.3 Removing the scuttle cover

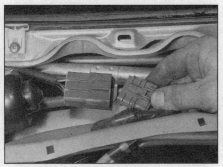

20.4 Disconnecting the wiring multiplug from the wiper motor

20.5a Unscrew the mounting bolts . . .

20.5b . . . and remove the wiper motor and linkage from the bulkhead

Refitting

7 Refitting is a reversal of removal, but tighten the mounting bolts to the specified torque.

21 Windscreen/tailgate washer system components - removal and refitting

1 The windscreen washer reservoir is situated beneath the right-hand (RHD) or left-hand (LHD) wheel arch with its filler neck protruding into the engine compartment. The washer system pump is mounted on the side of the reservoir. On Hatchback models, the reservoir is also used to supply the tailgate washer system via a second pump.

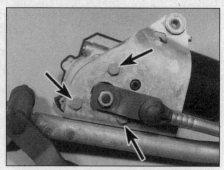

20.6 Bolts securing the motor to the wiper linkage

Windscreen washer reservoir

Removal

2 Remove the appropriate headlamp as described in Section 7. This procedure includes the removal of the front bumper.
3 Disconnect the wiring connector(s) and plastic tubing from the pump(s) (see illustrations).
4 Unscrew the mounting bolts and withdraw the reservoir from the front valance (see illustration).
5 Empty the washer fluid from the reservoir.
6 Remove the pumps as described later in this Section.

Refitting

7 Refitting is a reversal of removal. Ensure that the washer tubes are not trapped when

refitting the reservoir and note that the connectors for the pumps are colour-coded to aid correct reconnection on reassembly. Refill the reservoir with the correct washer solution on completion (see "Lubricants and fluids").

Pump

Removal

8 Carry out the procedure given in paragraphs 2 and 3 earlier in this Section.
9 Carefully ease the pump from the rubber grommet using a twisting action (see illustration).
10 Use a screwdriver to prise the grommet from the reservoir (see illustration).

Refitting

11 Refitting is a reversal of removal.

> **HAYNES HiNT** *Apply a little lubricant (such as washing-up liquid) to the rubber grommet to help it locate in the reservoir.*

Windscreen washer jet

Removal

12 Open the bonnet and disconnect the plastic tube from the bottom of the jet.
13 Using pliers, squeeze together the tabs and release the jet from the bonnet. Recover the gasket (see illustrations).

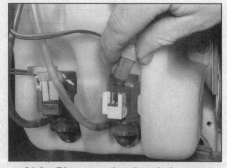

21.3a Disconnecting the windscreen washer pump wiring . . .

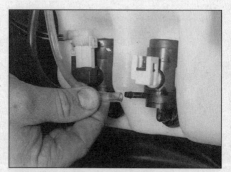

21.3b . . . and tubing from the pump

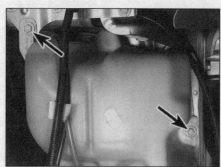

21.4 Windscreen washer reservoir mounting bolts

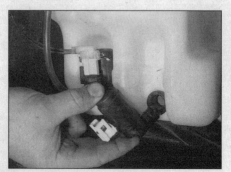

21.9 Removing the pump . . .

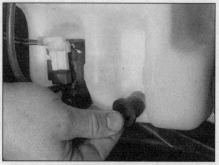

21.10 . . . and grommet from the washer reservoir

21.13a Squeeze together the tabs . . .

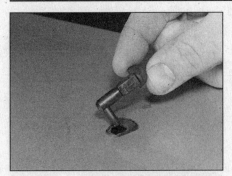

21.13b . . . and remove the windscreen washer jet from the bonnet

Refitting

14 Refitting is a reversal of removal. On completion operate the washers and check that the jet is directed to the top of the screen. If necessary, use a pin or suitable instrument to adjust the jet.

Tailgate washer jet (Hatchback models)

Removal

15 The washer jet is located at the top of the tailgate, and is retained with a tab located directly below the jet position (ie the bottom rear face).

16 Taking care not to damage the paintwork, use a thin screwdriver or similar tool to depress the tab, then release the jet from the tailgate.

17 Pull out the plastic tubing only sufficiently to disconnect it from the jet. **Do not** pull it out further otherwise the tubing may be damaged. If necessary, use a clip to prevent the tubing falling back into the tailgate.

Refitting

18 Refitting is a reversal of removal. On completion, operate the washers and check that the jet is directed to the top of the screen. If necessary, use a pin or suitable instrument to adjust the jet.

22 Tailgate wiper motor - removal and refitting

Removal

1 Remove the tailgate wiper arm as described in Section 19.
2 Remove the rubber spindle cap **(see illustration)**.
3 Remove the interior trim from the tailgate with reference to Chapter 11.
4 Unscrew the spindle nut and remove the flat washer and rubber seal **(see illustrations)**.
5 Disconnect the wiring multiplug from the wiper motor **(see illustration)**.
6 Unscrew the mounting bolts and withdraw the wiper motor from the tailgate **(see illustrations)**.

Refitting

7 Refitting is a reversal of removal, but tighten all nuts and bolts to the specified torque.

23 Radio/cassette player - removal and refitting

Note: *The following removal and refitting procedure is for the range of radio/cassette units which Rover fit as standard equipment. Removal and refitting procedures of non-standard units may differ slightly.*

Removal

1 Disconnect the battery negative (earth) lead (see Chapter 5A). Switch off the ignition and remove the ignition key.
2 To remove the unit, two standard DIN extraction tools are required. These are two U-shaped rods which are inserted into the four small holes in the front of the unit to release the unit retaining clips. The tools may be obtained from a Rover dealer or any audio accessory outlet, or can be made out of 3.0 mm wire rod, such as welding rod. Using the tools, push back the clamps on the left and right-hand sides of the radio/cassette, then withdraw the unit and disconnect the wiring plugs and aerial **(see illustrations overleaf)**.

22.2 Removing the rubber cap from the tailgate wiper motor drive spindle

22.4a Unscrew the spindle nut . . .

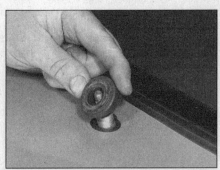

22.4b . . . and remove the flat washer and rubber seal

22.5 Disconnect the wiring . . .

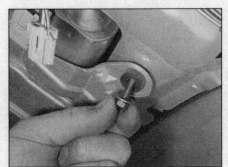

22.6a . . . then unscrew the mounting bolts . . .

22.6b . . . and remove the tailgate wiper motor

23.2a Withdraw the radio/cassette player from the facia . . .

23.2b . . . then disconnect the wiring plugs . . .

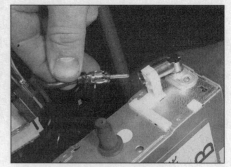

23.2c . . . and aerial lead

Refitting

3 Refitting is the reverse of the removal procedure. On completion, connect the battery negative lead and reactivate the security code.

24 Speakers -
removal and refitting

Front speaker

Removal

1 To remove a main speaker, remove the front door inner trim panel as described in Chapter 11, then undo the speaker retaining screws. Disconnect the speaker wiring connectors and remove the speaker from the door **(see illustrations)**.

2 To remove a tweeter, remove the door inner trim panel as described in Chapter 11, then carefully prise off the triangular panel at the front of the window aperture. Disconnect the wiring at the plug and release the wiring from the clips.

Refitting

3 Refitting is a reversal of removal.

Rear speaker (Hatchback models)

Removal

4 Open the tailgate then unhook the straps and remove the rear parcel shelf.

5 Undo the screws then unclip the parcel tray support from the side of the luggage compartment **(see illustration)**.

6 Undo the screws and withdraw the speaker from its mounting, then disconnect the wiring **(see illustrations)**.

Refitting

7 Refitting is a reversal of removal.

Rear speaker (Saloon models)

Removal

8 Open the boot lid. Reach under the rear shelf and disconnect the wiring from the rear speaker.

9 Unscrew the nuts securing the speaker to the rear shelf.

10 Inside the passenger compartment, withdraw the speaker.

Refitting

11 Refitting is a reversal of removal.

24.1a Undo the front speaker retaining screws . . .

24.1b . . . withdraw the speaker . . .

24.1c . . . and disconnect the wiring

24.5 Remove the parcel tray support . . .

24.6a . . . then undo the screws . . .

24.6b . . . and disconnect the wiring from the rear speaker

25 Radio aerial -
removal and refitting

Removal

1 Prise the lens from the interior light located at the front of the headlining.
2 Unscrew and remove the screws and withdraw the light assembly.
3 Unscrew the nut and disconnect the lead from the aerial **(see illustration)**.
4 Unscrew the mounting nuts and remove the aerial from the roof.
5 Removal of the aerial lead involves removal of the radio/cassette unit as described in Section 23, together with removal of interior trim.

Refitting

6 Refitting is a reversal of removal.

26 Alarm system -
general

1 All models are fitted with an anti-theft alarm/immobiliser system which employs an infra-red handset and receiver unit. The system incorporates indicators in the front door inner trim panels, a bonnet switch, alarm horn (on the scuttle in front of the windscreen), tailgate/bootlid switch, ECU and starter cut out relay **(see illustration)**, receiver unit, and door switches. If necessary, the vehicle can be locked using only the key, but in this case the internal movement sensor is inoperative. If the infra-red handset is used to lock the vehicle, it must also be used to disarm the system and disable the engine immobiliser. The engine immobiliser is activated when the car is locked using either the handset or the key, and also 30 seconds after the ignition has been switched off with the driver's door open. The handset must be used to de-activate the engine immobiliser; using the key to unlock the car will not de-activate the immobiliser.
2 If the handset fails to operate, the engine may be mobilised using the following procedure provided the four-digit key access code is known. First insert the key in the driver's door and turn to the locked position for 5 seconds, then release.

Turn the key to the unlock position the number of times corresponding to the first digit of the key access code.

Turn the key to the lock position the number of times corresponding to the second digit of the key access code.

Turn the key to the unlock position the number of times corresponding to the third digit of the key access code.

Turn the key to the lock position the number of times corresponding to the fourth digit of the key access code.

Finally, turn the key once to the unlock position. The passengers doors will now unlock and the engine will be fully mobilised. Note that if the incorrect number is entered three times, it will be necessary to wait 10 minutes before attempting to re-enter the number.
3 The handset contains a battery which should last for approximately 3 years. When it requires renewal, the indicator warning lights on the front doors will flash rapidly before the doors are opened and the operating range will reduce considerably. To renew the battery, use a small screwdriver or coin to prise off the handset cover then remove the battery from its clip. Press each button for a minimum of 5 seconds to drain any remaining power from the handset, then fit the new battery taking care not to touch the contact surfaces with the fingers. Make sure the new battery is correctly located with the positive (+) side facing downwards into the battery compartment. Press on the cover, then unlock the car using the key and operate the lock button on the handset at least four times.
4 Any suspected faults with the system should be referred to a Rover dealer.

27 Cruise control system -
general

1 The cruise control system is a vacuum operated system; the main components being a vacuum actuator unit mounted near the throttle housing, a vacuum control unit located under the battery mounting bracket, a control relay and ECU located on the side of the passenger footwell, a main switch located on the instrument panel surround, and a set/resume switch located on the steering wheel.

Electronic control unit (ECU)

Removal

2 Disconnect the battery negative (earth) lead (see Chapter 5A).
3 Inside the car remove the side trim panel from the passenger (left-hand) footwell.
4 Unscrew the ECU mounting nuts, then disconnect the wiring multiplug and remove the ECU.

Refitting

5 Refitting is a reversal of removal.

Set/resume switch

Removal

6 Remove the airbag module from the steering wheel as described in Section 16.
7 Remove the horn push switches from the steering wheel.
8 Undo the screws and disconnect the wiring then remove the set/resume switch.

Refitting

9 Refitting is a reversal of removal.

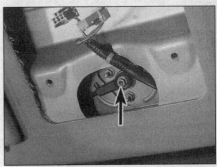

25.3 Aerial lead (arrowed) and aerial mounting nuts (shown with interior light removed)

Cruise control main switch

Removal

10 Carefully prise the switch from the instrument surround using a small screwdriver.
11 Disconnect the wiring multiplug.

Refitting

12 Refitting is a reversal of removal.

Cruise control relay

Removal

13 Disconnect the battery negative (earth) lead (see Chapter 5A).
14 Inside the car remove the side trim panel from the passenger (left-hand) footwell.
15 Unclip the base from the body, then disconnect the multiplug and remove the relay.

Refitting

16 Refitting is a reversal of removal.

Vacuum control unit

Removal

17 Remove the battery and air cleaner as described in Chapters 5A and 4.
18 Unbolt the battery tray from the mounting bracket.
19 Unbolt the air intake hose support from the battery mounting bracket.
20 Loosen the mounting bolts and release the bracket from the body.

26.1 Central door locking and alarm ECU (located beneath the centre of the facia)

12

21 Disconnect the multiplugs from the dim dip resistor and cruise control vacuum control unit.

22 Disconnect the vacuum hose and remove the bracket complete with vacuum control unit from the engine compartment.

23 Release the mounting rubbers and remove the control unit from the bracket. If necessary, remove the rubbers from the control unit.

Refitting

24 Refitting is a reversal of removal.

Cruise control actuator unit

Removal

25 Disconnect the battery negative (earth) lead (see Chapter 5A).

26 Disconnect the actuator pull rod from the lever on the throttle housing.

27 Disconnect the vacuum hose from the actuator unit.

28 Unscrew the mounting nut and remove the actuator unit from the engine compartment.

Refitting

29 Refitting is a reversal of removal.

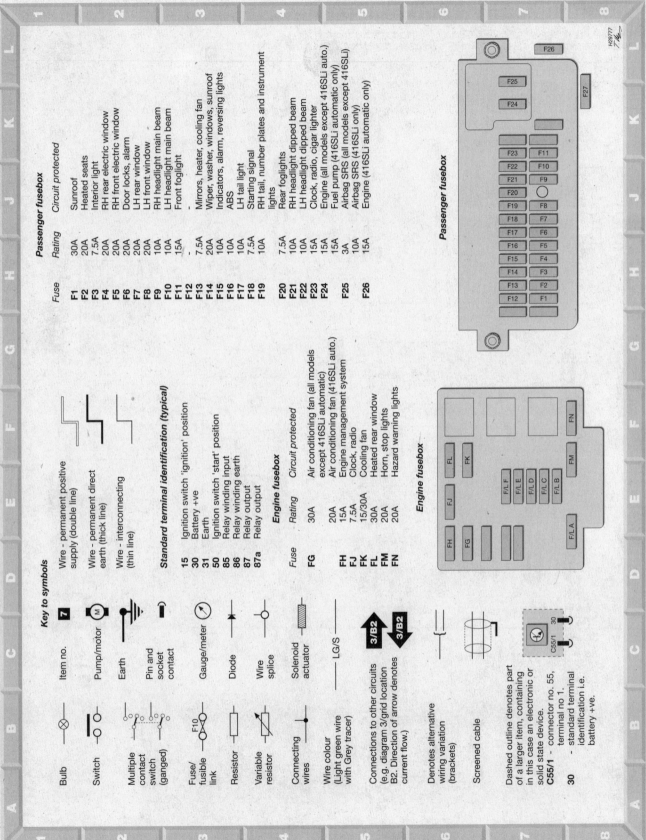

Key to symbols

Bulb	Bulb
Switch	Switch
Multiple contact switch (ganged)	Multiple contact switch (ganged)
Fuse/ fusible link	Fuse/fusible link
Resistor	Resistor
Variable resistor	Variable resistor
Connecting wires	Connecting wires
Wire colour (Light green wire with Grey tracer)	LG/S
Connections to other circuits (e.g. diagram 3/grid location B2. Direction of arrow denotes current flow.)	3/B2
Denotes alternative wiring variation (brackets)	
Screened cable	
Dashed outline denotes part of a larger item, containing in this case an electronic or solid state device. C55/1 – connector no. 55, terminal no 1. 30 – standard terminal identification i.e. battery +ve.	
Item no.	7
Pump/motor	M
Earth	
Pin and socket contact	
Gauge/meter	
Diode	
Wire splice	
Solenoid actuator	

Standard terminal identification (typical)

15	Ignition switch 'ignition' position
30	Battery +ve
31	Earth
50	Ignition switch 'start' position
85	Relay winding input
86	Relay winding earth
87	Relay output
87a	Relay output

Passenger fusebox

Fuse	Rating	Circuit protected
F1	30A	Sunroof
F2	20A	Heated seats
F3	7.5A	Interior light
F4	20A	RH rear electric window
F5	20A	RH front electric window
F6	20A	Door locks, alarm
F7	20A	LH rear window
F8	20A	LH front window
F9	10A	RH headlight main beam
F10	10A	LH headlight main beam
F11	15A	Front foglight
F12	–	–
F13	7.5A	Mirrors, heater, cooling fan
F14	20A	Wiper, washer, windows, sunroof
F15	10A	Indicators, alarm, reversing lights
F16	10A	ABS
F17	10A	LH tail light
F18	7.5A	Starting signal
F19	10A	RH tail, number plates and instrument lights
F20	7.5A	Rear foglights
F21	10A	RH headlight dipped beam
F22	10A	LH headlight dipped beam
F23	15A	Clock, radio, cigar lighter
F24	15A	Engine (all models except 416SLi auto.)
F25	3A	Fuel pump (416SLi automatic only)
	10A	Airbag SRS (all models except 416SLi)
F26	15A	Airbag SRS (416SLi only)
		Engine (416SLi automatic only)

Engine fusebox

Fuse	Rating	Circuit protected
FG	30A	Air conditioning fan (all models except 416SLi automatic)
	20A	Air conditioning fan (416SLi auto.)
FH	15A	Engine management system
FJ	7.5A	Clock, radio
FK	15/30A	Cooling fan
FL	30A	Heated rear window
FM	20A	Horn, stop lights
FN	20A	Hazard warning lights

Passenger fusebox

F26, F25, F24, F27

F23 F11
F22 F10
F21 F9
F20 F8
F19 F7
F18 F6
F17 F5
F16 F4
F15 F3
F14 F2
F13 F1
F12

Engine fusebox

FL, FK, FJ, FH, FG
F/L.F, F/L.E, F/L.D, F/L.C, F/L.B
FN, FM, F/L.A

Diagram 1 : Information for wiring diagrams

H29777

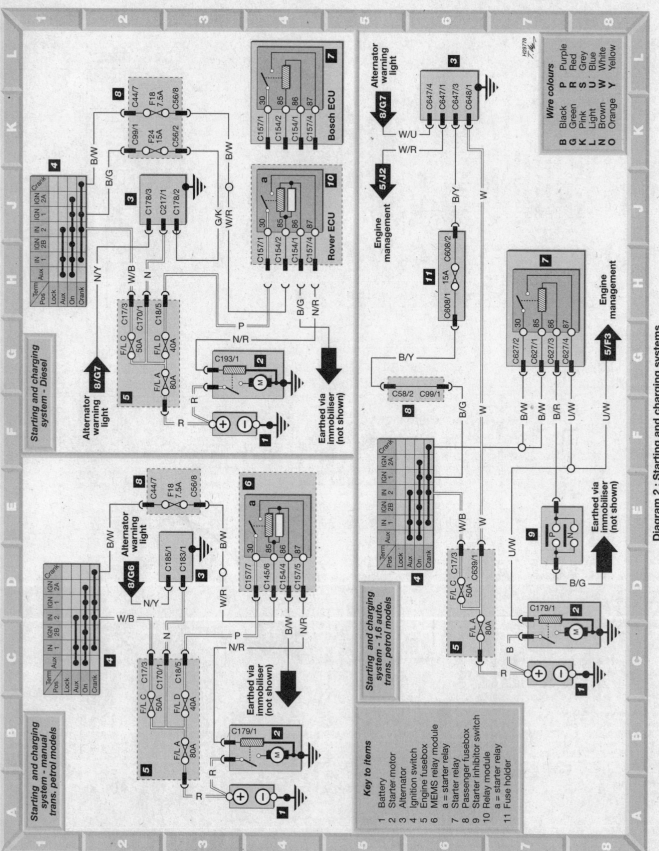

Diagram 2 : Starting and charging systems

Wire colours

B	Black	P	Purple
G	Green	R	Red
K	Pink	S	Grey
L	Light	U	Blue
N	Brown	W	White
O	Orange	Y	Yellow

Key to items

1 Battery
2 Starter motor
3 Alternator
4 Ignition switch
5 Engine fusebox
6 MEMS relay module
   a = starter relay
7 Starter relay
8 Passenger fusebox
9 Starter inhibitor switch
10 Relay module
   a = starter relay
11 Fuse holder

Starting and charging system - Diesel

Starting and charging system - manual trans. petrol models

Starting and charging system - 1.6 auto. trans. petrol models

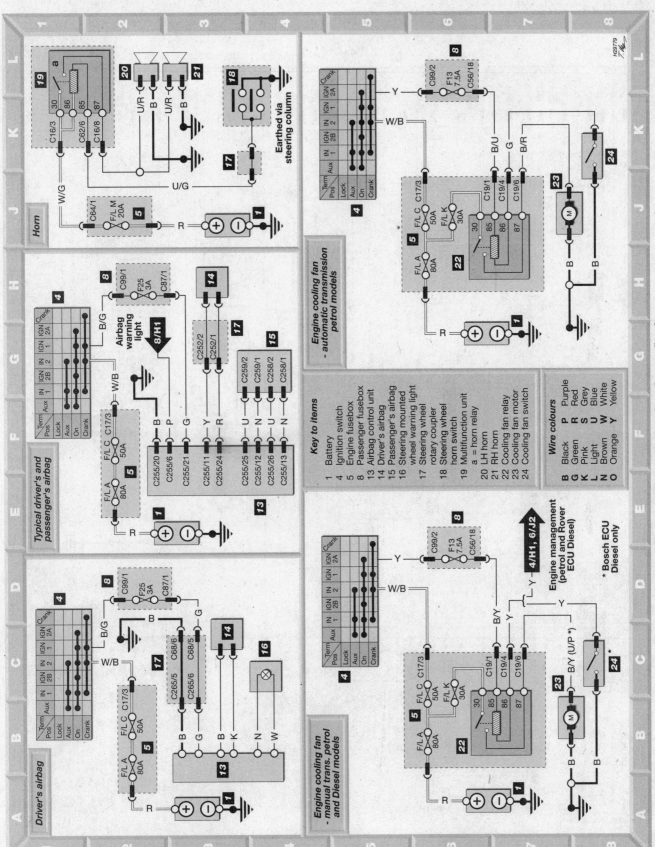

Diagram 3 : Airbag, horn and engine cooling fan

Horn

Typical driver's and passenger's airbag

Driver's airbag

Engine cooling fan – automatic transmission petrol models

Engine cooling fan – manual trans. petrol and Diesel models

Engine management (petrol and Rover ECU Diesel)

* Bosch ECU Diesel only

Airbag warning light

Earthed via steering column

Key to items

1 Battery
4 Ignition switch
5 Engine fusebox
8 Passenger fusebox
13 Airbag control unit
14 Driver's airbag
15 Passenger's airbag
16 Steering mounted wheel warning light
17 Steering wheel rotary coupler
18 Steering wheel horn switch
19 Multifunction unit
    a = horn relay
20 LH horn
21 RH horn
22 Cooling fan relay
23 Cooling fan motor
24 Cooling fan switch

Wire colours

B Black
G Green
K Pink
L Light
N Brown
O Orange
P Purple
R Red
S Grey
U Blue
W White
Y Yellow

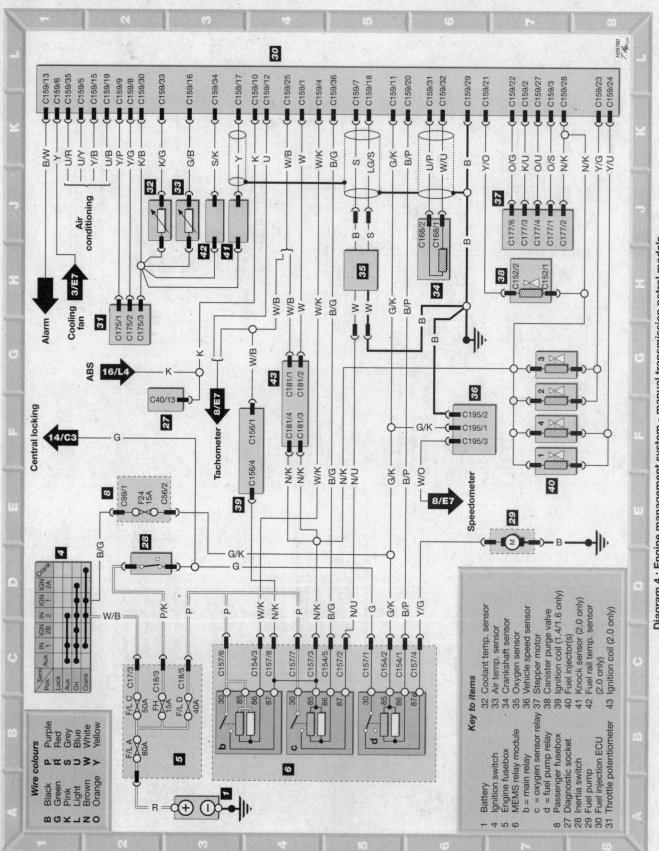

Diagram 4 : Engine management system - manual transmission petrol models

Wire colours

B	Black	**P**	Purple
G	Green	**R**	Red
K	Pink	**S**	Grey
L	Light	**U**	Blue
N	Brown	**W**	White
O	Orange	**Y**	Yellow

Key to items

1	Battery	32	Coolant temp. sensor
4	Ignition switch	33	Air temp. sensor
5	Engine fusebox	34	Crankshaft sensor
6	MEMS relay module	35	Oxygen sensor
	b = main relay	36	Vehicle speed sensor
	c = oxygen sensor relay	37	Stepper motor
	d = fuel pump relay	38	Canister purge valve
8	Passenger fusebox	39	Ignition coil (1.4/1.6 only)
27	Diagnostic socket	40	Fuel injector(s)
28	Inertia switch	41	Knock sensor (2.0 only)
29	Fuel pump	42	Fuel rail temp. sensor (2.0 only)
30	Fuel injection ECU	43	Throttle potentiometer
31	Fuel injection ECU		Ignition coil (2.0 only)

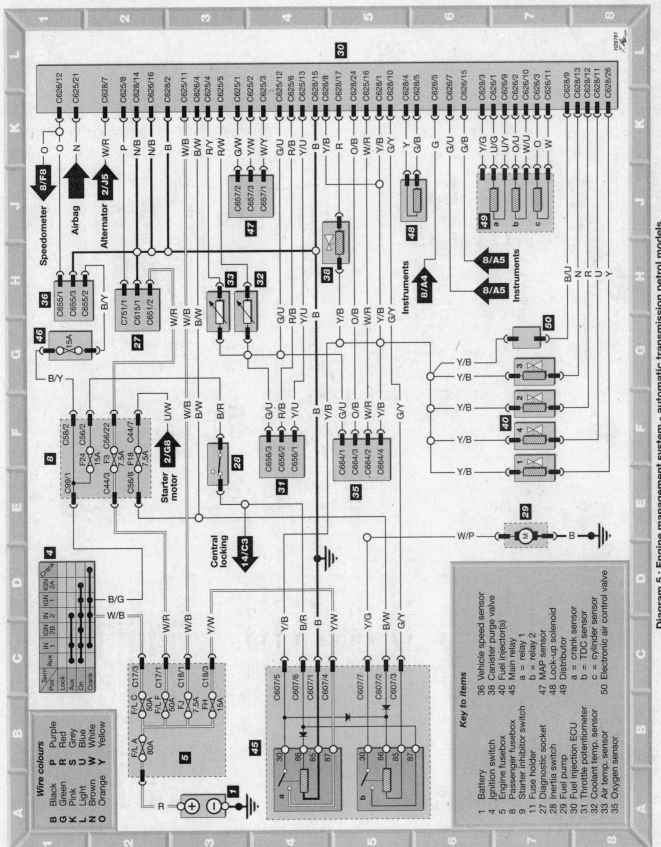

Diagram 5 : Engine management system - automatic transmission petrol models

Wire colours

B	Black	P	Purple
G	Green	R	Red
K	Pink	S	Grey
L	Light	U	Blue
N	Brown	W	White
O	Orange	Y	Yellow

Key to items

1	Battery
4	Ignition switch
5	Engine fusebox
8	Passenger fusebox
9	Starter inhibitor switch
11	Fuse holder
27	Diagnostic socket
28	Inertia switch
29	Fuel pump
30	Fuel injection ECU
31	Throttle potentiometer
32	Coolant temp. sensor
33	Air temp. sensor
35	Oxygen sensor
36	Vehicle speed sensor
38	Canister purge valve
40	Fuel injector(s)
45	Main relay
	a = relay 1
	b = relay 2
47	MAP sensor
48	Lock-up solenoid
49	Distributor
	a = crank sensor
	b = TDC sensor
	c = cylinder sensor
50	Electronic air control valve

12

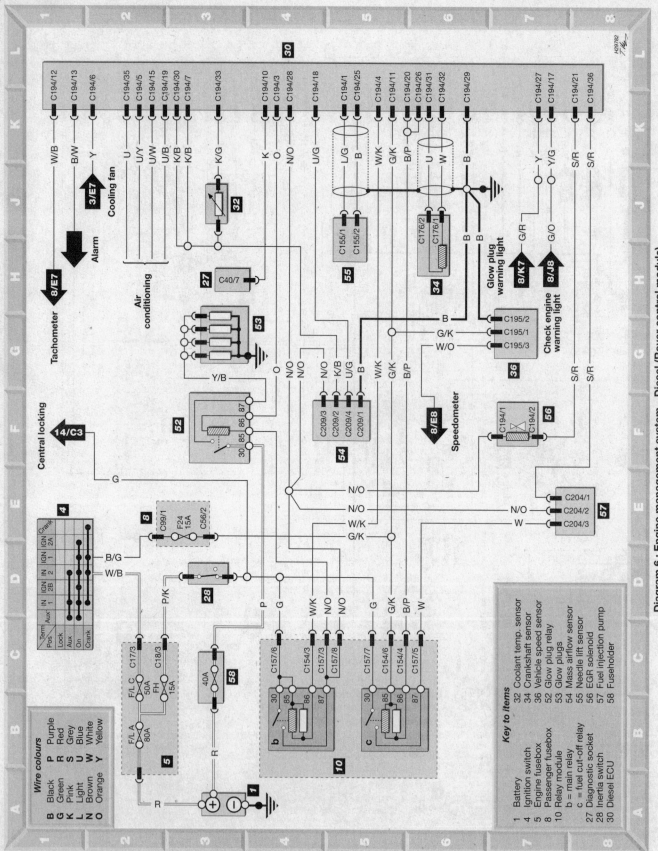

Diagram 6 : Engine management system - Diesel (Rover control module)

Wire colours

B	Black	P	Purple
G	Green	R	Red
K	Pink	S	Grey
L	Light	U	Blue
N	Brown	W	White
O	Orange	Y	Yellow

Key to items

1	Battery
4	Ignition switch
5	Engine fusebox
8	Passenger fusebox
10	Relay module
	b = main relay
	c = fuel cut-off relay
27	Diagnostic socket
28	Inertia switch
30	Diesel ECU
32	Coolant temp. sensor
34	Crankshaft sensor
36	Vehicle speed sensor
52	Glow plug relay
53	Glow plugs
54	Mass airflow sensor
55	Needle lift sensor
56	EGR solenoid
57	Fuel injection pump
58	Fuseholder

H29782

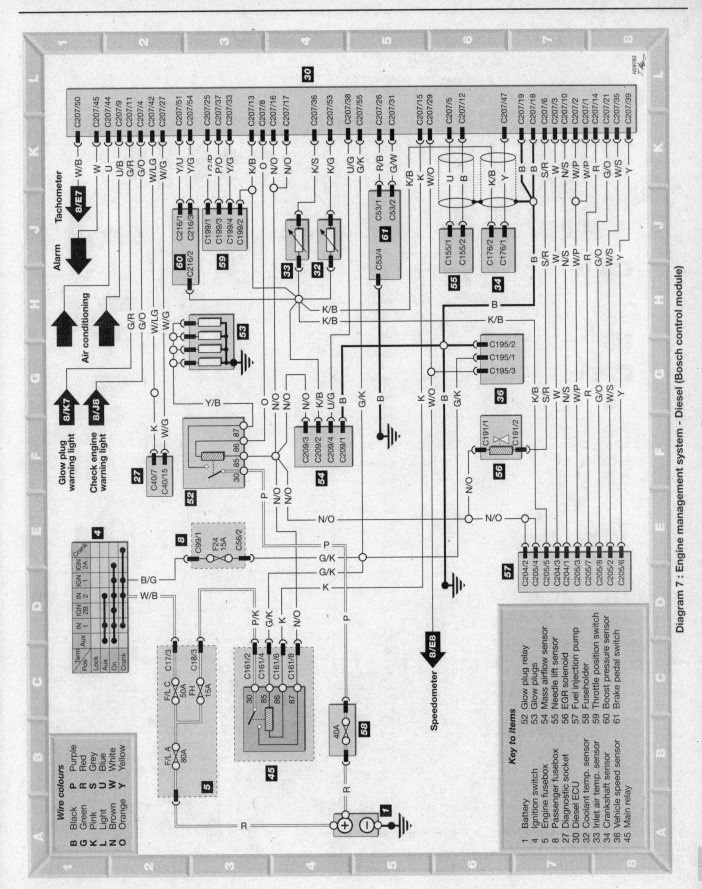

Diagram 7 : Engine management system - Diesel (Bosch control module)

Wire colours

B	Black	**P**	Purple
G	Green	**R**	Red
K	Pink	**S**	Grey
L	Light	**U**	Blue
N	Brown	**W**	White
O	Orange	**Y**	Yellow

Key to items

1	Battery
4	Ignition switch
5	Engine fusebox
8	Passenger fusebox
27	Diagnostic socket
30	Diesel ECU
32	Coolant temp. sensor
33	Inlet air temp. sensor
34	Crankshaft sensor
36	Vehicle speed sensor
45	Main relay
52	Glow plug relay
53	Glow plugs
54	Mass airflow sensor
55	Needle lift sensor
56	EGR solenoid
57	Fuel injection pump
58	Fuseholder
59	Throttle position switch
60	Boost pressure sensor
61	Brake pedal switch

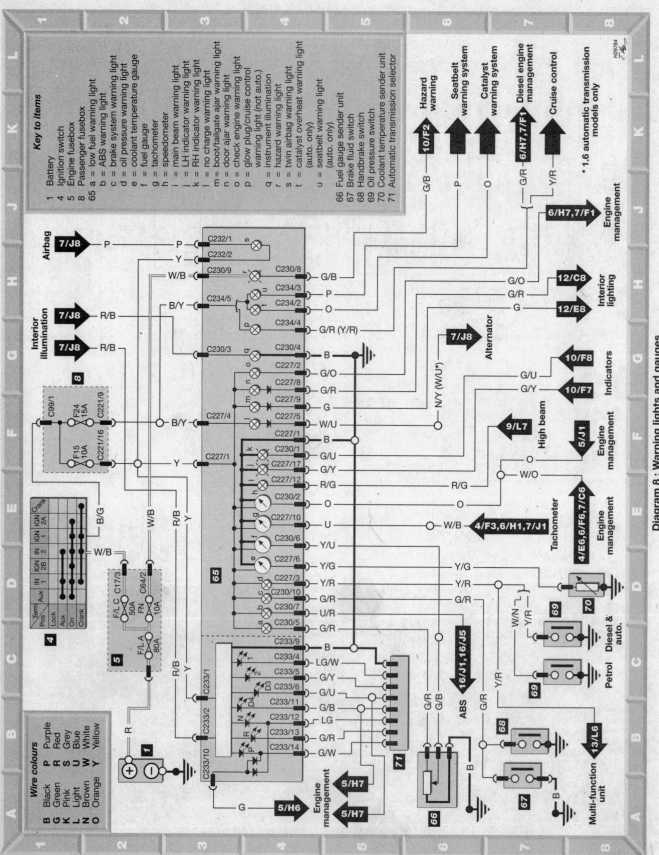

Key to items

1 Battery
4 Ignition switch
5 Engine fusebox
8 Passenger fusebox
65 a = low fuel warning light
b = ABS warning light
c = brake system warning light
d = oil pressure warning light
e = coolant temperature gauge
f = fuel gauge
g = tachometer
h = speedometer
i = main beam warning light
j = LH indicator warning light
k = RH indicator warning light
l = no charge warning light
m = boot/tailgate ajar warning light
n = door ajar warning light
o = check engine warning light
p = glow plug/cruise control warning light (not auto.)
q = instrument illumination
r = hazard warning light
s = twin airbag warning light
t = catalyst overheat warning light (auto. only)
u = seatbelt warning light (auto. only)
66 Fuel gauge sender unit
67 Brake fluid switch
68 Handbrake switch
69 Oil pressure switch
70 Coolant temperature sender unit
71 Automatic transmission selector

Wire colours

B	Black	P	Purple
G	Green	R	Red
K	Pink	S	Grey
N	Brown	U	Light
O	Orange	W	White
		Y	Yellow

Diagram 8 : Warning lights and gauges

H29784

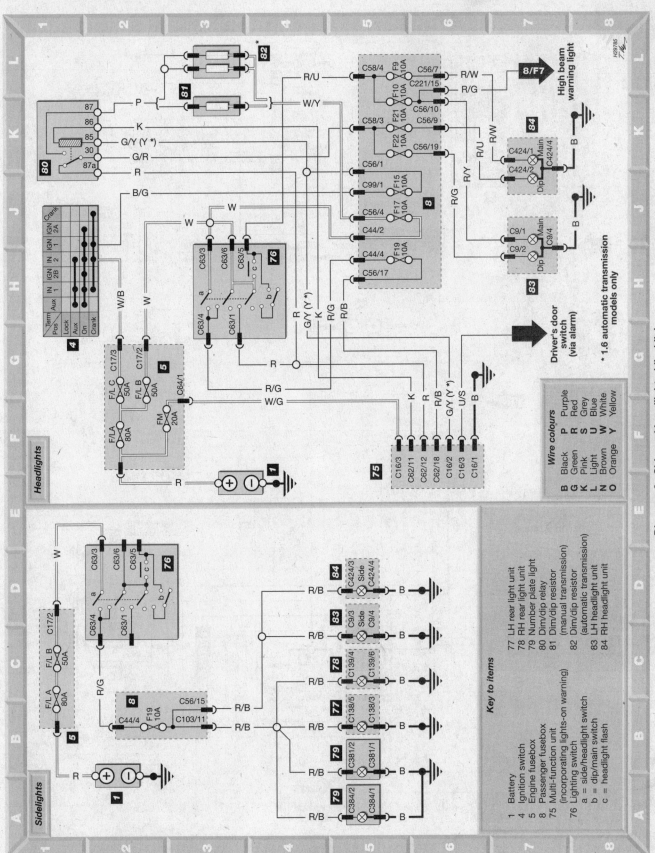

Diagram 9 : Side and headlights (dim/dip)

Headlights

Sidelights

High beam warning light

8/F7

Driver's door switch (via alarm)

* 1.6 automatic transmission models only

Wire colours

B	Black	P	Purple
G	Green	R	Red
K	Pink	S	Grey
L	Light	U	Brown
N	Brown	W	White
O	Orange	Y	Yellow

Key to items

1 Battery
4 Ignition switch
5 Engine fusebox
8 Passenger fusebox
75 Multi-function unit (incorporating lights-on warning)
76 Lighting switch
  a = side/headlight switch
  b = dip/main switch
  c = headlight flash

77 LH rear light unit
78 RH rear light unit
79 Number plate light
80 Dim/dip relay
81 Dim/dip resistor (manual transmission)
82 Dim/dip resistor (automatic transmission)
83 LH headlight unit
84 RH headlight unit

12

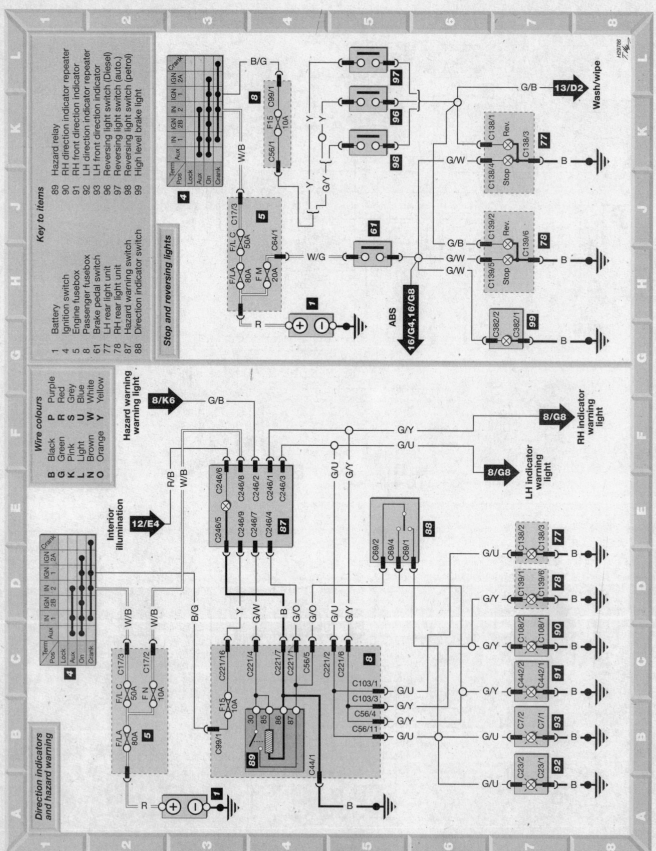

Key to items

89	Hazard relay
90	RH direction indicator repeater
91	RH front direction indicator
92	LH direction indicator repeater
93	LH front direction indicator
96	Reversing light switch (Diesel)
97	Reversing light switch (auto.)
98	Reversing light switch (petrol)
99	High level brake light

1	Battery
4	Ignition switch
5	Engine fusebox
8	Passenger fusebox
61	Brake pedal switch
77	LH rear light unit
78	RH rear light unit
87	Hazard warning switch
88	Direction indicator switch

Stop and reversing lights

Wire colours

B	Black	P	Purple
G	Green	R	Red
K	Pink	S	Grey
L	Light	U	Blue
N	Brown	W	White
O	Orange	Y	Yellow

Direction indicators and hazard warning

Diagram 10 : Direction indicators/hazard warning, stop and reversing lights

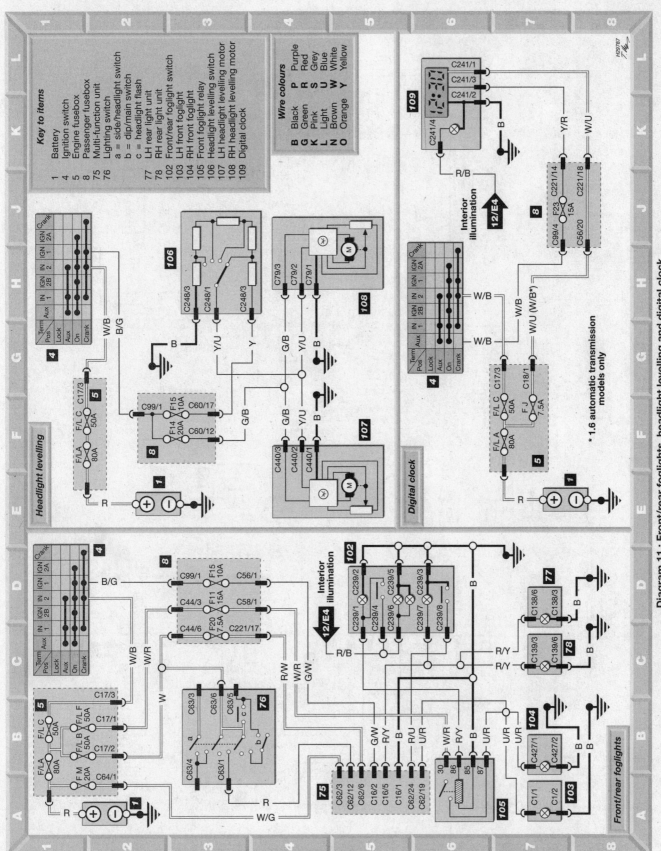

Key to items

1 Battery
4 Ignition switch
5 Engine fusebox
8 Passenger fusebox
75 Multi-function unit
76 Lighting switch
  a = side/headlight switch
  b = dip/main switch
  c = headlight flash
77 LH rear light unit
78 RH rear light unit
102 Front/rear foglight switch
103 LH front foglight
104 RH front foglight
105 Front foglight relay
106 Headlight levelling switch
107 LH headlight levelling motor
108 RH headlight levelling motor
109 Digital clock

Wire colours

B Black
G Green
K Pink
L Light
N Brown
O Orange
P Purple
R Red
S Grey
U Blue
W White
Y Yellow

Headlight levelling

Interior illumination

12/E4

Digital clock

* 1.6 automatic transmission models only

Interior illumination

12/E4

Front/rear foglights

Diagram 11 : Front/rear foglights, headlight levelling and digital clock

12

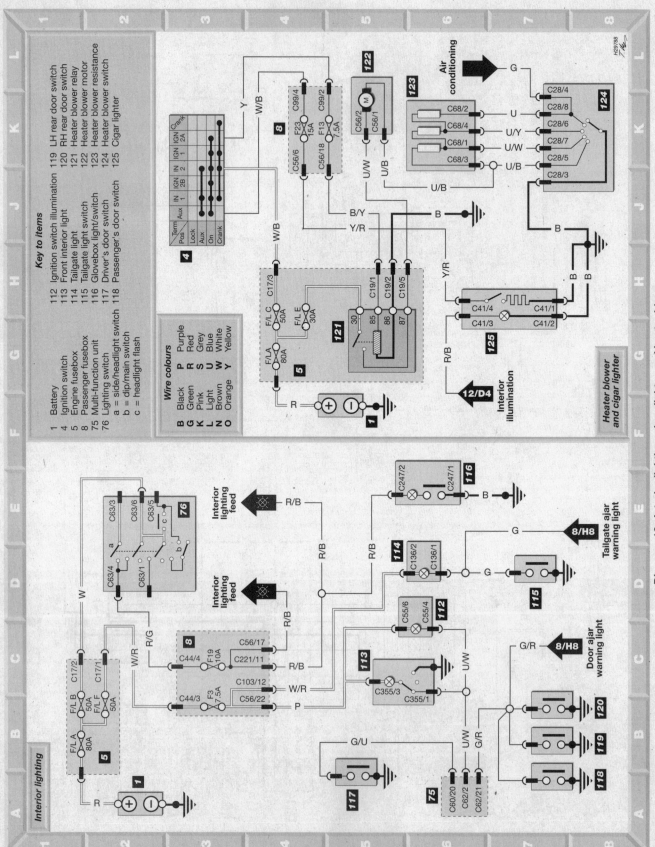

Key to items

1	Battery
4	Ignition switch
5	Engine fusebox
8	Passenger fusebox
75	Multi-function unit
76	Lighting switch

a = side/headlight switch
b = dip/main switch
c = headlight flash

112	Ignition switch illumination
113	Front interior light
114	Tailgate light
115	Tailgate light switch
116	Glovebox light/switch
117	Driver's door switch
118	Passenger's door switch
119	LH rear door switch
120	RH rear door switch
121	Heater blower relay
122	Heater blower motor
123	Heater blower resistance
124	Heater blower switch
125	Cigar lighter

Wire colours

B	Black	P	Purple
G	Green	R	Red
K	Pink	S	Grey
L	Light	U	Blue
N	Brown	W	White
O	Orange	Y	Yellow

Air conditioning

Interior illumination

12/D4

Heater blower and cigar lighter

Interior lighting feed

Interior lighting feed

Tailgate ajar warning light

8/H8

Door ajar warning light

8/H8

Interior lighting

Diagram 12 : Interior lighting, cigar lighter and heater blower

H29788

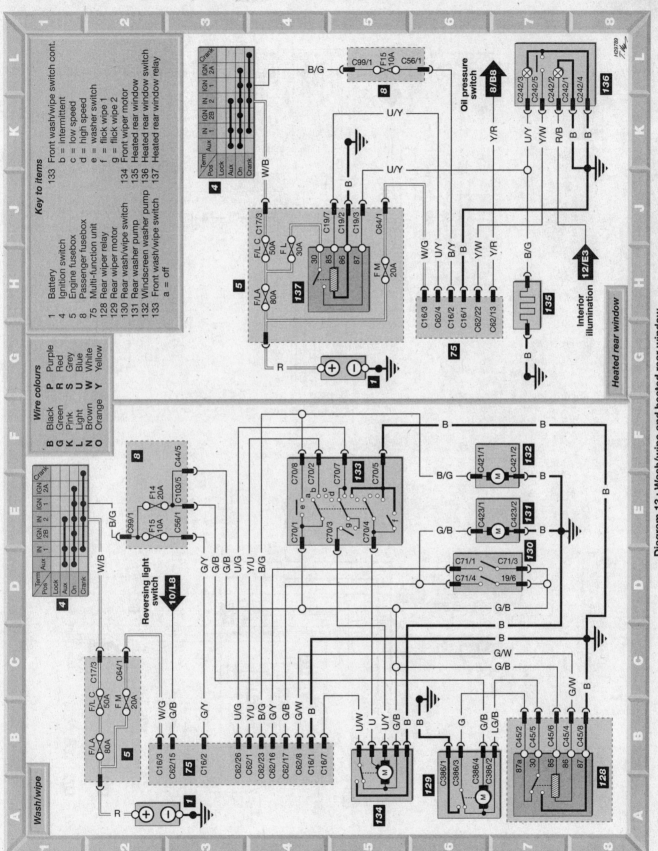

Key to items

1	Battery
4	Ignition switch
5	Engine fusebox
8	Passenger fusebox
75	Multi-function unit
128	Rear wiper relay
129	Rear wiper motor
130	Rear wash/wipe switch
131	Rear washer pump
132	Windscreen washer pump
133	Front wash/wipe switch

133 Front wash/wipe switch cont.
b = intermittent
c = low speed
d = high speed
e = washer switch
f = flick wipe 1
g = flick wipe 2
a = off

134 Front wiper motor
135 Heated rear window
136 Heated rear window switch
137 Heated rear window relay

Wire colours

B	Black	P	Purple
G	Green	R	Red
K	Pink	S	Grey
L	Light	U	Blue
N	Brown	W	White
O	Orange	Y	Yellow

Wash/wipe

Heated rear window

Interior illumination

Oil pressure switch

Reversing light switch

Diagram 13 : Wash/wipe and heated rear window

12

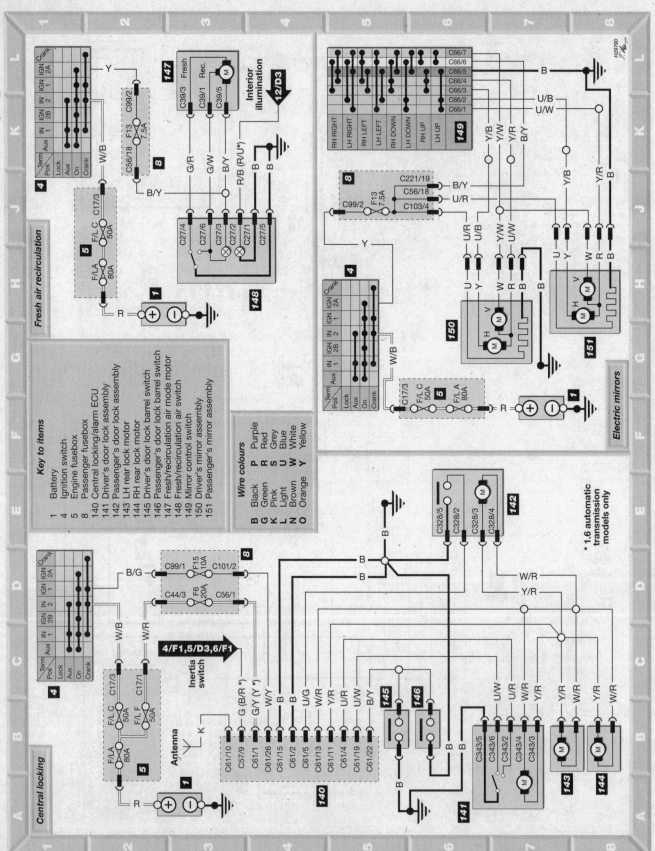

Diagram 14 : Central locking, electric mirrors and fresh air recirculation

Fresh air recirculation

Electric mirrors

Central locking

Key to items

1   Battery
2   Ignition switch
5   Engine fusebox
8   Passenger fusebox
140 Central locking/alarm ECU
141 Driver's door lock assembly
142 Passenger's door lock assembly
143 LH rear lock motor
144 RH rear lock motor
145 Driver's door lock barrel switch
146 Passenger's door lock barrel switch
147 Fresh/recirculation air mode motor
148 Fresh/recirculation air switch
149 Mirror control switch
150 Driver's mirror assembly
151 Passenger's mirror assembly

Wire colours

B	Black	P	Purple
G	Green	R	Red
K	Pink	S	Grey
L	Light	U	Blue
N	Brown	W	White
O	Orange	Y	Yellow

* 1.6 automatic transmission models only

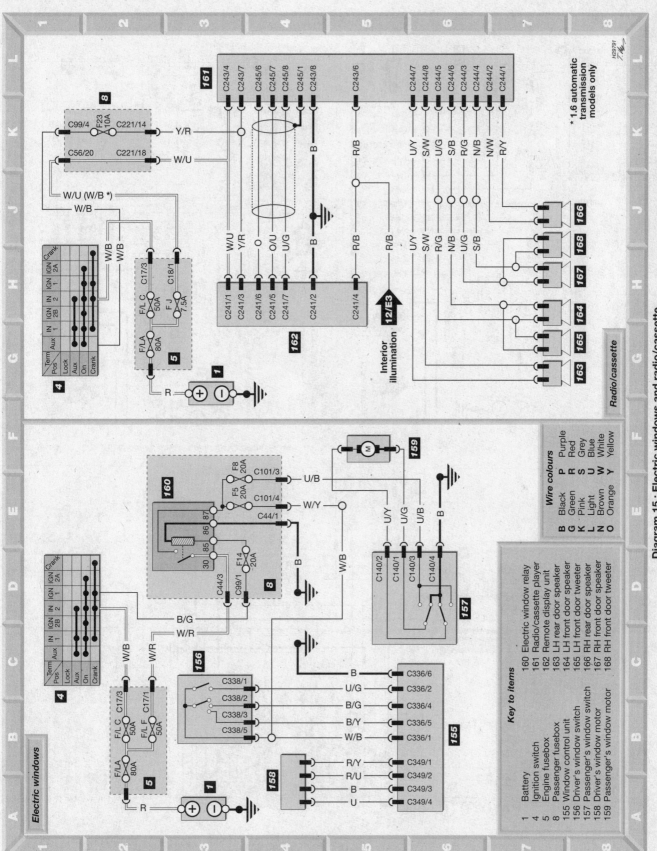

Diagram 15 : Electric windows and radio/cassette

* 1.6 automatic transmission models only

Interior illumination

Radio/cassette

Electric windows

Wire colours

B	Black	P	Purple
G	Green	R	Red
K	Pink	S	Grey
L	Light	U	Blue
N	Brown	W	White
O	Orange	Y	Yellow

Key to items

1	Battery
4	Ignition switch
5	Engine fusebox
8	Passenger fusebox
155	Window control unit
156	Driver's window switch
157	Passenger's window switch
158	Driver's window motor
159	Passenger's window motor
160	Electric window relay
161	Radio/cassette player
162	Remote display unit
163	LH rear door speaker
164	LH front door speaker
165	LH front door tweeter
166	RH rear door speaker
167	RH front door speaker
168	RH front door tweeter

12

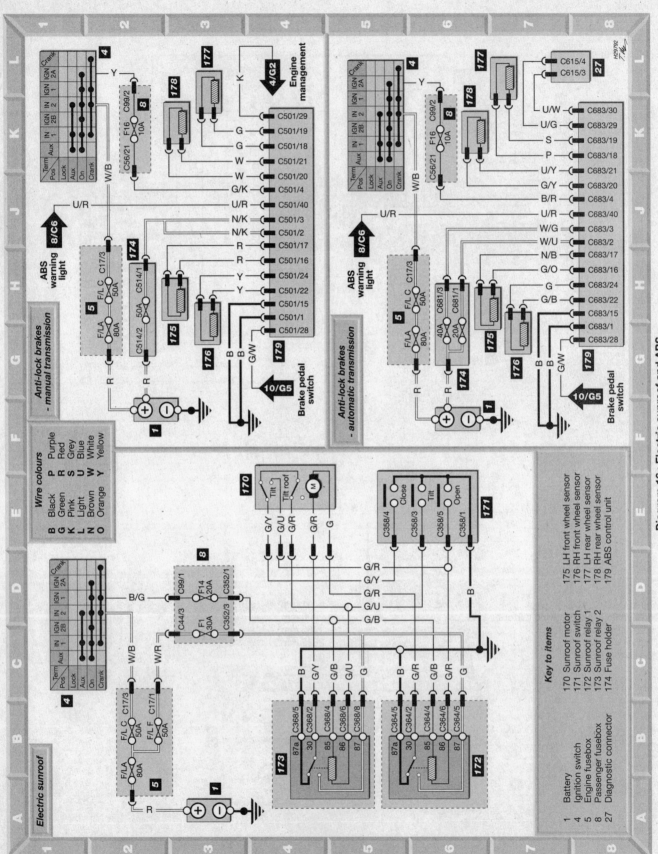

Diagram 16 : Electric sunroof and ABS

Wire colours

B Black	**P** Purple
G Green	**R** Red
K Pink	**S** Grey
L Light	**U** Blue
N Brown	**W** White
O Orange	**Y** Yellow

Key to items

1 Battery	170 Sunroof motor
4 Ignition switch	171 Sunroof switch
5 Engine fusebox	172 Sunroof relay 1
8 Passenger fusebox	173 Sunroof relay 2
27 Diagnostic connector	174 Fuse holder
	175 LH front wheel sensor
	176 RH front wheel sensor
	177 LH rear wheel sensor
	178 RH rear wheel sensor
	179 ABS control unit

Anti-lock brakes - manual transmission

Anti-lock brakes - automatic transmission

Electric sunroof

Engine management

Brake pedal switch

ABS warning light

Dimensions and weights

Note: *All figures are approximate, and may vary according to model. Refer to manufacturer's data for exact figures.*

Dimensions

Overall length:
  Hatchback . . . . 4316 mm
  Saloon . . . . 4491 mm
Overall width (including wing mirrors) . . . . 2000 mm
Overall height (unladen) . . . . 1385 mm
Wheelbase . . . . 2622 mm
Track width:
  Front . . . . 1475 mm
  Rear . . . . 1465 mm

Weights

Kerb weight (with full fuel tank):
  414i and Si . . . . 1120 kg
  416i and Si . . . . 1125 kg
  416 SLi . . . . 1135 kg
  420i and Si . . . . 1230 kg
  420SLi . . . . 1235 kg
  420GSi . . . . 1245 kg
  420D, SD and SDi . . . . 1240 kg
  420SLDi . . . . 1250 kg
  420GSDi . . . . 1280 kg
Maximum towing weight . . . . 1000 kg
Maximum roof rack load . . . . 65 kg

Conversion factors

Length (distance)

Inches (in)	x 25.4	= Millimetres (mm)	x 0.0394	= Inches (in)
Feet (ft)	x 0.305	= Metres (m)	x 3.281	= Feet (ft)
Miles	x 1.609	= Kilometres (km)	x 0.621	= Miles

Volume (capacity)

Cubic inches (cu in; in³)	x 16.387	= Cubic centimetres (cc; cm³)	x 0.061	= Cubic inches (cu in; in³)
Imperial pints (Imp pt)	x 0.568	= Litres (l)	x 1.76	= Imperial pints (Imp pt)
Imperial quarts (Imp qt)	x 1.137	= Litres (l)	x 0.88	= Imperial quarts (Imp qt)
Imperial quarts (Imp qt)	x 1.201	= US quarts (US qt)	x 0.833	= Imperial quarts (Imp qt)
US quarts (US qt)	x 0.946	= Litres (l)	x 1.057	= US quarts (US qt)
Imperial gallons (Imp gal)	x 4.546	= Litres (l)	x 0.22	= Imperial gallons (Imp gal)
Imperial gallons (Imp gal)	x 1.201	= US gallons (US gal)	x 0.833	= Imperial gallons (Imp gal)
US gallons (US gal)	x 3.785	= Litres (l)	x 0.264	= US gallons (US gal)

Mass (weight)

Ounces (oz)	x 28.35	= Grams (g)	x 0.035	= Ounces (oz)
Pounds (lb)	x 0.454	= Kilograms (kg)	x 2.205	= Pounds (lb)

Force

Ounces-force (ozf; oz)	x 0.278	= Newtons (N)	x 3.6	= Ounces-force (ozf; oz)
Pounds-force (lbf; lb)	x 4.448	= Newtons (N)	x 0.225	= Pounds-force (lbf; lb)
Newtons (N)	x 0.1	= Kilograms-force (kgf; kg)	x 9.81	= Newtons (N)

Pressure

Pounds-force per square inch (psi; lbf/in²; lb/in²)	x 0.070	= Kilograms-force per square centimetre (kgf/cm²; kg/cm²)	x 14.223	= Pounds-force per square inch (psi; lbf/in²; lb/in²)
Pounds-force per square inch (psi; lbf/in²; lb/in²)	x 0.068	= Atmospheres (atm)	x 14.696	= Pounds-force per square inch (psi; lbf/in²; lb/in²)
Pounds-force per square inch (psi; lbf/in²; lb/in²)	x 0.069	= Bars	x 14.5	= Pounds-force per square inch (psi; lbf/in²; lb/in²)
Pounds-force per square inch (psi; lbf/in²; lb/in²)	x 6.895	= Kilopascals (kPa)	x 0.145	= Pounds-force per square inch (psi; lbf/in²; lb/in²)
Kilopascals (kPa)	x 0.01	= Kilograms-force per square centimetre (kgf/cm²; kg/cm²)	x 98.1	= Kilopascals (kPa)
Millibar (mbar)	x 100	= Pascals (Pa)	x 0.01	= Millibar (mbar)
Millibar (mbar)	x 0.0145	= Pounds-force per square inch (psi; lbf/in²; lb/in²)	x 68.947	= Millibar (mbar)
Millibar (mbar)	x 0.75	= Millimetres of mercury (mmHg)	x 1.333	= Millibar (mbar)
Millibar (mbar)	x 0.401	= Inches of water (inH₂O)	x 2.491	= Millibar (mbar)
Millimetres of mercury (mmHg)	x 0.535	= Inches of water (inH₂O)	x 1.868	= Millimetres of mercury (mmHg)
Inches of water (inH₂O)	x 0.036	= Pounds-force per square inch (psi; lbf/in²; lb/in²)	x 27.68	= Inches of water (inH₂O)

Torque (moment of force)

Pounds-force inches (lbf in; lb in)	x 1.152	= Kilograms-force centimetre (kgf cm; kg cm)	x 0.868	= Pounds-force inches (lbf in; lb in)
Pounds-force inches (lbf in; lb in)	x 0.113	= Newton metres (Nm)	x 8.85	= Pounds-force inches (lbf in; lb in)
Pounds-force inches (lbf in; lb in)	x 0.083	= Pounds-force feet (lbf ft; lb ft)	x 12	= Pounds-force inches (lbf in; lb in)
Pounds-force feet (lbf ft; lb ft)	x 0.138	= Kilograms-force metres (kgf m; kg m)	x 7.233	= Pounds-force feet (lbf ft; lb ft)
Pounds-force feet (lbf ft; lb ft)	x 1.356	= Newton metres (Nm)	x 0.738	= Pounds-force feet (lbf ft; lb ft)
Newton metres (Nm)	x 0.102	= Kilograms-force metres (kgf m; kg m)	x 9.804	= Newton metres (Nm)

Power

Horsepower (hp)	x 745.7	= Watts (W)	x 0.0013	= Horsepower (hp)

Velocity (speed)

Miles per hour (miles/hr; mph)	x 1.609	= Kilometres per hour (km/hr; kph)	x 0.621	= Miles per hour (miles/hr; mph)

Fuel consumption*

Miles per gallon (mpg)	x 0.354	= Kilometres per litre (km/l)	x 2.825	= Miles per gallon (mpg)

Temperature

Degrees Fahrenheit = (°C x 1.8) + 32   Degrees Celsius (Degrees Centigrade; °C) = (°F - 32) x 0.56

It is common practice to convert from miles per gallon (mpg) to litres/100 kilometres (l/100km), where mpg x l/100 km = 282

Spare parts are available from many sources, including maker's appointed garages, accessory shops, and motor factors. To be sure of obtaining the correct parts, it will sometimes be necessary to quote the vehicle identification number. If possible, it can also be useful to take the old parts along for positive identification. Items such as starter motors and alternators may be available under a service exchange scheme - any parts returned should be clean.

Our advice regarding spare parts is as follows.

Officially appointed garages

This is the best source of parts which are peculiar to your car, and which are not otherwise generally available (eg, badges, interior trim, certain body panels, etc). It is also the only place at which you should buy parts if the vehicle is still under warranty.

Accessory shops

These are very good places to buy materials and components needed for the maintenance of your car (oil, air and fuel filters, light bulbs, drivebelts, greases, brake pads, tough-up paint, etc). Components of this nature sold by a reputable shop are of the same standard as those used by the car manufacturer.

Besides components, these shops also sell tools and general accessories, usually have convenient opening hours, charge lower prices, and can often be found close to home. Some accessory shops have parts counters where components needed for almost any repair job can be purchased or ordered.

Motor factors

Good factors will stock all the more important components which wear out comparatively quickly, and can sometimes supply individual components needed for the overhaul of a larger assembly (eg, brake seals and hydraulic parts, bearing shells, pistons, valves). They may also handle work such as cylinder block reboring, crankshaft regrinding, etc.

Tyre and exhaust specialists

These outlets may be independent, or members of a local or national chain. They frequently offer competitive prices when compared with a main dealer or local garage, but it will pay to obtain several quotes before making a decision. When researching prices, also ask what 'extras' may be added - for instance fitting a new valve and balancing the wheel are both commonly charged on top of the price of a new tyre.

Other sources

Beware of parts or materials obtained from market stalls, car boot sales or similar outlets. Such items are not invariably sub-standard, but there is little chance of compensation if they do prove unsatisfactory. In the case of safety-critical components such as brake pads, there is the risk not only of financial loss, but also of an accident causing injury or death.

Second-hand components or assemblies obtained from a car breaker can be a good buy in some circumstances, but his sort of purchase is best made by the experienced DIY mechanic.

Vehicle identification

Modifications are a continuing and unpublicised process in vehicle manufacture, quite apart from major model changes. Spare parts manuals and lists are compiled upon a numerical basis, the individual vehicle identification numbers being essential to correct identification of the component concerned.

When ordering spare parts, always give as much information as possible. Quote the car model, year of manufacture, body and engine numbers as appropriate.

The *vehicle identification plate* is situated at the bottom of the left-hand door B-pillar. It gives the VIN (vehicle identification number), vehicle weight information and paint and trim colour codes. The *vehicle identification number* is also repeated in the form of stamped numbers on the centre of the engine compartment bulkhead and on a plate visible through the lower left-hand corner of the windscreen **(see illustrations)**.

The *body number* is stamped onto a plate fixed to the side of the spare wheel well, in the luggage compartment **(see illustration)**.

The *engine number* is stamped on the front of the cylinder block adjacent to the gearbox on 1.4 and 1.6 litre engines, on the front of the cylinder block above No 4 cylinder block core plug on 2.0 litre petrol engines, and on the front of the cylinder block adjacent to the alternator on 2.0 litre diesel engines.

Other identification numbers or codes are stamped on major items such as the gearbox, etc. These numbers are unlikely to be needed by the home mechanic.

The *vehicle identification plate* is situated at the bottom of the left-hand door B-pillar

The *vehicle identification number* is also repeated in the form of stamped numbers on the centre of the engine compartment bulkhead

The *body number* is stamped onto a plate fixed to the side of the spare wheel well

Whenever servicing, repair or overhaul work is carried out on the car or its components, observe the following procedures and instructions. This will assist in carrying out the operation efficiently and to a professional standard of workmanship.

Joint mating faces and gaskets

When separating components at their mating faces, never insert screwdrivers or similar implements into the joint between the faces in order to prise them apart. This can cause severe damage which results in oil leaks, coolant leaks, etc upon reassembly. Separation is usually achieved by tapping along the joint with a soft-faced hammer in order to break the seal. However, note that this method may not be suitable where dowels are used for component location.

Where a gasket is used between the mating faces of two components, a new one must be fitted on reassembly; fit it dry unless otherwise stated in the repair procedure. Make sure that the mating faces are clean and dry, with all traces of old gasket removed. When cleaning a joint face, use a tool which is unlikely to score or damage the face, and remove any burrs or nicks with an oilstone or fine file.

Make sure that tapped holes are cleaned with a pipe cleaner, and keep them free of jointing compound, if this is being used, unless specifically instructed otherwise.

Ensure that all orifices, channels or pipes are clear, and blow through them, preferably using compressed air.

Oil seals

Oil seals can be removed by levering them out with a wide flat-bladed screwdriver or similar implement. Alternatively, a number of self-tapping screws may be screwed into the seal, and these used as a purchase for pliers or some similar device in order to pull the seal free.

Whenever an oil seal is removed from its working location, either individually or as part of an assembly, it should be renewed.

The very fine sealing lip of the seal is easily damaged, and will not seal if the surface it contacts is not completely clean and free from scratches, nicks or grooves. If the original sealing surface of the component cannot be restored, and the manufacturer has not made provision for slight relocation of the seal relative to the sealing surface, the component should be renewed.

Protect the lips of the seal from any surface which may damage them in the course of fitting. Use tape or a conical sleeve where possible. Lubricate the seal lips with oil before fitting and, on dual-lipped seals, fill the space between the lips with grease.

Unless otherwise stated, oil seals must be fitted with their sealing lips toward the lubricant to be sealed.

Use a tubular drift or block of wood of the appropriate size to install the seal and, if the seal housing is shouldered, drive the seal down to the shoulder. If the seal housing is unshouldered, the seal should be fitted with its face flush with the housing top face (unless otherwise instructed).

Screw threads and fastenings

Seized nuts, bolts and screws are quite a common occurrence where corrosion has set in, and the use of penetrating oil or releasing fluid will often overcome this problem if the offending item is soaked for a while before attempting to release it. The use of an impact driver may also provide a means of releasing such stubborn fastening devices, when used in conjunction with the appropriate screwdriver bit or socket. If none of these methods works, it may be necessary to resort to the careful application of heat, or the use of a hacksaw or nut splitter device.

Studs are usually removed by locking two nuts together on the threaded part, and then using a spanner on the lower nut to unscrew the stud. Studs or bolts which have broken off below the surface of the component in which they are mounted can sometimes be removed using a stud extractor. Always ensure that a blind tapped hole is completely free from oil, grease, water or other fluid before installing the bolt or stud. Failure to do this could cause the housing to crack due to the hydraulic action of the bolt or stud as it is screwed in.

When tightening a castellated nut to accept a split pin, tighten the nut to the specified torque, where applicable, and then tighten further to the next split pin hole. Never slacken the nut to align the split pin hole, unless stated in the repair procedure.

When checking or retightening a nut or bolt to a specified torque setting, slacken the nut or bolt by a quarter of a turn, and then retighten to the specified setting. However, this should not be attempted where angular tightening has been used.

For some screw fastenings, notably cylinder head bolts or nuts, torque wrench settings are no longer specified for the latter stages of tightening, "angle-tightening" being called up instead. Typically, a fairly low torque wrench setting will be applied to the bolts/nuts in the correct sequence, followed by one or more stages of tightening through specified angles.

Locknuts, locktabs and washers

Any fastening which will rotate against a component or housing during tightening should always have a washer between it and the relevant component or housing.

Spring or split washers should always be renewed when they are used to lock a critical component such as a big-end bearing retaining bolt or nut. Locktabs which are folded over to retain a nut or bolt should always be renewed.

Self-locking nuts can be re-used in non-critical areas, providing resistance can be felt when the locking portion passes over the bolt or stud thread. However, it should be noted that self-locking stiffnuts tend to lose their effectiveness after long periods of use, and should then be renewed as a matter of course.

Split pins must always be replaced with new ones of the correct size for the hole.

When thread-locking compound is found on the threads of a fastener which is to be re-used, it should be cleaned off with a wire brush and solvent, and fresh compound applied on reassembly.

Special tools

Some repair procedures in this manual entail the use of special tools such as a press, two or three-legged pullers, spring compressors, etc. Wherever possible, suitable readily-available alternatives to the manufacturer's special tools are described, and are shown in use. In some instances, where no alternative is possible, it has been necessary to resort to the use of a manufacturer's tool, and this has been done for reasons of safety as well as the efficient completion of the repair operation. Unless you are highly-skilled and have a thorough understanding of the procedures described, never attempt to bypass the use of any special tool when the procedure described specifies its use. Not only is there a very great risk of personal injury, but expensive damage could be caused to the components involved.

Environmental considerations

When disposing of used engine oil, brake fluid, antifreeze, etc, give due consideration to any detrimental environmental effects. Do not, for instance, pour any of the above liquids down drains into the general sewage system, or onto the ground to soak away. Many local council refuse tips provide a facility for waste oil disposal, as do some garages. If none of these facilities are available, consult your local Environmental Health Department, or the National Rivers Authority, for further advice.

With the universal tightening-up of legislation regarding the emission of environmentally-harmful substances from motor vehicles, most vehicles have tamperproof devices fitted to the main adjustment points of the fuel system. These devices are primarily designed to prevent unqualified persons from adjusting the fuel/air mixture, with the chance of a consequent increase in toxic emissions. If such devices are found during servicing or overhaul, they should, wherever possible, be renewed or refitted in accordance with the manufacturer's requirements or current legislation.

OIL CARE — FOLLOW THE CODE

OIL BANK LINE
0800 66 33 66

Note: It is antisocial and illegal to dump oil down the drain. To find the location of your local oil recycling bank, call this number free.

The jack supplied with the vehicle tool kit should only be used for changing the roadwheels - see "Wheel changing" at the front of this manual. When carrying out any other kind of work, raise the vehicle using a hydraulic trolley jack, and always supplement the jack with axle stands positioned under the vehicle jacking points.

When using a trolley jack or axle stands, always position the jack head or axle stand head under, or adjacent to one of the relevant wheel changing jacking points under the sills (see illustration). Use a block of wood between the jack or axle stand and the sill.

Do not attempt to jack the vehicle under the front crossmember, the sump, or any of the suspension components.

Never work under, around, or near a raised vehicle, unless it is adequately supported in at least two places.

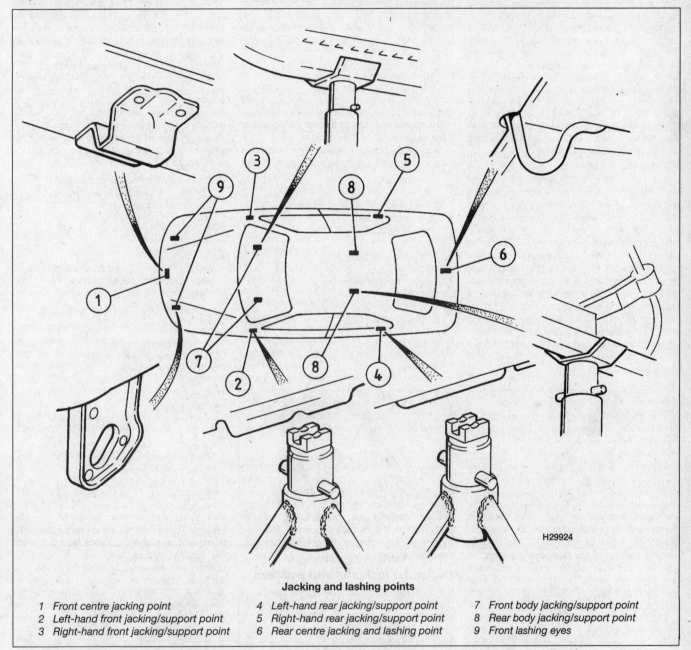

H29924

Jacking and lashing points

1 Front centre jacking point
2 Left-hand front jacking/support point
3 Right-hand front jacking/support point
4 Left-hand rear jacking/support point
5 Right-hand rear jacking/support point
6 Rear centre jacking and lashing point
7 Front body jacking/support point
8 Rear body jacking/support point
9 Front lashing eyes

Radio/cassette unit anti-theft system - precaution

The radio/cassette unit fitted as standard equipment by Rover is equipped with a built-in security code to deter thieves. If the power source to the unit is cut, the anti-theft system will activate. Even if the power source is immediately reconnected, the radio/cassette unit will not function until the correct security code has been entered. Therefore, if you do not know the correct security code for the unit, do not disconnect the battery negative lead, or remove the radio/cassette unit from the vehicle.

The procedure for reprogramming a unit that has been disconnected from its power supply varies from model to model. Consult the handbook supplied with the unit for specific details or refer to your Rover dealer.

Introduction

A selection of good tools is a fundamental requirement for anyone contemplating the maintenance and repair of a motor vehicle. For the owner who does not possess any, their purchase will prove a considerable expense, offsetting some of the savings made by doing-it-yourself. However, provided that the tools purchased meet the relevant national safety standards and are of good quality, they will last for many years and prove an extremely worthwhile investment.

To help the average owner to decide which tools are needed to carry out the various tasks detailed in this manual, we have compiled three lists of tools under the following headings: *Maintenance and minor repair*, *Repair and overhaul*, and *Special*. Newcomers to practical mechanics should start off with the *Maintenance and minor repair* tool kit, and confine themselves to the simpler jobs around the vehicle. Then, as confidence and experience grow, more difficult tasks can be undertaken, with extra tools being purchased as, and when, they are needed. In this way, a *Maintenance and minor repair* tool kit can be built up into a *Repair and overhaul* tool kit over a considerable period of time, without any major cash outlays. The experienced do-it-yourselfer will have a tool kit good enough for most repair and overhaul procedures, and will add tools from the *Special* category when it is felt that the expense is justified by the amount of use to which these tools will be put.

Maintenance and minor repair tool kit

The tools given in this list should be considered as a minimum requirement if routine maintenance, servicing and minor repair operations are to be undertaken. We recommend the purchase of combination spanners (ring one end, open-ended the other); although more expensive than open-ended ones, they do give the advantages of both types of spanner.

☐ *Combination spanners:*
  Metric - 8 to 19 mm inclusive
☐ *Adjustable spanner - 35 mm jaw (approx.)*
☐ *Spark plug spanner (with rubber insert) - petrol models*
☐ *Spark plug gap adjustment tool - petrol models*
☐ *Set of feeler gauges*
☐ *Brake bleed nipple spanner*
☐ *Screwdrivers:*
  Flat blade - 100 mm long x 6 mm dia
  Cross blade - 100 mm long x 6 mm dia
☐ *Combination pliers*
☐ *Hacksaw (junior)*
☐ *Tyre pump*
☐ *Tyre pressure gauge*
☐ *Oil can*
☐ *Oil filter removal tool*
☐ *Fine emery cloth*
☐ *Wire brush (small)*
☐ *Funnel (medium size)*

Repair and overhaul tool kit

These tools are virtually essential for anyone undertaking any major repairs to a motor vehicle, and are additional to those given in the *Maintenance and minor repair* list. Included in this list is a comprehensive set of sockets. Although these are expensive, they will be found invaluable as they are so versatile - particularly if various drives are included in the set. We recommend the half-inch square-drive type, as this can be used with most proprietary torque wrenches.

The tools in this list will sometimes need to be supplemented by tools from the *Special* list:

☐ *Sockets (or box spanners) to cover range in previous list (including Torx sockets)*
☐ *Reversible ratchet drive (for use with sockets)*
☐ *Extension piece, 250 mm (for use with sockets)*
☐ *Universal joint (for use with sockets)*
☐ *Torque wrench (for use with sockets)*
☐ *Self-locking grips*
☐ *Ball pein hammer*
☐ *Soft-faced mallet (plastic/aluminium or rubber)*
☐ *Screwdrivers:*
  Flat blade - long & sturdy, short (chubby), and narrow (electrician's) types
  Cross blade – Long & sturdy, and short (chubby) types
☐ *Pliers:*
  Long-nosed
  Side cutters (electrician's)
  Circlip (internal and external)
☐ *Cold chisel - 25 mm*
☐ *Scriber*
☐ *Scraper*
☐ *Centre-punch*
☐ *Pin punch*
☐ *Hacksaw*
☐ *Brake hose clamp*
☐ *Brake/clutch bleeding kit*
☐ *Selection of twist drills*
☐ *Steel rule/straight-edge*
☐ *Allen keys (inc. splined/Torx type)*
☐ *Selection of files*
☐ *Wire brush*
☐ *Axle stands*
☐ *Jack (strong trolley or hydraulic type)*
☐ *Light with extension lead*

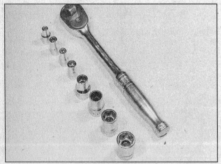

Sockets and reversible ratchet drive

Valve spring compressor

Spline bit set

Piston ring compressor

Clutch plate alignment set

Special tools

The tools in this list are those which are not used regularly, are expensive to buy, or which need to be used in accordance with their manufacturers' instructions. Unless relatively difficult mechanical jobs are undertaken frequently, it will not be economic to buy many of these tools. Where this is the case, you could consider clubbing together with friends (or joining a motorists' club) to make a joint purchase, or borrowing the tools against a deposit from a local garage or tool hire specialist. It is worth noting that many of the larger DIY superstores now carry a large range of special tools for hire at modest rates.

The following list contains only those tools and instruments freely available to the public, and not those special tools produced by the vehicle manufacturer specifically for its dealer network. You will find occasional references to these manufacturers' special tools in the text of this manual. Generally, an alternative method of doing the job without the vehicle manufacturers' special tool is given. However, sometimes there is no alternative to using them. Where this is the case and the relevant tool cannot be bought or borrowed, you will have to entrust the work to a dealer.

☐ Valve spring compressor
☐ Valve grinding tool
☐ Piston ring compressor
☐ Piston ring removal/installation tool
☐ Cylinder bore hone
☐ Balljoint separator
☐ Coil spring compressors (where applicable)
☐ Two/three-legged hub and bearing puller
☐ Impact screwdriver
☐ Micrometer and/or vernier calipers
☐ Dial gauge
☐ Stroboscopic timing light
☐ Dwell angle meter/tachometer
☐ Universal electrical multi-meter
☐ Cylinder compression gauge
☐ Hand-operated vacuum pump and gauge
☐ Clutch plate alignment set
☐ Brake shoe steady spring cup removal tool
☐ Bush and bearing removal/installation set
☐ Stud extractors
☐ Tap and die set
☐ Lifting tackle
☐ Trolley jack

Buying tools

Reputable motor accessory shops and superstores often offer excellent quality tools at discount prices, so it pays to shop around.

Remember, you don't have to buy the most expensive items on the shelf, but it is always advisable to steer clear of the very cheap tools. Beware of 'bargains' offered on market stalls or at car boot sales. There are plenty of good tools around at reasonable prices, but always aim to purchase items which meet the relevant national safety standards. If in doubt, ask the proprietor or manager of the shop for advice before making a purchase.

Care and maintenance of tools

Having purchased a reasonable tool kit, it is necessary to keep the tools in a clean and serviceable condition. After use, always wipe off any dirt, grease and metal particles using a clean, dry cloth, before putting the tools away. Never leave them lying around after they have been used. A simple tool rack on the garage or workshop wall for items such as screwdrivers and pliers is a good idea. Store all normal spanners and sockets in a metal box. Any measuring instruments, gauges, meters, etc, must be carefully stored where they cannot be damaged or become rusty.

Take a little care when tools are used. Hammer heads inevitably become marked, and screwdrivers lose the keen edge on their blades from time to time. A little timely attention with emery cloth or a file will soon restore items like this to a good finish.

Working facilities

Not to be forgotten when discussing tools is the workshop itself. If anything more than routine maintenance is to be carried out, a suitable working area becomes essential.

It is appreciated that many an owner-mechanic is forced by circumstances to remove an engine or similar item without the benefit of a garage or workshop. Having done this, any repairs should always be done under the cover of a roof.

Wherever possible, any dismantling should be done on a clean, flat workbench or table at a suitable working height.

Any workbench needs a vice; one with a jaw opening of 100 mm is suitable for most jobs. As mentioned previously, some clean dry storage space is also required for tools, as well as for any lubricants, cleaning fluids, touch-up paints etc, which become necessary.

Another item which may be required, and which has a much more general usage, is an electric drill with a chuck capacity of at least 8 mm. This, together with a good range of twist drills, is virtually essential for fitting accessories.

Last, but not least, always keep a supply of old newspapers and clean, lint-free rags available, and try to keep any working area as clean as possible.

Micrometer set

Dial test indicator ("dial gauge")

Stroboscopic timing light

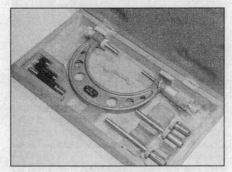

Compression tester

Stud extractor set

This is a guide to getting your vehicle through the MOT test. Obviously it will not be possible to examine the vehicle to the same standard as the professional MOT tester. However, working through the following checks will enable you to identify any problem areas before submitting the vehicle for the test.

Where a testable component is in borderline condition, the tester has discretion in deciding whether to pass or fail it. The basis of such discretion is whether the tester would be happy for a close relative or friend to use the vehicle with the component in that condition. If the vehicle presented is clean and evidently well cared for, the tester may be more inclined to pass a borderline component than if the vehicle is scruffy and apparently neglected.

It has only been possible to summarise the test requirements here, based on the regulations in force at the time of printing. Test standards are becoming increasingly stringent, although there are some exemptions for older vehicles. For full details obtain a copy of the Haynes publication Pass the MOT! (available from stockists of Haynes manuals).

An assistant will be needed to help carry out some of these checks.

The checks have been sub-divided into four categories, as follows:

1 Checks carried out **FROM THE DRIVER'S SEAT**

2 Checks carried out **WITH THE VEHICLE ON THE GROUND**

3 Checks carried out **WITH THE VEHICLE RAISED AND THE WHEELS FREE TO TURN**

4 Checks carried out on **YOUR VEHICLE'S EXHAUST EMISSION SYSTEM**

1 Checks carried out **FROM THE DRIVER'S SEAT**

Handbrake

☐ Test the operation of the handbrake. Excessive travel (too many clicks) indicates incorrect brake or cable adjustment.

☐ Check that the handbrake cannot be released by tapping the lever sideways. Check the security of the lever mountings.

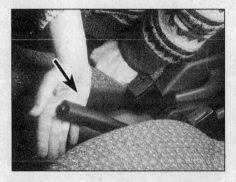

Footbrake

☐ Depress the brake pedal and check that it does not creep down to the floor, indicating a master cylinder fault. Release the pedal, wait a few seconds, then depress it again. If the pedal travels nearly to the floor before firm resistance is felt, brake adjustment or repair is necessary. If the pedal feels spongy, there is air in the hydraulic system which must be removed by bleeding.

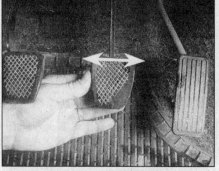

☐ Check that the brake pedal is secure and in good condition. Check also for signs of fluid leaks on the pedal, floor or carpets, which would indicate failed seals in the brake master cylinder.

☐ Check the servo unit (when applicable) by operating the brake pedal several times, then keeping the pedal depressed and starting the engine. As the engine starts, the pedal will move down slightly. If not, the vacuum hose or the servo itself may be faulty.

Steering wheel and column

☐ Examine the steering wheel for fractures or looseness of the hub, spokes or rim.

☐ Move the steering wheel from side to side and then up and down. Check that the steering wheel is not loose on the column, indicating wear or a loose retaining nut. Continue moving the steering wheel as before, but also turn it slightly from left to right.

☐ Check that the steering wheel is not loose on the column, and that there is no abnormal

movement of the steering wheel, indicating wear in the column support bearings or couplings.

Windscreen and mirrors

☐ The windscreen must be free of cracks or other significant damage within the driver's field of view. (Small stone chips are acceptable.) Rear view mirrors must be secure, intact, and capable of being adjusted.

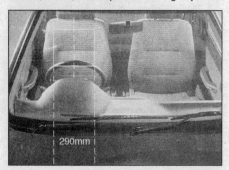

290mm

Seat belts and seats

Note: *The following checks are applicable to all seat belts, front and rear.*

☐ Examine the webbing of all the belts (including rear belts if fitted) for cuts, serious fraying or deterioration. Fasten and unfasten each belt to check the buckles. If applicable, check the retracting mechanism. Check the security of all seat belt mountings accessible from inside the vehicle.

☐ The front seats themselves must be securely attached and the backrests must lock in the upright position.

Doors

☐ Both front doors must be able to be opened and closed from outside and inside, and must latch securely when closed.

2 Checks carried out WITH THE VEHICLE ON THE GROUND

Vehicle identification

☐ Number plates must be in good condition, secure and legible, with letters and numbers correctly spaced – spacing at (A) should be twice that at (B).

☐ The VIN plate and/or homologation plate must be legible.

Electrical equipment

☐ Switch on the ignition and check the operation of the horn.

☐ Check the windscreen washers and wipers, examining the wiper blades; renew damaged or perished blades. Also check the operation of the stop-lights.

☐ Check the operation of the sidelights and number plate lights. The lenses and reflectors must be secure, clean and undamaged.

☐ Check the operation and alignment of the headlights. The headlight reflectors must not be tarnished and the lenses must be undamaged.

☐ Switch on the ignition and check the operation of the direction indicators (including the instrument panel tell-tale) and the hazard warning lights. Operation of the sidelights and stop-lights must not affect the indicators - if it does, the cause is usually a bad earth at the rear light cluster.

☐ Check the operation of the rear foglight(s), including the warning light on the instrument panel or in the switch.

Footbrake

☐ Examine the master cylinder, brake pipes and servo unit for leaks, loose mountings, corrosion or other damage.

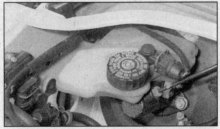

☐ The fluid reservoir must be secure and the fluid level must be between the upper (**A**) and lower (**B**) markings.

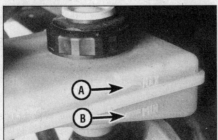

☐ Inspect both front brake flexible hoses for cracks or deterioration of the rubber. Turn the steering from lock to lock, and ensure that the hoses do not contact the wheel, tyre, or any part of the steering or suspension mechanism. With the brake pedal firmly depressed, check the hoses for bulges or leaks under pressure.

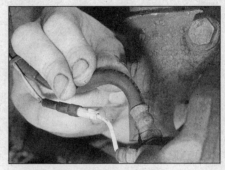

Steering and suspension

☐ Have your assistant turn the steering wheel from side to side slightly, up to the point where the steering gear just begins to transmit this movement to the roadwheels. Check for excessive free play between the steering wheel and the steering gear, indicating wear or insecurity of the steering column joints, the column-to-steering gear coupling, or the steering gear itself.

☐ Have your assistant turn the steering wheel more vigorously in each direction, so that the roadwheels just begin to turn. As this is done, examine all the steering joints, linkages, fittings and attachments. Renew any component that shows signs of wear or damage. On vehicles with power steering, check the security and condition of the steering pump, drivebelt and hoses.

☐ Check that the vehicle is standing level, and at approximately the correct ride height.

Shock absorbers

☐ Depress each corner of the vehicle in turn, then release it. The vehicle should rise and then settle in its normal position. If the vehicle continues to rise and fall, the shock absorber is defective. A shock absorber which has seized will also cause the vehicle to fail.

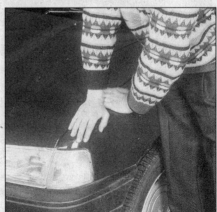

Exhaust system

☐ Start the engine. With your assistant holding a rag over the tailpipe, check the entire system for leaks. Repair or renew leaking sections.

3 Checks carried out WITH THE VEHICLE RAISED AND THE WHEELS FREE TO TURN

Jack up the front and rear of the vehicle, and securely support it on axle stands. Position the stands clear of the suspension assemblies. Ensure that the wheels are clear of the ground and that the steering can be turned from lock to lock.

Steering mechanism

☐ Have your assistant turn the steering from lock to lock. Check that the steering turns smoothly, and that no part of the steering mechanism, including a wheel or tyre, fouls any brake hose or pipe or any part of the body structure.
☐ Examine the steering rack rubber gaiters for damage or insecurity of the retaining clips. If power steering is fitted, check for signs of damage or leakage of the fluid hoses, pipes or connections. Also check for excessive stiffness or binding of the steering, a missing split pin or locking device, or severe corrosion of the body structure within 30 cm of any steering component attachment point.

Front and rear suspension and wheel bearings

☐ Starting at the front right-hand side, grasp the roadwheel at the 3 o'clock and 9 o'clock positions and shake it vigorously. Check for free play or insecurity at the wheel bearings, suspension balljoints, or suspension mountings, pivots and attachments.
☐ Now grasp the wheel at the 12 o'clock and 6 o'clock positions and repeat the previous inspection. Spin the wheel, and check for roughness or tightness of the front wheel bearing.

☐ If excess free play is suspected at a component pivot point, this can be confirmed by using a large screwdriver or similar tool and levering between the mounting and the component attachment. This will confirm whether the wear is in the pivot bush, its retaining bolt, or in the mounting itself (the bolt holes can often become elongated).

☐ Carry out all the above checks at the other front wheel, and then at both rear wheels.

Springs and shock absorbers

☐ Examine the suspension struts (when applicable) for serious fluid leakage, corrosion, or damage to the casing. Also check the security of the mounting points.
☐ If coil springs are fitted, check that the spring ends locate in their seats, and that the spring is not corroded, cracked or broken.
☐ If leaf springs are fitted, check that all leaves are intact, that the axle is securely attached to each spring, and that there is no deterioration of the spring eye mountings, bushes, and shackles.

☐ The same general checks apply to vehicles fitted with other suspension types, such as torsion bars, hydraulic displacer units, etc. Ensure that all mountings and attachments are secure, that there are no signs of excessive wear, corrosion or damage, and (on hydraulic types) that there are no fluid leaks or damaged pipes.
☐ Inspect the shock absorbers for signs of serious fluid leakage. Check for wear of the mounting bushes or attachments, or damage to the body of the unit.

Driveshafts (fwd vehicles only)

☐ Rotate each front wheel in turn and inspect the constant velocity joint gaiters for splits or damage. Also check that each driveshaft is straight and undamaged.

Braking system

☐ If possible without dismantling, check brake pad wear and disc condition. Ensure that the friction lining material has not worn excessively, (A) and that the discs are not fractured, pitted, scored or badly worn (B).

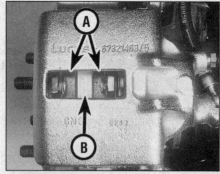

☐ Examine all the rigid brake pipes underneath the vehicle, and the flexible hose(s) at the rear. Look for corrosion, chafing or insecurity of the pipes, and for signs of bulging under pressure, chafing, splits or deterioration of the flexible hoses.
☐ Look for signs of fluid leaks at the brake calipers or on the brake backplates. Repair or renew leaking components.
☐ Slowly spin each wheel, while your assistant depresses and releases the footbrake. Ensure that each brake is operating and does not bind when the pedal is released.

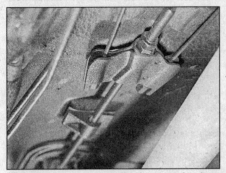

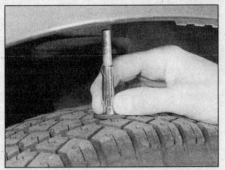

☐ Examine the handbrake mechanism, checking for frayed or broken cables, excessive corrosion, or wear or insecurity of the linkage. Check that the mechanism works on each relevant wheel, and releases fully, without binding.

☐ It is not possible to test brake efficiency without special equipment, but a road test can be carried out later to check that the vehicle pulls up in a straight line.

Fuel and exhaust systems

☐ Inspect the fuel tank (including the filler cap), fuel pipes, hoses and unions. All components must be secure and free from leaks.

☐ Examine the exhaust system over its entire length, checking for any damaged, broken or missing mountings, security of the retaining clamps and rust or corrosion.

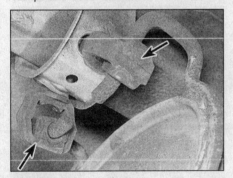

Wheels and tyres

☐ Examine the sidewalls and tread area of each tyre in turn. Check for cuts, tears, lumps, bulges, separation of the tread, and exposure of the ply or cord due to wear or damage. Check that the tyre bead is correctly seated on the wheel rim, that the valve is sound and

properly seated, and that the wheel is not distorted or damaged.

☐ Check that the tyres are of the correct size for the vehicle, that they are of the same size and type on each axle, and that the pressures are correct.

☐ Check the tyre tread depth. The legal minimum at the time of writing is 1.6 mm over at least three-quarters of the tread width. Abnormal tread wear may indicate incorrect front wheel alignment.

Body corrosion

☐ Check the condition of the entire vehicle structure for signs of corrosion in load-bearing areas. (These include chassis box sections, side sills, cross-members, pillars, and all suspension, steering, braking system and seat belt mountings and anchorages.) Any corrosion which has seriously reduced the thickness of a load-bearing area is likely to cause the vehicle to fail. In this case professional repairs are likely to be needed.

☐ Damage or corrosion which causes sharp or otherwise dangerous edges to be exposed will also cause the vehicle to fail.

4 Checks carried out on YOUR VEHICLE'S EXHAUST EMISSION SYSTEM

Petrol models

☐ Have the engine at normal operating temperature, and make sure that it is in good tune (ignition system in good order, air filter element clean, etc).

☐ Before any measurements are carried out, raise the engine speed to around 2500 rpm, and hold it at this speed for 20 seconds. Allow

the engine speed to return to idle, and watch for smoke emissions from the exhaust tailpipe. If the idle speed is obviously much too high, or if dense blue or clearly-visible black smoke comes from the tailpipe for more than 5 seconds, the vehicle will fail. As a rule of thumb, blue smoke signifies oil being burnt (engine wear) while black smoke signifies unburnt fuel (dirty air cleaner element, or other carburettor or fuel system fault).

☐ An exhaust gas analyser capable of measuring carbon monoxide (CO) and hydrocarbons (HC) is now needed. If such an instrument cannot be hired or borrowed, a local garage may agree to perform the check for a small fee.

CO emissions (mixture)

☐ At the time of writing, the maximum CO level at idle is 3.5% for vehicles first used after August 1986 and 4.5% for older vehicles. From January 1996 a much tighter limit (around 0.5%) applies to catalyst-equipped vehicles first used from August 1992. If the CO level cannot be reduced far enough to pass the test (and the fuel and ignition systems are otherwise in good condition) then the carburettor is badly worn, or there is some problem in the fuel injection system or catalytic converter (as applicable).

HC emissions

☐ With the CO emissions within limits, HC emissions must be no more than 1200 ppm (parts per million). If the vehicle fails this test at idle, it can be re-tested at around 2000 rpm; if the HC level is then 1200 ppm or less, this counts as a pass.

☐ Excessive HC emissions can be caused by oil being burnt, but they are more likely to be due to unburnt fuel.

Diesel models

☐ The only emission test applicable to Diesel engines is the measuring of exhaust smoke density. The test involves accelerating the engine several times to its maximum unloaded speed.

Note: *It is of the utmost importance that the engine timing belt is in good condition before the test is carried out.*

☐ Excessive smoke can be caused by a dirty air cleaner element. Otherwise, professional advice may be needed to find the cause.

Engine

- ☐ Engine fails to rotate when attempting to start
- ☐ Engine rotates, but will not start
- ☐ Engine difficult to start when cold
- ☐ Engine difficult to start when hot
- ☐ Starter motor noisy or excessively-rough in engagement
- ☐ Engine starts, but stops immediately
- ☐ Engine idles erratically
- ☐ Engine misfires at idle speed
- ☐ Engine misfires throughout the driving speed range
- ☐ Engine hesitates on acceleration
- ☐ Engine stalls
- ☐ Engine lacks power
- ☐ Engine backfires
- ☐ Oil pressure warning light illuminated with engine running
- ☐ Engine runs-on after switching off
- ☐ Engine noises

Cooling system

- ☐ Overheating
- ☐ Overcooling
- ☐ External coolant leakage
- ☐ Internal coolant leakage
- ☐ Corrosion

Fuel and exhaust systems

- ☐ Excessive fuel consumption
- ☐ Fuel leakage and/or fuel odour
- ☐ Excessive noise or fumes from the exhaust system

Clutch

- ☐ Pedal travels to floor - no pressure or very little resistance
- ☐ Clutch fails to disengage (unable to select gears)
- ☐ Clutch slips (engine speed increases, with no increase in vehicle speed)
- ☐ Judder as clutch is engaged
- ☐ Noise when depressing or releasing clutch pedal

Manual transmission

- ☐ Noisy in neutral with engine running
- ☐ Noisy in one particular gear
- ☐ Difficulty engaging gears
- ☐ Jumps out of gear
- ☐ Vibration
- ☐ Lubricant leaks

Driveshafts

- ☐ Vibration when accelerating or decelerating
- ☐ Clicking or knocking noise on turns (at slow speed on full-lock)

Braking system

- ☐ Vehicle pulls to one side under braking
- ☐ Noise (grinding or high-pitched squeal) when brakes applied
- ☐ Excessive brake pedal travel
- ☐ Brake pedal feels spongy when depressed
- ☐ Excessive brake pedal effort required to stop vehicle
- ☐ Judder felt through brake pedal or steering wheel when braking
- ☐ Pedal pulsates when braking hard
- ☐ Brakes binding
- ☐ Rear wheels locking under normal braking

Steering and suspension

- ☐ Vehicle pulls to one side
- ☐ Wheel wobble and vibration
- ☐ Excessive pitching and/or rolling around corners, or during braking
- ☐ Wandering or general instability
- ☐ Excessively-stiff steering
- ☐ Excessive play in steering
- ☐ Lack of power assistance
- ☐ Tyre wear excessive

Electrical system

- ☐ Battery will not hold a charge for more than a few days
- ☐ Ignition/no-charge warning light remains illuminated with engine running
- ☐ Ignition/no-charge warning light fails to come on
- ☐ Lights inoperative
- ☐ Instrument readings inaccurate or erratic
- ☐ Horn inoperative, or unsatisfactory in operation
- ☐ Windscreen/tailgate wipers inoperative, or unsatisfactory in operation
- ☐ Windscreen/tailgate washers inoperative, or unsatisfactory in operation
- ☐ Electric windows inoperative, or unsatisfactory in operation
- ☐ Central locking system inoperative, or unsatisfactory in operation

Introduction

The vehicle owner who does his or her own maintenance according to the recommended service schedules should not have to use this section of the manual very often. Modern component reliability is such that, provided those items subject to wear or deterioration are inspected or renewed at the specified intervals, sudden failure is comparatively rare. Faults do not usually just happen as a result of sudden failure, but develop over a period of time. Major mechanical failures in particular are usually preceded by characteristic symptoms over hundreds or even thousands of miles. Those components which do occasionally fail without warning are often small and easily carried in the vehicle.

With any fault-finding, the first step is to decide where to begin investigations.

Sometimes this is obvious, but on other occasions, a little detective work will be necessary. The owner who makes half a dozen haphazard adjustments or replacements may be successful in curing a fault (or its symptoms), but will be none the wiser if the fault recurs, and ultimately may have spent more time and money than was necessary. A calm and logical approach will be found to be more satisfactory in the long run. Always take into account any warning signs or abnormalities that may have been noticed in the period preceding the fault - power loss, high or low gauge readings, unusual smells, etc - and remember that failure of components such as fuses or spark plugs may only be pointers to some underlying fault.

The pages which follow provide an easy-reference guide to the more common problems which may occur during the operation of the vehicle. These problems and their possible causes are grouped under headings denoting various components or systems, such as Engine, Cooling system, etc. The Chapter and/or Section which deals with the problem is also shown in brackets. Whatever the fault, certain basic principles apply. These are as follows:

Verify the fault. This is simply a matter of being sure that you know what the symptoms are before starting work. This is particularly important if you are investigating a fault for someone else, who may not have described it very accurately.

Don't overlook the obvious. For example, if the vehicle won't start, is there fuel in the tank? (Don't take anyone else's word on this particular point, and don't trust the fuel gauge either!) If an electrical fault is indicated, look for loose or broken wires before digging out the test gear.

Cure the disease, not the symptom. Substituting a flat battery with a fully-charged one will get you off the hard shoulder, but if the underlying cause is not attended to, the new battery will go the same way. Similarly, changing oil-fouled spark plugs for a new set will get you moving again, but remember that the reason for the fouling (if it wasn't simply an incorrect grade of plug) will have to be established and corrected.

Don't take anything for granted. Particularly, don't forget that a 'new' component may itself be defective (especially if it's been rattling around in the boot for months), and don't leave components out of a fault diagnosis sequence just because they are new or recently-fitted. When you do finally diagnose a difficult fault, you'll probably realise that all the evidence was there from the start.

Engine

Engine fails to rotate when attempting to start

- [ ] Battery terminal connections loose or corroded (see *"Weekly checks"*).
- [ ] Battery discharged or faulty (Chapter 5A).
- [ ] Broken, loose or disconnected wiring in the starting circuit (Chapter 5A).
- [ ] Defective starter solenoid or switch (Chapter 5A).
- [ ] Defective starter motor (Chapter 5A).
- [ ] Starter pinion or flywheel ring gear teeth loose or broken (Chapters 2 and 5A).
- [ ] Engine earth strap broken or disconnected (Chapter 5A).

Engine rotates, but will not start

- [ ] Fuel tank empty.
- [ ] Battery discharged (engine rotates slowly) (Chapter 5A).
- [ ] Battery terminal connections loose or corroded (see *"Weekly checks"*).
- [ ] Ignition components damp or damaged - petrol models (Chapters 1A and 5B).
- [ ] Broken, loose or disconnected wiring in the ignition circuit - petrol models (Chapters 1A and 5B).
- [ ] Worn, faulty or incorrectly-gapped spark plugs - petrol models (Chapter 1A).
- [ ] Pre-heating system faulty - diesel models (Chapter 5C).
- [ ] Fuel injection system faulty - petrol models (Chapter 4A).
- [ ] Stop solenoid faulty - diesel models (Chapter 4B).
- [ ] Air in fuel system - diesel models (Chapter 4B).
- [ ] Major mechanical failure (eg camshaft drive) (Chapter 2).

Engine difficult to start when cold

- [ ] Battery discharged (Chapter 5A).
- [ ] Battery terminal connections loose or corroded (see *"Weekly checks"*).
- [ ] Worn, faulty or incorrectly-gapped spark plugs - petrol models (Chapter 1A).
- [ ] Pre-heating system faulty - diesel models (Chapter 5C).
- [ ] Fuel injection system faulty - petrol models (Chapter 4A).
- [ ] Other ignition system fault - petrol models (Chapters 1A and 5B).
- [ ] Low cylinder compressions (Chapter 2).

Engine difficult to start when hot

- [ ] Air filter element dirty or clogged (Chapter 1).
- [ ] Fuel injection system faulty - petrol models (Chapter 4A).
- [ ] Low cylinder compressions (Chapter 2).

Starter motor noisy or excessively-rough in engagement

- [ ] Starter pinion or flywheel ring gear teeth loose or broken (Chapters 2 and 5A).
- [ ] Starter motor mounting bolts loose or missing (Chapter 5A).
- [ ] Starter motor internal components worn or damaged (Chapter 5A).

Engine starts, but stops immediately

- [ ] Loose or faulty electrical connections in the ignition circuit - petrol models (Chapters 1A and 5B).

- [ ] Vacuum leak at the throttle body or inlet manifold - petrol models (Chapter 4A).
- [ ] Blocked injector/fuel injection system fault - petrol models (Chapter 4A).

Engine idles erratically

- [ ] Air filter element clogged (Chapter 1).
- [ ] Vacuum leak at the throttle body, inlet manifold or associated hoses - petrol models (Chapter 4A).
- [ ] Worn, faulty or incorrectly-gapped spark plugs - petrol models (Chapter 1A).
- [ ] Uneven or low cylinder compressions (Chapter 2).
- [ ] Camshaft lobes worn (Chapter 2).
- [ ] Timing belt incorrectly fitted (Chapter 2).
- [ ] Blocked injector/fuel injection system fault - petrol models (Chapter 4A).
- [ ] Faulty injector(s) - diesel models (Chapter 4B).

Engine misfires at idle speed

- [ ] Worn, faulty or incorrectly-gapped spark plugs - petrol models (Chapter 1A).
- [ ] Faulty spark plug HT leads - petrol models (Chapter 1A).
- [ ] Vacuum leak at the throttle body, inlet manifold or associated hoses - petrol models (Chapter 4A).
- [ ] Blocked injector/fuel injection system fault - petrol models (Chapter 4A).
- [ ] Faulty injector(s) - diesel models (Chapter 4B).
- [ ] Uneven or low cylinder compressions (Chapter 2).
- [ ] Disconnected, leaking, or perished crankcase ventilation hoses (Chapter 4C).

Engine misfires throughout the driving speed range

- [ ] Fuel filter choked (Chapter 1).
- [ ] Fuel pump faulty, or delivery pressure low - petrol models (Chapter 4A).
- [ ] Fuel tank vent blocked, or fuel pipes restricted (Chapter 4).
- [ ] Vacuum leak at the throttle body, inlet manifold or associated hoses - petrol models (Chapter 4A).
- [ ] Worn, faulty or incorrectly-gapped spark plugs - petrol models (Chapter 1A).
- [ ] Faulty spark plug HT leads - petrol models (Chapter 1A).
- [ ] Faulty injector(s) - diesel models (Chapter 4B).
- [ ] Faulty ignition coil - petrol models (Chapter 5B).
- [ ] Uneven or low cylinder compressions (Chapter 2).
- [ ] Blocked injector/fuel injection system fault - petrol models (Chapter 4A).

Engine hesitates on acceleration

- [ ] Worn, faulty or incorrectly-gapped spark plugs - petrol models (Chapter 1A).
- [ ] Vacuum leak at the throttle body, inlet manifold or associated hoses - petrol models (Chapter 4A).
- [ ] Blocked injector/fuel injection system fault - petrol models (Chapter 4A).
- [ ] Faulty injector(s) - diesel models (Chapter 4B).

Engine (continued)

Engine stalls

- ☐ Vacuum leak at the throttle body, inlet manifold or associated hoses - petrol models (Chapter 4A).
- ☐ Fuel filter choked (Chapter 1).
- ☐ Fuel pump faulty, or delivery pressure low - petrol models (Chapter 4A).
- ☐ Fuel tank vent blocked, or fuel pipes restricted (Chapter 4).
- ☐ Blocked injector/fuel injection system fault - petrol models (Chapter 4A).
- ☐ Faulty injector(s) - diesel models (Chapter 4B).

Engine lacks power

- ☐ Timing belt incorrectly fitted or tensioned (Chapter 2).
- ☐ Fuel filter choked (Chapter 1).
- ☐ Fuel pump faulty, or delivery pressure low - petrol models (Chapter 4A).
- ☐ Uneven or low cylinder compressions (Chapter 2).
- ☐ Worn, faulty or incorrectly-gapped spark plugs - petrol models (Chapter 1A).
- ☐ Vacuum leak at the throttle body, inlet manifold or associated hoses - petrol models (Chapter 4A).
- ☐ Blocked injector/fuel injection system fault - petrol models (Chapter 4A).
- ☐ Faulty injector(s) - diesel models (Chapter 4B).
- ☐ Injection pump timing incorrect - diesel models (Chapter 4B).
- ☐ Brakes binding (Chapters 1 and 9).
- ☐ Clutch slipping (Chapter 6).

Engine backfires

- ☐ Timing belt incorrectly fitted or tensioned (Chapter 2).
- ☐ Vacuum leak at the throttle body, inlet manifold or associated hoses - petrol models (Chapter 4A).
- ☐ Blocked injector/fuel injection system fault - petrol models (Chapter 4A).

Oil pressure warning light illuminated with engine running

- ☐ Low oil level, or incorrect oil grade (see "*Weekly checks*").
- ☐ Faulty oil pressure sensor (Chapter 5A).
- ☐ Worn engine bearings and/or oil pump (Chapter 2).
- ☐ High engine operating temperature (Chapter 3).
- ☐ Oil pressure relief valve defective (Chapter 2).
- ☐ Oil pick-up strainer clogged (Chapter 2).

Engine runs-on after switching off

- ☐ Excessive carbon build-up in engine (Chapter 2).
- ☐ High engine operating temperature (Chapter 3).
- ☐ Fuel injection system faulty - petrol models (Chapter 4A).
- ☐ Faulty stop solenoid - diesel models (Chapter 4B).

Engine noises

Pre-ignition (pinking) or knocking during acceleration or under load

- ☐ Ignition system fault - petrol models (Chapters 1A and 5B).
- ☐ Incorrect grade of spark plug - petrol models (Chapter 1A).
- ☐ Incorrect grade of fuel (Chapter 4).
- ☐ Vacuum leak at the throttle body, inlet manifold or associated hoses - petrol models (Chapter 4A).
- ☐ Excessive carbon build-up in engine (Chapter 2).
- ☐ Blocked injector/fuel injection system fault - petrol models (Chapter 4A).

Whistling or wheezing noises

- ☐ Leaking inlet manifold or throttle body gasket - petrol models (Chapter 4A).
- ☐ Leaking exhaust manifold gasket or pipe-to-manifold joint (Chapter 4).
- ☐ Leaking vacuum hose (Chapters 4 and 9).
- ☐ Blowing cylinder head gasket (Chapter 2).

Tapping or rattling noises

- ☐ Worn valve gear or camshaft (Chapter 2).
- ☐ Ancillary component fault (coolant pump, alternator, etc) (Chapters 3, 5A, etc).

Knocking or thumping noises

- ☐ Worn big-end bearings (regular heavy knocking, perhaps less under load) (Chapter 2).
- ☐ Worn main bearings (rumbling and knocking, perhaps worsening under load) (Chapter 2).
- ☐ Piston slap (most noticeable when cold) (Chapter 2).
- ☐ Ancillary component fault (coolant pump, alternator, etc) (Chapters 3, 5A, etc).

Cooling system

Overheating

- ☐ Insufficient coolant in system (see "*Weekly checks*").
- ☐ Thermostat faulty (Chapter 3).
- ☐ Radiator core blocked, or grille restricted (Chapter 3).
- ☐ Electric cooling fan or thermostatic switch faulty (Chapter 3).
- ☐ Inaccurate temperature gauge sender unit (Chapter 3).
- ☐ Airlock in cooling system (Chapter 3).
- ☐ Expansion tank pressure cap faulty (Chapter 3).

Overcooling

- ☐ Thermostat faulty (Chapter 3).
- ☐ Inaccurate temperature gauge sender unit (Chapter 3).

External coolant leakage

- ☐ Deteriorated or damaged hoses or hose clips (Chapter 1).

- ☐ Radiator core or heater matrix leaking (Chapter 3).
- ☐ Pressure cap faulty (Chapter 3).
- ☐ Coolant pump internal seal leaking (Chapter 3).
- ☐ Coolant pump-to-housing seal leaking (Chapter 3).
- ☐ Boiling due to overheating (Chapter 3).
- ☐ Core plug leaking (Chapter 2).

Internal coolant leakage

- ☐ Leaking cylinder head gasket (Chapter 2).
- ☐ Cracked cylinder head or cylinder block (Chapter 2).

Corrosion

- ☐ Infrequent draining and flushing (Chapter 1).
- ☐ Incorrect coolant mixture or inappropriate coolant type (see "*Weekly checks*").

Fuel and exhaust systems

Excessive fuel consumption

☐ Air filter element dirty or clogged (Chapter 1).
☐ Fuel injection system faulty - petrol models (Chapter 4A).
☐ Faulty injector(s) - diesel models (Chapter 4B).
☐ Ignition system faulty - petrol models (Chapters 1A and 5B).
☐ Tyres under-inflated (see "*Weekly checks*").

Fuel leakage and/or fuel odour

☐ Damaged or corroded fuel tank, pipes or connections (Chapter 4).

Excessive noise or fumes from the exhaust system

☐ Leaking exhaust system or manifold joints (Chapters 1 and 4).
☐ Leaking, corroded or damaged silencers or pipe (Chapters 1 and 4).
☐ Broken mountings causing body or suspension contact (Chapter 1).

Clutch

Pedal travels to floor - no pressure or very little resistance

☐ Faulty master or slave cylinder (Chapter 6).
☐ Faulty hydraulic release system (Chapter 6).
☐ Broken clutch release bearing or arm (Chapter 6).
☐ Broken diaphragm spring in clutch pressure plate (Chapter 6).

Clutch fails to disengage (unable to select gears)

☐ Faulty master or slave cylinder (Chapter 6).
☐ Faulty hydraulic release system (Chapter 6).
☐ Clutch disc sticking on gearbox input shaft splines (Chapter 6).
☐ Clutch disc sticking to flywheel or pressure plate (Chapter 6).
☐ Faulty pressure plate assembly (Chapter 6).
☐ Clutch release mechanism worn or incorrectly assembled (Chapter 6).

Clutch slips (engine speed increases, with no increase in vehicle speed)

☐ Faulty hydraulic release system (Chapter 6).
☐ Clutch disc linings excessively worn (Chapter 6).
☐ Clutch disc linings contaminated with oil or grease (Chapter 6).
☐ Faulty pressure plate or weak diaphragm spring (Chapter 6).

Judder as clutch is engaged

☐ Clutch disc linings contaminated with oil or grease (Chapter 6).
☐ Clutch disc linings excessively worn (Chapter 6).
☐ Faulty or distorted pressure plate or diaphragm spring (Chapter 6).
☐ Worn or loose engine or gearbox mountings (Chapter 2).
☐ Clutch disc hub or gearbox input shaft splines worn (Chapter 6).

Noise when depressing or releasing clutch pedal

☐ Worn clutch release bearing (Chapter 6).
☐ Worn or dry clutch pedal pivot (Chapter 6).
☐ Faulty pressure plate assembly (Chapter 6).
☐ Pressure plate diaphragm spring broken (Chapter 6).
☐ Broken clutch friction plate cushioning springs (Chapter 6).

Manual transmission

Noisy in neutral with engine running

☐ Input shaft bearings worn (noise apparent with clutch pedal released, but not when depressed) (Chapter 7).*
☐ Clutch release bearing worn (noise apparent with clutch pedal depressed, possibly less when released) (Chapter 6).

Noisy in one particular gear

☐ Worn, damaged or chipped gear teeth (Chapter 7).*

Difficulty engaging gears

☐ Clutch faulty (Chapter 6).
☐ Worn or damaged gear linkage (Chapter 7).
☐ Worn synchroniser units (Chapter 7).*

Jumps out of gear

☐ Worn or damaged gear linkage (Chapter 7).
☐ Worn synchroniser units (Chapter 7).*
☐ Worn selector forks (Chapter 7).*

Vibration

☐ Lack of oil (Chapter 1).
☐ Worn bearings (Chapter 7).*

Lubricant leaks

☐ Leaking oil seal (Chapter 7).
☐ Leaking housing joint (Chapter 7).*
☐ Leaking input shaft oil seal (Chapter 7).*

Although the corrective action necessary to remedy the symptoms described is beyond the scope of the home mechanic, the above information should be helpful in isolating the cause of the condition, so that the owner can communicate clearly with a professional mechanic.

Driveshafts

Vibration when accelerating or decelerating

- [ ] Worn inner constant velocity joint (Chapter 8).
- [ ] Bent or distorted driveshaft (Chapter 8).

Clicking or knocking noise on turns (at slow speed on full-lock)

- [ ] Worn outer constant velocity joint (Chapter 8).
- [ ] Lack of constant velocity joint lubricant, possibly due to damaged gaiter (Chapter 8).

Braking system

Note: *Before assuming that a brake problem exists, make sure that the tyres are in good condition and correctly inflated, that the front wheel alignment is correct, and that the vehicle is not loaded with weight in an unequal manner. Apart from checking the condition of all pipe and hose connections, any faults occurring on the anti-lock braking system should be referred to a Rover dealer for diagnosis.*

Vehicle pulls to one side under braking

- [ ] Worn, defective, damaged or contaminated front or rear brake pads/shoes on one side (Chapters 1 and 9).
- [ ] Seized or partially-seized front or rear brake caliper/wheel cylinder piston (Chapter 9).
- [ ] A mixture of brake pad/shoe lining materials fitted between sides (Chapter 9).
- [ ] Brake caliper or rear brake backplate mounting bolts loose (Chapter 9).
- [ ] Worn or damaged steering or suspension components (Chapters 1 and 10).

Noise (grinding or high-pitched squeal) when brakes applied

- [ ] Brake pad/shoe friction lining material worn down to metal backing (Chapters 1 and 9).
- [ ] Excessive corrosion of brake disc or drum - may be apparent after the vehicle has been standing for some time (Chapters 1 and 9).
- [ ] Foreign object (stone chipping, etc) trapped between brake disc and shield (Chapters 1 and 9).

Excessive brake pedal travel

- [ ] Faulty rear drum brake self-adjust mechanism (Chapter 9).
- [ ] Faulty master cylinder (Chapter 9).
- [ ] Air in hydraulic system (Chapter 9).
- [ ] Faulty vacuum servo unit (Chapter 9).
- [ ] Faulty vacuum pump - diesel models (Chapter 9).

Brake pedal feels spongy when depressed

- [ ] Air in hydraulic system (Chapter 9).
- [ ] Deteriorated flexible rubber brake hoses (Chapters 1 and 9).
- [ ] Master cylinder mountings loose (Chapter 9).
- [ ] Faulty master cylinder (Chapter 9).

Excessive brake pedal effort required to stop vehicle

- [ ] Faulty vacuum servo unit (Chapter 9).
- [ ] Disconnected, damaged or insecure brake servo vacuum hose (Chapters 1 and 9).
- [ ] Faulty vacuum pump - diesel models (Chapter 9).
- [ ] Primary or secondary hydraulic circuit failure (Chapter 9).
- [ ] Seized brake caliper or wheel cylinder piston(s) (Chapter 9).
- [ ] Brake pads/shoes incorrectly fitted (Chapter 9).
- [ ] Incorrect grade of brake pads/shoes fitted (Chapter 9).
- [ ] Brake pads/shoe linings contaminated (Chapter 9).

Judder felt through brake pedal or steering wheel when braking

- [ ] Excessive run-out or distortion of brake disc(s) or drum(s) (Chapter 9).
- [ ] Brake pad/shoe linings worn (Chapters 1 and 9).
- [ ] Brake caliper or rear brake backplate mounting bolts loose (Chapter 9).
- [ ] Wear in suspension or steering components or mountings (Chapters 1 and 10).

Pedal pulsates when braking hard

- [ ] Normal feature of ABS (where fitted) - no fault

Brakes binding

- [ ] Seized brake caliper/wheel cylinder piston(s) (Chapter 9).
- [ ] Incorrectly-adjusted handbrake mechanism (Chapter 9).
- [ ] Faulty master cylinder (Chapter 9).

Rear wheels locking under normal braking

- [ ] Rear brake pad/shoe linings contaminated (Chapters 1 and 9).
- [ ] Rear brake discs/drums warped (Chapters 1 and 9).

Steering and suspension

Note: *Before diagnosing suspension or steering faults, be sure that the trouble is not due to incorrect tyre pressures, mixtures of tyre types, or binding brakes.*

Vehicle pulls to one side

- [ ] Defective tyre (see *"Weekly checks"*).
- [ ] Excessive wear in suspension or steering components (Chapters 1 and 10).
- [ ] Incorrect front wheel alignment (Chapter 10).
- [ ] Accident damage to steering or suspension components (Chapters 1 and 10).

Wheel wobble and vibration

- [ ] Front roadwheels out of balance (vibration felt mainly through the steering wheel) (Chapter 10).
- [ ] Rear roadwheels out of balance (vibration felt throughout the vehicle) (Chapter 10).
- [ ] Roadwheels damaged or distorted (Chapter 10).
- [ ] Faulty or damaged tyre (see *"Weekly checks"*).
- [ ] Worn steering or suspension joints, bushes or components (Chapters 1 and 10).
- [ ] Wheel nuts loose (Chapter 1 and 10).

Excessive pitching and/or rolling around corners, or during braking

- [ ] Defective shock absorbers (Chapters 1 and 10).
- [ ] Broken or weak coil spring and/or suspension component (Chapters 1 and 10).
- [ ] Worn or damaged anti-roll bar or mountings (Chapter 10).

Wandering or general instability

- [ ] Incorrect front wheel alignment (Chapter 10).
- [ ] Worn steering or suspension joints, bushes or components (Chapters 1 and 10).
- [ ] Roadwheels out of balance (Chapter 10).
- [ ] Faulty or damaged tyre (see "Weekly checks").
- [ ] Wheel nuts loose (Chapter 10).
- [ ] Defective shock absorbers (Chapters 1 and 10).

Excessively-stiff steering

- [ ] Seized track rod end balljoint or suspension balljoint (Chapters 1 and 10).
- [ ] Broken or incorrectly adjusted auxiliary drivebelt (Chapter 1).
- [ ] Incorrect front wheel alignment (Chapter 10).
- [ ] Steering gear damaged (Chapter 10).

Excessive play in steering

- [ ] Worn steering column universal joint(s) (Chapter 10).
- [ ] Worn steering track rod end balljoints (Chapters 1 and 10).
- [ ] Worn steering gear (Chapter 10).
- [ ] Worn steering or suspension joints, bushes or components (Chapters 1 and 10).

Lack of power assistance

- [ ] Broken or incorrectly-adjusted auxiliary drivebelt (Chapter 1).
- [ ] Incorrect power steering fluid level (see "Weekly checks").
- [ ] Restriction in power steering fluid hoses (Chapter 10).
- [ ] Faulty power steering pump (Chapter 10).
- [ ] Faulty steering gear (Chapter 10).

Tyre wear excessive

Tyres worn on inside or outside edges

- [ ] Tyres under-inflated (wear on both edges) (see "Weekly checks").
- [ ] Incorrect camber or castor angles (wear on one edge only) (Chapter 10).
- [ ] Worn steering or suspension joints, bushes or components (Chapters 1 and 10).
- [ ] Excessively-hard cornering.
- [ ] Accident damage.

Tyre treads exhibit feathered edges

- [ ] Incorrect toe setting (Chapter 10).

Tyres worn in centre of tread

- [ ] Tyres over-inflated (see "Weekly checks").

Tyres worn on inside and outside edges

- [ ] Tyres under-inflated (see "Weekly checks").
- [ ] Worn shock absorbers (Chapter 10).

Tyres worn unevenly

- [ ] Tyres/wheels out of balance (see "Weekly checks").
- [ ] Excessive wheel or tyre run-out (Chapter 10).
- [ ] Worn shock absorbers (Chapters 1 and 10).
- [ ] Faulty tyre (see "Weekly checks").

Electrical system

Note: For problems associated with the starting system, refer to the faults listed under "Engine" earlier in this Section.

Battery will not hold a charge for more than a few days

- [ ] Battery defective internally (Chapter 5A).
- [ ] Battery electrolyte level low - where applicable.
- [ ] Battery terminal connections loose or corroded (see "Weekly checks").
- [ ] Auxiliary drivebelt worn - or incorrectly adjusted, where applicable (Chapter 1).
- [ ] Alternator not charging at correct output (Chapter 5A).
- [ ] Alternator or voltage regulator faulty (Chapter 5A).
- [ ] Short-circuit causing continual battery drain (Chapters 5 and 12).

Ignition/no-charge warning light remains illuminated with engine running

- [ ] Auxiliary drivebelt broken, worn, or incorrectly adjusted (Chapter 1).
- [ ] Internal fault in alternator or voltage regulator (Chapter 5A).
- [ ] Broken, disconnected, or loose wiring in charging circuit (Chapter 5A).

Ignition/no-charge warning light fails to come on

- [ ] Warning light bulb blown (Chapter 12).
- [ ] Broken, disconnected, or loose wiring in warning light circuit (Chapter 12).
- [ ] Alternator faulty (Chapter 5A).

Lights inoperative

- [ ] Bulb blown (Chapter 12).
- [ ] Corrosion of bulb or bulbholder contacts (Chapter 12).
- [ ] Blown fuse (Chapter 12).
- [ ] Faulty relay (Chapter 12).
- [ ] Broken, loose, or disconnected wiring (Chapter 12).
- [ ] Faulty switch (Chapter 12).

Instrument readings inaccurate or erratic

Instrument readings increase with engine speed

- [ ] Faulty voltage regulator (Chapter 12).

Fuel or temperature gauges give no reading

- [ ] Faulty gauge sender unit (Chapters 3 and 4).
- [ ] Wiring open-circuit (Chapter 12).
- [ ] Faulty gauge (Chapter 12).

Fuel or temperature gauges give continuous maximum reading

- [ ] Faulty gauge sender unit (Chapters 3 and 4).
- [ ] Wiring short-circuit (Chapter 12).
- [ ] Faulty gauge (Chapter 12).

Electrical system (continued)

Horn inoperative, or unsatisfactory in operation

Horn operates all the time

☐ Horn contacts permanently bridged or horn push stuck down (Chapter 12).

Horn fails to operate

☐ Blown fuse (Chapter 12).
☐ Cable or cable connections loose, broken or disconnected (Chapter 12).
☐ Faulty horn (Chapter 12).

Horn emits intermittent or unsatisfactory sound

☐ Cable connections loose (Chapter 12).
☐ Horn mountings loose (Chapter 12).
☐ Faulty horn (Chapter 12).

Windscreen/tailgate wipers inoperative, or unsatisfactory in operation

Wipers fail to operate, or operate very slowly

☐ Wiper blades stuck to screen, or linkage seized or binding (see "Weekly checks" and Chapter 12).
☐ Blown fuse (Chapter 12).
☐ Cable or cable connections loose, broken or disconnected (Chapter 12).
☐ Faulty relay (Chapter 12).
☐ Faulty wiper motor (Chapter 12).

Wiper blades sweep over too large or too small an area of the glass

☐ Wiper arms incorrectly positioned on spindles (Chapter 12).
☐ Excessive wear of wiper linkage (Chapter 12).
☐ Wiper motor or linkage mountings loose or insecure (Chapter 12).

Wiper blades fail to clean the glass effectively

☐ Wiper blade rubbers worn or perished (see "Weekly checks").
☐ Wiper arm tension springs broken, or arm pivots seized (Chapter 12).
☐ Insufficient windscreen washer additive to adequately remove road film (see "Weekly checks").

Windscreen/tailgate washers inoperative, or unsatisfactory in operation

One or more washer jets inoperative

☐ Blocked washer jet (Chapter 12).
☐ Disconnected, kinked or restricted fluid hose (Chapter 12).
☐ Insufficient fluid in washer reservoir (see "Weekly checks").

Washer pump fails to operate

☐ Broken or disconnected wiring or connections (Chapter 12).
☐ Blown fuse (Chapter 12).
☐ Faulty washer switch (Chapter 12).
☐ Faulty washer pump (Chapter 12).

Washer pump runs for some time before fluid is emitted from jets

☐ Faulty one-way valve in fluid supply hose (Chapter 12).

Electric windows inoperative, or unsatisfactory in operation

Window glass will only move in one direction

☐ Faulty switch (Chapter 12).

Window glass slow to move

☐ Regulator seized or damaged, or in need of lubrication (Chapter 11).
☐ Door internal components or trim fouling regulator (Chapter 11).
☐ Faulty motor (Chapter 11).

Window glass fails to move

☐ Blown fuse (Chapter 12).
☐ Faulty relay (Chapter 12).
☐ Broken or disconnected wiring or connections (Chapter 12).
☐ Faulty motor (Chapter 12).

Central locking system inoperative, or unsatisfactory in operation

Complete system failure

☐ Blown fuse (Chapter 12).
☐ Faulty relay (Chapter 12).
☐ Broken or disconnected wiring or connections (Chapter 12).
☐ Faulty motor (Chapter 11).

Latch locks but will not unlock, or unlocks but will not lock

☐ Faulty switch (Chapter 12).
☐ Broken or disconnected latch operating rods or levers (Chapter 11).
☐ Faulty relay (Chapter 12).
☐ Faulty motor (Chapter 11).

One solenoid/motor fails to operate

☐ Broken or disconnected wiring or connections (Chapter 12).
☐ Faulty motor (Chapter 11).
☐ Broken, binding or disconnected lock operating rods or levers (Chapter 11).
☐ Fault in door lock (Chapter 11).

A

ABS (Anti-lock brake system) A system, usually electronically controlled, that senses incipient wheel lockup during braking and relieves hydraulic pressure at wheels that are about to skid.

Air bag An inflatable bag hidden in the steering wheel (driver's side) or the dash or glovebox (passenger side). In a head-on collision, the bags inflate, preventing the driver and front passenger from being thrown forward into the steering wheel or windscreen.

Air cleaner A metal or plastic housing, containing a filter element, which removes dust and dirt from the air being drawn into the engine.

Air filter element The actual filter in an air cleaner system, usually manufactured from pleated paper and requiring renewal at regular intervals.

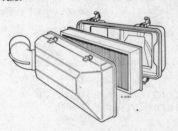

Air filter

Allen key A hexagonal wrench which fits into a recessed hexagonal hole.

Alligator clip A long-nosed spring-loaded metal clip with meshing teeth. Used to make temporary electrical connections.

Alternator A component in the electrical system which converts mechanical energy from a drivebelt into electrical energy to charge the battery and to operate the starting system, ignition system and electrical accessories.

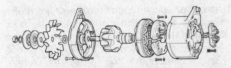

Alternator (exploded view)

Ampere (amp) A unit of measurement for the flow of electric current. One amp is the amount of current produced by one volt acting through a resistance of one ohm.

Anaerobic sealer A substance used to prevent bolts and screws from loosening. Anaerobic means that it does not require oxygen for activation. The Loctite brand is widely used.

Antifreeze A substance (usually ethylene glycol) mixed with water, and added to a vehicle's cooling system, to prevent freezing of the coolant in winter. Antifreeze also contains chemicals to inhibit corrosion and the formation of rust and other deposits that would tend to clog the radiator and coolant passages and reduce cooling efficiency.

Anti-seize compound A coating that reduces the risk of seizing on fasteners that are subjected to high temperatures, such as exhaust manifold bolts and nuts.

Anti-seize compound

Asbestos A natural fibrous mineral with great heat resistance, commonly used in the composition of brake friction materials. Asbestos is a health hazard and the dust created by brake systems should never be inhaled or ingested.

Axle A shaft on which a wheel revolves, or which revolves with a wheel. Also, a solid beam that connects the two wheels at one end of the vehicle. An axle which also transmits power to the wheels is known as a live axle.

Axle assembly

Axleshaft A single rotating shaft, on either side of the differential, which delivers power from the final drive assembly to the drive wheels. Also called a driveshaft or a halfshaft.

B

Ball bearing An anti-friction bearing consisting of a hardened inner and outer race with hardened steel balls between two races.

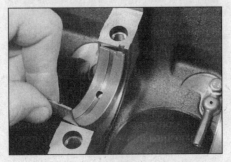

Bearing

Bearing The curved surface on a shaft or in a bore, or the part assembled into either, that permits relative motion between them with minimum wear and friction.

Big-end bearing The bearing in the end of the connecting rod that's attached to the crankshaft.

Bleed nipple A valve on a brake wheel cylinder, caliper or other hydraulic component that is opened to purge the hydraulic system of air. Also called a bleed screw.

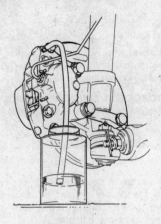

Brake bleeding

Brake bleeding Procedure for removing air from lines of a hydraulic brake system.

Brake disc The component of a disc brake that rotates with the wheels.

Brake drum The component of a drum brake that rotates with the wheels.

Brake linings The friction material which contacts the brake disc or drum to retard the vehicle's speed. The linings are bonded or riveted to the brake pads or shoes.

Brake pads The replaceable friction pads that pinch the brake disc when the brakes are applied. Brake pads consist of a friction material bonded or riveted to a rigid backing plate.

Brake shoe The crescent-shaped carrier to which the brake linings are mounted and which forces the lining against the rotating drum during braking.

Braking systems For more information on braking systems, consult the *Haynes Automotive Brake Manual*.

Breaker bar A long socket wrench handle providing greater leverage.

Bulkhead The insulated partition between the engine and the passenger compartment.

C

Caliper The non-rotating part of a disc-brake assembly that straddles the disc and carries the brake pads. The caliper also contains the hydraulic components that cause the pads to pinch the disc when the brakes are applied. A caliper is also a measuring tool that can be set to measure inside or outside dimensions of an object.

Camshaft A rotating shaft on which a series of cam lobes operate the valve mechanisms. The camshaft may be driven by gears, by sprockets and chain or by sprockets and a belt.

Canister A container in an evaporative emission control system; contains activated charcoal granules to trap vapours from the fuel system.

Canister

Carburettor A device which mixes fuel with air in the proper proportions to provide a desired power output from a spark ignition internal combustion engine.

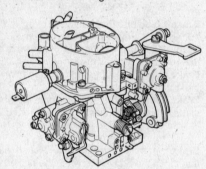

Carburettor

Castellated Resembling the parapets along the top of a castle wall. For example, a castellated balljoint stud nut.

Castellated nut

Castor In wheel alignment, the backward or forward tilt of the steering axis. Castor is positive when the steering axis is inclined rearward at the top.

Catalytic converter A silencer-like device in the exhaust system which converts certain pollutants in the exhaust gases into less harmful substances.

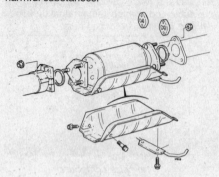

Catalytic converter

Circlip A ring-shaped clip used to prevent endwise movement of cylindrical parts and shafts. An internal circlip is installed in a groove in a housing; an external circlip fits into a groove on the outside of a cylindrical piece such as a shaft.

Clearance The amount of space between two parts. For example, between a piston and a cylinder, between a bearing and a journal, etc.

Coil spring A spiral of elastic steel found in various sizes throughout a vehicle, for example as a springing medium in the suspension and in the valve train.

Compression Reduction in volume, and increase in pressure and temperature, of a gas, caused by squeezing it into a smaller space.

Compression ratio The relationship between cylinder volume when the piston is at top dead centre and cylinder volume when the piston is at bottom dead centre.

Constant velocity (CV) joint A type of universal joint that cancels out vibrations caused by driving power being transmitted through an angle.

Core plug A disc or cup-shaped metal device inserted in a hole in a casting through which core was removed when the casting was formed. Also known as a freeze plug or expansion plug.

Crankcase The lower part of the engine block in which the crankshaft rotates.

Crankshaft The main rotating member, or shaft, running the length of the crankcase, with offset "throws" to which the connecting rods are attached.

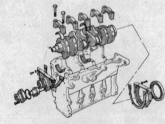

Crankshaft assembly

Crocodile clip See Alligator clip

D

Diagnostic code Code numbers obtained by accessing the diagnostic mode of an engine management computer. This code can be used to determine the area in the system where a malfunction may be located.

Disc brake A brake design incorporating a rotating disc onto which brake pads are squeezed. The resulting friction converts the energy of a moving vehicle into heat.

Double-overhead cam (DOHC) An engine that uses two overhead camshafts, usually one for the intake valves and one for the exhaust valves.

Drivebelt(s) The belt(s) used to drive accessories such as the alternator, water pump, power steering pump, air conditioning compressor, etc. off the crankshaft pulley.

Accessory drivebelts

Driveshaft Any shaft used to transmit motion. Commonly used when referring to the axleshafts on a front wheel drive vehicle.

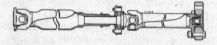

Driveshaft

Drum brake A type of brake using a drum-shaped metal cylinder attached to the inner surface of the wheel. When the brake pedal is pressed, curved brake shoes with friction linings press against the inside of the drum to slow or stop the vehicle.

Drum brake assembly

E

EGR valve A valve used to introduce exhaust gases into the intake air stream.

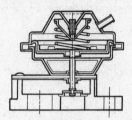

EGR valve

Electronic control unit (ECU) A computer which controls (for instance) ignition and fuel injection systems, or an anti-lock braking system. For more information refer to the *Haynes Automotive Electrical and Electronic Systems Manual.*

Electronic Fuel Injection (EFI) A computer controlled fuel system that distributes fuel through an injector located in each intake port of the engine.

Emergency brake A braking system, independent of the main hydraulic system, that can be used to slow or stop the vehicle if the primary brakes fail, or to hold the vehicle stationary even though the brake pedal isn't depressed. It usually consists of a hand lever that actuates either front or rear brakes mechanically through a series of cables and linkages. Also known as a handbrake or parking brake.

Endfloat The amount of lengthwise movement between two parts. As applied to a crankshaft, the distance that the crankshaft can move forward and back in the cylinder block.

Engine management system (EMS) A computer controlled system which manages the fuel injection and the ignition systems in an integrated fashion.

Exhaust manifold A part with several passages through which exhaust gases leave the engine combustion chambers and enter the exhaust pipe.

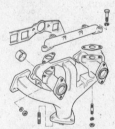

Exhaust manifold

F

Fan clutch A viscous (fluid) drive coupling device which permits variable engine fan speeds in relation to engine speeds.

Feeler blade A thin strip or blade of hardened steel, ground to an exact thickness, used to check or measure clearances between parts.

Feeler blade

Firing order The order in which the engine cylinders fire, or deliver their power strokes, beginning with the number one cylinder.

Flywheel A heavy spinning wheel in which energy is absorbed and stored by means of momentum. On cars, the flywheel is attached to the crankshaft to smooth out firing impulses.

Free play The amount of travel before any action takes place. The "looseness" in a linkage, or an assembly of parts, between the initial application of force and actual movement. For example, the distance the brake pedal moves before the pistons in the master cylinder are actuated.

Fuse An electrical device which protects a circuit against accidental overload. The typical fuse contains a soft piece of metal which is calibrated to melt at a predetermined current flow (expressed as amps) and break the circuit.

Fusible link A circuit protection device consisting of a conductor surrounded by heat-resistant insulation. The conductor is smaller than the wire it protects, so it acts as the weakest link in the circuit. Unlike a blown fuse, a failed fusible link must frequently be cut from the wire for replacement.

G

Gap The distance the spark must travel in jumping from the centre electrode to the side

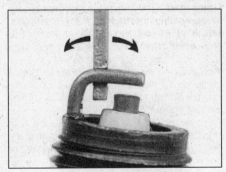

Adjusting spark plug gap

electrode in a spark plug. Also refers to the spacing between the points in a contact breaker assembly in a conventional points-type ignition, or to the distance between the reluctor or rotor and the pickup coil in an electronic ignition.

Gasket Any thin, soft material - usually cork, cardboard, asbestos or soft metal - installed between two metal surfaces to ensure a good seal. For instance, the cylinder head gasket seals the joint between the block and the cylinder head.

Gasket

Gauge An instrument panel display used to monitor engine conditions. A gauge with a movable pointer on a dial or a fixed scale is an analogue gauge. A gauge with a numerical readout is called a digital gauge.

H

Halfshaft A rotating shaft that transmits power from the final drive unit to a drive wheel, usually when referring to a live rear axle.

Harmonic balancer A device designed to reduce torsion or twisting vibration in the crankshaft. May be incorporated in the crankshaft pulley. Also known as a vibration damper.

Hone An abrasive tool for correcting small irregularities or differences in diameter in an engine cylinder, brake cylinder, etc.

Hydraulic tappet A tappet that utilises hydraulic pressure from the engine's lubrication system to maintain zero clearance (constant contact with both camshaft and valve stem). Automatically adjusts to variation in valve stem length. Hydraulic tappets also reduce valve noise.

I

Ignition timing The moment at which the spark plug fires, usually expressed in the number of crankshaft degrees before the piston reaches the top of its stroke.

Inlet manifold A tube or housing with passages through which flows the air-fuel mixture (carburettor vehicles and vehicles with throttle body injection) or air only (port fuel-injected vehicles) to the port openings in the cylinder head.

J

Jump start Starting the engine of a vehicle with a discharged or weak battery by attaching jump leads from the weak battery to a charged or helper battery.

L

Load Sensing Proportioning Valve (LSPV) A brake hydraulic system control valve that works like a proportioning valve, but also takes into consideration the amount of weight carried by the rear axle.

Locknut A nut used to lock an adjustment nut, or other threaded component, in place. For example, a locknut is employed to keep the adjusting nut on the rocker arm in position.

Lockwasher A form of washer designed to prevent an attaching nut from working loose.

M

MacPherson strut A type of front suspension system devised by Earle MacPherson at Ford of England. In its original form, a simple lateral link with the anti-roll bar creates the lower control arm. A long strut - an integral coil spring and shock absorber - is mounted between the body and the steering knuckle. Many modern so-called MacPherson strut systems use a conventional lower A-arm and don't rely on the anti-roll bar for location.

Multimeter An electrical test instrument with the capability to measure voltage, current and resistance.

N

NOx Oxides of Nitrogen. A common toxic pollutant emitted by petrol and diesel engines at higher temperatures.

O

Ohm The unit of electrical resistance. One volt applied to a resistance of one ohm will produce a current of one amp.

Ohmmeter An instrument for measuring electrical resistance.

O-ring A type of sealing ring made of a special rubber-like material; in use, the O-ring is compressed into a groove to provide the sealing action.

O-ring

Overhead cam (ohc) engine An engine with the camshaft(s) located on top of the cylinder head(s).

Overhead valve (ohv) engine An engine with the valves located in the cylinder head, but with the camshaft located in the engine block.

Oxygen sensor A device installed in the engine exhaust manifold, which senses the oxygen content in the exhaust and converts this information into an electric current. Also called a Lambda sensor.

P

Phillips screw A type of screw head having a cross instead of a slot for a corresponding type of screwdriver.

Plastigage A thin strip of plastic thread, available in different sizes, used for measuring clearances. For example, a strip of Plastigage is laid across a bearing journal. The parts are assembled and dismantled; the width of the crushed strip indicates the clearance between journal and bearing.

Plastigage

Propeller shaft The long hollow tube with universal joints at both ends that carries power from the transmission to the differential on front-engined rear wheel drive vehicles.

Proportioning valve A hydraulic control valve which limits the amount of pressure to the rear brakes during panic stops to prevent wheel lock-up.

R

Rack-and-pinion steering A steering system with a pinion gear on the end of the steering shaft that mates with a rack (think of a geared wheel opened up and laid flat). When the steering wheel is turned, the pinion turns, moving the rack to the left or right. This movement is transmitted through the track rods to the steering arms at the wheels.

Radiator A liquid-to-air heat transfer device designed to reduce the temperature of the coolant in an internal combustion engine cooling system.

Refrigerant Any substance used as a heat transfer agent in an air-conditioning system. R-12 has been the principle refrigerant for many years; recently, however, manufacturers have begun using R-134a, a non-CFC substance that is considered less harmful to the ozone in the upper atmosphere.

Rocker arm A lever arm that rocks on a shaft or pivots on a stud. In an overhead valve engine, the rocker arm converts the upward movement of the pushrod into a downward movement to open a valve.

Rotor In a distributor, the rotating device inside the cap that connects the centre electrode and the outer terminals as it turns, distributing the high voltage from the coil secondary winding to the proper spark plug. Also, that part of an alternator which rotates inside the stator. Also, the rotating assembly of a turbocharger, including the compressor wheel, shaft and turbine wheel.

Runout The amount of wobble (in-and-out movement) of a gear or wheel as it's rotated. The amount a shaft rotates "out-of-true." The out-of-round condition of a rotating part.

S

Sealant A liquid or paste used to prevent leakage at a joint. Sometimes used in conjunction with a gasket.

Sealed beam lamp An older headlight design which integrates the reflector, lens and filaments into a hermetically-sealed one-piece unit. When a filament burns out or the lens cracks, the entire unit is simply replaced.

Serpentine drivebelt A single, long, wide accessory drivebelt that's used on some newer vehicles to drive all the accessories, instead of a series of smaller, shorter belts. Serpentine drivebelts are usually tensioned by an automatic tensioner.

Serpentine drivebelt

Shim Thin spacer, commonly used to adjust the clearance or relative positions between two parts. For example, shims inserted into or under bucket tappets control valve clearances. Clearance is adjusted by changing the thickness of the shim.

Slide hammer A special puller that screws into or hooks onto a component such as a shaft or bearing; a heavy sliding handle on the shaft bottoms against the end of the shaft to knock the component free.

Sprocket A tooth or projection on the periphery of a wheel, shaped to engage with a chain or drivebelt. Commonly used to refer to the sprocket wheel itself.

Starter inhibitor switch On vehicles with an

automatic transmission, a switch that prevents starting if the vehicle is not in Neutral or Park.

Strut See MacPherson strut.

T

Tappet A cylindrical component which transmits motion from the cam to the valve stem, either directly or via a pushrod and rocker arm. Also called a cam follower.

Thermostat A heat-controlled valve that regulates the flow of coolant between the cylinder block and the radiator, so maintaining optimum engine operating temperature. A thermostat is also used in some air cleaners in which the temperature is regulated.

Thrust bearing The bearing in the clutch assembly that is moved in to the release levers by clutch pedal action to disengage the clutch. Also referred to as a release bearing.

Timing belt A toothed belt which drives the camshaft. Serious engine damage may result if it breaks in service.

Timing chain A chain which drives the camshaft.

Toe-in The amount the front wheels are closer together at the front than at the rear. On rear wheel drive vehicles, a slight amount of toe-in is usually specified to keep the front wheels running parallel on the road by offsetting other forces that tend to spread the wheels apart.

Toe-out The amount the front wheels are closer together at the rear than at the front. On front wheel drive vehicles, a slight amount of toe-out is usually specified.

Tools For full information on choosing and using tools, refer to the *Haynes Automotive Tools Manual*.

Tracer A stripe of a second colour applied to a wire insulator to distinguish that wire from another one with the same colour insulator.

Tune-up A process of accurate and careful adjustments and parts replacement to obtain the best possible engine performance.

Turbocharger A centrifugal device, driven by exhaust gases, that pressurises the intake air. Normally used to increase the power output from a given engine displacement, but can also be used primarily to reduce exhaust emissions (as on VW's "Umwelt" Diesel engine).

U

Universal joint or U-joint A double-pivoted connection for transmitting power from a driving to a driven shaft through an angle. A U-joint consists of two Y-shaped yokes and a cross-shaped member called the spider.

V

Valve A device through which the flow of liquid, gas, vacuum, or loose material in bulk may be started, stopped, or regulated by a movable part that opens, shuts, or partially obstructs one or more ports or passageways. A valve is also the movable part of such a device.

Valve clearance The clearance between the valve tip (the end of the valve stem) and the rocker arm or tappet. The valve clearance is measured when the valve is closed.

Vernier caliper A precision measuring instrument that measures inside and outside dimensions. Not quite as accurate as a micrometer, but more convenient.

Viscosity The thickness of a liquid or its resistance to flow.

Volt A unit for expressing electrical "pressure" in a circuit. One volt that will produce a current of one ampere through a resistance of one ohm.

W

Welding Various processes used to join metal items by heating the areas to be joined to a molten state and fusing them together. For more information refer to the *Haynes Automotive Welding Manual*.

Wiring diagram A drawing portraying the components and wires in a vehicle's electrical system, using standardised symbols. For more information refer to the *Haynes Automotive Electrical and Electronic Systems Manual*.

Note: *References throughout this index are in the form - "Chapter number" • "page number"*

Haynes Manuals – The Complete List

Title	Book No.
ALFA ROMEO	
Alfa Romeo Alfasud/Sprint (74 - 88) up to F	0292
Alfa Romeo Alfetta (73 - 87) up to E	0531
AUDI	
Audi 80 (72 - Feb 79) up to T	0207
Audi 80, 90 (79 - Oct 86) up to D & Coupe (81 - Nov 88) up to F	0605
Audi 80, 90 (Oct 86 - 90) D to H & Coupe (Nov 88 - 90) F to H	1491
Audi 100 (Oct 82 - 90) up to H & 200 (Feb 84 - Oct 89) A to G	0907
Audi 100 & A6 Petrol & Diesel (May 91 - May 97) H to P	3504
Audi A4 (95 - Feb 00) M to V	3575
AUSTIN	
Austin A35 & A40 (56 - 67) *	0118
Austin Allegro 1100, 1300, 1.0, 1.1 & 1.3 (73 - 82)*	0164
Austin Healey 100/6 & 3000 (56 - 68) *	0049
Austin/MG/Rover Maestro 1.3 & 1.6 (83 - May 95) up to M	0922
Austin/MG Metro (80 - May 90) up to G	0718
Austin/Rover Montego 1.3 & 1.6 (84 - 94) A to L	1066
Austin/MG/Rover Montego 2.0 (84 - 95) A to M	1067
Mini (59 - 69) up to H	0527
Mini (69 - Oct 96) up to P	0646
Austin/Rover 2.0 litre Diesel Engine (86 - 93) C to L	1857
BEDFORD	
Bedford CF (69 - 87) up to E	0163
Bedford/Vauxhall Rascal & Suzuki Supercarry (86 - Oct 94) C to M	3015
BMW	
BMW 1500, 1502, 1600, 1602, 2000 & 2002 (59 - 77)*	0240
BMW 316, 320 & 320i (4-cyl) (75 - Feb 83) up to Y	0276
BMW 320, 320i, 323i & 325i (6-cyl) (Oct 77 - Sept 87) up to E	0815
BMW 3-Series (Apr 91 - 96) H to N	3210
BMW 3- & 5-Series (sohc) (81 - 91) up to J	1948
BMW 520i & 525e (Oct 81 - June 88) up to E	1560
BMW 525, 528 & 528i (73 - Sept 81) up to X	0632
CITROËN	
Citroën 2CV, Ami & Dyane (67 - 90) up to H	0196
Citroën AX Petrol & Diesel (87 - 97) D to P	3014
Citroën BX (83 - 94) A to L	0908
Citroën C15 Van Petrol & Diesel (89 - Oct 98) F to S	3509
Citroën CX (75 - 88) up to F	0528
Citroën Saxo Petrol & Diesel (96 - 01) N to X	3506
Citroën Visa (79 - 88) up to F	0620
Citroën Xantia Petrol & Diesel (93 - 98) K to S	3082
Citroën XM Petrol & Diesel (89 - 00) G to X	3451
Citroën Xsara Petrol & Diesel (97 - Sept 00) R to W	3751
Citroën ZX Diesel (91 - 98) J to S	1922
Citroën ZX Petrol (91 - 98) H to S	1881
Citroën 1.7 & 1.9 litre Diesel Engine (84 - 96) A to N	1379
FIAT	
Fiat 126 (73 - 87) *	0305
Fiat 500 (57 - 73) up to M	0090
Fiat Bravo & Brava (95 - 00) N to W	3572
Fiat Cinquecento (93 - 98) K to R	3501
Fiat Panda (81 - 95) up to M	0793
Fiat Punto Petrol & Diesel (94 - Oct 99) L to V	3251
Fiat Regata (84 - 88) A to F	1167
Fiat Tipo (88 - 91) E to J	1625
Fiat Uno (83 - 95) up to M	0923
Fiat X1/9 (74 - 89) up to G	0273
FORD	
Ford Anglia (59 - 68) *	0001
Ford Capri II (& III) 1.6 & 2.0 (74 - 87) up to E	0283

Title	Book No.
Ford Capri II (& III) 2.8 & 3.0 (74 - 87) up to E	1309
Ford Cortina Mk III 1300 & 1600 (70 - 76) *	0070
Ford Cortina Mk IV (& V) 1.6 & 2.0 (76 - 83) *	0343
Ford Cortina Mk IV (& V) 2.3 V6 (77 - 83) *	0426
Ford Escort Mk I 1100 & 1300 (68 - 74) *	0171
Ford Escort Mk I Mexico, RS 1600 & RS 2000 (70 - 74)*	0139
Ford Escort Mk II Mexico, RS 1800 & RS 2000 (75 - 80)*	0735
Ford Escort (75 - Aug 80) *	0280
Ford Escort (Sept 80 - Sept 90) up to H	0686
Ford Escort & Orion (Sept 90 - 00) H to X	1737
Ford Fiesta (76 - Aug 83) up to Y	0334
Ford Fiesta (Aug 83 - Feb 89) A to F	1030
Ford Fiesta (Feb 89 - Oct 95) F to N	1595
Ford Fiesta (Oct 95 - 01) N-reg. onwards	3397
Ford Focus (98 - 01) S to Y	3759
Ford Granada (Sept 77 - Feb 85) up to B	0481
Ford Granada & Scorpio (Mar 85 - 94) B to M	1245
Ford Ka (96 - 02) P-reg. onwards	3570
Ford Mondeo Petrol (93 - 99) K to T	1923
Ford Mondeo Diesel (93 - 96) L to N	3465
Ford Orion (83 - Sept 90) up to H	1009
Ford Sierra 4 cyl. (82 - 93) up to K	0903
Ford Sierra V6 (82 - 91) up to J	0904
Ford Transit Petrol (Mk 2) (78 - Jan 86) up to C	0719
Ford Transit Petrol (Mk 3) (Feb 86 - 89) C to G	1468
Ford Transit Diesel (Feb 86 - 99) C to T	3019
Ford 1.6 & 1.8 litre Diesel Engine (84 - 96) A to N	1172
Ford 2.1, 2.3 & 2.5 litre Diesel Engine (77 - 90) up to H	1606
FREIGHT ROVER	
Freight Rover Sherpa (74 - 87) up to E	0463
HILLMAN	
Hillman Avenger (70 - 82) up to Y	0037
Hillman Imp (63 - 76) *	0022
HONDA	
Honda Accord (76 - Feb 84) up to A	0351
Honda Civic (Feb 84 - Oct 87) A to E	1226
Honda Civic (Nov 91 - 96) J to N	3199
HYUNDAI	
Hyundai Pony (85 - 94) C to M	3398
JAGUAR	
Jaguar E Type (61 - 72) up to L	0140
Jaguar MkI & II, 240 & 340 (55 - 69) *	0098
Jaguar XJ6, XJ & Sovereign; Daimler Sovereign (68 - Oct 86) up to D	0242
Jaguar XJ6 & Sovereign (Oct 86 - Sept 94) D to M	3261
Jaguar XJ12, XJS & Sovereign; Daimler Double Six (72 - 88) up to F	0478
JEEP	
Jeep Cherokee Petrol (93 - 96) K to N	1943
LADA	
Lada 1200, 1300, 1500 & 1600 (74 - 91) up to J	0413
Lada Samara (87 - 91) D to J	1610
LAND ROVER	
Land Rover 90, 110 & Defender Diesel (83 - 95) up to N	3017
Land Rover Discovery Petrol & Diesel (89 - 98) G to S	3016
Land Rover Series IIA & III Diesel (58 - 85) up to C	0529
Land Rover Series II, IIA & III Petrol (58 - 85) up to C	0314
MAZDA	
Mazda 323 (Mar 81 - Oct 89) up to G	1608
Mazda 323 (Oct 89 - 98) G to R	3455
Mazda 626 (May 83 - Sept 87) up to E	0929
Mazda B-1600, B-1800 & B-2000 Pick-up (72 - 88) up to F	0267
Mazda RX-7 (79 - 85) *	0460

Title	Book No.
MERCEDES-BENZ	
Mercedes-Benz 190, 190E & 190D Petrol & Diesel (83 - 93) A to L	3450
Mercedes-Benz 200, 240, 300 Diesel (Oct 76 - 85) up to C	1114
Mercedes-Benz 250 & 280 (68 - 72) up to L	0346
Mercedes-Benz 250 & 280 (123 Series) (Oct 76 - 84) up to B	0677
Mercedes-Benz 124 Series (85 - Aug 93) C to K	3253
Mercedes-Benz C-Class Petrol & Diesel (93 - Aug 00) L to W	3511
MG	
MGA (55 - 62) *	0475
MGB (62 - 80) up to W	0111
MG Midget & AH Sprite (58 - 80) up to W	0265
MITSUBISHI	
Mitsubishi Shogun & L200 Pick-Ups (83 - 94) up to M	1944
MORRIS	
Morris Ital 1.3 (80 - 84) up to B	0705
Morris Minor 1000 (56 - 71) up to K	0024
NISSAN	
Nissan Bluebird (May 84 - Mar 86) A to C	1223
Nissan Bluebird (Mar 86 - 90) C to H	1473
Nissan Cherry (Sept 82 - 86) up to D	1031
Nissan Micra (83 - Jan 93) up to K	0931
Nissan Micra (93 - 99) K to T	3254
Nissan Primera (90 - Aug 99) H to T	1851
Nissan Stanza (82 - 86) up to D	0824
Nissan Sunny (May 82 - Oct 86) up to D	0895
Nissan Sunny (Oct 86 - Mar 91) D to H	1378
Nissan Sunny (Apr 91 - 95) H to N	3219
OPEL	
Opel Ascona & Manta (B Series) (Sept 75 - 88) up to F	0316
Opel Ascona (81 - 88) (Not available in UK see Vauxhall Cavalier 0812)	3215
Opel Astra (Oct 91 - Feb 98) (Not available in UK see Vauxhall Astra 1832)	3156
Opel Astra & Zafira Diesel (Feb 98 - Sept 00) (See Astra & Zafira Diesel Book No. 3797)	
Opel Astra & Zafira Petrol (Feb 98 - Sept 00) (See Vauxhall/Opel Astra & Zafira Petrol Book No. 3758)	
Opel Calibra (90 - 98) (See Vauxhall/Opel Calibra Book No. 3502)	
Opel Corsa (83 - Mar 93) (Not available in UK see Vauxhall Nova 0909)	3160
Opel Corsa (Mar 93 - 97) (Not available in UK see Vauxhall Corsa 1985)	3159
Opel Frontera Petrol & Diesel (91 - 98) (See Vauxhall/Opel Frontera Book No. 3454)	
Opel Kadett (Nov 79 - Oct 84) up to B	0634
Opel Kadett (Oct 84 - Oct 91) (Not available in UK see Vauxhall Astra & Belmont 1136)	3196
Opel Omega & Senator (86 - 94) (Not available in UK see Vauxhall Carlton & Senator 1469)	3157
Opel Omega (94 - 99) (See Vauxhall/Opel Omega Book No. 3510)	
Opel Rekord (Feb 78 - Oct 86) up to D	0543
Opel Vectra (Oct 88 - Oct 95) (Not available in UK see Vauxhall Cavalier 1570)	3158
Opel Vectra Petrol & Diesel (95 - 98) (Not available in UK see Vauxhall Vectra 3396)	3523
PEUGEOT	
Peugeot 106 Petrol & Diesel (91 - 01) J to X	1882
Peugeot 205 Petrol (83 - 97) A to P	0932
Peugeot 206 Petrol and Diesel (98 - 01) S to X	3757
Peugeot 305 (78 - 89) up to G	0538

* Classic reprint

CL13.4/02

Preserving Our Motoring Heritage

< *The Model J Duesenberg Derham Tourster. Only eight of these magnificent cars were ever built – this is the only example to be found outside the United States of America*

Almost every car you've ever loved, loathed or desired is gathered under one roof at the Haynes Motor Museum. Over 300 immaculately presented cars and motorbikes represent every aspect of our motoring heritage, from elegant reminders of bygone days, such as the superb Model J Duesenberg to curiosities like the bug-eyed BMW Isetta. There are also many old friends and flames. Perhaps you remember the 1959 Ford Popular that you did your courting in? The magnificent 'Red Collection' is a spectacle of classic sports cars including AC, Alfa Romeo, Austin Healey, Ferrari, Lamborghini, Maserati, MG, Riley, Porsche and Triumph.

A Perfect Day Out

Each and every vehicle at the Haynes Motor Museum has played its part in the history and culture of Motoring. Today, they make a wonderful spectacle and a great day out for all the family. Bring the kids, bring Mum and Dad, but above all bring your camera to capture those golden memories for ever. You will also find an impressive array of motoring memorabilia, a comfortable 70 seat video cinema and one of the most extensive transport book shops in Britain. The Pit Stop Cafe serves everything from a cup of tea to wholesome, home-made meals or, if you prefer, you can enjoy the large picnic area nestled in the beautiful rural surroundings of Somerset.

John Haynes O.B.E., Founder and Chairman of the museum at the wheel of a Haynes Light 12.

< *Graham Hill's Lola Cosworth Formula 1 car next to a 1934 Riley Sports.*

The Museum is situated on the A359 Yeovil to Frome road at Sparkford, just off the A303 in Somerset. It is about 40 miles south of Bristol, and 25 minutes drive from the M5 intersection at Taunton.

Open 9.30am - 5.30pm (10.00am - 4.00pm Winter) 7 days a week, *except Christmas Day, Boxing Day and New Years Day*

Special rates available for schools, coach parties and outings Charitable Trust No. 292048